W9-BEI-009

THE BICENTENNIAL EDITION

OF THE

WORKS OF JOHN WESLEY

General Editor RICHARD P. HEITZENRATER

Textual Editor FRANK BAKER

The Directors of the Bicentennial Edition of
the Works of John Wesley
gratefully acknowledge the financial support of
The Methodist Church in Great Britain
and
The Wesley Memorial United Methodist Church
High Point, North Carolina
in the preparation of this volume

THE WORKS OF
JOHN WESLEY

VOLUME 9

THE METHODIST SOCIETIES

HISTORY, NATURE, AND DESIGN

EDITED BY

RUPERT E. DAVIES

ABINGDON PRESS

NASHVILLE

1989

The Works of John Wesley, Volume 9
THE METHODIST SOCIETIES: HISTORY, NATURE, AND DESIGN

Copyright © 1989 by Abingdon Press

All rights reserved.
No part of this book may be reproduced in any manner whatsoever without written permission of the publisher except brief quotations embodied in critical articles or reviews. For information address Abingdon Press, Nashville, Tennessee.

Library of Congress Cataloging in Publication Data

(Revised for vol. 9)

Wesley, John, 1703-1791.
The works of John Wesley.

Vol. 9 edited by Rupert E. Davies.
Includes bibliographical references and indexes.
Contents: v. 1. Sermons I, 1-33 — v. 2. Sermons II, 34-70 — [etc.] — v. 9. The Methodist societies: history, nature, and design.
1. Methodist Church—Doctrines. 2. Theology—18th century. I. Outler, Albert Cook, 1908- II. Davies, Rupert Eric, 1909- . III. Title.
BX8217.W5 1984 252′.07 83-22434

ISBN 0-687-46214-2 (v. 9)
ISBN 0-687-46221-5 (v. 18)
ISBN 0-687-46213-4 (v. 4)
ISBN 0-687-46212-6 (v. 3)
ISBN 0-687-46211-8 (v. 2)
ISBN 0-687-46210-X (v. 1)

THE MONOGRAM USED ON THE CASE AND HALF-TITLE IS ADAPTED BY RICHARD P. HEITZENRATER FROM ONE OF JOHN WESLEY'S PERSONAL SEALS

MANUFACTURED BY THE PARTHENON PRESS AT NASHVILLE, TENNESSEE, UNITED STATES OF AMERICA

THE BICENTENNIAL EDITION OF THE WORKS OF JOHN WESLEY

THIS edition of the works of John Wesley reflects the quickened interest in the heritage of Christian thought that has become evident during the last half-century. A fully critical presentation of Wesley's writings had long been a desideratum in order to furnish documentary sources illustrating his contribution to both catholic and evangelical Christianity.

Several scholars, notably Professor Albert C. Outler, Professor Franz Hildebrandt, Dean Merrimon Cuninggim, and Dean Robert E. Cushman, discussed the possibility of such an edition. Under the leadership of Dean Cushman, a Board of Directors was formed in 1960 comprising the deans of four sponsoring theological schools of Methodist-related universities in the United States: Drew, Duke, Emory, and Southern Methodist. They appointed an Editorial Committee to formulate plans, and enlisted an international and interdenominational team of scholars for the Wesley Works Editorial Project.

The works were divided into units of cognate material, with a separate editor (or joint editors) responsible for each unit. Dr. Frank Baker was appointed textual editor for the whole project, with responsibility for supplying each unit editor with a critically developed, accurate Wesley text for his consideration and use. The text seeks to represent Wesley's thought in its fullest and most deliberate expression, in so far as this can be determined from the available evidence. Substantive variant readings in any British edition published during Wesley's lifetime are shown in appendices to the units, preceded by a summary of the problems faced and the solutions reached in the complex task of securing and presenting Wesley's text. The aim throughout is to enable Wesley to be read with maximum ease and understanding, and with minimal intrusion by the editors.

This edition includes all Wesley's original or mainly original prose works, together with one volume devoted to his *Collection of Hymns* (1780) and another to his extensive work as editor and publisher of extracts from the writings of others. An essential feature of the project is a Bibliography outlining the historical settings of the works published by Wesley and his brother Charles, sometimes jointly, sometimes separately. The Bibliography also offers full analytical data for identifying each of the two thousand editions of these 450 items that were published during the lifetime of John Wesley, and notes the location of copies. An index is supplied for each unit, and a General Index for the whole edition.

The Delegates of the Oxford University Press agreed to undertake publication, but announced in June 1982 that because of severe economic problems they would regretfully be compelled to withdraw from the enterprise with the completion in 1983 of Vol. 7, the *Collection of Hymns*. The Abingdon Press offered its services, beginning with the publication of the first volume of the *Sermons* in 1984, the bicentennial year of the formation of American Methodism as an autonomous church. The new title now assumed, however, refers in general to the bicentennial of Wesley's total activities as author, editor, and publisher, from 1733 to 1791, especially as summarized in the first edition of his collected works in thirty-two volumes, 1771–74.

Dean Robert E. Cushman of Duke University undertook general administration and promotion of the project until 1971, when he was succeeded as President by Dean Joseph D. Quillian, Jr., of Southern Methodist University, these two universities having furnished the major support and guidance for the enterprise. During the decade 1961–70, an Editorial Committee supervised the task of setting editorial principles and procedures, and general editorship was shared by Dr. Eric W. Baker, Dean William R. Cannon, and Dean Cushman. In 1969 the Directors appointed Dr. Frank Baker, early attached to the project as bibliographer and textual editor for Wesley's text, as Editor-in-Chief also. Upon Dean Quillian's retirement in 1981, he was succeeded as President of the project by Dean James E. Kirby, Jr., also of Southern Methodist University. In 1986 the Directors appointed Richard P. Heitzenrater as General Editor to begin the chief editorship of the project with the *Journal and Diaries* unit.

Other sponsoring bodies have been successively added to the original four: The United Methodist Board of Higher Education and Ministry, The Commission on Archives and History of The United Methodist Church, and Boston University School of Theology. For the continuing support of the sponsoring institutions the Directors express their profound thanks. They gratefully acknowledge also the encouragement and financial support that have come from the Historical Societies and Commissions on Archives and History of many Annual Conferences, as well as the donations of The World Methodist Council, The British Methodist Church, private individuals, and foundations.

On June 9, 1976, The Wesley Works Editorial Project was incorporated in the State of North Carolina as a nonprofit corporation. In 1977, by-laws were approved governing the appointment and duties of the Directors, their Officers, and their Executive Committee.

The Board of Directors

President: James E. Kirby, Dean of Perkins School of Theology, Southern Methodist University, Dallas, Texas
Vice-President: Dennis M. Campbell, Dean of The Divinity School, Duke University, Durham, North Carolina
Secretary: Donald H. Treese, Associate General Secretary of The Division of the Ordained Ministry, The United Methodist Board of Higher Education and Ministry, Nashville, Tennessee
Treasurer: Thomas A. Langford, The Divinity School, Duke University, Durham, North Carolina
General Editor: Richard P. Heitzenrater, Perkins School of Theology, Southern Methodist University, Dallas, Texas
Textual Editor: Frank Baker, The Divinity School, Duke University, Durham, North Carolina
Joe Hale, General Secretary of The World Methodist Council, Lake Junaluska, North Carolina
Robert C. Neville, Dean of Boston University School of Theology, Boston, Massachusetts
Thomas W. Ogletree, Dean of The Theological School of Drew University, Madison, New Jersey
William K. Quick, Detroit, Michigan
Kenneth E. Rowe, Drew University, Madison, New Jersey
Jim L. Waits, Dean of Candler School of Theology, Emory University, Atlanta, Georgia
David L. Watson, Board of Discipleship, Nashville, Tennessee
Charles Yrigoyen, Jr., Executive Secretary of The Commission on Archives and History of The United Methodist Church, Drew University, Madison, New Jersey

PREFACE

If it was one of the major contributions of John Wesley to the inner life of the church at large to create and order close-knit companies of ordinary men and women who were committed to the pursuit of holiness, bound together by a common discipline, and engaged in the loving service of their fellows, then this volume can claim a special place in the corpus of John Wesley's *Works*.

It contains the *General Rules of the United Societies;* without the study of these it is impossible to appreciate the basic principles of the Methodist societies or to distinguish them from the other religious societies of the day. It contains also several descriptions by Wesley of the kind of person he conceived and expected a Methodist to be, as well as his answers to many criticisms of his work and of the people whom he influenced. It brings the reader back on several occasions to the burning question of the relation of the Methodist Societies to the Church of England, from which the Wesleys never wished to separate. Also included are Wesley's responses to those who encouraged or allowed actual physical persecution of the Methodists; these take the form of appeals to justice and reasonableness.

Many of the writings are of necessity controversial and afford examples of Wesley's almost always courteous but often devastating methods of argument (though some examples of dubious reasoning have to be pointed out). His opponents are seen to be sometimes worthy of his steel, but often not; they all receive full and careful treatment until the point is reached at which debate ceases to be profitable.

In the work of editing I needed and received a generous amount of help. My thanks are due to Hamby Barton, who assisted me in the early stages; to many correspondents in England and Ireland who enlightened me on matters in which they had a special competence; to Mrs. Ann Weeks and Mrs. Christine Lillington, who typed a great deal from my illegible handwriting; to the staff of the Abingdon Press; to John Vickers, the indexer; to Mrs. Enid Hickingbotham, the assistant copy-editor; and above and beyond all to Frank Baker, the textual editor, who combined so many functions in his own person, scholarship, and friendly advice that I am convinced that if the time had been available, he (as no one else, probably, in the world) could have performed the total task alone.

Rupert E. Davies

CONTENTS

APPENDICES

INDEXES

ILLUSTRATIONS *facing page*

SIGNS, SPECIAL USAGES, ABBREVIATIONS

[ ]	Indicate editorial insertions or substitutions in the original text, or (with a query) doubtful readings.
< >	Indicate conjectural readings in manuscripts where the original text is defective.
. . .	Indicate a passage omitted by the writer from the original and so noted by Wesley, usually by a dash.
[. . .]	Indicate a passage omitted silently by Wesley from a text he was quoting, to which the present editor is drawing attention; the brackets are not used in editorial annotations and introductions.
(( ))	Enclose passages within a manuscript struck through for erasure.
[[ ]]	Enclose passages supplied by the present editors from cipher or shorthand, from an abstract or similar document in the third person, or reconstructed from secondary evidence.
a, b, c,	Small superscript letters indicate footnotes supplied by Wesley.
1, 2, 3,	Small superscript figures indicate footnotes supplied by the editor.
Cf.	Before a scriptural or other citation by Wesley, indicates that he was quoting with more than minimal inexactness, yet nevertheless displaying the passage as a quotation.
See	Before a scriptural citation indicates an undoubted allusion, or a quotation which was not displayed as such by Wesley, and which is more than minimally inexact.

Wesley's publications. Where a work by Wesley was first published separately, its title is italicized; where it first appeared within a different work such as a collected volume, the title appears within quotation marks.

Book-titles in Wesley's text are italicized if accurate, and given in roman type with capitals if inaccurate. If a title consists of only one generic word which forms a major part of the original title, it is italicized; but if it is inaccurate (such as 'Sermons' for a volume entitled *Discourses*), it is printed in lower case roman.

Abbreviations. In addition to many common and fairly obvious abbreviations, the following are used in the notes: *A[nswer],* Conf[erence], Meth[odis]m, Meth[odist], *Q[uestion],* Wes[leyan].

Works and institutions frequently cited are abbreviated thus:

BCP	The Book of Common Prayer, London, 1662.
Bibliography	Frank Baker, *A Descriptive and Analytical Bibliography of the Publications of John and Charles Wesley,* Vols. 33–34 of this edition (in preparation).

JWJ	Wesley, John, *Journal,* Vols. 18–24 of this edition.
OED	*The Oxford English Dictionary on Historical Principles*, 11 vols., Oxford, Clarendon Press, 1933.
Works [1771–74]	John Wesley, *The Works of the Rev. John Wesley,* 32 vols., Bristol, Pine, 1771–74.

INTRODUCTION

I. WESLEY'S WRITINGS ON METHODISM

The writings contained in this volume exhibit at first sight a somewhat miscellaneous character. While they all refer, at least obliquely, to the 'history, nature, and design' of the Methodist societies founded by John Wesley, and some of them, in fact, deal directly with the principles and practices of those societies, it cannot be claimed that taken together they offer a systematic treatment, under suitable headings, of the themes contained in the title of this volume.

The reason for this is that Wesley himself did not often set out to deal with these themes in the orderly manner that makes it easy for later historians to study them, and when he did, it was on a small scale. The small, but definitive, treatises that resulted are here included. More frequently Wesley dealt with these themes as they arose in the context of a situation in the Methodist connexion with which he had to deal, or as he sought to remove a misunderstanding in the minds of individuals, or as he rebutted criticisms that had arisen in certain quarters. The writings which appeared in such circumstances throw great but incidental light on the Methodist societies and find a legitimate place here. Moreover, even when Wesley entitles one of his works here included 'A Short History of the People called Methodists' (1781), it is soon apparent that what he gives us is not exactly what the title suggests, but rather a largely personal account, and that this is so at least partly because Wesley had been moved to write it by the inclusion of George Whitefield and himself in a list of heretics drawn up by a Scottish Presbyterian divine[1] and was not primarily concerned with historiography.

This volume then brings together Wesley's writings that deal with the character of a Methodist and those that set out the rules by which the life of Methodist societies with their classes and bands were governed.[2] It includes a number of Wesley's replies to various clerical authors who had publicly criticized Methodism

[1] Archibald Maclaine; see p. 426, n. 3.

[2] *The Character of a Methodist;* see intro., pp. 31-32; *The Principles of a Methodist,* p. 47; *The Nature, Design, and General Rules of the United Societies,* p. 67; and *Advice to the People called Methodists,* p. 123.

out of ignorance, misunderstanding, or malice.[3] There are, in addition, narratives of some of the ill-treatment Wesley and his followers experienced, both in England and Ireland, with an earnest appeal for more understanding and justice.[4] Then there are two careful expositions—addressed in this case mainly to the Methodists—of Wesley's strongly held reasons for not separating from the Church of England.[5] These, of course, shed light on Wesley's 'design' for his societies. At the end are samples of his views on the holding of Methodist property and on his own right to choose the preachers for Methodist preaching places. Here his conception of his own relationship to his societies becomes apparent.

The arrangement of these writings is chronological, not thematic. A thematic arrangement would indeed have been virtually impossible for the reasons given above and because each writing touches on so many themes. The chronological method may give the reader the impression that he is inconsequently leaping from one subject to another, but it will certainly help him to follow the development of Wesley's thinking about his societies, as well as about other major topics which recur throughout the volume.

II. THE ORIGINS OF THE EARLY METHODIST SOCIETIES

If we are to elucidate the history of the Methodist societies from the available material, we must begin by freeing ourselves from the notion, popularized and *to some extent* substantiated in the sociological treatises of Weber and Troeltsch,[6] that all Christian communions fall into two categories, churches and sects. This classification serves a useful purpose, no doubt, in respect of the

[3] *An Answer to the Rev. Mr. Church's Remarks*, p. 80; *The Principles of a Methodist Farther Explained*, p. 160; *A Letter to a Clergyman*, p. 247; *A Letter to the Rev. Mr. Baily of Cork*, p. 288; *A Letter to the Rev. Dr. Free*, p. 315; *A Second Letter to the Reverend Dr. Free*, p. 321; *A Letter to the Reverend Mr. Downes*, p. 350; *A Letter to the Reverend Dr. Rutherforth*, p. 373; *A Letter to the Rev. Mr. Fleury*, p. 389; *A Letter to the Rev. Mr. Thomas Maxfield*, p. 416; and 'Some Remarks on Article X of Mr. Maty's *New Review*', p. 522.

[4] *Modern Christianity: Exemplified at Wednesbury*, p. 132; and *A Short Address to the Inhabitants of Ireland*, p. 281.

[5] *Reasons against a Separation from the Church of England*, p. 332; and 'Farther Thoughts on Separation from the Church', p. 538.

[6] Set out in its most lucid and persuasive form by Ernst Troeltsch in *Die Soziallehre der christlichen Kirchen* (Eng. trans. by Olive Wyon as *The Social Teaching of the Christian Churches* [London, 1931]). See espec. 1:334-82 in the Eng. trans.

majority of Christian bodies, but it is misleading if it is held to apply universally and without exception. It deceived Troeltsch, e.g., whose knowledge of Methodism was no doubt largely derived from its German expression, into classifying Methodism as a sect that cultivated an inner-worldly asceticism, and this classification has dominated and confused much of European writing about Methodism until the present day.

There is in fact a third category of Christian communion, which may be said to fall between the other two and to evince some of the characteristics of each of them: the category of 'society'. A 'church' claims to confess objectively the width and depth of catholic tradition, to guarantee the grace of the sacraments, and to comprehend all genuine varieties of worship, spirituality, and faith within its generous embrace. A 'sect' cuts itself off from the life of the church as just defined—it may be the 'established' church in certain countries, or the 'folk-church', i.e., the church which receives the total or partial allegiance of the people of a region or country, or a 'free church' which is equipped with catholic tradition, ministry, and sacraments—on the grounds of possessing the totality of Christian truth (or so near the totality as makes no matter) and of embodying the only authentic form of Christian discipleship. A 'society' acknowledges the truths proclaimed by the universal church and has no wish to separate from it, but claims to cultivate, by means of sacrament and fellowship, the type of inward holiness, which too great an objectivity can easily neglect and of which the church needs constantly to be reminded. A society does not unchurch the members of either church or sect, or repudiate their sacraments; it calls its own members within the larger church to a special personal commitment which respects the commitment of others.

The two most notable examples of society in church history are the Unitas Fratrum, commonly called the Moravians,[7] within the Lutheran folk-church, and the Methodist United Societies, within the Anglican folk-church. There may, indeed, be no other living examples. Because of circumstances only partly within their control, both societies in due course became separate from their mother churches and were thus forced to take on the characteristics of a church. Their society origin has therefore been largely forgotten even by their own members, but both have

[7] Their chequered history and distinguishing characteristics are briefly described by C. W. Towlson in *Moravian and Methodist* (London, 1957), pp. 21-35.

retained distinct traces of that origin. For instance, the Methodists of Britain still insist, at least in theory, on a particular discipline of life for members and claim the right to exclude from membership those who do not reach the standards required or who absent themselves from public worship for a considerable time without due reason. However, they do not regard persons so excluded as excommunicate. Methodist ministers are both 'received into full connexion' with the Conference, which is at this point the embodiment of the Methodist society, and ordained with the laying on of hands by the president or a former president into the ministry of the Holy Catholic Church (American Methodist ministers are ordained by one of their bishops).

In contemporary and later descriptions of eighteenth-century Methodism, the word 'society' was usually employed in the sense of the local company of Methodist Christians—these societies being united into a 'connexion' that owed allegiance to John Wesley and then to the 'Legal Hundred' that succeeded him. But the description of the whole connexion as a society gradually came into use alongside the distinctively Methodist words 'connexion' and, in the nineteenth century, 'body'.

With these sociological considerations in mind, we are in a position to look at the historical and religious antecedents of the Methodist society and societies. Historians of Methodism have frequently drawn attention to the societies under that name (but not with the technical meaning indicated above) which predated the mission of John Wesley. Some of them do not share much with the later Methodist society apart from the name, and the name is obviously usable for a large variety of organizations that bring people together for a particular purpose. Fairly near in spirit, and to some extent in modes of operation (such as the encouragement of local groups for spiritual instruction), are the Society for Promoting Christian Knowledge, founded in 1698 by Thomas Bray with the twin aims of starting schools in London for teaching the church catechism and of promoting religion in the American plantations by the dissemination of literature, and the Society for the Propagation of the Gospel in Foreign Parts, founded by the same Thomas Bray in 1701, with the purposes of ministering to the spiritual needs of British people overseas and of evangelizing non-Christian races who were subject to Britain. Although like Methodism in their evangelistic purpose, they were not real precursors of Wesley's societies in providing the kind of inward spiritual fellowship without which Methodism would not have been what it was.

In his *Short History of Methodism*, John Wesley traces the origin of the movement to the Oxford Methodists, young men who met in college rooms for devotions and conversation, first attracted the sobriquet 'Methodist', and came to be known more popularly than accurately as the Holy Club. For John and Charles the convictions and experiences that brought these men together and were deepened by their meetings and observances formed a vital stage in their spiritual development; without such a stage the two brothers might not have gone on to live and to preach as they did after the events of May 1738.[8]

But it is not the case that the Oxford Methodists formed the model for the later Methodist societies either in their theology or their practice, though of course some similarities can be observed. The Oxford Methodists organized their common life specifically with the object of pursuing their own personal holiness, and there is no evidence that their vision or their beliefs stretched very far beyond their own religious world. The regimen they worked out was designed for their own practice in the particular situation of a university, a university they believed to be riddled with irreligion, idleness, and corruption.

They borrowed parts of their discipline from other self-styled religious societies, of which the first was founded in or about the year 1676 by Anthony Horneck.[9] One of the books specified for their reading was *The Country Parson's Advice to his Parishioners*, written anonymously by a member of a religious society who recommended the practice of mutual help to 'the good men of the church' as the most effectual means of supporting 'our tottering and sinking church'. In a limited sense the Holy Club was a religious society.

The religious societies proper have a much better claim, however, than the Oxford Methodists to a place among the antecedents of the Methodist societies. The rules of these societies were no doubt slightly different in each case, but those

[8] See Richard P. Heitzenrater, *The Elusive Mr. Wesley*, 2 vols. (Nashville, 1984), 1:63-103.

[9] See the life of Anthony Horneck in Richard B. Hone, *Lives of Eminent Christians*, 3 vols. (London, 1839–42), 1:309-10. His societies are described in Josiah Woodward, *Account of the Rise and Progress of the Religious Societies in the City of London* (2nd edn., London, 1698; 4th edn., 1712).

drawn up by Horneck for his own society seem to have formed the model for later ones. The basic principle was that 'all that enter the society shall resolve upon a holy and serious life.' Only those confirmed by a bishop could belong, and a minister of the Church of England was prescribed as the director. There was not to be much discussion at the meetings of the society, and none at all of disputed theological points or of ecclesiastical or any other kind of politics; even the discussion of personal spiritual concerns was not obligatory or regular. Most of the time was spent in prayer and devotional readings. The subscription was sixpence a week (reduced to threepence for those not present). The society of Josiah Woodward in Poplar, founded in the early eighteenth century, extended the rules as laid down by Horneck to the encouragement of charity and moderation towards Dissenters 'of good conversation', though such persons were not eligible for membership unless they attached themselves to the Church of England. It also allowed more time for spiritual discussion. There is reason for thinking that the Society for Promoting of Christian Knowledge and the Society for the Propagation of the Gospel owed their existence partly to the influence of religious societies on Thomas Bray and his friends.[10]

There is one clear historical connection between the religious societies and Methodism. When John Wesley returned dispirited from Georgia to England in 1737, he helped his friend James Hutton to form a society that met at first in Hutton's house and later in a house in Fetter Lane. This followed the lines of earlier religious societies, but with the rules simplified and reduced in number to two, with the effect that a set pattern of devotion was avoided and non-Anglicans, in this case including Moravians, could be invited to share in the proceedings. The society was later divided into two 'companies' or 'orders', one of single and one of married men, and later still into several 'bands of little societies', each with a membership of five to ten with a leader. Another society was formed by James Hutton in Aldersgate Street and was subdivided as was the one in Fetter Lane, and it was in this society that Wesley was worshipping on the evening of May 24, 1738. The resemblances between these societies and the subsequent Methodist societies do not need to be pointed out, and it could

[10] See W. K. Lowther Clarke, *Eighteenth Century Piety* (London, 1944), pp. 96-100, for light on this question.

indeed be said that we can here see one kind of society merging into the other.

After less than two years, the Fetter Lane Society came under the powerful influence of Philip Henry Molther, who taught a particular form of Moravianism according to which the means of grace are unnecessary for those who live under grace, and the essential element in the religion of believers is 'stillness'. It was as a result of Molther's aberrations and influence that Wesley left the fellowship of the Fetter Lane Society for the Foundery, taking many of his friends with him. But he certainly did not entirely cast off the lessons and experiences of Fetter Lane when he came to work on his own enterprises.

It may well be that the Moravians exercised an even greater influence on him than the religious societies. The fact that he disagreed vigorously with the Moravian Molther is not significant in this regard, for Molther's views were not typical of Moravianism. Wesley was predisposed to look on the Moravian theological and disciplinary system with favour, a predisposition brought about by the demeanour of the Moravian emigrants on the voyage to America in 1735, by the searching help given him by Spangenberg in Georgia, by the impressive educational and philanthropic work done by the Moravians in that colony, and perhaps most of all by the personal and pastoral counsel of Peter Böhler after his own Georgian mission had failed. Soon after May 24, 1738, he paid a protracted visit to the Moravian communities in Marienborn and Herrnhut in order to acquaint himself with the ways of thought and life to be found there, and although he did not approve of everything he saw he was plainly impressed by much of it. He returned to England with the double intention of putting into effect, as opportunity offered, the good practices he had observed and of emending, if necessary, the less satisfactory ones.

The Moravianism which Wesley had encountered in his counsellors and guides from that communion in America and England, and later in Herrnhut, was strongly marked by the personality of Count Zinzendorf.[11] The original Unitas Fratrum was founded by Peter of Chelcic as a means of retiring from

[11] See A. J. Lewis, *Zinzendorf, the Ecumenical Pioneer* (London, 1962), espec. pp. 124-32, which sets out Zinzendorf's concept of unity and his disinclination to separate the Moravians from their mother churches.

national life into apostolic simplicity during the wars that followed the execution of John Hus. In spite of its seclusion this peaceful community, after it had broken away from the Papacy, was savagely persecuted and reduced to a very small number. Even so, it produced the notable educationalist, J. A. Comenius (1592–1670). Life in the countries of their origin—Moravia, Bohemia, and Austria—became so intolerable for the brethren, although they sought peace by greater and greater withdrawal from society, that they willingly accepted an invitation from Zinzendorf to form a settlement on his estate in Saxony in 1722.

Up to this time their principal aim had been to live in Christian love with each other without any special ministry or organization. Zinzendorf transformed them into a closely knit group of residential communities with set practices and strict rules. Each community was divided, for both spiritual and secular purposes, into eleven 'choirs', composed of married men, widowers, single brethren, youths, boys, married women, widows, single sisters, young women, girls, and even infants in arms. There were also voluntary groups of those at a similar stage of spiritual development, which were irrespective of the 'choirs'. These were called 'bands', at any rate at first, and consisted of five to ten people. The sexes were segregated at public worship. When the whole community came together, the Agape was celebrated with rye bread and water, except when the Lord's Supper was taken, and hymn-singing was an integral part of all their worship. After a period without an ordained ministry, one of their number, David Nitschmann, was consecrated bishop by Bishop Jablonsky, who claimed succession from the apostles (a claim accepted by Archbishop Potter of Canterbury in 1737, but not yet fully accepted by the Church of England). Thereafter preaching and the conduct of worship were restricted to ordained ministers.

III. DEVELOPMENTS WITHIN THE EARLY SOCIETIES

In the light of these many antecedents on the English scene and in Germany, it is not hard to account for and trace the origin and growth of Wesley's Methodist societies, so long as it is remembered that he never adopted the practices of others, or his own earlier ones, without strict scrutiny or without modification for his purposes. He was certainly a pragmatist, in the sense that he was always open to consider and use what was suggested to him in the form of ideas and activities. But he did not fail to put his own stamp on anything he proceeded to borrow.[12]

This is conspicuously true of the bands, which he took from the Moravians. He had experimented with them in Georgia under Moravian influence. Both at Savannah and at Frederica a religious society was first formed, and then the most serious members of the society were divided into smaller groups 'for a more intimate union with each other', and these groups met three times weekly. After his return from America, the newly created Fetter Lane Society, guided by Peter Böhler and John Wesley, was soon subdivided into bands, first of all as an experiment and then on a permanent basis. Shortly afterwards John Wesley made his journey to Herrnhut and formed many impressions of Moravian life, most of them favourable. On his return he was more than ever convinced of the value of the bands, and in December 1738 he drew up the *Rules of the Band Societies*. Of members it was required that they answer eleven questions about their spiritual state on entering their band and from time to time afterwards, and at every meeting five additional questions were put to them, based on James 5:16 ('confess your faults one to another'). They were very stringent.

1. What known sins have you committed since our last meeting?
2. What temptations have you met with?
3. How was you delivered?
4. What have you thought, said, or done, of which you doubt whether it be sin or not?
5. Have you nothing you desire to keep secret?

So Wesley's use of bands antedated the formation of the first specifically Methodist society that he created. This was in Bristol. The evangelistic work there and in neighbouring Kingswood was begun by George Whitefield and continued by John Wesley, both in company with Whitefield and after Whitefield had departed on his further travels. In one of the letters urging Wesley to come to Bristol, written a few days before he actually set out, Whitefield

[12] The most fully documented account of the development and design of the societies is that of Frank Baker in Rupert Davies and Gordon Rupp, *A History of the Methodist Church in Great Britain* (2nd edn., London, 1983), 1:213-55. He has, however, made certain amendments to this account in the *Bibliography* in this edn.

says of those to whom he had been preaching: 'Many are ripe for bands. I leave that entirely to you—I am but a novice.'[13] It is not quite clear whether he was writing of colliers in Kingswood or ordinary citizens of Bristol. Probably they were Bristolians, for we soon learn that Wesley formed two bands in the societies already existing there in Baldwin Street, Bristol, which was at this time the base of his operations. He added several more in the next few months.

But there was not yet a *Methodist* society either in Bristol or in Kingswood. The Baldwin Street Society and the Nicholas Street Society (not far away) were almost certainly religious societies of the old sort, although we have little information about their principles and practices. In the summer of 1739, Wesley purchased a piece of land in the Horsefair in Bristol and built the first 'New Room'[14] there. This was to provide accommodation for both the Baldwin Street and the Nicholas Street societies, as well as for those who had been converted or strongly influenced by Whitefield's and Wesley's preaching in the churches and open places of Bristol. It was on July 11, 1739, in the presence of Whitefield and Wesley, that the first distinctively Methodist society was born (under the name, at least for the time being, of the United Society), and Wesley was able to put into full effect the *Rules of the Band Societies* that he had drawn up in London in 1738 (no doubt they were an elaboration of the prescriptions drawn up not long before for the Fetter Lane Society).

After many visits to London and many conversations and disputes, John Wesley took his final leave of the Fetter Lane Society in July 1740. He had acquired in November of the previous year the lease of the disused and ruined King's Foundery near Upper Moorfields and adapted it to his purposes. It was here that the first Methodist society in London was founded in December 1739. This was strongly reinforced on July 23, 1740, by the seventy-five who had followed Wesley from Fetter Lane, where the society was now to be reconstituted on wholly Moravian lines as they were understood by Molther.

Both of these prototypal Methodist societies were from their beginning wider in their membership than any of the religious societies or any of the Moravian societies. They were open to all

[13] *Letters* (25:612 in this edn.).

[14] Sometimes, understandably, called the 'Old Room'.

who declared 'a desire to flee from the wrath to come, to be saved from their sins'. There was no credal basis at all, even though Wesley himself believed and sedulously taught the faith of the creeds. But this did not mean a lack of discipline. On the contrary, the members of the societies were retained in membership only if they continued to evince signs of their first desire, and this meant a considerable strictness of life.

Within the larger fellowship of the society there were the close fellowship and stricter obligations of the bands. These met from time to time as the 'united bands' or (rather confusingly for us) as the 'band society', and it was to this meeting that the names of the members of the society were referred if charges of indiscipline were brought against them, and by this meeting that they were confirmed in their membership or placed on further trial or, if necessary, excluded. The band society formed the inner circle, the core, of the society.

The years 1740–43 witnessed a series of events indicating both the value and the difficulties of the discipline that had been introduced. At a meeting of the band society in Bristol in early 1741, the names of all the members of the United Society were read out by Wesley. Objections to any on grounds of 'disorderly walking' were considered, and forty persons were excluded ('I trust only for a season,' writes Wesley in his *Journal*); others were put on probation. A few days later a similar purge took place at Kingswood.

In April 1741, the band society in London met for the same purpose, and at Christmas 1743 this was repeated. By the time of the latter meeting, the bands that met were ninety-three in number and mustered a total membership of five hundred. Meanwhile, a visitation of the societies in the north of England and the discovery of lax discipline among them had led Wesley to formulate and publish in the course of the year *The Nature, Design, and General Rules of the United Societies in London, Bristol, Kingswood, and Newcastle upon Tyne*. By doing this Wesley expressed his definitive intentions for all his societies.

The next development of the societies after the calling together of the band society also took place in Bristol. Not by any means for the last time in the history of Methodism the precipitating cause was financial. Money was needed to pay the debt incurred by the building of the New Room, and all the members of the United Society were summoned by Wesley to a meeting to consider means of obtaining it. The historic suggestion of the otherwise unknown Captain Foy was that every member should give a penny a week towards the liquidation of the debt; and he offered to call on eleven of the poorest members weekly to obtain their contribution and to make good any deficiency. Others made similar offers, and Foy's suggestion was approved. The society was divided into 'little companies or classes' of eleven or twelve; and the contributions of each class were brought by an appointed person from the class to the stewards of the society each week. Within two years it became the practice, not for the 'leader' (as the appointed person soon came to be called) to visit the homes of the members of his class, but for the members of the class to meet him in his home or in the New Room or in some other convenient place. This change was no doubt due partly to its obvious economy of time for the leaders, but more to the opportunity Wesley saw for spiritual fellowship in the form of prayer, hymn-singing, the interchange of confession and Christian experience, and pastoral counsel and leadership. The leaders, of course, were to visit the homes of those absent from the weekly meeting for fellowship, whatever the reason.

All members of the United Society were allocated to classes. It was in the classes that the practice of issuing tickets as a certification of membership probably originated, though the evidence on this point is not conclusive.[15] Those who absented themselves from the class-meeting without good reason after a visit from their leader were regarded as having 'ceased to meet'. Their tickets were withheld, and they were no longer members of the society. The later issue of band-tickets was no doubt a development from the practice of the classes.

Wesley soon recognized what he called 'the unspeakable usefulness of the institution' of the class-meeting and established it in the Foundery Society in London, and then over the years in every Methodist society that came into existence throughout the land. There is no doubt that the cellular structure of the Methodist organism, introduced almost accidentally in Bristol, does much to account for the dynamism and growth of Wesley's mission.

The bands continued to exist alongside the classes and were, in

[15] The evidence is in the article by J. H. Verney, in the *Proceedings of the Wesley Historical Society* (1957), 31:1-9, 15, 34-38, 70-73.

fact, intertwined with them. In 1744 a new set of strict *Directions* for band-members was issued. Those who could not or would not carry out these *Directions*—or the revisions introduced from time to time—were downgraded from band membership to society membership.

Wesley, it must be acknowledged, had a tendency towards the proliferation of small groups. As if bands and classes were not enough, he set up, at least at the Foundery and perhaps in other large societies, 'select societies', one in each society, comprising the inner circle of the bands as the bands were already the inner circle of the society. It was made up of those in the bands who showed plain signs of growth in grace and who could consequently be urged with good prospect of success to press on to perfection. The select societies also served as sounding boards of Wesley's ideas for the spiritual direction of his people. The rules of the select society insist on confidentiality, a feature that survives in the tradition today when Methodists discussing intimate matters among themselves remind each other that they are speaking 'in band'.

A still further complication was the formation of groups of 'penitents', band members who had fallen away from the faith and later repented; they were to meet separately with the purpose of rebuilding their faith.

But such complexity of organization could not be sustained, and the intricate distinctions between various spiritual states and grades came to be seen as impracticable. The movement was in danger of being clogged up by over-organization. So the select societies and the groups of penitents gradually ceased in most cases to operate as such, and places were found for their members in the bands and classes. The whole elaborate organization that Wesley had favoured in the early years lingered on, however, until the 1780s in many areas.

The bands, in spite of their great value and effectiveness among the religious societies, the Moravians, and the early Methodists, did not last a great deal longer than the select societies and the penitents. Their history is not altogether clear, but it seems that, while the importance of the classes increased, that of the bands decreased throughout Wesley's later years and that at the end of his life they were retained only in the larger societies. But Wesley himself never ceased to urge their establishment and retention, and they survived into the nineteenth century both in England and in America. Perhaps their decline is evidence in Methodism of that gradual drop in the spiritual temperature liable to be experienced in all movements of religious renewal as time goes on, or perhaps it was just spiritual common sense.

Wesley did not suppose that the spiritual gifts of the class-leaders and the devotion of the individual members of the societies would be adequate by themselves to ensure the continuance of his mission. From almost the first days of the societies in the Foundery and the New Room, he chose men with some skill in temporal matters to relieve him of the burden of financial administration and the upkeep of property, and he called them 'stewards' according to the practice of the religious societies. Stewards were soon found to be useful for multitudinous purposes: receiving the class-money from the leaders, giving alms to the poor, keeping accounts, ensuring that the premises were clean and tidy and that the appropriate rules were kept therein, telling the 'helpers' and 'assistants' if they went wrong in teaching or life—and even meeting with Wesley himself at the annual Conference, if he felt that they had sound advice to give. The larger societies had two stewards as the system developed, and the smaller societies one.

Rather surprisingly, Wesley, as is evident from time to time in his writings, placed the stewards on a higher level of status and responsibility than the leaders of the bands and the classes, though below the assistants and the other preachers.

The organization of the Methodist societies into bands and classes and the appointment of stewards were not, as we have seen, a complete innovation in English Christianity. But when the societies with their subdivisions began to appear and take root in many parts of the country—in fact, almost wherever John Wesley preached—a new religious phenomenon had in fact occurred. The religious societies before Wesley had been recruited almost entirely from the spiritual élite, from those who for profound spiritual reasons were dissatisfied with the ministrations of the Church of England and wished to create for themselves a context in which they could help each other to grow in faith and love. But the Methodist societies were open to all and sundry, and were to be found in places and among groups of people where spiritual growth had never been expected or found before.

They even seemed to many observers to verge on democracy,

since ordinary men and women of the people were drawn into consultation and asked to express themselves publicly in words and actions. Indeed, as many people now think, and as the course of later history seems to confirm, they contained the seeds of democracy and were leading by stages inexorably towards it. But nothing of this sort was in Wesley's mind, though the fact that he was at least once forced to repudiate any tendency to 'republicanism' shows that it was present in the minds of some. For him, the authority for each society lay firmly in his own hands. In the early days he himself admitted people to membership of the society and of the bands, and he himself excluded anyone from membership who needed to be thus disciplined. He appointed the stewards, the band-leaders, and the class-leaders, and he replaced them by others if he judged it right to do so. He made it a practice, though not an invariable one, to consult the band society from time to time, and at times just the band-leaders, as to who should be admitted or retained as members; but he took the decisions himself. (In certain places his brother Charles was authorized by him to act similarly.)

IV. THE RISE OF ITINERANT PREACHING AND THE CIRCUIT SYSTEM

BUT even Wesley could not be everywhere always, and delegation became imperative. The obvious persons to be appointed as delegates were those ordained clergymen of the Church of England who supported him, but they were thin on the ground and, in any case, confined to their parishes for the greater part of the year. So laymen were brought into service—not in this case the lay stewards and class-leaders, but the steadily increasing group of full-time itinerant lay preachers. It may be that in the thinking of Wesley, and indeed according to his deepest convictions, the authority of the Word was transmitted in fuller measure to the preachers of the Word than to any other kind of Christian. The temporary disagreement of Wesley with his mother about the desirability of appointing Thomas Maxfield as a preacher—a disagreement resolved with lasting consequences by Susanna's assertion that Maxfield had a truly divine call—should not obscure the fact that Wesley had requested John Cennick, a layman, to preach in Kingswood (Cennick later defected, first to Whitefield's predestinarianism and then to the Moravians; he was therefore not a very encouraging precedent). But Cennick was an occasional, part-time preacher who never received a permanent status. Maxfield was welcomed and appointed as a full-time regular preacher, liable to be instructed by Wesley to fulfil that calling in the society of Wesley's choice.

The increase in the number of such preachers was rapid, rising to perhaps as many as fifty in 1745. Wesley forestalled a chaotic state of affairs by naming fifteen of these as assistants in that year; the rest were called helpers. After the Conference of 1749 only those who had the oversight of a 'circuit' or 'round' were designated as assistants.

The circuit was the area throughout which the assistant was commanded to travel; and the Conference of 1749 carefully laid down the duties of the assistant in each place in his circuit. He was to visit and regulate the bands and the classes, deliver the class-tickets, hold quarterly meetings of all the societies, care for and watch over the helpers, supply books, and keep careful accounts of financial transactions.

In this way Wesley had in effect delegated his authority in the matter of the admission, testing, and expulsion of members of a society and of band-leaders and class-leaders to the assistants. They were assistants, of course, to Mr. Wesley, and it was right and proper that after his death they were renamed 'superintendents'. Even during his lifetime, as his work carried him widely over a country that lacked all modern means of speedy communication (except that letters did not always arrive much less quickly than they do today),[16] the assistants wielded a much greater, though delegated, authority than their modest title suggests. This is true in spite of the fact that the assistants were itinerant, not only in the sense of travelling widely within their own circuits—with long absences from home and one-night sojourns in society after society—but also in the sense of travelling at Wesley's behest to a new circuit every year, or at most every two years, to prevent their sermons from becoming either stale or repetitive. Yet in a mysterious way, the authority of Wesley himself never ceased to breathe through the authority of his delegates.

The helpers were also itinerant preachers; it was from their number that the assistants were selected. There was normally,

[16] *Letters* (25:20-28 in this edn.).

and perhaps invariably, only one assistant in each circuit; and if an assistant for any reason moved to a circuit where there was one already, he reverted to the status, or more accurately the functions, of a helper. The helpers were in fact the rank and file of the itinerant preachers.[17]

As the assistants came from the ranks of the helpers, so the helpers came from the ranks of those called local preachers, whose role is sufficiently indicated by their name. They were first described (in 1747) as those who 'assist us only in one place'. The number of preachers grew rapidly as Methodism increased its range. Their activities were not carefully regulated by John Wesley, and there was even the charge that some of them might have been admitted too hastily into the ranks of the itinerancy, because of the greatness of the need. In 1751 Charles urged John to lay it down that the local preachers should be examined by the assistant and only on his recommendation be admitted as helpers by the brothers Wesley.[18] John Wesley experimented with the preparation of circuit preaching plans in 1754, initially for the itinerants in the large London Circuit, and especially those assembling for the Conference there. Preaching plans developed only slowly, however, and the first printed example seems to have been that for the London Circuit covering the months October 1786 to January 1787.[19] Local preachers' affairs were at first dealt with in the Circuit Quarterly Meeting, but separate meetings for local preachers began just before, and were regularized shortly after, the death of Wesley.

The steady acquisition of property for Methodist worship and fellowship necessitated another set of officers for each society. Wesley himself held the lease for the Foundery, and was at first the proprietor of the land and building in the Horsefair for the Bristol Society. But it was clearly impossible for him to own and

[17] There is a curious case of James Barry, who was listed as an assistant (at Brecon) in the 1773 *Minutes*, again in South Wiltshire in 1774 (though not specifically listed as such), yet was not listed as being 'admitted' (i.e., into full connexion) until 1775. There may have been other cases, but all such are exceptional.

[18] *Letters*, 26:469n., 470n., 471n., 472n., 473 in this edn., together with Frank Baker, *Charles Wesley as Revealed by his Letters*, ch. 7, 'Purging the Preachers', espec. pp. 83-87.

[19] This antedates the date of 1789 given in Alan Rose's otherwise excellent article on 'The Evolution of the Circuit Plan', in the *Proceedings of the Wesley Historical Society* (1969), 37:50-54; see also Frank Baker, 'the Circuit Plan', *Library Notes*, Dec. 1979 (Duke Univ. Library, Durham, N.C.), No. 49, pp. 9-28. On the 1754 experiment see *Wesleyan Methodist Magazine* (1855), 78:223-26. The 1786–87 London plan is in the Methodist Archives, Manchester.

administer personally all the preaching-houses that might be built; yet he did not wish to resign all his rights in respect of them. So a complex scheme was worked out in the 1740s, and in 1746 the New Room in Bristol and the preaching-houses in Kingswood and Newcastle upon Tyne were secured on a deed that set up in each case a body of trustees obliged to keep the property in good repair (presumably in cooperation with the stewards, whose functions Wesley did not very clearly differentiate from those of the trustees) and also to ensure that those who preached there should not propagate anything but authentic Methodist doctrine. But a clause was added according to which the trustees were bound to permit John Wesley (and after his death Charles Wesley) or his nominees to have free use of the premises and to 'expound God's Holy Word'. This clause was to have no further validity after both brothers were dead.

John Wesley, of course, appointed the original trustees in each case and was no doubt careful to select men of high integrity and intelligence as well as proved business ability. But it is by no means clear why Wesley gave to this particular group in each chapel an authority greater than any of the assistants possessed—in effect, the authority to determine what was Methodist doctrine—and so set up a body of people who could not be dislodged from office without great difficulty unless they ceased to be Methodists altogether. We almost seem to be in an area of checks and balances analogous to those of the American Constitution. Certainly his provision in this matter led to endless conflicts between various parties on matters both of doctrine and of property for the powerful reason that those who were supposed to work together sometimes came to work against each other.

The deed drawn up for the three preaching-houses in 1746 was at the time intended to be a model for all preaching-houses.[20]

[20] The subsequent developments and difficulties are set out by E. Benson Perkins in *Methodist Preaching Houses and the Law* (London, 1952), pp. 31-83. Legal difficulties arose also in relation to the relief granted to Dissenters by the Toleration Act of 1689 from penalties imposed by the Conventicle Act of 1664. Wesley was insistent that Methodists were not Dissenters and that Methodist buildings should be called preaching-houses, not meeting-houses, the name given to places where Dissenters met for worship. But what was the relation of Methodist preaching-houses (or, as they were later often called, chapels) to the Toleration Act? In 1748 a trustee of the rebuilt New Room in Bristol applied for and gained a certificate authorizing the use of the building for Dissenting worship. John Wesley was not pleased but was gradually forced to the conclusion that such action was necessary, though unpleasant, and in 1787 he agreed that all preaching-houses should be licensed under the Act of Toleration. See Perkins, pp. 13-16.

But it had to be revised, as Wesley came to see, especially in relation to the appointment of preachers. So in 1763 it was enacted by the Conference that the deed for Birchin Lane preaching-house in Manchester should be the model for all. This, in the form finally authorized by the Conference, appointed the Rev. William Grimshaw as the eventual successor of John and Charles in charge of all the Methodist societies, with the same reserved privileges in relation to property as the two brothers held in respect of the New Room, Kingswood, and Newcastle (Grimshaw, however, died soon afterwards). It also laid down that the trustees were authorized to allow the use of the preaching-house only to those 'appointed at the yearly Conference', and that those so appointed should 'preach no other doctrine than is contained in Mr. Wesley's *Notes upon the New Testament* and four volumes of sermons'.

This measure did not clear up the matter by any means, as two of the writings contained in this volume abundantly illustrate.[21] They show, for instance, that the trustees of a new building in Birstall, Yorkshire, in 1782, were not willing to forego the sole right to appoint preachers, and a new deed had to be drawn up to give that right to the Conference.

Such conflicts, and others that might be expected in the future, especially after the death of John Wesley, furnished a powerful motive for the drawing up and legalization of the *Deed of Declaration* of 1784. Before we come to the detailed provisions of that deed we need to consider the other tendencies in the societies that led up to it.

As Wesley was opposed to the introduction of the democratic principle into Methodism, so also he allowed no vestige of congregationalism. From the start he took every opportunity of uniting individual societies for purposes of consultation and mutual support, and the Quarterly Meeting already referred to was an early product of this way of thinking. The first such meeting, assembled at Todmorden Edge in 1748 under the leadership of William Grimshaw, and the second very soon after in Woodley, Cheshire, under that of John Bennet—the proponent of the idea of Quarterly Meetings. The Conference of 1749 made it obligatory for all assistants to hold such meetings for the purpose of inquiring into 'the spiritual and temporal state of each society' and, as was convenient, to keep a roll of the

[21] *The Case of Birstall House* (p. 505) and *The Case of Dewsbury House* (p. 512).

membership of each society for the assistant to present to the ensuing Conference.

But of course no power for formulating and settling policy, even in local matters, was delegated to Quarterly Meetings. They functioned strictly for consultation and conversation on matters both spiritual and temporal.

V. THE METHODIST CONFERENCE

THE same consultative function applies on a larger scale to the Conference, which Wesley summoned for the first time in 1744. It cannot be too strongly or too frequently pointed out that during his lifetime Wesley was in all respects (as he described himself in 1769) 'under God a centre of union to all our travelling as well as local preachers'. On his relation to the members of the Conference, Wesley wrote in 1766: 'I sent for them to *advise* not *govern* me. Neither did I at any of these times divest myself of any part of the power above described, which the Providence of God had cast upon me, without any design or choice of mine.' He *was* Methodism, in person and in power.

The 1744 Conference in the Foundery consisted of the brothers Wesley, four sympathetic Anglican clergymen, and four unordained preachers. The second and third Conferences were held in the New Room, Bristol, the next three in the Foundery. Later, Leeds and Manchester—but only these before the end of the century—were added to the Conference's places of assembly. The number of Anglican clergymen present did not increase, the number of unordained preachers did, very rapidly. From 1746, it was agreed that 'as many of the preachers as conveniently can' should attend the Conference; in practice, Wesley decided by his issue of invitations to which preachers this phrase applied. All the assistants were expected either to be present, if invited, or to send an account of their spiritual and financial stewardship.

The scope of the agenda grew with Methodism. Doctrine dominated the proceedings of the first few years, and in later years came to the fore from time to time, as in the years leading up to 1770, when the controversy with the antinomian Calvinists reached its height. For the rest, administrative arrangements, such as those for the establishment and maintenance of Kingswood School, and the conditions of life for the travelling preachers needed more and more time and more and more complex discussion as the years went by. The matters concerning the preachers came to be dealt with in the first few days in private session, as we should now call it; after these were settled, respected lay people other than preachers, from the neighbourhood or from further afield, were invited to come in. The procedure was for a series of questions (in the literal sense) to be asked and discussed—and then for Mr. Wesley to deliver the definitive answer. In 1749 Wesley published two pamphlets to summarize the doctrinal and disciplinary decisions so far reached. About 1753 the disciplinary decisions were codified in a work known as the 'Large' *Minutes*, and this was regularly revised until 1797. From 1765 on the *Minutes* of the Conference were published yearly. Wesley stationed the preachers himself (but after consultation with the members of the Conference) at the same time as the Conference was held, and the annual *Minutes* included the stations of the preachers, the membership and financial returns, and an account of any new legislation.

From time to time Wesley mentioned to the Conference the unwelcome prospect of his own demise and its consequences. When he raised the matter for the first time in 1769, the Conference agreed to his suggestion that a small committee be appointed by the Conference at his death, each member to serve in turn as moderator. In the same year and several times thereafter, he called upon all the preachers to pledge themselves to preserve the unity of Methodism by preaching the doctrines and preserving the discipline already agreed upon; and the preachers responded in the way that he expected.

It was in 1784 that the decisive step was taken.[22] Wesley was coming up to his eighty-second birthday. The ownership of Methodist property needed to be put on a proper legal footing lest after Wesley's death some or all revert to the sole disposition of the trustees. The continuance of Wesley's work after his death, the preaching of Methodist doctrine and the practice of Methodist discipline, needed to be assured by the appointment of

[22] It was in this year, of course, that at the Christmas Conference in Baltimore, American Methodism began quite definitely to diverge from the British form and norm for reasons created by the completely different circumstances in which Americans found themselves. Wesley in his 'Letter to our Brethren in America' of Sept. 10, 1784, had acknowledged that 'the case is widely different between England and North America.' He did, however, persuade the Americans to accept his *Sunday Service of the Methodists* (Vol. 8 in this edn.). Even before 1784 it is probable that the Methodist societies in America by no means followed exactly the prescriptions of Wesley for the societies in Britain.

suitable preachers, rather than simply promised by men of goodwill and sound purpose who were themselves mortal. So on legal advice a deed poll, known as the Deed of Declaration, was drawn up, approved by the Conference, and deposited in Chancery. The deed named a hundred preachers, chosen of course by Wesley himself from all generations of the itinerant ministry, to whom as a body all the powers exercised by Wesley would pass after his death. The Legal Hundred, as they were soon called, were to meet annually, elect a president and secretary from among their number (neither officer had to be an ordained clergyman), fill any gaps in their ranks, carry out the business which the Conference had been transacting for many years, and other matters which would in future arise. In particular the Hundred had the powers, previously reserved to the Wesleys, to acquire and dispose of property through duly appointed bodies of trustees. The preachers not appointed to the Hundred were eligible to attend their meetings from time to time, but legally and actually the Hundred now constituted the Conference.

One very important function of the Conference had been, and still was, the receiving of preachers as full-time itinerants, i.e., as helpers. This followed a carefully directed period of trial, usually of one year's duration, but sometimes extended to as much as four years. When this probation was satisfactorily completed in the judgment of the Conference, the man was solemnly 'admitted into Full Connexion', sometimes with the laying on of hands, but usually without (the laying on of hands did not become an accepted part of the procedure until 1836).

Other matters connected with the itinerant preachers were then taken in order (including the cases of those who ceased to travel through age, illness, or other causes, and the appointment of those who were to act as assistants during the ensuing year). The stationing of the preachers had been in Wesley's hands, but it had been annually brought to the Conference during his lifetime and was, of course, in the hands of the Conference after his death. All these ministerial matters were taken early in the sittings of the Conference. When they had been discharged, the temporal affairs of the societies, and not least of Kingswood School, came under consideration as in Wesley's own earlier conferences.

Thus the idea of a connexion of the societies, which Wesley had long ago conceived and steadily developed, was now fully embodied. Essential to this connexionalism, though not always noticed or honoured as such, is what is now called in ecumenical language the 'episcopé', defined as pastoral rule and care and the safeguarding of doctrine, exercised by Wesley himself in his lifetime and thereafter by the Conference. Episcopé at Wesley's death passed from a person to an assembly; the 'personal bishop' became a 'corporate bishop', by Wesley's express wish and intention. The Conference, at least in Great Britain and in the countries where British influence remains strong, is still today the corporate bishop of Methodism. It is hard to find any function exercised by the bishop in episcopal churches, such as the Church of England, that is not exercised by the Conference, either directly during its sessions or by its delegates between the sessions. In fact, it is probably true to say that the Conference exercises a greater authority in discipline and administration, as well as in doctrinal matters, than any Anglican bishop or House of Bishops; in pastoral matters the personal bishop may well have an advantage.[23]

VI. THE NATURE AND DESIGN OF THE UNITED SOCIETIES

We have exhibited the nature and design of the Methodist societies in a large measure by outlining their history in Wesley's lifetime. It should now be more than ever apparent why it is impossible to characterize Wesley's societies as forming either a church or a sect. Wesley was neither the founder of a church nor a schismatic, still less was he a sectarian. Nor were he or his followers Nonconformists, still less Dissenters; such names

[23] The episcopal character of the Conference in Britain became increasingly evident during the course of the Anglican-Methodist Conversations (1956–72). 'Methodism has *episcopé* in the corporate form. Episcopal functions in British Methodism are distributed among various officers, most notably the President, the Chairmen of Districts, particularly in their pastoral care of the ministry and the administration of their districts, and superintendent ministers. But they act as representatives of the Conference, the governing body of the Church which exercises other episcopal functions, such as the authorization of ordination. This is the significance of the word *connexion*, a familiar description of Methodism as a whole before the word *Church* came into general use. The word and its derivative adjective *connexional* still persist in many quarters, being applied to individuals or committees, or indeed other institutions, which act on behalf of Methodism as a whole. It is with the Conference that these individuals or other bodies are 'connected', so that the idea of connexion in Methodism is not dissimilar from that of the episcopate for the Anglican.' (*Conversations between the Church of England and the Methodist Church; a Report*, 1963, p. 26; see also *London Quarterly & Holborn Review*, July 1963). The report was approved by the Methodist Conference in 1965.

could be applied to them, and then inaccurately, only during a period of the nineteenth century when Nonconformist influences were strong. Indeed, serious harm has been done to the understanding of Wesley, and of Methodism in general, and to church relations in the last century and this, by lumping together Methodists and Nonconformists. Each is an honourable term derived from conscientious convictions; but they refer to distinct and different forms of church life.

Wesley created a society within the Church of England and was its perpetual president, and in a non-technical but valid sense, its 'episcopos'. He himself came to speak of a connexion fairly frequently in his later years and to use the word 'society' of the local group of Methodists. But the local society was the microcosm of the whole; the connexion was the local society writ large, and the local society was the connexion writ small. The Methodist Connexion is also properly styled 'the Society of people called Methodists'.

It may be asked why the category of society, in the particular sense in which it applies to the Methodists, is so small as to be represented in church history only by the Moravians and the Methodists. The answer may be that religious societies in general, because of the very intensity of their devotion, tend to become either exclusive or obsessive, i.e., they either confine their membership to those who show a similar degree of commitment to that of their founders or concentrate narrowly on one or two particular aims. They tend to become spiritually élitist, as in the case of the Society of Jesus, or to disparage the objectives of any society except their own, as in the case of the Society of Friends (in its formative years; a considerable process of mellowing has taken place since).[24] Wesley indeed pursued a single objective and urged all Methodists to follow a single objective, that of scriptural holiness, and it was to promote this above all else that he created his societies in the first place; but this objective as he conceived it was all-embracing in its scope for each person and included social life as well as personal life. So he was exempt from the danger of obsessiveness. On the other side, he threw open his societies to all who desired to be saved from

[24] This evaluation of the Quakers may incense some of their number, but the writings and utterances of George Fox and his first followers brook no other interpretation. Modern Quakers evince a very different attitude to their fellow-Christians but do not retract their objections to Creeds and Sacraments.

their sins—there was no further test of original suitability for membership than that and no test for continued membership except a manner of life consistent with the first desire, however strictly that test was applied. Thus he combined depth of personal commitment with openness of welcome in a way that has proved so far in Christian history to be almost unique.

This combination had a strong theological basis. When Wesley rejected Whitefield's predestinarianism in favour of a doctrine of 'free grace', he was rejecting far more than an important element in Calvin's theology. Although in his exposition of the divine grace he went, as he himself acknowledged, to the very brink of Calvinism, nevertheless, by denominating that grace as *free*—free for all and free for each—he ruled out the possibility of overstepping that brink and ensured that in the rest of his thinking his distance from Calvinism was sedulously maintained.[25] With this position the invitation to all and sundry—so long as they desired to be saved from their sins—was wholly consistent.

Wesley's invitation to all was accompanied by insistence on holiness. Holiness he defined in many different ways, some of them not necessarily attractive to ordinary people, we might think. But he also interpreted holiness in terms of love, and perfection in terms of perfect love; and this, it may be surmised but cannot be demonstrated, was the most persuasive language he used.

So he broke down the theological barrier of Calvinistic exclusiveness. Nor should we neglect the sociological overtones of his message and practice. English society in the mid-eighteenth century was rigidly divided into classes and was keenly class-conscious. The landowners formed the top class, small and proud, reckoning to govern the country in perpetuity; below them were the people with a university education (which they were expected to use in the service of the landowners)—chiefly the clergy and the lawyers—together with the lesser landed gentry, the squirearchy, whose interests were the same as those of their 'betters'. Below these two groups were the tradespeople, the artisans, the peasants, and the industrial poor. In Wesley's lifetime the Industrial Revolution was already modifying, and then drastically changing, this pattern by creating the additional

[25] In *An Answer to Mr. Rowland Hill's Tract* (p. 402), most of the heads of the dispute between Wesley and the Calvinists are reviewed—courteously by Wesley in response to the vitriolic abuse of his opponents.

class of successful manufacturers. At the same time it was vastly increasing the proportion of urban, landless workers in whose minds the seeds of revolution were already suspected of germinating, even before the French Revolution made the suspicion inevitable; but class-consciousness remained.

Wesley, by preaching a salvation available to all—and by meaning those words quite literally—struck right across this class structure both in its original and in its modified form. The landowners were not much moved by such a gospel, though they were often alarmed by it. The squirearchy and its clerical supporters saw its dangerous possibilities and resisted it by all means in their power. The people to whom its appeal went home were the scarcely educated tradespeople and artisans and superior farm-workers in the first place—people until then deemed to be capable of grasping only the elementary principles of Christianity, those usually identified with the Ten Commandments—and through them to the wholly illiterate peasants and urban 'labouring classes'—people thought to be capable of nothing more than blind obedience to their masters. All these people, women no less than men, were now offered the status of children of God, heirs of all God's promises and responsible members of a community that granted both their natural rights as human beings and their supernatural rights as aspirants by the help of the Holy Spirit to Christian perfection. And they knew that if they entered that community they would have the further chance, if they were not too shy or too ill-equipped to take it, of leading classes, preaching from pulpits, and receiving a hitherto undreamed-of measure of education in the fulfilment of their office.

It is a gross caricature of early Methodism (except in some instances) to suggest that its really attractive power was the promise of compensation in heaven for the hardships of earth.[26] The promise of heaven was inescapable and certainly included in the gospel Wesley preached, but if that had been the only, or even the chief, ingredient, why should the holders of local or national power have been afraid of Methodists as the agents of revolution? The truth is that Methodists were offered a double and interrelated citizenship of both earth and heaven, not one without

[26] This charge is made *in extenso* by E. P. Thompson, *The Making of the English Working Class* (London, 1968) and rebutted by B. Semmel, *The Methodist Revolution* (New York, 1973).

the other. This was the 'exaltation of the humble and meek', and this was the breach in the class barrier through which the Methodists poured when they heard the 'pure word of general grace'.

In the second half of the eighteenth century, by reason of the creation and development of the Methodist Connexion, there were two powerful Christian institutions in England: on the one hand, the Church of England, ramshackle but all-pervasive, and established by law; on the other, the Methodist society, small but compact and growing, tightly organized, and inspired by more than ordinary spiritual zeal. Both institutions professed the same Christian faith (though no doubt with different emphases) and observed the same Christian ordinances. The second, the Methodist society, was within the first, the Church of England. This is not to be understood in the legal sense of being authorized and registered by the authorities of the Church (such authorization and registration were not customary anyway) but in the more important sense that its leader, John Wesley, laid upon all its members the duties of professing the faith of the Church of England, of attending the parish church (and therefore of not holding their own services at times which conflicted with this duty), of obeying their bishop and the Book of Common Prayer, of disowning all thought of separation, and the additional higher duty of working and praying for the reform of the Church in matters where it was defective or corrupt. In all of these he was supported by his followers, some a little reluctantly, and by their official governing body, the Conference.

From the standpoint of the present day, it seems absurd to suppose that this situation could remain unchanged forever in view of its inherent tensions, quite apart from the local frustrations, irritations, and confrontations it frequently engendered, with bad faults on both sides. Yet Wesley firmly believed for a very long time that it could persist and always hoped that it would. He made what he intended to be adequate arrangements for it to do so after his death—while at the same time, by such provisions as the Deed of Declaration, preparing for the opposite outcome. Even his own ordinations for America, Scotland, and ultimately for parts of England, though apparently acts of canonical disobedience, did not seem to him necessarily to disrupt the existing relationship. For him, they were in accordance with Scripture as he (and other Anglican divines) had long interpreted it, embodying a principle on which he had refrained from acting in order to maintain peace in the Church of England, and which now, in the American emergency and later similar emergencies in these islands, demanded to be put into practice.

The only thing that is clear about the attitude of the Church of England to these issues is that no corporate attitude was ever reached or formulated. Some of the bishops, no doubt, reckoned that the church was nourishing a viper, or at least a potentially rebellious child, in its bosom. Others were generally sympathetic with the work that Wesley was doing, though very doubtful about the methods he was employing. The rest do not seem to have regarded it as necessary to have any opinion or take any action at all. In any case, in the absence of a meeting of Convocation, there was no council of the church in which the matter could be discussed or decided.

While the two institutions were visibly drifting apart, and the tenuous link that joined them was being stretched more and more, Wesley maintained and repeatedly expressed his complete rejection of all arguments for separation from the Church of England. His frequent repetition of his own views indicates that many of his followers saw no point in remaining within the Established Church, and needed to be reminded of its advantages. It also indicates Wesley's intense desire that no one outside the Methodist society should be able justly to charge him with schism, which he held to be among the worst possible sins.

His grounds throughout his career for rejecting separation are fundamentally scriptural and theological, but he was also influenced by the grievous inexpediency of exhibiting division to the world and giving an occasion for offence, of dividing the Methodists among themselves, and of raising up strife within the nation at large. He was also influenced by a deep love for the Church of England as an integral part of the English nation and by an intense desire to renew its life and witness. One of the last treatises in this volume, 'Farther Thoughts on Separation from the Church', gives in summary his final and definitive views on the matter, hammering home what he had often said before. Even if during his last years there are hints that he was reluctantly coming to believe that separation was inevitable, this did not affect his fundamental conviction that it was wrong.

In the event, one of his greatest hopes for the Society of people called Methodists in Britain was disappointed, and the society was compelled eventually to become a church; while in America the society became a church before Wesley's death and apparently, in the different circumstances of America, with his consent and aid. In spite of that disappointment, his design for a Methodist society that would enable its members to spread the quest for scriptural holiness throughout the land proved to be a remarkably appropriate ground plan for the Methodist churches pursuing the same aim throughout the world. The 'nature' of Methodism has thus in large measure enabled it to fulfil its 'design'.

THE

CHARACTER

OF A

METHODIST.

By *JOHN WESLEY*, M.A.

FELLOW of *Lincoln* College, in OXFORD.

Not as tho'. I had already attained.

BRISTOL:

Printed by *Felix Farley*, and sold at his Printing-Office in *Castle-Green*, and by *J. Wilson* in *Wine-street:* In LONDON, by *Thomas Trye*, near *Gray's-Inn-Gate* and *Thomas Harris* on the Bridge; and at the *Foundery*. M. D. CC. XLII. [Price *Two Pence*.

1

THE CHARACTER OF A METHODIST (1742)

AN INTRODUCTORY COMMENT

Wesley tells us in a much later work (A Plain Account of Christian Perfection) *that this was the first tract he ever wrote expressly on the subject of perfection, but that he had avoided the word 'perfection' in the title in order not to arouse prejudice.*

His purpose in writing it was threefold. First, he wished to demonstrate that Methodism is just genuine Christianity, not some newfangled theory. He attains this end by describing the 'practices and principles' of Methodism in terms that everyone would recognize as scriptural; and, for good measure, he slips in an answer to those of his critics who say that the mere statement of Methodist principles is not enough by adding that a Methodist 'not only aims at' what he is describing 'but actually attains it'. He is thus able to reinforce his contention that if others practised their faith, and not only professed it, the existence of Methodism would be unnecessary.

Second, he wished to put into more scriptural terms the description of a perfect Christian he had found in the Stromateis *(or Miscellanies) of Clement of Alexandria (150–215). Clement, in the seventh book of this work, was concerned to contrast the true, i.e., the Christian, Gnostic with the bogus kind produced by the various Gnostic sects that abounded in the eastern part of the Roman Empire. He speaks of true 'gnosis' as being, not the acquisition of wisdom, but the knowledge of God in the heart through faith. Wesley greatly welcomed this account of a genuine Christian and echoes it at some length in the present work.*

Third, he wishes to give the proper meaning to the term 'Methodist', which, he points out, was not one that the Methodists had assumed, but one that had been thrust upon them in Oxford at the time of the Holy Club.

In the course of the argument Wesley makes use of a distinction vital for the understanding of his 'practical divinity' and his 'catholic spirit': the distinction between central articles of faith and opinions. 'Opinions' in Wesley's use of the term are considered and deliberate convictions on matters of faith and practice held by churches and individuals, which do not affect fundamental matters of faith; they are to be treated with respect, but should not divide Christians from one another. For Wesley's most striking use of this distinction see his sermon on a 'Catholic Spirit', (Sermon 39, 2:81-95 in this edn.).

For a summary of the nineteen English editions published during Wesley's lifetime, a stemma illustrating the transmission of the text, and a list of the substantive variant readings from the edited text (based on the 1st edn., Bristol, Farley, 1742), see Appendix A, pp. 541ff. For full bibliographical details see Bibliography, *No. 57 in this edition.*

The Character of a Methodist

Not as tho' I had already attained.[1]

To the Reader

1. Since the name first came abroad into the world, many have been at a loss to know what a 'Methodist' is; what are the *principles* and the *practice* of those who are commonly called by that name; and what the *distinguishing marks* of this 'SECT which is everywhere spoken against'.[2]

2. And it being generally believed that I was able to give the clearest account of these things (as having been one of the first to whom that name was given, and the person by whom the rest were supposed to be directed), I have been called upon, in all manner of ways, and with the utmost earnestness, so to do. I yield at last to the continued importunity both of friends and enemies, and do now give the clearest account I can, in the presence of the Lord and Judge of heaven and earth, of the *principles* and *practice* whereby those who are called 'Methodists' are distinguished from other men.

3. I say 'those who are called Methodists', for let it be well observed that this is not a name which they take to themselves, but one fixed upon them by way of reproach, without their approbation or consent. It was first given to three or four young men at Oxford, by Mr. John Bingham, then Student of Christ

[1] Phil. 3:12*a*.

[2] Cf. Acts 28:22. Here and in §17 Wesley prints 'sect' in small capitals as if to emphasize the falseness of the charge.

Church[3]—either in allusion to the ancient sect of physicians so called[4] (from their teaching that almost all diseases might be cured by a specific *method* of diet and exercise), or from their observing a more regular *method* of study and behaviour than was usual with those of their age and station.

4. I should still rejoice (so little ambitious am I to be the head[5] of any sect or party) if the very name might never be mentioned more, might[6] be buried in eternal oblivion. But if that cannot be, at least let those who *will* use it, know the meaning of the word they use. Let us not always be fighting in the dark. Come, and let us look one another in the face. And perhaps some of you who hate *what I am called* may love what *I am* (by the grace of God);[7] or rather, what 'I follow after, if that I may apprehend that for which also I am apprehended of Christ Jesus'.[8]

* * * * * * * * * * * * *

1. The *distinguishing marks* of a Methodist are not his *opinions*[9] of any sort. His assenting to this or that scheme of religion, his embracing any particular set of notions, his espousing the judgment of one man or of another, are all quite wide of the point. Whosoever therefore imagines that a Methodist is a man of such or such an *opinion* is grossly ignorant of the whole affair; he mistakes the truth totally. We believe, indeed, that 'all Scripture is

[3] John Bingham (1709–35) was the second son of Richard Bingham of Bingham Melcombe, Dorset, by his wife Penelope. On both sides their families were old and distinguished. In 1721, at the age of twelve, John had been King's Scholar at Westminster School, whence he matriculated in 1725 at Christ Church, graduated B.A. in 1729, proceeded M.A. on Mar. 23, 1731/32, and died Aug. 17, 1735. During their early months he occasionally shared in the sessions of the Oxford Methodists (see Heitzenrater, 'John Wesley and the Oxford Methodists, 1725–35', Ph.D. diss., Duke Univ. 1972, pp. 96n., 110). Bingham's name was omitted from all editions of the pamphlet except the first, reading instead 'by a Student of Christ Church'.

[4] Cf. Samuel Johnson's *Dictionary* (1755): '1. A physician who practised by theory. "Our wariest physicians, not only chemists but *methodists,* Give it inwardly in several constitutions and distempers." *Boyle.* 2. One of a new kind of puritans lately arisen, so called from their profession to live by rules and in constant method.' Cf. *OED:* 'The distinctive epithet of one of the three ancient schools of physicians, holding views intermediate between those of the Dogmatic and the Empiric school'—with a reference to 'Thessalus, the Head of the Methodick sect in the Reign of Nero'.

[5] B onwards, 'at the head'.

[6] From the 6th edn. (H, 1747) onwards, 'but'.

[7] 1 Cor. 15:10.

[8] Phil. 3:12*b*.

[9] For a discussion of Wesley's 'sharp distinction between essential doctrines and non-essential opinions' see this edn., 1:86-87, and 11:22-23.

given by inspiration of God';[10] and herein are we distinguished from Jews, Turks, and infidels. We believe this written Word of God to be the *only and the sufficient*[11] rule both of Christian faith and practice; and herein we are fundamentally distinguished from those of the Romish Church. We believe Christ to be the Eternal Supreme God; and herein are we distinguished from the Socinians and Arians. But as to all opinions which do not strike at the root of Christianity we 'think and let think'.[12] So that whatsoever they are, whether right or wrong, they are no 'distinguishing marks' of a Methodist.

2. Neither are *words* or *phrases* of any sort. We do not place our religion, or any part of it, in being attached to any peculiar mode of speaking, any quaint or uncommon set of expressions. The most obvious, easy, common words wherein our meaning can be conveyed we prefer before others, both on ordinary occasions, and when we speak of the things of God. We never therefore willingly or designedly deviate from the most usual way of speaking, unless when we express Scripture truths in Scripture words—which, we presume, no Christian will condemn. Neither do we affect to use any particular expressions of Scripture more frequently than others, unless they are such as are more frequently used by the inspired writer themselves. So that it is as gross an error to place the marks of a Methodist in his *words* as in *opinions* of any sort.

3. Nor do we desire to be distinguished, by *actions, customs,* or *usages* of an *indifferent* nature. Our religion does not lie in doing what God has not enjoined, or abstaining from what he hath not forbidden. It does not lie in the form of our apparel, in the posture of our body, or the covering our heads; nor yet in abstaining from marriage, nor from meats and drinks, which are all good if received with thanksgiving. Therefore neither will any man who knows whereof he affirms fix the mark of a Methodist here, in any

[10] 2 Tim. 3:16.

[11] From the 5th edn. (G, 1745) onwards, '*only and sufficient*'—as also in the French translation of 1743 (F), 'la seule et suffisante régle'. The italicization of these words is probably for the sake of emphasis and does not indicate a quotation, since the words 'sole and sufficient' are not to be found in the Book of Common Prayer or the Homilies in this connection. The words are no doubt intended by Wesley to be a summary of Art. VI ('Of the Sufficiency of the Holy Scriptures for Salvation') and the question put to those about to be ordained as priests and to those about to be consecrated as bishops in the 1662 Ordinal: 'Are you persuaded that the Holy Scriptures contain sufficiently all doctrine required of necessity for eternal Salvation through faith in Jesus Christ?'

[12] Cf. the proverb, 'Live and let live.'

actions or customs purely indifferent, undetermined by the Word of God.

4. Nor, lastly, is he to be distinguished by laying the *whole stress* of religion on any *single part* of it. If you say, 'Yes, he is; for he thinks *we are saved by faith alone*.'[13] I answer, You do not understand the terms. By *salvation* he means holiness of heart and life. And this he affirms to spring from true *faith alone*. Can even a nominal Christian deny it? Is this placing a part of religion for the whole? 'Do we then make void the law through faith? God forbid! Yea, we establish the law.'[14] We do not place the whole of religion (as too many do, God knoweth) either in doing no harm, or in doing good, or in using the ordinances of God.[15] No, nor in all of them together, wherein we know by experience a man may labour many years, and at the end have no true religion at all, no more than he had at the beginning. Much less in any one of these; or, it may be in a scrap of one of them—like her who fancies herself a *virtuous* woman only because she's not a prostitute; or him who dreams he is an *honest* man merely because he does not rob or steal. May the Lord God of my fathers preserve me from such a poor, starved religion as this! Were this the mark of a Methodist I would sooner choose to be a *sincere* Jew, Turk, or pagan.

5. 'What then is the mark? Who is a Methodist, according to your own account?' I answer: a Methodist is one who has 'the love of God shed abroad in his heart by the Holy Ghost given unto him';[16] one who 'loves the Lord his God with all his heart, and with all his soul, and with all his mind, and with all his strength'.[17] God is the joy of his heart, and the desire of his soul, which is constantly crying out, 'Whom have I in heaven but thee? and there is none upon earth that I desire beside thee!'[18] My God and my all! Thou art the strength of my heart, and my portion for ever![19]

6. He is therefore happy in God, yea, always happy, as having in him 'a well of water springing up into everlasting life',[20] and 'overflowing his soul with peace and joy'.[21] 'Perfect love' having now 'cast out fear',[22] he 'rejoices evermore'.[23] He 'rejoices in the Lord always',[24] even 'in God his Saviour';[25] and in the Father,

[13] See Eph. 2:8.
[14] Rom. 3:31.
[15] See the basic divisions of Wesley's *General Rules*, §§4-6 (see below, pp. 70-73).
[16] Cf. Rom. 5:5.
[17] Cf. Mark 12:30.
[18] Ps. 73:25.
[19] See Ps. 73:26.
[20] John 4:14.
[21] Cf. Rom. 15:13.
[22] Cf. 1 John 4:18.
[23] Cf. 1 Thess. 5:16.
[24] Cf. Phil. 4:4.
[25] Cf. Luke 1:47.

'through our Lord Jesus Christ, by whom he hath now received the atonement'.[26] Having found 'redemption through his blood, the forgiveness of his sins',[27] he cannot but rejoice whenever he looks back on the horrible pit out of which he is delivered, when he sees 'all his transgressions blotted out as a cloud, and his iniquities as a thick cloud'.[28] He cannot but rejoice whenever he looks on the state wherein he now is, 'being justified freely',[29] and 'having peace with God through our Lord Jesus Christ'.[30] For 'he that believeth hath the witness' of this 'in himself';[31] being now 'the son of God' by FAITH, 'because he is a son, God hath sent forth the Spirit of his Son into his heart, crying out, Abba, Father.'[32] And 'the Spirit itself beareth witness with his spirit that he is a child of God.'[33] He rejoiceth also, whenever he looks forward, 'in hope of'[34] 'the glory that shall be revealed'.[35] Yea, this his joy is full, and all his bones cry out, 'Blessed be the God and Father of our Lord Jesus Christ, who, according to his abundant mercy, hath begotten *me* again to a living hope . . . of an inheritance incorruptible, undefiled, and that fadeth not away, reserved in heaven for *me*.'[36]

7. And he who hath his 'hope' thus 'full of immortality'[37] 'in everything giveth thanks', as knowing that 'this' (whatsoever it is) 'is the will of God in Christ Jesus concerning him.'[38] From him therefore he cheerfully receives all, saying 'Good is the will of the Lord';[39] and whether the Lord giveth or taketh away, equally 'blessing the name of the Lord'.[40] For he hath 'learned in whatsoever state he is, therewith to be content'.[41] He knoweth 'both how to be abased, and how to abound. Everywhere and in all things he is instructed, both to be full and to be hungry, both to abound and to suffer need.'[42] Whether in ease or pain, whether in sickness or health, whether in life or death, he giveth thanks from the ground of the heart to him who orders it for good; knowing that as 'every good gift cometh from above', so none but good can come 'from the Father of lights',[43] into whose hands he has wholly

[26] Cf. Rom. 5:11.
[27] Cf. Eph. 1:7.
[28] Cf. Isa. 44:22.
[29] Rom. 3:24.
[30] Cf. Rom. 5:1.
[31] 1 John 5:10.
[32] Cf. Gal. 4:5-7.
[33] Cf. Rom. 8:16.
[34] Rom. 5:2.
[35] 1 Pet. 5:1.
[36] Cf. 1 Pet. 1:3-4.
[37] Wisd. 3:4.
[38] Cf. 1 Thess. 5:18.
[39] Cf. 2 Kgs. 20:19; Isa. 39:8.
[40] Cf. Deut. 21:5, etc.
[41] Cf. Phil. 4:11.
[42] Cf. Phil. 4:12.
[43] Cf. Jas. 1:17.

committed his body and soul, 'as into the hands of a faithful Creator'.[44] He is therefore 'careful' (anxiously or uneasily careful) 'for nothing';[45] as having 'cast all his care on him that careth for him',[46] and 'in all things' resting on him, after 'making his requests known to him with thanksgiving'.[47]

8. For indeed he 'prays without ceasing'.[48] It is given him 'always to pray, and not to faint'.[49] Not that he is always in the house of prayer—though he neglects no opportunity of being there. Neither is he always on his knees, although he often is, or on his face, before the Lord his God. Nor yet is he always crying aloud to God, or calling upon him in words. For many times 'the Spirit maketh intercession for him, with groans that cannot be uttered.'[50] But at all times the language of his heart is this: 'Thou brightness of the eternal glory, unto thee is my mouth,[51] though without a voice, and my silence speaketh unto thee.' And this is true prayer, the lifting up the heart to God. This is the essence of prayer, and this alone.[52] But his heart is ever lifted up to God, at all times, and in all places. In this he is never hindered, much less interrupted, by any person or thing. In retirement or company, in leisure, business, or conversation, his heart is ever with the Lord. Whether he lie down or rise up, 'God is in all his thoughts';[53] he 'walks with God'[54] continually, having the loving eye of his mind still fixed upon him, and everywhere 'seeing him that is invisible'.[55]

9. And while he thus always exercises his love to God, by prayer without ceasing, rejoicing evermore, and in everything giving thanks,[56] this commandment is written in his heart, that 'he who loveth God, loves his brother also.'[57] And he accordingly 'loves his neighbour as himself';[58] he loves every man as his own soul.[59] His heart is full of love to all mankind, to every child of 'the Father of the spirits of all flesh'.[60] That a man is not personally

[44] Cf. 1 Pet. 4:19.
[45] Phil. 4:6.
[46] Cf. 1 Pet. 5:7.
[47] Cf. Phil. 4:6.
[48] Cf. 1 Thess. 5:17.
[49] Luke 18:1.
[50] Cf. Rom. 8:26.
[51] Both the printed errata and Wesley's MS alterations in his own copy of the 1772 *Works* replace the original 'mouth' with 'heart'.
[52] 1772 *Works* reduces the two sentences to one: 'And this is true prayer, and this alone.'
[53] Cf. Ps. 10:4.
[54] Cf. Gen. 6:9.
[55] Heb. 11:27.
[56] See 1 Thess. 5:16-18.
[57] 1 John 4:21.
[58] Cf. Mark 12:33.
[59] See 1 Sam. 18:1, 3, etc.
[60] Cf. Num. 16:22; 27:16; Heb. 12:9.

known to him is no bar to his love. No, nor that he is known to be such as he approves not, that he repays hatred for his goodwill. For he 'loves his enemies'; yea, and the enemies of God, 'the evil and the unthankful'.[61] And if it be not in his power to do good to them that hate him, yet he ceases not to pray for them, though they continue to spurn his love and still 'despitefully use him and persecute him'.[62]

10. For he is 'pure in heart'.[63] The love of God has purified his heart from all revengeful passions, from envy, malice, and wrath, from every unkind temper or malign affection. It hath cleansed him from pride and haughtiness of spirit, whereof alone cometh contention.[64] And he hath now 'put on bowels of mercies, kindness, humbleness of mind, meekness, long-suffering';[65] so that he 'forbears and forgives, if he had a quarrel against any; even as God in Christ hath forgiven him'.[66] And indeed all possible ground for contention,[67] on his part, is utterly cut off. For none can take from him what he desires; seeing he 'loves not the world, nor' any of 'the things of the world';[68] being now 'crucified to the world, and the world crucified to him';[69] being dead to all that is in the world, both to 'the lust of the flesh, the lust of the eye, and the pride of life'.[70] For 'all his desire is unto God', and to the remembrance of his name.[71]

11. Agreeable to this his one desire is the one design of his life, namely, 'not to do his own will, but the will of him that sent him'.[72] His one intention at all times and in all things is, not to please himself, but him whom his soul loveth. He has a single eye. And because 'his eye is single, his whole body is full of light'.[73] Indeed where the loving eye of the soul is continually fixed upon God, there can be no darkness at all, but 'the whole is light; as when the bright shining of a candle doth enlighten the house.'[74] God then reigns alone. All that is in the soul is holiness to the Lord.[75] There is not a motion in his heart but is according to his will. Every thought that arises points to him, and is in obedience to the law of Christ.[76]

[61] Cf. Luke 6:35.
[62] Cf. Matt. 5:44.
[63] Matt. 5:8.
[64] See Prov. 13:10.
[65] Col. 3:12.
[66] Cf. Col. 3:13.
[67] After 'ground for', H, L, M, insert 'pride and haughtiness of spirit, whereof alone cometh'—apparently a compositor's error, repeating the second sentence in this section.
[68] Cf. 1 John 2:15.
[69] Cf. Gal. 6:14.
[70] 1 John 2:16.
[71] Cf. Isa. 26:8.
[72] Cf. John 6:38.
[73] Cf. Matt. 6:22; Luke 11:34.
[74] Cf. Luke 11:36.
[75] See Exod. 28:36, etc.
[76] See 2 Cor. 10:5.

12. And the tree is known by its fruits.[77] For as he loves God, so 'he keeps his commandments.'[78] Not only some, or most of them, but all, from the least to the greatest. He is not content to 'keep the whole law, and offend in one point',[79] but has in all points 'a conscience void of offence towards God and towards man'.[80] Whatever God has forbidden he avoids; whatever God has enjoined he doth—and that whether it be little or great, hard or easy, joyous or grievous to the flesh. He 'runs the way of God's commandments, now he hath set his heart at liberty'.[81] It is his glory, I say,[82] so to do; it is his daily crown of rejoicing to 'do the will' of God 'on earth, as it is done in heaven';[83] knowing it is the highest privilege of 'the angels of God, of those that excel in strength, to fulfil his commandments, and hearken to the voice of his word'.[84]

13. All the commandments of God he accordingly keeps, and that with all his might. For his obedience is in proportion to his love, the source from whence it flows. And therefore, loving God with all his heart, he serves him with all his strength.[85] He continually presents his soul and body a living sacrifice, holy, acceptable to God;[86] entirely and without reserve devoting himself, all he has, and all he is, to his glory. All the talents he has received he constantly employs according to his Master's will; every power and faculty of his soul, every member of his body. Once he 'yielded' them 'unto sin' and the devil, 'as instruments of unrighteousness'; but now, 'being alive from the dead, he yields' them all 'as instruments of righteousness unto God'.[87]

14. By consequence, whatsoever he doth, it is all to the glory of God.[88] In all his employments of every kind he not only *aims* at this (which is implied in having a single eye)[89] but actually *attains* it. His business and refreshments, as well as his prayers, all serve to this great end. Whether he sit in his house or walk by the way, whether he lie down or rise up,[90] he is promoting in all he speaks

77 See Matt. 12:33.

78 Cf. John 14:21.

79 Cf. Jas. 2:10.

80 Cf. Acts 24:16.

81 Cf. Ps. 119:32 (BCP).

82 See §6 above. Possibly not understanding this reference, the 1743 Newcastle edn. and others changed 'I say' to 'and joy', which later edns. (from 1763 onwards) omitted completely (see Appendix A for details).

83 Cf. Matt. 6:10.

84 Cf. Ps. 103:20 (BCP).

85 See Mark 12:30, etc.

86 See Rom. 12:1.

87 Cf. Rom. 6:13.

88 See 1 Cor. 10:31.

89 Matt. 6:22, etc.; see §11 above.

90 See Deut. 6:7; 11:19.

or does the one business of his life; whether he put on his apparel, or labour, or eat and drink, or divert himself from too wasting labour, it all tends to advance the glory of God by peace and goodwill among men. His one invariable rule is this: 'Whatsoever ye do in word or deed, do it all in the name of the Lord Jesus, giving thanks to God and the Father by him.'[91]

15. Nor do the customs of the world at all hinder his 'running the race which is set before him'.[92] He knows that vice does not lose its nature, though it become ever so fashionable; and remembers that 'every man is to give an account of himself to God.'[93] He cannot, therefore, even 'follow a multitude to do evil'.[94] He cannot 'fare sumptuously every day',[95] or 'make provision for the flesh, to fulfil the lusts thereof'.[96] He cannot 'lay up treasures upon earth',[97] any[98] more than he can take fire into his bosom.[99] He cannot 'adorn himself' (on any pretence) 'with gold or costly apparel'.[1] He cannot join in or countenance any diversion which has the least tendency to vice of any kind. He cannot *speak evil* of his neighbour, any more than he can lie, either for God or man. He cannot utter an unkind word of anyone; for love keeps the door of his lips.[2] He cannot speak *idle words;* 'no corrupt communication ever comes out of his mouth,' as is all that 'which is' not 'good to the use of edifying', not 'fit to minister grace to the hearers'.[3] But 'whatsoever things are pure, whatsoever things are lovely, whatsoever things are' justly 'of good report',[4] he thinks, and speaks, and acts, 'adorning the gospel of our Lord Jesus Christ in all things'.[5]

[91] Cf. Col. 3:17.
[92] Cf. Heb. 12:1.
[93] Cf. Rom. 14:12.
[94] Cf. Exod. 23:2.
[95] Cf. Luke 16:19.
[96] Cf. Rom. 13:14.
[97] Cf. Matt. 6:19.
[98] Orig., here and three lines below, 'no', altered by Wesley both in the printed errata to his *Works*, 1772, and in his own corrected copy thereof, to 'any'.
[99] See Prov. 6:27.
[1] Cf. 1 Tim. 2:9.
[2] See Ps. 141:3.
[3] Cf. Eph. 4:29.
[4] Phil. 4:8.
[5] Cf. Titus 2:10; for this translation see Wesley's *Explanatory Notes upon the New Testament* (henceforth *Notes*). N.B. Wesley's *Plain Account of Christian Perfection*, §10 (1766), incorporates an abridged and slightly revised version of §§5-15 of *The Character of a Methodist*.

16. Lastly, as he has time, he 'does good unto all men'[6]—unto neighbours, and strangers, friends, and enemies. And that in every possible kind; not only to their bodies, by 'feeding the hungry, clothing the naked, visiting those that are sick or in prison',[7] but much more does he labour to do good to their souls, as of the ability which God giveth:[8] to awaken those that sleep in death; to bring those who are awakened to the atoning blood, that 'being justified by FAITH'[9] they may have peace with God; and to provoke those who have peace with God to abound more in love and in good works. And he is willing to 'spend and to be spent herein',[10] even to 'be offered upon the sacrifice and service of their faith',[11] so they may 'all come unto the measure of the stature of the fullness of Christ'.[12]

17. These are the *principles* and *practices* of our SECT; these are the *marks* of a true Methodist.[13] By these alone do those who are in derision so called desire to be distinguished from other men. If any man say, 'Why, these are[14] only the common, fundamental principles of Christianity'—'Thou hast said.'[15] So I mean. This is the very truth. I know they are no other, and I would to God both thou and all men knew that I, and all who follow my judgment, do vehemently refuse to be distinguished from other men by any but the common principles of Christianity—the plain, old Christianity that I teach, renouncing and detesting all other marks of distinction. And whosoever *is* what I *preach* (let him be *called* what he will; for names change not the nature of things) he is a Christian, not in *name* only, but in *heart* and in *life*. He is inwardly and outwardly conformed to the will of God, as revealed in the written Word. *He thinks, speaks, and lives according to the* 'method' *laid down in the revelation of Jesus Christ.*[16] His soul is 'renewed after the image of God',[17] 'in righteousness and in all true holiness'.[18] And 'having the mind that was in Christ'[19] he 'so walks as' Christ 'also walked'.[20]

[6] Cf. Gal. 6:10.
[7] Cf. Matt. 25:35-36.
[8] 1 Pet. 4:11.
[9] Rom. 5:1.
[10] Cf. 2 Cor. 12:15.
[11] Cf. Phil. 2:17.
[12] Cf. Eph. 4:13.
[13] See Pref. 1.
[14] 1st edn., 'are these'.
[15] Matt. 26:64.
[16] Cf. §14 above.
[17] Cf. Col. 3:10.
[18] Cf. Eph. 4:24.
[19] Cf. Phil. 2:5.
[20] Cf. 1 John 2:6.

18. By these *marks*, by these fruits of a living faith, do we labour to *distinguish* ourselves from the unbelieving world, from all those whose minds or lives are not according to the gospel of Christ. But from real Christians, of whatsoever denomination they be, we earnestly desire not to be distinguished at all. Nor from any who sincerely follow after what they know they have not yet attained. No: 'Whosoever doth the will of my Father which is in heaven, the same is my brother and sister and mother.'[21] And I beseech you, brethren, by the mercies of God,[22] that we be in no wise divided among ourselves. 'Is thy heart right, as my heart is with thine?' I ask no farther question. 'If it be, give me thy hand.'[23] For opinions, or terms, let us 'not destroy the work of God'.[24] Dost thou love and serve God? It is enough. I give thee the right hand of fellowship.[25] 'If there be any consolation in Christ, if any comfort of love, if any fellowship of the Spirit, if any bowels and mercies',[26] let us 'strive together for the faith of the gospel';[27] 'walking worthy of the vocation wherewith we are called, with all lowliness and meekness, with long-suffering, forbearing one another in love, endeavouring to keep the unity of the Spirit in the bond of peace'; remembering, 'there is one body and one Spirit, even as we are called with one hope of our calling;[28] one Lord, one faith, one baptism; one God and Father of all, who is above all, and through all, and in you all!'[29]

[21] Cf. Matt. 12:50.
[22] See Rom. 12:1.
[23] Cf. 2 Kgs. 10:15, and Sermon 39, 'Catholic Spirit' (1750).
[24] Cf. Rom. 14:20.
[25] For this characteristic phrase cf. JWJ, Mar. 28, 1741; 'A Short History of the People called Methodists' (1781), §131; and JWJ, Oct. 16, 1787.
[26] Phil. 2:1.
[27] Cf. Phil. 1:27.
[28] A-D (surely in error) read 'with hope of our one calling'; E, G, H, M, 'with hope of our calling' (one copy of M adding the MS correction 'one'); F, 'Comme il y a une esperance de notre seule vocation' ('As there is one hope of our one calling'); L, 'with the hope of our calling'; I-K, P-U (including Wesley's own copy of his *Works*) the text as presented.
[29] Cf. Eph. 1:4-6.

The Whole Armour of God[30]

Ephesians 6

1. Soldiers of Christ, arise,
And put your armour on,
Strong in the strength which God supplies
Through his eternal Son;
Strong in the Lord of Hosts,
And in his mighty power,
Who in the strength of Jesus trusts
Is more than conqueror.

2. Stand then in his great might,
With all his strength endued,
And take, to arm you for the fight,
The panoply of God;
That having all things done,
And all your conflicts passed,
Ye may o'ercome through Christ alone,
And stand entire at last.

3. Stand then against your foes
In close and firm array;
Legions of wily fiends oppose
Throughout the evil day;
But meet the sons of night,
But mock their vain design,
Armed in the arms of heavenly light,
In righteousness divine.[31]

4. Leave no unguarded place,
No weakness of the soul,
Take every virtue, every grace,
And fortify the whole;
Indissolubly joined,
To battle all proceed,
But arm yourselves with all the mind
That was in Christ your head.

5. Let truth the girdle be
That binds your armour on;

[30] The title is from Eph. 6:13. This poem by Charles Wesley appears only as an appendix to the first three Bristol editions of the pamphlet, A, B, and D. It was also published about the same time as a broadsheet, and included by Charles Wesley in his *Hymns and Sacred Poems* (1749), I.236-39. John Wesley published it also in his *Select Hymns* of 1761 (*Bibliography,* No. 244.ii), and (with some omissions) in his *Collection of Hymns for the Use of the People called Methodists,* Hymns 258-60 (see 7:399-403 in this edn.).

[31] Broadsheet, 'And righteousness'; 1749, 1780, 'of righteousness'.

In faithful firm sincerity
To Jesus cleave alone;
Let faith and love combine
To guard your valiant breast;
The plate be righteousness divine,
Imputed and impressed.

6. Still let your feet be shod,
Ready his will to do,
Ready in all the ways of God
His glory to pursue:
Ruin is spread beneath,
The gospel greaves put on,
And safe through all the snares of death
To life eternal run.

7. But above all, lay hold
On *faith's* victorious shield;
Armed with that adamant and gold
Be sure to win the field;
If faith surround your heart,
Satan shall be subdued,
Repelled his every fiery dart,
And quenched with Jesu's blood.

8. Jesus hath died for you!
What can his love withstand?
Believe, hold fast your shield, and who
Shall pluck you from his hand?
Believe that Jesus reigns,
All power to him is giv'n;
Believe, till freed from sin's remains,
Believe yourselves to heaven.

9. Your Rock can never shake:
Hither, he saith, come up!
The helmet of salvation take,
The confidence of hope:
Hope for his perfect love,
Hope for his people's rest,
Hope to sit down with Christ above
And share the marriage feast.

10. Brandish in faith till then
The Spirit's two-edged sword,
Hew all the snares of fiends and men
In pieces with the Word;
'Tis *written;* this applied
Baffles their strength and art;
Spirit and soul with this divide,
And joints and marrow part.

11. To keep your armour bright
Attend with constant care,
Still walking in your Captain's sight,
And watching unto prayer;
Ready for all alarms,
Steadfastly set your face,
And always exercise your arms,
And use your every grace.

12. Pray, without ceasing pray
(Your Captain gives the word),
His summons cheerfully obey,
And call upon the Lord;
To God your every want
In instant prayer display,
Pray always; pray, and never faint;
Pray, without ceasing pray.

13. In fellowship, alone,
To God with faith draw near;
Approach his courts, besiege his throne
With all the power of prayer;
Go to his temple, go,
Nor from his altar move;[32]
Let every house his worship know,
And every heart his love.

14. To God your spirits dart,
Your souls in words declare,
Or groan, to him who reads the heart,
Th' unutterable prayer.
His mercy now implore
And now show forth his praise,
In shouts, or silent awe, adore
His miracles of grace.

15. Pour out your souls to God,
And bow them with your knees,
And spread your hearts and hands abroad,
And pray for Zion's peace;
Your guides and brethren bear
Forever on your mind;
Extend the arms of mighty prayer
Ingrasping all mankind.[33]

[32] Broadsheet, 'table'.

[33] All the early edns. agree in this coining of the word 'ingrasping' by Wesley, rather than in its division into two words, which occurred in later edns.

16. From strength to strength go on,
Wrestle, and fight, and pray;
Tread all the powers of darkness down,
And win the well-fought day;
Still let the Spirit cry
In all his soldiers, 'Come!'
Till Christ the Lord descends from high.
And takes the conqu'rors home.

2

THE PRINCIPLES OF A METHODIST (1742)

AN INTRODUCTORY COMMENT

This is a direct reply to the long pamphlet of Josiah Tucker, A Brief History of the Principles of Methodism, wherein the Rise and Progress, together with the Causes of the several Variations, Divisions, and present Inconsistencies of this Sect are attempted to be traced out, and accounted for *(published in July 1742). For this see Richard Green,* Anti-Methodist Publications *(London, Kelly, 1902), No. 150.*

Josiah Tucker (1712–99) was a formidable opponent. He was an undergraduate at Oxford during the heyday of the Holy Club and after ordination had become Vicar of All Saints, Bristol, and Chaplain to the Bishop of Bristol (Joseph Butler), who had picked him out as a man of distinct promise for the future. In 1758 he became Dean of Gloucester, without relinquishing his cure in Bristol, and remained so until his death.

He became well known in Bristol and beyond for his writings on trade and economics, though his larger works on the subject were published after his death. Indeed the claim has been made for him that he anticipated many of the ideas of Adam Smith; certainly he predicted the independence and development of America, accompanied by the decline of the European powers.

His work on Methodism was commissioned by Hugh Boulter (1672–1742), translated from the see of Bristol in 1724 to become Archbishop of Armagh. The most recent Bishop of Bristol (from 1738) was Joseph Butler (1692–1752), who had already crossed swords with Wesley. Just after the meeting on July 16, 1739, between Wesley and the bishop, in which Wesley was advised by Butler to leave his diocese, and Wesley refused, Tucker preached a sermon in All Saints which seemed to Wesley to proclaim justification 'on account of our own righteousness'. This was reported by Wesley to the bishop. On July 19 Wesley was interviewed by the bishop with Tucker in attendance to defend himself. The interview was inconclusive (see Frank Baker, 'John Wesley and Bishop Joseph Butler', WHS, 42:93-100).

In The Principles of Methodism *Tucker pointed out Wesley's dependence on William Law and the Moravians, his combination of Calvinist and Arminian ideas, and charged him with serious inconsistency.*

Acknowledging that Tucker's argument was cool and dispassionate, Wesley in his reply sets out in full his teaching on salvation and Christian perfection, claims that Tucker has overestimated his dependence on Law and the Moravians, and criticizes in detail Tucker's summary of his beliefs.

Apart from its controversial aspect, the treatise sheds great light on Wesley's relations with his Moravian teachers, who perhaps influenced him more than he is willing to concede.

For a summary of the seven British editions published during Wesley's lifetime, a stemma illustrating the transmission of the text, and a list of the substantive variant readings from the edited text (based on the 1st edn., Bristol, Farley, 1742), see Appendix A, pp. 541ff. For fuller bibliographical details see Bibliography, *No. 67.*

The Principles of a Methodist

To the Reader

1. I have often wrote on *controverted points* before; but not with an eye to *any* particular person. So that this is the first time I have appeared in *controversy* properly so called. Indeed I have not wanted occasion to do it before. Particularly when, after many stabs in the dark, I was publicly attacked, not by an open enemy, but by 'my own familiar friend'.[1] But I *could* not answer *him.* I could only cover my face and say, καὶ σύ ἐκείνων; καὶ σύ, τέκνον;[2] 'Art thou also among them? Art thou, my son?'

2. I now tread an untried path with fear and trembling—fear, not of my adversary, but of myself. I fear my own spirit, lest I 'fall,

[1] Ps. 41:9 (BCP).

[2] According to Suetonius, *Lives of the Twelve Caesars: The Deified Julius,* 82, the words of Julius Caesar as Brutus stabbed him. Cf. *The Doctrine of Original Sin* (Bristol, Farley, 1757), VI.vi (Vol. 12 in this edn.); and Charles Wesley to JW, Mar. 16-17, 1741 (26:54 in this edn.).

where many mightier have been slain'.[3] I never knew one (or but one) man write controversy with what I thought a right spirit. Every disputant seems to think (as every soldier) that he *may* hurt his opponent as much as he *can;* nay, that he ought to *do his worst* to him, or he cannot *make the best* of his own cause; that, so he do not belie or wilfully misrepresent him, *he must expose* him as far as he is able. It is enough, we suppose, if we do not show heat or passion against our adversary. But not to despise him, or endeavour to make others do so, is quite a work of supererogation.

3. But ought these things to be so? (I speak on the Christian scheme.) Ought we not to love our neighbour as ourselves?[4] And does a man cease to be our neighbour because he is of a different opinion? Nay, and declares himself so to be? Ought we not, for all this, to do to him as we would he should do to us?[5] But do we ourselves love to be *exposed* or *set in the worst light?* Would we willingly be treated with contempt? If not, why do we treat others thus? And yet who scruples it? Who does not hit every blot[6] he can, however foreign to the merits of the cause? Who, in controversy, casts the mantle of love over the nakedness of his brother? Who keeps steadily and uniformly to the question, without ever striking at the person? Who shows in every sentence that he loves his brother, only less than the truth?[7]

4. I have made a little faint essay towards this. I have a brother who is as my own soul.[8] My desire is in every word I say to look upon Mr. Tucker[9] as in his place; and to speak no tittle concerning the one in any other spirit than I would speak concerning the other. But whether I have attained this or no, I know not; for my heart is 'deceitful and desperately wicked'.[10] If I

[3] This is surely a line from a poem, but the source seems to be irrecoverable. For the sentiment cf. 2 Sam. 1:10. For a repeated use see *The Principles of a Methodist Farther Explained,* §3, p. 162 below.

[4] See Lev. 19:18; Matt. 5:43, etc.

[5] See Matt. 7:12; Luke 6:31.

[6] To take an exposed piece in backgammon. Altered in 1777, 1789, to 'hit every blow'.

[7] All except the opening clause of §§2-3 are repeated by Wesley in *The Principles of a Methodist Farther Explained,* §§3-4 (see below, pp. 162-63).

[8] See 1 Sam. 18:1. John here seems to refer to his brother Charles.

[9] Tucker's *A Brief History of the Principles of Methodism, wherein the Rise and Progress, together with the Causes of the several Variations, Divisions, and present Inconsistencies of this Sect are attempted to be traced out, and accounted for* (Oxford, Fletcher), 51 pp., was dedicated to the Archbishop of Armagh, who had commissioned him in June 1741, to 'get him an authentic account of the divisions and quarrels of the Methodists', and then desired its publication.

[10] Jer. 17:9.

have spoken anything in another spirit I pray God it may not be laid to my charge![11] And that it may not condemn me in that day when the secrets of all hearts shall be made manifest![12] Meanwhile my heart's desire and prayer to God is that both I and all who think it their duty to oppose me may 'put on bowels of mercies, kindness, humbleness of mind, meekness, long-suffering; forbearing one another, and forgiving one another, even as God for Christ's sake hath forgiven us'.[13]

* * * * * * * * * * * *

1. There has lately appeared in the world a tract entitled, *A Brief History of the Principles of Methodism.*[14] I doubt not but the writer's design was good, and believe he has a real desire to know the truth. And the manner wherein he pursues that design is generally calm and dispassionate. He is indeed in several mistakes; but as many of these are either of small consequence in themselves, or do not immediately relate to me, it is not my concern to mention them. All of any consequence which relates to me, I think, falls under three heads:

First, that I believe justification by faith alone;

Secondly, that I believe sinless perfection; and

Thirdly, that I believe inconsistencies—Of each of these I will speak as plainly as I can.

2. First, that I believe *justification by faith alone.*[15] This I allow. For I am firmly persuaded that every man of the offspring of Adam is very far gone from original righteousness, and is, of his own nature, inclined to evil; that this corruption of our nature, in every person born into the world, deserves God's wrath and damnation; that therefore if ever we receive the remission of our sins and are accounted righteous before God, it must be only for the merits of Christ, by faith, and not for our own works or deservings of any kind. Nay, I am persuaded that all works done

[11] See Ps. 35:11; 2 Tim. 4:16.

[12] See 1 Cor. 14:25.

[13] Cf. Col. 3:12-13.

[14] See above, n. 9.

[15] See *Brief History*, pp. 32-36, where (having recounted Wesley's spiritual history from his *Journal*) Tucker summarizes from the *Journal* the 'system (or rather the *medley*) of principles' with which he returned to England from Germany, under the headings, 'Of the Assurances of Justification', 'Of the Conditions of Justification', and 'Of the Effects of Justification'.

before justification have in them the nature of sin; and that, consequently, till he is justified a man has no power to do any work which is pleasing and acceptable to God.

3. To express my meaning a little more at large. I believe three things must go together in our justification: upon God's part, his great mercy and grace; upon Christ's part, the satisfaction of God's justice by the offering his body and shedding his blood, 'and fulfilling the law of God perfectly'; and upon our part, true and living faith in the merits of Jesus Christ. So that in our justification there is not only God's mercy and grace, but his justice also. And so the grace of God does not shut out the righteousness of God in our justification, but only shuts out the righteousness of man, that is the righteousness of our works.[16]

4. And therefore St. Paul requires nothing on the part of man but 'only a true and living faith'.[17] Yet this faith does not shut out repentance, hope, and love, which are joined with faith in every man that is justified. But it shuts them out from the office of justifying. So that although they are all present together in him that is justified, yet they justify not all together.[18]

5. Neither does faith shut out good works, necessarily to be done afterwards. But 'we may not do them to this intent, to be justified by doing them.' Our justification comes freely, of the mere mercy of God. For whereas all the world was not able to pay any part towards their ransom it pleased him, without any of our deserving, to prepare for us Christ's body and blood, whereby our ransom might be paid, 'his law fulfilled, and his justice satisfied'. Christ therefore is now the righteousness of all them that truly believe in him. 'He for them paid the ransom by his death. He for them fulfilled the law in his life.' So that now in him, and by him, every believer may be called a fulfiller of the law.[19]

16 *Certain Sermons or Homilies appointed by the King's Majesty* (1547), one of Wesley's major documents in proving that Methodism set forth the genuine teaching of the Church of England (cf. §10 below); henceforth, 'Homilies, "Of Salvation", Pt. I', etc., abridged by Wesley in *The Doctrine of Salvation, Faith, and Good Works,* I.5, of which this paragraph is almost a reprint, with the addition of the phrase quoted from the Homily: 'with fulfilling of the law perfectly and throughly' (for this pamphlet see *Bibliography,* No. 11, and Vol. 12 in this edn.).

17 Homilies, 'Of Salvation', Pt. I, a quotation, as the whole paragraph is in effect, of Wesley's *Doctrine of Salvation,* I.6.

18 1777, 1789, 'altogether'.

19 Homilies, 'Of Salvation', Pt. I, the whole paragraph being a summary of the closing passage, with Wesley indicating (by italics) three passages as being specific quotations, though in fact much of the remainder is also quoted with fair accuracy and fullness. From his *Works,* 1772, Wesley omitted the last two sentences.

6. But let it be observed, the true sense of those words, 'We are justified by faith in Christ only,'[20] is not that this our own act 'to believe in Christ', or this our faith which is within us justifies us (for that were to account ourselves to be justified by some act or virtue that is within us); but that, although we have faith, hope, and love within us, and do never so many good works, yet we must renounce the merit of all, of faith, hope, love, and all other virtues and good works, which we either have done, shall do, or can do, as far too weak to deserve our justification; for which therefore we must trust only in God's mercy and the merits of Christ. For it is he alone that taketh away our sins. To him alone are we to go for this; forsaking all our virtues, good words, thoughts, and works, and putting our trust in Christ only.

7. In strictness, therefore, neither our faith nor our works justify us, i.e., deserve the remission of our sins. But God himself justifies us, of his own mercy, through the merits of his Son only. Nevertheless, because by faith we embrace the promise of God's mercy and of the remission of our sins, therefore the Scripture says that *faith does justify*, yea, *faith without works*. And as it is all one to say, 'faith without works', and 'faith alone justifies us,' therefore the ancient fathers from time to time speak thus: 'Faith alone justifies us.' And because we receive faith through the only merits of Christ, and not through the merit of any virtue we have, or work we do; therefore in that respect we renounce, as it were, again, faith, works, and all other virtues. For our corruption through original sin is so great that all our faith, charity, words, and works, cannot merit or deserve any part of our justification for us. And therefore we thus speak, humbling ourselves before God, and giving Christ all the glory of our justification.[21]

8. But it should also be observed what that faith is whereby we are justified. Now that faith which brings not forth good works is not a living faith, but a dead and devilish one. For even the devils believe that 'Christ was born of a virgin, that he wrought all kind of miracles, declaring himself to be very God, that for our sakes he died and rose again and ascended into heaven, and at the end of the world shall come again to judge the quick and the dead.'[22]

[20] Cf. Homilies, 'Of Salvation', Pt. II, the closing section, incorporating in the whole paragraph slightly more than in I.10 of Wesley's *Doctrine of Salvation.*

[21] Ibid., Pt. III; and Wesley, *Doctrine of Salvation,* I.12.

[22] Ibid., Pt. III; cf. for the whole paragraph Wesley, *Doctrine of Salvation,* I.13. The Homily paraphrases the Nicene Creed.

This the devils believe, and so they believe all that is written in the Old and New Testament. And yet still, for all this faith, they are but devils. They remain still in their damnable estate, lacking the true Christian faith.

9. The true Christian faith is not only to believe the Holy Scriptures and the articles of our faith are true, but also to have 'a sure trust and confidence to be saved from everlasting damnation by Christ', whereof doth follow a loving heart, to obey his commandments.[23] And this faith neither any devil hath, nor any wicked man. No ungodly man hath, or can have, this 'sure trust and confidence in God that, by the merits of Christ, his sins are forgiven and he reconciled to the favour of God'.[24]

10. This is what I believe (and have believed for some years) concerning *justification by faith alone*. I have chose to express it in the words of a little treatise, published several years ago; as being the most authentic proof, both of my past and present sentiments.[25] If I err herein, let those who are better informed calmly point out my error to me. And I trust I shall not shut my eyes against the light, from whatsoever side it comes.

11. The second thing laid to my charge is that *I believe sinless perfection*.[26] I will simply declare what I do believe concerning this also, and leave unprejudiced men to judge.

12. My last and most deliberate thoughts on this head were published but a few months[27] since, in these words:[28]

(1). Perhaps the general prejudice against *Christian perfection* may chiefly arise from a misapprehension of the *nature* of it. We willingly allow, and continually declare, there is no *such* perfection in this life as implies either a dispensation from doing good and attending all the ordinances of God; or a freedom from ignorance, mistake, temptation, and a thousand infirmities necessarily connected with flesh and blood.

(2). First, we not only allow, but 'earnestly contend' (as 'for the faith once delivered to the saints'),[29] that there is no such perfection in this life as implies

[23] Ibid. Cf. Wesley, *Doctrine of Salvation*, I.14, the whole sentence, italicized throughout, forming the complete paragraph.

[24] Ibid. Cf. Wesley, *Doctrine of Salvation*, I.15. The latter became one of Wesley's favourite definitions of faith. Cf. *An Earnest Appeal*, §59 (11:69 in this edn.).

[25] *The Doctrine of Salvation* . . . , as noted above, p. 51, n. 16.

[26] See Tucker, *Brief History*, pp. 9-12, 37-43.

[27] The regular edns. from 1756 onwards change this to 'published a few years since'.

[28] In the following six paragraphs Wesley quotes the whole (almost exactly) of his preface to the *Hymns and Sacred Poems*, published by him and his brother Charles earlier in 1742 (see *Bibliography*, No. 54, and Vol. 12 in this edn.).

[29] Cf. Jude 3.

any dispensation from attending all the ordinances of God, or from 'doing good unto all men, while we have time', though 'especially unto the household of faith'.[30] And whosoever they are who have taught otherwise, we are convinced, are not 'taught of God'.[31] We dare not 'receive' them, 'neither bid them God speed', lest we be 'partakers of their evil deeds'.[32] We believe that not only the 'babes in Christ',[33] who have newly found redemption in his blood, but those also who are grown up 'unto perfect men, unto the measure of the stature of the fullness of Christ',[34] are indispensably obliged (and that they are obliged thereto is their 'glory and crown of rejoicing'),[35] as oft as they have opportunity, to eat bread and drink wine 'in remembrance of him';[36] to 'search the Scriptures';[37] by fasting (as well as temperance) to 'keep their bodies under, and bring them into subjection';[38] and above all to pour out their souls in prayer, both 'secretly' and 'in the great congregation'.[39]

(3). We secondly believe, and therefore speak, and that unto 'all men',[40] and 'with much assurance',[41] that there is no *such* perfection in this life as implies an entire deliverance either from ignorance or mistake in things not essential to salvation, or from manifold temptations, or from numberless infirmities, wherewith the corruptible body, more or less, presses down the soul.[42] This is the same thing which we have spoken from the beginning. If any teach otherwise, 'they are not of us.'[43] We cannot find any ground in Scripture to suppose that any inhabitant of an house of clay[44] is wholly exempt either from bodily infirmities, or from ignorance of many things; or to imagine any mere man is incapable of mistake, or of falling into divers temptations. No: 'The disciple is not above his master, nor the servant above his Lord.'[45] 'It is enough that everyone who is perfect shall be as his Master.'[46]

(4). But what then, it may be asked, do you mean by 'one that is perfect', or 'one that is as his Master'? We mean, one in whom is 'the mind which was in Christ',[47] and who so 'walketh as he also walked';[48] a man that 'hath clean hands and a pure heart';[49] or that is 'cleansed from all filthiness of flesh and spirit';[50] one 'in whom there is no occasion of stumbling',[51] and who accordingly 'doth not commit sin'.[52] To declare this a little more particularly, we understand by that scriptural expression 'A PERFECT MAN',[53] one in whom God hath fulfilled his faithful word, 'From all your filthiness and from all your idols will I cleanse you . . . I will also save you from all your uncleannesses.'[54] We understand hereby one whom God hath 'sanctified throughout', even in 'body, soul, and spirit';[55] one who 'walketh in the light, as he is in the light',[56] in whom 'is no darkness at all, the blood of Jesus Christ his Son having cleansed him from all sin'.[57]

[30] Cf. Gal. 6:10. [31] John 6:45. [32] 2 John 10-11.
[33] 1 Cor. 3:1. [34] Cf. Eph. 4:13. [35] Cf. 1 Thess. 2:19.
[36] Cf. Luke 22:19; 1 Cor. 11:24, 25. [37] John 5:39.
[38] Cf. 1 Cor. 9:27. [39] Cf. Ps. 111:1 (BCP). [40] Acts 22:15.
[41] 1 Thess. 1:5. [42] Cf. Wisd. 9:15. [43] Cf. 1 John 2:19.
[44] See Job 4:19. [45] Matt. 10:24; cf. Luke 6:40.
[46] Luke 6:40; cf. Matt. 10:25. [47] Cf. Phil. 2:5.
[48] Cf. 1 John 2:6. [49] Ps. 24:4.
[50] Cf. 2 Cor. 7:1. [51] Cf. 1 John 2:10.
[52] 1 John 3:9. [53] Job 8:20, etc. Cf. closing paragraph.
[54] Ezek. 36:25, 29. [55] Cf. 1 Thess. 5:23.
[56] Cf. 1 John 1:7. [57] 1 John 1:5, 7.

(5). This man can now testify to all mankind, 'I am crucified with Christ: nevertheless I live; yet not I, but Christ liveth in me.'[58] He is 'holy, as God who hath called him is holy', both in heart and 'in all manner of conversation'.[59] He 'loveth the Lord his God with all his heart', and 'serveth him with all his strength'.[60] He 'loveth his neighbour (every man) as himself';[61] yea, 'as Christ loved us'[62]—them in particular that 'despitefully use him and persecute him',[63] because 'they know not the Son, neither the Father'.[64] Indeed his soul is all love, filled with 'bowels of mercies, kindness, meekness, gentleness, long-suffering'.[65] And his life agreeth thereto, full of 'the work of faith, the patience of hope, the labour of love'.[66] And 'whatsoever he doth, either in word or deed', he doth 'it all in the name', in the love and power, 'of the Lord Jesus'.[67] In a word, he doth the will of God 'on earth as it is done in heaven'.[68]

This it is to be 'a perfect man', to be 'sanctified throughout',[69] 'created anew in Christ Jesus';[70] even 'to have a heart so all-flaming with the love of God' (to use Archbishop Ussher's words), 'as continually to offer up every thought, word, and work as a spiritual sacrifice, acceptable unto God through Christ'.[71] In every thought of our hearts, in every word of our tongues, in every work of our hands, 'to show forth his praise who hath called us out of darkness into his marvellous light'![72] O that both we and all who seek the Lord Jesus in sincerity, may thus 'be made perfect in one'![73]

13. If there be anything unscriptural in these words, anything wild or extravagant, anything contrary to the analogy of faith,[74] or the experience of adult Christians, let them 'smite me friendly and reprove me';[75] let them impart to me of the clearer light God has given them. How knowest thou, O man, 'but thou mayst gain thy brother'?[76] But he may at length come to the knowledge of the truth? And thy labour of love, shown forth with meekness of wisdom,[77] may not be in vain!

[58] Gal. 2:20.
[59] Cf. 1 Pet. 1:15. [60] Cf. Mark 12:30, etc.
[61] Ibid. [62] Cf. Eph. 5:2. [63] Cf. Matt. 5:44, etc.
[64] Cf. John 8:19. [65] Cf. Col. 3:12. [66] Cf. 1 Thess. 1:3.
[67] Cf. Col. 3:17. [68] Cf. Matt. 6:10. [69] See §12(4) above.
[70] Cf. 2 Cor. 5:17; Eph. 2:10.

[71] James Ussher (1581–1656), Archbishop of Armagh. The exact passage has not been identified in any of his voluminous writings, but cf. *A Body of Divinitie* (5th edn., London, Owsley and Lillicrap, 1658), p. 176: 'We receive an high degree of felicity by the second Adam . . . , who carrieth us as our Head unto the highest degree of happiness in the kingdom of heaven, where we shall lead, not a natural life, . . . but a spiritual life in all unspeakable manner and glory. . . . Being sanctified by him . . . we have freedom and boldness to draw near and offer ourselves, souls, and bodies, and all that we have, as a reasonable sacrifice to God the Father . . . made acceptable unto God . . . by the merit and intercession of the same our High Priest.' Cf. Wesley's *Letter to the Bishop of London*, 1747, §8, which quotes much of this same preface (see 11:339-40 in this edn.).

[72] Cf. 1 Pet. 2:9. [73] John 17:23.

[74] The general sense of Scripture. See Sermon 5, 'Justification by Faith', §2, and lengthy note (1:183 and n. 4 in this edn.).

[75] Ps. 141:5 (BCP). [76] Cf. Matt. 18:15. [77] Jas. 3:13.

14. There remains yet another charge against me, that I believe *inconsistencies,* that my tenets, particularly concerning justification, are *contradictory to themselves;*[78] that Mr. Wesley, 'since his return from Germany, has *improved* in the spirit of *inconsistency*. For then he published [extracts of] two treatises of Dr. Barnes's, the Calvinist, or Dominican rather, who suffered in 1541': (Let us spare the ashes of the dead. Were I *such* a Dominican as he was, I should rejoice too to die in the flames)—'the first on *Justification by Faith Only,* the other on *The Sinfulness of Man's Natural Will, and his utter Inability to do Works acceptable to God, until he be justified.* Which principles if added to his former tenets' (Nay, they need not be *added to* them, for they are the very same) 'will give the whole a *new vein of inconsistency,* and make the *contradictions* more gross and glaring than before.'[79]

15. It will be necessary to speak more largely on this head than on either of the preceding. And, in order to speak as distinctly as I can, I propose taking the paragraphs one by one as they lie before me.

16. (1). It is 'asserted that Mr. Law's system was the *creed* of the Methodists'.[80] But it is not *proved.* I had been eight years at Oxford before I read any of Mr. Law's writings.[81] And when I did

[78] Cf. Tucker, *Brief History,* p. 35: 'I believe an hundred other *absurdities* might be fully and fairly made out. . . . Only let me observe that upon his return from Germany he seemed to *improve* in the spirit of inconsistency.' In the following pages Tucker claimed that 'Mr. Wesley has made an essay towards reconciling these *jarring elements,* and reducing them into some kind of order and uniformity', by describing three spiritual stages: 'before *justification*', 'after *justification*', and '*sanctification,* the last and highest state of perfection in this life'.

[79] Ibid., p. 35. Tucker refers to *Two Treatises. The first, On Justification by Faith only. . . . The second, On the Sinfulness of Man's natural Will* (London, Lewis, 1739), from the works of Robert Barnes (1495–1540), together with an extract of his life from Foxe's *Book of Martyrs;* see *Bibliography,* No. 16.

[80] Tucker, p. 21: 'Having before laid down Mr. Law's system and asserted that it was the *creed* of the Methodists, I can come now directly to observe that Mr. John Wesley seemed to have set out for Georgia without any alterations at all.' (For Tucker's account of how the Oxford Methodists 'chose to put themselves chiefly under the direction of the writings of Mr. William Law', see pp. 7-21, dealing espec. with Whitefield.)

The subsidiary sectional number, '(1)', like the '(2)' used for I.18, and others later, refers to the section numbers in the second part of Tucker's work, 1-20 (pp. 21-51).

[81] Wesley entered Oxford in the summer of 1720, and began to prescribe Law's *Serious Call* to his students in 1730. There is no solid evidence about Wesley's own first reading of Law, his diary being missing from Feb. 1727 to Apr. 1729; his name does not occur in the extant diaries from 1726 to 1730. Although the argument from silence is inconclusive, Wesley's memory for dates was notoriously erratic, and the implication of his *Journal* (May 24, 1738, §5), 'In 1727 I read Mr. Law's *Christian Perfection* and *Serious Call,*' is clearly incorrect, for the latter work was not published until 1728. (For a discussion between

I was so far from making them my 'creed' that I had objections to almost every page. But all this time my manner was to spend several hours a day in reading the Scripture in the original tongues. And hence my system (so termed) was wholly drawn according to the light I then had.

17. It was in my passage to Georgia I met with those Moravian teachers who *would* have taught me the way of God more perfectly.[82] But I understood them not. Neither 'on my arrival there' did they 'infuse' any 'particularities into me' either 'about justification' or anything else. For I came back with the same notions I went. And this I have explicitly acknowledged in my second *Journal*, where some of my words are these:

> When Peter Böhler,[83] as soon as I came to London, affirmed of true faith in Christ (which is but one) that it had these two fruits inseparably attending it, 'dominion over sin, and constant peace from a sense of forgiveness', I was quite amazed, and looked upon it as a *new gospel*. If this was so, it was clear I had no faith. But I was not willing to be convinced of this. Therefore I disputed with all my might, and laboured to prove that faith might be where these were not; especially where that sense of forgiveness was not. For all the Scriptures relating to this I had been long since taught to construe away, and to call all 'Presbyterians' who spoke otherwise. Besides, I well saw no one could (in the nature of things) have such a sense of forgiveness, and not *feel* it. But I felt it not. If then there was no faith without this, all my pretensions to faith dropped at once.[a]

18. (2). Yet it was not Peter Böhler who convinced me that *conversion* (I mean, justification) *was* an *instantaneous work*.[84] On the contrary, when I was convinced of the nature and fruits of justifying faith, still,

> I could not comprehend what he spoke of *an instantaneous work*. I could not understand how this faith should be given in a moment; how a man could *at once*

[a] Page 32 [i.e., May 24, 1738, §11, with some minor changes].

Frank Baker and Frederick Hunter on the date of Wesley's introduction to Law see *Proceedings of the Wesley Historical Society* (1969–70), 37:78-82, 143-45, 173-77.)

[82] Tucker, p. 21: 'But upon his arrival there [in Georgia], he met with some Moravian teachers, who infused strange particularities into him about the *assurances of grace* and *justification*.'

[83] Peter Böhler, the Moravian, who had studied at the University of Jena and lectured in Latin at Oxford, was introduced to Wesley on his return from Georgia by John Gambold, who had interpreted for him at Oxford.

[84] Tucker, §2, p. 22: 'And upon his return to England, having conversed with Peter Böhler, another Moravian teacher, who, it seems, convinced him that conversion was an instantaneous work. . . .'

be thus turned from darkness to light, from sin and misery to righteousness and joy in the Holy Ghost. I searched the Scriptures again touching this very thing, particularly the Acts of the Apostles; but to my utter astonishment I found scarce any instances there of other than *instantaneous* conversions—scarce any other so slow as that of St. Paul, who was three days in the pangs of the new birth. I had but *one* retreat left; viz., '*Thus*, I grant, God wrought in the *first ages* of Christianity; but the times are changed. What reason have I to believe he works in the same manner *now*?'

But on Sunday 22 I was beat out of this retreat too, by the concurring evidence of several living witnesses who testified God *had thus wrought in themselves;* giving them *in a moment* such a faith in the blood of his Son as translated them out of darkness into light, out of sin and fear into holiness and happiness. Here ended my disputing. I could now only cry out, 'Lord, help thou my unbelief.'[b]

The remaining part of this section, with the third and fourth, contain my own words, to which I still subscribe.

And if there is a mistake in the fifth it is not material.

19. (6). It is true that 'on Wednesday, July 12, the Count spoke to this effect:

1. Justification is the forgiveness of sins.
2. The moment a man flies to Christ he is justified.
3. And has peace with God, but not always joy.
4. Nor perhaps may he know he is justified till long after.
5. For the assurance of it is distinct from justification itself.
6. But others may know he is justified by his power over sin, by his seriousness, his love of the brethren, and his hunger and thirst after righteousness, which alone proves the spiritual life to be begun.
7. To be justified is the same thing as to be born of God. When a man is awakened he is begotten of God, and his fear and sorrow and sense of the wrath of God are the pangs of the new birth.'[85]

20.[86] It is true also that I then recollected 'what P[eter] Böhler had often said on this head, which was to this effect':

1. When a man has living faith in Christ, then he is justified.
2. This is always given in a moment.
3. And in that moment he has peace with God.
4. Which he cannot have without knowing that he has it.
5. And being born of God, he sinneth not:

[b] Second *Journal*, page 19 [Apr. 21-22, 1738].

---

[85] Quoted in Tucker, §6, pp. 24-25, from JWJ, July 12, 1738.

[86] There is some confusion in the numbering from 18 (which is in 1742 numbered 17) onwards, while 19 is numbered 20 in 1742 and 1746. The final numbering of 1756 not only made the alterations in the earlier sections, but introduced the number 20 here.

6. Which deliverance from sin he cannot have without knowing that he has it.[87]

21. I did not apprehend it possible for any man living to have imagined that I believed both these accounts, the words whereof I had purposely so ranged and divided into short sentences that the gross, irreconcilable difference between them might be plain to the meanest reader. I cannot therefore but be a little surprised at the strength of that prejudice which could prevent anyone's seeing that in opposition to the Count's opinion (which in many respects I wholly disapproved of) I quoted the words of one of his own church, which, if true, overturn it altogether.

22. I have nothing to object to the quotations made in the seventh, eighth, and ninth sections. In the tenth are these words:

'Now since Mr. Wesley went so far to gather such materials together, let us see what was the *system* (or rather the *medley*) of principles he had to return with to England.'

Of the assurance[s] *of justification.*

I believe that conversion is an instantaneous work. And that the moment a man is converted, or has living faith in Christ, he is justified. Which faith a man cannot have without knowing that he hath it.

Yet I believe he may not know that he is justified (i.e., that he has living faith) till a long time after.

I believe also that the moment a man is justified, he has peace with God.

Which he cannot have without knowing that he has it.

Yet I believe he may not know that he is justified (i.e., that he has peace with God) till a long time after.

I believe to be justified is the same thing as to be born of God.[88]

And 'being born of God he sinneth not'.

Which deliverance from sin he cannot have without knowing it.

Yet I believe he may not know that he is justified (i.e., delivered from sin) till a long time after.

Though I believe that others may know that he is justified by his power over sin, his seriousness, and love of the brethren.

23. *Of the* conditions *of justification.*

I believe that *Christ formed in us* subordinately to Christ *given for us* (i.e., our own *inherent* righteousness subordinate to Christ's *merits*) ought to be insisted upon, as necessary to our justification.

And it is just and right that a man should be humble and penitent, and have a broken and contrite heart (i.e., should have Christ *formed in him*) before he can expect to be justified.

And that this penitence and contrition is the work of the Holy Ghost.

[87] Tucker, pp. 25-26, quoting JWJ, July 12, 1738, a continuation of the previous passage.

[88] *Works*, 1772, 'I believe when a man is justified, he is born of God.'

Yet I believe that all this is nothing towards, and has no influence on our justification.

Again, I believe that, in order to justification, I must go straight to Christ with all my ungodliness, and plead nothing else.

Yet I believe that we should not insist upon anything we *do* or *feel*, as if it were necessary[89] *previous* to justification.

24. *Of the* effects *of justification.*

I believe that justification is the same thing as to be born of God. Yet a man may have a *strong assurance* that he is justified, and not be able to affirm that he is born of God.

A man may be fully assured that his sins are forgiven, yet may not be able to tell the hour or day when he received this full assurance, because it may grow up in him by degrees . . . Though he can remember that from the time this full assurance was confirmed in him he never lost it, no, not for a moment.

A man may have a weak faith at the same time that he hath peace with God, *not one uneasy thought*, and freedom from sin, *not one unholy desire.*

A man may be justified (i.e., born of God) who has not a clean heart (i.e., is not sanctified).

He may be justified (i.e., born of God) and not have the indwelling of the Spirit.[90]

25. I entirely agree that the foregoing creed is '*a very extraordinary and odd composition*'.[91] But it is not mine. I neither composed it, nor believe it—as I doubt not every impartial reader will be fully convinced, when we shall have gone over it once more, step by step.

The parts of it which I do believe I shall barely repeat: on the others it will be needful to add a few words.

Of the assurances *of justification.*

'I believe that conversion' (meaning thereby justification) 'is an instantaneous work, and that the moment a man has living faith in Christ he is converted or justified.' (So the proposition must be expressed to make it sense.) 'Which faith he cannot have without knowing that he has it.'

[89] The 2nd edn. onwards changed this to 'necessarily', though Tucker correctly quoted Christian David's account from JWJ as 'necessary'.

[90] This long series of quotations under three headings is reproduced with fair accuracy from Tucker, pp. 32-34, though Wesley omits Tucker's citation of the source for each one, sometimes from previous paragraphs of the *Brief History*, sometimes from Wesley's *Journal*, including the narratives of the Moravians whom he met in Germany. Both Wesley and Tucker (in accordance with common practice) silently omit words and phrases which they believe do not alter the sense, but simply its literary expression. When Wesley came to discuss each statement in detail he frequently made slightly different selections, and italicized many passages for emphasis which are not so italicized in JWJ.

[91] Tucker, p. 32.

'Yet I believe he may not know that he has it till long after.' This I deny; I believe no such thing.

'I believe, the moment a man is justified he has peace with God.

'Which he cannot have without knowing that he has it.

'Yet I believe he may not know that he has it till long after.' This again I deny. I believe it not. Nor Michael Linner[92] neither. To clear whom entirely one need only read his own words:

> About fourteen years ago I was more than ever convinced that I was wholly different from what God required me to be. I consulted his Word again and again; but it spoke nothing but condemnation; till at last I could not read, nor indeed do anything else, having no hope and no spirit left in me. I had been in this state for several days when, being musing by myself, those words came strongly into my mind, 'God so loved the world that he gave his only-begotten Son, to the end that all who believe in him should not perish but have everlasting life.' I thought, '*All?* Then I am one. Then he is given for *me.* But I am a sinner. And he came to save sinners.' Immediately my burden dropped off, and my heart was at rest.
>
> But the full assurance of faith I had not yet; nor for the two years I continued in Moravia. When I was driven out thence by the Jesuits I retired hither, and was soon after received into the church. And here after some time it pleased our Lord to manifest himself more clearly to my soul, and give me that full sense of acceptance in him which excludes all doubt and fear.
>
> Indeed the leading of the Spirit is different in different souls. His more usual method, I believe, is to give in one and the same moment forgiveness of sins and a full assurance of that forgiveness. Yet in many he works as he did in me—giving first the remission of sins, and after some weeks or months or years the full assurance of it.[c]

All I need observe is that the *first sense of forgiveness* is often mixed with doubt or fear. But the 'full assurance of faith'[93] excludes all doubt and fear, as the very term implies.

Therefore instead of 'He may not know that he has peace with God till long after,' it should be (to agree with Michael Linner's words), 'He may not have till long after that full assurance of faith which excludes all doubt and fear.'

'I believe to be justified is the same as to be born of God.[94]

'And he that is born of God, sinneth not.

'Which deliverance from sin he cannot have without knowing that he has it.

[c] Second *Journal*, pages 65-66 [Aug. 1738, 18:281-82 in this edn.].

---

[92] For Michael Linner (1692–1760) see 18:270 in this edn.

[93] Heb. 10:22.

[94] *Works*, 1772, 'I believe a man is justified at the same time that he is born of God.'

'Yet I believe he may not know it till long after.' This also I utterly deny.

26. *Of the* conditions *of justification.*

'I believe that "Christ formed in us" ought to be *insisted on, as necessary to our justification.*'

I no more believe this than Christian David[95] does, whose words concerning it are these:

> It pleased God to show me that *Christ in us* and *Christ for us* ought indeed to be both insisted on;
>
> But I clearly saw *we ought not to insist on* anything *we feel*, any more than anything *we do*, as if it were *necessary* previous to *our justification.*

'And before a man can expect to be justified, he should be humble and penitent, and have a broken and contrite heart, that is, should have "Christ formed in him".' No; that is quite another thing. I believe every man is *penitent* before he is *justified;* he *repents* before he *believes* the gospel. But it is never *before,* and generally *long after,*[96] he is justified, that 'Christ is formed in him'.[97]

'And that this penitence and contrition is the work of the Holy Ghost.

'Yet I believe that all this is nothing towards, and has no influence on our justification.'

Christian David's words are: 'Observe, this is not the foundation. It is not this by which' (for the sake of which) 'you are justified. This is not the righteousness, this is no part of the righteousness, by which you are reconciled to God. You grieve for your sins. You are deeply humbled. Your heart is broken. Well. But *all this is nothing to your justification.*' (The words immediately following fix the sense of this otherwise exceptionable sentence.) 'The remission of your sins *is not owing to this cause*, either in whole or in part. Your humiliation *has no influence on that.*' Not *as a cause*; so the very last words explain it.

'Again, I believe that in order to obtain justification I must go

[95] Christian David, born in 1690 in Senftleben, Moravia, and baptized in the Roman Catholic Church, became disaffected with Catholicism, and while serving in the army was received into the Lutheran Church. After discharge from the army on health grounds, he pursued the trade of a journeyman carpenter in Görlitz, and in 1717 crossed the frontier back into his own country secretly in order to evangelize. Zinzendorf offered asylum to him with his Moravian friends who looked for the restoration of the old Unitas Fratrum; he cut the first tree for the building of the Herrnhut settlement, and was a founding father of the renewed Unitas Fratrum, the Moravian Church.

[96] *Works,* 1772, omits 'and generally long after'.

[97] Cf. Gal. 4:19.

straight to Christ, with all my ungodliness, and plead *nothing else.*'[98]

'Yet I believe we should not insist upon anything we *do* or *feel*, as if it were necessary previous to justification.'[99] No, not on anything *else*. So the whole tenor of Christian David's words implies.

27. *Of the* effects *of justification.*

'I believe a man may have a strong assurance he is justified, and not be able to affirm he is a child of God.'

Feder's[1] words are these: 'I found my heart at rest, *in good hope that my sins were forgiven;* of which I had a stronger assurance six weeks after.' (True, *comparatively stronger*, though still mixed with doubt and fear.) 'But I dare not affirm I am a child of God.' I see no inconsistency in all this. Many such instances I know at this day. I myself was one, for some time.

'A man may be fully assured that his sins are forgiven, yet may not be able to tell the day when he received this full assurance, because it grew up in him by degrees.' (Of this also I know a few other instances.) 'But from the time this full assurance *was confirmed in him* he never lost it.' Very true, and I think, consistent.

Neisser's own words are: 'In him I found true rest to my soul, being fully assured that all my sins were forgiven. Yet I cannot tell the hour or day when I first received that full assurance. For it was not given me at first, neither at once' (not in its fullness), 'but grew up in me by degrees. And *from the time it was confirmed in me* I have never lost it, having never since doubted, no, not for a moment.'[2]

'A man may have a weak faith at the same time that he has "peace with God", and no unholy desires.'[3]

'A man may be justified, who has not a clean heart, neither the indwelling of the Spirit.'[4] Not in the full sense of the word.[5]

[98] Wesley quotes Christian David's sermon, from JWJ, Aug. 10, 1738; see 18:271-72 in this edn. (cf. Tucker, pp. 33-34).

[99] Here Tucker returns to Wesley's lengthy conference with David on Aug. 10, recounted later in JWJ for Aug. 1738 (cf. 18:280 in this edn.).

[1] Albinus Theodorus Feder, a student at Herrnhut; see JWJ, Aug. 11, 1738 (cf. 18:284 in this edn.).

[2] The testimony of Augustin Neisser, a knifesmith, Aug. 11, in JWJ, Aug. 1738 (18:285 in this edn.). Both here and in the *Journal* Wesley spells the name 'Neusser'.

[3] Tucker cites (p. 34), as 'The Case of Mr. Wesley'; cf. 18:253 in this edn.

[4] Tucker cites (p. 34), 'The Case of Zacharias Neusser' (i.e., Neisser), from JWJ, Aug. 1738 (cf. 18:287 in this edn., lines 28-29, 'justifying the ungodly'; there is no obvious quotation). The *Works*, 1772, abridges and alters to, 'A man may be justified who has not a clear heart.'

[5] This sentence is added in Wesley's *Works*, 16:37, after the beginning of the following section, '28. (11)', where it hardly makes sense. It appears almost certain that it was

28. (11).[6] This I do verily believe is *sound* divinity, agreeable both to Scripture and experience. And, I believe, it is consistent with itself. As to the 'hundred other absurdities' which '*might be* fully and fairly made out', it will be time enough to consider them when they are produced.

29. (12, 13). But whether I have succeeded in attempting to reconcile these things or no, I verily think Mr. Tucker has. I desire not a more consistent account of my principles than he has himself given in the following words:

> Our spiritual state should be considered distinctly[7] under each of these views.
>
> 1. Before *justification;* in which state we may be said to be *unable* to do anything *acceptable* to God, because then we can *do nothing but come to Christ.* Which ought not to be considered as *doing* anything, but as *supplicating* (or waiting)[8] to receive a *power of doing* for the time to come. For the preventing grace of God, which is common to all, is sufficient to *bring* us to Christ, though it is not sufficient to carry us any *further* till we are justified.[9]
>
> 2. After *justification.* The moment a man comes to Christ (by faith)[10] he is justified, and born again; that is, he is born again in the[11] *imperfect* sense (for there are two [if not more][12] degrees of regeneration). And he has *power over* all the stirrings and motions of sin, but not a total *freedom from* them. He has Christ *with* him, but not Christ *in* him.[13] Therefore he hath not yet, in the full and proper sense, a *new* and *clean heart*, or the *indwelling* of the Spirit.[14] But being exposed to various temptations he may and will fall again from this condition, if he doth not attain to a more excellent gift.[d]

[d] 'Mr. Charles Wesley' (the note says) 'was not persuaded of the truth of the Moravian faith till some time after his brother's return from Germany.' There is a great mistake in this. I returned not from Germany till Saturday, September 16. Whereas my brother was fully persuaded of the truth of the 'Moravian faith' (so called) on Wednesday, May 3, preceding. The note adds, 'This (i.e., justifying faith) he received but very lately.' This also is a mistake. What we believe to be justifying faith he received May 21, 1738. See Second *Journal*, pages 20, 26 [May 1, 19, 1738].

---

intended by Wesley as a comment on the previous sentence, but that the printer misplaced it, and the error was not discovered and corrected in the errata or Wesley's MS notes.

[6] After reciting the series of apparently contradictory quotations on justification from JWJ, Tucker continued (p. 11): '11. This is the *sound* and *orthodox* divinity Mr. Wesley so much longed after, and took such pains to acquire—And were it necessary, I believe an hundred other *absurdities* might be fully and fairly made out, by deducing one article from another, and comparing them together.'

[7] 1st and later edns., 'and distinctly'. The 'and' does not occur in Tucker (p. 36), and is omitted from Wesley's *Works* (1772).

[8] JW's parenthetic addition.

[9] Tucker adds, 'and born of the Spirit'.

[10] JW's parenthetic addition.

[11] Tucker, 'in an imperfect'.

[12] JW's parenthetic addition.

[13] *Works* (1772), omits this sentence.

[14] *Works* (1772), omits 'the *indwelling* of the Spirit'.

3. Sanctification, the last and highest state of *perfection* in this life. For then are the faithful born again in the full and perfect sense. Then have they the indwelling of the Spirit.[15] Then is there given unto them a new and clean[16] heart; and the struggle between the old and *new* man is over.[e]

30. (14). That I may say many things which have been said before, and perhaps by Calvin or Arminius, by Montanus or Barclay,[17] or the Archbishop of Cambrai,[18] is highly probable. But it cannot thence be inferred that I hold 'a *medley* of all their principles—Calvinism, Arminianism, Montanism, Quakerism, Quietism, all thrown together'.[19] There might as well have been added Judaism, Mahometanism, paganism. It would have made the period rounder, and been full as easily *proved*—I mean *asserted*. For other proof is not yet produced.

31. I pass over the smaller mistakes which occur in the fifteenth and sixteenth paragraphs, together with the prophecy or prognostication concerning the approaching divisions and downfall of the Methodists. What follows to the end, concerning the ground of our hope, is indeed of greater importance. But we have not as yet the strength of the cause. The dissertation

[e] The next note runs thus: 'Mr. Wesley has such a *peculiar turn* and *tendency* toward inconsistencies in his principles that in his preface to *Haliburton's Life* (wrote February 9, 1738–39, *just after* his return from Germany) he contradicts all that he has said elsewhere for this *sinless perfection*, viz., "But it may be said, *the gospel covenant does not promise entire freedom from sin.*" What do you mean by the word sin? The infection of nature? Or those numberless weaknesses and follies, sometimes (improperly) termed *sins of infirmity?* If you mean only this, you say most true. We shall not put off these, but with our bodies. But if you mean, it does not promise entire freedom from sin, in its proper sense, or from committing sin; this is by no means true, unless the Scripture be false. *For thus it is written,* "Whosoever is born of God, doth not commit sin," (unless he lose the spirit of adoption, if not finally, yet for a while, as did this child of God) "for his seed remaineth in him, and he cannot sin, because he is born of God" [1 John 3:9]. He cannot sin, "so long as he keepeth himself", for then "the wicked one toucheth him not" [1 John 5:18].'

The question is not whether this be right or wrong; but whether it contradict anything I have said elsewhere. Thrice I have spoken expressly on this subject—in a sermon, and in two prefaces. If in any of these I have contradicted what I said before, I will own the former assertion as a mistake. [The whole passage is quoted from Tucker, *Brief History*, pp. 36-37, Wesley omitting the closing sentence of para. 3, ('And the time of their *probation* is ended,' and a following lengthy paragraph on Christian perfection quoted by Tucker from the preface to *Hymns and Sacred Poems*, 1740, to which Tucker added the lengthy footnote from which Wesley here gives an extract.]

---

[15] *Works* (1772), omits this sentence.

[16] *Works* (1772), 'clear'.

[17] Robert Barclay (1648–90), Scottish Quaker theologian.

[18] I.e., François de Salignac de la Mothe Fénelon (1651–1715), friend of Madame Guyon, the quietist, though Fénelon later repudiated quietism.

[19] Tucker, p. 39.

promised is still behind. Therefore, as my work is great, and my time short, I waive that dispute for the present. And perhaps, when I shall have received farther light, I may be convinced that 'gospel holiness' (as Mr. Tucker believes) is 'a necessary qualification, antecedent to justification'[20] and that Christ did not *in any degree* fulfil the terms of justification *in our stead*, but having purchased for us sufficient powers and abilities to perform them, then left us to fulfil them ourselves.'[21] This appears to me now to be directly opposite to the gospel of Christ. But I will endeavour, impartially, to consider what shall be advanced in defence of it. And may he who knoweth my simpleness teach me his way, and give me a right judgment in all things![22]

[20] Tucker, pp. 46-47.

[21] Ibid., p. 50; this passage Wesley omitted from *Works* (1772).

[22] For the closing phrase see BCP, Collect for Whit Sunday.

3–4

GENERAL RULES AND RULES OF THE BAND SOCIETIES

AN INTRODUCTORY COMMENT

Wesley drew up his Rules of the Band Societies *(see pp. 77-79 below) in December 1738, before the emergence of the distinctively Methodist societies in Bristol and London. The Methodist societies attracted and included, not only those who were willing to meet 'in band', but also a much larger and less homogeneous group of people who expressed a desire to be saved from their sins, but did not necessarily understand the full implications of belonging to the societies. From 1741 discipline was exercised by renewing or withholding the quarterly ticket of membership, but something more was needed. This became apparent after Wesley had interviewed every member of the societies in London, Bristol, Kingswood, and Newcastle upon Tyne. In Newcastle he had felt himself bound to exclude fifty members out of eight hundred for non-performance of their Methodist obligations.*

So he published these General Rules *in Newcastle in early 1743. They were intended to illustrate the ways in which the three principles—'doing no harm', 'doing good', and 'attending upon all the ordinances of God'—were expected by Wesley to work out in practical living. He claimed that both the principles and their application were based on the New Testament and the practice of the apostolic church (for his understanding of which he placed great faith in William Cave's* Primitive Christianity*).*

In earlier and later editions during his lifetime Charles Wesley's hymn 'A Prayer for those who are convinced of Sin' (beginning 'O most compassionate High Priest') was added as an appendix, and in some editions the Rules of the Band Societies *were included. The* General Rules *(which became the usual name for this work) have been frequently revised and republished since Wesley's time.*

For a summary of the thirty-nine editions of the General Rules *published during Wesley's lifetime, a stemma illustrating the transmission of the text, and a list of the substantive variant readings from the edited text (based on the 1st edn., Newcastle, Gooding, 1743), see Appendix A, pp. 541ff. For fuller bibliographical details see*

THE

NATURE, DESIGN,

AND

GENERAL RULES,

OF THE

United Societies,

IN

London, Briſtol, King's-wood, and *Newcaſtle upon Tyne.*

NEWCASTLE UPON TYNE,
Printed by JOHN GOODING, on the *Side.*
[Price One Penny.]

MDCCXLIII.

Bibliography, *No. 73. For a stemma of the nineteen editions of the* Rules of the Band Societies *see Appendix A, pp. 541ff., and see also* Bibliography, *No. 81.*

The Nature, Design, and General Rules of the United Societies

in London, Bristol, Kingswood, and Newcastle upon Tyne (1743)

1. In the latter end of the year 1739 eight or ten persons came to me in London who appeared to be deeply convinced of sin, and earnestly groaning for redemption. They desired (as did two or three more the next day) that I would spend some time with them in prayer, and advise them how to flee from the wrath to come,[1] which they saw continually hanging over their heads. That we might have more time for this great work I appointed a day when they might all come together, which from thenceforward they did every week, namely, on Thursday, in the evening. To these, and as many more as desired to join with them (for their number increased daily), I gave those advices from time to time which I judged most needful for them; and we always concluded our meeting with prayer suited to their several necessities.[2]

2. This was the rise of the United Society, first at London, and then in other places.[3] Such a Society is no other than 'a company of men "having the form, and seeking the power of godliness",[4] united in order to pray together, to receive the word of exhortation, and to watch over one another in love, that they may help each other to work out their salvation'.[5]

3. That it may the more easily be discerned whether they are indeed working out their own salvation, each Society is divided into smaller companies, called Classes, according to their

[1] Matt. 3:7.
[2] Cf. *Plain Account,* I.6, p. 256 below.
[3] 18th edn. (New York, Ross, 1788), 'first in Europe, and then in America'.
[4] Cf. 2 Tim. 3:5.
[5] See Phil. 2:12.

respective places of abode. There are about twelve persons in every class, one of whom is styled *the Leader*. It is his business:

(1). To see each person in his class once a week at the least; in order

To receive what they are willing to give toward the relief of the poor;[6]

To inquire how their souls prosper;

To advise, reprove, comfort, or exhort, as occasion may require.

(2). To meet the Minister and the stewards of the Society once a week, in order:

To pay in to the stewards what they have received of their several classes in the week preceding;

To show their account of what each person has contributed; and

To inform the Minister of any that are sick, or of any that walk disorderly and will not be reproved.[7]

4. There is one only condition previously required in those who desire admission into these societies, 'a desire to flee from the wrath to come,[8] to be saved from their sins'.[9] But wherever this is really fixed in the soul it will be shown by its fruits. It is therefore expected of all who continue therein that they should continue to evidence their desire of salvation,

First, By doing no harm, by avoiding evil in every kind—especially that which is most generally practised. Such is:

The taking the name of God in vain.[10]

The profaning the day of the Lord, either by doing ordinary work thereon, or by buying or selling.

Drunkenness, *buying or selling spirituous liquors;* or *drinking them* (unless in cases of extreme necessity).[11]

[6] Some early Irish edns., beginning with that of Dublin, Powell, 1747, here add, 'and the necessary expenses of the Society'. The 18th edn. (New York, Ross, 1788) reads, 'towards the relief of the church and poor', and adds the footnote: 'These parts refer wholly to towns and cities, where the poor are generally numerous, and church expenses considerable.' The added section sign shows that this footnote applied also to the class receipts noted in the second paragraph of *General Rules*, §3(2). (For many minor variants in the American edn. see Appendix A, pp. 541ff. below.)

[7] The 1788 New York edn. omits para. 3 and reverses the order of paras. 2 and 4.

[8] Matt. 3:7, etc. The 1788 New York edn. adds here, 'i.e., a desire'.

[9] Cf. Matt. 1:21, etc.

[10] See Exod. 20:7, etc.

[11] The 4th edn. of the *Discipline* (Kollock, 1788) included, as the first of the 'useful pieces annexed', the 19th American edn. of the *Rules* and added as an extension: '. . . drinking them; especially the buying or selling the bodies and souls of men, women, or

Fighting, quarrelling, brawling; brother 'going to law'[12] with brother; returning evil for evil,[13] or railing for railing; the 'using many words'[14] in buying or selling.

The *buying or selling uncustomed goods*.

The *giving or taking things on usury*.[15]

Uncharitable or *unprofitable* conversation, especially *speaking evil of ministers or those in authority*.[16]

Doing to others as we would not they should do unto us.[17]

Doing what we know is not for the glory of God, as,

The 'putting on of gold or costly apparel', particularly *the wearing of calashes*,[18] *high-heads, or enormous bonnets*;[19]

The *taking such diversions* as cannot be used in the name of the Lord Jesus,

The *singing* those *songs*, or *reading* those *books*, which do not tend to the knowledge or love of God;

Softness, and needless self-indulgence;

Laying up treasures upon earth;

children, with an intention to enslave them'. In the 1789 and subsequent edns. of the *Discipline* this addition became a separate rule, with the omission of 'especially the'. Slave-holding was prohibited by the 'Christmas Conference' of 1784–85, a prohibition vigorously supported by Thomas Coke and Francis Asbury, but its enforcement seemed impracticable under the prevailing conditions, and it became a dead letter. This rule does not appear in the separately printed 18th edn. of the *Rules* (New York, Ross, 1788), and the history of its insertion remains a mystery, though one suspects that it was done on the initiative of Thomas Coke. It appears only in the reprint of the *Rules* in the 5th edn. of the *Discipline* (New York, Ross, 1789); cf. J. J. Tigert, *A Constitutional History of American Episcopal Methodism* (6th edn., Nashville, 1916), p. 252; cf. also David Sherman, *History of the Revisions of the Discipline of the Methodist Episcopal Church* (New York, 1874), pp. 113-18.

12 Cf. 1 Cor. 6:6. The 1st edn. read 'going to law', the fuller version appearing first in the 7th Bristol edn. (1762) and the 8th London edn. (1764), and frequently thereafter where these editions were the progenitors of others. The alteration probably resulted from the review of this work on Aug. 26, 1756, at Wesley's Bristol Conference (see Vol. 10 in this edn.).

13 See 1 Pet. 3:9.

14 Cf. Ecclus. 20:8, 'He that useth many words shall be abhorred;' see also Ecclus. 13:11.

15 Cf. Lev. 25:36; Isa. 24:2, etc.

16 'especially . . . authority' was first added in the 4th edn. (London, Strahan, 1744), certainly by Wesley himself. This was altered in the 7th edn., (Dublin, Powell, 1747) and a few which derived their text from this, to 'especially speaking evil of magistrates or of ministers', whose opening word was altered to 'particularly' in the 7th edn. (Bristol, Pine, 1762), and those stemming from it. In some editions 'of' was inserted before 'ministers'. For the relations between the many editions, the stemma showing their relationships, and the other variant readings, see Appendix A, pp. 541ff. below.

17 See Matt. 7:12, etc.

18 A 'calash' is a woman's hooped silk hood.

19 Cf. 1 Pet. 3:3. 'particularly . . . *bonnets*' was first added (apparently by Wesley) in the 17th edn. (London, Paramore, 1781), and remained a regular part of the text.

Borrowing without a probability of paying: or taking up goods without a probability of paying for them.[20]

5. It is expected of all who continue in these societies that they should continue to evidence their desire of salvation,

Secondly, By doing good, by being in every kind merciful after their power, as they have opportunity doing good of every possible sort and as far as is possible to all men:[21]

To their bodies, of the ability which God giveth, by giving food to the hungry, by clothing the naked, by visiting or helping them that are sick, or in prison.[22]

To their souls, by instructing, *reproving*, or exhorting all they[23] have any intercourse with; trampling under foot that enthusiastic doctrine of devils, that 'we are not to do good unless *our heart be free to it*.'[24]

By doing good especially to them that are of the household of faith,[25] or groaning so to be; employing them preferably to others, buying one of another, helping each other in business—and that so much the more because the world will love its own, and them only.

By all possible *diligence and frugality*, that the gospel be not blamed.

By running with patience the race that is set before them;[26] 'denying themselves, and taking up their cross daily';[27] submitting to bear the reproach of Christ, to be as the filth and offscouring of the world;[28] and looking that men should 'say all manner of evil of them falsely, for their Lord's sake'.[29]

6. It is expected of all who desire to continue in these societies that they should continue to evidence their desire of salvation,

[20] This paragraph was first added by Wesley in the 7th edn. (Bristol, Pine, 1762), and continued as his authorized text. In the 1st edn. it closed, 'paying them'; in which 'for' was first inserted in the 17th edn. (London, Paramore, 1781).

[21] See Gal. 6:10.

[22] See Matt. 25:35-39.

[23] The first three editions read 'we', the correction being made in the major revision of 1744, but only surviving in the 5th (Cork, Harrison, 1748?), the 5th (Limerick, Welsh, 1748?), and Wesley's *Works*, 1772.

[24] Cf. Wesley's lengthy challenge to the Moravians, Aug. 5-8, 1740, espec. §16, in refusing to encourage good works, but saying only: 'If you find yourself moved, if your heart is free to it, then reprove, exhort, relieve' (26:30 in this edn.).

[25] See Gal. 6:10.

[26] See Heb. 12:1.

[27] Cf. Luke 9:23.

[28] See 1 Cor. 4:13.

[29] Cf. Matt. 5:11.

Thirdly, By attending upon all the ordinances of God. Such are:

The public worship of God;
The ministry of the Word, either read or expounded;
The Supper of the Lord;
Family and private prayer;[30]
Searching the Scriptures;[31] and
Fasting, or abstinence.

7. These are the General Rules of our societies; all which we are taught of God to observe, even in his written Word, the only rule, and the sufficient rule, both of our faith and practice. And all these we know his Spirit writes on every truly awakened heart. If there be any among us who observe them not, who habitually break any one of them,[32] let it be made known unto them who watch[33] over that soul, as they that must give account. We will admonish him of the error of his ways. We will bear with him for a season. But if then he repent not, he hath no more place among us. We have delivered our own souls.[34]

John Wesley
Charles Wesley

May 1, 1743[35]

A Prayer for those who are convinced of Sin[36]

1. O most compassionate High Priest,
   Full of all grace we know thou art;
Faith puts its hand upon thy breast,
   And feels beneath thy panting heart.

30 'Family and' were first added to Wesley's orig. 'Private prayer' in the major 1744 revision.

31 See John 5:39; Acts 17:11.

32 From 1764 this became in most edns., 'any of them'.

33 The 1st edn. and its reprint in 1743 (A, B), both have 'unto him who watches', i.e., John Wesley, 'as one that must give account', 'I' to begin the following sentences, and the signature of JW only.

34 See Ezek. 3:19, etc.

35 The 1st edn. is signed by JW only, and dated 'Feb. 23, 1742/3'. Several edns. from the 8th (London, n.p., 1764), are dated 'May 1, 1764'. The extant American edns. are signed 'Thomas Coke, Francis Asbury', and dated 'May 28, 1787'.

36 This composition by Charles Wesley was published in his *Hymns and Sacred Poems* (Bristol, Farley, 1749), II.89-91. The poem was included in all the English edns. of the *General Rules* except the 4th, 1744 (which contained the Band Rules), and that in Wesley's *Works*.

2. Thy panting heart for sinners bleeds;
 Thy mercies and compassions move;
Thy groaning Spirit intercedes,
 And yearn the bowels of thy love.

3. Hear then the pleading Spirit's prayer
 (The Spirit's will to thee is known)
For all who now thy sufferings share,
 And still for full redemption groan.

4. Poor tempted souls, with tempests tossed,
 And strangers to a moment's peace,
Disconsolate, afflicted, lost—
 Lost in an howling wilderness.

5. Torn with an endless war within,
 Vexed with the flesh and spirit's strife,
And struggling in the toils of sin,
 And agonizing into life.

6. O let the pris'ners' mournful cries
 As incense in thy sight appear,
Their humble wailings pierce the skies,
 If haply they may feel thee near!

7. The captive exiles make their moans,
 From sin impatient to be free;
Call home, call home thy banished ones!
 Lead captive their captivity!

8. Show them the blood that bought their peace,
 The anchor of their steadfast hope,
And bid their guilty terrors cease,
 And bring the ransomed pris'ners up.

9. Out of the deep regard their cries,
 The fallen raise, the mourners cheer;
O Sun of righteousness, arise,
 And scatter all their doubt and fear!

10. Pity the day of feeble things;
 O gather ev'ry halting soul,
And drop salvation from thy wings,
 And make the contrite sinner whole.

11. Stand by them in the fiery hour,
 Their feebleness of mind defend;
And in their weakness show thy power,
 And make them patient to the end.

12. O satisfy their soul in drought;
 Give them thy saving health to see,
And let thy mercy find them out;
 And let thy mercy reach to me.

13. Hast thou the work of grace begun,
    And brought them to the birth in vain?
O let thy children see the sun!
    Let all their souls be born again!

14. Relieve the souls whose cross we bear,
    For whom thy suffering members mourn,
Answer our faith's effectual prayer,
    Bid ev'ry struggling child be born.

15. Hark how thy turtle-dove complains,
    And see us weep for Zion's woe!
Pity thy suffering people's pain;
    Avenge us of our inbred foe.

16. Whom thou hast bound, O Lord, expel,
    And take his armour all away;
The man of sin, the child of hell,
    The devil in our nature slay.

17. Him and his works at once destroy,
    The *being* of all sin erase,
And turn our mourning into joy,
    And clothe us with the robes of praise.

18. Then when our sufferings all are past,
    O let us pure and perfect be,
And gain our calling's prize at last,
    For ever sanctified in thee.

May 1750.

If ye love me, keep my Commandments.

John xiv. 15.

B

Josiah Dornford

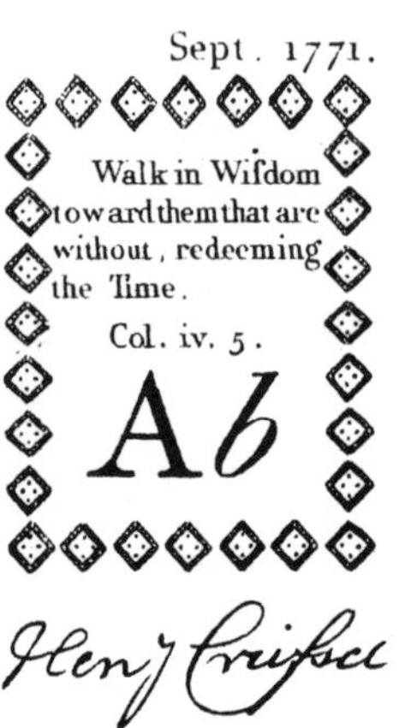

4

Rules of the Band Societies

Drawn up Dec. 25, 1738

The design of our meeting is to obey that command of God, 'Confess your faults one to another, and pray one for another that ye may be healed.'[1]

To this end we intend:

1. To meet once a week, at the least.
2. To come punctually at the hour appointed, without some extraordinary reason.
3. To begin (those of us who are present) exactly at the hour, with singing or prayer.
4. To speak, each of us in order, freely and plainly the true state of our souls, with the faults we have committed in thought, word, or deed, and the temptations we have felt since our last meeting.
5. To end every meeting with prayer, suited to the state of each person present.
6. To desire some person among us to speak *his*[2] own state first, and then to ask the rest in order as many and as searching questions as may be concerning their state, sins, and temptations.

Some of the questions proposed to every one before *he* is admitted amongst us may be to this effect:

1. Have you the forgiveness of your sins?
2. Have you peace with God, through our Lord Jesus Christ?[3]
3. Have you the witness of God's Spirit with your spirit that you are a child of God?[4]
4. Is the love of God shed abroad in your heart?[5]
5. Has no sin, inward or outward, dominion over you?[6]

[1] Jas. 5:16.

[2] The italics are used here and similarly elsewhere in this document to indicate that the alternative 'her' may be substituted as necessary.

[3] Rom. 5:1.

[4] See Rom. 8:16.

[5] See Rom. 5:5.

[6] See Rom. 6:14.

6. Do you desire to be told of your faults?

7. Do you desire to be told of all your faults, and that plain and home?

8. Do you desire that every one of us should tell you from time to time whatsoever is in *his* heart concerning you?

9. Consider! Do you desire we should tell you whatsoever we think, whatsoever we fear, whatsoever we hear, concerning you?

10. Do you desire that in doing this we should come as close as possible, that we should cut to the quick, and search your heart to the bottom?

11. Is it your desire and design to be on this and all other occasions entirely open, so as to speak everything that is in your heart, without exception, without disguise, and without reserve?[7]

Any of the preceding questions may be asked as often as occasion offers; the five[8] following at every meeting:[9]

1. What known sins[10] have you committed since our last meeting?

2. What temptations have you met with?

3. How was you delivered?

4. What have you thought, said, or done, of which you doubt whether it be sin[11] or not?

5. Have you nothing you desire to keep secret?[12]

[7] The remainder of p. 9 is blank (having space for about eight lines), as is the whole of the following page, and the top one-third of p. 11—clearly in order to allow further questions or rules to be added by hand. The remainder follows without any break. This pattern was followed exactly in the 1748 Newcastle edn. of the *Rules*, except that the following five questions were also omitted.

[8] All the early edns. have five rules, but the later ones omit the fifth, and here read 'four'—all except one, which reads 'five' but actually contains four.

[9] In 1744 the preceding six words are set off in a separate line.

[10] Orig., 'sin'.

[11] Orig., 'a sin'.

[12] This question is dropped from the later edns., beginning about 1779 or 1780.

Directions given to the Band Societies
Dec. 25, 1744

You are supposed to have the 'faith that overcometh the world'.[13] To you therefore it is not grievous,

I. Carefully to abstain from doing evil; in particular,

1. Neither to *buy nor sell* anything at all on the Lord's Day.
2. To taste no spirituous liquor, *no dram* of any kind, unless prescribed by a physician.
3. To be *at a word* both in buying and selling.
4. To *pawn nothing*, no, not to save life.
5. Not to *mention the fault* of any *behind his back*, and to stop those short that do.
6. To wear no *needless ornaments*, such as rings, ear-rings, necklaces, lace, ruffles.
7. To use no *needless self-indulgence*, such as taking snuff or tobacco, unless prescribed by a physician.

II. Zealously to maintain good works; in particular,

1. To *give alms* of such things as you possess, and that to the uttermost of your power.
2. To *reprove* all that sin in your sight, and that in love, and meekness of wisdom.[14]
3. To be patterns of *diligence* and *frugality*, of *self-denial*, and taking up the cross daily.[15]

III. Constantly to attend on all the ordinances of God; in particular,

1. To be at church, and at the Lord's table, every week, and at every public meeting of the bands.
2. To attend the ministry of the Word every morning, unless distance, business, or sickness prevent.
3. To use private prayer every day, and family prayer if you are the head of a family.
4. To read the Scriptures, and meditate thereon, at every vacant hour. And,
5. To observe as days of fasting or abstinence all *Fridays* in the year.

[13] Cf. 1 John 5:4.
[14] Jas. 3:13.
[15] See Luke 9:23.

5

AN ANSWER TO THE REV. MR. CHURCH'S *REMARKS* (1745)

AN INTRODUCTORY COMMENT

Thomas Church, Vicar of Battersea and Prebendary of St. Paul's, had attacked the fourth extract from Wesley's Journal, *published in July 1744. The content and purpose of the attack are revealed by the protracted and somewhat supercilious title of Church's 'Letter':* Remarks on the Rev. John Wesley's last Journal, wherein he gave an Account of the Tenets and Proceedings of the Moravians, especially those in England, and of the Divisions and Perplexities of the Methodists: showing by the Confessions of Mr. Wesley himself the many Errors relating both to Faith and Practice which have already arisen among these deluded People, and in a particular Manner explaining the very fatal Tendency of denying good Works to be Conditions of our Justification *(see Green,* Anti-Methodist, *No. 185*).

Wesley's reply does not impugn the character or ability of Mr. Church, and proceeds by rebutting his contentions that Wesley praised the Moravians unduly, was heretical in the matter of justification, and was guilty of gross enthusiasm.

It is worth noticing that Wesley was probably less willing to condemn the Moravians than others with whom he had less disagreement, no doubt because they had helped him at an important stage in his own development. On one major issue of dispute between Church and himself, good works as a condition of justification, Wesley had to wrestle with friends and critics all through his life (e.g., in the Minutes *of 1771).*

For a summary of the three English editions published during Wesley's lifetime, a stemma illustrating the transmission of the text, and a list of the substantive variant readings from the edited text (based on the 1st edn., Bristol, Farley, 1745), see Appendix A, pp. 541ff. For full bibliographical details see Bibliography, *No. 97.*

An Answer to the Rev. Mr. Church's Remarks on the Rev. Mr. John Wesley's Last Journal

Reverend sir,

1. My first desire (and prayer to God) is that I may live peaceably with all men. My next, that if I must dispute at all it may be with a man of understanding. Thus far therefore I rejoice on the present occasion. I rejoice also in that I have confidence of your sincerity, of your real desire to promote the glory of God by peace and goodwill among men.[1] I am likewise thankful to God for your calm manner of writing (a few paragraphs excepted); and yet more for this, that *such* an opponent should by writing in *such* a manner give me an opportunity of explaining myself on those very heads whereon I wanted an occasion so to do.

2. I do not want indeed (though perhaps you think I do) to widen the breach between us, or to represent the difference of the doctrines we severally teach as greater than it really is. So far from it that I earnestly wish there were none at all, or if there must be some, that it may be as small as possible; being fully persuaded that could we once agree in doctrines, other differences would soon fall to the ground.

3. In order to contribute as I am able to this, it will be my endeavour to acknowledge what I think you have spoken right, and to answer what I cannot think right as yet, with what brevity and clearness I can. I desire to do this in as inoffensive a manner as the nature of the thing will bear, and consistently with that brotherly love which I can't deny you without wronging my own soul.

4. You sum up your charge thus:

> You have now, sir, my sentiments. . . . It is impossible for you to put an entire stop to the enormities of the Moravians while you still, (1), too much commend these men, (2), hold principles in common with them, from which these

[1] See Luke 2:14.

enormities naturally follow, and (3), maintain other errors more than theirs, and are guilty of enthusiasm to the highest degree.[a]

I. 1. You first charge me with 'too much commending' the Moravians. That the case may be fully understood I will transcribe the passages which you cite from the *Journal* concerning them, and then give a general answer.

She told me Mr. Molther had advised her, till she received faith, to be still, 'ceasing from outward works'. . . . In the evening Mr. Bray also was highly commending the being *still*. . . . He likewise spoke largely of the *great danger* that attended the doing of *outward works*, and of the *folly* of people that keep *running about to Church* and Sacrament.[b]

Sun. Nov. 4. Our society met, and continued *silent* till eight.[c]

Sun. June 22. I spoke thus: eight or nine months ago certain men arose who affirmed that there is no such thing as any 'Means of Grace', . . . and that we ought to leave off these 'Works of the Law'.[d]

You (Mr. Molther) believe that the way to attain faith is, not to go to Church, not to communicate, not to fast, not to use *so much* private prayer. Not to read the Scripture; not to do temporal good, or attempt to do spiritual good.[e]

You undervalue *good works*, especially works of *outward mercy*, never publicly insisting on the necessity of them.[f]

Some of our brethren asserted, (1), that till they had true faith they ought to be *still*, that is (as they explained themselves), to abstain from the 'Means of

[a] [Thomas Church], *Remarks* [*on the Reverend Mr. John Wesley's Last Journal*, London, Cooper, 1745], pp. 73-74. [As usual in his quotations from other works which he is discussing or answering, Wesley does not quote exactly, but gives a summary of the section with occasional verbatim passages; some of the material is rearranged, and Wesley here adds the numbering of the points. At the foot of p. 2 Wesley added the note: 'N.B. The sentences quoted from the *Remarks* are all printed in italics.' In this edn. these have been printed in roman, either within quotation marks or in smaller type.]

[b] [John Wesley], 4th *Journal* [Nov. 1, 1739–Sept. 3, 1741, London, Strahan, 1744], p. 7 [Nov. 3, 1739. To this Church briefly referred in his *Remarks*, p. 5, as one source of his statement that the Moravians 'have a cant word among them into which they resolve almost everything. This is "stillness". Their notion of this is, that it is "ceasing from all outward works", and leaving off the works of the Christian law; that this is the way to attain faith, not to pray, fast, receive the sacraments, read the Gospel, go to church, do temporal good, or attempt to do spiritual good. . . .' Wesley documents Church's summary from some of the passages briefly listed by page number in the margins of the *Remarks*, pp. 5-7. For *Journal* 4 see Vol. 19 in this edn.].

[c] Ibid. [, Nov. 4].

[d] [Ibid.,] pp. 41-42 [June 22, 1740]. [In Wesley's own footnotes the normal practice is to insert any additions within square brackets, but on occasion this can become over-complex. Thus for the comfort both of reader and publisher, in this volume square brackets are not inserted to indicate minimal changes in the sometimes defective page numbers of Wesley's own citations. Thus 'p. 42' here is given as 'pp. 41-42' rather than '[p. 41-] p. 42' or 'p [p. 41-]42'.]

[e] [Ibid.,] p. 20 [Dec. 31, 1739].

[f] [Ibid.,] p. 108 [letter of Aug. 8, 1740, §14].

Grace', as they are called, the Lord's Supper in particular; (2), that the ordinances are not *means of grace*, there being no other means than Christ.[g]

I could not agree either that none has any faith so long as he is liable to any doubt or fear, or that till we have it we ought to abstain from the ordinances of God.[h]

Mr. *Br——n* speaks so slightingly of the *means of grace* that many are much grieved to hear him. But others are greatly delighted with him. Ten or fourteen of them meet at our Brother Clark's, with Mr. Molther, and make a mere jest of going to Church or to the Sacrament.[i]

You (Mr. Molther) believe it is impossible for a man to 'use these means' without 'trusting in them'.[j]

Believers (said Mr. Simpson) are *not subject* to ordinances, and unbelievers have nothing to do with them.[k]

Believers *need not* and unbelievers *may not* use them. These *do not* sin when they *abstain* from them; but those *do sin* when they do not abstain.[l]

For one who is not born of God to read the Scriptures, or to pray, or to communicate, or to do any outward work, is *deadly poison*. . . . If he does any of these things he *destroys* himself.[m]

Mr. Bell earnestly defended this.

At eight the society (at Nottingham) met. I could not but observe . . . that not one who came in used any prayer at all. . . . I looked for one of our hymn-books, but both that and the Bible were vanished away, and in the room thereof lay the Moravian Hymns and the Count's Sermons.[n]

One of our English brethren, joined with you, said in his public expounding, 'As many go to hell by *praying* as by *thieving*.' Another: 'I knew one who, leaning over the back of a chair, received a great gift. But he must kneel down to give God thanks. So he lost it immediately. And I know not whether he will ever have it again.' And yet another, 'You have lost your first joy. Therefore you pray. That is the devil. You read the Bible. That is the devil. You communicate. That is the devil.'[o]

They affirmed that there is *no commandment* in the New Testament but to *believe*; that no other *duty* lies upon us; and that when a man does believe he is not *bound* or *obliged* to do anything which is commanded there.[p]

Mr. *St*[onehouse] told me, No one has *any degree* of faith till he is 'perfect as God is perfect'.[q]

[g] [Ibid.,] p. 8 [Nov. 4, 1739].
[h] [Ibid.,] p. 8 [Nov. 7, 1739].
[i] [*Journal* 4,] p. 17 [Dec. 13, 1739].
[j] [Ibid.,] p. 20 [Dec. 31, 1739].
[k] [Ibid.,] p. 34 [Apr. 21, 1740].
[l] [Ibid.,] p. 43 [June 24, 1740].
[m] [Ibid.,] p. 48 [July 16, 1740].
[n] [Ibid.,] pp. 87-88 [June 11, 1741].
[o] [Ibid.,] p. 106 [letter of Aug. 8, 1740, §9].
[p] [Ibid.,] p. 41 [June 22, 1740].
[q] [Ibid.,] p. 35 [Apr. 30, 1740].

You believe there are *no degrees* in faith.[r]

I have heard Mr. Molther affirm that there is no justifying faith where there is ever any doubt.[s]

The moment a man is justified, he is sanctified wholly. Thenceforth, till death, he is neither more nor less holy.[t]

We are to grow in grace, but not in holiness.[u]

2. I have frequently observed that I wholly disapprove of all these positions: 'that there are *no degrees* in faith', 'that in order to attain faith we must *abstain* from all the ordinances of God', 'that a believer does not *grow in holiness*', and 'that he is not *obliged* to keep the commandments of God'. But I must also observe: (1). That you ought not to charge the Moravian Church with the first of these, since in the very page from which you quote those words, 'There is no justifying faith where there is ever any doubt' that note occurs, 'In the Preface to the 2nd *Journal* the Moravian Church is cleared from this mistake.'[2] (2). That with respect to the ordinances of God their practice is better than their principle. They do use them themselves, I am a witness, and that with reverence and godly fear.[3] Those expressions, however, of our own countrymen are utterly indefensible; as, I think, are Mr. Molther's also, who was quickly after recalled into Germany. The great fault of the Moravian Church seems to lie in not openly disclaiming all he had said, which in all probability they would have done had they not leaned to the same opinion. I must, (3), observe, that I never knew one of the Moravian Church but that single person affirm that 'a believer does not grow in holiness'. And perhaps he would not affirm it on reflection. But I am still afraid their whole Church is tainted with *quietism, universal*

[r] Ibid. [p. 34, Apr. 25, 1740; cf. also p. 105, letter of Aug. 8, 1740, §5].

[s] [Ibid.,] p. 105 [letter of Aug. 8, 1740, §5].

[t] [Ibid.,] p. 100 [Oct. 3, 1741, a part of Wesley's conversation with Count Zinzendorf, which he gave in Latin in his *Journal*, and of which in this same year he published a partial translation to English in *A Short View of the Difference between the Moravian Brethren, lately in England, and the Reverend Mr. John and Charles Wesley* (*Bibliography*, No. 100; see Vol. 13 in this edn.)]. The original Latin of Zinzendorf's statement on this occasion was: 'Eo momento quo justificatur, sanctificatur penitus. Exin, neque magis sanctus est, neque minus sanctus, ad mortem usque.'

[u] [Ibid.,] p. 101 [Oct. 3, 1741, as last, the Latin original being:
'W[esley]: Putavi, Crescendum esse in gratia!
Z[inzendorf]: Certe. Sed non in sanctitate. . . '].

[2] See *Journal* 4, p. 105, letter of Aug. 8, 1740, §5, and footnote thereto. (In fact Church cited for this teaching, on p. 7 of his *Remarks*, p. 35 of the *Journal* rather than p. 105.)

[3] See Heb. 12:28.

salvation, and *antinomianism*—'I speak' (as I said elsewhere) 'of antinomian *opinions,* abstracted from practice, good or bad.'[4]

3. But I should rejoice if there lay no other objection against them than that of erroneous opinions. I know in some measure how to have compassion on the ignorant; I know the incredible force of prepossession. And God only knows what ignorance or error (all things considered) is invincible, and what allowance his mercy will make in such cases to those who desire to be led into all truth. But how far what follows may be imputed to invincible ignorance or prepossession I cannot tell.

Many of 'you greatly, yea, above measure, exalt yourselves (as a Church) and despise others':[v]

> I have scarce heard one Moravian brother own *his Church* to be wrong in anything.
>
> Many of you I have heard speak of it as if it were infallible.
>
> Some of you have set it up as the judge of all the earth, of all persons as well as doctrines.
>
> Some of you have said that there is no *true Church* but yours; yea, that there are no *true Christians* out of it.
>
> And your own members you require to have *implicit faith* in her decisions, and to pay *implicit* obedience to her directions.

I can in no degree justify these things. And yet neither can I look upon them in the same light that you do, as 'some of the very worst things which are objected to the Church of Rome'.[w] They are exceeding great mistakes. Yet in as great mistakes have holy men both lived and died—Thomas à Kempis,[5] for instance, and Francis Sales.[6] And yet I doubt not they are now in Abraham's bosom.[7]

4. I am more concerned for their 'despising and decrying

[v] [Wesley,] 4th *Journal,* pp. 107-8 [letter of Aug. 8, 1740, §11. In Church's *Remarks,* pp. 7-9, the following passages are summarized and cited in the margins].

[w] *Remarks,* p. 7.

---

[4] Cf. Lev. 19:18.

[5] Thomas Hemerken (*c.* 1380–1471; known as Thomas à Kempis) probable author of the *Imitation of Christ,* was born in Kempen, near Cologne, entered the House of the Canons Regular (later known as the Augustinian Canons) at the Agnietenberg, near Zwolle in 1399, and lived there for the rest of his life.

[6] Born at the Castle of Sales in Savoy in 1567, he gave up brilliant personal prospects to be ordained, and was Bishop of Geneva from 1602 until his death in 1622. He is credited with winning back the Chablais from Calvinism to Roman Catholicism and is recognized as one of the leaders of the Counter-Reformation. His most famous writings are *Introduction to the Devout Life* (1609) and *Treatise on the Love of God* (1616).

[7] Luke 16:22.

self-denial';[x] for their 'extending Christian liberty beyond all warrant of Holy Writ',[y] for their 'want of zeal for good works';[z] and above all for their supposing that 'we may on some accounts use guile'.[a] In consequence of which they do 'use guile or dissimulation in many cases'.[b] 'Nay, in many of them I have found' (not in all, nor in most) 'much subtlety, much evasion and disguise, so "becoming all things to all men" as to take the colour and shape of any that were near them.'[c]

I can neither defend nor excuse those among the Moravians whom I have found guilty of this. But neither can I condemn *all* for the sake of *some*. 'Every man shall give an account of himself to God.'[8]

But you say:

> Your protesting against some of their opinions is not sufficient to discharge you. . . . Have you not prepared the way for these Moravians by . . . countenancing and commending them? And by still speaking of them as if they were in the main the best Christians in the world, and only deluded or mistaken in a few points?[d]

I cannot speak of them otherwise than I think. And I still think, (1), that God has some thousands in our own Church who have the faith and love which is among them, without those errors either of judgment or practice; (2), that next to these, 'the body' of the Moravian Church, however 'mistaken' 'some of them' are, are 'in the main', of all whom I have seen, the 'best Christians' in the world.[9]

5. Because I am continually charged with inconsistency herein, even by the Moravians themselves, it may be 'needful to give a short account of what has occurred between us from the beginning'.[10]

[x] [Wesley,] *Journal,* p. 80 [Apr. 21, 1741, quoting a letter of that date written to his brother Charles, cited in Church, *Remarks,* p. 8].

[y] P. 80.

[z] Ibid.

[a] P. 21 [cited in *Remarks,* pp. 8-9, from JWJ, Dec. 31, 1739].

[b] P. 111 [*Journal,* unfinished letter of Sept. (27-28), 1738].

[c] P. 104 [*Journal,* letter of Aug. 8, 1740, §4(3)].

[d] [Church,] *Remarks,* pp. 11-12.

---

[8] Cf. Rom. 4:12.

[9] Cf. Church, *Remarks,* pp. 19-20, quoted below, I.6.

[10] JWJ 4, p. 109, Sept. 3, 1741, after presenting his letter of Aug. 8, 1740, the quotations continuing to p. 111, to the end of I.5 of this *Answer.*

'My first acquaintance with the Moravian Brethren began in my voyage to Georgia.[e] Being then with many of them in the same ship, I narrowly observed their whole behaviour. And I greatly approved of all I saw.' (The particulars are related in the first *Journal.*)

From Feb. 14, 1735, to Dec. 2, 1737, being with them (except when I went to Frederica or Carolina) twice or thrice every day, I loved and esteemed them more and more. *Yet a few things I could not approve of.* These I mentioned to them from time to time, and then commended the cause to God.

In February following I met with Peter Böhler. My heart clave to him as soon as he spoke. And the more we conversed, so much the more did I esteem both him and the Moravian Church. So that I had no rest in my spirit till I executed the design which I had formed long before, till after a short stay in Holland I hastened forward, first to Marienborn, and then to Herrnhut.

It may be observed that I had before seen 'a few things' in the Moravians 'which I could not approve of'. In this journey I saw *a few more,* in the midst of many excellent things. In consequence whereof,

In Sept. 1738, soon after my return to England, I began the following letter to the Moravian Church. But being fearful of trusting my own judgment, I determined to wait yet a little longer, and so laid it by unfinished:

'My dear brethren,

'I cannot but rejoice in your steadfast faith, in your love to our blessed Redeemer, your deadness to the world, your meekness, temperance, chastity, and love of one another. I greatly approve of your conferences and bands,[f] of your methods of instructing children; and in general of your great care of the souls committed to your charge.

'But of some other things I stand in doubt, which I will mention in love and meekness. And I wish that, in order to remove those doubts, you would on each of those heads, first, plainly answer whether the fact be as I suppose, and if so, secondly, consider whether it be right.

'Is not the Count all in all among you?

'Do you not magnify your own church too much?

'Do you not use guile and dissimulation in many cases?

'Are you not of a close, dark, reserved temper and behaviour? . . .'

'It may easily be seen that my objections then were nearly the same as now.' (Only with this difference; I was not then assured that the facts were as I supposed.) 'Yet I cannot say my affection was lessened at all (for I did not dare to determine anything). But from Nov. 1 I could not but see more and more things which I could not reconcile with the Gospel.'

[e] These are the words of the 4th *Journal,* p. 109, etc. [i.e., under date Sept. 3, 1741].

[f] The Band Society in London began May 1, some time before I set out for Germany.

'These I have set down with all simplicity. . . . Yet do I this because I love them not? God knoweth: Yea, and *in part* I esteem them still. Because I verily believe, they have a sincere desire to serve God; because many of them have tasted of his love, and some retain it in simplicity; because they love one another; because they have *so much* of the truth of the gospel, and *so far* abstain from outward sin. And lastly, because their discipline is, *in most respects*, so truly excellent'[11]—(notwithstanding that visible blemish, the paying *too much* regard to their great patron and benefactor, Count Zinzendorf).

6. I believe if you coolly consider this account you will not find either that it is inconsistent with itself, or that it lays you under any necessity of speaking in the following manner:

> What charms there may be in a demure look and a sour behaviour I know not. But sure they must be in your eye very extraordinary, as they can be sufficient to cover such a multitude of errors and crimes, and keep up the same regard and affection for the authors and abettors of them. I doubt your regard for them was not lessened till they began to interfere with what you thought your province. . . . You was influenced not by a just resentment to see the honour of religion and virtue so injuriously and scandalously trampled upon, but by a fear of losing your own authority.[g]

I doubt, there is scarce one line of all these which is consistent either with truth or love. But I will transcribe a few more before I answer.

> How could you so long and so intimately converse with, so much commend, and give such countenance to such desperately wicked people as the Moravians, according to your own account, were known by you to be? . . . And you still speak of them as if they were in the main the best Christians in the world. . . . In one place you say, 'A few things I could not approve of.' But, in God's name, sir, is the contempt of almost the whole of our duty, of every Christian ordinance, to be so gently touched? Can detestation in such a case be too strongly expressed? Either they are some of the vilest wretches in the world, or you are the falsest accuser in the world. Christian charity has scarce an allowance to make for them as you have described them. If you have done this truly, they ought to be discouraged, by all means that can be imagined.[12]

7. Let us now weigh these assertions. 'They' (i.e., 'the charms of their *sour* behavior') 'must be in your eye very extraordinary.'

[g] [Church,] *Remarks*, pp. 18-19.

---

[11] JWJ 4, pp. 109-11, Sept. 3, 1741.
[12] Church, *Remarks*, pp. 19-20.

. . . Do not you stumble at the threshold? The Moravians [so] excel in *sweetness* of behaviour—'as they can be sufficient to cover, such a *multitude* of *errors* and *crimes*'—'Such a *multitude* of *errors* and *crimes*'! I believe, as to errors, they hold *universal salvation*, and are partly *antinomians* (in opinion) and partly *quietists*. And for this cause I cannot join with them. But where is the *multitude* of errors? Whosoever knows two or three hundred more, let him please to mention them.

Such a *multitude* of *crimes*, too! That some of them have used guile, and are of a close, reserved behaviour, I know. And I excuse them not. But to this *multitude* of *crimes* I am an utter stranger. Let *him* prove this charge upon them who *can*. For *me*, I declare I *cannot*.

'To keep up *the same* regard and affection'. . . . Not so. I say my affection was 'not lessened' till after September 1739, till I had proof of what I had *feared* before. But I had not the *same degree* of regard for them when I saw the dark as well as the bright side of their character. 'I doubt your regard for them was not lessened till they began to interfere with what you thought your province.' If this were only a *doubt*, it were not much amiss; but it presently shoots up into an *assertion*, equally groundless; for my *regard* for them *lessened* even while I was in Georgia. But it increased again after my return from thence, especially while I was at Herrnhut. And it gradually *lessened* again for some years as I saw more and more which I approved not. How then does it 'appear' that I was 'influenced herein by a fear of losing my own authority, not by a just resentment to see the honour of religion and virtue so scandalously trampled upon'—'Trampled upon'! By whom? Not by the Moravians. I never saw any such thing among them.

But what do you mean by a just resentment? I hope you do not mean what is *commonly* called 'zeal'—a flame which often 'sets on fire the whole course of nature, and is itself set on fire of hell'![13]—'Rivers of water run from my eyes, because men keep not thy law.'[14] This resentment on such an occasion I understand. From all other may God deliver me!

8. You go on. 'How could you so long and so intimately converse with . . . such desperately wicked people as the Moravians, according to *your own account*, were known by you to

[13] Cf. Jas. 3:6.
[14] Cf. Ps. 119:136 (BCP).

be?' O sir, what another assertion is this! 'The Moravians, according to your *own account*, were *known* by you to be desperately wicked people while you intimately conversed with them!' Utterly false and injurious. I never gave any such account. I conversed intimately with them, both at Savannah and Herrnhut. But neither then nor at any other time did I *know* or think or say, they were desperately wicked people. I think and say—nay, you blame me for saying—just the reverse, viz., that though I soon 'found among them a few things which I could not approve',[15] yet I believe they are 'in the main some of the best Christians in the world'.[16]

You surprise me yet more in going on thus: 'In God's name, sir, is the contempt of almost the whole of our duty, of every Christian ordinance, to be so very gently touched?' Sir, this is not the case. This charge no more belongs to the Moravians than that of murder. Some of our countrymen spoke very wicked things. The Moravians did not sufficiently disavow them. These are the premises. By what art can you extort so dreadful a conclusion from them?

'Can detestation, in such a case, be too strongly expressed?'—Indeed it can; even were the case as you suppose.—'Either they are some of the vilest wretches in the world, or you are the falsest accuser in the world.'—Neither one nor the other; though I prove what I allege, yet they may be in the main, good men.—'Charity has scarce an allowance to make for them, as you have described them.'—I have described them as of a mixed character, with much evil among them, but more good. Is it not a strange kind of charity which cannot find an allowance to make in such a case?—'If you have described them truly, they ought to be discouraged by all means that can be imagined.'—By all means? I hope not by fire and faggot—though the *House of Mercy*[17] imagines these to be of all means most effectual.

9. You proceed.

[15] Church, *Remarks*, p. 19.

[16] Ibid.

[17] Presumably an ironic reference to the Inquisition, founded in 1232 by Pope Gregory IX. It imposed torture and, in the case of the impenitent, the 'handing over' of the accused 'to the secular arm'—which meant death at the stake. The Spanish Inquisition was set up separately in 1479 to deal with Marranos and Moriscos, converts from Judaism and Islam respectively; in the following centuries it was also put to use in the treatment of Protestants, employing the same practices as the original Inquisition. This may be what was specifically in Wesley's mind.

How can you justify the many good things you say of the Moravians, notwithstanding this character? . . . You say, they love God. . . . But how can this be when they even plead against keeping most of his commandments? . . . You say you believe they have a sincere desire to serve God. . . . How then can they despise his service in so many instances? . . . You declare some of them much holier than any people you had yet known. Strange, if they fail in so many prime points of Christian duty, and this not only habitually and presumptuously, but even to the denying their use and necessity. You praise them for trampling under foot the lust of the flesh, the lust of the eye, and the pride of life. . . . And yet you make them a close, reserved, insincere, deceitful people.[h]

'How you will explain those things, I know not.'—By nakedly declaring each thing as it is. They are, I believe, the most self-inconsistent people now under the sun. And I describe them just as I find them, neither better nor worse, but leaving the good and bad together. Upon this ground I can very easily justify the saying 'many good things' of them, as well as bad. For instance. I am still persuaded that 'they' (many of them) 'love God', although many others of them ignorantly 'plead against the keeping', not *most*, but 'some of his commandments'. I believe 'they have a sincere desire to serve God.' And yet in several instances some of them (I think) 'despise' that manner 'of serving him' which I know God hath ordained. I believe 'some of them are much holier than any people I had known' in August 1740. Yet sure I am that others among them 'fail', not indeed in the 'prime points of Christian duty' (for these are faith and the love of God and man) but in several points of no small importance. Not that they herein sin 'presumptuously', neither; for they are 'fully' (though erroneously) 'persuaded in their own minds'.[18] From the same persuasion they act when they (in some sense) 'deny the use or necessity' of those ordinances. How far that persuasion will justify or excuse them I leave to him who knoweth their hearts. Lastly, I believe 'they trample under foot', in a good degree, the 'lust of the flesh, the lust of the eye, and the pride of life.' And yet many of them 'use reserve', yea, 'guile'. Therefore my soul mourns for them in secret places.[19]

10. But 'I must observe', you say, 'that you fall not only into inconsistencies, but into direct contradictions':

[h] [Church,] *Remarks*, pp. 20-21.

---

[18] Cf. Rom. 14:5.

[19] See Jer. 13:17.

You commend them for 'loving one another in a manner the world knoweth not of'. And yet you charge them with being 'in the utmost confusion, biting and devouring one another'. You say, 'They caution us against natural love of one another. . . . And had wellnigh destroyed brotherly love from among us.'

You praise them, for 'using no diversions but such as become saints', and for 'not regarding outward adorning'. Yet you say they 'conform to the world in wearing gold and costly apparel; and by joining in worldly diversions in order to do good'.

You call their discipline 'in most respects, truly excellent'. I wish you had more fully explained yourself. I am sure it is no sign of good discipline to permit such abominations. And you tell them yourself, 'I can show you such a subordination as answers all Christian purposes, and yet is as distant from that among you as the heavens are from the earth.'

You mention it as a good effect of their discipline that 'everyone knows and keeps his proper rank.' Soon after, as if it were with a design to confute yourself, you say, 'Our brethren have neither wisdom enough to guide, nor prudence enough to let it alone.'[i]

'And now, sir, how can you reconcile these opposite descriptions?'[20] Just as easily as those before, by simply declaring the thing as it is. 'You commend them (the Moravians) for loving one another.[j] And yet charge them with biting and devouring one another.'[k] Them! Whom? Not the Moravians; but the *English* brethren of Fetter Lane, before their union with the Moravians. Here then is no shadow of contradiction, for the two sentences do not relate to the same persons.

You say, 'They had wellnigh destroyed brotherly love from among us,' partly by 'cautions against natural love'.[l] It is a melancholy truth—so they had. But *we* had then no connexion with *them*.[21] Neither therefore does this contradict 'their "loving one another" in a manner the world knoweth not of'.

'You praise them for using no diversions but such as become saints,[m] and yet say'—I recite the whole sentence—'I have heard some of you affirm that Christian salvation implies liberty to conform to the world, by joining in worldly diversions in order to

[i] [Church,] *Remarks*, pp. 20-21 [citing the passages from JWJ which follow].
[j] [Wesley,] *Journal*, p. 4 [Pref. 5].
[k] [Ibid.,] p. 18 [Dec. 19, 1739].
[l] [*Journal* 4], p. 108 [letter of Aug. 8, 1740, §12].
[m] [Ibid.,] p. 5 [Pref. 6].

---

[20] Church, *Remarks*, p. 23.
[21] Wesley and his adherents formally withdrew from the Fetter Lane Society on July 20, 1740.

do good.'[n] And both these are true. The Moravians, in general, 'use no diversions but such as become saints'. And yet I have heard some of them affirm (in contradiction to their own practice) that 'one then mentioned did well when he joined in *playing at tennis* in order to do good.'

11. 'You praise them for not "regarding outward adorning".'[o] So I do, the bulk of the congregation. 'And yet you say' (I again recite the whole sentence) 'I have heard some of you affirm that Christian salvation implies liberty to conform to the world by putting on of gold and costly apparel.'[p] I have so. And I blame them the more because they are condemned by the general practice of their own church.

'You call their discipline "in most respects truly excellent".[q] I could wish you had more fully explained yourself.'[22]—I have, in the second *Journal*, from the 44th to the 82nd page.[23] 'It is no sign of good discipline to permit such abominations'[24] (i.e., error in opinion, and guile in practice). True, 'tis not; nor is it any demonstration against it. For there may be 'good discipline' even in a College of Jesuits.—Another fault is, too great a deference to the Count. And yet, 'in most respects their discipline is truly excellent.'

'You mention it as a good effect of their discipline that "everyone knows and keeps his proper rank."[r] Soon after, as it were with a design to confute yourself, you say, "Our brethren have neither wisdom enough to guide nor prudence enough to let it alone." '[s] Pardon me, sir, I have no design either to confute or to contradict myself in these words. The former sentence is spoken of the *Moravian* brethren, the latter of the *English* brethren of Fetter Lane.

12. You need not therefore 'imagine that either the strong pretences and warm professions of the Moravians', or their 'agreeing with me in some favourite topics' (for my love to them

[n] [Ibid.,] p. 103 [in fact pp. 102-3, letter of Aug. 8, 1740, §4. 'Christian salvation' is understood from §3].
[o] [Ibid.,] p. 5 [Pref. 6].
[p] [Ibid.,] p. 103 [letter of Aug. 8, 1740, §4].
[q] Ibid. [i.e., p. 103 of *Journal* 4, though it is in fact from p. 111].
[r] P. 5 [i.e., of *Journal* 4, §7].
[s] P. 17 [i.e., of *Journal* 4, Dec. 13, 1739. Church's *Remarks*, p. 22, gives these citations].

[22] Church, *Remarks*, p. 22, citing 'p. 5, 111' (i.e., of Wesley's 4th *Journal* extract).
[23] I.e., Aug. 4-14, 1738.
[24] Ibid.

was antecedent to any such *agreement*) 'induce me to overlook their iniquity', and 'to forgive their other crimes'.[t] No. I love them upon quite different grounds—even because I believe (notwithstanding all their faults) they 'love the Lord Jesus in sincerity',[25] and have a measure of 'the mind that was in him'.[26] And I am 'in' great 'earnest when I declare' once more that I have a deep, abiding conviction, by how many degrees the good which is among them overbalances the evil; that I cannot speak of them but with 'tender affection', were it only for the benefits I have received from them; and that at this hour 'I desire union with them' (were those stumbling-blocks once put away which have hitherto made that desire ineffectual) 'above all things under heaven.'[27]

II. 1. Your second charge is 'that I hold in common with them principles from which their errors naturally follow'.[28] You mean, justification by faith alone. To set things in the clearest light I can I will first observe what I hold, and what you object, and then inquire what the consequences have been.

First, as to what I hold, my latest thoughts upon justification are expressed in the following words:

> Justification sometimes means our acquittal at the last day. But this is out of the present question—that justification whereof our Articles and Homilies speak, meaning present . . . pardon, and acceptance with God, who therein 'declares his righteousness and mercy', by or 'for the remission of the sins' that are past. . . .
>
> I believe, the condition of this is faith. I mean, not only that without faith we cannot be justified, but also that as soon as anyone has true faith, in that moment he is justified.
>
> *Good works* follow this faith, but cannot go before it: much less can sanctification, which implies a continued course of good works springing from holiness of heart. But entire sanctification goes before our justification at the last day.

[t] [Church,] *Remarks*, p. 23.

---

[25] Eph. 6:24.

[26] Cf. Phil. 2:5.

[27] Cf. Church, *Remarks*, p. 23: 'With what tender affection do you yet speak of them! One can scarce think you in earnest when you declare that you loved them and desire union with them above all things under heaven.'

[28] Cf. Church, *Remarks*, p. 24: '[Consider] whether their mischievous opinions . . . be not the plain and evident consequence of what you still teach. . . . And it will be but vain and idle for you to resent the conclusion while you hold the principle from which it flows. . . .'

It is allowed that repentance and 'fruits meet for repentance' go before faith. Repentance *absolutely* must go before faith; 'fruits meet for it' if there be opportunity. By *repentance* I mean conviction of sin, producing real desires and sincere resolutions of amendment; and by 'fruits meet for repentance' forgiving our brother, ceasing from evil, doing good, using the ordinances of God, and in general obeying him according to the measure of grace which we have received. But these I cannot as yet term 'good works', because they do not spring from faith and the love of God.

2. Faith, in general, is a divine, supernatural ἔλεγχος (evidence or conviction) of things not seen, not discoverable by our bodily senses, as being either past, future, or spiritual. Justifying faith implies, not only a divine ἔλεγχος that 'God was in Christ reconciling the world unto himself,' but a sure trust and confidence that Christ died for *my* sins, that he loved *me*, and gave himself for *me*. And the moment a *penitent* sinner *thus* believes, God *pardons* and absolves him.[u]

Now it being allowed,

that both inward and outward holiness are the stated conditions of final justification, . . . what more can you desire, who have hitherto opposed *justification by faith alone,* merely upon a principle of conscience, because you was zealous for holiness and good works? Do I not effectually secure these from contempt at the same time that I defend the doctrines of the Church? I not only allow, but vehemently contend, that none shall ever enter into glory who is not holy on earth, as well in heart as 'in all manner of conversation'. I cry aloud, 'Let all that have believed be careful to maintain good works'; and, 'Let every one that nameth the name of Christ depart from all iniquity.' I exhort even those who are conscious they do not believe, 'Cease to do evil, learn to do well'; 'The kingdom of heaven is at hand'; therefore, repent, and 'bring forth fruits meet for repentance.' Are not these directions the very same in substance which you yourself would give to persons so circumstanced? . . .

3. Many of those who are perhaps as zealous of good works as you, think I have allowed you too much. Nay, my brethren, but how can we help allowing it, if we allow the Scriptures to be from God? For is it not written, and do not you yourselves believe, 'Without holiness no man shall see the Lord'? And how, then, without fighting about words, can we deny that holiness is a condition of final acceptance? And, as to the first acceptance or pardon, does not all experience as well as Scripture prove that no man ever yet truly 'believed the gospel' who did not first *repent*? . . . Repentance therefore we cannot deny to be necessarily previous to faith. Is it not equally undeniable that the running back into wilful, known sin (suppose it were drunkenness or uncleanness) stifles that repentance or conviction? And can that repentance come to any good issue in his soul, who resolves not to forgive his brother? Or who obstinately refrains from what God convinces him is right, whether it be prayer or hearing his Word? Would you scruple yourself to tell one of these . . . , 'Unto him that hath shall be given; but from him that hath not (i.e., uses it not) shall be taken even that

[u] *A Farther Appeal to Men of Reason and Religion,* pp. 1-2 [i.e., Pt. I, I.2, 4, abr.; see 11:105-7 in this edn. for the scriptural allusions in this passage].

which he hath.' Would you scruple to say this? . . . But in saying this you allow all which I have said, viz., that previous to justifying faith there *must* be repentance, and if opportunity permit, 'fruits meet for repentance'.

And yet I allow you this, that although both repentance and the fruits thereof are in *some sense* necessary before justification, yet neither the one nor the other is necessary in the *same sense* or in the *same degree* with faith. Not in the *same degree;* for in whatever moment a man believes (in the Christian sense of the word) he is justified, his sins are blotted out, 'his faith is counted to him for righteousness.' But it is not so at whatever moment he repents, or brings forth any or all the fruits of repentance. Faith alone therefore justifies, which repentance alone does not, much less any outward work. And consequently none of these are necessary to justification in the *same degree* with faith.

Nor in the *same sense.* For none of these has so direct, immediate a relation to justification as faith. This is *proximately* necessary thereto; repentance, *remotely*, as it is necessary to the increase or continuance of [. . .] repentance.[29] And even in this sense these are only necessary on supposition—if there be time and opportunity for them; for in many instances there is not, but God cuts short his work, and faith prevents the fruits of repentance. So that the general proposition is not overthrown, but clearly established by these concessions; and we conclude still . . . that faith alone is the proximate condition of justification.[v]

4. This is what I hold concerning justification. I am next, briefly to observe what you object. 'If faith', say you, 'is the sole condition of justification, then it is our sole duty.'[w] I deny the consequence. Faith may be (in the sense above described) the sole condition of justification, and yet not only repentance be our duty *before*, but all obedience *after* we believe.

You go on. 'If good works are not conditions of our justification, they are not conditions of our (final) salvation.'[x] I deny the consequence again. 'Good works' (properly so called) cannot be the conditions of justification, because it is impossible to do any good work *before* we are justified. And yet, notwithstanding, good works may be (and are) conditions of final

[v] Ibid., pp. 13-15 [i.e., *A Farther Appeal*, Pt. I, II.8-11, abr.; see 11:115-17 in this edn. for the scriptural allusions in this passage].

[w] [Church,] *Remarks*, p. 25.

[x] Ibid.

[29] This, of course, is nonsense, coming from the 1st edn. of *A Farther Appeal*, which omitted a whole line from the manuscript, replacing it in an erratum slip, which did not find its way into any subsequent edn. until that of 1976. The original manuscript read, 'repentance, *remotely*, as it is necessary to the increase or continuance of faith: and the fruits of repentance still more remotely, as they are necessary to repentance.' The omission of 'faith' and the following thirteen words, leaving 'repentance' to conclude the sentence, made no sense, of course. When Wesley prepared his next edn. (not having a copy of the erratum by him), he altered the closing 'repentance' to 'faith', which removed the nonsense but did not restore the original sense (see 11:117 in this edn.).

salvation. For who will say it is impossible to do any good work before we are finally saved?

You proceed. 'Can we be saved in the contemptuous neglect of repentance, prayer, etc.?'[y] No, nor justified neither; but while they are previous to faith, these are not allowed to be 'good works'.

You afterwards argue from my own concessions, thus:

> Your notion of true stillness is, 'a patient waiting upon God by lowliness, meekness, and resignation, in all the ways of his holy law, and the works of his commandments'. . . . But how is it possible to reconcile to this the position that these duties are not conditions of our justification? If we are justified without them, we may be saved without them. . . . This consequence cannot be too often repeated.[z]

Let it be repeated ever so often, it is good for nothing. For, far other qualifications are required in order to our standing before God in glory than were required in order to his giving us faith and pardon. In order to this nothing is *indispensably* required but repentance, or conviction of sin. But in order to the other it is indispensably required that we be fully 'cleansed from all sin';[30] that the 'very God of peace'[31] sanctify us wholly, even τὸ ὁλόκληρον ἡμῶν, our entire body, soul, and spirit.[32] It is not necessary, therefore (nor indeed possible), that we should *before* justification 'patiently wait upon God by lowliness, meekness, and resignation, in all the ways of his holy law'. And yet it is necessary in the highest degree that we should thus wait upon him *after* justification. Otherwise, how shall we be 'meet to be partakers of the inheritance of the saints in light'?

5. Soon after you add:

> In the passages last cited you plead for the necessity of a good life. But in others the force of your principles shows itself. . . . An answer approved by you is, 'My heart is desperately wicked. But I have no doubt or fear. I know my Saviour loves me, and I love him.' Both these particulars are impossible if the Scripture be true.[a]

[y] [Church, *Remarks*,] p. 26.
[z] [Ibid.,] p. 26 [i.e., p. 28].
[a] [Church,] *Remarks*, pp. 29-30 [quoting *Journal* 4, Apr. 29, 1740, the words of Rev. George Stonehouse].

---

[30] Cf. 1 John 1:7.
[31] 1 Thess. 5:23.
[32] Ibid.

You amaze me! Is it possible you should be ignorant that *your own* heart is 'desperately wicked'?[33] Yet I dare not say either that God does not love *you*, or that you do not love *him*.

'Again, you say "you described the state of those who have forgiveness of sins, but not a clean heart"' (not in the *full, proper* sense). Very true. But even then they had power over both inward and outward *corruptions*—far from being, as you suppose, 'still wedded to their vices, and resolved to continue in them'.[b]

> In another place, after having observed that 'Sin does *remain* in one that is justified, though it has not *dominion* over him,' you go on, 'But fear not, though you have an evil heart. Yet a little while and you shall be endued with power from on high, whereby ye may purify yourselves, even as he is pure.' . . . Sinners, if they believe this, may be quite secure, and imagine they have nothing to fear, though they continue in their iniquities. . . . For God's sake, sir, speak out. . . . If they that have an evil heart have not, who has reason to fear?[c]

All who have not *dominion* over sin. All who 'continue in their iniquities'. You, for one, if any sin has dominion over you. If so, I testify against you this day (and you will not be 'quite secure', 'if you believe me'), 'The wrath of God abideth on you!'[34]

'What do you mean by "Sin remains in one that is justified"? That he is guilty of any known, wilful, habitual sin?'[d] Judge by what has gone before. I mean the same as our Church means by 'Sin remains in the regenerate.'[35]

6. You proceed to another passage, which in the *Journal* stands thus:

> After we had wandered many years in the *new path* of *salvation by faith and works*, about two years ago it pleased God to show us the *old way* of *salvation by faith only*. And many soon tasted of *this salvation*, being justified freely, having *peace* with God, *rejoicing* in hope of the glory of God, and having his *love* shed abroad in their hearts.[e]

Thus I define what I mean by *this salvation*, viz., 'righteousness, and peace, and joy in the Holy Ghost'.[36]

[b] [Church, *Remarks*,] p. 30. [c] [Ibid.,] pp. 30-31.
[d] [Ibid.,] pp. 31-32. [e] [Wesley, *Journal* 4,] p. 41 [June 22, 1740].

[33] Jer. 17:9.
[34] Cf. John 3:36.
[35] Cf. Art. IX, '*Of Original or Birth Sin:* . . . this infection of nature doth remain, yea, in them that are regenerated. . . .' See also Albert C. Outler's introduction to and notes on Wesley's *On Sin in Believers* (2:314-16 in this edn.), Art. IX being quoted on p. 318.
[36] Rom. 14:17.

But you object, 'Here you deny the necessity of good works in order to salvation'.[f]—I deny the necessity, nay possibility, of *good works* as previous to *this* salvation, as previous to faith or those fruits of faith, righteousness and peace and joy in the Holy Ghost. This is my *'real sentiment'*, not 'a slip of my pen', neither any proof of my want of accuracy.[37]

7. 'I shall now, you say, consider the account you give in this *Journal*, of the doctrine of justification.'[g]

I will recite the whole, just as it stands, together with the occasion of it.

In the afternoon I was informed how many who cannot, in terms, *deny* it—*explain* justification by faith. They say (1), justification is *twofold;* the *first* in this life, the *second* at the last day. (2). Both these are by *faith alone,* that is, by *objective faith,* or, by the merits of Christ, which are the object of our faith. And this, they say, is all that St. Paul and the Church mean, by 'We are justified by faith only.' But they add, (3), we are not justified by *subjective faith alone,* that is, by the faith which is in us. But good works also must be added to this faith, as a *joint* condition both of the *first* and *second* justification.

In flat opposition to this I cannot but maintain (at least till I have a clearer light), (1), that the justification which is spoken of by St. Paul to the Romans, and in our Articles, is *not twofold.* It is one, and no more. It is the present remission of our sins, or our first acceptance with God. (2). It is true that the merits of Christ are the sole cause of this our justification. But it is not true that this is all which St. Paul and our Church mean by our being justified by faith only; neither is it true that either St. Paul or the Church mean[s] by faith the merits of Christ. But, (3), by our being justified by faith only both St. Paul and the Church mean that the condition of our justification is faith alone, and not good works; inasmuch as all works done before justification have in them the nature of sin. Lastly, that faith which is the sole condition of justification is the faith which is in us[38] by the grace of God. It is a sure trust which a man hath that Christ hath loved *him* and died for *him.*[h]

8. To the first of these propositions you object, 'that justification is not only twofold, but manifold. For a man may possibly sin many times, and as many times be justified or forgiven.'[i]

[f] [Church, *Remarks,*] p. 33.
[g] [Church,] *Remarks,* p. 30 [i.e., pp. 36-37].
[h] [Wesley,] *Journal* [4,] pp. 16-17 [i.e., Dec. 13, 1739].
[i] [Church,] *Remarks,* pp. 37-39.

[37] Cf. Church, *Remarks,* p. 33, 'unless, which I charitably hope, the sentence before me be only a slip of your pen, and do[es] not contain your real sentiments. In which case, however, you are obliged to [confess] your want of judgment and accuracy. . . .'

[38] The edition in Wesley's *Works* (1772) was revised to read 'wrought in us', though 'wrought' was not present in the original.

I grant it. I grant also that justification sometimes means a *state* of acceptance with God. But all this does not in the least affect my assertion, that '*that justification* which is spoken of by St. Paul to the Romans, and by our Church in the 11th, 12th, and 13th Articles, is not *our acquittal* at the last day, but the *present remission* of our sins'.[39]

You add,

> You write in other places so variously about this matter that I despair to find any consistency. . . . Once you held[40] 'a degree of justifying faith short of "the full assurance" of faith, the "abiding witness" of the Spirit, or the clear perception that Christ abideth in him'. . . . And yet you afterwards 'warned all not to think they were justified before they had a clear assurance that God had forgiven their sins'. . . . What difference there is between this 'clear assurance' and the former 'full assurance' and 'clear perception' I know not.[j]

Let us go on step by step, and you will know. 'Once you held "a *degree* of justifying faith, short of the *full assurance* of faith, *the abiding* witness of the Spirit, or the *clear perception* that Christ abideth in him."' And so I hold still, and have done for some years. 'And yet you afterwards warned all not to think they were justified before they had a clear assurance that God had forgiven their sins.'—I did so. 'What difference there is between this *clear assurance*, and that *full assurance* and *clear perception*, I know not.'—Sir, I will tell you. The one is an *assurance* that *my* sins are forgiven, *clear* at first, but soon clouded with doubt or fear. The other is, such a *plerophory* or *full assurance* that I am forgiven, and so clear a perception that Christ 'abideth in me'[41] as utterly excludes all doubt and fear, and leaves them no place, no, not for an hour. So that the difference between them is as great as the difference between the light of the morning and that of the midday sun.

9. On the second proposition you remark, (1), that I ought to have said, 'The merits of Christ are (not the *sole* cause, but) the *sole meritorious* cause of this our justification; (2), that St. Paul and the Church, by justifying faith, mean faith in the gospel and

[j] [Church, *Remarks*,] p. 40.

[39] See JWJ, Dec. 13, 1739, and cf. above, II.7.
[40] Orig. 'hold', revised in Wesley's *Works* (1772).
[41] John 15:5.

merits of Christ.'[k] The very thing. So I contend, in flat opposition to those who say they mean *only the object* of this faith.

Upon the third proposition, 'By our being justified by faith only both St. Paul and the Church mean that the condition of our justification is *faith alone,* and not good works,' you say: 'Neither of them mean any such thing. You greatly wrong them in ascribing so mischievous a sentiment to them.'[l] Let me beg you, sir, to have patience, and calmly to consider: (1). What I mean by this proposition. Why should you any longer run as uncertainly, and fight as one that beateth the air?[42] (2). What is advanced touching the sentiments of the Church in the tract referred to above.[43] Till you have done this it would be mere loss of time to dispute with you on this head.

I waive therefore for the present the consideration of some of your following pages. Only I cannot quite pass over that (I believe, new) assertion, that 'the 13th Article, entitled,

Of Works done before Justification

does not speak of works done *before justification,* but of works *before grace,* which is a very different thing!'[m]—I beseech you, sir, to consider the 11th, 12th, and 13th Articles, just as they lie, in one view. And you cannot but see that it is as absolutely impossible to maintain that proposition as it is to prove that the 11th and 12th Articles 'speak not of Justification' but of some 'very different thing'.

10. Against that part of the fourth proposition, 'Faith is a sure trust which a man hath that Christ loved *him* and died for *him,*' you object: 'This definition is absurd, as it supposes that such a sure trust can be in one who does not repent of his sins.'[n]—I suppose quite the contrary, as I have declared over and over; nor therefore is there any such 'danger' as you apprehend.

But you say, 'There is nothing distinguishing enough in this to point out the true justifying faith.'[o] I grant it—supposing a man were to write a book and say this of it, and no more. But did you ever see any treatise of mine wherein I said this of faith, and no

[k] [Church,] *Remarks,* p. 41 [again citing p. 17 of Wesley, *Journal* 4].
[l] Ibid. [citing Wesley, ibid.].
[m] [Church, *Remarks,*] p. 45.
[n] [Ibid.,] p. 48.
[o] Ibid.

---

[42] See 1 Cor. 9:26.
[43] *A Farther Appeal,* Pt. I; see II.1 above, pp. 94-95.

more? Nothing whereby to distinguish *true* faith from *false*? Touching this *Journal* your own quotations prove the contrary. Yea, and I everywhere insist that we are to distinguish them by *their* fruits, by inward and outward *righteousness*, by the *peace* of God filling and ruling the heart, and by patient active *joy* in the Holy Ghost.[44]

You conclude this point: 'I have now, sir, examined at large your account of justification, and I hope fully refuted the several articles in which you have comprised it.'[p]—We differ in our judgment. I do not apprehend you have 'refuted' any one proposition of the four. You have indeed amended the second, by adding the word 'meritorious'; for which I give you thanks.

11. You next give what you style '*The* Christian Scheme'[q] of justification, and afterwards point out the consequences which you apprehend to have attended the preaching justification by faith—the third point into which I was to inquire.

You open the cause thus:

> The denying the necessity of good works as the condition of justification directly draws after it, or rather includes in it, all manner of impiety and vice. . . . It has often perplexed and disturbed the minds of men, and in the last century occasioned great confusions in this nation. . . . These are points which are ever liable to misconstructions, and have ever yet been more or less attended with them. And it appears from what you have lately published that since you have preached the doctrine it has had its old consequences, or rather worse ones: it has been more misunderstood, more perverted and abused, than ever.[r]

'The denying the necessity of good works as the condition of justification draws after it, or rather includes in it, all manner of impiety and vice.' Here stands the proposition. But where is the proof? Till that appears I simply say, 'It does not.'

'It has often perplexed and disturbed the minds of men.' And so have many other points in St. Paul's epistles.

But 'these are points which are ever liable to misconstructions, and have ever yet, more or less, been attended with them.'—And what points of *revealed* religion are those which are not 'ever liable to misconstructions'? Or of what material point can we say that it has not 'ever yet, more or less, been attended with them'?

[p] [Ibid.,] p. 49.
[q] [Ibid.,] p. 50.
[r] [Ibid.,] pp. 1-2.

[44] See Rom. 14:17.

'In the last century it occasioned great confusions in this nation.'—'*It* occasioned'? No; in no wise. It is demonstrable, the occasions of those confusions were quite of another kind.

'And it appears . . . that since you have preached the doctrine it has had its old consequences, or rather worse. It has been more misunderstood, more perverted and abused than ever.'—What! Worse consequences than *regicide* (which you say was the old one) and making our whole land a *field of blood*? Or 'has it been more perverted and abused' than when (in *your* account) it overturned the whole frame both of church and state?

12. You go on: 'The terms of the gospel are, repentance toward God, and faith toward our Lord Jesus Christ. . . . But when we undervalue either of these terms we involve the consciences of the weak in fatal perplexities; we give a handle to others to justify their impieties; we confirm the enemies of religion in their prejudices.'[s]

All this I grant. But it affects not me. For I do not undervalue either faith or repentance.

> Was not irreligion and vice already prevailing enough in the nation, but we must . . . throw snares in people's way, and root out the remains of piety and devotion in the weak and well-meaning? That this has been the case your own confessions put beyond all doubt. And you even now hold and teach the principles from which these dangerous consequences do plainly and directly follow.[t]

'Was not irreligion and vice already prevailing enough' (whether I have increased them we will consider by and by) '. . . but we must throw snares in people's way?'—God forbid! My whole life is employed in taking those snares out of people's way which the world and the devil have thrown there.—'And root out the remains of piety and devotion in the weak and well-meaning.' Of whom speaketh the prophet this? Of himself? Or of some other man?[45]—'Your own confessions put this beyond all doubt.'—What? That I 'root out the remains of piety and devotion'? Not so. The sum of them all (recited above) amounts to this and no more: that 'while my brother and I were absent from London many weak men were tainted with wrong opinions, most of whom we recovered at our return. But even those who

[s] [Church,] *Remarks*, p. 2.

[t] [Ibid.,] p. 3.

[45] Cf. John 18:34.

continued therein did notwithstanding continue to live a holier life than ever they did before they heard us preach.'[46] 'And you even now hold the principles from which these dangerous consequences do plainly and directly follow.'—But I know not where to find 'these consequences'—unless it be in your title-page. There indeed I read of 'the very fatal tendency' of justification by faith only, 'the divisions and perplexities of the Methodists', and 'the many errors relating both to faith and practice, which' (as you conceive) 'have already arisen among these deluded people'.

However, 'you charitably believe I was not aware of these consequences at first.'[u] No, nor am I yet; though 'tis strange I should not if they 'so naturally succeed that doctrine'.[47] I will go a step farther. I do not know, neither believe, that they ever did 'succeed that doctrine'. Unless perhaps *accidentally*, as they might have succeeded any doctrine whatsoever. And till the contrary is proved those consequences cannot 'show' that 'these principles are not true'.[48]

13. Another consequence which you charge on my preaching justification by faith is the introducing the errors of the Moravians. 'Had the people', say you, 'gone on in a quiet and regular practice of their duty, as most of them did before you deluded them, it would have been impossible for the Moravian tenets to have prevailed among them. . . . But when they had been long and often used to hear good works undervalued . . . I cannot wonder . . . that they should plunge into new errors, . . . and wax worse and worse.'[v]

This is one string of mistakes. 'Had the people gone on in a quiet and regular practice of their duty, as most of them did before you deluded them.'—'Deluded them'! Into what? Into the love of God and all mankind, and a zealous care to keep his commandments. I would to God this delusion (if such it is accounted) may spread to the four corners of the earth! But how did 'most of them' go on 'before they were' thus 'deluded'? Four in five, by a moderate computation? Even as other baptized

[u] [Church,] *Remarks*, p. 4.
[v] [Ibid.,] p. 12.

[46] Cf. I.9 above.
[47] Church, *Remarks*, p. 4.
[48] Cf. ibid.

heathens—in the works of the devil,[49] in all the wretchlessness[50] of unclean living. 'In a quiet and regular practice of their duty!'—What duty? The duty of cursing and swearing? The duty of gluttony and drunkenness? The duty of whoredom and adultery? Or of beating one another, and any that came in their way? In this (not very 'quiet' or 'regular') 'practice, did most of' *those* 'go on before' they heard us, who have now 'put off the old man with his deeds',[51] and are holy in all manner of conversation.[52]

Have these, think you, 'been long and often used to hear good works undervalued'? Or are they 'prepared for' receiving the Moravian errors by the knowledge and love of God?[53] O sir, the Moravians know, if you do not, that there is no such barrier under heaven against their tenets as those very people whom you suppose just prepared for receiving them.

But 'complaints' (you say) 'of their errors come very ill from you, because you have occasioned them.'[54] Nay, if it were so, for that very cause they ought to 'come' from me. If I had 'occasioned' an evil, surely I am the very person who ought to 'remove' it as far as I can—to recover, if possible, those who are hurt already, and to caution others against it.

14. On some of those complaints (as you term them) you remark as follows: 'Many of those who once knew in whom they had believed' (these are my words) 'were thrown into idle reasonings, and thereby filled with doubts and fears.'[w] 'This', you add, 'it is to be feared, has been too much the case of the Methodists in general. . . . Accordingly we find in this *Journal* several instances not barely of doubts and fears, but of the most desperate despair. This is the consequence of resting so much on sensible impressions. . . . Bad men may be led into presumption thereby, an instance of which you give, p. 66.'[55]

[w] [Ibid.,] p. 13 [citing Wesley, *Journal* 4, p. 8, i.e., Nov. 7, 1739].

---

[49] 1 John 3:8.

[50] Orig., 'wretchlessness', altered in *Works*, 1772, to 'wretchedness', but corrected back to 'wretchlessness' in the errata and in Wesley's manuscript revisions in his own copy. *OED* shows that the word was 'an erroneous form of *retchlessness*, obsolete variation of *recklessness*'. Wesley was in fact alluding to Art. XVII of the Thirty-nine Articles: '. . . for curious and carnal persons, lacking the Spirit of Christ, to have continually before their eyes the sentence of God's predestination is a most dangerous downfall, whereby the devil doth thrust them either into desperation or into wretchlessness of most unclean living, not less perilous than desperation.'

[51] Col. 3:9.

[52] 1 Pet. 1:15.

[53] BCP, Communion, Blessing.

[54] Church, *Remarks*, p. 13.

[55] Ibid., pp. 13-14.

That instance will come in our way again. 'Many of those who once knew in whom they had believed were thrown' (by the antinomians) 'into idle reasonings, and thereby filled with doubts and fears.' 'This', you fear, 'has been the case with the Methodists in general.' You must mean (to make it a parallel case) 'that the generality of the people now termed Methodists were true believers till they heard us preach, but were *thereby* 'thrown into idle reasonings, and filled with' *needless* 'doubts and fears'. Exactly contrary to truth in every particular. For, (1), they lived in open sins 'till they heard us preach', and consequently were no better 'believers' than their father, the devil.[56] (2). They were not then thrown into 'idle reasonings', but into 'serious thought' how to flee from the wrath to come.[57] Nor, (3), were they filled with 'needless doubts and fears', but with such as were *needful* in the highest degree—such as actually issued in repentance toward God, and faith in our Lord Jesus Christ.

'Accordingly we find in this *Journal* several instances of the most desperate despair—pages 24, 38, 63.'[58]

Then I am greatly mistaken. But I will set down at length the several instances you refer to.

Page 24. 'I was a little surprised in going out of the Room at one who catched hold of me, and said abruptly, "I must speak with you, and will. I have sinned against light and against love."' (N.B. She was soon after, if not at that very time, a common prostitute.) '"I have sinned beyond forgiveness. I have been cursing you in my heart, and blaspheming God, ever since I came here. I am damned. I know it. I feel it. I am in hell. I have hell in my heart." I desired two or three who had confidence in God to join in crying to him on her behalf. Immediately that horrible dread was taken away, and she began to see some dawnings of hope.'[59]

Page 38. 'The attention of all was soon fixed on poor L[ucretia] S[mith]. One so violently and variously torn of the evil one did I never see before. Sometimes she laughed till almost strangled; then broke out into cursing and blaspheming; then stamped and struggled with incredible strength, so that four or five could scarce hold her; then cried out, "O eternity! Eternity. O that I had no soul! O that I had never been born." At last she faintly called

[56] See John 8:44.
[57] Matt. 3:7.
[58] Church, *Remarks*, p. 13 (citing Wesley, *Journal* 4).
[59] Jan. 22, 1740.

on Christ to help her. And the violence of her pangs ceased.'[60]

(It should be remembered that from that time to this her conversation has been as becometh the gospel.[61])

Page 63. 'Thursday, Dec. 25 [1740]. I met with such a case as I do not remember either to have known or heard of before. L[ucretia] S[mith]' (the same person) 'after many years of mourning' (long before she heard of us) 'was filled with peace and joy in believing. In the midst of this, without any discernible cause, such a cloud suddenly overwhelmed her that she could not believe her sins were ever forgiven at all, nor that there was any such thing as forgiveness of sins. She could not believe that the Scriptures were true, that there was any heaven, or hell, or angel, or Spirit, or any God. One more I have since found in the same state.' (But observe, neither of these continued therein—nor did I ever know one that did.) 'So sure it is that all faith is the gift of God, which the moment he withdraws, the evil heart of unbelief will poison the whole soul.'

Which of these is an 'instance of the most desperate despair'? Surely the 'most desperate' of any, yea, the only one which is properly said to be desperate at all, is that which produces instant self-murder, which causes a poor wretch, by a sin which he cannot repent of, to rush straight through death into hell. But that was not the case in any of these instances; in all which we have already 'seen the end of the Lord'.[62]

15. That I raise separate 'Societies against the Church',[x] is a charge which I need not examine till the evidence is produced. You next cite a Moravian's words to me (an Englishman joined with the Moravians): 'You have eyes full of adultery, and cannot cease from sin; you take upon you to guide unstable souls, and lead them in the way of damnation'—and remark, 'This is only returning some of your own treatment upon yourself. Here also you set the pattern.'[63] At what time and place? When and where were 'such abuses as these thrown out' by me 'against our universities, and against our regular clergy, not the highest or the worthiest excepted'?[64] I am altogether clear in this matter, as often

[x] [Ibid.,] p. 14 [citing JWJ for Feb. 18, 1741].

[60] May 21, 1740.

[61] See Phil. 1:27.

[62] Jas. 5:11.

[63] Church, *Remarks*, p. 14 (citing Wesley, *Journal* 4 for July 22, 1740).

[64] Ibid., pp. 14-15.

as it has been objected. Neither do I desire to receive any other treatment from the clergy than they have received from me to this day.

You have a note at the bottom of this page which runs thus: 'See page 71, 77, and 73, where some Methodists said they had heard both your brother and you many times preach popery.'[65]

I am afraid you advance here a wilful untruth, purely *ad movendam invidiam*.[66] For you cannot but know, (1), that there is not one word of 'preaching popery' either in the 71st or 77th page; and, (2), that when Mr. C[ennick] and two other *predestinarians* (as is related, page 73)[67] affirmed, they 'had heard both my brother and me many times preach popery', they meant neither more nor less thereby than the doctrine of *universal redemption*.

16. You proceed:

> Kingswood you call 'you own house'. And when one Mr. C[ennick] opposed you there you reply to him, 'You should not have supplanted me in *my own house*, stealing the hearts of the people.'. . . The parochial clergy may call their several districts their *own houses* with much more propriety than you could call Kingswood *yours*. And yet how have you supplanted them therein, and laboured to steal the hearts of the people. . . . You have suffered by the same ways you took to discharge your spleen and malice against your brethren.
>
> Your brother's words to Mr. C[ennick] are . . . 'Whether his doctrine is true or false is not the question. But you ought first to have fairly told him, "I preach contrary to you. Are you willing notwithstanding that I should continue *in your house* gainsaying you? . . . Shall I stay here opposing you, or shall I depart?"'. . . Think you hear this spoken to *you* by *us*. . . . What can you justly reply? . . . Again, if Mr. C[ennick] had said thus to you, and you had refused him leave to stay; I ask you whether, in such a case, he would have had reason to resent such a refusal? I think you can't say he would. And yet how loudly have you objected our refusing our pulpits to you![a]

So you judge these to be exactly parallel cases. It lies therefore upon me to show that they are not parallel at all—that there is, in many respects, an essential difference between them.

(1). 'Kingswood you call your own house.' So I do, that is, the school-house there. For I bought the ground where it stands, and paid for the building it, partly from the contribution of my friends

[a] [Ibid.,] pp. 15-16 [citing JWJ, Feb. 18, Mar. 8, 1741].

---

[65] Ibid., p. 14.

[66] 'To provoke hostility'.

[67] JWJ, Feb. 28, 1741.

(one of whom contributed fifty pounds), partly from the income of my own fellowship. No clergyman therefore can call his parish 'his own house' with 'more propriety' than I can call this house *mine*.

(2). 'Mr. C[ennick] opposed you there.' True. But who was Mr. C[ennick]? One I had sent for to *assist me there*—a friend that was as my own soul,[68] that even while he opposed me lay in my bosom. What resemblance then does Mr. *C[ennick], thus* opposing *me*, bear to *me* opposing (if I really did) a *parochial minister*?

(3). 'You said to Mr. C[ennick]: "You should not have supplanted me in my house, stealing the hearts of the people." Yet you have supplanted the clergy in their own houses.'—What, in the *same manner* as Mr. C[ennick] did *me*? Have I done to any of *them* as he has done to *me*? You may as justly say I have cut their throats!—'Stealing the hearts of their people.'—Nor are these 'their' people in the *same sense* wherein those were *mine*, viz., servants of the devil brought through my ministry to be servants and children of God.—'You have suffered by the same ways you took to discharge your spleen and malice against your brethren.' —'To discharge your spleen and malice'! Say, your muskets and blunderbusses. I have just as much to do with one as with the other.

(4). 'Your brother said to Mr. C[ennick]: "You ought to have told my brother fairly, I preach contrary to you. Are you willing I should continue in your house, gainsaying you? Shall I stay here opposing you, or shall I depart?" Think you hear this spoken to *you* by *us*. . . . What can you justly reply?'—I can justly reply: 'Sir, Mr. C[ennick]'s case totally differs from *yours*. Therefore it makes absolutely nothing for your purpose.'

17. A farther consequence (you think) of my preaching this doctrine is 'the introducing that of absolute predestination. And whenever these errors', say you, 'gain ground, there can be no wonder that confusion, presumption, and despair, many very shocking instances of all which you give us among your followers, should be the consequences.'[b]—You should by all means have specified a few of those instances, or at least the pages where they occur. Till this is done I can look upon this assertion as no other than a flourish of your pen.

[b] [Ibid.,] p. 52 [and pp. 54-55].

---

[68] See Deut. 13:6.

To conclude this head. You roundly affirm once for all: 'The grossest corruptions have ever followed the spreading of this tenet. The greatest heats and animosities have been raised thereby. The wildest errors have been thus occasioned. And in proportion to its getting ground it has never failed . . . to perplex the weak, to harden the wicked, and to please the profane. Your *Journal* is a proof that these terrible consequences have of late prevailed, perhaps more than ever.'[c]—Suppose that *Journal* gives a true account of facts (which you seem not to deny) could you find there no other fruits of my preaching than these terrible ones you here mention?

O who so blind as he that *will* not see![69]

18. But that we may not still talk at large, let us bring this question into as narrow a compass as possible. Let us go no farther as to time than seven years last past; as to place than London and the parts adjoining; as to persons than you and me—*Thomas Church* preaching one doctrine, *John Wesley* the other. Now then let us consider with meekness and fear, What have been the consequences of each doctrine?

You have preached *justification by faith and works* at Battersea and St. Ann's, Westminster, while I preached *justification by faith alone* near Moorfields and at Short's Gardens. I beseech you then to consider, in the secret of your heart, How many sinners have you converted to God? By their fruits we shall know them.[70] This is a plain rule. By this test let them be tried. How many outwardly and habitually wicked men have you brought to uniform habits of outward holiness? 'Tis an awful thought! Can you instance in a hundred? In fifty? In twenty? In ten?—If not, take heed unto yourself and to your doctrine. It cannot be that both are right before God.

Consider now (I would not speak; but I dare not refrain) what have been the consequences of even my preaching the other doctrine. By the fruits shall we know those of whom I speak—even the cloud of witnesses[71] who at this hour experience

[c] [Ibid.,] pp. 51-52.

[69] Although Wesley presents this as if it were a line of verse, this proverbial expression had been in currency in various forms for about a century, and appears in both Matthew Henry's *Commentary* (on Jer. 20) and in Swift's *Polite Conversation*, 1738, dial. 3.

[70] See Matt. 7:20, etc.

[71] Heb. 12:1.

the gospel I preach to be the power of God unto salvation.[72] The habitual drunkard, that was, is now temperate in all things.[73] The whoremonger now flees fornication. He that stole, steals no more, but works with his hands. He that cursed or swore, perhaps at every sentence, has now learned to serve the Lord with fear, and rejoice unto him with reverence.[74] Those formerly enslaved to various habits of sin are now brought to uniform habits of holiness. These are demonstrable facts. I can name the men, with their several places of abode. One of them was an avowed *atheist* for many years; some were *Jews;* a considerable number, *Papists*—the greatest part of them as much strangers to the form as to the power of godliness.[75]

When you have weighed these things touching the consequences of *my preaching*, on the one hand (somewhat different from those set down in your *Remarks*), and of *your preaching* on the other, I would earnestly recommend the following words to your deepest consideration: 'Beware of false prophets. Ye shall know them by their fruits. Do men gather grapes of thorns, or figs of thistles? Even so every good tree' (every true prophet or teacher) 'bringeth forth good fruit. . . . Every tree that bringeth not forth good fruit is hewn down and cast into the fire.'[d]

III. 1. Having spoke more largely than I designed on the principle I 'hold in common with the Moravians' I shall touch very briefly on 'those errors' (so called) which, you say, I 'hold more than theirs'.[e]

You name, as the first, my holding 'that a man may have a *degree* of justifying faith before he has, in the *full, proper* sense, a new, a *clean heart*'.[76]

I have so often explained this that I cannot throw away time in adding any more now, only this, that the moment a sinner is justified, his *heart* is *cleansed* in a *low degree*. But yet he has not a *clean heart*, in the *full, proper* sense, till he is made *perfect in love*.[77]

[d] Matt. 7:15-19 [orig., 'Matt. vi.15, &c'.].
[e] [Church,] *Remarks*, p. 55.

---

[72] Rom. 1:16.
[73] 1 Cor. 9:25.
[74] Ps. 2:11 (BCP).
[75] See 2 Tim. 3:5.
[76] Citing JWJ, June 22, 1740.
[77] 1 John 4:18.

2. Another error you mention is this *doctrine of perfection.*[f] To save you from a continued *ignoratio elenchi,*[78] I waive disputing on this point also till you are better acquainted with my real sentiments. I have declared them on that head again and again; particularly in the sermon on *Christian Perfection.*[79]

3. Into this fallacy you plunge from the beginning to the end of what you speak on my third *error* (so you term it), relating to the Lord's Supper, confuting as mine notions which I know not.[g] I cannot think any farther answer is needful here than the bare recital of my own words:

> Fri. June 27 [1740]. I preached on 'Do this in remembrance of me.'. . . It has been diligently taught among us that none but those who are *converted,* who have 'received the Holy Ghost', who are believers in the full sense, ought to communicate.
>
> But experience shows the gross falsehood of that assertion that the Lord's Supper is not a *converting* ordinance. Ye are the witnesses. For many now present know, the very beginning of your *conversion* to God (perhaps, in some the first, deep *conviction*) was wrought at the Lord's Supper. Now one single instance of this kind overthrows that whole assertion.
>
> The falsehood of the other assertion appears both from Scripture—precept and example. Our Lord commanded those very men who were then *unconverted,* who had *not* yet 'received the Holy Ghost', who (in the full sense of the word) were not *believers,* to 'do this in remembrance of him'. Here the precept is clear. And to these he delivered the elements with his own hands. Here is example, equally indisputable.
>
> Sat. 28. I showed at large, (1), that the Lord's Supper was ordained by God to be a *means of conveying* to men either *preventing,* or *justifying,* or *sanctifying grace,* according to their several necessities; (2), that the persons for whom it was ordained are all those who know and feel that they *want* the *grace* of God, either to *restrain* them from sin, or to *show their sins forgiven,* or to *renew their souls* in the image of God; (3), that inasmuch as we come to his table, not to *give* him anything, but to *receive* whatsoever he sees best for us, there is *no previous preparation* indispensably necessary, but *a desire* to receive whatsoever he pleases to give; and (4), that *no fitness* is required at the time of communicating, but *a sense of our state,* of our utter sinfulness and helplessness; everyone who knows he is *fit for hell* being just *fit to come to Christ,* in this as well as all other ways of his appointment.[h]

4. 'A stoical insensibility', you add, 'is the next error I have to charge you with. . . . You say, "the servants of God suffer

[f] [Ibid.,] p. 60.
[g] [Ibid.,] pp. 56-57 [citing Wesley's letter of Aug. 8, 1740, and JWJ, June 28, 1740].
[h] *Journal,* pp. 46-47.

---

[78] 'Ignorance of the argument', i.e., refuting what one's opponent does not assert.
[79] See No. 40 (1741), 2:97-121 in this edn.; cf. *Bibliography,* No. 53.

nothing," and suppose that we ought to be here so free as in the strongest pain not once to desire to have a moment's ease.'

'At the end of one of your hymns you seem to carry this notion to the very height of extravagance and presumption. You say:

> Doom, if thou canst, to endless pains,
> And drive me from thy face.'[i]

'A stoical insensibility is the next error I have to charge you with.'—And how do you support the charge? Why, thus—You say, 'The servants of God suffer nothing.'[j] And can you possibly misunderstand these words if you read those that immediately follow? 'His body was wellnigh torn asunder with pain. But God made all his bed in his sickness. So that he was continually giving thanks to God, and making his boast of his praise.'

'You suppose we ought to be so free as in the strongest pain not once to desire to have a moment's ease.'—O sir, with what eyes did you read those words?

'I dined with one who told me in all simplicity: Sir, I thought last week there could be no such rest as you describe; none in this world wherein we should be so free as not to desire ease in pain. But God has taught me better. For on Friday and Saturday, when I was in the strongest pain, I never once had one moment's desire of ease, but only that the will of God might be done.'[k] Do I say here that 'we ought not, in the strongest pain, once to desire to have a moment's ease'? What a frightful distortion of my words is this. What I say is, 'A serious person affirmed to me that God kept her for two days in such a state.' And why not? Where is the absurdity?

'At the end of one of your hymns you seem to carry this notion to the very height of extravagance and presumption. You say:

> Doom, if thou canst, to endless pains,
> And drive me from thy face.'

'If thou canst'—i.e., *If thou canst* deny thyself, *if thou canst* forget to be gracious, *if thou canst* cease to be truth and love. So the lines both preceding and following fix the sense. I see nothing of

[i] [Church,] *Remarks*, pp. 58-59 [citing *Journal*, pp. 51, 59, 117, i.e., Aug. 4, Oct. 19, 1740, and the appended poem, 'The Means of Grace', pp. 88-90].

[j] *Journal*, p. 59.

[k] [Ibid.,] p. 51 [Monday, Aug. 4, 1740].

'stoical insensibility', neither of 'extravagance'[80] or 'presumption' in this.

5. Your last charge is that I am 'guilty of enthusiasm to the highest degree. Enthusiasm', you say,

> is a false persuasion of an extraordinary divine assistance, which leads men on to such conduct as is only to be justified by the supposition of such assistance. . . . An enthusiast is then sincere, but mistaken. His intentions are good—but his actions most abominable. Instead of making the Word of God the rule of his actions he follows only that secret impulse which is owing to a warm imagination. . . . Instead of judging of his spiritual estate by the improvement of his heart, he rests only on ecstasies, etc. He is very liable to err, as not considering things coolly and carefully. He is very difficult to be convinced by reason and argument, as he acts upon a supposed principle superior to it, the direction of God's Spirit. Whoever opposes him is charged with rejecting[81] the Spirit. His own dreams must be regarded as oracles. . . . Whatever he does is to be accounted the work of God. Hence he talks in the style of inspired persons, and applies Scripture phrases to himself, without attending to their original meaning, or once considering the difference of times and circumstances.[1]

You have drawn, sir (in the main), a true picture of an *enthusiast*. But it is no more like *me* than I am like a centaur. Yet you say, 'They are these very things which have been charged upon you, and which you could never yet disprove.' I will try for once; and to that end will go over these articles one by one.

Enthusiasm is 'a false persuasion of an extraordinary divine assistance, which leads men on to such conduct as is only to be justified by the supposition of such assistance'.—Before this touches *me* you are to prove (which I conceive you have not done yet) that *my* conduct is such as is only to be justified by the supposition of an extraordinary divine assistance. 'An enthusiast is then sincere, but mistaken.' That I am *mistaken* remains also to be proved.—'His intentions are good; but his actions most abominable.' Sometimes they are, yet not *always*. For there may be *innocent* madmen. But what actions of mine are 'most abominable'? I wait to learn. 'Instead of making the Word of God

[1] [Church,] *Remarks*, pp. 60-62.

---

[80] Orig., 'extravagancy'; Wesley quotes the passages correctly earlier in III.4.

[81] Church's original text was, 'resisting or rejecting the Spirit'. All the contemporary edns. of Wesley's *Answer* have 'rejecting', but in his own copy of his *Works* (1772), and in the errata to that volume, he altered this to 'resisting', and made the same alteration when three paragraphs later he came to discuss this passage. (The reason for this later alteration—when Wesley almost certainly did not have Church's *Remarks* on hand—was that 'resist the spirit' was scriptural, see Acts 6:10; 7:51.)

the rule of his actions he follows only his secret impulse.'—In the whole compass of language there is not a proposition which less belongs to me than this. I have declared again and again that I make the Word of God the rule of all my actions; and that I no more follow any 'secret impulse' instead thereof than I follow Mahomet or Confucius.

> Not even a word or look
>   Do I approve or own,
> But by the model of thy Book,
>   Thy Sacred Book alone.[82]

'Instead of judging of his spiritual estate by the improvement of his heart, he rests only on ecstasies.'—Neither is this my case. I rest not on them at all. Nor did I ever experience any. I do judge of my spiritual estate by the improvement of my heart and the tenor of my life, conjointly. 'He is very liable to err.'—So indeed I am. I find it every day more and more. But I do not yet find that this is owing to my want of 'considering things coolly and carefully'. Perhaps you do not know many persons (excuse my simplicity in speaking it) who more carefully consider every step they take. Yet I know, I am not cool or careful enough. May God supply this and all my wants! 'He is very difficult to be convinced by reason and argument, as he acts upon a supposed principle superior to it, the direction of God's Spirit.'—I am very difficult to be convinced by dry blows or hard names (both of which I have not wanted); but not by reason and argument. At least that difficulty cannot spring from the cause you mention. For I claim no other direction of God's Spirit than is common to all believers. 'Whoever opposes him is charged with rejecting[83] the Spirit.'—What, whoever opposes *me, John Wesley?* Do I charge every such person with rejecting the Spirit? No more than I charge him with robbing on the highway. I cite you yourself, to confute your own words. For

[82] Adapted by Wesley from George Herbert's 'Discipline', in *The Temple* (Cambridge, 1633):

> Not a word or look
> I affect to own
>   But by book
> And the Book alone.

This Wesley had altered into a hymn in his *Hymns and Sacred Poems* of 1739, pp. 77-78 (cf. *Poet. Wks.*, I. 70).

[83] See above, n. 81.

do I charge *you* with rejecting the Spirit? 'His own dreams must be regarded as oracles.'—Whose? I desire neither my dreams nor my waking thoughts may be regarded at all, unless just so far as they agree with the oracles of God. 'Whatever he does is to be accounted the work of God.' You strike quite wide of *me* still. I never said so of what I do. I never thought so. Yet I trust what I do is pleasing to God. 'Hence he talks in the style of *inspired* persons.'—No otherwise inspired than you are, if you love God. 'And applies Scripture phrases to himself, without attending to their original meaning, or once considering the difference of times and circumstances.'—I am not conscious of anything like this, I apply no Scripture phrase either to myself or any other, without carefully considering both the[84] *original* meaning, and the *secondary* sense wherein (allowing for different times and circumstances) it may be applied to ordinary Christians.

6. So much for the bulk of your charge. But it concerns me likewise to gather up the fragments of it. You say, 'We desire no more than to try your sentiments and proceedings by the written Word.'[85]—Agreed. Begin when and where you please. 'We find there good works as strongly insisted on as faith.'—I do as strongly insist on them as on faith. But each in its own order. 'We find all railing, etc., condemned therein.'—True; and so you may in all I write or preach. 'We are assured that the doing what God commands is the sure way of knowing that we have received his Spirit.'—We have doubtless received it if we love God (as he commands) with all our heart, mind, soul, and strength;[86] 'and not by any sensible impulses or feelings whatsoever'.—'Any sensible impulses whatsoever'! Do you then exclude *all* 'sensible impulses'? Do you reject 'inward feelings' *toto genere?*[87] Then you reject both the *love* of God and of our neighbour. For if these cannot be *inwardly felt,* nothing can. You reject all *joy* in the Holy Ghost.[88] For if we cannot be *sensible*[89] of this, it is no joy at all. You reject the *peace* of God, which if it be not *felt* in the *inmost soul* is a dream, a notion, an empty name. You therefore reject the whole *inward kingdom* of God, that is, in effect, the whole gospel of Jesus Christ.

[84] Orig., 'their' in all contemporary edns., but altered in Wesley's own copy of his *Works* (1772) and in the errata to that volume.

[85] Church, *Remarks,* pp. 62-63.

[86] See Luke 10:27.

[87] 'Of every kind'.

[88] Rom. 14:17.

[89] The primary meaning of this word in Wesley's day, of course, was 'affecting the senses' rather than 'making sense'.

You have therefore yourself abundantly shown (what I do not *insinuate*, but proclaim on the housetop) that I am charged with *enthusiasm* for *asserting the power* (as well as the form) *of godliness*.[90]

7. You go on, 'The character of the enthusiast above drawn will fit, I believe, all such of the Methodists as can be thought sincere.'[m]—I believe not. I have tried it on one, and it fitted him just as Saul's armour did David. However, 'a few instances' of enthusiasm you undertake to show 'in this very *Journal*'.

And first 'you give us one' (these are your words) 'of a private revelation, which you seem to pay great credit to.'[91] You partly relate this, and then remark, 'What enthusiasm is here! To represent the conjectures of a woman whose brain appears to have been too much heated as if they had been owing to a particular and miraculous spirit of prophecy!' Descant, sir, as you please on this *enthusiasm;* on the *credit* I paid to this private revelation; and my 'representing the conjectures' of this brain-sick woman as owing to the miraculous 'power of the Spirit of God'. And when you have done I will desire you to read that passage once more, where you will find my express words are (introducing this account): 'Sunday, 11. I met with a surprising instance of the *power of the devil*.'[n] Such was the *credit* I paid to this revelation! All which I ascribe to 'the Spirit of God' is the enabling her to strive against 'the power of the devil', and at length restoring peace to her soul.

8. As a second instance of enthusiasm you cite those words: 'I expounded out of the fullness which was given me.'[o] The whole sentence is, 'Out of the fullness that was given me I expounded those words of St. Paul (indeed of every true believer), "To me to live is Christ, and to die is gain."' I mean, I had then a *fuller*, deeper sense of that great truth than I *ordinarily* have. And I still think it right to ascribe this, not to myself, but to the Giver of 'every good and perfect gift'.[92]

You relate what follows as a third 'very extraordinary instance of enthusiasm':[p]

[m] [Ibid.,] pp. 63.
[n] *Journal*, pp. 66 [i.e., Jan. 11, 1741].
[o] [Ibid.,] p. 65 [i.e., Jan. 1, 1741].
[p] [Church,] *Remarks*, p. 65.

[90] See 2 Tim. 3:5.
[91] Church, *Remarks*, p. 64, citing JWJ, Jan. 11-12, 1741.
[92] Jas. 1:17.

> Tuesday, Feb. 17, I left London. In the afternoon I reached Oxford, and leaving my horse there (for he was tired, and the horse-road exceeding bad, and my business admitted of no delay), set out on foot for Stanton Harcourt. The night overtook me in about an hour, accompanied with heavy rain. Being wet and weary, and not well knowing my way, I could not help saying in my heart (though ashamed of my want of resignation to God's will), O that thou wouldst 'stay the bottles of heaven'! Or at least give me light, or an honest guide, or some help in the manner thou knowest! Presently the rain ceased; the moon broke out, and a friendly man overtook me, who set me on his own horse, and walked by my side till we came to Mr. Gambold's door.[q]

Here you remark, 'If you would not have us look on this as miraculous, there is nothing in it worthy of being related.'—It may be so; let it pass then as a trifle not worth relating. But still it is no proof of enthusiasm. For I 'would not have you look on it as miraculous'. I do not myself look upon it as such, but as a signal instance of God's *particular providence* over all those who call upon him.

9. 'In the same spirit of enthusiasm' (you go on, citing this as a fourth instance) 'you describe heaven as executing judgments, immediate punishments, on those who oppose you. You say, "Mr. Molther was taken ill this day. I believe it was the hand of God that was upon him."'[r] I do. But I do not say, as a 'judgment from God', for opposing me. That *you* say for me. 'Again, you tell us of "one who was exceeding angry at those who pretended to be in fits, and was just going to kick one of them out of the way when she dropped down herself, and was in violent agonies for an hour." . . . And you say you left her . . . under a deep sense of the "just judgment" of God.'[93] So she termed it, and so I believe it was. But observe. Not for 'opposing me'.—'Again, you mention as an awful providence the case of a poor wretch who was last week cursing and blaspheming, and had boasted to many that he would come again on Sunday, and no man should stop his mouth then.' (His mouth was stopped before, in the midst of the most horrid blasphemies, by asking him if he was stronger than God.) 'But on Friday God laid his hand upon him, and on Sunday he was buried.'[94]—I do look on this as a manifest judgment of God on a hardened sinner, for his complicated wickedness.—'Again,

[q] *Journal*, pp. 69-70 [i.e., Feb. 17, 1741].
[r] [Church,] *Remarks*, p. 66 [citing JWJ, Apr. 21, 1740].

---

[93] Church, *Remarks*, p. 66, citing JWJ, Aug. 16, 1740.
[94] Ibid., pp. 66-67, citing JWJ, Oct. 23, 1740.

"One being just going to beat his wife (which he frequently did), God smote him in a moment, so that his hand dropped, and he fell down upon the ground, having no more strength than a new-born child."'[s] And can you, sir, 'consider this as one of the common dispensations of providence'? Have you known a parallel one in your life? But it was never cited by me, as it is by you, as *an immediate punishment* on a man for *opposing me.* You have no authority from any sentence or word of mine for putting such a construction upon it—no more than you have for that strange intimation (How remote both from justice and charity!) that I 'parallel these cases with those of Ananias and Sapphira, or of Elymas the sorcerer'!

10. You proceed to what you account a fifth instance of enthusiasm. 'With regard to people's falling in fits, it is plain you look upon both the disorders and the removals of them to be supernatural.'—It is not quite plain. I look upon some of these cases as wholly natural, on the rest as mixed, both the disorder and the removal being partly natural and partly not. Six of these you pick out from, it may be, two hundred, and add, 'From all which you leave no room to doubt that you would have these cases considered as those of the demoniacs in the New Testament, in order, I suppose, to parallel your supposed cures of them with the highest miracles of Christ and his disciples.'[t]—I should once have wondered at your making such a supposition. But I now wonder at nothing of this kind. Only be pleased to remember, till this supposition is made good it is no 'confirmation' at all 'of my enthusiasm'.

You then attempt to account for those fits by 'obstructions or irregularities of the blood and spirits; hysterical disorder; watchings, fastings; closeness of rooms, great crowds, violent heat'. And lastly by 'terrors, perplexities, and doubts, in weak and well-meaning men', which you think, in many of the cases before us, have 'quite overset their understandings'.

As to each of the rest, let it go as far as it can go. But I require proof of the last way whereby you would account for these disorders. Why, 'The instances', you say, 'of religious madness have much increased since you began to disturb the world.'[u]—I doubt the fact. Although if these instances had increased lately,

[s] [Ibid.,] p. 67 [citing JWJ, Aug. 12, 1741].

[t] [Church,] *Remarks*, p. 68.

[u] [Ibid.,] p. 69.

'tis easy to account for them another way. 'Most have heard of or known several of the Methodists thus driven to distraction.'—You may have *heard* of five hundred. But how many have you *known*? Be pleased to name eight or ten of them. I cannot find them, no, not one of them to this day, either man, woman, or child. I find some indeed whom *you told* they 'would be distracted' if they continued to follow these men; and whom at that time you threw into much 'doubt' and 'terror' and 'perplexity'. But though they did continue to hear them ever since, they are not distracted yet.

As for 'the abilities, learning, and experience'[v] of Dr. M[onro], if you are personally acquainted with him, you do well to testify them. But if not, permit me to remind you of the old advice:

> *Qualem commendes, etiam atque etiam aspice, ne mox*
> *Incutiant aliena tibi peccata pudorem.*[95]

In endeavouring to account for the people's recovery from those disorders you say, 'I shall not dispute how far prayer may have naturally a good effect.' (Nay, I am persuaded, you will not dispute but it may have *supernatural* good effects also.) 'However, there is no need of supposing these recoveries miraculous.'[w]—Who affirms there is? I have set down the facts just as they were, passing no judgment upon them myself (consequently here is no foundation for the charge of 'enthusiasm'), and leaving every man else to judge as he pleases.

11. The next passage you quote as a proof of my *enthusiasm*, taking the whole together, runs thus: 'After communicating at St. James's, our parish church, I visited several of the sick. Most of them were ill of the spotted fever; which, they informed me, had been extremely mortal, few persons recovering from it. But God had said, "Hitherto shalt thou come. . . ." I believe there was not one with whom we were but recovered.'[x]—On which you comment thus: 'Here is indeed no intimation of anything miraculous.'[96]—No? Not so much as an intimation? Then why is

[v] [Ibid.,] p. 70 [citing JWJ, Sept. 21, 1739 (the 'last *Journal*') and Aug. 23, Sept. 17, 1740].

[w] [Ibid.,] p. 71.

[x] *Journal*, p. 61 [i.e., Nov. 16, 1740].

---

[95] Horace, *Epistles*, I.xvii.76-77: 'What sort of person you introduce, consider again and again, lest by and by the other's failings strike you with shame' (Loeb Classical Library).

[96] Church, *Remarks*, p. 72.

this cited as an instance of my *enthusiasm?* Why, 'You seem to desire to have it believed that an extraordinary blessing attended your prayers; whereas I believe they would not have failed of an equal blessing and success had they had the prayers of their own parish ministers.'[97]—I believe this argument will have *extraordinary success* if it convince anyone that I am an *enthusiast.*

12. You add, 'I shall give but one account more, and this is what you give of yourself.'[y] The sum whereof is, 'At two several times, being ill and in violent pain, I prayed to God and found immediate ease.' I did so. I assert the fact still. 'Now if these' (you say) 'are not miraculous cures, all this is rank *enthusiasm*'.[98]

I will put your argument in form:

He that believes those are miraculous cures which are not so is a rank enthusiast:

But you believe those to be miraculous cures which are not so:

Therefore you are a rank enthusiast.

Before I answer I must know what you mean by 'miraculous'. If you term everything so which is *not strictly accountable for by the ordinary course of natural causes,*[99] then I deny the latter part of the minor proposition. And unless you can make this good, unless you can prove the effects in question are strictly accountable for by the *ordinary course* of natural causes, your argument is nothing worth.

You conclude this head with: '*Can you work miracles?* . . . All your present pretences to the Spirit, till they are proved by miracles, cannot be excused or acquitted from *enthusiasm.*'[z]

My short answer is this: I 'pretend to the Spirit' just so far as is essential to a state of salvation. And cannot I be 'acquitted from enthusiasm' till I 'prove by miracles' that I am in a state of salvation?

13. We now draw to a period. 'The consequences of Methodism,' you say, i.e., of our preaching this doctrine, 'which have hitherto appeared, are bad enough to induce you to leave it. It has

[y] [Church,] *Remarks*, p. 72.
[z] [Ibid.,] p. 73.

---

[97] Ibid.
[98] Ibid., p. 73.
[99] Throughout pp. 60-73 of his *Remarks*, in which Church charges Wesley with enthusiasm, and in effect with claiming miraculous powers, he does not define miracles. Wesley himself wrote at length about miracles, including a similar definition in *A Farther Appeal*, Pt. III, III.29, published about this time (11:310-11 in this edn.).

in fact introduced many disorders, enthusiasm, antinomianism, Calvinism, a neglect and contempt of God's ordinances, and almost all other duties.'[a]

That whenever God revives his work upon earth many 'tares will spring up with the wheat',[1] both the Word of God gives us ground to expect, and the experience of all ages. But where, sir, have you been, that you have heard of the tares only? And that you rank among the consequences of *my* preaching 'a neglect and contempt of God's ordinances, and almost of all duties'? Does not the very reverse appear, at London, at Bristol, at Kingswood, at Newcastle? In every one of which places multitudes of those (I am able to name the persons) who before lived in a thorough 'neglect' and 'contempt' of God's ordinances and all duties do now zealously discharge their duties to God and man, and walk in all his ordinances blameless.[2]

And as to those drunkards, whoremongers, and other servants of the devil, as they were before, who heard us awhile and then fell to the Calvinists or Moravians, are they not even now in a far better state than they were before they heard us? Admit they are in error, yea, and die therein, yet who dares affirm they will perish everlastingly? But had they died in those sins, we are sure they had fallen into 'the fire that never shall be quenched'.[3]

I hope, sir, you will rejoice in considering this, how much their gain still outweighs their loss. As well as in finding the 'sentiments you could not reconcile together clearly and consistently explained'.[4] I am very willing to consider whatever farther you have to offer. May God give us both a right judgment in all things![5] I am persuaded you will readily join in this prayer with,

Reverend sir,
Your servant for Christ's sake,
John Wesley

Bristol, Feb. 2, 1744/45

[a] [Ibid.,] p. 75.

[1] Cf. Matt. 13:26. [2] See Luke 1:6. [3] Mark 9:43, 45.

[4] See Church, *Remarks*, p. 75: 'And if I have not . . . been able to reconcile what you say in different parts of your Journal together, I shall yet rejoice to find you explain your sentiments so clearly and consistently that they may no longer be a snare and an offence to the weak and ignorant.'

[5] BCP, Collect for Whit Sunday.

6

ADVICE TO THE PEOPLE CALLED METHODISTS

(1745)

AN INTRODUCTORY COMMENT

The purpose and content of the Advice *are immediately obvious. It needs only to be added that this is another claim that Methodism is simply 'genuine Christianity', with a warning that those who practice it must expect persecution, and react to it with simplicity, tolerance, and faith.*

For a summary of the nine British editions published during Wesley's lifetime, a stemma illustrating the transmission of the text, and a list of the substantive variant readings from the edited text (based on the 1st ed., Newcastle, Gooding, 1745) see *Appendix A, pp. 541ff.* *For full bibliographical details see* Bibliography, *No. 108.*

Advice to the People called Methodists

Disce, docendus adhuc quae censet amiculus.

Horace[1]

[1.] It may be needful to specify whom I mean by this ambiguous term, since it would be lost labour to speak to Methodists, so called, without first describing those to whom I speak.

[2.] By Methodists I mean a people who profess to pursue (in whatsoever measure they have attained) holiness of heart and life, inward and outward conformity in all things to the revealed will of God; who place religion in an[2] uniform resemblance of the great

[1] Horace, *Epistles*, I.xvii.3—'Yet learn the views of your humble friend, who still needs some teaching' (Loeb Classical Library).

[2] 'an' not present in A, F-H.

Object of it; in a steady imitation of him they worship in all his imitable perfections; more particularly in justice, mercy, and truth,[3] or universal love filling the heart and governing the life.

[3.] You to whom I now speak believe this love of humankind cannot spring but from the love of God. You think there can be no instance of one whose tender affection embraces every child of man (though not endeared to him either by ties of blood or by any natural or civil relation) unless that affection flow from a grateful, filial love to the common Father of all; to God, considered not only as his Father, but as the Father of the spirits of all flesh;[4] yea, as the general parent and friend of all the families both of heaven and earth.

[4.] This filial love you suppose to flow only from faith, which you describe as a supernatural evidence (or conviction) of things not seen,[5] so that to him who has this principle,

> The things unknown to feeble sense,
> Unseen by reason's glimm'ring ray,
> With strong, commanding evidence
> Their heav'nly origin display.
>
> Faith lends its realizing light,
> The clouds disperse, the shadows fly;
> Th' Invisible appears in sight,
> And God is seen by mortal's eye.[6]

[5.] You suppose this faith to imply an evidence that God is merciful to me a sinner;[7] that he is reconciled to me by the death of his Son,[8] and now accepts me, for his sake. You accordingly describe the faith of a real Christian as, 'A sure *trust* and confidence' (over and above his *assent* to the sacred Writings) 'which he hath in God, that his sins are forgiven; and that he is, through the merits of Christ, reconciled to the favour of God'.[9]

[6.] You believe, farther, that both this faith and love are wrought in us by the Spirit of God; nay, that there cannot be in

[3] See Ps. 89:14.

[4] See Num. 16:22; 27:16.

[5] Heb. 11:1.

[6] John and Charles Wesley, *Hymns and Sacred Poems,* 1740, p. 7, sts. 5-6 of the section on 'Verse 1' of Charles Wesley's poem, 'The Life of Faith', pp. 6-20. See also No. 92 in *A Collection of Hymns,* 1780 (7:194-95 in this edn.). In the 2nd to 5th and 1787 edns. the last line reads, 'And God is seen by mortal eye.'

[7] See Luke 18:13.

[8] See Rom. 5:10.

[9] See above, p. 53, for this definition from the Homilies.

any man one good temper or desire, or so much as one good thought, unless it be produced by the almighty power of God, by the inspiration or influence of the Holy Ghost.[10]

[7.] If you walk by this rule, continually endeavouring to know, and love, and resemble, and obey the great God and Father of our Lord Jesus Christ,[11] as the God of love, of pardoning mercy; if from this principle of loving, obedient faith, you carefully abstain from all evil,[12] and labour, as you have opportunity, to do good to all men,[13] friends or enemies; if, lastly, you unite together to encourage and help each other in thus working out your salvation, and for that end watch over one another in love—you are they whom I mean by Methodists.

[8.] The first general advice which one who loves your souls would earnestly recommend to every one of you, is: *Consider, with deep and frequent attention, the peculiar circumstances wherein you stand.*

[9.] One of these is, that you are a *new* people. Your *name* is new (at least as used in a religious sense), not heard of till a few years ago either in our own or any other nation. Your *principles* are new, in this respect, that there is no other set of people among us (and possibly not in the Christian world) who hold them all in the same degree and connexion; who so strenuously and continually insist on the absolute necessity of universal holiness both in heart and life; of a peaceful, joyous love of God; of a supernatural evidence of things not seen; of an inward witness that we are the children of God; and of the inspiration of the Holy Ghost, in order to any good thought or word or work. And perhaps there is no other set of people (at least not visibly united together) who lay *so much*, and yet *no more* stress than you do, on rectitude of *opinions*,[14] on outward *modes of worship*, and the use of those *ordinances* which you acknowledge to be of God. *So much* stress you lay even on right *opinions* as to profess that you earnestly desire to have a right judgment in all things,[15] and are glad to use every means which you know or believe may be conducive thereto; and yet *not so much* as to condemn any man upon earth

[10] See BCP, Communion, Collect.
[11] 2 Cor. 11:31, etc.
[12] 1 Thess. 5:22.
[13] See Gal. 6:10.
[14] On the meaning and importance of 'opinions', cf. *The Character of a Methodist*, §1 (pp. 33-34 above).
[15] BCP, Collect for Whit Sunday.

merely for thinking otherwise than you do, much less to imagine that God condemns him for this, if he be upright and sincere of heart. On those outward *modes of worship* wherein you have been bred up you lay *so much* stress as highly to approve them, but not so much as to lessen your love to those who conscientiously dissent from you herein. You likewise lay *so much* stress on the use of those *ordinances* which you believe to be of God as to confess, there is no salvation for *you* if you wilfully neglect them. And yet you do not judge them that are otherwise minded; you determine nothing concerning those who, not believing those ordinances to be of God, do, out of principle, abstain from them.

[10.] Your *strictness* of life, taking the whole of it together, may likewise be accounted new. I mean, your making it a rule to abstain from fashionable *diversions*, from *reading* plays, romances, or books of humour, from *singing* innocent songs, or *talking* in a merry, gay, diverting manner; your *plainness* of dress; your *manner of dealing* in trade; your exactness in observing the *Lord's day;* your scrupulosity as to things that have *not paid custom;* your total abstinence from *spirituous liquors* (unless in cases of extreme necessity);[16] your rule 'not to mention the fault of an absent person, in particular, of *ministers,* or of *those in authority*',[17] may justly be termed new. Seeing although some are scrupulous in some of these things, and others are strict with regard to other particulars, yet we do not find any other body of people who insist on all these rules together. With respect therefore both to your *name, principles,* and *practice,* you may be considered as a *new* people.

[11.] Another peculiar circumstance of your present situation is that you are *newly united* together; that you are just gathered, or (as it seems) gathering, rather, out of all other societies or congregations; nay, and that you have been hitherto, and do still subsist, without *power* (for you are a low, insignificant people), without *riches* (for you are poor, almost to a man, having no more than the plain necessaries of life), and without either any extraordinary gifts of *nature* or the advantages of *education,* most even of your teachers being quite unlearned and (in other things) ignorant men.

[16] A, F-H, 'of necessity'.

[17] Here, as in earlier passages, Wesley clearly has in mind the *General Rules* of his societies; see above, p. 71 and n. 16, where it is shown that the passage 'speaking evil of ministers', etc., was added to the 4th edn. of 1744.

[12.] There is yet another circumstance which is quite peculiar to yourselves. Whereas every other *religious set* of people, as soon as they were joined to each other, *separated themselves* from their former societies or congregations, you, on the contrary, do not; nay, you *absolutely disavow* all desire of separating from them. You openly and continually declare you have not, nor ever had, such a design. And whereas the congregations to which those separatists belonged have generally spared no pains to prevent that separation, those to which you belong spare no pains (not to prevent, but) to occasion this *separation*, to drive you from them, to force you on that division to which you declare you have the strongest aversion.

[13.] Consider these peculiar circumstances wherein you stand, and[18] you will see the propriety of a *second* advice I would recommend to you: *Do not imagine you can avoid giving offence.* Your very *name* renders this impossible. Perhaps not one in a hundred of those who use the term 'Methodist' have any idea of what it means. To ninety-nine of them it is still heathen Greek. Only they think it means something very bad, either a Papist, an heretic, an underminer of the Church, or some unheard-of monster; and, in all probability, the farther it goes it must gather up more and more evil. It is vain, therefore, for any that is called a Methodist ever to think of not giving offence.

[14.] And as much offence as you give by your *name*, you will give still more by your *principles*. You will give offence to the *bigots for* opinions, modes of worship, and ordinances, by laying *no more* stress upon them; to the *bigots against* them, by laying *so much;* to *men of form*, by insisting so frequently and strongly on the inward *power* of religion; to *moral men* (so called) by declaring the absolute necessity of *faith* in order to acceptance with God. To men of *reason* you will give offence by talking of inspiration and receiving the Holy Ghost; to drunkards, sabbath-breakers, common swearers, and other *open sinners*, by refraining from their company, as well as by that disapprobation of their behaviour which you will often be obliged to express. And indeed your life must give them continual offence; your sobriety is grievously offensive to a drunkard; your serious conversation is equally intolerable to a gay impertinent; and, in general, that 'you are

[18] Wesley's *Works* (1773) omitted the 'and'; Wesley corrected this, not by restoring the original text, but by a manuscript note in his personal copy and by an entry in the errata for Vol. 18 which changed the opening word from 'Consider' to 'Considering'.

grown so precise and *singular*, so monstrously *strict*, beyond all sense and reason, that you *scruple* so many harmless things, and fancy you are *obliged* to do so many others which you need not,'[19] cannot but be an offence to abundance of people, your friends and relations in particular. Either therefore you must consent to give up your *principles*, or your fond hope of pleasing men.

[15.] What makes even your *principles* more offensive is this *uniting* of yourselves *together*, because this union renders you more *conspicuous*, placing you more in the eye of men; more *suspicious*—I mean, liable to be suspected of carrying on some sinister design (especially by those who do not, or *will* not, know your inviolable attachment to his present Majesty King George);[20] more *dreadful* to those of a fearful temper who imagine you have any such design; and more *odious* to men of zeal, if their zeal be any other than fervent love to God and man.

[16.] This offence will sink the deeper because you are gathered out of so many other congregations. For the warm[21] men in each will not easily be convinced that you do not *despise* either them or their teachers; nay, will probably imagine that you utterly *condemn* them, as though they could not be saved. And this occasion of offence is now at the height, because you are just gathered, or gathering rather,[22] so that they know not where it will end; but the fear of losing (so they account it) more of their members gives an edge to their zeal, and keeps all their anger and resentment in its strength.

[17.] Add to this that you *do not leave* them quite, you still rank yourselves[23] among their members, which, to those who know not that you do it for conscience' sake, is also a provoking circumstance. 'If you would but get out of their sight!' But you are a continual thorn in their side as long as you remain with them.

[18.] And (which cannot but anger them the more) you have neither *power*, nor *riches*, nor *learning;* yet, with all their power and money and wisdom, they can gain no ground against you.

[19] Although Wesley may be quoting a passage from some letter or printed work, it is more probable that he is summarizing the kind of criticism frequently levelled at Methodists; and the probability is increased by the presence of the imaginary quotation in §17 below.

[20] 'King George' added in edns. B-E, I.

[21] This frequently means 'rich' (*OED*, adj. 8), but here it more probably implies 'excitable' (10) or 'hot-tempered' (11).

[22] Cf. §11 above.

[23] D, E, I, 'yourself'.

[19.] You cannot but expect that the offence continually arising from such a variety of provocations will gradually ripen into hatred, malice, and all other unkind tempers. And as they who are thus affected will not fail to represent you to others in the same light as you appear to them, sometimes as madmen and fools, sometimes as wicked men, fellows not fit to live upon the earth; the consequence, humanly speaking, must be that, together with your reputation, you will lose, first, the love of your friends, relations, and acquaintance, even those who once loved you the most tenderly; then your business—for many will employ you no longer, nor 'buy of such an one as you are'; and, in due time (unless he who governs the world interpose), your health, liberty, and life.

[20.] What further advice can be given to a person[24] in such a situation? I can but advise you, thirdly: *Consider deeply with yourself, Is the God whom I serve able to deliver me?*[25] I am not able to deliver myself out of these difficulties; much less am I able to bear them. I know not how to give up my reputation, my friends, my substance, my liberty, my life. *Can* God give me to rejoice in doing this? And may I depend upon him that he *will?* Are the hairs of my head all numbered?[26] And does he never fail them that trust in him? Weigh this thoroughly; and if you can trust God with your all, then go on, in the power of his might.[27]

[21.] Go on, I would earnestly advise you, fourthly: *Keep in the very path wherein you now tread. Be true to your principles.*[28] Never rest again in the dead *formality* of religion. Pursue with your might inward and outward holiness, a steady imitation of him you worship, a still increasing resemblance of his imitable perfections, his justice, mercy, and truth.[29]

[22.] Let this be your manly, noble, generous religion, equally remote from the meanness of *superstition* (which places religion in doing what God hath not enjoined, or abstaining from what he hath not forbidden) and from the unkindness of *bigotry* (which confines our affection to our own party, sect, or opinion). Above

[24] 1st edn., followed by F, G, and H, reads 'to persons'.
[25] See Dan. 3:17.
[26] See Matt. 10:30; Luke 12:7.
[27] Eph. 6:10.
[28] In the orig., 'Keep . . . tread', is not italicized, as one would expect upon the precedents of §§8, 13, and 20.
[29] Cf. §2 above.

all, stand fast in obedient faith,[30] faith in the God of pardoning mercy, in the God and Father of our Lord Jesus Christ,[31] who hath loved *you*, and given himself for you.[32] Ascribe to him all the good you find in yourself, all your peace, and joy, and love, all your power to do and suffer his will, through the Spirit of the living God. Yet in the meantime carefully avoid *enthusiasm*. Impute not the dreams of men to the all-wise God; and expect neither light nor power from him but in the serious use of all the means he hath ordained.

[23.] Be true also to your principles touching opinions, and the externals of religion. Use every *ordinance* which you believe is of God, but beware of narrowness of spirit towards those who use them not. Conform yourself to those *modes of worship* which you approve, yet love, as brethren, those who cannot conform. Lay so much stress on *opinions* that all your own (if it be possible) may agree with truth and reason; but have a care of anger, dislike, or contempt toward those whose opinions differ from yours. You are daily accused of this (and, indeed, what is it whereof you are not accused?); but beware of giving any ground for such an accusation. Condemn no man for not thinking as you think. Let everyone enjoy the full and free liberty of thinking for himself. Let every man use his own judgment, since every man must give an account of himself to God.[33] Abhor every approach, in any kind or degree, to the spirit of *persecution*. If you cannot *reason* or *persuade* a man into the truth, never attempt to *force* him into it. If love will not compel him to come in,[34] leave him to God, the Judge of all.[35]

[24.] Yet expect not that others will deal thus with you. No. Some will endeavour to *fright* you out of your principles, some to *shame* you into a more popular religion, to laugh and rally you out of your singularity. But from none of these will you be in so great danger as from those who assault you with quite different weapons—with softness, good nature, and earnest professions of (perhaps real) goodwill. Here you are equally concerned to avoid the very appearance of anger, contempt, or unkindness, and to hold fast the whole truth of God, both in principle and in practice.

[25.] This indeed will be interpreted as unkindness. Your former acquaintance will look upon this, that you will not *sin* or *trifle* with them, as a plain proof of your coldness toward them; and this burden you must be content to bear. But labour to avoid

[30] See 1 Cor. 16:3. [31] 2 Cor. 11:31, etc. [32] See Gal. 2:20.
[33] Rom. 14:12. [34] See Luke 14:23. [35] Heb. 12:23.

all real unkindness, all disobliging words, or harshness of speech, all shyness or strangeness of behaviour. Speak to them with all the tenderness and love, and behave with all the sweetness and courtesy you can, taking care not to give any needless offence, to neighbour or stranger, friend or enemy.

[26.] Perhaps on this very account I might advise you, fifthly, *Not to talk much of what you suffer*, 'of the *persecution* you endured at such a time, and the wickedness of your *persecutors*'. Nothing more tends to exasperate them than this; and therefore (although there is a time when these things must be mentioned, yet) it might be a general rule to do it as seldom as you can with a safe conscience. For (besides its tendency to inflame them) it has the appearance of evil,[36] of ostentation, of magnifying yourselves. It also tends to puff you up with pride, and to make you think yourselves some great ones, as it certainly does to excite or increase in your heart ill will, anger, and all unkind tempers. It is, at best, loss of time; for instead of the wickedness of men you might be talking of the goodness of God. Nay, it is, in truth, an open, wilful sin; it is talebearing, backbiting, evil-speaking—a sin you can never be sufficiently watchful against, seeing it steals upon you in a thousand shapes. Would it not be far more profitable for your souls, instead of speaking against them, to pray for them? To confirm your love towards those unhappy men whom you believe to be fighting against God by crying mightily to him in their behalf, that he may open their eyes and change their hearts?

[27.] I have now only to commend you to the care of him who hath all power in heaven and in earth; beseeching him that in every circumstance of life you may stand 'firm as the beaten anvil to the stroke';[37] desiring nothing on earth, accounting all things but dung and dross, that you may win Christ,[38] and always remembering, 'It is the part of a good champion to be flayed[39] alive, and to conquer!'[40]

October 10, 1745

[36] 1 Thess. 5:22.

[37] Samuel Wesley, Jun., *Poems on Several Occasions* (London, 1736), p. 66 ('The Parish Priest', *l.* 28): 'Firm as the beaten anvil to the Stroke'. Cf. Ignatius, *Epistle to Polycarp,* §3 (as given in Wesley's *Christian Library,* I.64 [1749]): 'Stand firm as a beaten anvil.'

[38] See Phil. 3:8.

[39] Orig., 'flead'.

[40] See Ignatius, *Epistle to Polycarp,* §3 (as in n. 37): 'It is the part of a brave combatant to be torn in pieces, and yet to conquer.' Cf. Wesley's letter to Ebenezer Blackwell, July 20, 1752: 'A good soldier desires "to be flayed alive and to conquer"' (26:497 in this edn.).

7

MODERN CHRISTIANITY: EXEMPLIFIED AT WEDNESBURY

(1745)

AN INTRODUCTORY COMMENT

The short title, which may be sardonic, of this writing tends to conceal the fact that it gives first-hand evidence, of a virtually unimpeachable kind, of the riots which are recognised as the classic example of physical opposition to Methodism in its early years. It is true that if we had well-authenticated testimony from those who instigated and shared in the harassment of the Methodists, a different picture might possibly emerge, but it would probably be only slightly different.

Modern Christianity *is a series of documents, in the form of affidavits requested by Wesley, presented verbatim by him, with only three comments of his own, two brief (§§17 and 21), one lengthy (§§30, 31), and concluded with an account of his own experience in the area of Wednesbury and a dedication of himself to God's purposes.*

Wesley omitted the closing section from Modern Christianity *in Vol. 18 of his* Works, *and also from the summary of the riots given in* A Farther Appeal to Men of Reason and Religion, *Pt. III (1745), II. 5-14 (see 11:282-89 in this edn.).*

Only some of the numerous problems of the identification of individuals have so far been solved. The generally accepted modern spelling of place-names is here used; personal names with the best textual evidence are retained as in the original, except when a modern spelling can be confidently substituted.

For a stemma showing the transmission of the text through the four editions published during Wesley's lifetime, and variants therein from the edited text, based on the first edition of Newcastle, 1745, see Appendix A, pp. 541ff. For fuller details see Bibliography, *No. 110.*

Modern Christianity: Exemplified at Wednesbury
and Other Adjacent Places in Staffordshire[1]

Tua res agitur paries quum proximus ardet.[2]

Advertisement

It was our desire and design that the following accounts, drawn up long since, should have slept for ever; but the gross misrepresentations of these facts, which are still spread abroad from day to day, constrain us at length to speak the naked truth, in as plain a manner as we are able. And now let any man of common humanity judge whether these things ought to be so.[3]

1. I, John Eaton, of[4] Wednesbury, in Staffordshire, heard the Rev. Mr. Charles Wesley, in the latter end of the year 1742, preach salvation by faith, in the Coalpit Field.[5] I and many others rejoiced to hear it, particularly many of the poor people at Darlaston,[6] some of whom soon after began to meet together in the evenings, to sing, and pray, and read the Bible.

Some of Wednesbury[7] used to go and meet with them; but one evening the mob at Darlaston rose, pelted them with clods and stones, and broke all the windows of the house where they had been.

[1] This series of documents is presented verbatim by Wesley, without enclosure within quotation marks, and in this we have followed him. Sects. 1-29, 32-33 seem to be copies of written affidavits prepared by the sufferers for Wesley—see §26: 'According to your request I send you some account of what the mob did on Shrove Tuesday.' For a valuable account of the Wednesbury Riots see J. Leonard Waddy, *The Bitter Sacred Cup* (London, Pinhorns, for the World Methodist Historical Society, 1976).

[2] Horace, *Epistles*, I.xvii.84—''Tis your own safety that's at stake when your neighbour's wall is in flames' (Loeb Classical Library). Wesley also used this as the motto for *Serious Thoughts occasioned by the Earthquake at Lisbon* (1755), *Bibliography*, No. 213, published in Vol. 15 of this edn.

[3] See Jas. 3:10.

[4] John Eaton, the Wednesbury constable, was a Methodist and about fifty at this time. He died in 1753.

[5] Orig., 'Colepit Field'.

[6] Orig., 'Darleston', as throughout the work.

[7] Orig., 'Wensbury', as in most references to the town.

On the 30th of May, 1743, John Adams[8] (whose house it was) fetched a warrant to carry some of the rioters before Justice P[ersehouse][9] of Walsall.[10] He desired some of us of Wednesbury to go with him; so four or five of us went. But the mob at Walsall immediately rose upon us, so that we were obliged to take shelter in a public house. Here we were kept close prisoners till it was dark, several of us having been much hurt and abused. When it was night we escaped one or two at a time. Francis Ward[11] and I went last.

On the 21st of June, 1743, a large mob came to my house at Wednesbury. I was then constable, so I went to the door with my constable's staff, and began reading the Act of Parliament against riots.[12] But the stones flew so thick about my head that I was forced to leave off reading and retire; so they broke about half my windows and went away. But some hours after they came again, and broke all the rest, and the door of my house, and the clock to pieces. This is a short account of the first damage that was done to me.

John Eaton

2. On the 30th of May, I, James Jones,[13] went with John Eaton and some others to Walsall. As we were going to and from the justice's house the mob pelted us with dirt and stones. They raged more and more, till Francis Ward desired the justice, who was present, to quiet them. But instead of that he swung his hat round his head twice, and cried, 'Huzza!' On which encourage-

[8] John Adams of Darlaston was one of the founding Methodists there. (See Waddy, pp. 3, 9-10.)

[9] William Persehouse (1691–1749), of Reynolds Hall, Walsall, belonged to an old Staffordshire family, which had held the Reynolds Hall estates for two centuries. In his *Journal* of Oct. 20, 1743, Wesley includes an order to all officers of the peace in Staffordshire 'to make diligent search after the said Methodist preachers, and to bring him or them before some of us his said Majesty's Justices of the Peace, to be examined concerning their unlawful doings'. This was dated Oct. 12, 1743, and signed by J. Lane and W. Persehouse.

[10] Orig., 'Walsal', as usual with Wesley.

[11] Francis Ward (1707–82) was at this time churchwarden at Wednesbury and also a prominent Methodist.

[12] The Riot Act (1 Geo. I, stat. 2, c. 5) provided that if twelve or more persons should unlawfully or riotously assemble and refuse to disperse within an hour after the reading of a specified portion of the act by a competent authority, they should be considered felons. It was prompted by many disturbances in the early months of 1715.

[13] Possibly the James Jones who was born in Tipton, became one of Wesley's itinerant preachers for a time, and remained a local preacher in Staffordshire until his death in Birmingham in 1783.

ment they grew so outrageous that we were forced to take shelter in a public house, and to stay there till it was dark.

On the 21st of June a great multitude gathered together in Wednesbury churchyard; among them was Harvey Walklet of Wednesbury, and Richard Dorset of Darlaston. Harvey said to Richard Dorset, 'Methinks they are not so well armed as I would have them.' Richard answered, 'There are many pretty fellows from Darlaston. I know them to be good blood.' Harvey replied, 'There is John Baker[14] with the oak bough in his hat; he will break the first pane of Mr. Eaton's windows.' Accordingly they went to Mr. Eaton's first, and from thence to other houses. Here are above fourscore houses in and about Wednesbury, in many of which there are not three panes of glass left.

Wednesbury, June 29 James Jones

3. I, Jonathan Jones, in the county of Stafford, farmer, am willing to pay the King and country their due, might I be at peace, and go about my lawful occasions as I ought to do.

On the 20th of June, at my neighbour Adams's house, two or three were singing a hymn, and a parcel of 'prentices and others, in a very rude manner, came and threw many stones through the windows; in particular Mr. Richard Taylor's 'prentice. So my neighbour John Adams goes to Squire P[ersehouse] and brings a warrant for him; but Mr. Taylor goes to Walsall to the justice before the offenders were brought; and he was with Squire P[ersehouse] when we came, who would not act at his own hall, but sent us down into the town, where a great mob was waiting for our coming.

So the constable gave him the warrant; and he said, 'What! I understand you are Methodists! I will not act for you.' Then he went to the door, and told a great mob they might do what they would; and took off his hat, and swung it about, and went away. They gave a great shout, and some of them swore bitterly they would murder us all. We sent for the constable to help us out of the town, but he was not to be found. So we stayed in the house about two hours, till we thought the mob was gone; but as soon as we came out some began to hollow, and the street was quickly full. They beat and bruised us very much; but through God's mercy we escaped with our lives.

[14] John Baker was known as 'the man who whacked his father'; he seems to have drowned himself a year or two later. Thomas Jackson, ed., *The Journal of the Rev. Charles Wesley*, 2 vols. (London, 1849), 2:442.

About a week after there arose a great mob at Darlaston, and broke me nine large windows, and many of my goods. The same day my man was coming home with my team; and they met him, and beat him, and much abused my horses. At night they came to break the rest of my goods; but I gave them money, and they went away.

So I was at Richard Dorset's, our churchwarden, and many of the mob came in and said, 'Come now, d——n you, Dorset; we have done our work; pay us our wages.' And I saw the drink come in, in large jugs; and everyone drank what he would.

What I have here said I am ready to make oath of.

Jonathan Jones

4. I, Francis Ward, of Wednesbury, went to Walsall May 30 with John Eaton, to see if we could have justice done to the rioters, who had abused our neighbours at Darlaston. We went to Benjamin Westley's,[15] at the sign of the George, when one Mr. Taylor,[16] Curate of Walsall, came with the mob to the house, and in our hearing encouraged them to insult us. Accordingly they pelted us with dirt and stones, all the way we went to the justice's gate. The justice came out, and said we must go down into the town, and then he would hear our complaint. But as we went the mob continued to pelt us, though the justice was with us. I desired he would be pleased to read the Act of Parliament against riots; but he would not. When we came to Benjamin Westley's the justice would have had a hearing in the streets, among the mob; but at last he was prevailed with to go into the house. Then he called for John Adams, or his wife, and, without hearing them speak, said, 'What, you are Methodists!' or words to that purpose, and immediately went out to the mob. We stayed in the house a considerable time, hoping they would disperse; but as soon as ever we came out they gathered round us again, and beat and pelted us with whatever they could find. One of them came to me, and struck me on the eye, and cut it so that I expected to lose my sight. I got into a shop, and had my eye dressed, and then returned to my friends. The mob pursued me again, fetched me out of the house, and beat me very much; but with much difficulty I got from them again, and escaped a second time into the house. They fetched me out again, and dragged me along the street, and

[15] The innkeeper (Waddy, p. 10).

[16] Apparently the Rev. Richard Taylor (ibid., pp. 9-10).

through the kennel,[17] to and fro, till I had quite lost my strength, and was so weak I was not able to get up. There came a poor woman, and said to the mob, 'Will ye kill the man?' and lifted me up. With much ado I got home; but the abuse I there received threw me into a fever.

5. About Whitsuntide I, Joshua Constable, of Darlaston, had all my windows broke by the mob, and many of my goods damaged or spoiled, and so had many of my neighbours; in particular, John Cotterell, smith, Thomas Butler, Thomas Wilkinson, Aaron Longmore, William Powell,[18] Anne Evans, Walter Carter, Samuel Foster, and Thomas Wilks, had their windows all broke.

Edward Martin, Anne Low, Joan Fletcher, Edward Horton, Mumford Wilks, Jos. Yardly, and Robert Deacon, had all their windows broke twice.

James Foster, nailer, Sarah Hires, widow, and Jonathan Jones, had their windows broke, and money extorted to save their houses.

John Foster, nailer, and Joyce Wood, had their windows broke, and their goods broken and spoiled.

Jos. Spittle, collier, had his windows broke, his house broke open, some goods taken, and some lost.

William Woods, brick-maker, had his windows broke twice, and was compelled to go along with the rioters.

Elizabeth Lingham, a widow with five children, had her goods spoiled, her spinning-wheel (the support of her family) broke, and her parish allowance reduced from 2*s*. 6*d*. to 1*s*. 6*d*. a week.

Valentine Ambersly,[19] collier, had his windows broke twice, his wife, big with child, abused and beat with clubs.[20]

George Wynn had his windows and goods broke, and, to save his house, was forced to give them drink.

Thomas Day had his windows and goods broke, and was forced to remove from the town.

[17] The gutter.

[18] Some of the names appear with various spellings both in Wesley's writings and in local records. Without stronger evidence for one than the other we have preferred the more familiar spelling, as in Powell rather than Powel, Onions rather than Oniens, Stubbs rather than Stubs.

[19] *A Farther Appeal,* II.6, 'Amberley'.

[20] *Works,* 'a club'.

Jos. Stubbs had his windows broke twice, and his wife so frighted that she miscarried.

6. On June 20 John Baker, Thomas Griffiths, and Daniel Onions,[21] at the head of a large mob, came to my house, Jonas Turner by name, at West Bromwich[22] near Wednesbury, and asked whether I would keep from these men and go to the church. I answered, 'I go to the church very often, but I never see any of you there.' Presently Daniel Onions, with a great club, broke great part of my windows at one blow. Others laid hold of me, and said, 'You shall go along with us.' I told them I would not. They dragged me by force about sixty yards, and then I got loose from them. Afterwards they broke all my windows, and threw into my house three basketful of stones, to break my goods.

7. Some time in June, about four in the afternoon, a mob came to my house at West Bromwich; I was within, and my two daughters without. They threw in stones and bricks so fast that I thought I should have been knocked on the head. Whereupon I opened the door and ran out amongst them. One of my daughters cried out, 'My mother will be killed.' On which they fell to throwing stones at her. She ran into a neighbour's house; but before she could shut the door they broke the bottom off with a brick-end. They followed my other daughter with stones, and one with a great stake. She ran into another house, much frighted, expecting to be murdered. I asked them how they could come and abuse us thus. Upon which one came with a large club, and swore if I spoke another word he would knock me on the head and bury me in the ditch. Then he went to the window, and broke two or three panes of glass, which were all that were left. A woman then came with a club, and broke to pieces part of the tiling of the house.

Of this I am ready to make oath.

Mary Turner

8. On the 19th of June James Yeoman of Walsall saw me in my father's house at Wednesbury, and swore, 'By G——, you are there now, but we will break the windows and kill you tomorrow.' Accordingly he came with a mob the next day; and after they had

[21] Orig., 'Oniens'.

[22] Orig., 'Bramwick', as usual with Wesley.

broke all the windows he took up a stone, and said, 'Now, by G——, I will kill you.' He threw it, and struck me on the side of the head. The blood gushed out, and I dropped down immediately.

Mary Bird

9. June 20, the mob came to the house of me, John Bird, and demanded five shillings of my wife, or they would break all the windows. She offered them some money, which they snatched out of her hand, and then broke ten windows in front, the sash frames, shutters, cases, chest of drawers, and hanging-press, and damaged the ceiling, doors, dresser, and many other things.

John Bird

10. On the 20th of June the mob came to my house. John Baker by name came first. They threw in stones and bricks as fast as they could throw them, so that we within were afraid of our lives. They broke all the windows I had in my house, and likewise the casements and the ceiling; and when there was no more damage for them to do one of them cried out, 'I suppose now you will go to your dear Jesus's wounds, and see them opened for you.'

John Turner

11. June 20, 1743, one Daliston, my neighbour at Wednesbury, after some words, took me by the throat, swore he would be the death of me, gave me a great swing, and threw me on the ground. As soon as I arose Equal Baker, a collier, gave me a blow on the eye, and knocked me down again. When I got up he came after me to my house, and said, 'You dog, I will kill you.' I went in, got a proper application to my eye, and lay down on the bed. In about half an hour there came a large mob to my house, and broke all the windows except about twenty panes. The kitchen windows they cleared, lead, bars, and all, and broke the window posts, and threw them into the house. My shop was shut up; but they soon broke it open, broke all my pots and bottles, and destroyed almost all my medicines. They broke also the shelves and drawers in the shop to pieces, and many of my household goods.

That day and the next they broke the windows and goods in more than fourscore houses.

Humphrey Hands

12. In the latter end of June 1743 I, John Griffiths,[23] of Wednesbury, with Francis Ward, went to Mr. D[olphin], Justice of the Peace.[24] We told him what condition we and our neighbours were in, our houses broken, and our goods spoiled. He replied, 'I suppose you follow these parsons that come about.' So he talked to us very roughly, refused us a warrant, and said, 'I will neither meddle nor make.' And after he and some gentlewomen that were with him had made as much game at us as they thought fit, we came away without any justice at all.

13. I, Mumford Wilks, heard the Rev. Mr. E[gginton][25] say to the mob at Darlaston (after they had committed these outrages), 'Well, my lads, he that has done it *out of pure zeal for the Church,* don't blame him. My lads, I hope you will let us *settle our affairs in our own parish ourselves.* But if these men should come, and they should follow them, then *your help will be needful.*'

14. Line and Mare's Green have been long noted for wickedness of every kind, for cursing and swearing, sabbath-breaking, idleness, and all manner of debauchery. Few thereabouts used to go to church, or trouble themselves about religion, till some of them heard Mr. John and Charles Wesley, who then had a desire to flee from the wrath to come.[26] In order to this they set apart one evening in a week to meet and encourage one another, by reading a chapter, singing a psalm or hymn, and praying and conversing together.

The revellers, finding their old companions had forsaken them, were enraged at them more and more; insomuch that they came one evening when they were met, in November 1743, and unroofed the shop that was aside the house, and thrust down the walls.

The next time we met they came in more fury than before, threw great stones, broke the windows and looking-glass, and made the roof of the house to crack and sink, and seem every moment as if it would break in upon us; insomuch that we were obliged to press out in the dark, in the midst of a shower of stones.

[23] Griffiths was the brother-in-law of John Eaton.

[24] John Dolphin became Sheriff in 1760.

[25] The Rev. Edward Egginton, Vicar of Wednesbury, for whom see JWJ, Jan. 9 and Apr. 15-17, 1743, and his letter to 'John Smith', June 25, 1746, §10 (26:204-5 in this edn.).

[26] See *General Rules,* above, pp. 69-70, nn.1, 8.

We thought it would be best afterwards to meet in the day, and accordingly we did. Immediately they blew a horn to gather their company together. When they had gathered fifty or sixty, they went from one house to another, threatening to kill those who would not go along with them. They went together to a house where were things of value, with a great shout, swearing they would plunder. The woman of the house went out and asked what they wanted. They did not make much reply, but part of them immediately went into the garden, and dashed in pieces things which cost several pounds.

We made complaint hereof to a justice, Mr. W[illiam] G[ough].[27] He took a warrant to fill up, and asked us what number there was in all. We told him, about sixty. He then said, 'What, you are Methodists! Get about your business; you shall have no warrant! I am informed you are the vilest men that live.'

George Hadley
Samuel Hadley
Jos. Moore

15. Upon January 13, 1744, I, Jonathan Jones, of Darlaston, about eight or nine at night, met in the street a great company of rioters, who told me they were going to destroy the rest of my goods, and pull my house down, as they had done Joshua Constable's. So I asked for Thomas Tonks,[28] who was called the captain of the mob, and gave him many good words, and he took of me 2*s*. 6*d*., and some others I treated with ale; so they persuaded the rest to let me alone for that time.

The next day came John Stokes, with a great club, and wanted good money, or he said he would break my windows; but I put him away for the present with some drink. The same night, about six o'clock, came John Bagot and John Linyard, with each a great club, and said, 'You have given money to others, and we will have some too; or else we will call the rest of our company, and serve you as we have done your neighbours.' So I gave them some money, and they went off about nine or ten o'clock. About six or eight with clubs and staffs came after, and John Wilks with a short gun; but my neighbours and I, with giving them some drink, persuaded them to go away.

[27] Waddy, pp. 26, 28-30, offers little more information.

[28] Orig., 'Tunks'. It was he who forced the door of the warehouse with an ax (Waddy, p. 32).

It was sometime before, just after the great mob had broken all our windows, that the Rev. Mr. [Egginton], with others, met at Thomas Foreshew's, at the sign of the Crown, and made a writing, and the mob was sent to bring as many as they had a mind to sign it. They declared, whoever did not come and sign this, they would immediately pull his house down. It was to this effect, that they would 'never read, or sing, or pray together again, nor hear Mr. Wesley preach'.

16. In the month of January I, Sarah Longmore, late of Darlaston, was coming to Wednesbury, with my brother and sister-in-law, and about thirty men stopped us in the fields, and asked where we were going. We said, 'About our business.' Without any more to-do they began to throw dirt and stones at us, and then went before us, and stopped us at the stile. Seeing a gap in the hedge, we offered to go through there; but they would not let us. I was knocked down only once, but was bruised in many places.

Some time before this happened the mob rose at Darlaston, to near a thousand people. They took me by force out of my mother's house, gave me a club in my hand, and said, if I did not go with them, and pull down Joseph Spittle's house, they would murder me. William Corfield was the man who put the club in my hand, and haled[29] me along the street. I threw down the club, and when I came to the place, saw them break open the house, and bring out some of the goods, the people belonging to it being fled for their lives.

The same day the Rev. Mr. E[gginton] came to Darlaston; and Nicholas Winspur, the common crier of the town, gave notice, ringing his bell, that all the people belonging to the society must come to Mr. Foreshew's house, and there set their hands to a paper, signifying that they would not hear these men any more; but if they did not come and set their hands, they must expect to have their houses pulled down.

When I came Mr. Foreshew asked me if I could write, I said, 'No.' Then he bid me make my mark; so, through fear, I did. I then laid down a penny, which they made every one of us do, to make the mob drink.

[29] In its original transitive sense of draw or pull, later superseded by 'haul', which is found in the 2nd edn. and Wesley's *Works* (though spelled 'hawl').

17. About Candlemas my wife was going to Wednesbury, and a mob met her in the road, and threw her down several times, and abused her sadly.

(The manner is too horrible to write. The nearest to a parallel case is that of the woman abused by the men of Gibeah;[30] although in this case are many circumstances exceeding that.)[31]

I got a warrant for some of them from Justice G[ough]. As soon as this was known the mob rose and broke all my windows again. All who were served with the warrant escaped, but one the constable took, and brought before the justice, who came back and told his companions that the justice bid them go home about their business. So they went home and told the mob; and then they came to my house, broke some goods, and went away for a little time; but when they came again they broke and destroyed all the necessary goods we had in the house. They likewise broke and spoiled all my shop tools; threw the tiles off of[32] the roof of the house, [and] pulled down one room, the joist of which they carried away with them. Many things they took away, particularly all my gun-locks, both them that were filed, and them that were in the rough. They tore to pieces all my wife's linen, cut the bed and bedstead, so that it was good for nothing, broke her box into little bits, and tore her Bible and Common Prayer Book all to pieces. We retired to a friend's house; but one telling them we were there, they swore they would tear it down if he let us stay any longer. So we went out in the frost and snow, not knowing where to lay our head.

18. John Allen, of Wednesbury, in the county of Stafford; John Darby, of Brierley,[33] in the said county; and James Constable, of Wednesbury aforesaid, jointly and severally make oath and say: And first, John Allen for himself saith, that on Monday, the 6th day of this instant February, being informed that the mob would come the next day to plunder several of his friends and acquaintance, he went to the house of one Francis Ward, of Wednesbury, and assisted in removing goods and furniture; and that on Tuesday morning (being Shrove Tuesday) this deponent, hearing the mob was come to the town, assisted in removing

[30] Judg. 19:22-30.

[31] This paragraph, of course, is Wesley's comment.

[32] Wesley removes this dialect form from his *Works* by omitting 'of'.

[33] Orig., 'Brereley'.

divers other goods; and that afterwards, on the same day, he met about three hundred persons assembled together in a riotous manner; and that presently after one George Winspur, of Darlaston, and divers others, broke and entered the house of Francis Ward, broke down the fire-grate fixed therein, and then pulled down, took, and carried away all such goods as were left there, and which they were able to carry. After which one John Baker, of Wednesbury, and a great number of other riotous persons, came to the house of Francis Ward, and broke the windows; and then the said Baker, with divers others, entered the same, and broke to pieces and destroyed the bedsteads and other goods and furniture.

The said riotous company then went to another village, called West Bromwich, and returned back again to Wednesbury, where this deponent saw one Thomas Horton, of Darlaston, with divers others, go in a riotous manner to the house of John Griffiths of Wednesbury; and saw Thomas Horton, with a sledge-hammer, break open the door of that house, which he, with others, entered and destroyed, and broke to pieces divers of the household goods, and took and carried away the remainder, or the greatest part thereof.

19. And the said John Darby for himself saith, that on the said 6th day of February he heard a great many people making a noise; that he went thereupon into his own house, and locked and bolted the door; that in about a quarter of an hour about sevenscore persons came up to this deponent's house, nine or ten of whom bade him give them money, else they would break the door; that John Hammersley, of Darlaston, and several others, with a great rail of wood, broke down the door, and entered the house, and caught up a large ax, and broke to pieces and destroyed this deponent's goods and windows. After which they destroyed five stalls of bees, and killed and took away all his hens, and threw the hay out of his barn; and carrying away what they thought proper, went to the house of Samuel Smith, a quarter of a mile further, and broke his windows. Thence they went in a riotous manner to Bilston, and in the morning to Wednesbury.

20. James Constable saith, that on Monday, the 6th instant, Henry Old, Thomas Adams, and Francis Longmore, all of Darlaston, came to Wednesbury, and with oaths and curses, in

this deponent's hearing, protested that they would 'come the next day and pull down the house' of one Benjamin Constable, and 'have his heart and his liver out'; that accordingly the next day, about ten in the morning, he heard a great huzza in the town street, and went to see what was the matter, when he, this deponent, was immediately, by one Samuel Cotterell of Darlaston and three others, seized by the collar, and forced to go into a great concourse of people (about three hundred persons), who had just broken into the house of one John Bird, and were throwing the goods of the said John Bird out of the windows of his house; that those who held this deponent, then letting him go, and running to get their share of the plunder, he went to the house of Benjamin Constable; and about two or three o'clock the same day the said riotous persons came up to the house, which was locked and bolted; and as this deponent stood on the outside he saw Thomas Horton with a large hammer strike at the door, in order to break it open; which he not being able to do, Joseph Page, of Darlaston, broke the window, and forced out the iron bars of the said window with a pike, and afterwards broke and entered the same, and, unbolting the door, let the other rioters in; that Thomas Tonks, of Darlaston, and divers others, with an ax, wrenched and forced open the door of Benjamin Constable's warehouse, riotously entered into the same, and broke to pieces and destroyed the goods therein, spilt the liquors therein placed, plundered and destroyed such goods as they could not carry away, both household goods and grocery goods, and also chandler's ware; that afterwards they went to this deponent's house, broke to pieces all the windows of his house, plundered the same from top to bottom, broke to pieces many of his goods, and carried a great part of them away; that thence they went to the house of Daniel Constable, broke open and plundered it in the like manner, and from thence to the house of Thomas Atherley, which they also damaged and plundered.

John Allen
John Darby
James Constable

All three sworn at Serjeants Inn,
London, on Feb. 24, 1743,
before William Chapple.

21. Monday, February 6, we kept as a fast. Sixty or more of us met at one, and joined in prayer. About eight we heard the mob was at John Griffiths', the elder, breaking the house and spoiling

his goods. This put some of us on removing our most portable goods. When I came home my wife had awakened my youngest girls, and carried them to a neighbour's house. We then laid down, and committed our own souls to God.

Next morning, February 7 (Shrove Tuesday), all things were pretty still till ten. We were all very cheerful. The greatest fear we had was lest we should deny our Master; for they had got a paper, which if anyone would subscribe, his house was not to be plundered. But the far greater part, by the grace of God, chose rather the loss of all things.

About half an hour after ten great numbers of men were gathered together on the Church Hill. We could see them march down, some armed with swords, some with clubs, and some with axes. They first fell upon Benjamin Watson's house, and broke many of the tiles, and all the windows. Next they came to Mr. Addingbrook's, broke a fine clock, with many of his goods, and stole all the things they could carry away; among which were writings of importance, and papers relating to the land-tax. The next house was Jane Smith's, whose windows they broke, with what little goods she had. The next was Mr. Bird's, where they destroyed everything they found, except what they carried away, cutting the beds in pieces, as they did all the beds they could anywhere find. Thence they went to Mr. Edge's house. He was ill of a fever; so, for a sum of money, they passed it over. The next house was mine. They were going by it, but one who used to be my familiar friend called them back. They broke my counter, boxes, and drawers, to chips, and all that ax or hammer could break, except my bedsteads. They spilt all my drugs and chemical medicines, and stole everything they could carry, even all my wife's wearing apparel and mine, besides what we had on.

Mr. Eaton's house was next. They broke all his windows, and all his inside doors in pieces, cut the lead off his house, destroyed or stole whatever they could lay their hands on. The gentlemen offered to stop them, if he would set his hand to the recantation paper. But he told them, he had felt already what a wounded conscience was; and, by the grace of God, he would wound his conscience no more.

The next day they came with another mob, and said, if he did not sign it, they would level his house to the ground. He told them, they might do as they pleased; but he would not sign it if they tore him bit from bit.

The mob on Tuesday, after they had done at Mr. Eaton's, plundered several other houses in Wednesbury, and several in West Bromwich. It is impossible to describe the outrages they have committed. We keep meeting together morning and evening, are in great peace and love with each other, and in nothing terrified by our adversaries. God grant we may endure to the end.

February 26 Humphrey Hands

22. On Tuesday, January 31, 1744, Henry Old came to John Griffiths Senior's house, saying, if they did not leave following 'this way',[34] he had a hundred men at his command, who should come and pull the house down. Soon after, he brought seven or eight men with him, swearing what he would do unless they gave him a guinea. She said, a guinea was not so soon shaken out of poor folk's sleeves. Then he said he would go and fetch the mob; but the neighbours gave him money, and sent him away for that time.

Monday, February 6, between seven and eight at night, came part of the same company. Hearing them afar off, John and his wife fastened the door, and left the house. Some of the neighbours going in soon after found them destroying all they could. Two chairs and several bundles of linen were laid upon the fire. They did not dare to touch them, but persuaded the men all they could to go home. After they had destroyed what they could, they loaded themselves with clothes and meat, and went their way.

John Griffiths, Sen.

23. My father sending me word that the mob had been at his house, and broke many of his goods, and stole many, I removed as many as I could of mine, before they plundered my house. And hearing they would force me to go with them, I sent my wife and children before, and then followed them to her father's; but he did not care to receive us. My wife wept: I was full of love, and not at all moved. At last their hearts relented, and they took us in. This indeed was the case with many of us. We were driven out of our own houses, and our friends did not dare to receive us into theirs. The reason for which my old companions have the greatest

[34] Acts 9:2; 22:4.

spite to me is because I will not drink and game, and break the Sabbath with them, as I used to do.

John Griffiths, Jun.

24. I, Edward Smith, of Wednesbury, standing by my own door, on Shrove Tuesday, there came a great mob, and broke into and plundered Benjamin Constable's house. Then they came to my house, and the foremost of them, Thomas Horton, with a great hammer, broke open the door. I begged them to let me unlock the door; but he swore, if I did not get away he would knock me down. At the same time Richard Adams, with a large iron bar, broke the house window, and got through. A great number of them followed both ways, and plundered the house, breaking some goods, and stealing others, several neighbours endeavouring to save them, but to no purpose.

25. I, Edward Slater, of Wednesbury, was informed the night before that the mob designed to plunder my house the next day. And between ten and eleven on Tuesday, standing in the fields, I saw them come down the town with clubs and other weapons, to Mr. Eaton's house. Then the colliers, by themselves, swinging their clubs round their heads, gave a great shout and a jump together. Then they began breaking his windows; and those who first broke into the house and went upstairs threw the goods out of the chamber windows, which Henry Old cut to pieces with an ax. I saw some come out with their pockets, and waistcoats, and breeches, loaded with goods. I went down the field towards my own house, got into a valley, read part of a chapter, and prayed for them. Then I got up, and saw the light through my own house, both doors and windows being knocked to pieces. After they had plundered some other houses, I saw them go up the street, laden with brass, pewter, and linen.

26. According to your request I send you some account of what the mob did on Shrove Tuesday. When I heard they were in town, and broke and stole all before them, I got out our beds and wearing apparel, and hid them in the hedges, and went and stood aside of a hedge about sixty yards off my own house.

When the mob came they began with breaking the windows. They then broke and stole all they could lay hands on. They searched and found the beds and linen which I had hid, and took all they thought worth carrying away. I waded through the brook, to try if I could save some of my goods, which a man was pulling out of the ditch where I had hid them. His name was David Garrington. He told me it would 'be the same here as it was in Ireland', for 'there would be a *massacre* very quickly, and he wished it was *now*'.

When they were gone my wife and I and two children came home. Our house was all laid open, for both the doors were gone, and all the windows and the middle posts were broke out. Being wet and very cold, we gathered up some of the chips (for our goods were mostly broke into chips and strewed about the rooms), and made a fire; but the wind blew the smoke so about that we could not bear to sit by it. We knew not what to do, till one of our neighbours sent us word we might come to his house. But one went to Walsall the next day and told the landlord, who came and told them that received us, they must turn [us] out; and we expected there would not be an house to receive a Methodist in the whole country.

On Ash Wednesday I was helping Mr. Eaton to remove some corn[35] which they had not found the day before, when Mr. William Horton came with a paper in his hand, and about a hundred persons with him. He pressed Mr. Eaton to sign it, who refused. Then they laid hold of me, and swore I should. I told them I would not. They caught hold of my collar, shook me, tore my shirt and waistcoat, pushed me from one to another, and asked again, 'Will you sign the paper yet?' I told them, No. They then got a cord, put it about my neck, and swore they would hang me out of hand. Others cried out, 'Draw him through the brook.' But one of them snatched away the cord, and said, if I would not set my hand I might go about my business. They followed me, however, with many stones; but by the providence of God I was not hurt.

March 5, 1744 John Turner

27. Having notice that the mob was coming I, William Sitch, of West Bromwich, and my wife (who had been delivered but a fortnight), thought it best to go out of the house and leave it to them. My wife, with her young child, was forced to stay in the fields, none daring to take her into their house. At length one man

[35] 2nd edn., followed by *Works*, 'iron'.

did; but he was in a little time persuaded to turn her out again.

The rioters plundered my house three several times, and did all the mischief they could. But, blessed be God, I could rejoice therein. He has said, 'As thy day is, so thy strength shall be.' And never did I find his promise fulfilled more than at that time.

William Sitch

28. On Shrove Tuesday, after two large mobs were passed by, came four or five men to my next neighbour, Jonas Turner's house. I and another woman followed them, to see what they would do. They first broke the windows, then broke down the door, and went into the house. Soon after they were in, they flung out a box at the chamber window, and swore, if any touched it they would murder them. Soon after they flung out a Bible, and one of them came out, and in great rage cut it into pieces with his ax.

Mary Turner, of West Bromwich

29. The first that came to my house[36] (Thomas Parkes, of West Bromwich)[37] on Tuesday, February 7, were five with great clubs, whom I met at the door. They demanded whether I would deny hearing these parsons. I told them, No, for I believed they spoke the truth as it is in Jesus, and if I were to deny them I should deny him that sent them. They told me, if I would not, they would plunder my house. I replied, they must answer it at God's bar, and I would meet them there. I asked whether I had done them any harm. They said, No; but they would have me keep to the Church. I told them, 'Some of you may know that I worship among the Dissenters; but I love a good man, let him go where he will; for there is but one church of Christ; and if you do not belong to that church, you had better never have been born.'

I told them, 'God has allowed me liberty of conscience, and so have the King and Parliament, and I hope my neighbours will, too; but if not, a day is coming when the persecuted and the persecutor shall stand together; and if you wrong me now, God will right me then.'

While I was speaking I caught hold of their clubs, and the words seemed to have some influence on them. But by this time

[36] 2nd edn., 'They first that came to my house; *Works*, 'They that came to my house first'.

[37] Parkes, of course, is the suffering Methodist.

there was a great body of them gathered together; so they broke my windows, and then the door, and flocked into my house, and began to break my goods. But here the Lord suffered them not to go so far as they had done in other places; for they soon fell to plundering, and loading themselves with the things I had provided[38] for myself, a wife, and seven children.

However, in a while I had prevailed with some of them to stop. But then they said I must set my hand to their paper. I told them they were cloaked over with the name of Protestants; but none but a popish spirit would tie men's consciences. So I commended my cause to God, and withdrew from my house and them.

As I went along, one who thinks herself a Christian said, now I might see God was against me. I told her I did now feel that God was for me, and that he loved me never the less for this; for God loved Job on the dunghill with only a potsherd as well as he did in all his plenty. I thought she, in effect, bid me curse God and die. May the Lord make her a Christian indeed!

When I returned to my house, and saw it in ruins, I found nothing in my heart towards my persecutors but love. Neither could I doubt of God's love to my soul. All that is within me, bless his holy name!

One day six or eight of the mob got me amongst them, and said they were going to make a law, and we should all set our hands to it. I told them I would submit to the laws of God and my Prince, but I could not to the laws of the devil. One of them swore he would break my windows again. I asked him if ever he heard of Jesus Christ doing so, and how he durst, when he must answer it at his bar. At which he stood silent.

30.[39] On Shrove Tuesday, about eleven o'clock, Sarah, the wife of John Sheldon, of West Bromwich, being told the mob was coming to her house, went and met them at the gate. Mr. S———, Mr. J———, and Mr. S[amuel] L[owe], cornet, were at the head of them. She asked John Baker, who was captain of the mob, what they were come here for. He answered, if she would have nothing more to do with these people, not a pennyworth of her goods should be hurt. She made no reply. Then they broke the door open, and began breaking and plundering the goods.

[38] This word is supplied only in Wesley's *Works*, 1773.

[39] §§30-31 consists of narratives and a summary by Wesley.

One coming out with a fire-shovel, she begged him not to take it away. He swore, if she spoke another word he would beat her brains out.

After they had rifled the house, they went to search the barn. Some goods were hid there, which she thought would now go with the rest; so she went and sat contentedly down in the ruined house. But a man of their own, as bitter as the rest till then, desired they would not pull up the cow's stakes; so they looked no further, but seeing a calf, they beat and lamed it in such a manner that they were obliged to kill it.

John Sheldon was this while[40] helping Thomas Parkes to hide his goods, though he knew by the noise they were breaking his own in pieces. Between two and three he came to his house with William Sitch. William asked Sarah how she did, saying, for his part he took joyfully the spoiling of his goods. She answered that, seeing so much wickedness, she could not rejoice; but she blessed God she could bear it patiently, and found not the least anger in her. John Sheldon, seeing the spoil they had made, smiled, and said, 'Here is strange work.' His wife told him, if she had complied with their terms, not one pennyworth would have been hurt. He replied that if she had complied to deny the truth, and he had found his goods whole on that account, he should never have been easy as long as he lived; but he blessed God that she had rather chose to suffer wrong.

31. The mob continued to rise for six days together. The damage they did in and about Wednesbury, at the very lowest computation, is as follows:

	£.	s.	d.
Benjamin Constable	103	0	0
Humphrey Hands	44	6	7
John Eaton	43	11	0
John Bird	43	0	0
Richard Bolton	40	0	0
Francis Ward	22	14	6
Godfrey Ward	22	6	4
John Turner	20	0	0
William Mason	19	0	4
Thomas Parkes	14	0	0

[40] 1790, 'at this time'.

	£.	s.	d.
John Sheldon	9	6	6
John Griffiths	3	15	8
Lydia Partridge	2	0	0
Joseph Perry	1	10	0
John Darby	8	13	6
Jonas Turner	3	12	0
Richard Spittle	2	17	0
Joseph Spittle	1	5	0
Edward Holdbury	4	10	0
Humphrey Hadley	13	11	0
John Griffiths	6	6	0
Benjamin Watson	2	11	0
Thomas Smith	7	15	6
Edward Smith	2	5	0
William Sitch	5	6	0
Daniel Constable	2	13	5
Henry Addin[g]brook	15	14	4
Joshua Constable	14	11	0
Joseph Stubbs, and Robert Dakin	2	0	0
Jonathan Jones	3	0	0
William Small	4	12	7
Thomas Edwardly	5	0	0
Edward Slater	9	12	10
	£ 504	7	1

32. I, Benjamin Constable, was induced to go to a Justice of Peace, on account of a warrant fetched by the wife of Joshua Constable for abuse done to her, as she went over the field betwixt Wednesbury and Darlaston. She swore against five men before Mr. G[ough]. The warrant was executed upon one of them; but the justice would not act anything against him unless the other four were brought before him. The man, returning home, raised a mob the same evening, went to the house of Joshua Constable, pulled part of it down, and destroyed his goods. This I thought proper to acquaint the justice of.

A second thing which induced me was that on the last day of January there came to my house Henry Old, Francis Longmore, and Thomas Baylis, and demanded money; else, they said, they would break my goods. But it being daytime, and their strength small (though they had large clubs in their hands), I refused.

I sent to the constable of Darlaston, to know if he would execute his warrant on the other four. He sent me word, he durst not do it, for fear of having his house pulled down.

I went on February 2 to Mr. G[ough] and gave him the above account; and withal told him that on the Tuesday following, February 7, they threatened to rise and pull down our houses. He answered me in a rough manner, and asked what I would have him to do: he could do no more than give out his warrant; and if the constable would not, or could not, execute it, he could not help it. I desired him that he would write a line to the officers of Wednesbury and Darlaston, to exert themselves for the discouraging any rising on Tuesday; but he refused, and told me, if we could not agree among one another, we must 'go to the devil which way we would'.

33. John Bird, of Wednesbury, in the County of Stafford, carpenter, is ready to make oath that he, together with William Mumford and Mary Bird, on the 10th day of this instant April, went to the house of W[illiam] G[ough], Esq., Justice of the Peace, in order to have a warrant for some of the principal rioters, who had lately done great damage to this deponent, and divers other persons; but the said justice refused to grant any warrant against them; that William Mumford then demanded a warrant against some of the said rioters, who had done damage to him; to which the said justice said they were Methodists, and after several other words refused to grant it; that on the 13th instant this deponent, together with William Mumford and Mary Bird, went to the house of J[ohn] D[olphin], Esq., a Justice of the Peace in the said county, and requested the said justice to grant him a warrant to take up some of the rioters, which the said justice refused to do; that on the 17th instant this deponent, together with Mary Bird, went to the house of W[illiam] P[ersehouse], Esq., a Justice of the Peace for the said county, and requested a warrant to take up some of the rioters; to which the said justice answered him roughly that he should have no warrant; and farther said that he and the rest of the justices in the neighbourhood had concluded and agreed to grant us no warrants. And this deponent further saith that he himself hath sustained damage by the rioters to the value of fifty pounds and upwards; and that neither he nor any other person who hath

sustained damage by them are able to bring the said rioters to justice, because not any of the above-mentioned Justices of the Peace will grant any warrant to apprehend them.

Such is the liberty of conscience which Protestants grant one another! Does not he that is higher than the highest regard it?[41]

34. Wednesday, October 19, 1743,[42] I, John Wesley, came to Birmingham, in my way to Newcastle. Thursday, October 20, several persons from Wednesbury earnestly desired me to call there. I yielded to their importunity, and went. I was sitting and writing at Francis Ward's, in the afternoon, when the cry arose that the Darlaston mob had beset the house. I called together those that were in the house, and prayed that God would 'scatter the people that delight in war'.[43] And it was so: one went one way, and one another, so that in half an hour the house was clear on every side. But before five they returned with greater numbers. The cry of all was, 'Bring out the minister.'

I desired one to bring the captain of the mob into the house. After a few words interchanged the lion was as a lamb.[44] I then desired him to bring in one or two more of the most angry of his companions. He did so; and in two minutes their mind was changed too. I then bade them who were in the room make way, that I might go out among the people. As soon as I was in the midst of them I said, 'Here I am. What do you want with me?' Many cried out, 'We want you to go with us to the justice.' I told them, 'That I will, with all my heart.' So I walked before, and two or three hundred of them followed, to Bentley Hall, two miles from Wednesbury. But a servant came out and told them Justice Lane was not to be spoken with.[45] Here they were at a stand, till one advised to go to Justice Persehouse, at Walsall. Above seven

[41] This comment is added by Wesley. The *Works* (1773) ends at this point. The following section contains an account of Wesley's own experience in Wednesbury, varying slightly from that under the date Oct. 20., 1743, in the *Journal* (which was not published until 1749).

[42] 1st edn., '1744'.

[43] Ps. 68:30.

[44] A frequent theme in Wesley's *Journal*, possibly based on Isa. 11:6-7. Cf. Apr. 7, 1744, etc.

[45] The *Journal* narrative has Lane replying to the messengers, 'What have I to do with Mr. Wesley? Go and carry him back again.' When the main body arrived a servant told them that he was in bed, and then his son seems to have brought a message from him, 'to go home, and be quiet'. John Lane (1699–1748) was the grandson of the man who had sheltered King Charles II at Bentley Hall after the Battle of Worcester.

we came to his house; but he also sent word that he was in bed, and could not be spoken with.

All the company were now pretty well agreed to make the best of their way home; but we had not gone a hundred yards when the mob of Walsall came pouring in like a flood. The Darlaston mob stood against them for a while; but in a short time, some being knocked down, and others much hurt, the rest ran away, and left me in their hands.

To attempt to speak was vain, the noise being like that of taking a city by storm. So they dragged me along till we came to the town, at a few hundred yards' distance; where, seeing the door of a large house open, I endeavoured to go in; but a man, catching me by the hair (my hat having been caught away at the beginning), pulled me back into the middle of the mob, who were as so many ramping and roaring lions. They hurried me from thence, through the main street, from one end of the town to the other. I continued speaking all the time to those within hearing, feeling no pain or weariness. At the west end of the town, seeing a door half open, I made towards it, and would have gone in; but a gentleman in the shop would not suffer me, saying, they would 'pull the house down' if I did. However, here I stood, and asked, 'Are you willing to hear me speak?' Many cried out, 'No, no. Knock his brains out.' Others said 'Nay, but we *will* hear him speak first.' I began asking, 'What hurt have I done you? Whom among you have I wronged in word or deed?' And continued speaking till my voice failed. Then the floods lifted up their voice[46] again, many crying out, 'Bring him away, bring him away.'

Feeling my strength renewed, I spoke again, and broke out aloud into prayer. And now one of the men, who had headed the mob before, turned and said, 'Sir, follow me; not a man shall touch a hair of your head.' Two or three more confirmed his words. At the same time the mayor (for it was he that stood in the shop) cried out, 'For shame, for shame! Let him go!' An honest butcher spoke to the same effect, and seconded his words by laying hold of four or five, one after another, who were running on the most fiercely. The people then dividing to the right and left, those three or four men who had spoken before took me between them, and carried me through the midst, bitterly protesting[47] they

[46] See Ps. 93:3.

[47] 2nd edn., 'professing'.

would 'knock down any that touched him'. But on the bridge the mob rallied again. We therefore went on one side, over a mill dam, and thence through the meadows, till a little after ten God brought me safe to Wednesbury, having lost only a part of my waistcoat, and a little skin from one of my hands.

I never saw such a chain of providences before, so many convincing proofs that the hand of God is on every person and thing, overruling all as it seemeth him good.

Among these I cannot but reckon the circumstances that follow: (1). That they endeavoured, abundance of times, to trip me up, as we went downhill over the wet, slippery grass, to the town; as well judging that if I was once on the ground I should hardly rise again. But I made no slip, nor the least stumble at all, till I was entirely out of their hands. (2). That although many strove to lay hold on my collar, or clothes, they could not fasten at all; their fingers, I cannot tell how, slipping along, without fixing once. Only one man seized the flap of my waistcoat, and took it away with him; the other flap, in the pocket of which was a twenty pound bank note, was torn but half off. (3). That a lusty man, just behind, struck at me many time with a large oaken stick; with which if he had struck me once on the back of the head I should probably have preached no more; but every time the blow was turned aside, I know not how, for I could not move to the right hand or left. (4). That another man came rushing through the press, raised his arm to strike, let it sink again, and, stroking my head, said, 'What soft hair he has! I can't find in my heart to hurt him.' (5). That I went as straight to the mayor's door, when I was a little loosed for a few moments, as if I had known it (which they probably thought I did), and found him standing in the shop; which gave the first check to the fury of the people. (6). That no creature (at least within my hearing) laid anything to my charge, either true or false; having in the hurry, it seems, forgot to provide themselves with an accusation of any kind. And, lastly, that they were equally at a loss what to do with me, none proposing any determinate thing. The cry of most was 'Away with him, away with him.' Of others, 'Kill him at once.' But none so much as once mentioned how; only one or two (I almost tremble to relate it) screamed out (with what meaning I cannot tell), 'Crucify the dog, crucify him.'

By how gentle degrees does God prepare us either for doing or suffering his will! Two years since, one threw at me a piece of

brick, which grazed on my shoulder, but hurt me not. It was a year after that another threw a stone, which struck me between the eyes; but the hurt was soon healed. And still no man had power to lay a hand upon me. At St. Ives, last month, I received one blow, the first I ever had, on the side of the head; and this night two, one before we came into the town, and one after I was gone out into the meadows. But though one man struck me on the breast with all his might, and the other on the mouth, so that the blood gushed out, I felt no more pain from either of the blows than if they had touched me with a straw.
October 22, 1743

'Lo, I come', if this soul and body may be useful to anything, 'to do thy will, O God.'[48] And if it please thee to use the power thou hast over dust and ashes,[49] over weak flesh and blood,[50] over a brittle vessel of clay,[51] over the work of thine own hands,[52] lo, here they are, to suffer also thy good pleasure. If thou please to visit me either with pain or dishonour, I will 'humble myself' under it, and, through thy grace, be 'obedient unto death, even the death upon the cross'.[53] Whatsoever may befall me, either from neighbours or strangers, since it is thou employest them, though they know it not (unless thou help me to some lawful means of redressing the wrong), I will not 'open my mouth before the Lord',[54] who smiteth me, except only to 'bless the Lord'.[55] Hereafter no man can take away anything from me, no life, no honour, no estate, since I am ready to lay them down as soon as I perceive thou requirest them at my hands. Nevertheless, 'O Father, if thou be willing, remove this cup from me; but if not, thy will be done.'[56] Whatever sufferings hereafter may trouble my flesh, or whatever agonies may trouble my spirit, 'O Father, into thy hand will I commend'[57] my life, and all that concerneth it. And if thou be pleased, either that I live yet awhile, or not, I will, with my Saviour, 'bow down my head';[58] I will humble myself under thy hand; I will give up all thou art pleased to ask, until at last I 'give up the ghost'.[59]

[48] Heb. 10:7.
[49] Gen. 18:27, etc.
[50] Matt., 16:17, etc.
[51] See Jer. 18:4.
[52] Ps. 138:8.
[53] Cf. Phil. 2:8.
[54] Cf. Judg. 11:35-36.
[55] Ps. 103:1, etc.
[56] Cf. Luke 22:42.
[57] Cf. Luke 23:46.
[58] Cf. John 19:30.
[59] Ibid.

THE
PRINCIPLES
OF A
METHODIST
FARTHER EXPLAIN'D:

Occasioned by the

Reverend Mr. CHURCH's Second LETTER to Mr. WESLEY:

In a Second LETTER to that Gentleman.

By JOHN WESLEY, M. A.
Fellow of LINCOLN-COLLEGE, OXFORD.

LONDON:
Printed by W. STRAHAN; And Sold by T. TRYE, near *Gray's-Inn Gate, Holborn*; H. BUTLER, in *Bow-Church-Yard, Cheapside*; and at the *Foundary* near *Upper-Moorfields*. MDCCXLVI.

[Price Eight-Pence.]

8

THE PRINCIPLES OF A METHODIST FARTHER EXPLAINED

(1746)

AN INTRODUCTORY COMMENT

Wesley did not have many months of waiting for the Rev. Mr. Church's reply to his Answer to the Rev. Mr. Church's Remarks on the Rev. Mr. John Wesley's Last Journal *(pp. 80-122 above). In 1746 appeared* Some Farther Remarks on the Rev. Mr. John Wesley's Last Journal, together with a few considerations on his Farther Appeal; showing the inconsistency of his Conduct and Sentiments with the Constitution and Doctrine of the Church of England, and explaining the Articles relating to Justification. To which is annexed a Vindication of the Remarks, being a Reply to Mr. Wesley's answer, in a second Letter to that Gentleman. By Thomas Church, A.M., Vicar of Battersea, and Prebendary of St. Paul's *(see Green,* Anti-Methodist, *No. 205*).

The Vindication *comprises nine sections: I. Concerning the Moravians; II. Concerning Justification by Faith; III. The Instances of Despair reviewed; IV. Abuses of the Clergy, etc., considered; V. Of Predestination, and other bad Consequences of excluding good Works as Conditions of Justification; VI. Of Perfection and a clean Heart; VII. Of the Lord's Supper; VIII. Of a Stoical Insensibility; and IX. Of Enthusiasm and Presumption.*

The elaborate title of Church's work and the chapter headings of the Vindication *indicate clearly what we may expect from John Wesley's response,* The Principles of a Methodist Farther Explain'd. *All such expectations are abundantly fulfilled, since Wesley deals in order and in detail with almost all the points that Church makes. Rather confusingly, he borrows his title from his reply to Josiah Tucker (pp. 47-66 above), part of which, indeed, he quotes in the present work (§3 of his preamble is based on §4 of* The Principles of a Methodist, *and §4 is an exact replica of the former §3). Other repetitions from other works are to be found here from time to time.*

Of general importance for an assessment of Wesley's defence of his doctrine and practices against his critics are several positions taken up by him at length in this writing: (a) his undiminished claim to be a minister of the Church of England; (b) his vindication of his methods through 'miracles' and 'special providences'; (c) his argument in favour of his divine calling and encouragement from the success of Methodist preaching and the way of life in many areas of the country both rural and industrial.

Mr. Church issued no reply to this treatise. He died in 1756. That Wesley believed that he had done all that was needed is shown by his letter to 'John Smith' (26:251 in this edn.).

For the details of the two editions of the work and variants introduced in Wesley's Works (1772, Vol. 16), see Appendix A, pp. 541ff. See also Bibliography, *No. 123.*

The Principles of a Methodist Farther Explained

Occasioned by the Rev. Mr. Church's Second Letter to Mr. Wesley: In a Second Letter to that Gentleman

Reverend sir,

1. At the time that I was reading your former letter[1] I expected to hear from you again. And I was not displeased with the expectation; believing it would give me a fresh opportunity of weighing the sentiments I might have too lightly espoused, and the actions which perhaps I had not enough considered. Viewing things in this light I cannot but esteem you, not an enemy, but a friend; and one in some respects better qualified to do me real service than those whom the world accounts so, who may be hindered by their prejudice in my favour either from observing what is reprovable, or from using that freedom and plainness of speech which are requisite to convince me of it.

2. It is at least as much with a view to learn myself as to show others (what I think) the truth that I intend to set down a few

[1] See *Answer to the Rev. Mr. Church's Remarks* (1745), pp. 81-122 above.

reflections on some parts of the tract you have lately published.[2] I say, *some* parts, for it is not my design to answer every sentence in this, any more than in the former. Many things I pass over because I think them true; many more because I think them not material; and some because I am determined not to engage in an useless, if not hurtful, controversy.

3. Fear indeed is one cause of my declining this—fear (as I said elsewhere)[a] not of my *adversary*, but of *myself*. I fear my own spirit, lest 'I fall where many mightier have been slain'.[3] I never knew one (or but one) man write controversy with what I thought a right spirit. Every disputant seems to think (as every soldier) that he may hurt his opponent as much as he can; nay, that he *ought* to do his worst to him, or he cannot make the best of his own cause; that, so he do not belie or wilfully misrepresent him, he must expose him as much as he is able. It is enough, we suppose, if we do not show heat or passion against our adversary. But not to despise him, or endeavour to make others do so, is quite a work of supererogation.

4. But ought these things to be so? (I speak on the Christian scheme.) Ought we not to love our neighbour as ourselves? And does a man cease to be our neighbour because he is of a different opinion? Nay, and declares himself so to be? Ought we not, for all this, to do to him as we would he should do to us? But do we ourselves love to be *exposed* or set in the worst light? Would we willingly be treated with contempt? If not, why do we treat others thus? And yet who scruples it? Who does not hit every blot he can, however foreign to the merits of the cause? Who, in controversy,

[a] In the Preface to the Answer to Mr. Tucker [i.e., *The Principles of a Methodist* (pp. 48-50 above), of which Wesley quotes verbatim here almost the whole of §§2-3, which see for annotations].

---

[2] *Some Farther Remarks on the Rev. Mr. John Wesley's Last Journal* (London, Cooper, 1746), see Intro. above. Pp. 78-134 are given over to 'A Vindication of the *Remarks*, or, a Reply to your *Answer*'. This begins (p. 78):

'The foregoing letter was begun before your *Farther Appeal* came to my hands, and a good part of it was wrote before I received your *Answer* to my *Remarks*. I find, I had fortunately obviated some of your strongest objections. However I will once more review the whole, and consider what you have replied to me, only referring to what I have said above on such points which have been already examined.'

Church's own copy of Wesley's *Answer* is in Lambeth Palace Library, and contains his manuscript annotations in the margins, many of which have been written up more fully and incorporated in this 'Vindication'.

[3] See *The Principles of a Methodist*, pp. 48-49 and n. 3 above.

casts the mantle of love over the nakedness of his brother? Who keeps steadily and uniformly to the question, without ever striking at the person? Who shows in every sentence that he loves his brother, only less than the truth?

5. I fear neither you nor I have attained to this. I believe brotherly love might have found a better construction than that of 'unfairness', 'art', or 'disingenuity',[4] to have put either on my not answering *every part* of your book (a thing which never once entered my thoughts) or on my not reciting *all the words* of those parts which I did answer. I cannot yet perceive any blame herein. I still account it *fair* and *ingenuous* to pass over both what I believe is right, and what I believe is not dangerously wrong. Neither can I see any *disingenuity* at all in quoting only *that part* of any sentence against which I conceive the objection lies; nor in *abridging* any part of any treatise to which I reply, whether in the author's or in my own words.

6. If indeed it were so abridged as to alter the sense, this would be *unfair*. And if this were designedly done, it would be *artful* and *disingenuous*. But I am not conscious of having done this at all, although you speak as if I had done it a thousand times. And yet I cannot undertake now either to transcribe your whole book, or every page or paragraph which I answer. But I must generally abridge before I reply; and that not only to save time (of which I have none to spare) but often to make the argument clearer, which is best understood when couched in few words.

7. You complain also of my mentioning, all at once, sentences which you placed at a distance from each other. I do so; and I think it quite *fair* and *ingenuous*, to lay together what was before scattered abroad. For instance: you now speak of the conditions of justification in the 18th and following pages; again from the 89th to the 102nd; and yet again in the 127th page. Now I have not leisure to follow you to and fro. Therefore what I say on one head I set in one place.

[4] See Church's 'Vindication', pp. 81, 83-84 of his *Farther Remarks:* 'Before I proceed, this may be a proper place to mention one great and just complaint which I have to make. This is in regard to your method of citing my words. You alter them at your pleasure. You leave out what you think fit, once at least whole pages, without any line or the least mark of omission. And this perpetually, nay several times in the same sentence. Though some of these changes and omissions may be of no consequence, yet others are. I may remind you of some of these hereafter. I own I was astonished at such unfair treatment, when I compared your *Answer* with my *Remarks.*'

I. 1. This premised, I come to the letter itself. I begin, as before, with the case of the Moravians, of whom you say:[b]

I collected together the character which you had given of these men [. . .], the errors and vices which you had charged upon them, and the mischiefs . . . they had done among your followers. And I proved that in several respects you had been the occasion of this mischief, and are therefore in some measure accountable for it. Let us see what answer you give to all this.

With regard to the denying degrees in faith, you mentioned that the Moravian Church was cleared from this mistake.[5] But did you not mention this as one of the tenets of the Moravians? Do you not say that you could not agree with Mr. Spangenberg, 'that none has any faith so long as he is liable to any doubt or fear'?[6] Do not you represent Mr. Molther and other Moravians in England as teaching the same?[7] In short, I have not charged the Moravian Church with anything, but only repeat after you. And if you have accused them when you knew them to be guiltless, you must bear the blame.

'They do use the ordinances of God with reverence and godly fear.'[8]—You have charged Mr. Spangenberg and Mr. Molther with teaching that we ought to abstain from them. And the same you say in general of the Moravian Brethren in your letter to them.—But 'Mr. Molther was quickly after recalled into Germany.' This might be on other accounts. You do not say it was out of any dislike of his doctrines or proceedings. Nor indeed can you, consistently with your next words: 'The great fault of the Moravian Church seems to lie in not openly disclaiming all he had said—which in all probability they would have done, had they not leaned to the same opinion.'

You 'never knew but one of the Moravian Church affirm that a believer does not grow in holiness'. But who was this? No less a person than Count Zinzendorf, their great bishop and patron, whose authority is very high, all in all with them, and to whom you think 'they pay *too much* regard'.[c]

[b] Mr. Church's words are printed in *italics* [in this edn. within quotation marks]. [It is probably desirable at this point to say something about Wesley's documentation of this complex work, with its interwoven quotations from and cross-references to five distinct publications, and our editorial treatment of it. To indicate the sources of the passages which he quotes (often imperfectly) he uses verbal clues—'You remark', 'I answer', 'You reply'—and abbreviated titles and page numbers, both in the text and in footnotes. In our editorial notes (those prefixed by figure cues) we have been able to make these much more specific. This is much more difficult to do in reproducing Wesley's own notes (prefixed by letter cues) without the profuse and confusing use of square brackets. We have tried to simplify this for the reader's sake. We have extended abbreviated titles, filled out (and sometimes corrected) the page numbers, and made the necessary styling alterations, without using square brackets to inform the reader exactly what we were doing about these mechanical minutiae. Further details and illustrations of this process will be found in Appendix A.]

[c] Second Letter [i.e., Church, *Farther Remarks,* and so henceforth], p. 79.

---

[5] Here Church cited Wesley's *Answer,* p. 4, viz., I.2(1).

[6] Church cites Wesley's *Journal* 4, p. 8, viz., Nov. 7, 1741.

[7] Citing ibid., pp. 19, 105, i.e., Dec. 31, 1739, and letter of Aug. 8, 1740, §5.

[8] Church cites Wesley's *Answer,* pp. 4-5.

2. This is the whole of your reply to this part of my answer. I will now consider it, part by part.

First, 'With regard to the denying degrees in faith, you mentioned that the Moravian Church was cleared from this mistake. But did you not mention this as one of the tenets of the Moravians?'—No; not of the Moravians in general.—'Do you not say that you could not agree with Mr. Spangenberg, "that none has any faith so long as he is liable to any doubt or fear"?'—I do say so still. But Mr. Spangenberg is not the Moravian Church.—'Do you not represent Mr. Molther and other Moravians in England as teaching the same?'—I do; three or four in all. But neither are these the Moravian Church.—'In short, I have not charged the Moravian Church with anything, but only repeat after you.'—Indeed you have, in the very case before us. You charge them 'with denying degrees in faith'. I do not charge them herewith. I openly cleared them from any such charge near six years ago.—'If therefore you have accused them when you knew them to be guiltless, you must bear the blame.'—In this case, I must entreat *you* to bear it in my stead. For I have not 'accused them' (the Moravian Church). It is *you* that have accused them. I have again and again declared, they are *not guilty*.

Secondly, '"They do use the ordinances of God with reverence and godly fear."—You have charged Mr. Spangenberg and Mr. Molther with teaching that we ought to abstain from them.'—That *we*? No. That *unbelievers* ought. The assertion relates to them only.—'And the same you say in general of the Moravian Brethren in your letter.'—I say, they hold that 'unbelievers ought to abstain from them'. But yet I know and bear witness, they use them themselves, and that with reverence and godly fear.—'"Mr. Molther was quickly after recalled to Germany." This might be on other accounts. You do not say it was out of any dislike of his doctrines or proceedings.'—I do not say so, because I am not sure; but I believe it was out of a dislike to *some* of his proceedings, if not of his doctrines too.—'Nor indeed can you, consistently with your next words: "The great fault of the Moravian Church seems to lie in not openly disclaiming all he had said"' (relating to this head).—They did *privately disclaim* what he had said, of degrees in faith. But I think, that was not enough. And I still believe, they would have done more 'had they not leaned themselves to the same opinion' touching the ordinances.

Thirdly, 'you "never knew but one of the Moravian Church affirm that a believer does not grow in holiness".—But who was this? No less a person than Count Zinzendorf, their great bishop and patron, whose authority is very high, all in all with them, and to whom you think "they pay too much regard"'.—Do you apprehend where the stress of the argument lies? I never heard one Moravian affirm this, but the Count alone; and him only once; and that once was in the heat of dispute. And hence I inferred, It is not a doctrine of the Moravian Church. Nay, I doubt whether it be the Count's own settled judgment.

3. But I may not dismiss this passage yet. It is now my turn to complain of unfair usage, of the exceeding lame, broken, imperfect manner wherein you cite my words. For instance, your citation runs thus: You 'never knew but one of the Moravian Church affirm that a believer does not grow in holiness'.—Whereas my words are these, 'I never knew one of the Moravian Church but that single person affirm that a believer does not grow in holiness. And perhaps he would not affirm it on reflection.'—Now why was the former part of the sentence changed, and the latter quite left out?—Had the whole stood in your tract just as it does in mine, it must have appeared, I do not here charge the Moravian Church.

I complain also of your manner of replying to the first article of this very paragraph. For you do not cite so much as one line of that answer to which you profess to reply. My words are, 'You ought not to charge the Moravian Church with the first of these (errors), since in the very page from which you quote those words, "There is no justifying faith where there is ever any doubt" that note occurs, (viz., 4th *Journal*, p. 105) "In the Preface to the 2nd *Journal* the Moravian Church is cleared from this mistake."'—If you had cited these words, could you possibly have subjoined, 'I have not charged the Moravian Church with anything; but only repeat after you'?

4. [A]. I have now considered one page of your reply in the manner you seem to require. But sure you can't expect I should follow you thus, step by step, through an hundred and forty pages! If you should then think it worth while to make a second reply, and to follow me in the same manner, we might write indeed; but who would read?—I return therefore to what I proposed at first, viz., to touch only on what seems of the most importance, and leave the rest just as it lies.

4. [B]. You say, 'With regard to subtlety, evasion, and disguise, you *now* would have it thought that you only found this "in many of them, not in all, nor in most".'[d]—'You *now* would have it thought'! Yes, and *always*, as well as *now*. For my original charge was, 'I have found this in many of you', i.e., 'much subtlety, much evasion, and disguise'.[e]—But you add:

> Let the reader judge from the following passages whether you did not charge the Moravians in general with these crimes. 'I had a long conference with those whom I esteem very highly in love. But I could not yet understand them in one point, Christian openness and plainness of speech. They pleaded for such a reservedness and closeness of conversation. . . . Yet I scarce knew what to think, considering they had the practice of the whole Moravian Church on their side.

True, in pleading for such a *reservedness* of conversation as I could not in any wise[9] approve of, but not in using 'much subtlety, much evasion, and disguise'. This I dare not charge on the whole Moravian Church. Those words also, 'There is darkness and closeness in all their behaviour, and guile in almost all their words,'[10] I spoke, not of all the Moravians, nor of most; but of those who were then in England. I could not speak it of them all; for I never found any guile in Christian David, Michael Linner,[11] and many others.

5. 'We are next to see how you get over the objection I made good in three several particulars, that you have prepared the way for [the] spreading of these tenets. The first you say nothing to here . . . ; the second you quote very partially thus, "by countenancing and commending them". And why would you not add, "and being the occasion of so many of them coming over among us"?'—Because I was not the occasion. I was indeed the first Englishman that ever was at Herrnhut.[12] But before I was at

[d] P. 80 [i.e., of Church's *Farther Remarks,* continuing his 'Vindication' from Wesley's *Answer,* begun p. 78, and citing the *Answer,* p. 6, i.e., I.4].

[e] 4th *Journal,* p. 104 [i.e., Wesley's letter of Aug. 8, 1740, §4].

---

[9] Orig., both edns., 'any ways', corrected in the errata and in Wesley's own copy of his *Works*.

[10] Quoted by Church, p. 80, citing p. 80 of Wesley's *Journal* 4, i.e., Apr. 21, 1741.

[11] Linner's spiritual autobiography immediately follows that of Christian David in JWJ, Aug. 10, 1738.

[12] A difficult claim to substantiate or refute; it was presumably based on statements made to him at the time.

Herrnhut (I find on later enquiry), the Count himself had been in England.[13]

'You "still think that, next to some thousands in our own church, the body of the Moravian Church, however mistaken some of them are, [are] in the main the best Christians in the world".'[f] I do—'of all whom I have seen'. (You should not omit these words.)—'Those dreadful errors and crimes are here softened into mistakes.' (I term them 'errors of judgment and practice'.) 'I have proved, that you have charged the body with such.'—At present the proof does not amount to demonstration. There needs a little farther proof that I charge any 'dreadful crimes' on 'the body of the Moravians'.

I see no manner of inconsistency still in those accounts of my intercourse with the Moravians which you suppose irreconcilable with each other. Let anyone read them in the *Journal*, and judge.

6. 'You had said your "objections then were nearly the same as now".' You now add,

> 'only with this difference; I was not then assured that the facts were as I supposed. I did not dare to determine anything.' No, not when by conversing among them you saw these things? As indeed the facts are of such a nature that you could not but be assured of them if they were true. Nor do the questions in your letter really imply any doubt of their truth, but are so many appeals to their consciences, and equivalent to strong assertions. And if you had not been assured, if you did not dare to determine anything concerning what you saw, your writing bare suspicions to a body of men in such a manner was inexcusable. This excuse therefore will not serve you.[g]

I apprehend it will. 'I was not then (in September 1738) assured that the facts were as I supposed. (Therefore) I did not (then) dare to determine anything.' Be pleased to add the immediately following words: 'But from November 1 (1739) I *saw*

[f] P. 81.
[g] P. 83 [citing p. 8 of Wesley's *Answer,* i.e., I.5].

---

[13] Zinzendorf visited London on Jan. 20, 1737, to inquire of John Potter, Archbishop Elect of Canterbury, whether the Moravian episcopacy was valid. Potter declared that no one with any knowledge of church history could doubt the Moravian succession. (It has never, however, been officially acknowledged by the Church of England, in spite of frequent discussions between the two Churches. See A. J. Lewis, *Zinzendorf, The Ecumenical Pioneer* [S.C.M., 1962]; Report of the committee appointed by the Archbishop of Canterbury to consider the Orders of the Unitas Fratrum, or Moravians [London, 1907], p. 55. The matter came up, but was not settled, 1979–82 in connection with the Covenanting Proposals for the visible unity of the Churches of England.) In Feb. 1737, Zinzendorf established a Diaspora Society in London (Lewis, p. 125).

more and more things which I could not reconcile with the gospel.'

If you had not omitted these words, you could have had no colour to remark on my saying, 'I did not dare to determine anything'—'No, not when by conversing among them you *saw* these things?'—No. I did not 'dare to determine', in September 1738, from what I saw in November 1739.—'But the facts are of such a nature that you could not but be assured of them if they were true.'—I cannot think so. 'Is not the Count all in all among you? Do not you magnify your own church too much? Do you not use guile and dissimulation in many cases?' These 'facts' are by no means of 'such a nature' as that whoever converses (even intimately) among the Moravians 'cannot but be assured of them'.—'Nor do the questions in your letter really imply any doubt of their truth.'—No? Are not my very words prefixed to those questions: 'Of some other things I stand in *doubt*. . . . And I wish that, *in order to remove those doubts*, you would . . . plainly answer whether the fact be as I suppose.'—'But (these questions) are so many appeals to their consciences.'—True.—'And equivalent to strong assertions.'—Utterly false.—'If you had not been assured, if you did not dare to determine anything concerning what you saw' (fifteen months after), 'your writing bare suspicions to a body of men in such a manner was inexcusable.'—They were *strong presumptions* then; which yet I did not 'write to a body of men' whom I so highly esteemed, no, not even in the *tenderest* manner, till I was *assured* they were not groundless.

7. 'In a note at the bottom of p. 8 you observe, "The Band Society in London began May 1, some time before I set out for Germany." Would you insinuate here that you did not set it up in imitation of the Moravians?'[14]—Sir, I will tell you the naked truth. You had remarked thus: 'You took the trouble of a journey to Germany to them, and were so much in love with their methods that at *your return* hither you set up their Bands among your disciples.'[h] This was an entire mistake. For that Society was set up, not only before I *returned*, but before I *set out*. And I designed that note to *insinuate* this to *you*, without telling your mistake to all the world.

[h] P. 17 [i.e., of Church's original *Remarks*, 1745].

[14] Church, *Farther Remarks*, p. 83.

'I imagined, that supposing your account of the Moravians true, it would be impossible for any serious Christian to doubt of their being very wicked people.'—I know many serious Christians who suppose it true, and yet believe they are, in the main, good men.—'A much worse character, take the whole body together, cannot be given of a body of men.'—Let us try. 'Here is a body of men who have not one spark either of justice, mercy, or truth, among them; who are lost to all sense of right and wrong; who have neither sobriety, temperance, nor chastity; who are, in general, liars, drunkards, gluttons, thieves, adulterers, or murderers.'[15] I cannot but think that this is a 'much worse character' than that of the Moravians, take it how you will.—'Let the reader judge how far you are *now* able to defend them.'—Just as far as I did at first. Still I dare not condemn what is good among them; and I will not excuse what is evil.

8. '"The Moravians excel in sweetness of behaviour." What, though they use guile and dissimulation?'—Yes.—'"Where is their multitude of errors?" In your own Journal. . . . I have taken the pains to place them in one view in my *Remarks*, the justness of which with all your art you cannot disprove.'—You have taken the pains to transcribe many words, all which together amount to this, that they (generally) hold *universal salvation*, and are partly *antinomians* (in opinion) partly *quietists*. The justness of some of your remarks, if I mistake not, has[16] been pretty fully disproved. As to what you speak of my 'art', 'subtlety', and so on, in this and many other places, I look upon it as neither better nor worse than a civil way of *calling names*.

'"To this multitude of crimes I am also an utter stranger." Then you have charged them wrongfully.—What do you account guile, etc.?'[i]—I account guile despising self-denial, even in the smallest points, and teaching that those who have not the assurance of faith may not use the ordinances of God, the Lord's Supper in particular (this is the real unaggravated charge), to be faults which cannot be excused. But I do not account them all together a 'multitude of crimes'. I conceive this is a vehement hyperbole.

[i] Second Letter, p. 84 [citing Wesley's *Answer*, p. 10, i.e., I.7].

---

[15] The words 'let us try' indicate that Wesley is composing a sentence for the sake of his immediate argument, not quoting a specific source.

[16] Orig., 'have', corrected in the errata and Wesley's MS revisions in his *Works*.

'The honour of religion', said you, 'and virtue trampled upon?' I answered, 'By whom? Not by the Moravians.'—You reply, 'And yet you have accused some of these as decrying all the means of grace.'—No. What I accused them of was teaching that an unbeliever (in their sense) ought to abstain from them.—' "Neither did I know or think or say, they were desperately wicked people." Your *Journal* is before the world, to whom I appeal whether this has not so represented them.'—But how do you here represent your remark, and my answer? My paragraph runs thus:

You go on:

'How could you so long and so intimately converse with . . . such desperately wicked people as the Moravians, according to your own account, were known by you to be?' O sir, what another assertion is this! 'The Moravians, according to your *own account*, were *known* by you to be desperately wicked people, while you intimately conversed with them.' Utterly false and injurious! I never gave any such account. I conversed with them intimately both at Savannah and Herrnhut. But neither then nor at any other time did I *know* or think or say, they were desperately wicked people. I think and say . . . just the reverse, viz., that though I soon 'found among them a few things which I could not approve', yet I believe they are, 'in the main, some of the best Christians in the world'.

After this are *you* the person who complains of *me* for imperfect and partial quotations?

I added, 'You surprise me yet more in going on thus: "In God's name, sir, is the contempt of almost the whole of our duty, of every Christian ordinance to be so very gently touched?" Sir, this is not the case. This charge no more belongs to the Moravians than that of murder.'[j]

You reply, 'Mr. Spangenberg and Mr. Molther are accused by name. If falsely, I am sorry both for them and you.' Accused? True. But of what? Of the contempt of every Christian ordinance, of almost the whole of our duty? By no means. The plain case is, I accuse them of one thing, viz., 'teaching that an unbeliever should abstain from the ordinances'. You accuse them of another, 'condemning every Christian ordinance, and almost the whole of our duty'.[17] And this you would father upon me. I desire to be excused.

9. As to what I said in my letter to the Moravian Church, 'You can hinder this if you will, . . . therefore if you do not prevent

[j] P. 11 [of Wesley's *Answer*, i.e., I.8].

---

[17] Church, *Farther Remarks*, p. 84.

their speaking thus you do in effect speak thus yourselves,' it may be observed: (1), that this letter is dated August 8, 1740;[18] (2), that from that time the Moravian Church did in great measure prevent any of their members speaking thus.

You proceed:

> You distinguish between the English Brethren and the Moravians. These English Brethren, I presume, were your followers. Afterwards you represent them as perverted by the Moravians. Before they had spoke these wicked things, you say, they had joined these men, and acted under their direction. If they did not learn them from these new teachers, from whom did they learn them? Not, sure, from yourself, or any other Methodists. You cannot therefore bring off the Moravians without condemning your own people. Here therefore you have certainly overshot yourself.[k]

—Perhaps not.—'These English Brethren were, I presume, your followers.'—No; this is your first mistake. I was but a single private member of that Society.—'Afterwards you represent them as perverted by the Moravians.'—I do—but not yet connected with them.—'Before they spoke these wicked things they had joined these men, and acted under their direction.'—This is another mistake. They did not join these men, nor act by their direction, till long after.—'If they did not learn them from these new teachers, from whom did they learn them? . . . You can't bring off the Moravians, without condemning your own people.'—They learned them from Mr. Molther chiefly: whom I am not at all concerned to 'bring off'.—Now let all men judge which of us two has 'overshot himself'.

10. 'In answer to my objections against the inconsistent accounts you have given of the Moravians . . . you say, "They are, I believe, the most self-inconsistent people under the sun." Would not one imagine that you here speak of the same persons, or of the whole body of them in general?'[19]—I do, thus far: I ascribe the good to the body of them in general, the evil to part only of that body, to *some* of those 'same persons'.

'Your method of getting over the contradictions I had charged upon you is much the same, to distinguish either between the Moravians and the English Brethren, though these had been their disciples . . . ' (this has been abundantly answered) 'or

[k] Pp. 84-85.

[18] Orig., '1741'.

[19] *Farther Remarks,* p. 85, citing Wesley's *Answer,* p. 12, i.e., I.9.

between some of the Moravians and others.'[l]—I think a very good method, for propositions are not contradictory unless they both speak of the same persons.

However, since you persist to affirm that I am 'guilty of the contradictions you charged upon me',[m] I think there cannot be a sufficient reply without reciting the several instances.

11. First, 'You commend them' (the Moravians) 'for loving one another; and yet charge them with biting and devouring one another.'—I answered, 'Them! Whom? Not the Moravians, but the English Brethren of Fetter Lane, before their union with the Moravians. Herein then is no shadow of contradiction. For the two sentences do not relate to the same persons.'[20]

You reply, 'Would you then have us think that so much anger and contradiction reigned among your Methodists?'—I would have you think this is nothing to the purpose. Prove the contradiction, and you speak to the point.—'It is plain they had before this been perverted by the Moravians, and that . . . they were unwilling to be taught by any others.'—'They'—that is, nearly half of the society.[21] But here is no proof of the contradiction still.

(2). 'You say they "had wellnigh destroyed brotherly love from among us, partly by cautions against natural love" (partly by occasioning almost continual disputes); . . . So they had. But *we* had then no connexion with *them*. Neither therefore does this contradict their loving one another.'[22] You reply, 'As if they can truly love each other who teach you not to do it, and stir up divisions and disturbances among you.'—You should say, if you would *repeat after me*, 'who caution you against natural love, and occasion many disputes among you'. Well, allowing they do this (which is utterly wrong), yet where is the contradiction? Yet they may love one another.

(3). 'You "praise them for using no diversions but such as become saints, and yet say" (I recite the whole sentence) "I have heard some of you affirm that Christian salvation implies liberty

[l] P. 86 [of Church, *Farther Remarks*].
[m] P. 87.

---

[20] Wesley, *Answer,* I.10; cf. Church, *Farther Remarks,* p. 87.

[21] Wesley apparently refers to those who withdrew from the Fetter Lane Society with him on July 20, 1740.

[22] Church, *Farther Remarks,* p. 87, quoting Wesley's *Answer,* I.10.

to conform to the world, by joining in worldly diversions, in order to do good." And both these are true. The Moravians, in general, "use no diversions but such as become saints". And yet I have heard some of them affirm (in contradiction to their own practice) that "one then mentioned did well when he joined in playing at tennis in order to do good".'[23] To this you make no reply. Silence then consents that there is no contradiction here.

(4). 'You "praise them for not regarding outward adorning". So I do, the bulk of the congregation. "And yet you say" (I again recite the whole sentence) "I have heard some of you affirm that Christian salvation implies liberty to conform to the world by putting on gold and costly apparel." I have so. And I blame them the more because they are condemned by the general practice of their own church.'[24]—To this also you reply not. So I must count this the fourth contradiction which you have charged upon me but have not proved.

(5). '"You call their discipline, *in most respects*, truly excellent. I could wish you had more fully explained yourself."—I have, in the 2nd *Journal*, from the 44th to the 82nd page. "It is no sign of good discipline to permit such abominations" (i.e., error in opinion, and guile in practice). True; 'tis not; nor is it any demonstration against it. For there may be good discipline even in a College of Jesuits. Another fault is, too great deference to the Count. And yet, "*in most respects* their discipline is truly excellent."'[25]

You reply, 'Such excellent discipline, for all that I know, they may have,' (i.e., as the Jesuits), 'but I cannot agree . . . that this is scarce inferior to that of the apostolic age.'—It may be, for anything you advance to the contrary.—'Here I cited some words of yours condemning their subordination, which you prudently take no notice of.'[n]—Yes; I had just before taken notice of their too great deference to the Count. But, the contradiction. Where is the contradiction?

(6). 'You mention it as a good effect of their discipline that everyone knows and keeps his proper rank. Soon after, as it were with a design to confute yourself, you say, Our brethren have

[n] P. 88 [actually pp. 87-88 of Church's *Farther Remarks*, quoting Wesley's *Answer*, I.11].

---

[23] Wesley's *Answer*, I.10.
[24] Ibid., I.11.
[25] Ibid.

neither wisdom enough to guide nor prudence enough to let it alone.'[26]—I answered, 'Pardon me, sir, I have no design either to confute or contradict myself in these words. The former sentence is spoken of the *Moravian* brethren, the latter of the *English* brethren of Fetter Lane'—not then united with the Moravians, neither acting by their direction. To this likewise you do not reply. Here is then a sixth contradiction, alleged against me, but not proved.

12. However you add:

> Had you . . . shown me mistaken in any points you have attempted to reply to, still . . . you confess errors and wickedness enough among the Moravians to render your account of them very inconsistent. But you have not succeeded in any one answer. You have not shown that I have in any one instance misquoted you, or misunderstood the character you had given of them, or argued falsely from what you had said of them. And truly, sir, all you have done has been cavilling at a few particulars. But the argument I was urging all this while you quite forgot.[27]

Sir, if it be so, you do me too much honour in setting pen to paper again. But is it so? Have I 'all this while quite forgot the argument you was urging'? I hope not. I seem to remember you 'was urging' some argument to prove that I 'fall not only into inconsistencies, but direct contradictions';[o] and that I 'showed you mistaken' not only in *one*, but in *every* point which you advanced as such; that I did not confess any such 'errors' or 'wickedness' of the Moravians as rendered my account of them 'self-inconsistent'; that I 'succeeded' in more than 'one answer' to the objections you had urged against it; and that I 'showed' you had 'misquoted or misunderstood the character I had given of them, or argued falsely from it', not properly 'in one instance', but from the beginning to the end.

Yet this I think it incumbent upon me to say, that whereinsoever I have contributed, directly or indirectly, to the spreading of anything evil, which is, or has been, among the Moravians, I am sorry for it, and hereby ask pardon both of God and all the world.

II. 1. I think it appears by what you have yourself observed, that on the second head, justification by faith, I allow, in the

[o] *Remarks*, p. 21, answered by Wesley in *Answer*, I.10.

---

[26] Wesley, *Answer*, I.11.

[27] Church, *Farther Remarks*, p. 88.

beginning of the *Farther Appeal*, almost as much as you contend for.

I desire leave to cite part of that passage again, that we may come as near each other as possible. I would just subjoin a few words in each head, which I hope may remove more difficulties out of the way.

'That justification whereof our Articles and Homilies speak means present pardon and acceptance with God, who therein "declares his righteousness" or mercy by or "for the remission of the sins that are past".'[28]

I say *past*. For I cannot find anything in the Bible of the remission of sins past, present, and to come.

'I believe the condition of this is faith: I mean, not only that without faith we cannot be justified, but also that as soon as anyone has true faith, in that moment he is justified.'[29]

You take the word 'condition'[30] in the former sense only, as that without which we cannot be justified. In this sense of the word I think we may allow that there are several conditions of justification.

'Good works follow this faith, but cannot go before it. Much less can sanctification, which implies a continued course of good works, springing from holiness of heart.'[31]

Yet such a course is without doubt absolutely necessary to our continuance in a *state* of *justification*.

'It is allowed that repentance and "fruits meet for repentance" go before faith. Repentance *absolutely must* go before faith; *fruits meet for it*, if there be opportunity. By *repentance* I mean conviction of sin, producing real desires and sincere resolutions of amendment; and by "fruits meet for repentance", forgiving our brother, ceasing from evil, doing good, using the ordinances of God, and, in general, obeying him according to the measure of grace which we have received. But these I cannot as yet term good works, because they do not spring from faith and the love of God.'[32] Although the same works are then good when they are performed by *those who have believed*.

[28] Wesley, *A Farther Appeal*, Pt. I, I.2 (11:105 in this edn.), abridged, as are some others of the following quotations from the same work.

[29] Ibid.

[30] I.e., Church, in his *Farther Remarks*, pp. 89-104, the second section of the 'Vindication', entitled, 'Concerning Justification by Faith'.

[31] *A Farther Appeal*, Pt. I, I.2 (11:105-6 in this edn.).

[32] Ibid.

'Faith in general is a divine supernatural ἔλεγχος' (evidence, or conviction) 'of things not seen, not discoverable by our bodily senses, as being either past, future, or spiritual. Justifying faith implies, not only a divine ἔλεγχος, that God was in Christ, reconciling the world unto himself, but a sure trust and confidence, that Christ died for *my* sins, that he loved *me*, and gave himself for *me*. And the moment a *penitent* sinner *thus* believes, God pardons and absolves him.'[33]

I say, a *penitent* sinner; because justifying faith cannot exist without previous *repentance*.

'Yet although both repentance and the fruits thereof are in *some sense* necessary before justification, neither the one nor the other is necessary in the *same sense*, or in the *same degree* with faith. Not in the *same degree:* for in whatever moment a man believes (in the Christian sense of the word), he is justified. . . . But it is not so at whatever moment he repents, or brings forth any or all the fruits of repentance. . . . Consequently none of these are necessary to justification, in the same degree with faith.'

'Nor in the *same sense:* for none of these has so direct, immediate a relation to justification as faith. This is *proximately* necessary thereto; repentance *remotely*, as it is necessary to faith' (so the error of the press is to be corrected);[34] 'and the fruits of repentance still *more remotely*, as they are necessary to the increase or continuance of repentance. And even in this sense they are only necessary on supposition—if there be time and opportunity for them. For in many instances there is not, but God cuts short his work, and faith prevents the fruits of repentance.'[35]

2. Thus far I believe we are nearly agreed. But on those words, 'Far other qualifications are required in order to our standing before God in glory than were required in order to his giving us faith and pardon: in order to this nothing is *indispensably* required but repentance or conviction of sin; but in order to the other it is

[33] Ibid., I.4.

[34] A line of type had been omitted from the 1st edn. of *A Farther Appeal,* leading to the nonsensical reading, 'repentance *remotely,* . . . as it is necessary to repentance'. Without consulting his original manuscript (probably destroyed), or discovering the overlooked erratum slip, for his *Answer,* II.3, Wesley patched up something which made sense, though not his original sense. Here, however, under the pressure of Church's criticism, he has apparently discovered the erratum slip and correctly restored the missing passage, though when he came to publish subsequent edns. of the *Appeal* the correct reading was again overlooked (see 11:117 in this edn.).

[35] *A Farther Appeal,* Pt. I, II.11 (11:117 in this edn.).

indispensably required that we be fully cleansed from all sin'[36] you remark: 'Here I apprehend are two great mistakes: (1). You make too little necessary before pardon. (2). Too much afterward. You confine repentance within too narrow limits, and extend holiness beyond its just bounds.'

'First, by repentance you mean only conviction of sin. But this is a very partial account of it. Every child that has learned his catechism can tell that forsaking of sin is also included in it; . . . living in obedience to God's will, when there is opportunity; and even when there is not, a sincere desire and purpose to do so, . . . and a faith in God's mercies through Christ Jesus.'[p]

I had said, 'In order to God's giving us faith and pardon nothing is indispensably required but repentance,' i.e., 'conviction of sin producing real desires and sincere resolutions of amendment.' But you 'apprehend that I am here in a great mistake', that I give a 'very partial account of repentance'; that I ought to 'include therein a sincere desire and purpose' to obey God.—I do. I have said so expressly.—And 'living in obedience to God's will where there is opportunity'.—Very well; but I here speak of what is 'indispensably required', i.e., whether there is opportunity of actual obedience or no.—'And a faith in God's mercies through Christ Jesus'.—A very great mistake indeed! My not including faith in that 'repentance' which I say is *indispensably* required—*in order* to faith!

'Secondly, you make sinless perfection necessary after justification, in order to make us meet for glory.'—And who does not? Indeed men do not agree in the time. Some believe it is attained before death; some, in the article of death; some, in an after-state; in the *mystic*, or the *popish* purgatory. But all writers whom I have ever seen till now (the Romish themselves not excepted) agree that we must be 'fully cleansed from all sin' before we can enter into glory.

3. After what has already been allowed I cannot think it needful to dispute farther on the head of justification.—Rather suffer me to close this part of our debate by transcribing what I assent to from that clear recapitulation of your sentiments which you have given in your 45th and 46th pages.[37]

[p] P. 92 [i.e., of Church, *Farther Remarks*].

---

[36] Wesley, *Answer,* II.4.

[37] In his *Farther Remarks* Church had just quoted Wesley's *Farther Appeal,* Pt. I, II.8, as

First, justification is the act of God, pardoning our sins, and receiving us again to his favour. This was free in him, because undeserved by us; undeserved, because we had transgressed his law, and could not, nor even can now, perfectly fulfil it.

(2). We cannot therefore be justified by our works, because this would be to be justified by some merit of our own. Much less can we be justified by an external show of religion, or by any superstitious observances.

(3). The life and death of our Lord is the sole meritorious cause of this mercy, which must be firmly believed and trusted in by us. Our faith therefore in him, though not more meritorious than any other of our actions, yet has a nearer relation to the promises of pardon through him, and is the mean and instrument whereby we embrace and receive them.

(4). True faith must be lively and productive of good works, which are its proper fruits, the marks whereby it is known.

(5). Works really good are such as are commanded by God (springing from faith),[38] done by the aid of his Holy Spirit, with good designs, and to good ends. These may be considered as internal or external.

(6). The inward ones, such as [repentance], hope, trust, fear, and love of God and our neighbour, which may be more properly termed *good dispositions* and (are branches of)[39] sanctification, must always be joined with faith, and consequently be *conditions present* in justification, . . . though they are not the means or instruments of receiving it.

(7). The outward . . . (which are more properly termed good works)[40] though there be no immediate opportunity of practising them, and therefore a sincere desire and resolution to perform them be sufficient for the present, yet must follow after as soon as occasion offers, and will then be necessary conditions of preserving our justification.[41]

(8). There is a justification conveyed to us in our baptism, or properly, this state is then[42] begun. But . . . should we fall into sins, . . . we cannot regain it without true faith and repentance, which implies (as its fruits)[43] a forsaking of our sins, and amendment of (our whole) life.[44]

I have only one circumstance farther to add, namely, that I am not *newly* convinced of these things. For this is the doctrine which

'what you call the doctrine of the Church of England', claiming that it was 'falsely ascribed to her'. He went on to set forth 'a juster account of her sentiments', pp. 45-46, which Wesley here quotes approvingly, though with some minor alterations.

[38] Wesley's added comment, in square brackets in the original.

[39] Wesley here places within square brackets his modification of Church's original: 'which may be more properly good dispositions or principles, and surely contain some degree of sanctification'.

[40] Church, 'The outward virtues, which are more especially good works'.

[41] Church continues: 'and rendering this of any service and consequence to us'.

[42] Wesley's original reads 'thus', altered in *Works* (1772), to Church's 'then'.

[43] Wesley's insertion within square brackets.

[44] Wesley inserts '[our whole]' within Church's 'of life'. Church continues: 'which contains restitution, alms, and the forgiveness of enemies; which last the Church expressly calls a *condition* of our pardon. And, (9). These are the same conditions of our present justification and future reward.'

I have continually taught for eight or nine years last past—only I abstained from the word *condition*, perhaps more scrupulously than was needful.

4. With regard to the *consequences* of my teaching this doctrine, I desire any who will not account it lost labour to consult with his own eyes, seriously and in the fear of God, the 3rd and 4th *Journals*. And if he pleases he may farther read over and compare from the 25th to the 29th page of my *Answer*,[45] with your reply, from the 101st (inclusive) to the 104th page.

Among the consequences you reckoned (in your *Remarks*), besides 'introducing predestination', 'confusion, presumption, and despair, many very shocking instances of all which' (your words are) 'you give us among your followers'.[q]—I answered, 'You should have specified a few of those instances; at least the pages where they occur.' (Suppose, only three of each sort, out of any, or all the four *Journals*.) 'Till this is done, I can look upon this assertion as no other than a flourish of your pen.'[46]

Upon this you exclaim, 'I must beg the reader to observe your method of citing my words. Many instances of omissions he has had already. But here is such a one as I believe few controversies can parallel. . . . Would not anyone imagine from the view of these words' ('predestination, confusion, presumption, and despair') 'that they occurred all together in the page 52 of my *Remarks*, and that I observed nothing farther concerning this point? Could it be thought that anything intervened between the page referred to and the last sentence? And yet so it is, that near three pages intervene!'[r]—Ha! do 'near three pages intervene'? Prodigious indeed!—'And this is called an *Answer!*'—So it is, for want of a better.

'Your business was to show that the Calvinistical notions have not prevailed among the Methodists, or that they were no consequences of unconditional justification.'—No, sir, it was not my business to show this. It was not my business to prove the negative; but yours, to prove the affirmative. Mr. Whitefield is himself a Calvinist. Such therefore doubtless are many of his followers. But Calvinism has not prevailed at all among any other

[q] [Church, *Remarks*,] pp. 52, 55.
[r] [Church, *Farther Remarks*,] p. 111.

---

[45] I.e., *Answer*, II.11-14, pp. 102-7 above.
[46] See Wesley's *Answer*, II.17, p. 109 above.

of the Methodists (so called), nor is it to this day any consequence of unconditional justification, in the manner wherein I preach it.

5. You next 'take the pains to lay before the reader an instance or two of confusion, etc.' The first I read thus:

> 'While we were at the room, Mrs. J[one]s, sitting at home, took the Bible to read; but on a sudden threw it away, saying, "I am good enough. I will never read or pray more." She was in the same mind when I came, often repeating, "I used to think I was full of sin, and that I sinned in everything I did. But now I know better. I am a good Christian. I never did any harm in my life. I don't desire to be any better than I am." She spoke many things to the same effect, plainly showing that the spirit of pride and of lies had the full dominion over her. . . . I asked, "Do you desire to be healed?" She said, "I am whole." "But do you desire to be saved?" She replied, "I am saved. I ail nothing. I am happy."' . . . This is one of the fruits of the present salvation and sinless perfection, taught by you among the weak and ignorant.'[s]

I should wonder if the scarecrow of *sinless perfection* was not brought in some way or other. But to the point. You here repeat a relation as from me, and that 'in confirmation', you say, 'of your own veracity', and yet leave out both the beginning of that relation, part of the middle, and the end of it.

It begins thus: 'Sun. 11. I met with a surprising instance of the power of the devil.'[t] These words, of all others, should not have been left out, being a key to all that follows. In the middle of the relation, immediately after the words, 'I am happy,' I add: 'Yet it was easy to discern, she was in the most violent agony, both of body and mind; sweating exceedingly, notwithstanding the severe frost, and not continuing in the same posture a moment.' A plain proof that this was no instance of *presumption*, nor a *natural* fruit of any teaching whatever.

It ends thus. 'About a quarter before six the next morning, after lying quiet awhile, she broke out, "Peace be unto thee (her husband). Peace be unto this house. The peace of God is come to my soul. I know that my Redeemer liveth." And for several days her mouth was filled with his praise, and her talk was wholly of his wondrous works.'—Had not these words been left out, neither could this have passed for an instance of *despair*.—Though still I do not know but it might have stood for an 'instance of confusion, etc.'.

[s] [Church, *Farther Remarks*,] pp. 11-12 [quoting JWJ, Jan. 11-12, 1741].

[t] 4th *Journal*, p. 66.

I must not forget that this was cited at first as a proof of my *enthusiasm*, as an instance of 'a private revelation, which' (you say) I 'seemed to pay great credit to', 'representing the conjectures of a woman . . . whose brain appears to have been too much heated as if they had been owing to a particular and miraculous spirit of prophecy'.[u] I answered, 'Descant, sir, as you please on this "enthusiasm"; on the "credit" I paid to this "private revelation"; and my representing the "conjectures" of this brain-sick woman as owing to a miraculous power of the "spirit of prophecy". And when you have done I will desire you to read the passage once more, where you will find my express words are (introducing this account): "Sunday 11. I met with a surprising instance of the *power of the devil*." Such was the credit I paid to this revelation! All which I ascribe to the spirit of God is the enabling her to strive against "the power of the devil", and at length restoring peace to her soul.'[v]

I was in hopes you had done with this instance. But I am disappointed. For in your 2nd letter I read thus:

'The instances of enthusiasm and presumption which your last *Journal* had furnished me with remain now to be reviewed. The first was of a private revelation which you appeared to pay great credit to. You had represented everything the woman had spoken in her agony as coming to pass.'[w]—But I had not represented anything she spoke then, whether it came to pass or no, as coming 'from the Spirit of God', but 'from the devil'.

You say, 'When I read this first I was amazed, and . . . impatient to look again into your *Journal*. But I had no sooner done this but I was still more astonished. For you have very grievously misrepresented the case.'—If I have, then I will bear the blame, but if not it will light on *your* head.

'It is not *this* account which you had thus introduced, but another, and a very different one, of what happened a day or two before. Sunday, you mention her as being guilty of gross presumption . . . , which you attribute to the power of the devil. But on Monday and Tuesday the supposed revelations happened, which . . . you relate without the least mark of diffidence or blame.'[x]

[u] [Church,] *Remarks*, p. 64.
[v] *Answer*, pp. 40-41 [III.7].
[w] [Church, *Farther Remarks*,] pp. 130-31.
[x] [Ibid.,] p. 131.

I am grieved that you constrain me to say any more. In the 66th and 67th pages of the last *Journal* I give an account of Mrs. Jones which I term, 'a surprising instance of the power of the devil'. It includes the occurrences of three days. This you brought as a proof of my enthusiasm. I answer, 'The very words that introduce this account' prove it is no instance of enthusiasm—meaning by 'this account' (as I suppose is plain to every reader) the following account of Mrs. Jones. You reply: 'It is not *this* account which you had thus introduced, but another, and a very different one, of what happened a day or two before.' Sir, it is the whole account of Mrs. Jones which I thus introduce; and not 'another', not a 'very different' one. And I attribute the agony which she (Mrs. Jones) was in, and most of the words which she spoke, both on Sunday, Monday, and Tuesday, not to the Spirit of God, but to the 'power of the devil'.

6. The next instance which you relate as an instance of despair is that of a young woman of Kingswood, which you break off with, 'Take me away, etc.'[y] But why did you not decipher that 'etc.'? Why did you not add the rest of the paragraph? Because it would have spoiled your whole argument. It would have shown what the end of the Lord was in permitting that severe visitation. The words are: 'We interrupted her by calling again upon God, on which she sunk down as before (as one asleep); and another young woman began to roar as loud as she had done. My brother now came in, it being about nine a clock. We continued in prayer till past eleven; when God in a moment spoke peace into the soul, first, of the first tormented, and then of the other. And they both joined in singing praises to him who had stilled the enemy and the avenger.'[z]

7. I am sorry to find you still affirm that with regard to the Lord's Supper also I 'advance many injudicious, false, and dangerous things. Such as, (1), that a man ought to communicate without a sure trust in God's mercy through Christ.'[a] You mark[47]

[y] [Church, *Farther Remarks*,] pp. 112-13.
[z] *Journal* III, p. 93 (i.e., Oct. 23, 1739).
[a] [Church, *Farther Remarks*,] p. 117.

[47] I.e., by placing them within quotation marks, rather than by italicizing, which was Wesley's own declared (but not invariable) practice. The *Works* (1772) alters to 'make'. It seems clear that the words are (as Wesley says) not his, but are Church's rephrasing of Wesley's statement in his *Journal*, quoted in his *Answer*, III.3(2), that the Lord's Supper 'was ordained' for 'all those who know and feel that they want [i.e., 'need'] the grace of God . . . to show their sins forgiven'.

these as my words; but I know them not. (2). 'That there is no previous preparation *indispensably* necessary, but a desire to receive whatsoever God pleases to give.'—But I include abundantly more in that 'desire' than you seem to apprehend, even a willingness to know and do the whole will of God.—(3). 'That no fitness is required at the time of communicating' (I recite the whole sentence)[48] 'but a sense of our state, of our utter sinfulness and helplessness, everyone who knows he is fit for hell being just fit to come to Christ, in this as well as in all other ways of his appointment.'—But neither can this sense of our utter sinfulness and helplessness subsist without earnest desires of universal holiness.—'There was another passage' (you say) 'which you chose to omit.'[b] Which this was I do not understand.[49] Nor do I perceive any one of these 'dreadful positions'[50] (as you style them) to be contrary to the Word of God.

8. You will likewise at all hazards stand your ground as to the charge of 'stoical insensibility'. I answered before: 'How do you support the charge? Why, thus—You say, "The servants of God suffer nothing."—And can you possibly misunderstand these words if you read those that immediately follow? "His body was wellnigh torn asunder with pain. But God made all his bed in his sickness. So that he was continually giving thanks to God, and making his boast of his praise."'[c]

You reply: 'If you meant no more than that a man under the sharpest pains may be thankful to God, why did you call this a strange truth?'[d]—Because I think it is so. I think it exceeding strange that one in such a degree of pain should be continually giving thanks to God. Not that I suppose him 'insensible of his torments'. 'His body', I say, 'was wellnigh torn asunder with pain.' But the love of God so abundantly overbalanced all pain that it was as nothing to him.

[b] [Ibid.,] p. 118.
[c] [*Answer,*] p. 36 [III.4].
[d] [Church, *Farther Remarks,*] p. 118.

---

[48] I.e., the whole sentence from Wesley's *Answer,* III.3, itself quoted from his *Journal,* and in Church's *Farther Remarks* (p. 117) abridged to, 'that everyone who knows he is fit for hell being just fit to come to Christ'.

[49] In quoting his *Journal* for June 27-28, 1740, in his *Answer,* III.3, Wesley omitted the opening paragraph, asserting the practice of daily Communion in the apostolic church, and it seems most likely that Church refers to this omission.

[50] Church, *Farther Remarks,* p. 118.

'The next instance is as follows. One told you, sir, I thought last week there could be no such rest as you describe; none in this world wherein we should be so free as not to desire ease in pain. But God has taught me better. For on Friday and Saturday, when I was in the strongest pain, I never once had one moment's desire of ease'[51] (add, 'but only that the will of God might be done').

Neither has this any resemblance of 'stoical insensibility'. I never *supposed*, that this person did not *feel* pain. (Nor indeed that there is any state on earth wherein we shall not feel it.) But that her soul was filled with the love of God, and thankfully resigned to his will.

'Another instance is taken from one of your hymns, where are these lines:

> Doom, if thou canst, to endless pains,
> And drive me from thy face.'[e] (add,
> 'But if thy stronger love constrains,
> Let me be saved by grace.')

'This I thought the height of insensibility, extravagance and presumption. . . . You see nothing of these in it. And yet you explain yourself thus, "If thou canst deny thyself, if thou canst forget to be gracious, if thou canst cease to be truth and love." All which in my opinion is fixing the charge most strongly upon you. For the supposition that Christ *can* do these things—.' Are you in earnest, sir? Are you really ignorant that expressions of this kind do not suppose he *can*, but quite the reverse? That they are one of the strongest forms of obtestation, of adjuring God to show mercy, by all his grace and truth and love? So far is this also from proving the charge of 'stoical insensibility'.

III. 1. I come now to consider the point of Church communion, of which you have spoke in the beginning of your treatise. In the entrance you say: 'We teach no other doctrine than has always been taught in our church. . . . Our sentiments concerning justification are reconcilable to our Articles, Homilies, and Service. . . . This I apprehend several of the Methodists have been convinced of, and have *therefore* left our communion entirely. You give us more instances than one of this in your last *Journal*.'[f]—No, not one. Nor did I ever yet know one

[e] [Church, *Farther Remarks*,] p. 119.

[f] [Church, *Farther Remarks*,] p. 2.

[51] Church, *Farther Remarks*, p. 119.

man who 'therefore left the communion of the Church', because he was 'convinced' that either her Articles, Homilies, or Liturgy opposed his 'sentiments concerning justification'. Poor Mr. St[onehouse][52] and Mr. Simpson[53] were induced to leave it by reasons of quite another kind.

You add, 'We cannot wonder that some Methodists have withdrawn from her, . . . while they have been used to hear doctrines which, they must have been sensible, have no place in her Articles and Service.'—So far from it that all I know of them are deeply 'sensible', the 'doctrines they have been used to hear' daily are no other than the genuine doctrines of the Church, as expressed both in her Articles and Service.

2. But our present question turns not on doctrine but discipline.—'My first business' (you say) 'is to consider some very lax notions of Church communion which I find in your last *Journal*. Page 26[54] you say, "Our twentieth Article defines a true church, 'a congregation of faithful people, wherein the true Word of God is preached, and the sacraments duly administered'".'[g] The use I would willingly make of this definition (which, observe is not mine, be it good or bad) is to stop the boasting of ungodly men by cutting off their pretence to call themselves, 'of the Church'. But you think they may call themselves so still. Then let them. I will not contend about it.

But you cannot infer from hence that my notions of Church communion are either lax or otherwise. The definition which I occasionally cite shows nothing of my sentiments on that head. And for anything which occurs in this page they may be strict or loose, right or wrong.

You add: 'It will be requisite, in order to approve yourself a

[g] [Ibid.,] p. 3.

---

[52] Church quoted a passage from JWJ, June 6, 1740, in which the Rev. George Stonehouse said that he intended to sell his church living because the Book of Common Prayer was 'full of horrid lies'. He was Vicar of Islington, and sold the living (of which he held the advowson) to join the Moravians with his wife, who was the adopted daughter of Zinzendorf. JWJ, Jan. 5, 1746, expresses Wesley's view that the change had adversely affected his way of life.

[53] Church quoted from JWJ, June 10, 1741, a passage referring to John Simpson 'drawing people from the Church, and advising them to leave off prayer'. He was one of the Oxford Methodists, and after ordination held a living in Leicestershire. He sold it and joined the Moravians. (See 25:700 in this edn.)

According to JWJ, Apr. 3, 1740, the Countess of Huntingdon, who thought highly of Simpson, tried hard, but in vain, to win him back to the Methodists.

[54] I.e., Feb. 6, 1740.

minister of our church, that you follow her rules and orders, . . . that you constantly conform to the method of worship she has prescribed, and study to promote her peace.'[h] All this is good and fit to be done. But it properly belongs to the following question.

'What led you into such very loose notions of Church communion, I imagine, might be your being conscious to yourself that according to the strict, just account of the Church of England, you could not with any grace maintain your pretensions to belong still to her.'[55]—Sir, I have never told you yet what my notions of Church communion are. They may be wrong, or they may be right, for all you know. Therefore, when you are first *supposing* that I have told you my notions, and then assigning the reasons of them, what can be said but that you 'imagine' the whole matter?

3. How far I have 'acted agreeably to the rules and orders of our church'[56] is a farther question. You think I have acted contrary thereto, first, by using 'extemporary prayer'[57] in public. 'The Church', you say, 'has strongly declared her mind on this point by appointing her excellent Liturgy, which you have solemnly promised to use—and no other.'[58] I know not when or where.—'And whoever . . . does not worship God in the manner she prescribes . . . must be supposed to slight and contemn her Offices and rules, and therefore can be no more worthy to be called her minister.'[i]

I do not 'slight or contemn the Offices' of the Church. I esteem them very highly. And yet I 'do not', at all times, 'worship God', even in public, in the very terms of those Offices. Nor yet do I knowingly 'slight or contemn her rules'. For it is not clear to my apprehension that she has any rule which forbids using 'extemporary prayer', suppose between the Morning and Evening Service. And if I am 'not worthy to be called her minister' (which I dare by no means affirm myself to be) yet *her minister I am*, and must always be, unless I should be judicially deposed from my ministry.

Your second argument is this. 'If you suppose the Scripture

[h] [Ibid.,] p. 5.

[i] [Ibid.,] p. 7.

[55] Church, *Farther Remarks*, p. 6.

[56] Ibid.

[57] Ibid. Church has 'extempore'.

[58] Ibid., pp. 6-7.

enjoins you to use extemporary prayer, then you must suppose our Liturgy to be inconsistent with Scripture, and consequently unlawful to be used.'[59] That does not follow—unless I supposed the Scripture to enjoin, to use extemporary prayer, *and no other.* Then it would follow that a form of prayer was 'inconsistent with Scripture'. But this I never did suppose.

Your third argument is to this effect: 'You act contrary to the rule of the Church. Allow, she is in the wrong. Yet while you break her rule, how do you act as her minister?'[60] It ought to be expressed, 'How are you her minister?' For the conclusion to be proved is that I am not her minister.

I answer, (1). I am not convinced, as I observed before, that I do hereby *break her rule.* (2). If I did, yet should I not *cease* to be her minister unless I were formally *deprived.* (3). I now *actually do* continue in her communion, and hope that I always shall.

4. You object farther that I 'disobey the governors of the Church'. I answer, I both do and will obey them in all things where I do not apprehend there is some particular law of God to the contrary.—'Here', say you, 'you confess that in some things you do not, and cannot obey your governors.'[j]—Did I 'confess' this? Then I spoke rashly and foolishly—for I granted more than I can make good.—I do certainly apprehend that the law of God requires me both to preach and (sometimes) to pray *extempore.* Yet I do not know that I disobey the governors of the Church herein. For I do not know that they have forbidden me to do either.

But your 'behaviour and method of teaching is irregular. . . . Have you any warrant from Scripture'[61] for preaching up and down thus?—I think I have. I think God hath called me to this work by 'the laying on of the hands of the presbytery',[62] which directs me how to obey that general command, 'While we have time, let us do good unto all men.'[63]

'But we ought to do this agreeably to our respective situations, and not break in upon each other's provinces. . . . Every private man may take upon himself the office of a magistrate, . . . and

[j] [Ibid.,] p. 8.

---

[59] Wesley paraphrases Church's argument on p. 7 of *Farther Remarks.*

[60] Church, *Farther Remarks,* pp. 7-8.

[61] Ibid., p. 8.

[62] 1 Tim. 4:14.

[63] Cf. Gal. 6:10.

quote this text as justly as you have done.'[k] No. The private man is not called to the office of a *magistrate;* but I am, to the office of preacher.—'You was indeed authorized to preach the gospel, but it was in the congregation to which you should be lawfully appointed. . . . Whereas you have many years preached in places whereunto you was not lawfully appointed; nay, which were entrusted to others, who neither wanted nor desired your assistance.'

Many of them wanted it enough, whether they desired it or no. But I shall not now debate that point. I rather follow you to the first part of the *Farther Appeal*, where this objection is considered.

5. 'Our church' (it was said) 'has provided against this preaching up and down, in the ordination of a priest, by *expressly limiting* the exercise of the powers then conferred upon him to "the *congregation* where he shall be lawfully appointed thereunto".'[64]

I answered, '(1). Your argument proves too much. If it be allowed just as you propose it, it proves that no priest has authority either to preach or administer the sacrament in any other than his own congregation.'[l]

You reply, 'Is there no difference between a thing's being done occasionally, . . . and its being done for years together?'[65] Yes, a great one. And more inconveniences may arise from the latter than from the former. But this is all wide—it does not touch the point. Still if our church does *expressly limit* the exercise of the sacerdotal powers to *that congregation* whereunto each priest shall

[k] [Ibid.,] p. 9.

[l] *Farther Appeal*, p. 84 [i.e., Pt. I, VI.9, quoting the Bishop of London's *Observations on the Conduct and Behaviour of a Certain Sect, usually distinguished by the Name of Methodists* (see 11:119, 183 in this edn.)].

---

[64] It is worth noticing that John Wesley in this passage, and in the arguments which follow in the next section, defends his preaching in other clergymen's parishes *not* (as before Bishop Butler in Bristol) on the grounds that as a Fellow of Lincoln College, Oxford, he has *ius ubique docendi* (a dubious argument anyway), but on the ground that he was ordained, and that the Church of England had put no restrictions on his preaching in earlier days.

This leads up to his contention in the next section that the phrase in the Ordinal 'the congregation to which you should be lawfully appointed', is not meant to restrict a man to his own congregation (since that would disqualify a large number of clergy), but simply to give him authority in his own congregation (which in his case was meaningless, as he had not a congregation when he was ordained). See also *A Farther Appeal* (11:183-84 and nn. in this edn.).

[65] Church, *Farther Remarks*, p. 9.

be appointed, this precludes him from exercising those powers *at all* in any other than *that congregation*.

I answered, '(2). Had the powers conferred been so *limited* when I was ordained priest, my ordination would have signified just nothing. For I was not *appointed to any congregation* at all, but was ordained as a member of that "College of Divines" (so our statutes express it) "founded to overturn all heresies, and defend the catholic faith".'[66]

You reply, 'I presume it was expected you should either continue at your College, or enter upon some regular cure.'[67]—Perhaps so; but I must still insist that if my sacerdotal powers had been then *expressly limited* to *that congregation* whereunto I should be *appointed*, my ordination would have *signified nothing*. I mean, I could never, in virtue of that ordination, have exercised those powers at all, seeing I never was appointed to any single congregation—at least, not till I went to Georgia.

I answered, '(3). For many years after I was ordained priest this limitation was never heard of. I heard not one syllable of it, by way of objection to my preaching up and down in Oxford or London or the parts adjacent; in Gloucestershire or Worcestershire; in Lancashire, Yorkshire, or Lincolnshire. Nor did the strictest disciplinarian scruple suffering me to exercise those powers wherever I came.'[68]

You reply, 'There is great difference between preaching occasionally . . . with the leave of the incumbents, and doing it constantly without their leave.'[69] I grant there is; and there are objections to the latter which do not reach the former case. But they do not belong to this head. They do not in the least affect this consequence, 'If every priest, when ordained, is *expressly limited* touching the exercise of the power then received to *that congregation* to which he shall be appointed, then is he precluded by this *express limitation* from preaching, with or without the incumbent's leave, in *any other congregation* whatever.'[70]

I answered, '(4). Is it not, in fact, universally allowed that every priest, as such, has a power, in virtue of his ordination, to preach

[66] Wesley, *A Farther Appeal*, Pt. I, VI.9(2); 11:183 in this edn.

[67] Church, *Farther Remarks*, p. 10.

[68] *A Farther Appeal*, Pt. I, VI.9(3); 11:183 in this edn.

[69] Church, *Farther Remarks*, p. 11, conflated by Wesley.

[70] A summary by Wesley of the conclusion which Church draws from his previous argument.

. . . in any congregation where the curate desires his assistance?'[71]

You reply to this by what you judge a parallel case. But it does not touch the *restriction* in question. Either this does or does not *expressly limit* the exercise of the powers conferred upon a priest in his ordination to *that congregation* whereunto he shall be appointed. If it does not I am not condemned by this, however faulty I may be on a thousand other accounts. If it does, then is every priest condemned who ever preaches out of the *congregation to which he is appointed.*

Your parallel case is this: 'Because a man does not offend against the law of the land, when I prevail upon him to teach my children, . . . *therefore* he is empowered to seize' (read, he does not offend against the law of the land in seizing) 'an apartment in my house, and against my will and approbation to continue therein, and to direct and dictate to my family!'[m]

An exact parallel indeed!—When therefore I came to live in St. Luke's parish,[72] was it just the same thing as if I had 'seized an apartment in Dr. Buckley's house'?[73] And was the 'continuing therein against his will and approbation' (supposing it were so) precisely the same as if I had continued 'in his house', whether he would or no? Is the one exactly the same 'offence against the law of the land' as the other? Once more. Is the warning *sinners in Moorfields* to flee from the wrath to come the very same with directing the Dr.'s *family, under his own roof?* I should not have answered this, but that I was afraid you would conclude it was unanswerable.

I answered the former objector, '(5). Before those words which you suppose to imply such a restraint . . . were those spoken without any restraint or limitation at all, which I apprehend to convey an indelible character: "Receive the Holy Ghost for the office and work of a priest in the Church of God, now committed unto thee by the imposition of our hands." '[74]

You reply, 'The question is not whether you are in orders or not.'[n]—I am glad to hear it; I really thought it was.—'But whether

[m] [Church, *Farther Remarks,*] p. 11.
[n] [Ibid.,] p. 12.

---

[71] *A Farther Appeal,* Pt. I, VI.9(4); 11:183-84 in this edn.
[72] I.e., at the Foundery, London.
[73] I.e., Benjamin Bulkeley, D.D. (Oxon.), assistant preacher at St. Luke's. Cf. 11:349 in this edn., and Wesley's letter to 'John Smith', Mar. 25, 1747, §12 (26:236 in this edn.).
[74] *A Farther Appeal,* Pt. I, pp. 85-86, i.e., VI.10 (11:184-85 in this edn.).

you have acted suitably to the directions or rules of the Church of England.'—Not suitably to that rule, if it were strictly to be interpreted of preaching only in a single congregation. But I have given my reasons why I think it can't be so interpreted. And those reasons I do not see that you have invalidated.

I would only add, if I am in orders, if I am a minister still, and yet not a minister of the Church of England, of what church am I a minister? Whoever is a minister at all is a minister of some particular church. Neither can he cease to be a minister of that church till he is cast out of it by a judicial sentence. Till therefore I am so cast out (which I trust will never be) I must style myself a minister of the Church of England.

6. Your next objection is: 'You not only erect Bands, which, after the Moravians, you call the United Society, but also give out tickets to those that continue therein.'—These Bands, you think, 'have had very bad consequences, . . . as was to be expected . . . when weak people . . . are made leaders . . . of their brethren, and are set upon expounding Scripture'.[o]

You are in some mistakes here. For, (1). The Bands are not called 'The United Society'. (2). The United Society was originally so called, not after the Moravians, but because it consisted of several smaller societies *united together*. (3). Neither the Bands, nor the leaders of them, as such, are 'set upon expounding Scripture'. (4). The good consequences of their meeting together *in Bands* I know; but the 'very bad consequences' I know not.

When any members of these, or of the United Society, are proved to live in known sin, we then mark and avoid them; we separate ourselves from every one that walks disorderly.[75] Sometimes, if the case be judged infectious (though rarely) this is openly declared. And this you style 'excommunication', and say, 'Does not everyone see a separate ecclesiastical society or communion?'[p]—No. This Society does not 'separate' from the 'communion' of the rest of the Church of England. They 'continue steadfastly' with them, both 'in the apostolical doctrine, and in the breaking of bread, and in prayers'[76] (which neither Mr.

[o] Ibid.
[p] [Ibid.,] p. 13.

[75] See 2 Thess. 3:6.
[76] See Acts 2:42.

St[onehouse] nor Mr. Si[mpson] does, nor the gentleman who writes to you in favour of the Moravians—who also writes pressingly to me, to *separate* myself from the Church). A Society 'over which you had appointed yourself a governor'.—No. So far as I governed them it was at their own entreaty.—'And took upon you all the spiritual authority which the very highest church governor could claim.'—What! At Kingswood? In February 1740–41?[77] Not so. I took upon me no other authority (then and there at least) than any steward of a Society exerts by the consent of the other members. I did neither more nor less than declare that they who had broken our rules were no longer of our Society.

'Can you pretend that you received this authority from our church?'—Not by ordination; for I did not exert it as a *priest*, but as one whom that Society had voluntarily chosen to be at the head of them.—'Or that you exercised it in subjection or subordination to her lawful governors?'—I think so; I am sure I did not exercise it in any designed opposition to them.—'Did you ever think proper to consult or advise with them about fixing the terms of your communion?'—If you mean about fixing the rules of admitting or excluding from our Society, I never did think it either needful or proper. Nor do I at this day.

'How then will you vindicate all these powers?'—All these are, 'declaring those are no longer of our Society'. 'Here is a manifest congregation. Either it belonged to the Church of England, or not. . . . If it did not . . . you set up a separate communion against her. And how then are you injured in being thought to have withdrawn from her?'[78]—I have nothing to do with this. The antecedent is false. Therefore the consequent falls of course.—'If it did belong to the Church, show where the Church gave you such authority of controlling and regulating it.'—Authority of putting disorderly members out of that Society? The Society itself gave me that authority. 'What private clergyman can plead her commission to be thus a judge and ordinary, even in his own parish?'—Any clergyman or layman, without pleading her commission, may be thus a judge and ordinary. 'Are not these powers inherent in her governors, and committed to the higher

[77] The form of 'excommunication' which Church quoted in his *Farther Remarks*, pp. 12-13, was the document read on Feb. 28, 1741, at the dismissal of John Cennick and others from the Kingswood Society.

[78] Church, *Farther Remarks*, p. 13.

order of her clergy?'—No; not the power of excluding members from a private Society, unless on supposition of some such rule as ours is, viz., 'That if any man separate from the Church, he is no longer a member of our Society.'[79]

7. But you have more proof yet. 'The Grand Jury in Georgia found that you had called yourself Ordinary of Savannah. Nor was this fact contradicted, even by those of the jury who you say wrote in your favour. So that it appears, you have long had an inclination to be independent and uncontrolled.'—This argument ought to be good; for it is farfetched. The plain case was this. That Grand Jury did assert, 'that in Mr. Causton's hearing I had called myself Ordinary of Savannah'. The minority of the jury, in their letter to the Trustees, refuted the other allegations particularly, but thought this so idle an one that they did not deign to give it any farther reply, than: 'As to the eighth Bill we are in doubt, as not well knowing the meaning of the word "Ordinary".'[q]

You add, 'I appeal to any reasonable man whether you had not acted as an *ordinary*, nay a *bishop*, in Kingswood.'—If you mean, in 'declaring those disorderly members were no longer of that Society', I admit your appeal, whether I therein acted as a *bishop*, or as any *steward* of a Society may. 'Nay, you have gone far beyond the generality of the Dissenters themselves, who do not commit the power of excommunication' (and 'appointing to preach'—that is another question) 'to the hands of any private minister.'—The 'powers of excommunication'—true; but this was not *excommunication*, but a quite different thing.

How far, in what circumstances, and in what sense, I have 'appointed men to preach' I have explained at large in the third part of the *Farther Appeal*.[80] But I wait for farther light; and am ready to consider, as I am able, whatever shall be replied to what is there advanced.

[q] See 1st *Journal*, pp. 47, 49 [N.B. Wesley quotes from the 2nd edn. of JWJ, for Aug. 22, 1737, whereas Church, in his *Farther Remarks*, p. 15, had cited 'p. 50', clearly using the 1st edn.].

---

[79] The import of this sentence is not immediately clear; certainly there was no rule in the Methodist societies that anyone who separated from the Church of England was to be excluded. We may suppose that Wesley is arguing thus: 'The power of excluding members from a private society does not belong to the Anglican authorities, though it would possess such power in our case if we had a rule that "if any man separate from the Church, he is no longer a member of our Society"; but we have no such rule.'

[80] *A Farther Appeal*, Pt. III, III.8-19 (11:294-304 in this edn.).

8. Your general conclusion is: 'Whatever your pretences or professions may be, you can be looked upon by serious and impartial persons (not as a *member*, much less a *minister* of the Church of England, but) as no other than an enemy to her constitution, worship, and doctrine, raising divisions and disturbances in her communion.'[r]—'And yet you say . . . , "I cannot have a greater regard to her rules. . . . I dare not renounce communion with her."'[s]

I do say so still. I cannot have a greater regard to any *human rules* than to follow them in all things, unless where I apprehend there is a *divine* rule to the contrary. I dare not 'renounce communion' with the Church of England. As a minister, I teach her doctrines. I use her offices. I conform to her rubrics. I suffer reproach for my attachment to her. As a private *member* I hold her doctrines. I join in her offices, in prayer, in hearing, in communicating. I *expect* every reasonable man, touching these facts, to *believe his own eyes and ears*.—But if these facts are so, how dare any man of common sense charge me with *renouncing* the Church of England?

9. Use ever so many exaggerations, still the whole of this matter is: (1). I often use extemporary prayer. (2). Wherever I can, I preach the gospel. (3). Those who desire to *live the gospel* I advise how to watch over each other, and to put from them such as walk disorderly. Now whether these things are, on other considerations, right or wrong, this single point I must still insist on: 'All this does not prove either that I am no *member* or that I am no *minister* of the Church of England.' Nay, nothing can prove that I am no *member* of the Church till I either am *excommunicated* or *renounce* her communion, and no longer join in her doctrine, and in the breaking of bread, and in prayer.[81] Nor can anything prove, I am no *minister* of the Church, till I either am *deposed* from my ministry or *voluntarily renounce* her, and wholly cease to teach her doctrines, use her offices, and obey her rubrics for conscience' sake.

However, I grant that whatsoever is 'urged on this head deserves my most serious consideration'.[82] And whensoever I am

[r] [Church, *Farther Remarks*,] p. 76 [rearranged].
[s] [Ibid.,] p. 15.

---

[81] Cf. Acts 2:42.
[82] Church, *Farther Remarks*, p. 15.

convinced that by taking any *methods* more or less *different* from those I now take I may better 'consult the honour of religion, and be able to do more in the world', by the grace of God I shall not persist in these one hour, but instantly choose the more excellent way.[83]

IV. 1. What you urge on the head of *enthusiasm* also, I think, 'deserves my most serious consideration'. (You may add, 'and presumption'.[84] I let it drop once more; because I do not love tautology, and because I look upon presumption to be essential to enthusiasm, and consequently contained therein.) I will therefore weigh what you advance concerning it, and explain myself something more at large.

'I am to examine', you say, 'how far you have cleared yourself of enthusiasm. My account of this you set down, making as many alterations and omissions as there are lines.'[t]—Perhaps more; for I never designed to recite the whole, but only the material part of it. 'If you did not wholly approve of it, why would you not let me know what you disliked in it?'—Because I do not love many words. Therefore when the argument stood thus: 'He that does this is an enthusiast: but you do this,' I was generally content with answering the second proposition, and leaving the first as I found it.

'I laid this charge against you and the Methodists in general. Between you every part of the character has been verified.'—I answer for one; let the rest answer for themselves—if they have not better employment.

That the question between us may be the more fully understood, I shall briefly compare together; (1), your *Remarks;* (2), my *Answer;* (3), your reply—though still I cannot promise to repeat your words at length.

2. You remark: 'Though you would be thought an enemy to enthusiasm and presumption, . . . yet in both you are far from being inferior to the Moravians, or indeed to any others.' (Strong assertions! Not 'inferior to' any others? Not to the French

[t] [Church, *Farther Remarks,*] p. 120.

---

[83] See 1 Cor. 12:31.

[84] Sect. I of Church's 'Vindication', pp. 120-43, was headed 'Of Enthusiasm and Presumption'.

Prophets,[85] or John of Leyden?)[86] (1). 'Enthusiasm is, a false persuasion of an extraordinary divine assistance, which leads men to such conduct as is only to be justified by the supposition of such assistance.'[u] I answer: 'Before this touches me you are to prove (which I conceive you have not done yet) that my conduct is such as is only to be justified by the supposition of such assistance.'[v] You reply, 'This, I think, is proved in the preceding Tract.'[w]—I think not. Let men of candour judge.—Yet I am persuaded, there was such an assistance at some times. You have also to prove that this was a[87] *false* persuasion.

You remark, (2), 'An enthusiast is then sincere, but mistaken.'[x] I answered, 'That I am mistaken remains to be proved.'[88] You reply, 'The world must judge.'[89] Agreed, if by the world you mean, men of reason and religion.

You remark, (3), 'His intentions must be good; but his actions will be most abominable.'[90] I answered, 'What actions of mine are

[u] [Church, *Remarks*,] pp. 60-61.
[v] [Wesley, *Answer*,] p. 38 [i.e., III.5, p. 114 above].
[w] [Church, *Farther Remarks*,] p. 120.
[x] [Church, *Remarks*,] p. 61.

---

[85] The so-called 'French prophets' (who included prophetesses) formed a group among the French Protestant immigrants who took refuge in England after the revocation of the Edict of Nantes in 1685. They claimed to speak under direct inspiration, as testified by the bodily agitations which accompanied their eloquence, and to reveal truths superior to those which were uttered by the biblical prophets. They attempted to take over the Baptist congregation in Broadmead, Bristol in 1720 and infiltrated both the Fetter Lane Society in London and the Methodist societies in Bristol in 1739 and 1740. Wesley, with his usual openness, interviewed one of the prophetesses in London but was not impressed. He noted that her 'motion [i.e., her convulsions] might be either hysterical or artificial' (JWJ, Jan. 1739). He later took steps to neutralize the influence of the 'French prophets' on his societies, and it seems to have disappeared.

[86] John of Leiden (otherwise called John Beukels, or John Bokelson) belonged to the Anabaptist sect called Melchiorites (from Melchior Hofmann), which believed that the kingdom of God, the New Israel, was to be set up on earth and control the whole life, political, economic, social, and spiritual, of those who entered it by the 'covenant seal' of re-baptism. After the city of Münster in Westphalia had accepted the Lutheran Reformation, Bernard Rothmann, who had led the reform, was pushed into Anabaptism by John Mathijs and later ousted by him. John Mathijs, after a short period of power, was killed by the episcopal forces besieging the city. John of Leiden succeeded him, was crowned king, restored the 'communism' of Acts 2 on his own lines, instituted polygamy, executed dissidents, and inspired the citizens to fight to the death against the combined Catholic and Protestant forces which assaulted the city. The Münsterite experiment ended in a holocaust of torture and slaughter, and John was burned with red-hot irons and executed.

[87] 'a' added in *Works* (1772) only.

[88] Wesley, *Answer*, III.5.

[89] Church, *Farther Remarks*, p. 120.

[90] *Remarks*, p. 61.

most abominable?'[91] You reply, 'The world must be judge . . . whether your public actions have not been . . . in many respects abominable.'[92] I am glad the charge softens. I hope by and by you will think they are only abominable in *some* respects.

You remark, (4), 'Instead of making the Word of God . . . the rule of his actions, he follows only secret persuasion or impulse.'[93]—I answered, 'I have declared again and again that I make the Word of God the rule of all my actions; and that I no more follow any "secret impulse" instead thereof than I follow Mahomet or Confucius.'[94] You reply: 'You fall again into your strain of boasting, as if declarations could have any weight against facts; assert that you "make the Word of God the rule of all your actions", and that I "perhaps do not know many persons".'[y]—Stop, sir. You are stepping over one or two points which I have not done with.

You remark, (5), 'Instead of judging of his spiritual estate by the improvement of his heart, he rests only on ecstasies, etc.'[95]—I answered, 'Neither is this my case. I rest not on them at all. . . . I judge of my spiritual estate by the improvement of my heart and the tenor of my life, conjointly.'[96] To this I do not perceive you reply one word. Herein then I am not an enthusiast.

You remark, (6), 'He is very liable to err, . . . not considering things coolly and carefully.'[97] I answered: 'So indeed I am. I find it every day more and more. But I do not yet find that this is owing to my want of "considering things coolly and carefully". Perhaps you do not know many persons (excuse my simplicity in speaking it) who more carefully consider every step they take. Yet I know I am not cool or careful enough. May God supply this and all my wants!'[z] You reply, 'Your private life I have nothing to do with:'—and then enlarge on my 'method of consulting Scripture',

[y] [Church, *Farther Remarks*,] p. 121.
[z] [Wesley, *Answer*,] p. 39 [i.e., III.5].

---

[91] *Answer*, III.5 (p. 114 above).
[92] *Farther Remarks*, p. 120.
[93] *Remarks*, p. 61.
[94] *Answer*, III.5 (p. 115 above).
[95] *Remarks*, p. 61. Although in this instance, as in others, the quotation is exactly the same as that given in Wesley's *Answer*, the evidence of the previous quotation from the *Remarks*, with its addition of 'secret persuasion', implied that Wesley did use all three printed pamphlets in preparing this reply.
[96] *Answer*, III.5 (p. 115 above).
[97] *Remarks*, p. 61.

and of 'using lots'.[98] Of both which by and by. But meantime, observe this does not affect the question. For I neither cast lots, nor use that method at all, till I have considered things with all the care I can. So that, be this right or wrong, it is no manner of proof that I do not 'carefully consider every step I take'.

But how little did I profit by begging your *excuse*, suppose I had spoken a word unguardedly?[99] O sir, you put me in mind of him who said, 'I know not to show mercy!'[1] You have need never to fight but when you are sure to conquer, seeing you are resolved neither to give nor take quarter.

You remark, (7), 'He is very difficult to be convinced by reason and argument, as he acts upon a supposed principle superior to it, the direction of God's Spirit.'[2] I answered, 'I am very difficult to be convinced by dry blows or hard names . . . , but not by reason or argument. At least that difficulty cannot spring from the cause you mention. For I claim no other direction of God's Spirit than is *common* to all believers.'[3]

You reply, 'I fear this will not be easily reconcilable to your past pretences and behaviour.'[a] I believe it will; in particular to what I speak of the light I received from God in that important affair.[b] But as to the directions in general of the Spirit of God, we very probably differ in this; you apprehend those directions to be *extraordinary* which I suppose to be *common* to all believers.

You remark, (8), 'Whoever opposes him will be charged with resisting or rejecting the Spirit.'[4] I answered, 'What, whoever opposes *me*, John Wesley? Do I charge every such person with "rejecting the Spirit"? No more than I charge him with robbing on the highway. . . . Do I charge *you* with rejecting the Spirit?'[5] You reply, 'You deny that you charge the opposers with rejecting the Spirit, and affirm that you never said or thought that what you

[a] [Church, *Farther Remarks*,] p. 124.

[b] 1st *Journal*, p. 37 [i.e., JWJ, Mar. 4, 1737, and 'the directions I received from God this day touching an affair of the greatest importance', to which Church refers in his *Farther Remarks*, p. 124].

---

[98] *Farther Remarks*, pp. 121, 123.

[99] Wesley appears to refer to his three conciliatory paragraphs at the beginning of his *Answer* (p. 81 above).

[1] It seems almost certain that Wesley was thinking of Shylock. See Shakespeare, *Merchant of Venice*, III.iii.1, 'Jailer, look to him; tell not me of mercy.'

[2] *Remarks*, p. 61.

[3] *Answer*, III.5 (p. 115 above).

[4] *Remarks*, p. 61.

[5] *Answer*, III.5 (pp. 115-16 above).

do is to be accounted the work of God.'[6] Here you blend different sentences together which I must consider apart, as they were written. And first, where do I charge *you* with rejecting the Spirit? If I charge whoever opposes me with this, undoubtedly I charge *you*. If I do not charge *you*, that proposition is false—I do not so charge whoever opposes me. Your next words are: 'You affirm that you never said or thought that what you do is to be accounted the work of God. . . . If it be the work of God, you need not deny the other point.'—Yes, sir. Whether it be or no, I must still deny that I ever charged *you* with rejecting the Spirit in opposing *me*.

You remark, (9), 'His own dreams must be regarded as oracles.'[7]—I answered, 'Whose? I desire neither my dreams nor my waking thoughts may be regarded at all, unless just so far as they agree with the oracles of God.'[8] To this also you make no reply.

You remark, (10), 'However wild . . . his behaviour may be, whatever he . . . does is to be accounted the work of God.'[9] It was to this I answered, 'I never said so of what I do. I never thought so.'[10] This answer was ill expressed. And I might have foreseen, you would hardly fail to make your advantage of it. I must therefore explain myself upon it a little farther. You said, 'An enthusiast accounts "whatever he does" to be the work of God.' I should have said, 'But I do not account "whatever I do" to be the work of God.' What that is which I do account his work will be considered by and by.

You remark, (11), 'He talks in the style of inspired persons.'[11] I answered, 'No otherwise inspired than you are, if you love God.'[12] You reply, 'The point was not whether you are actually inspired, but whether you have talked in the style of those who were so.'[c] That was so much the point that if it were allowed it would overturn your whole argument. For if I was inspired (in *your* sense) you could not term that inspiration enthusiasm without blasphemy. But you again mistake my words. The plain meaning of them is, that I talk in the style of those persons who are 'no otherwise inspired than you are, if you love God'.

[c] [*Farther Remarks*,] p. 126.

---

[6] *Farther Remarks*, p. 124, and cf. p. 125.

[7] *Remarks*, p. 61.

[8] *Answer*, III.5 (p. 116 above).

[9] *Remarks*, p. 61.

[10] *Answer*, III.5 (p. 116 above).

[11] *Remarks*, p. 61.

[12] *Answer*, III.5 (p. 116 above).

You remark, (12), 'He applies Scripture phrases to himself, without attending to their original meaning, or once considering the difference of times and circumstances.'[d] I answered, 'I am not conscious of anything like this. I apply no Scripture phrase either to myself or any other without carefully considering both the *original* meaning, and the *secondary* sense wherein, allowing for different times and circumstances, it may be applied to ordinary Christians.'[e] You reply: 'This also you deny to have done, holding however some *secondary* sense (what it is you have not told us) in which Scripture phrases may . . . be applied to ordinary Christians.' I have largely told you what I mean by a *secondary* sense, in the first part of the *Farther Appeal*. You add: 'Many things which were truly written of the preaching of Christianity at first you have vainly applied to yourselves.'[f] Sir, I am to answer only for myself, as I will for that expression, 'Behold, the day of the Lord is come; he is again visiting and redeeming his people!'[13]

3. I come now to what you expatiate upon at large as the two grand instances of my enthusiasm. The first is plainly this. At some rare times, when I have been in great distress of soul, or in utter uncertainty how to act, in an important case, which required a speedy determination, after using all other means that occurred, I have cast lots, or opened the Bible.[14] And by this means I have been relieved from that distress, or directed in that uncertainty.

Instances of this kind occur in the 12th, 14th, 15th, 28th, and 88th page of the third *Journal*, as also in the 27th, 28th, and 80th page of the last *Journal*.[15] I desire any who would understand this matter thoroughly to read those passages as they stand at length.

As to the particular instances, I would observe, (1), that with regard to my first journey to Bristol you should in any wise have set down those words that preface the Scriptures there recited: 'I was entreated in the most pressing manner to come to Bristol

[d] [Church, *Remarks*,] pp. 61-62.
[e] [Wesley, *Answer*,] p. 39 [i.e., III.5].
[f] [Church, *Farther Remarks*,] p. 126.

---

[13] See Luke 1:68, quoted in Church's *Farther Remarks*, p. 126, as misapplied by Wesley to Methodism.

[14] To these practices Church had drawn attention earlier, and Wesley had deferred consideration (IV.2[6]; see n. 7).

[15] Viz., JWJ, Oct. 29, Nov. 23, Dec. 3, 1738; Mar. 28, Oct. 12, 1739; and Feb. 21, Apr. 20, 1740. Church cited these examples in his condemnation of the use of lots and bibliomancy in his *Farther Remarks*, pp. 121-24.

without delay. This I was not at all forward to do; and perhaps a little the less inclined to it . . . because of the remarkable Scriptures which offered as often as we inquired touching the consequence of this removal; though whether this was permitted only for the trial of our faith, God knoweth, and the event will show.'[16]—From the Scriptures afterwards recited some inferred that the event they apprehended was yet afar off.—I infer nothing at all. I still know not how to judge, but leave the whole to God.—This only I know, that the continual expectation of death was then an unspeakable blessing to me, that I did not dare, knowingly, to waste a moment, neither to throw away one desire on earthly things; those words being ever uppermost in my thoughts, and indeed frequently on my tongue:

> E'er long, when Sovereign Wisdom wills,
> My soul an unknown path shall tread,
> Shall strangely leave, who strangely fills
> This frame, and waft me to the dead.
> O what is death? 'Tis life's last shore,
> Where vanities are vain no more;
> Where all pursuits their goal obtain,
> And life is all retouched again. . . . [17]

I observe, (2), that in two other of those instances it is particularly mentioned that I 'was troubled', and that by the seasonable application of those Scriptures that trouble was entirely removed.[g] The same blessing I received (so I must term it still) from the words set down in the 88th page,[18] and in a yet higher degree from the exceeding apposite Scripture mentioned in the 80th page of the last *Journal*.[19]

I observe, (3), that at the times to which your other citations refer I was utterly uncertain how to act, in points of great importance, and such as required a speedy determination, and that by this means my uncertainty was removed, and I went on my

[g] 3rd *Journal*, pp. 12 and 14 [i.e., Oct. 29, Nov. 23, 1738].

---

[16] This passage, from JWJ, Mar. 28, 1739, had been ridiculed by Church in his *Farther Remarks*, p. 122.

[17] John Gambold, 'The Mystery of Life', st. 6, included in John and Charles Wesley, *Hymns and Sacred Poems* (1739), p. 8, and John Wesley, *A Collection of Moral and Sacred Poems* (1744), III.194—where it is identified as by the former Oxford Methodist. In both cases the 3rd line reads, 'And strangely leave'.

[18] I.e., JWJ, Oct. 12, 1739.

[19] I.e., JWJ, Apr. 20, 1740.

way rejoicing—*Journal* III, pp. 12, 15; *Journal* IV, pp. 27-28.[20]

My 'own experience' therefore, which you 'think' should 'discourage me for the future'[21] from anything of this kind, does on the contrary greatly encourage me herein, since I have found much benefit and no inconvenience, unless perhaps this be one, that you 'cannot acquit me of enthusiasm'[22]—add, if you please, and presumption.

But you ask, 'Has God ever commanded us to do thus?'[23] I believe he has neither commanded nor forbidden it in Scripture. But then remember 'that Scripture' (to use the words which you cite from 'our learned and judicious Hooker') 'is *not* the only rule of all things which in this life may be done by men'.[24]—All I affirm concerning this is, *that it may be done;* and that I have in fact received *assistance* and *direction* thereby.

4. I give the same answer to your assertion that we are not ordered in Scripture to decide any point in question *by lots*.[h] You allow indeed, there are 'instances of this in Scripture', but affirm, these 'were miraculous, nor can we without presumption' (a species of enthusiasm) 'apply to this method'. I want proof of this. Bring one plain text of Scripture, and I am satisfied.—'This I apprehend you learned from the Moravians.'—I did; though 'tis true Mr. Whitefield thought I went too far therein.—'Instances of the same occur in your *Journals*. I will mention only one. It being debated when you should go to Bristol, you say, "We at length all agreed to decide it by lot. And by this it was determined, I should go."[i] Is this your way of carefully considering every step you take? Can there be greater rashness and extravagance? Reason is thus in a manner rendered useless. Prudence is set aside, and affairs of moment left to be determined by chance!'[j]

So this you give as a genuine instance of my proceedings—and, I suppose, of your own fairness and candour! 'We agreed at length to decide it by lot.' True, at *length*—after a debate of some hours; after carefully hearing and weighing coolly all the reasons which could be alleged on either side. 'Our brethren still continuing the dispute, without any probability of their coming to

[h] [*Farther Remarks*,] p. 123.
[i] *Journal* 3, p. 28 [i.e., JWJ, Mar. 28, 1739].
[j] [*Farther Remarks*,] p. 124.

---

[20] I.e., JWJ, Oct. 31, Dec. 3, 1738; Feb. 21, 1740.
[21] *Farther Remarks*, p. 122.
[22] Ibid., p. 123.
[23] Ibid.
[24] Ibid., p. 122.

one conclusion, "we at length (the night being now far spent) all agreed to this."' 'Can there be greater rashness and extravagance?'—I cannot but think there can. 'Reason is thus in a manner rendered useless.' No. We had used it as far as it could go, from Saturday, March 17 (when I received the first letter) to Wednesday 28, when the case was laid before the Society. 'Prudence is set aside.' Not so; but the arguments here were so equal that she saw not how to determine.—'And affairs of moment left to be determined by chance.' By chance? What a blunder then is that, 'The lot is cast into the lap; but the whole disposal thereof is of the Lord!'[25]

This I firmly believe is truth and reason, and will be to the end of the world. And I therefore still subscribe to that declaration of the Moravian Church (laid before the whole body of divines in the University of Württemberg, and not by them accounted *enthusiasm*): 'We have a peculiar esteem for *lots*, and accordingly use them both in public and private to decide points of importance, when the reasons brought on each side appear to be of equal weight. And we believe this to be then the only way of wholly setting aside our own will, of acquitting ourselves of all blame, and clearly knowing, what is the will of God.'[k]

5. You next 'remarked' several 'instances' of my enthusiasm. The first was that of Mrs. Jones. The next ran thus. 'Again, you say, "I expounded out of the fullness that was given me."'[l] I answered, 'I mean, I had then a *fuller*, deeper sense' (of what I spoke) 'than I *ordinarily* have.'[m] But if you still think 'it would have been more decent to have said, according to the best of my power and ability, with God's assistance, I expounded,'[26] I will say so another time.

With regard to the third 'instance' of enthusiasm you 'remarked': 'If you would not have us look on this as miraculous, there is nothing in it worthy of being related.'[n]—I answered, 'It

[k] *Journal* 2, p. 81 [i.e., Aug. 1738, the closing document presented by the *Journal*, 'An Extract of the Constitution of the Church of the Moravian Brethren at Herrnhut, laid before the Theological Order at Württemberg in the year 1733', §16. In both instances the original spelling is 'Wirtemmberg'. The *Journal* presents this section in the third person rather than the second].

[l] [Church, *Remarks*,] p. 64.

[m] [Wesley, *Answer*,] p. 41 [i.e., III.8].

[n] [*Remarks*,] p. 64 [i.e., pp. 65-66].

---

[25] Prov. 16:33.

[26] *Remarks*, p. 65.

may be so. Let it pass then as a trifle not worth relating. But still it is no proof of enthusiasm. For I would not have you look upon it as miraculous, . . . but as a signal instance of God's particular providence.'[o] How friendly and generous is your reply! 'You seem ashamed of it. . . . I am glad you give this fooling up, and hope for the future you will treat your readers better.'[p] Sir, I am not 'ashamed of it', nor shall I ever give 'this fooling' up till I give up the Bible. I still look upon this 'as a signal instance of God's particular providence'.—'But how is this consistent with yielding it to be a trifle?'[q] My words do not imply that I 'yield' it so to be. Being urged with the dilemma, 'Either this is related as miraculous (and then it is enthusiasm), or it is not worth relating' I answered (to avoid drawing the saw of controversy:[27] 'Let it pass then as a trifle not worth relating. But still' (if it be a trifle, which I *suppose*, not grant) 'it is no proof of enthusiasm. For I would not have you look upon it as miraculous.'

And yet I believe I yielded too much, and what might too much favour your assertion that 'there is a great difference between particular providences and such extraordinary interpositions.'[28] —Pray, sir, show me what this difference is. It is a subject that deserves your coolest thoughts.—'I know no ground . . . to hope or pray for such immediate reliefs. . . . These things must be represented either as common accidents or as miracles.'[29] I do not thoroughly understand your terms. What is a common *accident*? That a sparrow falls to the ground?[30] Or something more inconsiderable than the hairs of your head?[31] Is there no medium between accident and miracle? If there be, what is that medium?—When we are agreed with regard to these few points, I shall be glad to resume the subject.

6. The fourth instance of my enthusiasm was this, that I related judgments inflicted on my opposers.[32] As to Mr. Molther, I must observe once more, that I do believe there was a particular

[o] [*Answer*,] p. 42 [i.e., III.8].

[p] [Church, *Farther Remarks*,] p. 131.

[q] [Ibid.,] p. 132.

---

[27] A proverbial expression whose origin is so far unknown, frequently used by Wesley; cf. his *Letters* 25:411n. in this edn.

[28] Church, *Farther Remarks*, p. 132.

[29] Ibid.

[30] See Matt. 10:29.

[31] See Matt. 10:30.

[32] *Farther Remarks*, p. 132.

providence in his sickness. But I do not believe (nor did I design to insinuate), that it was a judgment for opposing *me.*[33]

You go on. 'Again, you mention as "an awful providence, the case of a poor wretch who was last week cursing and blaspheming, and had boasted to many that he would come again on Sunday, and no man should stop his mouth then.—But on Friday God laid his hand upon him, and on Sunday he was buried." '[r] I answered, 'I look on this as a manifest judgment of God on a hardened sinner for his complicated wickedness.'[s] You reply: 'Add, if you please, his "labouring with all his might to hinder the Word of God". Here therefore is a confessed judgment, for his opposition to you.'[t]—There is, for his *thus* opposing with curses and blasphemy. This was part of his complicated wickedness. Here then you 'think I plead guilty'.—Not of *enthusiasm*, till you prove, this was not 'an awful providence'.

'Again, "One was just going to beat his wife (which he frequently did) when God smote him in a moment, so that his hand dropped, and he fell down upon the ground, having no more strength than a new-born child." Have we any warrant either from Scripture or the common dispensations of providence to interpret misfortunes of this nature as judgments?'[u] I answered, 'Can you, sir, consider this as one of the common dispensations of providence? Have you known a parallel one in your life? But it was never cited by me (as it is by you) as an immediate punishment on a man for opposing me.'[v]—You reply: 'As if what is not common, or what I have not known, must be a miraculous judgment.'[34]—I believe it was, whether miraculous or no, a judgment mixed with mercy.

You now add to the rest the following instance:

> One John Haydon, a man of a regular life and conversation, being informed that 'people fell into strange fits at the societies', came to see and judge for himself. But he was still less satisfied than before; insomuch that he went about to his acquaintance one after another, and laboured above measure to convince them, it was a delusion of the devil. We were going home when one met us in the street and informed us that J. H. was fallen raving mad. It seems he had sat down

[r] [Church, *Remarks,*] pp. 66-67 [citing JWJ, Oct. 23, 1740].
[s] [Wesley, *Answer,*] p. 42 [i.e., III.9].
[t] [Church, *Farther Remarks,*] p. 133.
[u] [*Remarks,*] p. 67 [citing JWJ, Aug. 12, 1741].
[v] [*Answer,*] p. 42.

[33] Cf. Wesley, *Answer,* III.9.

[34] *Farther Remarks,* p. 133.

to dinner, but had a mind first to end the Sermon on *Salvation by Faith.* In reading the last page he changed colour, fell off his chair, and began screaming terribly, and beating himself against the ground. The neighbours were alarmed, and flocked into the house. I came in and found him upon the floor, the room being full of people, whom his wife would have kept without; but he cried aloud, 'No; let them all come; let all the world see the just judgment of God.' Two or three men were holding him as well as they could. He immediately fixed his eyes upon me, and cried. 'Ay, this is he, who I said was a deceiver of the people. But God has overtaken me. I said it was all a delusion. But this is no delusion.' He then roared out, 'O thou devil! Thou cursed devil! Yea, thou legion of devils! Thou canst not stay! Christ will cast thee out. I know his work is begun. Tear me to pieces if thou wilt, but thou canst not hurt me.' He then beat himself against the ground again, his breast heaving at the same time, as in the pangs of death, and great drops of sweat trickling down his face. We all betook ourselves to prayer. His pangs ceased, and both his body and soul were set at liberty.[w]

If you had pleased, you might have added from the next paragraph, 'Returning to J. H., we found his voice was lost, and his body weak as that of an infant. But his soul was in peace, full of love, and rejoicing in hope of the glory of God.'

You subjoin, 'This you may desire, for ought I know, to pass as a trifle too.'[x] No. It is so terrible an instance of the judgment of God (though at length 'mercy rejoiced over judgment')[35] as ought never to be forgotten by those who fear God, so long as the sun or moon endureth.

7. The account of people falling down in fits you cite as a fifth instance of my enthusiasm, it being 'plain', you say, that I 'look upon both the disorders and the removals of them to be supernatural'.[y] I answered, 'It is not quite plain. I look upon some of these cases as wholly natural, on the rest, as mixed, both the disorders and the removals being partly natural and partly not.'[z] You reply, 'It would have been kind to have let us know your rule, by which you distinguish these.'[36]—I will. I distinguish them by the circumstances that precede, accompany, and follow. 'However, some of these you here allow to be in part supernatural. Miracles therefore are not wholly ceased.'[37] Can you prove they are? By Scripture, or reason?—You then refer to

[w] [*Journal* 3, p. 44 [i.e., JWJ, May 2, 1739, quoted in Church's *Farther Remarks,* pp. 133-34].
[x] [*Farther Remarks,*] p. 134.
[y] [Church, *Remarks,*] p. 67.
[z] [Wesley, *Answer,*] p. 43 [i.e., III.10].

---

[35] Cf. Jas. 2:13.
[36] Church, *Farther Remarks,* p. 134.
[37] Ibid.

two or three cases related in the 42nd and 43rd pages of the third *Journal.*[38] I believe there was a *supernatural* power on the minds of the persons there mentioned, which occasioned their bodies to be so affected by the *natural* laws of the vital union. This point therefore you have to prove, or here is no enthusiasm—that there was no *supernatural* power in the case.

Hereon you remarked: 'You leave no room to doubt that you would have these cases considered as those of the demoniacs in the New Testament, in order, I suppose, to parallel your supposed cures of them with those highest miracles of Christ and his disciples, the casting out devils.'[a]—I answered: 'I should once have wondered at your making such a supposition. But I now wonder at nothing of this kind.'[39] You reply: 'Why so? What have I done lately to take off your surprise? Have I forfeited my character for ingenuous and fair dealing with you?'[b] Since you ask me the question I will answer it (I hope, in love and in the spirit of meekness). I scarce know, of all who have wrote against me, a less ingenuous dealer, or one who has shown a more steady, invariable disposition to put an ill construction on whatever I say.

'But why would you not particularly explain these cases?'[40]—I will explain myself upon them once for all. For more than three hundred years after Christ, you know demoniacs were common in the Church. And I suppose you are not unapprised that during this period (if not much longer) they were continually relieved by the prayers of the faithful. Nor can I doubt but demoniacs will remain so long as Satan is the 'god of this world'.[41] I doubt not but there are such at this day. And I believe John Haydon was one. But of whatever sort his disorder was, that it was removed by prayer is undeniable. Now, sir, you have only two points to prove, and then your argument will be conclusive: (1), that to think or say, 'there are demoniacs now, and they are now relieved by prayer', is enthusiasm; (2), that to say, 'demoniacs were or are relieved, on prayer made by Cyprian, or their parish minister,' is 'to parallel' the actions of Cyprian or that minister 'with the highest miracles of Christ and his disciples'.[42]

[a] *R[emarks,]* p. 68.
[b] Second Letter [i.e., *Farther Remarks,*] p. 135.

---

[38] JWJ, Apr. 25, 29, 1739.
[39] *Answer,* III.10.
[40] *Farther Remarks,* p. 135.
[41] 2 Cor. 4:4.
[42] *Farther Remarks,* p. 135.

8. You remarked, 'It will be difficult to persuade any sober person that there is anything supernatural in these disorders.'[c] The remainder of that paragraph I abridged thus. You attempt to account for those fits 'by obstructions or irregularities of the blood and spirits; hysterical disorders; watchings, fastings; closeness of rooms, great crowds, violent heat'. And lastly by 'terrors, perplexities, and doubts, in weak and well-meaning men; which' you think 'in many of the cases before us have quite overset their understandings'.

I answered: 'As to each of the rest, let it go as far as it can go.' (Let it be supposed to have *some* influence in *some* cases; perhaps, 'fully to account for' one in a thousand.) 'But I require proof of the last way whereby you would account for these disorders.'[d]—Why, 'the instances', you say, 'of religious madness have much increased since you began to disturb the world.'[43]—'I doubt the fact.'[44]—You reply, 'This no way disproves it.'[e]—Yes it does, till you produce some proof. For a bare negation is the proper and sufficient answer to a bare affirmation. I add, 'If these instances had increased daily, 'tis easy to account for them another way'[45] (as is done in the First Part of the *Farther Appeal*, at the 101st and following pages).[46] You say, 'Most have heard of or known several of the Methodists thus driven to distraction.'[47] I answered: '*You* may have *heard* of five hundred. But how many have you *known?* Be pleased to name eight or ten of them. I cannot find them, no, not one of them to this day, either man, woman, or child.'[f] You reply: 'This' (the naming them) 'would be very improper and unnecessary.'[g]—However, sir, it is extremely necessary that you should name them to me in private. I will then, if required, excuse you to the public, which till then I cannot do.

The person I mentioned whom you 'threw into much *doubt* and

[c] *Remarks*, pp. 68-69.

[d] *Answer*, p. 43 [i.e., III. 10; in this instance the citation is placed at the close of the previous paragraph, and incorrectly reads, '*R*[*emarks*], p. 43'].

[e] [*Farther Remarks*,] p. 137.

[f] [*Answer*,] p. 44.

[g] [*Farther Remarks*,] p. 138.

---

[43] *Remarks*, p. 69.

[44] *Answer*, p. 43.

[45] Ibid.

[46] VII.14-17 (11:198-201 in this edn.).

[47] *Remarks*, p. 69.

perplexity' then lived in the parish of St. Ann[e], Westminster. I related the case just as she related it to me. But she is able and ready to answer for herself.

9. You go on. 'It is the most charitable supposition we can make that many of the cases you have mentioned in your *Journals*, and some of which have been represented above, are of this kind', i.e., instances of madness.[h] O tender charity! But cannot your charity reach one hair's breadth farther than this?—No; for 'otherwise' (i.e., if those persons were not mad) 'the presumption and despair are terrible indeed.'—But what if you were to suppose John Haydon (to instance in one) was not mad, but under a temporary possession? And that others were deeply convinced of sin, and of the wrath of God abiding on them? I should think this supposition (be it true or false) was full as 'charitable' as the other.

I said 'I cannot find one such instance to this day.' You reply: 'Yet once you could not but be "under some concern, with regard to one or two persons, who *seemed* to be indeed *lunatic,* as well as sore vexed".'[48]—So they *seemed.* But it soon appeared, they *were not*. The very next paragraph mentions that one of these, within a few hours, was 'filled with the spirit of love, and of a sound mind'.[i]

But you are resolved, come what will, to carry this point, and so add: 'Toward the end of your *Farther Appeal* (the First Part, p. 101), you say you "have seen one instance of real, lasting madness". This was one whom you took with you to Bristol, who was afterwards prejudiced against you, and began a vehement invective both against your person and doctrines. "In the midst of this he was struck raving mad." '[49] Add, 'And so he continued till his friends put him into Bedlam; and probably laid *his* madness to *my* charge.'—If they did not, it is now done to their hands.

10. 'As to the cure of these fits, I observed' (so you, page 139, proceed) 'that you had frequently represented them as miraculous, as the instantaneous consequences of your prayers.'—My former answer to this was, 'I have set down the facts just as they were, passing no judgment upon them myself, and leaving every man else to judge as he pleases.'[50]

[h] Second Letter [*Farther Remarks,*] p. 138. [i] *Journal* 3, p. 88 [Oct. 12, 1739].

---

[48] *Farther Remarks,* p. 138, quoting JWJ, Oct. 12, 1739.
[49] Ibid., quoting *A Farther Appeal,* Pt. I, VII.14 (11:198-99 in this edn.).
[50] *Answer,* III.10.

I am glad you gave me an occasion of reviewing this answer; for upon reflection I do not like it at all. It grants you more than I can in conscience do. As it can be proved by abundance of witnesses that these cures were frequently (indeed almost always) the *instantaneous* consequence of prayer, your inference is just. I cannot, dare not, affirm that they were purely *natural.* I believe they were not. I believe many of them were wrought by the *supernatural* power of God. That of John Haydon in particular (I fix on this, and will join issue with you upon it when you please). And yet this is not 'barefaced enthusiasm'. Nor can you prove it any *enthusiasm* at all unless you can prove that this is *falsely* ascribed to a *supernatural* power.

'The next case', you say, 'relates to the spotted fever, which you represent as being extremely mortal; but . . . you believe there was not one with whom you were but recovered. I allowed that "here is no intimation of anything miraculous."[j] You ask, "Why then is this cited as an instance of my enthusiasm?"[k]—You sure cannot think that false pretences to miracles are the *whole* of enthusiasm.'[51] No; but I think they are *that part* of enthusiasm which you here undertook to prove upon me. You are here to prove that I 'boast of curing bodily distempers by prayer, without the use of any other means'.[l] But if 'there is no intimation' in my account 'of anything miraculous, or that proper remedies had not been applied', how is this a proof that I 'boast of curing bodily distempers, without applying' any 'remedies' at all?

But you seem to desire to have it believed that an extraordinary blessing attended your prayers. Whereas, if the circumstances could be particularly inquired into, most probably it would appear that either the fury of the distemper was abated, or the persons you visited were seized with it in a more favourable degree, or were by reason of a good constitution more capable of going through it. Neither do I believe that they would have failed of an equal blessing and success had they had the assistance and prayers of their own parish ministers.[52]

[j] *Remarks*, p. 72.
[k] *Answer*, p. 45 [III.11].
[l] *Remarks*, p. 71.

---

[51] *Farther Remarks*, p. 139.
[52] *Remarks*, p. 72, quoted in abridged form in Wesley's *Answer*, p. 45 (III.11), with both the original and the abridgement printed in parallel columns in Church's *Farther Remarks*, p. 140. (There are many such examples of quotations appearing three or four times throughout this controversy, in different forms.)

There, sir; now I have done as you require—I have quoted your whole remark. But does all this prove that I 'boast of curing bodily distempers by prayer, without the use of any other means'? If you say, although it does not prove this, it proves that 'you seem to desire to have it believed that an extraordinary blessing attended your prayers.' And this is another sort of enthusiasm.—'Tis very well. So it does not prove the conclusion you designed, but it proves another, which is as good!

11. The two last instances of my enthusiasm which you bring[m] I had summed up in two lines thus: 'At two several times, being ill and in violent pain, I prayed to God, and found immediate ease.'[n] But since you say, I 'must not hope to escape so; these instances must once more be laid before me particularly',[o] I must yield to necessity, and set them down from the beginning to the end.

Sat. March 21 [1741]. I explained in the evening the thirty-third chapter of Ezekiel; in applying which I was seized with such a pain in my side, I could not speak. I knew my remedy, and immediately kneeled down. In a moment the pain was gone.[p]

Friday, May 8 [1741]. I found myself much out of order. However, I made shift to preach in the evening. But on Saturday my bodily strength quite failed, so that for several hours I could scarce lift up my head. Sunday 10. I was obliged to lie down most part of the day, being easy only in that posture. . . . In the evening . . . , beside the pain in my back and head, and the fever which still continued upon me, just as I began to pray I was seized with such a cough that I could hardly speak. At the same time came strongly into my mind, 'These signs shall follow them that believe. . . .' I called on Jesus aloud to 'increase my faith', and to 'confirm the word of his grace'. While I was speaking my pain vanished away. The fever left me. My bodily strength returned. And for many weeks I felt neither weakness nor pain. 'Unto thee, O Lord, do I give thanks.'[q]

When you first cited these as proofs of enthusiasm I answered:

I will put your argument into form:

He that believes those are miraculous cures which are not so is a rank enthusiast; but,

You believe those are miraculous cures which are not so;

Therefore, you are a rank enthusiast.

. . . What do you mean by miraculous? If you term everything so which is 'not strictly accountable for by the ordinary course of natural causes', then I deny the latter part of the minor proposition. And unless you can make this good, unless

[m] *Remarks*, pp. 72-73.
[n] *Answer*, p. 45 [III.12].
[o] [*Farther Remarks*,] p. 140.
[p] *Journal* 4, p. 77.
[q] *Journal* 4, p. 83.

you can prove the effects in question are 'strictly accountable for by the ordinary course of natural causes', your argument is nothing worth.[53]

You reply:

Your answer to the objection is very evasive, though you pretend to put my argument in form. You mistake the major proposition, which should have been:

He that represents those cures as the immediate effects of his own prayers, and as miraculous, which are not so, is a rank enthusiast, if sincere;

But, This you have done: *Ergo,* etc.[54]

To this clumsy syllogism I rejoin, (1). That the words 'if sincere' are utterly impertinent;[55] for if *insincerity* be supposed, *enthusiasm* will be out of the question. (2). That those words 'as the effects of his own prayers' may likewise be pared off; for they are unnecessary and cumbersome, the argument being complete without them. (3). That with or without them the proposition is false, unless so far as it coincides with that you reject. For it is *the believing* those to be miracles which are not that constitutes an *enthusiast,* not the *representing* them one way or the other, unless so far as it implies such a *belief.*

12. Upon my answer to the syllogism first proposed you observe, 'Thus' (by denying the latter part of the minor) 'you clear yourself from the charge of enthusiasm by acknowledging the cures to be supernatural and miraculous. . . . Why then would you not speak out, and directly say that you can work real and undoubted miracles? This would put the controversy between you and your opposers on a short foot, and be an effectual proof of the truth of your pretences.'[r]

V. 1. I have in some measure explained myself on the head of miracles in the Third Part of the *Farther Appeal.*[56] But since you repeat the demand (though without taking any notice of the arguments there advanced) I will endeavour once more to give you a distinct, full, and determinate answer.

And first, I acknowledge that I have seen with my eyes, and heard with my ears, several things which, to the best of my

[r] [*Farther Remarks,*] p. 142.

---

[53] *Answer,* III.12.

[54] *Farther Remarks,* pp. 141-42.

[55] In its primary sense of not pertinent, irrelevant.

[56] *A Farther Appeal,* Pt. III, III.28-30 (11:310-12 in this edn.).

judgment, cannot be accounted for by the ordinary course of natural causes, and which I therefore believe ought to be 'ascribed to the extraordinary interposition of God'.[57] If any man choose to style these 'miracles' I reclaim[58] not. I have diligently inquired into the facts. I have weighed the preceding and following circumstances. I have strove to account for them in a *natural* way. I could not, without doing violence to my reason. Not to go far back, I am clearly persuaded that the sudden deliverance of John Haydon was one instance of this kind, and my own recovery on May the tenth another. I cannot account for either of these in a *natural* way. Therefore I believe they were both *supernatural.*

I must, secondly, observe, that the truth of these facts is supported by the same kind of proof as that of all other facts is wont to be, namely, the testimony of competent witnesses; and that the testimony here is in as high a degree as any reasonable man can desire. Those witnesses were many in number; they could not be deceived themselves, for the facts in question they saw with their own eyes, and heard with their own ears. Nor is it credible that so many of them would combine together with a view of deceiving others, the greater part being men that feared God, as appeared by the general tenor of their lives. Thus, in the case of John Haydon, this thing was not contrived and executed in a corner, and in the presence of his own family only, or three or four persons prepared for the purpose. No; it was in an open street of the city of Bristol, at one or two in the afternoon. And the doors being all open from the beginning, not only many of the neighbours from every side, but several others (indeed whosoever desired it) went in till the house could contain no more. Nor yet does the account of my own illness and recovery 'depend', as you suppose, 'on my bare word'.[59] There were many witnesses both of my disorder on Friday and Saturday, and of my lying down most part of Sunday (a thing which they were well satisfied could not be the effect of a slight indisposition). And all who saw me that evening plainly discerned (what I could not wholly conceal) that I was in pain, about two hundred of whom were present when I was seized with that cough which cut me short so that I could speak no more; till I cried out aloud, 'Lord, increase my faith. Lord,

[57] Church, *Farther Remarks*, p. 142.

[58] Apparently in the rare intransitive sense of 'exclaim' or 'protest' (see *OED*, II.7).

[59] *Remarks*, p. 73.

confirm the word of thy grace.' The same persons saw and heard that at that instant I changed my posture, and broke out into thanksgiving; that quickly after I stood upright (which I could not before), and showed no more sign either of sickness or pain.

Yet I must desire you well to observe, thirdly, that my will, or choice, or desire, had no place either in this, or any case of this kind that has ever fallen under my notice. Five minutes before I had no thought of this. I expected nothing else. I was willing to wait for a gradual recovery in the ordinary use of outward means. I did not look for any other cure till the moment before I found it. And it is my belief that the case was always the same with regard to the most 'real and undoubted miracles'.[60] I believe God never interposed his miraculous power but according to his own sovereign will—not according to the will of man, neither of him by whom he wrought, nor of any other man whatsoever. The wisdom as well as the power are his. Nor can I find that ever, from the beginning of the world, he lodged this power in any mere man, to be used whenever that man saw good. Suppose, therefore, there was a man now on earth who did work 'real and undoubted miracles', I would ask, By whose power doth he work these? And at whose pleasure? His own, or God's? Not his own; but God's. But if so, then your demand is not made on man, but on God. I cannot say it is modest, thus to challenge God; or well suiting the relation of a creature to his Creator.

2. However, I cannot but think, there have been already so many plain interpositions of divine power as will shortly leave you without excuse if you either deny or despise them. We desire no favour but the justice that diligent inquiry may be made concerning them. We are ready to name the persons on whom that power was shown which belongeth to none but God (not one or two, or ten or twelve only); to point out their places of abode. And we engage they shall answer every pertinent question fairly and directly; and, if required, shall give all those answers upon oath before any who are empowered so to receive them. It is our particular request that the circumstances which went before, which accompanied, and which followed after the facts under consideration, may be thoroughly examined, and punctually noted down. Let but this be done (and is it not highly needful it should, at least by those who would form an exact judgment?),

[60] Church, *Farther Remarks*, p. 141.

and we have no fear that any reasonable man should scruple to say, 'This hath God wrought!'[61]

As there have been already so many instances of this kind, far beyond what we had dared to ask or think,[62] I cannot take upon me to say whether or not it will please God to add to their number. I have not herein 'known the mind of the Lord', neither am I 'his counsellor'.[63] He may, or he may not; I cannot affirm or deny. I have no light, and I have no desire either way. 'It is the Lord, let him do what seemeth him good.'[64] I desire only to be as clay in his hand.

3. But what if there were not to be wrought ever so many 'real and undoubted miracles'? (I suppose you mean by 'undoubted' such as being sufficiently attested, ought not to be doubted of.) Why, this, you say, 'would put the controversy on a short foot, and be an effectual proof of the truth of your pretences'.[65] By no means. As common as this assertion is, there is none upon earth more false. Suppose a teacher were now, on this very day, to work 'real and undoubted miracles'. This would extremely little 'shorten the controversy' between him and the greater part of his opposers. For all this would not force them to believe, but many would still stand just where they did before—seeing men may 'harden their hearts'[66] against miracles, as well as against arguments.

So men have done from the beginning of the world, even against such signal, glorious miracles, against such interpositions of the power of God, as may not be again till the consummation of all things. Permit me to remind you only of a few instances, and to observe, that the argument holds *à fortiori:* for who will ever be empowered of God again to work *such* miracles as these were? Did *Pharaoh* look on all that Moses and Aaron wrought as an 'effectual proof of the truth of their pretences'? Even when 'the Lord made the sea to be dry land, and the waters were divided; when the children of Israel went into the midst of the sea, and the waters were a wall on the right and on the left'?[s] Nay,

[s] Exod. 14:21-22.

---

[61] Cf. Num. 23:23.
[62] See Eph. 3:20.
[63] Rom. 11:34.
[64] 1 Sam. 3:18.
[65] See IV.12 above.
[66] Cf. Josh. 11:20, etc.

The wounded dragon raged in vain;
  And fierce the utmost plague to brave,
Madly he dared the parted main,
  And sunk beneath th' o'erwhelming wave.[67]

Was all this 'an effectual proof of the truth of their pretences' to the Israelites themselves? It was not. 'They were' *still* 'disobedient at the sea, even at the Red Sea.'[68] Was the giving them day by day 'bread from heaven'[69] 'an effectual proof' to those 'two hundred and fifty princes of the assembly, famous in the congregation, men of renown', who said, with Dathan and Abiram, 'Wilt thou put out the eyes of these men? We will not come up.'[t] Nay, when 'the ground clave asunder that was under them, and the earth opened her mouth and swallowed them up',[u] neither was this an 'effectual proof' to those who saw it with their eyes, and heard the cry of those that went down into the pit; but the very next day they 'murmured against Moses and against Aaron, saying, Ye have killed the people of the Lord!'[v]

Was not the case generally the same with regard to the prophets that followed? Several of whom 'stopped the mouths of lions, quenched the violence of fire',[70] did many mighty works; yet their own people received them not. Yet 'they were stoned, they were sawn asunder, they were slain with the sword; they were destitute, afflicted, tormented!'[71]—utterly contrary to the commonly received supposition that the working 'real, undoubted miracles' must bring all controversy to an end, and convince every gainsayer.

Let us come nearer yet. How stood the case between our Lord himself and his opposers? Did he not work 'real and undoubted miracles'? And what was the effect? Still when 'he came to his own, his own received him not.'[72] Still 'he was despised and rejected of men.'[73] Still it was a challenge not to be answered, 'Have any of the rulers or of the Pharisees believed on him?'[74]—After this, how can you imagine that whoever works miracles must convince 'all men of the truth of his pretences'?

[t] Num. 16:[2,] 14. [u] Ver. 31-32. [v] Ver. 41.

[67] Charles Wesley, 'The Fifty-first Chapter of Isaiah', Pt. II, st. 4, in *Hymns and Sacred Poems* (1749), I.21 (*Poet. Wks.*, IV.303). Orig., 'While bold thine utmost plague to brave'.
[68] Ps. 106:7 (BCP).
[69] Exod. 16:4.
[70] Heb. 11:33-34.
[71] Heb. 11:37.
[72] John 1:11.
[73] Isa. 53:3.
[74] John 7:48.

I would just remind you of only one instance more. 'There sat a certain man at Lystra, impotent in his feet, being a cripple from his mother's womb, who never had walked. The same heard Paul speak; who steadfastly beholding him, and perceiving that he had faith to be healed, said with a loud voice, Stand upright on thy feet. And he leaped and walked.'—Here was so *undoubted a miracle* that the people 'lift up their voices, saying, . . . The gods are come down in the likeness of men.' But how long were even these convinced of 'the truth of his pretences'? Only till 'there came thither certain Jews from Antioch and Iconium'; and then they 'stoned him' (as they supposed) to death![w] So certain it is that no miracles whatever which were ever yet wrought in the world were *effectual* to *prove* the most glaring truth to those that hardened their hearts against it.

4. And it will equally hold in every age and nation. 'If they hear not Moses and the prophets, neither will they be convinced' (of what they desire not to believe) 'though one rose from the dead.'[75] Without a miracle, without one rising from the dead, ἐάν τις θέλῃ ποιεῖν, 'if any man be willing to do his will, he shall know of the doctrine whether it be of God.'[76] But if he is not willing to do his will he will never want an excuse, a plausible reason, for rejecting it. Yea, though ever so many miracles were wrought to confirm it. For let ever so much 'light come into the world', it will have no effect (such is the wise and just will of God) on those who 'love darkness rather than light'.[77] It will not convince those who do not simply desire to do the will of their Father which is in heaven.[78] Those who mind earthly things, who (if they do not continue in any gross outward sin, yet) love pleasure or ease, yet seek profit or power, preferment or reputation. Nothing will ever be an effectual proof to these of the holy and acceptable will of God, unless first their proud hearts be humbled, their stubborn wills bowed down, and their desires brought, at least in some degree, into obedience to the law of Christ.

Hence although it should please God to work anew all the wonders that ever were wrought on the earth, still these men, however 'wise and prudent'[79] they may be in things relating to the

[w] Acts 14:1, etc. [i.e., 8-11, 19].

---

[75] Luke 16:31.
[76] John 7:17.
[77] John 3:19.
[78] See Matt. 12:50.
[79] Matt. 11:25.

present world, would fight against God and all his messengers, and that in spite of all these miracles. Meanwhile God will reveal his truth 'unto babes',[80] unto those who are meek and lowly, whose desires are in heaven, who want to 'know nothing save Jesus Christ and him crucified'.[81]—These need no outward miracle to show them his will: they have a plain rule, the written Word. And 'the anointing which they have received of him abideth in them, and teacheth them of all things'.[x] Through this they are enabled to bring all doctrines 'to the law and to the testimony'.[82] And whatsoever is agreeable to this they receive, without waiting to see it attested by miracles. As, on the other hand, whatever is contrary to this they reject—nor can any miracles move them to receive it.

5. Yet I do not know that God hath any way precluded himself from thus exerting his sovereign power, from working miracles in any kind or degree, in any age to the end of the world. I do not recollect any Scripture wherein we are taught that miracles were to be confined within the limits either of the apostolic or the Cyprianic age—or of any period of time, longer or shorter, even till the restitution of all things.[83] I have not observed either in the Old Testament or the New any intimation at all of this kind. St. Paul says indeed once, concerning two of the miraculous gifts of the Spirit (so, I think, that text is usually understood), 'Whether there be prophecies, they shall fail; whether there be tongues, they shall cease.'[84] But he does not say either that these or any other miracles shall cease till faith and hope shall cease also, till they shall all be swallowed up in the vision of God, and love be all in all.

I presume you will allow, there is one kind of miracles (loosely speaking) which are not ceased, namely, *τέρατα ψεύδους*, lying wonders,[85] diabolical miracles, or works beyond the virtue of natural causes, wrought by the power of evil spirits. Nor can you easily conceive that these will cease, as long as the father of lies[86] is the prince of this world.[87] And why should you think that the God

[x] [Cf.] 1 John 2:27.

[80] Ibid.

[81] 1 Cor. 2:2.

[82] Isa. 8:20.

[83] Acts 3:21.

[84] 1 Cor. 13:8.

[85] 2 Thess. 2:9.

[86] See John 8:44.

[87] John 12:31, etc.

of truth is less active than him, or that he will not have his miracles also? Only, not as man wills, neither when he wills, but according to his own excellent wisdom and greatness.

6. But even if it were supposed that God does now work beyond the operation of merely natural causes, yet what impression would this make upon *you*, in the disposition your mind is now in? Suppose the trial were repeated, were made again tomorrow. One informs you the next day, 'While a clergyman was preaching yesterday, where I was, a man came who had been long ill of an incurable distemper. Prayer was made for him. And he was restored to perfect health.'

Suppose now that this were real fact, perhaps you would scarce have patience to hear the account of it, but would cut it short in the midst, with, 'Do you tell this as something *supernatural?* Then miracles are not ceased!' But if you should venture to ask, Where was this? And who was the person that prayed? And it was answered, 'At the Foundery near Moorfields; the person who prayed was Mr. Wesley.' What a damp comes at once! What a weight falls on your mind, at the very first setting out! 'Tis well if you have any heart or desire to move one step further. Or if you should, what a strong additional propensity do you now feel to deny the fact! And is there not a ready excuse for so doing? 'Oh, they who tell the story are doubtless *his own people*—most of whom, we may be sure, will *say* anything for him, and the rest will *believe* anything.'—But if you at length allowed the fact, might you not find means to account for it by *natural* causes? 'Great crowds, violent heats, with obstructions and irregularities of the blood and spirits', will do wonders.—If you could not but allow it was more than *natural*, might not some plausible reason be found for ranking it among the 'lying wonders', for ascribing it to the devil rather than God? And if, after all, you was convinced, it was the finger of God, must you not still bring every doctrine advanced to the law and to the testimony, the only sure and infallible test of all?—What then is the use of this continual demand, 'Show us a sign, and we will believe'? What will you believe? I hope no more than is written in the Book of God. And thus far you might venture to believe, even without a miracle.

7. Let us consider this point yet a little farther. 'What is it you would have us prove by miracles? The doctrines we preach?' We prove these by Scripture and reason; and, if need be, by antiquity. What else is it then we are to prove by miracles? At length we have

a distinct reply—'Wise and sober men will not otherwise be convinced' (i.e., unless you prove this by miracles) 'that God is, by the means of such teachers, and such doctrines, working a great and extraordinary work in the earth.'[y]

So then the determinate point which you, in their name, call upon us to prove by miracles, is this, 'that God is, by these teachers, working a great and extraordinary work in the earth'.

What I mean by a great and extraordinary work is the bringing multitudes of gross, notorious sinners, in a short space, to the fear, and love, and service of God, to an entire change of heart and life.

Now then, let us take a nearer view of the proposition, and see which part of it we are to prove by miracles.

> Is it, (1), that A.B. was for many years without God in the world, a common swearer, a drunkard, a sabbath-breaker?
>
> Or, (2), that he is not so now?
>
> Or, (3), that he continued so till he heard these men preach, and from that time was another man?
>
> Not so. The proper way to prove these facts is by the testimony of competent witnesses. And these witnesses are ready, whenever required, to give full evidence of them.
>
> Or would you have us prove by miracles,
>
> (4), that this was not done by our own power or holiness? That God only is able to raise the dead, to quicken those who are dead in trespasses and sins?[88]

Surely no. Whosoever believes the Scriptures will want no new proof of this.

Where then is the 'wisdom' of those men who demand miracles in proof of such a proposition? One branch of which, 'that such sinners are reformed by the means of these teachers', being a plain fact, can only be proved by testimony, as all other facts are; and the other, that this is a 'work of God' and a 'great and more than ordinary work', needs no proof, as carrying its own evidence to every thinking man.

8. To sum up this. No truly 'wise' or 'sober' man can possibly desire or expect miracles to prove, either, (1), that these *doctrines* are true—this must be decided by Scripture and reason; or, (2), that these *facts* are true—this can only be proved by testimony; or, (3), that to *change* sinners from darkness to light is the 'work of

[y] [Church, *Farther Remarks*,] Preface, p. vi.

---

[88] Wesley, *A Farther Appeal*, Pt. III, III.28 (11:310 in this edn.).

God' alone, only using what instruments he pleases—this is glaringly self-evident; or, (4), that such a change wrought in so many notorious sinners, within so short a time, is a 'great' and 'extraordinary' work of God—this also carries its own evidence. What then is it which remains to be proved by miracles? Perhaps you will say, it is this: 'that God hath *called* or *sent* you to do this.' Nay, this is implied in the third of the foregoing propositions. If God has actually *used* us therein, if *his work* hath in fact prospered in our hands, then he hath *called* or *sent* us to do this. I entreat reasonable men to weigh this thoroughly, whether the *fact* does not plainly prove the *call*; whether he who *enables* us thus to save souls alive does not *commission* us so to do? Whether by *giving* us the *power* to pluck these brands out of the burning,[89] he does not authorize us to exert it?

O that it were possible for you to consider calmly whether the *success* of the gospel of Jesus Christ, even as it is preached by us, the least of his servants, be not itself a *miracle*, never to be forgotten! One which cannot be denied, as being visible at this day, not in one but a hundred places; one which cannot be accounted for by the ordinary course of any *natural causes* whatsoever; one which cannot be ascribed with any colour of reason to *diabolical* agency; and lastly, one which will bear the infallible test, the trial of the written Word.

VI. 1. But here I am aware of abundance of objections. You object, first, that to speak anything of myself, of what I have done, or am doing now, is mere *boasting* and *vanity*. This charge you frequently repeat. So, p. 102, 'The following page is full of *boasting*'; p. 113, 'You *boast* very much of the numbers you have converted', and again, 'As to myself, I hope I shall never be led to imitate you in *boasting*.'—I think therefore it is needful, once for all, to examine this charge thoroughly, and to show distinctly what that *good* thing is which you disguise under this *bad* name.

From the year 1725 to 1729 I preached much, but saw no fruit of my labour. Indeed it could not be that I should, for I neither laid the foundation of *repentance*, nor of *believing the gospel*, taking it for granted that all to whom I preached were *believers*, and that many of them *needed no repentance*. (2). From the year 1729 to 1734, laying a deeper foundation of repentance, I saw a little fruit. But it was only a little; and no wonder. For I did not preach faith

[89] See Amos 4:11; Zech. 3:2.

in the blood of the covenant.[90] (3). From 1734 to 1738, speaking more of faith in Christ, I saw more fruit of my preaching and visiting from house to house than ever I had done before. Though I know not if any of those who were outwardly reformed were inwardly and thoroughly converted to God. (4). From 1738 to this time, speaking continually of Jesus Christ, laying him only for the foundation of the whole building, making him all in all, the first and the last;[91] preaching wholly on this plan, 'The kingdom of God is at hand; repent ye and believe the gospel,'[92] the 'Word of God ran' as fire among the stubble; it 'was glorified'[93] more and more; multitudes crying out, 'What must we do to be saved?'[94] And afterwards witnessing, 'By grace we are saved through faith.'[95] (5). I considered deeply with myself what I ought to do. Whether to declare the things I had seen or not? I consulted the most serious friends I had. They all agreed, I ought to declare them, that the work itself was of such a kind as ought in no wise to be concealed; and, indeed, that the unusual circumstances now attending it made it impossible that it should. (6). This very difficulty occurred: 'Will not my speaking of this be *boasting?* At least, will it not be accounted so?' They replied, 'If you speak of it as *your own* work it will be *vanity* and *boasting* all over; but if you ascribe it wholly to God, if you give him all the praise, it will not. And if, after this, some will account it so still, you must be content, and bear the burden.' (7). I yielded, and transcribed my papers for the press; only labouring as far as possible to 'render unto God the things which are God's',[96] to give him the praise of his own work.

2. But this very thing you improve into a fresh objection. If I ascribe anything to God it is *enthusiasm*. If I do not (or if I do) it is *vanity and boasting*, supposing me to mention it at all. What then can I do to escape your censure? 'Why, be silent, say nothing at all.' I cannot. I dare not. Were I thus to 'please men' I could 'not be the servant of Christ'.[97]

You do not appear to have the least idea or conception of what is in the heart of one whom it pleases him that worketh all in all[98]

[90] See Heb. 10:29; 13:20.
[91] Rev. 1:11; 22:13.
[92] Mark 1:15.
[93] Cf. 2 Thess. 3:1 *(Notes)*.
[94] Acts 16:30.
[95] Cf. Eph. 2:8.
[96] Cf. Luke 20:25.
[97] Gal. 1:10.
[98] 1 Cor. 12:6.

to employ in a work of this kind. He is in no wise forward to be at all employed therein; he starts back again and again. Not only because he readily foresees what shame, care, sorrow, reproach, what loss of friends and of all that the world accounts dear will inevitably follow. But much more because he (in some measure) knows himself. This chiefly it is which constrains him to cry out (and that many times, in the bitterness of his soul, when no human eye seeth him), 'O Lord! Send by whom thou wilt send![99] Only, send not me!—What am I? A worm! a dead dog![1] a man unclean in heart and lips!'—And when he dares no longer gainsay or resist, when he is at last 'thrust out into the harvest',[2] he looketh on the right hand, and on the left, he takes every step with fear and trembling, and with the deepest sense (such as words cannot express) of, 'Who is sufficient for these things?'[3] Every gift which he has received of God, for the furtherance of his Word, whether of nature or grace, heightens this fear, and increases his jealousy over himself; knowing that so much the stricter must the inquiry be when he gives an account of his stewardship.[4] He is most of all jealous over himself when the work of his Lord prospers in his hand. He is then amazed and confounded before God. Shame covers his face. Yet when he sees that he ought to 'praise the Lord for his goodness, and to declare the wonders which he doth for the children of men',[5] he is in a strait between two;[6] he knows not which way to turn; he cannot speak; he dares not be silent. It may be, for a time he 'keeps his mouth with a bridle, he holds his peace even from good. But his heart is hot within him,'[7] and constrains him at length to declare what God hath wrought.[8] And this he then doth in all simplicity, with 'great plainness of speech'[9] desiring only to commend himself to him who 'searcheth the heart and trieth the reins';[10] and (whether his words are the 'savour of life' or 'of death'[11] to others) to have that witness in himself, 'as of sincerity, as of God, in the sight of God speak we in

[99] See Exod. 4:13.
[1] 2 Sam. 9:8.
[2] Cf. Rev. 14:15.
[3] 2 Cor. 2:16.
[4] See Luke 16:2.
[5] Cf. Ps. 107:8, etc. (BCP).
[6] Phil. 1:23.
[7] Cf. Ps. 39:1-3.
[8] See Num. 23:23.
[9] 2 Cor. 3:12.
[10] Cf. Jer. 17:10.
[11] 2 Cor. 2:16.

Christ'.[12]—If any man counts this *boasting*, he cannot help it. It is enough that a higher judge standeth at the door.[13]

3. But you may say, 'Why do you talk of the *success* of the gospel in England, which was a Christian country before you was born?' Was it indeed? Is it so at this day? I would explain myself a little on this head also.

And, (1), none can deny that the people of England in general are *called* Christians. They are *called* so, a few only excepted, by others, as well as by themselves. But I presume no man will say that the *name* makes the *thing*, that men *are* Christians barely because they are *called* so. It must be, (2), allowed that the people of England, generally speaking, have been *christened* or baptized. But neither can we infer: these were once *baptized*, therefore they *are Christians* now. It is, (3), allowed, that many of those who were once *baptized*, and are *called Christians* to this day, *hear* the Word of God, attend *public prayers*, and partake of the *Lord's Supper*. But neither does this prove that they *are Christians*. For notwithstanding this some of them live in open sin; and others (though not conscious to themselves of *hypocrisy*, yet) are utter strangers to the *religion of the heart;* are full of pride, vanity, covetousness, ambition; of hatred, anger, malice, or envy; and consequently are no more *scriptural Christians* than the open drunkard or common swearer.

Now these being removed, where are the Christians from whom we may properly term England a 'Christian country'? The men who have the mind which was in Christ,[14] and who walk, as he also walked?[15] Whose inmost soul is renewed after the image of God, and who are outwardly holy, as he who hath called them is holy? There are doubtless a few such to be found. To deny this would be *want of candour*. But how few! How thinly scattered up and down! And as for a Christian, visible church, or a body of Christians, visibly united together, where is this to be seen?

> Ye different sects, who all declare,
> 'Lo! Here is Christ,' or 'Christ is there!'
> Your stronger proofs *divinely* give,
> And *show* me, where *the Christians* live![16]

[12] 2 Cor. 2:17.

[13] See Jas. 5:9.

[14] See Phil. 2:5.

[15] See 1 John 2:6.

[16] Charles Wesley, st. 9 of 'Primitive Christianity', appended to *An Earnest Appeal* (1743—see 11:91 in this edn.), an extract being reproduced as Hymn 16 in *A Collection of Hymns* (1780—see 7:99, ver. 6, in this edn.).

And what use is it of, what good end does it serve, to term England a 'Christian country'? (Although 'tis true most of the natives are *called* Christians, have been *baptized*, frequent the *ordinances;* and although a real Christian is here and there to be found, 'as a light shining in a dark place'.)[17] Does it do any honour to our great Master among those who are not *called* by his name? Does it recommend Christianity to the Jews, the Mahometans, or the avowed heathens? Surely no one can conceive it does. It only makes Christianity stink in their nostrils. Does it answer any *good end* with regard to those on whom this worthy name is called? I fear not; but rather an exceeding bad one. For does it not keep multitudes easy in their *heathen practice?* Does it not make or keep still greater numbers satisfied with their *heathen tempers?* Does it not directly tend to make both the one and the other imagine that they *are* what indeed they *are not?* That they *are* 'Christians', while they are utterly without Christ and without God in the world?[18]—To close this point: If men are not Christians till they are renewed after the image of Christ, and if the *people of England* in general are not thus renewed, why do we term them so? 'The God of this world hath *long* blinded their hearts.'[19] Let us do nothing to increase that blindness, but rather labour to recover them from that 'strong delusion',[20] that they may no longer 'believe a lie'.[21]

4. Let us labour to convince all mankind that to be a real Christian is to love the Lord our God with all our heart, and to serve him with all our strength; to love our neighbour as ourselves,[22] and therefore do unto every man as we would he should do unto us.[23] Nay, you say: 'Had you confined yourselves to these great points, there would have been no objection against your doctrine. But the doctrines you have distinguished yourselves by . . . are not the love of God and man, but many false and pernicious errors.'[z]

I have again and again, with all the plainness I could, declared what our constant doctrines are, whereby we are 'distin-

[z] [Church, *Farther Remarks*,] p. 104.

[17] Cf. 2 Pet. 1:19.
[18] Eph. 2:12.
[19] Cf. 2 Cor. 4:4.
[20] 2 Thess. 2:11.
[21] Ibid.
[22] See Luke 10:27, etc.
[23] See Matt. 7:12, etc.

guished'—only from heathens, or nominal Christians, not from any that worship God in spirit and in truth.[24] Our main doctrines, which include all the rest, are three, that of repentance, of faith, and of holiness. The first of these we account, as it were, the porch of religion; the next, the door; the third is religion itself.

That repentance, or conviction of sin, which is always previous to faith (either in a higher or lower degree, as it pleases God) we describe in words to this effect:

> When men *feel* in themselves the heavy burden of sin, see damnation to be the reward of it, behold with the eye of their mind the horror of hell, they tremble, they quake, and are inwardly touched with sorrowfulness of heart, and cannot but accuse themselves, and open their grief unto Almighty God, and call unto him for mercy. This being done seriously, their mind is so occupied, partly with sorrow and heaviness, partly with an earnest desire to be delivered from this danger of hell and damnation, that all desire of meat and drink is laid apart, and loathing of all worldly things and pleasure cometh in place. So that nothing then liketh them more than to weep, to lament, to mourn, and both with words and behaviour of body to show themselves weary of life.[25]

Now permit me to ask, What if before you had observed that these were the very words of our own church, one of *your* acquaintance or parishioners had come and told you that ever since he heard a sermon at the Foundery he 'saw damnation' before him, and 'beheld with the eye of his mind the horror of hell'? What if he had 'trembled and quaked', and been so taken up, 'partly with sorrow and heaviness, partly with an earnest desire to be delivered from the danger of hell and damnation', as to 'weep, to lament, to mourn, and both with words and behaviour to show himself weary of life'? Would you have scrupled to say, Here is another 'deplorable instance' of the 'Methodists driving men to distraction'! See into what 'excessive terrors, frights, doubts, and perplexities, they throw weak and well-meaning men! Quite oversetting their understandings and judgments, and making them liable to all these miseries.'[26]

I dare not refrain from adding one plain question, which I beseech you to answer, not to me, but to God. Have you ever experienced this *repentance* yourself? Did you ever 'feel in yourself that heavy burden of sin'? Of sin in general; more

[24] John 4:23-24.

[25] Homilies, 'Of Fasting, Pt. I', quoted also in *A Farther Appeal*, Pt. I, VII.12 (11:196-97 in this edn.).

[26] Cf. Church, *Remarks*, p. 69.

especially, inward sin? Of pride, anger, lust, vanity? Of (what is all sin in one) that carnal mind which is enmity, essential enmity against God?[27] Do you know by experience what it is to 'behold with the eye of the mind the horror of hell'? Was *your mind* ever so 'taken up, partly with sorrow and heaviness, partly with an earnest desire to be delivered from this danger of hell and damnation, that even all desire of meat and drink' was taken away, and you 'loathed all worldly things and pleasure'?—Surely if you had known what it is to have the 'arrows of the Almighty'[28] thus 'sticking fast in you'[29] you could not so lightly have condemned those who now cry out, 'The pains of hell come about me; the sorrows of death compass me, and the overflowings of ungodliness make me afraid.'[30]

5. Concerning the gate of religion (if it may be allowed so to speak), the true, Christian, saving faith, we believe it implies abundantly more than an assent to the truth of the Bible. 'Even the devils believe that Christ was born of a virgin; that he wrought all kind of miracles; that for our sakes he suffered a most painful death, to redeem us from death everlasting. These articles of our faith the very devils believe, and so they believe all that is written in the Old and New Testament. And yet for all this faith they be but devils. They remain still in their damnable estate, lacking the very true, Christian faith.

'The right and true Christian faith is, not only to believe that the Holy Scriptures and the articles of our faith are true, but also to have a sure trust and confidence, to be saved from everlasting damnation through Christ.'[31] Perhaps it may be expressed more clearly thus, 'a sure trust and confidence which a man hath in God, that by the merits of Christ his sins are forgiven, and he reconciled to the favour of God'.[32]

For giving this account of Christian faith (as well as the preceding account of repentance, both which I have here also purposely described in the very terms of the Homilies) I have been again and again, for near these eight years past, accused of *enthusiasm;* sometimes by those who spoke to my face, either in

[27] Rom. 8:7.
[28] Job 6:4.
[29] Cf. Ps. 38:2.
[30] Ps. 18:3, 4*a* (BCP).
[31] Homilies, 'Of Salvation, Pt. III', as quoted in *An Earnest Appeal,* §9 (11:68-69 in this edn.).
[32] Ibid., also quoted in §59 of *An Earnest Appeal.* Wesley's favourite definition; cf. above, p. 53.

conversation, or from the pulpit, but more frequently by those who chose to speak in my absence; and not seldom from the press. I wait for those who judge this to be enthusiasm to bring forth their strong reasons. Till then I must continue to account all these the words of truth and soberness.

6. Religion itself (I choose to use the very words wherein I described it long ago) we define: 'The loving God with all our heart, and our neighbour as ourselves, and in that love abstaining from all evil, and doing all possible good to all men.'[33] The same meaning we have sometimes expressed a little more at large, thus:

> Religion we conceive to be no other than love: the love of God and of all mankind; the loving God with all our heart[34] and soul and strength, as having first loved us, as the fountain of all the good we have received, and of all we ever hope to enjoy; and the loving every soul which God hath made, every man on earth, as our own soul.
>
> This love we believe to be the medicine of life, the never-failing remedy for all the evils of a disordered world, for all the miseries and vices of men. Wherever this is, there are virtue and happiness, going hand in hand. There is humbleness of mind, gentleness, long-suffering, the whole image of God, and at the same time, a peace that passeth all understanding, and joy unspeakable, full of glory:
>
> Eternal sunshine of the spotless mind;
> Each prayer accepted, and each wish resigned;
> Desires composed, affections ever even;
> Tears that delight, and sighs that waft to heaven.[35]
>
> This religion we long to see established in the world, a religion of love, and joy, and peace; having its seat in the heart, in the inmost soul, but ever showing itself by its fruits, continually springing forth, not only in all innocence—for love worketh no ill to his neighbour—but likewise in every kind of beneficence, spreading virtue and happiness all around it.[36]

If this can be proved by Scripture or reason to be enthusiastic or erroneous doctrine, we will then plead guilty to the indictment of 'teaching error and enthusiasm'. But if this be the genuine religion of Christ, then will all who advance this charge against us be found false witnesses before God[37] in the day when he shall judge the earth.[38]

7. However, with regard to the *fruits* of our teaching, you say,

[33] For this definition, with its allusions to Deut. 6:5, etc.; Lev. 19:18, etc.; 1 Thess. 5:22; and Gal. 6:10, see *A Farther Appeal*, Pt. I, III.2 (11:120 in this edn.).

[34] Orig., 'hearts', corrected in *Works* (1772).

[35] *Works* (1772), omits this quotation from Matthew Prior's 'Charity', *ll.* 5-8, which is present in *An Earnest Appeal.*

[36] *An Earnest Appeal,* §§2-4, with minor variations (11:45-46 in this edn.).

[37] See 1 Cor. 15:15.

[38] See Ps. 96:13; Acts 17:31.

'It is to be feared, the numbers of serious men who have been perplexed and deluded are much greater than the numbers of notorious sinners who have been brought to repentance and good life.'[a] 'Indeed, if you could prove . . . that the Methodists were in general very wicked people before they followed you, and that all you have been teaching them is the love of God and their neighbour, and a care to keep his commandments, which accordingly they have done since, you would . . . stop the mouths of any adversaries at once. But . . . we have great reason to believe that the generality of the Methodists, before they became so, were serious, regular, well-disposed people.'[b]

If the question were proposed, 'Which are greater, the numbers of serious men who have been perplexed and deluded, or of notorious sinners who have been brought to repentance and good life' by these preachers throughout England within seven years, it might be difficult for you to fix the conclusion. For England is a place of wide dimensions; nor is it easy to make a satisfactory computation unless you confine yourself within a smaller compass. Suppose then we were to contract the question, in order to make it a little less unwieldly?[39] We will bound our inquiry, for the present, within a square of three or four miles. It may be certainly known by candid men both what has been and what is now done within this distance. And from hence they may judge of those fruits elsewhere, which they cannot be so particularly informed of.

Inquire then, 'Which are greater, the numbers of serious men perplexed and deluded by these teachers, or of notorious sinners brought to repentance and good life', within the Forest of Kingswood? Many indeed of the inhabitants are nearly as they were, are not much better or worse for their preaching—because the neighbouring clergy and gentry have successfully laboured to deter them from hearing it. But between three and four hundred of those who would not be deterred are now under the care of those preachers. Now, what number of these were 'serious Christians' before? Were fifty? Were twenty? Were ten? Peradventure there might five such be found.[40] But 'tis a question

[a] [Church, *Farther Remarks*,] p. 113. [b] [Ibid.,] p. 103.

[39] Orig., 'unweildly', reproduced also in *Works* (1772). It seems clear that Wesley did intend the rare 'unwieldly', not its more familiar synonym, 'unwieldy' (see *OED*).

[40] Wesley seems deliberately to have patterned this passage on Abraham's plea for the few righteous men in Sodom, Gen. 18:23-32.

whether there could or no. The remainder were gross, open sinners, common swearers, drunkards, sabbath-breakers, whoremongers, plunderers, robbers, implacable, unmerciful, wolves and bears in the shape of men. Do you desire instances of more 'notorious sinners' than these? I know not if Turkey or Japan[41] can afford them. And what do you include in 'repentance and good life'? Give the strictest definition thereof that you are able, and I will undertake, these once notorious sinners shall be weighed in that balance, and not found wanting.[42]

8. Not that all the Methodists (so called) 'were very wicked people before they followed us'. There are those among them, and not a few, who are able to stop the boasting of those that despise them, and to say, 'Whereinsoever any of you is bold, I am bold also.'[43] Only they 'count all these things but loss, for the excellency of the knowledge of Christ Jesus'.[44] But these we found, as it were, when we sought them not. We went forth to 'seek that which was lost'[45] (more eminently lost); 'to call' the most flagrant, hardened, desperate 'sinners to repentance'.[46] To this end we preached in the Horse Fair at Bristol, in Kingswood, in Newcastle; among the colliers in Staffordshire, and the tinners in Cornwall; in Southwark, Wapping, Moorfields, Drury Lane, at London.[47] Did any man ever pick out such places as these in order to find 'serious, regular, well-disposed people'? How many such might then be in any of them I know not. But this I know, that four in five of those who are now with us were not of that number, but were wallowing in their blood[48] till God by us said unto them, *live*.

Sir, I willingly put the whole cause on this issue: What are the *general consequences* of this preaching? Are there more *tares* or *wheat?*[49] More *good men destroyed* (that is the proper question) or *wicked men saved?* The last place where we began constant preaching is a part of Wiltshire and Somersetshire, near Bath.

41 This is one of the very few references to Japan in Wesley's writings (cf. *A Letter to the Rev. Dr. Free*, §10). Probably he mentions it here just as an example of a heathen country (as is frequently the case with Turkey in Christian writing).

42 See Dan. 5:27.

43 2 Cor. 11:21.

44 Phil. 3:8.

45 Cf. Luke 15:4, etc.

46 Matt. 9:13, etc.

47 Orig. omits 'at', supplied in *Works* (1772).

48 Cf. 2 Sam. 10:12.

49 See Matt. 13:25, etc.

Now let any man inquire at Rode,[50] Bradford,[51] Wraxall,[52] or among the colliers at Coleford:[53] (1). What kind of people were those, 'before they followed these men'? (2). What are the *main doctrines* they have been teaching for this twelvemonth? (3). *What effect* have these doctrines upon their followers? What manner of lives do they lead now? And if you do not find, (1), that three in four of these were two years ago notoriously wicked men; (2), that the main doctrines they have heard since were, 'Love God and your neighbour, and carefully keep his commandments;'[54] and (3), that they have since exercised themselves herein, and continue so to do; I say, if you or any reasonable man who will be at the pains to inquire does not find this to be an unquestionable fact, I will openly acknowledge myself an enthusiast, or whatsoever else you shall please to style me.

Only one caution I would give to such an inquirer. Let him not ask the colliers of Coleford: 'Were' not 'the generality' of you, 'before you followed these men', 'serious, regular, well-disposed people'? Were you not 'offended at the profaneness and debauchery of the age'? And was it not 'this disposition which at first made you liable to receive these impressions'?[c] Because if he talk thus to some of those who do not yet 'follow these men', perhaps he will not live to bring back their answer.

9. But will this, or a thousand such instances as this, 'stop the mouths of adversaries at once'? O sir, would one expect such a thought as this in one that had read the Bible? What if you could convert as many sinners as St. Paul himself? Would that 'stop the mouths of all your adversaries'? Yea, if you could convert three thousand at one sermon, still you would be so far from 'stopping all their mouths at once' that the greater part of them would

[c] [Church, *Farther Remarks,*] p. 103.

---

[50] Orig., 'Rhode', between Frome (Somerset) and Bradford-on-Avon (Wiltshire). JWJ first records Wesley's preaching here on Sept. 23, 1746.

[51] Bradford-on-Avon, which had been one of Wesley's regular preaching centres since 1739.

[52] Orig., 'Rexal', apparently either South Wraxall, four miles east of Bath, or North Wraxall, seven miles north, neither of which does Wesley name in his *Journal,* though he may well have visited one or both, the *Journal* being by no means exhaustive, even for the dates which it mentions.

[53] Wesley first records visiting Coleford in Somerset on Jan. 31, 1745, and preached at the laying of the foundation stone for a preaching-house there on Feb. 3, 1746, when 'the colliers fell down amid unhewn stones and mortar'. Nehemiah Curnock, ed., *The Journal of the Rev. John Wesley,* 8 vols. (London, 1938), 3:161n.

[54] Church, *Farther Remarks,* p. 103.

'gnash upon' you 'with their teeth',[55] and cry, 'Away with such a fellow from the earth.'[56]

I never therefore expect to 'persuade the world', the majority of mankind, that I 'have been' for some years 'advancing nothing' but what has a clear immediate connection with 'the true knowledge and love of God'; that God hath been pleased to use me, a weak, vile worm, in 'reforming' many of my fellow-sinners, and making them, even at this day, living witnesses of 'inward and pure religion'; and that many of these, 'from living in all sin, are quite changed, are become' so far 'holy that', though they are not 'free from all sin', yet no sin hath dominion over them.[57] And yet I do firmly believe, 'it is nothing but downright prejudice to deny or oppose any of these particulars.'[d]

'Allow Mr. Wesley', you say, 'but these few points, and he will defend his conduct . . . beyond exception.'—That is most true. If I *have* indeed 'been advancing nothing but the true knowledge and love of God'; if God has made me an 'instrument' in 'reforming' many sinners, and bringing them to 'inward and pure religion'; and if many of these continue 'holy' to this day, and 'free from all' wilful sin, then may I, even I, use those awful words, 'He that despiseth me, despiseth him that sent me.'[58] But I never expect the world to allow me one of these points. However, I must go on, as God shall enable me. I must lay out whatsoever he entrusts me with (whether others will believe I do it or no), in advancing the true Christian knowledge of God, and the love and fear of God among men; in reforming (if so be it please him to use me still) those who are yet without God in the world;[59] and in propagating inward and pure religion, righteousness, peace, and joy in the Holy Ghost.[60]

10. But you believe I 'only corrupt those who were good Christians before, teaching them to revile and censure their neighbours, and to abuse the clergy, notwithstanding all their meekness and gentleness, as I do myself.'[61] 'I must declare' (say you) 'we have in general answered your pretence with all

[d] [Church, *Farther Remarks*,] Preface, p. v.

---

[55] Acts 7:54.
[56] Acts 22:22.
[57] See Rom. 6:14.
[58] Luke 10:16.
[59] Eph. 2:12.
[60] Rom. 14:17.
[61] This is presumably given as a quotation from Church's *Remarks*, or *Farther Remarks*, but the exact wording is not found in either treatise.

meekness and temper; . . . the railing and reviling has been chiefly on the side of the Methodists.'[e]

Your first charge ran thus: 'How have such abuses as these been thrown out by you . . . against our . . . regular clergy, not the highest or the worthiest excepted!'[f]—I answered: 'I am altogether clear in this matter, as often as it has been objected. Neither do I desire to receive any other treatment from the clergy than they have received from me to this day.'[g]

You reply: (1). 'One instance of your misrepresenting and injuring a preacher of our church I mentioned.'[h] Mentioned? Well. But did you *prove* it was an 'injury' or 'misrepresentation'? I know not that you once attempted it. (2). You next quote part of a letter from the third *Journal*[i] wherein (according to your account) 'the most considerable of our clergy are abused, and at once accused in a very gross manner.'[j] Set down the whole paragraph, and I will prove that this also is naked truth, and no abuse at all. You say, (3), 'you approved' of Whitefield's 'railing against the clergy'—i.e., I say, 'Mr. Whitefield preached, concerning the "Holy Ghost, which all who believe are to receive"; not without a just, though severe censure of those who preach as if there were no Holy Ghost.'[k] Nor is this *railing*, but melancholy *truth*. I have myself heard several preach in this manner. (4). You cite my words, 'Woe unto you, ye blind leaders of the blind! How long will ye pervert the right ways of the Lord.'[62]—And add, 'I appeal to yourself, whether you did not design this reflection against the clergy in general who differ from you?'[63] No more than I did against Moses and Aaron. I expressly specify whom I design: 'Ye who tell the mourners in Zion, much religion hath made you mad.' You say, (5) (with a N.B.), 'All the clergy who differ from you, you style so, p. 82, in which and the foregoing page you causelessly slander them as "speaking of our own holiness . . . as that for the sake of which, on account of which", we are justified before God.'[64]

[e] [Church, *Farther Remarks*,] p. 16.
[f] [Church,] *Remarks*, p. 15.
[g] [Wesley, *Answer*,] p. 30 [II.15].
[h] [*Farther Remarks*,] p. 105.
[i] P. 36 [i.e., JWJ, quoting JW's letter of Dec. 10, 1734, to his father, §21].
[j] [Church, *Farther Remarks*,] p. 106.
[k] *Journal* 3, p. 65 [i.e., July 6, 1739].

---

[62] JWJ, July 15, 1739.
[63] *Farther Remarks*, p. 106.
[64] Ibid., quoting JWJ, Sept. 13, 1739.

Let any serious person read over those pages. I therein 'slander' no man. I speak what I know, what I have both heard and read. The men are alive, and the books are extant. And the same conclusion I now defend touching that *part* of the clergy who preach or write thus, viz., 'If they preach the truth as it is in Jesus, I am found a false witness before God. But if I preach the way of God in truth, then they are blind leaders of the blind.'[65] (6). You quote those words, 'Nor can I be said to intrude into the labours of those who do not labour at all, but suffer thousands of those for whom Christ died to perish for lack of knowledge.'[l] I wrote that letter near Kingswood. I would to God the observation were not terribly true! (7). The first passage you cite from the *Earnest Appeal,*[m] evidently relates to *a few* only among the clergy; and if the charge be true but of one in five hundred it abundantly 'supports my reasoning'. (8). In the next, I address all those, and those only, who affirm that I preach for gain.[n]

You conclude: 'The reader has now before him the manner in which you have been pleased to treat the clergy. . . . And your late sermon . . . is too fresh an instance of . . . the like usage of the universities.'[o]—It is an instance of 'speaking the truth in love'.[66] So I desire all mankind may 'use' me. Nor could I have said less either to the university or the clergy without sinning against God and my own soul.

11. But I must explain myself a little on that practice which you so often term 'abusing the clergy'.[67] I have many times great sorrow and heaviness in my heart on account of these my brethren. And this sometimes constrains me to speak to them, in the only way which is now in my power; and sometimes (though rarely) to speak of them; of a few, not all, in general. In either case I take an especial care, (1), to speak nothing but the truth; (2), to speak this with all plainness; and, (3), with love and in the spirit of

[l] *Journal* 3, p. 69 [i.e., letter to Dr. Henry Stebbing (July 25, 1739), §2].

[m] P. 36 [i.e., §72, quoted in *Farther Remarks*, pp. 106-7, though Church cites pp. 40-41 in the 1st edn., Wesley p. 36 in the 2nd edn.].

[n] P. 47 [i.e., §94, cited from the 1st edn. (p. 54), in p. 107 of Church's *Farther Remarks,* but from the 2nd edn. by Wesley].

[o] [*Farther Remarks,*] p. 107.

---

[65] JWJ, Sept. 13, 1739.

[66] Eph. 4:15.

[67] As in Church's *Farther Remarks*, '§IV. Abuses of the Clergy, etc., considered', pp. 105-10.

meekness.[68] Now if you will call this 'abusing', 'railing', or 'reviling', you must. But still I dare not refrain from it. I must *thus rail, thus abuse* sinners of all sorts and degrees, unless I will perish with them.

When I first read your declaration that our brethren 'in general had treated us with all meekness and temper',[69] I had thoughts of spreading before you a few of the flowers which they have strewed upon us with no sparing hand. But on reflection I judged it better to forbear. Let them die and be forgotten!

As to those of the people called Methodists whom you suppose to 'rail at and abuse the clergy', and to 'revile' and 'censure' their neighbours,[70] I can only say, Which are they? Show me the men. And if it appear that any of those under my care habitually *censure* or *revile* others, whether clergy or laity, I will make them an example, for the benefit of all the rest.

Touching *you*, I believe I was *afraid* without cause. I do not think you advanced a 'wilful untruth'.[71] This was a rash word. I hereby openly retract it, and ask pardon of God and you.

To draw toward a conclusion. Whosoever they are that 'despise me, and make no account of my labours',[72] I know that they are 'not in vain in the Lord',[73] and that I have not 'fought as one that beateth the air'.[74] I still see (and I praise 'the Father of lights, from whom every good and perfect gift descendeth')[75] a continual increase of pure religion and undefiled,[76] of the love of God and man, of the 'wisdom' which is 'pure and peaceable, gentle, and easy to be entreated, full of mercy, and of good fruits'.[77] I see more and more of those 'who before lived in a thorough contempt of God's ordinances, and of all duties, now zealously discharging their duties to God and man, and walking in all his ordinances blameless'.[78] A few indeed I have seen draw back to perdition, chiefly through a fear of being 'righteous overmuch'.[79] And here

[68] See 1 Cor. 4:21.

[69] *Farther Remarks*, p. 16; cf. *Modern Christianity*, §20, pp. 144-45 above.

[70] See *Farther Remarks*, pp. 16, 109-10, etc.

[71] Wesley, *Answer*, II.15; cf. *Farther Remarks*, pp. 107-8.

[72] Cf. Wisd. 5:1.

[73] 1 Cor. 15:58.

[74] Cf. 1 Cor. 9:26.

[75] Cf. Jas. 1:17.

[76] Jas. 1:27.

[77] Jas. 3:17.

[78] Cf. Wesley, *Answer*, III.13.

[79] Eccles. 7:16. Probably a reference to the printed attack by the Rev. Joseph Trapp, *The Nature, Folly, Sin, and Danger of being Righteous Overmuch.* (London, 1739; cf. 11:75n. in this edn.)

and there one has fallen into Calvinism, or turned aside to the Moravians. But I doubt not these 'are in a better state than they were before they heard us. Admit they are in error, yea, and die therein, yet who dares affirm they will perish everlastingly? But had they died in gross sin, we are sure they had fallen into "the fire that never shall be quenched".'[80]

I have now considered, as far as my time would permit (not *everything* in your letter, 'whether of moment or no',[81] but) those points which I conceived to be of the greatest weight. That God may lead us both into all truth, and that we may not drop our love in the pursuit of it, is the continual prayer of,

Reverend sir,
Your Friend and Servant for
Christ's Sake,
John Wesley

June 17, 1746

[80] Wesley, *Answer*, III.13.

[81] See the complaint in Church's *Farther Remarks*, p. 81: 'You leave out what you think fit. . . . Though some of these changes and omissions may be of no consequence, yet others are. . . . I own I was astonished at such unfair treatment when I compared your *Answer* with my *Remarks*.' Wesley had already defended his practice in the Preface to this treatise, §§5-6.

9

GAIR I'R METHODIST

(1748)

AN INTRODUCTORY COMMENT

John Wesley visited Wales almost annually from 1739 onwards, usually for short periods, a total of thirty-five visits, as well as passing through the country on a further eighteen occasions. His Journal *and diary accounts, carefully and attractively edited, are set forth in A. H. Williams,* John Wesley in Wales, 1739–1790 *(Cardiff, University of Wales Press, 1971). On the whole he was well received, though inevitably there was some persecution. He traversed the Isle of Anglesey (en route to Dublin via Holyhead) no fewer than sixteen times, at a period when strong traditional loyalty to the Church of England was being threatened by the growth of evangelical Dissent as well as the disturbing influence of Methodism. Wesley's first journey through Anglesey, in August 1747, was uneventful; he did not preach. On the second occasion, however, snowy weather having delayed the ferry service, he remained for more than a week, preached to crowded congregations in Holyhead, and made preaching visits nearby. The local Anglican clergyman, the Rev. Thomas Ellis, asked him to write a pamphlet to 'advise the Methodists not to leave the Church, and not to rail at their ministers'. Wesley's* Journal *for February 27, 1748, records: 'I sat down immediately and wrote* A Word to a Methodist, *which Mr. E[llis] translated into Welsh, and printed.'*

Although Wesley planned to publish the pamphlet both in Welsh and English, in fact it seems to have been printed twice only, each time in Dublin, each time in Welsh, in 1748 and 1751. For fuller details of these editions see Bibliography, *No. 145. The Welsh text is here transcribed literally, with no attempt to style it in accordance with the principles adopted in this edition for English texts. Frank Baker acknowledges the generous co-operation of Miss Monica Davies of the National Library of Wales in preparing the basic translation into English, and of Mr. A. H. Williams and the Revs. George Lawton and Griffith T. Roberts in helping him to transform this into something as close as possible to Wesley's original manuscript.*

Gair i'r Methodist

1. A dderbyniwch chwi Gyngor? Ai nis derbyniech *Gyngor da*, ie gan un a'ch cafsâei? Pa faint mwy y derbyniwch hynny gan un a gâr eich Eneidiau, fel ei Enaid ei hun?

Fe am gelwir I yn Fethodist fel chwithau. A ydych chwi yn credu fod *Jesu Grist wedi ei wneuthur i ni gan DDUW yn Ddoethineb ac yn Gyfiawnder ac yn Sancteiddrwydd ac yn Brynnedigaeth*, I Cor. 1.30? A ydych chwi yn credu y *cyfiawnheir ni yn rhâd, trwy'r Prynnedigaeth sydd yn Ghrist Jesu*, Rhuf. 3.24? ac mai *trwy Râs*, Grâs yn unig, *yr ydych yn gadwedig trwy Ffydd*, Ephes. 2.8? Yr wyf finneu yn credu'r unrhyw. A ydych chwi yn dal fod *Yspryd DUW yn cyd-tystiolaethu ag Yspryd* pob gwir Gredadyn, ei fod ef yn *blentyn i DDUW*, Rhuf. 8.16? a bod *cariad DUW wedi ei dywallt ynghalonnau'r* cyfryw, ynghyd a chariad holl Ddynol[-]Ryw? Yr ydwyf fi fel chwithau yn cwblgredu mai Gwirionedd DUW yw hyn oll. A ydych chwi yn ei gyfrif *ef*, ac ef yn unig yn wir Gristion, *yn yr hwn y mae y meddwl a oedd yn Ghrist Jesu*, Philip, 2.5, ac a Sydd *yn rhodio megis ac y rhodioff Ef*, I Jo. 2.6? Yna y mae dy Galon di fel fy nghalon inneu: Moes i mi dy law, a bydded ini *ymannog i gariad a gweithredoedd da*, Hebr. 10.24.

2. Attolygaf i chwi gan hynny, er trugareddau DUW, na attalioch y Gwirionedd mewn Anghyfiawnder. *Megis y derbyniafoch Grist Jesu yr Arglwydd, felly rhodiwch ynddo*, Col. 2.6. *Megis y mae y neb a'ch galwodd chwi yn Sanctaidd, byddwch chwithau Sanctaidd ymbôb ymarweddiad*, I Pet. 1.15. Ymogelwch rhag Ffydd ddiffrwyth, farw: Bucheddwch yn attebol i'ch Crediniaeth: Herddwch Efengyl DUW ein Jachawdwr: *Lewyrched eich goleuni ger bron Dynion, fel y gwelont eich gweithredoedd da chwi*, Matt. 5.16, ac y gwyddont na chredasoch yn ofer.

3. A gâf fi fod cyn hyfed arnoch a chynnyg i chwi un neu ddau yn rhagor o Gynghorion peunodol? A dderbyniwch chwi hwynt yn garedig? Pwyswch ac ystyriwch hwynt ger bron yr Arglwydd: Ac os gwelwch eu bod yn rhai cywir a da, yna dilynwch hwynt.

Y mae rhai o honoch gwedi ymwrthod ag *Eglwys Loegr*, yn yr hon eich maethwyd. Yr ydych gwedi ymwrthod a'r Sacrament, a'r Gwasanaeth Eglwysig. Pa'm oedd raid wrth hyn? Gellwch, *heb* ymadael a'r Eglwys, lynu wrth holl wirioneddau mawrion a gogoneddus yr Efengyl: Ac *heb* droi eich cefnau ar na'r Sacrament na'r Gweddiau Eglwysawl, gellwch yn siwr fod yn sanctaidd ymhob ymarweddiad. Pa'm oedd raid i chwi gan hynny ymwrthod a'r Eglwys? Nid wyf yn medru deall hyn.

4. A ddywedwch chwi, 'Yr oedd[1] Pobl yn chwerthin am fy mhen ac yn fy llysenwi, pan awn i'r Eglwys'? Er y gwnelont hynny fyth, cyd-ddygwch a'r peth er mwyn Crist; ac nis gwna mo'r niwed i chwi. 'Eithr hwynt hwy a ddywedant wrthyf, nad oes gennyf ddim a wnelwyf yno, ac a berant imi fyned ymmaith.' Na ruswch yn hynny; gwyddoch yn eich Cydwybod *fod* gennych a wnelych yno. 'Ond yr wyf yn cael gwell cyssur wrth gadw draw.' Geill hynny fod; eithr y mae i chwi fwy bendith i'w chael, pan fyddoch lai eich cyssur; sef pan i'ch enllibir, pan fyddoch yn gofidio dros y sawl nad adwaenont DDUW, pan i'ch trallodir ac i'ch darostyngir ger bron yr Arglwydd.

5. Am hynny, nid oes ymma ddim Rheswm i chwi am ymwrthod a'r Eglwys; eithr y mae i chwi amryw Refymmau cedyrn i'r gwrthwyneb. Canys (1), Ai ni dderbyniasoch chwi fwy nag unwaith Fendith gan DDUW yno, yr amser a fu? (2). Ai ni dderbyniodd amryw rai eraill yr unrhyw, yn y Gweddiau a Swpper yr Arglwydd? Felly eglur yw, na wrthododd DUW mo'r Eglwys; a chan hynny paham y gwrthodech chwi Hi? (3). Os bydd ond dau neu dri yn yr holl Gynnulleidfa a adwaenant DDUW, yno y mae Crist yn eu canol hwynt: A lle y mae Ef, oni ddylei ei wâs ef fod yno hefyd? (4). Onid oedd Ef yno o'r blaen, ewch chwi y rhai a adwaenwch DDUW, a dygwch ei Fendith ef yno gyd a[2] chwi. (5). Os Crist'nogion ydych, chychwi yw *Halen y Ddaiar*, Matt. 5.13. Ond pa fôdd yr helltwch chwi rai eraill, oni ddeuwch i'w plith? Os Crist'nogion ydych, yr ydych megis ychydig lefein, a sydd i lefeinio yr holl does, I Cor. 5.6: Eithr oni chyffyrddwch a'r toes, pa fôdd y lefeinir ef? Ai nid ydis wrth hyn yn diddymmu graslawn fwriad DUW? Yn ola' man, ai nid ydych chwi, wrth ymwrthod a'r Eglwys, yn peri anair i'r gwirioneddau a ddelir neu a broffessir gennych? Je ac yn caledu calonnau pobl yn erbyn y gwirionedd; y rhai, oni b'ai hynny, a'i derbyniasent ef ynghariad yr unrhyw? O meddyliwch am hyn! Os cyfrgollir y rhai'n eu hanwiredd, ai ni bydd eu gwaed ar eich pennau chwi?

[1] 1748, 'Roedd'.
[2] 1748, 'gida'.

6. Eithr onid ydych etto yn canfod *grym* y Rhefymmau hyn yn erbyn eich ymadawiad oddiwrth yr Eglwys, o leiaf mi a attolygaf i chwi, na ddiystyroch ac na ddibrisioch mo'ni, ac na ossioch gynnyg iddi nag Anair nag amharch na llyfenwau: Canys nid yw hynny ddim amgen na *dwyn barn gablaidd* arni, yr hon nis dygei yr Archangel ar Ddiafol ei hun, Jud. 9: Pa faint llai y dygei neb o honom y cyfryw Farn yn erbyn *Eglwys Loegr*, yr hon yr ym yn dal ac yn glynu wrth ei Hathrawiaeth oll, yn caru ei Lyfr Gweddi-gyffredin, ac mewn cymmundeb a pha un y derbyniasom gynnifer o Fendithion gan DDUW?

Je, paham y dirmygech neu y dibrisiech yr *Adeilad* a elwir yn gyffredinol *yr Eglwys*? Y mae'n hoff gennych hyd yn oed y *Ty*, lle yr arferwch ymgyfarfod a'ch Cyfeillion: Ac oni hoffwch chwi y Ty hwnnw, lle y cyfarfuoch mor aml a'ch Cyfaill goreu? Siccr gennyf fod *Dafydd* (er bod ganddo yntef Dy o'r eiddo ei hun) yn hoffi ac yn parchu ie'r *Adeilad*, lle yr arferei ymddangos ger bron DUW: Ac am hynny y llefodd ef mor ddifrifol, *Mor hawddgar yw dy bebyll di, o Arglwydd y lluoedd! Fy enaid a hiraetha, ie ac a flysia am Gynteddau'r Arglwydd!* Ps. 84.1,2.

7. Goddeswch imi roi i chwi un gair o gyngor yn rhagor. *Ymddygwch yn hynaws tuag*[3] at yr Eglwyswyr, ie tuag at y sawl ac nad ydynt yn gyfryw ac y dymuner eu bod, ie tuag at y gwaethaf o honynt: Pe bwriech fod neb rhyw un nid yn unig yn wr anfucheddol, eithr hefyd yn gwrthwynebu y Gwirionedd a ddylei ef ei bregethu; ie pe bwriech ei fod ef yn drwg-siarad[4] yn erchyll, ac hefyd yn difenwi gwasanaethwyr y DUW goruchaf: Etto ai gweddus fyddai i *chwi* dalu drwg am ddrwg, neu senn am Senn? Na atto DUW. Beth bynnag a wnelo *ef*, y mae eich Rheol chwi yn amlwg; *Nac ymddielwch, rai anwyl; onid rhoddwch le i ddigofaint: Canys scrifennedig yw, i mi y mae dial, myfi a dalaf, medd yr Arglwydd*, Rhuf. 12.19.

8. O gweddiwch, a hynny yn ddifrifol, drosto ef, yr *hwn a wnêl niwed i chwi ac a'ch erlidio*, Matt. 5.44. Y scatfydd y meddalhâ DUW ei galon ef wrth hynny: O leiaf gwnâ hyn feddalhâu eich calon eich hun, a'ch gogwyddo i'w gyfarch ef yn barchus ac yn ostyngedig, ie pan fyddo waetha' ei foes tuag[5] attoch chwi. Felly ni *orchfychir di gan ddrygioni, eithr gorchfyga di ddrygioni trwy ddaioni*, Rhuf. 12.21.

[3] 1748, 'tuac', three times in this sentence.
[4] 1748, 'drwg-sariad'.
[5] 1748, 'tuac'.

9. Ond pe bwriech fod neb o honynt mo'r ddall a chyndyn a'r Pharisaeaid gynt, fe ddywed ein Harglwydd am y cyfryw, *gadewch iddynt, gadewch iddynt; tywysogion deillion i'r deillion ydynt,* Matt. 15.14. Nis geill dim fod eglurach na'r cyfarwyddiad ymma. Gwiliwch yn wir rhag *barnu gwâs un arall; i'w Arglwydd ei hun y mae efe yn sefyll neu yn syrthio,* Rhuf. 14.4. Bydded anhawdd gennych feddwl, chwaethach dywedyd, fod unrhyw Eglwyswyr yn gyfryw Pharisaeaid: Ond pe *baent* felly, *gadewch iddynt.* Os yw bossibl, na feddyliwch am danynt, oddigerth mewn Gweddi: Na soniwch am danynt o gwbl oll: Os rhydd neb i chwi hanes eu geiriau neu eu gweithredoedd beius, distêwch ef a'r atteb ymma, *gadewch iddynt.* Os digwydd i chwi eich hunan eu gweled neu eu clywed yn gwneuthur neu yn siarad ar *fai,* ymogelwch rhag adrodd y peth wrth arall: Eithr bydded y Gair hwnnw o eiddo ein Harglwydd yn argraphedig yn eich calon, *Beth yw hynny i Ti? Canlyn di Fyfi;* Joan 21.22.

A Word to a Methodist[1]

1. Will you accept advice? Would you not accept *good advice,* yes, even from one who hated you? Will you not then accept it more readily from one who loves your souls even as his own soul?

I am called a Methodist, like you. Do you believe that 'Jesus Christ is made unto us by God wisdom and righteousness and sanctification and redemption'?[a] Do you believe, 'We are freely justified by his grace, through the redemption that is in Christ Jesus'?[b] And that 'by grace', grace alone, 'you are saved, through faith'?[c] I believe the same. Do you hold that 'the Spirit of God beareth witness with the spirit' of every true believer that he is 'a child of God'?[d] And that 'the love of God is shed abroad in the hearts'[2] of such, together with the love of all mankind? Like you I firmly believe that all this is the truth of God. Do you count *him* and him only a true Christian 'in whom is the mind which was also in Christ Jesus',[e] and who 'walks even as he walked'?[f] Then thy heart is as my heart. Give me thy hand,[3] and let us 'provoke unto love and to good works'.[g]

2. Therefore I beseech you, by the mercies of God,[4] do not hinder the truth by unrighteousness. 'As ye have received Christ Jesus the Lord, so walk ye in him.'[h] 'But as he who hath called you is holy, so be ye yourselves also holy, in all manner of conversation.'[i] Beware of a faith which is unfruitful, dead. Live in accordance with your belief. Adorn the gospel of God our Saviour. 'Let your light so shine before men that they may see your good works.'[j] And know that you have not believed in vain.[5]

[a] [Cf.] 1 Cor. 1:30.
[b] Rom. 3:24.
[c] Eph. 2:8.
[d] Rom. 8:16.
[e] Phil. 2:5.
[f] 1 John 2:6.
[g] Heb. 10:24.
[h] Col. 2:6.
[i] 1 Pet. 1:15.
[j] Matt. 5:16.

---

[1] The Welsh is literally translated, 'A Word to the Methodist'.

[2] Rom. 5:5.

[3] Cf. 2 Kgs. 10:15, the text of the famous sermon which Wesley prepared a year later, 'Catholic Spirit' (2:79-95 in this edn.).

[4] Rom. 12:1.

[5] See 1 Cor. 15:2.

3. Let me be so free with you as to offer you one or two more particular advices. Will you receive them kindly? Weigh them and ponder them before the Lord. And if you find them right and proper, then follow them.

Some of you have turned away from the Church of England in which you were brought up; you have forsaken the sacrament and the Church service. Why was this necessary? Without leaving the Church you can adhere to all the great and glorious truths of the gospel; and without turning your backs on either the sacrament or the Church prayers you can certainly be holy in your conduct. Why then did you have to leave the Church? I cannot understand this.

4. Do you say, 'People were making sport of me and calling me nicknames when I went to church'? Even if they were to do this forever, endure it for the sake of Christ, and it will do you no harm. 'But they tell me that I have no right there, and send me away.' Do not be put out by that; you know in your conscience that you *have* a right to be there. 'But I get greater comfort when I stay away.' That may be; but the less your comfort, the greater your blessing, as when you grieve over those who know not God, when you are troubled and humbled before the Lord.

5. Therefore there is no reason for you to leave the Church, but there are many strong reasons to the contrary. For, (1). Have you not received a blessing from God there more than once in times past? (2). Have not many others received the same in the prayers and the Lord's Supper? (3). If there are but two or three in the whole congregation who know God, Christ is there in their midst. And where he is, should not his servant he also?[6] (4). Were he not there formerly, go you, who know God, and take his blessing there with you. (5). If you are Christians you are the 'salt of the earth';[k] but how can you season others unless you move among them.[7] If you are Christians you are like the little leaven which leavens the whole lump.[l] But if you do not come in contact with the dough, how will it be leavened? Are you not in this way making void the gracious purpose of God? Lastly, do you not, by leaving the Church, bring reproach upon the truths you hold or

[k] Matt. 5:13.
[l] 1 Cor. 5:6.

---

[6] See John 12:26.
[7] Cf. Wesley's Sermon 24, 'Sermon on the Mount, IV', I.7 (1:536-37 in this edn.).

profess? Yea, and harden people's hearts against the truth, those who but for that might accept it in love. O think on this! If these are accounted lost in their sins, will not their blood be upon your heads?

6. But if you do not yet perceive the strength of these reasons against your forsaking of the Church, at least, I beg of you, do not scorn or belittle her, do not offer her reproach or dishonour or abuse. For that is no less than bringing a 'railing accusation' against her, which the archangel would not bring against the devil himself.[m] How much less should any one of us bring an accusation against the Church of England, all of whose doctrines we subscribe and hold, whose Common Prayer Book we love, and in communion with whom we have received so many blessings from God.

Yea, why do you despise and belittle even the *building* commonly called 'the church'? You hold dear the *house* where you are used to meet with your friends; and do you not love that house where you meet so often with your best Friend? I am sure that David (though he possessed a house of his own), loved and honoured the *building* where he was accustomed to appear before God, and because of that he cried so earnestly, 'How amiable are thy dwellings, O Lord of Hosts! My soul longeth, yea, even fainteth, for the courts of the Lord!'[n]

7. Allow me to give you one further advice: 'Behave courteously towards the clergy'—yes, even to those who are not as they should be; yea, unto the worst of them—even if you suppose one of them is not only wicked, but also opposes the truth that he should be preaching; yea, even if you suppose him guilty of evil-speaking of the most horrible kind, and that he rebukes the servants of the most high God. Yet even so, is it proper for *you* to render evil for evil, or railing for railing?[8] God forbid![9] Whatever *he* does, your course is clear: 'Dearly beloved, avenge not yourselves, but rather give place unto wrath; for it is written, Vengeance is mine; I will repay, saith the Lord.'[o]

8. O pray for him, and that earnestly, for him 'who despitefully uses you, and persecutes you'.[p] Peradventure God will thereby

[m] Jude 9.
[n] Ps. 84:1-2.
[o] Rom. 12:19.
[p] Matt. 5:44.

[8] 1 Pet. 3:9.
[9] Rom. 3:4, etc.

soften his heart; at least it will soften your own heart, and incline you to greet him with courtesy and humility, yea, even when he behaves at his worst towards you. Thus 'be not overcome of evil, but overcome evil with good.'[q]

9. But even if you suppose one of them to be as blind and as stubborn as the Pharisee of old, our Lord said of such: 'Let them alone, let them alone; they be blind leaders of the blind.'[r] Nothing can be clearer than this rule. Beware lest ye 'judge another man's servant. To his own master he standeth or falleth.'[s] Do not readily think, let alone say, that any clergyman could be such a Pharisee. But if they *be* so, *let them alone.* If possible, think not of them, except in prayer. Do not speak of them at all. If anyone tells you about their conversation or their misdeeds, silence him with this answer, 'Let them alone.' If you yourself should happen to see them doing wrong, or hear them speaking ill, take care not to tell anyone else. Rather let that word of our Lord's be engraved on your heart, 'What is that to thee? Follow thou me.'[t]

[q] Rom. 12:21.
[r] Matt. 15:14.
[s] Rom. 14:4.
[t] John 21:22.

10

A LETTER TO A CLERGYMAN

(1748)

AN INTRODUCTORY COMMENT

The identity of the Irish recipient of this letter cannot be precisely established. Wesley's Journal *for May 3, 1748, shows that he rode the twenty miles from Athlone to Birr, preached in the street, and 'in the evening . . . rode to Ballyboy', where he also preached in the street, 'there being no house that could contain the congregation'. He preached there again in the morning to 'a considerable number' of people, with as great a blessing as he had met anywhere in Ireland. From the opening sentence of the* Letter, *it is clear that on the evening of May 3, almost certainly after preaching, he conversed with a critic of Methodism; and on the following morning wrote the* Letter. *From the evidence of his* Letter to the Rev. Mr. Fleury, *we know that the* Letter *'convinced [this] serious clergyman'.*

The parish of Ballyboy (also known as Kilcormac and Frankford) is in the diocese of Meath, and in the Minute Book of the vestry of that parish the Rev. Nicholas Tubbs appears as curate of Ballyboy and Killaghey from 1733 to 1756, and the Rev. Dan. Jackson as vicar from 1729 to 1755. Either of these clergymen may well have been Wesley's interlocutor on May 3, 1748, and the recipient of his letter of May 4. (I am grateful to Canon R. H. Boyle for telling me of the entry in the Parish Vestry Minutes. Ed.)

The matter at issue between Wesley and the clergyman is the authority, not of John Wesley himself, which was not disputed, but of unordained preachers who could point to the effect of their preaching in the saving of souls. Wesley makes his point by the use of an extended analogy between a physician and a pastor.

The five editions of this work are so alike in styling and in wording as to make the attempt to depict the transmission of the text somewhat uncertain, especially in ascertaining the edition used by Wesley as the prototype for his Works, *though the third of 1766 (in spite of two errors corrected in the* Works*) seems slightly preferable to either of the 1748 editions. For the probable stemma and the very few variants from the edited text (based on the Dublin edn. of 1748) see Appendix A, pp. 541ff. For fuller details see* Bibliography, *No. 146.*

A Letter to a Clergyman

Tullamore, May 4, 1748

Rev. sir,

I have at present neither leisure nor inclination to enter into a formal controversy; but you will give me leave just to offer a few loose hints relating to the subject of last[1] night's conversation.

[I.] 1. Seeing life and health are things of so great importance, it is without question highly expedient that physicians should have all possible advantages of learning and education.

2. That trial should be made of them by competent judges before they practise publicly.

3. That after such trial they be authorized to practise by those who are empowered to convey that authority;

4. And that while they are preserving the lives of others they should have what is sufficient to sustain their own.

5. But supposing a gentleman bred at the university in Dublin, with all the advantages of education; after he has undergone all the usual trials, and then been regularly authorized to practise;

6. Suppose, I say, this physician settles at ——[2] for some years, and yet makes no cures at all; but after trying his skill on five hundred persons cannot show that he has healed one; many of his patients dying under his hands, and the rest remaining just as they were before he came.

7. Will you condemn a man who, having some little skill in physic, and a tender compassion for those who are sick or dying all round him, cures many of those, without fee or reward, whom the doctor could not cure?

8. At least, *did* not (which is the same thing as to the case in hand)—were it only for this reason, because he did not go to them, and they would not come to him.

9. Will you condemn him[3] because he has not learning? Or has not had an university education?

[1] 1771, 'our last'.
[2] Leaving the recipient to supply his own residence, such as Ballyboy.
[3] I.e., of course, the untrained healer of §7.

What then? He cures those whom the man of learning and education cannot cure.

10. Will you object that he is no physician, nor has any authority to practise?

I cannot come into your opinion. I think he is a physician who heals—*medicus est qui medetur*[4]—and that every man has authority to save the life of a dying man.

But if you only mean he has no authority to take fees, I contend not—for he takes none at all.

11. Nay, and I am afraid it will hold, on the other hand, *medicus non est qui non medetur:* I am afraid, if we use propriety of speech, he is no physician who works no cure.

12. 'Oh, but he has taken his degree of Doctor of Physic, and therefore has authority.'

Authority to do what? 'Why, to heal all the sick that will employ him.' But (to waive the case of those who will not employ him—and would you have even *their* lives thrown away?) he does not heal those that do employ him. He that was sick before is sick still, or else he is gone hence, and is no more seen.[5]

Therefore his authority is not worth a rush; for it serves not the end for which it was given.

13. And surely he has not[6] authority to kill them, by hindering another from saving their lives!

14. If he either attempts or desires to hinder him, if he condemns or dislikes him for it, 'tis plain to all thinking men he regards his own fees more than the lives of his patients.

II. Now to apply. 1. Seeing life everlasting and holiness, or health of soul, are things of so great importance, it is highly expedient that ministers, being physicians of the soul, should have all advantages of education and learning.

2. That[7] full trial should be made of them, in all respects, and that by the most competent judges, before they enter on the public exercise of their office, the saving souls from death.[8]

3. That after such trial they be authorized to exercise that

[4] 'He is a physician who heals.' This does not seem to be a Roman proverb, but cf. Ovid (*Ars Amatoria,* ii.647-48): 'Quod medicorum est Promittunt medici.'

[5] See Ps. 39:15 (BCP).

[6] 1772, 'no'; cf. II.13 below.

[7] Here and at the beginning of II.3-4, the prefatory phrase from II.1, 'it is highly expedient', is understood.

[8] See Jas. 5:20.

office by those who are empowered to convey that authority. (I believe, bishops are empowered to do this, and have been so from the apostolic age.)

4. And that those whose souls they save ought meantime to provide them what is needful for the body.

5. But suppose a gentleman bred at the university in Dublin, with all the advantages of education, after he has undergone the usual trials, and been regularly authorized to save souls from death;

6. Suppose, I say, this minister settles at ——[9] for some years, and yet saves no souls at all; saves no sinners from their sins, but after he has preached all this time to five or six hundred persons, cannot show that he has converted one from the error of his ways;[10] many of his parishioners dying as they lived, and the rest remaining just as they were before he came.[11]

7. Will you condemn a man who, having compassion on dying souls, and some knowledge of the gospel of Christ, without any temporal reward saves many from their sins whom the minister could not save?

8. At least *did* not—nor ever was likely to do it, for he did not go to them, and they would not come to him.

9. Will you condemn such a preacher because he has not learning? Or has not had an university education?

What then? He saves those sinners from their sins whom the man of learning and education cannot save.

A peasant being brought before the College of Physicians at Paris, a learned doctor accosted him, 'What, friend, do you pretend to prescribe to people that have agues? Dost thou know what an ague is?'

He replied, 'Yes, sir. An ague is what I can cure and you can't.'

10. Will you object, 'But he is no minister, nor has any authority to save souls'?

I must beg leave to dissent from you in this. I think he is a true, evangelical minister, *διάκονος*, servant of Christ and his church, who *οὕτως διακονεῖ*,[12] so ministers as to save souls from death, to reclaim sinners from their sins; and that every Christian, if he is able to do it, has authority to save a dying soul.

[9] Ballyboy? Cf. I.6 above.

[10] See Jas. 5:20.

[11] In the orig. 'many of his parishioners' begins a new paragraph; but cf. I.6 above, noting the close (and deliberate) parallels of the two sections.

[12] 'thus ministers'.

But if you only mean he has no authority to take tithes, I grant it. He takes none. As he has freely received, so he freely gives.[13]

11. But to carry the matter a little farther, I am afraid it will hold, on the other hand, with regard to the soul as well as the body, *medicus non est qui non medetur*.[14] I am afraid reasonable men will be much inclined to think, he that saves no souls in no minister of Christ.

12. 'Oh, but he is ordained, and therefore has authority.'

Authority to do what? To save all the souls that will put themselves under his care. True. But (to waive the case of them that will not—and would you desire that even those should perish?) he does not, in fact, save them that are under his care. Therefore, what end does his authority serve? He that was a drunkard is a drunkard still. The same is true of the sabbath-breaker, the thief, the common swearer. This is the best of the case. For many have died in their iniquity, and their blood will God require at the watchman's hand.[15]

13. For surely he has no authority to murder souls, either by his neglect, by his smooth if not false doctrine, or by hindering another from plucking them out of the fire,[16] and bringing them to life everlasting.

14. If he either attempts or desires to hinder him, if he condemns or is displeased with him for it, how great reason is there to fear that he regards his own profit more than the salvation of souls!

I am, Rev. sir,
Your affectionate brother,
J. W.

[13] See Matt. 10:8.
[14] Cf. I.10, 11 above.
[15] See Ezek. 33:6.
[16] See Zech. 3:2.

A

Plain Account

OF

The PEOPLE called

METHODISTS.

IN A

LETTER

TO THE

Rev^d. Mr. *PERRONET*.

VICAR of *Shoreham* in *KENT*.

DUBLIN:

Printed by S. POWELL in *Crane-lane*.

M DCC XLIX.

[Price *Three-pence*.]

11

A PLAIN ACCOUNT OF THE PEOPLE CALLED METHODISTS

(1749)

AN INTRODUCTORY COMMENT

The Rev. Vincent Perronet, to whom this letter was addressed, belonged to a family of French refugees from Chateau d'Oex in Switzerland which made its home in England in 1680. He was vicar of Shoreham, Kent, for more than fifty years from 1728, and became a trusted friend of the Wesleys (Charles sometimes called him 'The Archbishop of the Methodists'). John visited him in 1789, when he was ninety-four years of age, and said of him: 'His bodily strength is gone, but his understanding is little impaired, and he appears to have more love than ever.'

His sons, Charles and Edward, became Methodist preachers, and Edward was the author of all but the first verse of the hymn 'All hail the power of Jesus' name'. The brothers, however, came to be in favour of separation from the Church of England and in the end separated from John Wesley.

In this classic account of Methodist societies Wesley narrates the origin and early history of many Methodist institutions, which in many cases started life in the provinces, not least in Bristol, and then were developed in London.

For a summary of the nine editions published during Wesley's lifetime, a stemma illustrating the transmission of the text, and a list of the substantive variant readings from the edited text (based on the 1st edn., Bristol, Farley, 1749), see Appendix A, pp. 541ff. For full bibliographical details see Bibliography, *No. 156.*

A Plain Account of the People called Methodists

In a Letter to the Rev. Mr. Perronet, Vicar of Shoreham in Kent

Rev. and dear sir,

1. Some time since you desired an account of the *whole economy* of the people commonly called Methodists. And you received a true (as far as it went), but not a full account. To supply what I think was wanting in that I send you this account, that you may know not only their *practice* on every head, but likewise the *reasons* whereon it is grounded, the *occasion* of every step they have taken, and the *advantages* reaped thereby.

2. But I must premise, that as they had not the least expectation at first of anything like what has since followed, so they had no previous design or plan at all, but everything arose just as the occasion offered. They saw or felt some impending or pressing evil, or some good end necessary to be pursued. And many times they fell unawares on the very thing which secured the good, or removed the evil. At other times they consulted on the most probable means, following only *common sense* and *Scripture*—though they generally found, in looking back, something in *Christian antiquity*, likewise, very nearly parallel thereto.

I. 1. Above ten years ago my brother and I were desired to preach in many parts of London. We had no view therein but so far as we were able (and we knew God *could* work by whomsoever it pleased him) to *convince* those who would hear what true Christianity was, and to *persuade* them to embrace it.

2. The points we chiefly insisted upon were four. First, that *orthodoxy*,[1] or *right opinions*, is at best but a very slender *part* of

[1] Wesley's definition of orthodoxy at this point is to be noted. He always asserted, of course, the importance of right *doctrine*—orthodoxy in a different sense.

religion, if it can be allowed to be any part of it at all; that neither does religion consist in *negatives*, in bare harmlessness of any kind; nor merely in *externals*, in doing good or[2] using the means of grace, in works of piety (so called) or of charity; that it is nothing short of or different from 'the mind that was in Christ',[3] 'the image of God'[4] stamped upon the heart, inward 'righteousness', attended with the 'peace' of God, and 'joy in the Holy Ghost'.[5] Secondly, that the only way under heaven to this religion is to 'repent, and believe the gospel',[6] or (as the Apostle words it) 'repentance towards God, and faith in our Lord Jesus Christ'.[7] Thirdly, that by this faith, 'he that worketh not, but believeth on him that justifieth the ungodly',[8] is 'justified freely by his grace, through the redemption which is in Jesus Christ'.[9] And, lastly, that 'being justified by faith',[10] we taste of the heaven to which we are going; we are holy and happy; we tread down sin and fear, and 'sit in heavenly places with Christ Jesus'.[11]

3. Many of those who heard this began to cry out that we brought 'strange things to their ears';[12] that this was doctrine which they never heard before, or at least never regarded. They 'searched the Scriptures, whether these things were so',[13] and acknowledged 'the truth as it is in Jesus'.[14] Their hearts also were influenced as well as their understandings, and they determined[15] to follow 'Jesus Christ and him crucified'.[16]

4. Immediately they were surrounded with difficulties. All the world rose up against them. Neighbours, strangers, acquaintance, relations, friends, began to cry out amain: "'Be not

[2] Wesley's MS alteration, 1772, 'good, in'.

[3] Cf. Phil. 2:5.

[4] Gen. 1:27; 9:6, etc., a favourite phrase with Wesley, who was familiar with the place of *imago Dei* ('the image of God') in the whole theological debate. Cf. 11:273n. in this edn.

[5] Rom. 14:17.

[6] Mark 1:16.

[7] Cf. Acts 20:21.

[8] Rom. 4:5.

[9] Rom. 3:24.

[10] Rom. 5:1.

[11] Cf. Eph. 2:6.

[12] Cf. Acts 17:20.

[13] Cf. Acts 17:11.

[14] Cf. Eph. 4:21.

[15] 1784, 1786, omit 'as well . . . determined', apparently through an error in copying from 1764.

[16] 1 Cor. 2:2.

righteous overmuch. Why shouldst thou destroy thyself?"[17] Let not "much religion make thee mad".'[18]

5. One and another and another came to us, asking what they should do, being distressed on every side, as everyone strove to weaken, and none to strengthen their hands in God.[19] We advised them: 'Strengthen you one another. Talk together as often as you can. And pray earnestly with and for one another, that you may "endure to the end and be saved".'[20] Against this advice we presumed there could be no objection, as being grounded on the plainest reason, and on so many Scriptures, both of the Old Testament and the New, that it would be tedious to recite them.

6. They said, 'But we want *you* likewise to talk with us often, to direct and quicken us in our way, to give us the advices which you well know we need, and to pray with us, as well as for us.' I asked, Which of you desires this? Let me know your names and places of abode. They did so. But I soon found, they were too many for me to talk with severally so often as they wanted it. So I told them, 'If you will all of you come together every Thursday, in the evening, I will gladly spend some time with you in prayer, and give you the best advice I can.'[21]

7. Thus arose, without any previous design on either side, what was afterwards called a *Society*—a very innocent name, and very common in London for any number of people *associating* themselves together. The thing proposed in their associating themselves together was obvious to everyone. They wanted to 'flee from the wrath to come',[22] and to assist each other in so doing. They therefore united themselves 'in order to pray together, to receive the word of exhortation, and to watch over one another in love, that they might help each other to work out their salvation'.[23]

8. 'There is one only condition previously required in those

[17] Eccles. 7:16. Dr. Joseph Trapp preached and published a series of sermons against the Methodists upon this text in 1739, which went through several editions and gave rise to other pamphlets (see p. 236 above, n. 79).

[18] Cf. Acts 26:24. This was another frequent charge, which Wesley answered in 1745 in *A Farther Appeal,* Pt. I, VII.11-17 (see 11:196-201 in this edn.).

[19] See 1 Sam. 23:26.

[20] Cf. Matt. 24:13.

[21] This describes the beginning of the Foundery Society in London in [Dec. ?] 1739; cf. above, p. 69. Thursday evening was the time allocated by Wesley's mother to his early education at Epworth.

[22] Matt. 3:7; Luke 3:7.

[23] *General Rules,* §2, p. 69 above.

who desire admission into this Society, "a desire to flee from the wrath to come, and to be saved from their sins".[24] But wherever this desire is fixed in the soul, it will be shown by its fruits. It is therefore expected of all who continue therein that they should continue to evidence their desire of salvation.'

First, By doing no harm, by avoiding evil in every kind—especially that which is most generally practised.

(Such as, the taking the name of God in vain; the profaning the day of the Lord; drunkenness; fighting, quarrelling, brawling; the buying or selling *uncustomed* goods; the doing to others as we would not they should do unto us; uncharitable or unprofitable conversation, particularly speaking evil of magistrates or ministers.)

Secondly, By doing good, by being in every kind merciful after their power; as they have opportunity doing good of every possible sort, and as far as it is possible to all men:

By all possible *diligence* and *frugality*, that the gospel be not blamed.

By submitting to bear the reproach of Christ, to be as 'the filth and offscouring of the world', and looking that men should 'say all manner of evil of them falsely, for their Lord's sake'.

Thirdly: By[25] attending upon all the ordinances of God:

Such as, the public worship of God, the Supper of the Lord, private prayer, searching the Scriptures, and fasting or abstinence.

They now likewise agreed that as many of them as had opportunity would meet together every Friday, and spend the dinner hour in crying to God, both for each other and for all mankind.[a]

9. It quickly appeared that their thus uniting together answered the end proposed therein. In a few months the far greater part of those who had begun to 'fear God and work righteousness',[26] but were not united together, grew faint in their

[a] See the rules of the United Societies. [The last paragraph of §8 is a footnote or addendum to the earlier ones; it does not appear in the *General Rules* of the United Societies. The 'agreement' refers to intercession days modelled on those which he had met among the Moravians at Ijsselstein (June 17, 1738) and Marienborn (July 15, 1738). Wesley's letter to James Hutton of May 28, 1739, shows that he was then holding 'intercession days', which were also the occasions for reading letters describing the experiences of witnessing Christians, especially missionaries. The Conferences from 1744 onwards made arrangements for such monthly occasions. For the monthly letter days cf. also V, pp. 265-66 below.]

---

[24] Ibid., §4. The edn. in Wesley's *Works* omits 'and' (as does the orig. *General Rules*), and also the following summary of §§4-6, which varies from the original in several respects, as well as being abridged.

[25] Orig. (in error), 'Be'.

[26] Cf. Acts 10:35.

minds, and fell back into what they were before. Meanwhile the far greater part of those who were thus united together continued 'striving to enter in at the strait gate',[27] and to 'lay hold on eternal life'.[28]

10. Upon reflection I could not but observe, This is the very thing which was from the beginning of Christianity. In the earliest times those whom God had sent forth 'preached the gospel to every creature'.[29] And the *οἱ ἀκροαταὶ*,[30] the body of hearers, were mostly either Jews or heathens. But as soon as any of these were so convinced of the truth as to forsake sin and seek the gospel salvation, they immediately joined them together, took an account of their names, advised them to watch over each other, and met these *κατηχοῦμενοι*[31] (catechumens, as they were then called) apart from the great congregation, that they might instruct, rebuke, exhort, and pray with them and for them, according to their several necessities.

11. But it was not long before an objection was made to this, which had not once entered into my thought: 'Is not this making a schism? Is not the joining these people together, *gathering churches out of churches?*'[32]

It was easily answered, If you mean only 'gathering people out of buildings called churches', it is. But if you mean dividing Christians from Christians, and so destroying Christian fellowship, it is not. For, (1), these were not Christians before they were thus joined. Most of them were barefaced heathens. (2). Neither are they Christians from whom you suppose them to be divided. You will not look at me in the face and say they are. What! Drunken Christians? Cursing and swearing Christians? Lying Christians? Cheating Christians? If these are Christians at all, they are *devil Christians* (as the poor Malabarians[33] term them).

[27] Luke 13:24.

[28] 1 Tim. 6:12, 19.

[29] Cf. Mark 16:15; Col. 1:23.

[30] Rom. 2:13, 'the hearers'.

[31] Cf. Rom. 2:18, etc.

[32] Probably this is an allusion to the 'gathered' (i.e., Independent and Baptist) churches of an earlier period.

[33] Wesley's father had offered himself as a missionary to the East Indies, and his mother had dedicated herself to a pastoral ministry in the winter of 1711/12 through the influence of a book found in her husband's library, *Propagation of the Gospel in the East, being an Account of the Success of two Danish Missionaries lately sent to the East Indies for the Conversion of the Heathens in Malabar.* This was translated by Anton Wilhelm Böhme (1673–1722)

(3). Neither are they divided any more than they were before, even from these wretched 'devil Christians'. They are as ready as ever to assist them, and to perform every office of real kindness toward them.[34] (4). If it be said, 'But there are some true Christians in the parish, and you destroy the Christian fellowship between these and them,' I answer, That which never existed cannot be destroyed. But the fellowship you speak of never existed. Therefore it cannot be destroyed.[35] Which of those true Christians had any such fellowship with these? Who watched over them in love? Who marked their growth in grace? Who advised and exhorted them from time to time? Who prayed with them and for them as they had need? This, and this alone is Christian fellowship. But alas! Where is it to be found? Look east or west, north or south; name what parish you please. Is this Christian fellowship there? Rather, are not the bulk of the parishioners a mere rope of sand?[36] What Christian connexion is there between them? What intercourse in spiritual things? What watching over each others' souls? What bearing of one another's burdens?[37] What a mere jest is it, then, to talk so gravely of *destroying* what never was! The real truth is just the reverse of this: we *introduce* Christian fellowship where it was *utterly destroyed*. And the fruits of it have been peace, joy, love,[38] and zeal for every good word and work.[39]

from the letters home of two German Pietists trained at Halle, Bartholomaeus Ziegenbalg (1683–1710) and Heinrich Plütschau (1678–1747). John Wesley may well have borrowed his father's copy of the first edn. of 1709 or the second of 1711 to read in Oxford in May 1730. On pp. xvii-xviii of the latter ('. . . the true character of a missionary')—quoted from a 1665 publication—he read: 'I have often heard the natives . . . say thus in broken English . . . : "Christian religion, devil religion; Christian much drunk; Christian much do wrong, much beat, much abuse others."' John Wesley found echoes among the American Indians in Georgia, represented by Tomochichi: 'Christian much drunk. Christian beat men, Christian tell lies, devil Christian! Me no Christian' (see 11:189 in this edn.).

[34] The 1749 Dublin edn. here adds: 'And they (generally speaking) continue to join in the same public worship they did before.'

[35] 1786 omits, 'But the . . . be destroyed'.

[36] Wesley made frequent use of the proverb about making a rope of sand, found in the Latin of Erasmus, in Burton's *Anatomy of Melancholy* (1621), and Butler's *Hudibras* (1662); cf. *Oxford Dictionary of English Proverbs*. Cf. a parallel passage in the *Farther Appeal*, Pt. III.[16] (11:301 in this edn.), though he there speaks of Christian discipline rather than fellowship: 'Are you the rector of a parish? . . . Does this order obtain there? Nothing less. Your parishioners are a rope of sand.'

[37] See Gal. 6:2.

[38] See Gal. 5:22.

[39] 2 Thess. 2:17.

II. 1. But as much as we endeavoured to watch over each other, we soon found some who did not 'live the gospel'.[40] I do not know that any hypocrites were crept in, for indeed there was no temptation. But several grew cold, and gave way to the sins which had long easily beset them.[41] We quickly perceived, there were many ill consequences of suffering these to remain among us. It was dangerous to others, inasmuch as all sin is of an infectious nature. It brought such a scandal on their brethren as exposed them to what was not properly 'the reproach of Christ'.[42] It laid a stumbling-block in the way of others, and caused the truth to be evil spoken of.[43]

2. We groaned under these inconveniences long, before a remedy could be found. The people were scattered so wide in all parts of the town,[44] from Wapping to Westminster, that I could not easily see what the behaviour of each person in his own neighbourhood was. So that several disorderly walkers did much hurt before I was apprised of it.

3. At length, while we were thinking of quite another thing, we struck upon a method for which we have cause to bless God ever since. I was talking with several of the society in Bristol concerning the means of paying the debts there,[45] when one stood up and said, 'Let every member of the society give a *penny* a week till all are paid.' Another answered, 'But many of them are poor, and cannot afford to do it.' 'Then', said he, 'put eleven of the poorest with me, and if they can give anything, well. I will call on them weekly, and if they can give nothing, I will give for them as well as for myself. And each of you, call on eleven of your neighbours weekly; receive what they give, and make up what is wanting.'[46] It was done. In a while some of these informed me,

[40] Cf. 1 Cor. 9:14.

[41] See Heb. 12:1.

[42] Heb. 11:26. Here (as occasionally), Wesley indicates that he thinks of this phrase as a quotation, not by displaying it in italics—his usual method for scriptural quotations—but by using capital letters, even for 'The', for the two first edns., though only for 'Reproach' in subsequent edns.; in 1772 this also was dropped, so that the fact of its being a quotation was lost.

[43] See 2 Pet. 2:2.

[44] I.e., London, which is the main source of Wesley's descriptions and examples, especially for the Rev. Vincent Perronet of Shoreham, who lived not far away, though Methodism in Bristol, Leeds, Newcastle, and elsewhere developed similar institutions—and indeed, as in the present instance, first pioneered them.

[45] Caused by the building of the first New Room in 1739.

[46] See JWJ, Feb. 15, 1742. The instigator of this fund was Captain Foy, for whom see *Proceedings of the Wesley Historical Society* (1901), 3:64-65, and p. 528 below.

they found such and such an one did not live as he ought. It struck me immediately. 'This is the thing, the very thing we have wanted so long.' I called together all the *Leaders* of the *Classes* (so we used to term them and their companies), and desired that each would make a particular inquiry into the behaviour of those whom he saw weekly. They did so. Many disorderly walkers were detected. Some turned from the evil of their ways. Some were put away from us. Many saw it with fear, and rejoiced unto God with reverence.

4. As soon as possible the same method was used in London and all other places. Evil men were detected, and reproved. They were borne with for a season. If they forsook their sins, we received them gladly; if they obstinately persisted therein, it was openly declared that they were not of us. The rest mourned and prayed for them, and yet rejoiced that, as far as in us lay, the scandal was rolled away from the Society.

5. It is the business of a Leader

(1) To see each person in his class once a week at the least; in order
To inquire how their souls prosper;
To advise, reprove, comfort, or exhort, as occasion may require.
To receive what they are willing to give toward the relief of the poor.

(2) To meet the Minister and the stewards of the Society in order:
To inform the minister of any that are sick, or of any that are disorderly and will not be reproved.
To pay to the stewards what they have received of their several classes in the week preceding.[47]

6. At first they visited each person at his own house; but this was soon found not so expedient. And that on many accounts. (1). It took up more time than most of the leaders had to spare. (2). Many persons lived with masters, mistresses, or relations, who would not suffer them to be thus visited. (3). At the houses of those who were not so averse, they had often no opportunity of speaking to them but in company. And this did not at all answer the end proposed, of exhorting, comforting, or reproving. (4). It frequently happened that one affirmed what another denied. And this could not be cleared up[48] without seeing them both together. (5). Little misunderstandings and quarrels of various kinds frequently arose among relations or neighbours, effectually to

[47] See *General Rules*, 1743, §3, rearranged and abridged.
[48] 'up' is added only in Wesley's hand in his own copy of his *Works*, 1772.

remove which it was needful to see them all face to face. Upon all these considerations it was agreed that those of each class should meet all together. And by this means a more full inquiry was made into the behaviour of every person. Those who could not be visited at home, or no otherwise than in company, had the same advantage with others. Advice or reproof was given as need required, quarrels made up, misunderstandings removed. And after an hour or two spent in this labour of love, they concluded with prayer and thanksgiving.

7. It can scarce be conceived what advantages have been reaped from this little prudential regulation. Many now happily experienced that Christian fellowship of which they had not so much as an idea before. They began to 'bear one another's burdens',[49] and 'naturally'[50] to 'care for each other'.[51] As they had daily a more intimate acquaintance with, so they had a more endeared affection for each other. And 'speaking the truth in love, they grew up into him in all things which is the head, even Christ; from whom the whole body, fitly joined together, and compacted by that which every joint supplied, according to the effectual working in the measure of every part, increased unto the edifying itself in love.'[52]

8. But notwithstanding all these advantages, many were at first extremely averse to meeting thus. Some, viewing it in a wrong point of light, not as a *privilege* (indeed an invaluable one) but rather a *restraint*, disliked it on that account, because they did not love to be restrained in anything. Some were *ashamed* to speak before company. Others honestly said, 'I don't know why; but I *don't like it*.'

9. Some objected, 'There were no such meetings when I came into the society first. And why should there now? I don't understand these things, and this changing one thing after another continually.' It was easily answered, 'Tis pity but they had been at first. But we knew not then either the need or the benefit of them. Why we use them you will readily understand if you read over the *Rules* of the Society. That with regard to these little prudential helps we are continually changing one thing after another, it is not a weakness or fault (as you imagine) but a

[49] Gal. 6:2.
[50] Phil. 2:20.
[51] Cf. 1 Cor. 12:25; Phil. 2:20.
[52] Cf. Eph. 4:15-16—'up' not present in the first two edns.

peculiar advantage which we enjoy. By this means we declare them all to be merely prudential, not essential, not of divine institution. We prevent, so far as in us lies, their growing formal and dead. We are always open to instruction, willing to be wiser every day than we were before, and to change whatever we can change for the better.

10. Another objection was, 'There is no Scripture for this, for classes and I know not what.' I answer, (1). There is no Scripture *against* it. You cannot show one text which forbids them. (2). There is much Scripture *for* it, even all those texts which enjoin the substance of those various duties, whereof this is only an indifferent circumstance, to be determined by reason and experience. (3). You seem not to have observed that the Scripture, in most points, gives only *general* rules, and leaves the *particular* circumstances to be adjusted by the common sense of mankind. The Scripture (for instance) gives that *general* rule, 'Let all things be done decently and in order.'[53] But common sense is to determine, on *particular* occasions, what order and decency require. So, in another instance, the Scripture lays it down as a *general* standing direction, 'Whether ye eat or drink, or whatsoever ye do, do all to the glory of God.'[54] But it is common prudence which is to make the application of this, in a thousand *particular* cases.

11. 'But these', said another, 'are all *man's inventions*.' This is but the same objection in another form. And the same answer will suffice for any reasonable person. These are man's inventions. And what then? That is, they are methods which men have found, by reason and common sense, for the more effectually applying several scriptural rules, couched in general terms, to particular occasions.

12. They spoke far more plausibly than these who said, 'The thing is well enough in itself. But the *leaders* are insufficient for the work. They have neither gifts nor grace for such an employment.' I answer, (1). Yet such leaders as they are, it is plain God has blessed their labour. (2). If any of these is remarkably wanting in gifts or grace, he is soon taken notice of and removed. (3). If you know any such, tell it to *me*, not to others, and I will endeavour to exchange him for a better. (4). It may be hoped, they

[53] 1 Cor. 14:40.
[54] 1 Cor. 10:31.

will all be better than they are, both by experience and observation, and by the advices given them by the minister every Tuesday night, and the prayer (then in particular) offered up for them.

III. 1. About this time I was informed that several persons in Kingswood frequently met together at the school, and (when they could spare the time) spent the greater part of the night in prayer and praise and thanksgiving. Some advised me to put an end to this. But upon weighing the thing thoroughly, and comparing it with the practice of the ancient Christians, I could see no cause to forbid it. Rather, I believed, it might be made of more general use. So I sent them word, I designed to watch with them on the Friday nearest the full moon, that we might have light thither and back again. I gave public notice of this the Sunday before, and withal, that I intended to preach; desiring they and they only would meet me there who could do it without prejudice to their business or families. On Friday abundance of people came. I began preaching between *eight* and *nine;* and we continued till a little beyond the noon of night, singing, praying, and praising God.[55]

2. This we have continued to do once a month ever since, in Bristol, London, and Newcastle, as well as Kingswood. And exceeding great are the blessings we have found therein. It has generally been an extremely solemn season, when the Word of God sunk deep into the heart, even of those who till then knew him not. If it be said, 'This was only owing to the novelty of the thing (the circumstance which still draws such multitudes together at those seasons), or perhaps to the awful silence of the night,' I am not careful to answer in this matter. Be it so. However, the impression then made on many souls has never since been effaced. Now, allowing that God did make use either of the novelty or any other indifferent circumstance in order to bring sinners to repentance, yet they are brought. And herein let us rejoice together.

3. Nay, may I not put the case farther yet? If I can probably conjecture that, either by the novelty of this *ancient* custom, or by any other indifferent circumstance, it is in my power to 'save a soul from death, and hide a multitude of sins',[56] am I clear before

[55] For what was almost certainly this first Methodist Watch-night see JWJ, Mar. 12, 1742.

[56] Jas. 5:20.

God if I do it not? If I do not snatch that brand out of the burning?[57]

IV. 1. As the society increased I found it required still greater care to separate the precious from the vile. In order to this I determined, at least once in three months, to talk with every member myself, and to inquire at their own mouths, as well as of their leaders and neighbors, whether they grew in grace and in the knowledge of our Lord Jesus Christ.[58] At these seasons I likewise particularly inquire whether there be any misunderstandings or differences among them, that every hindrance of peace and brotherly love may be taken out of the way.

2. To each of those of whose seriousness and good conversation I found no reason to doubt I gave a testimony under my own hand, by writing their name on a *ticket* prepared for that purpose; every ticket implying as strong a recommendation of the person to whom it was given as if I had wrote at length, 'I believe the bearer hereof to be one that fears God and works righteousness.'[59]

3. Those who bore these tickets (these *σὺμβολα* or *tesserae*,[60] as the ancients termed them, being of just the same force with the *συστατικαὶ*,[61] 'commendatory letters', mentioned by the Apostle), wherever they came, were acknowledged by their brethren, and received with all cheerfulness. These were likewise of use in other respects. By these it was easily distinguished when the society were to meet apart, who were members of it and who not. These also supplied us with a quiet and inoffensive method of removing any disorderly member. He has no new ticket at the quarterly visitation (for so often the tickets are changed); and hereby it is immediately known that he is no longer of this community.

V. The thing which I was greatly afraid of all this time, and which I resolved to use every possible method of preventing, was a

[57] See Amos 4:11. [58] See 2 Pet. 3:18. [59] Cf. Acts 10:35.

[60] Both the Greek *symbolon* and the Latin *tessera* were material objects with a special shape or marking which indicated some abstract value, a *token* of that value, whether material or immaterial. The Greek word came to refer especially to Christian belief, so that 'symbol' was a synonym for 'creed', and from it developed the verb 'symbolize'. The Roman *tessera* was used not only for numbered dice in gambling but also for small square tablets bearing military watchwords or private messages.

[61] Cf. 2 Cor. 3:1.

narrowness of spirit, a party zeal, a being straitened in our own bowels;[62] that miserable bigotry which makes many so unready to believe that there is any work of God but among themselves. I thought it might be a help against this frequently to read, to all who were willing to hear, the accounts I received from time to time of the work which God is carrying on in the earth, both in our own and other countries, not among us alone, but among those of various opinions and denominations. For this I allotted one evening in every month.[63] And I find no cause to repent my labour. It is generally a time of strong consolation to those who love God, and all mankind for his sake; as well as of breaking down the partition walls which either the craft of the devil or the folly of men has built up; and of encouraging every child of God to say (O when shall it once be?), 'Whosoever doth the will of my Father which is in heaven, the same is my brother and sister and mother.'[64]

VI. 1. By the blessing of God upon their endeavors to help one another, many found the pearl of great price.[65] Being justified by faith, they had 'peace with God, through our Lord Jesus Christ'.[66] These felt a more tender affection than before to those who were partakers of like precious faith; and hence arose such a confidence in each other that they poured out their souls into each other's bosom. Indeed they had great need so to do; for the war was not over, as they had supposed. But they had still to wrestle both with flesh and blood, and with principalities and powers;[67] so that temptations were on every side; and often temptations of such a kind as they knew not how to speak in a class, in which persons of every sort, young and old, men and women, met together.

2. These therefore wanted some means of closer union: they wanted to pour out of their hearts without reserve, particularly with regard to the sin which did still 'easily beset'[68] them, and the temptations which were most apt to prevail over them. And they were the more desirous of this when they observed, it was the

[62] See 2 Cor. 6:12.

[63] For these monthly letter days cf. the monthly intercession days, I.8 above (p. 257).

[64] Cf. Matt. 12:50.

[65] Matt. 13:46.

[66] Rom. 5:1.

[67] See Eph. 6:12.

[68] Heb. 12:1.

express advice of an inspired writer, 'Confess your faults one to another, and pray one for another, that ye may be healed.'[69]

3. In compliance with their desire I divided them into smaller companies; putting married or single men, and married or single women together.[70] The chief rules of these *Bands* (i.e., little companies; so that old English word signifies) run thus:

In order to 'confess our faults one to another, and pray one for another that we may be healed', we intend:

(1). To meet once a week, at the least.

(2). To come punctually at the hour appointed.

(3). To begin with singing or prayer.

(4). To speak, each of us in order, freely and plainly, the true state of our soul, with the faults we have committed in thought, word, or deed, and the temptations we have felt since our last meeting.

(5). To desire some person among us (thence called a *Leader*) to speak *his* own state first, and then to ask the rest in order as many and as searching questions as may be, concerning their state, sins, and temptations.[71]

4. That their design in meeting might be the more effectually answered, I desired all the men bands to meet me together every Wednesday evening, and the women on Sunday; that they might receive such particular instructions, and such[72] exhortations, as from time to time might appear to be most needful for them; that such prayers might be offered up to God as their necessities should require; and praise returned to the Giver of every good gift[73] for whatever mercies they had received.

5. In order to increase in them a grateful sense of all his mercies, I desired that one evening in a quarter all the men in band,[74] on a second, all the women, would meet; and on a third, both men and women together; that we might together 'eat bread' (as the ancient Christians did) 'with gladness and singleness of heart'.[75] At these *love-feasts* (so we termed them, retaining the

[69] Jas. 5:16.

[70] In describing bands as an offshoot of the institution of classes Wesley's memory fails him (as frequently), for he had introduced this development of the Moravian 'choirs' as early as 1738, four years earlier than the classes. The discovered value of their later function in the society-class-band nexus seems to have blinded him to their historical origins.

[71] An abridgement from the *Rules of the Band Societies* (pp. 77-79 above).

[72] In his own copy of his *Works* (1772), as well as in the errata, Wesley (surely in error) deleted 'such', which was the catchword at the foot of p. 212, and also occurred at the head of p. 213.

[73] See Jas. 1:17.

[74] 'in band' is added only in Wesley's *Works* (1772).

[75] Cf. Acts 2:46.

name, as well as the thing, which was in use from the beginning) our food is only a little plain cake and water. But we seldom return from them without being fed, not only with 'the meat which perisheth', but with 'that which endureth to everlasting life'.[76]

6. Great and many are the advantages which have ever since flowed from this closer union of the believers with each other. They prayed for one another, that they might be healed of the faults they had confessed—and it was so. The chains were broken, the bands were burst in sunder,[77] and sin had no more dominion over them. Many were delivered from the temptations out of which till then they found no way to escape. They were built up in our most holy faith. They rejoiced in the Lord more abundantly. They were strengthened in love, and more effectually provoked to abound in every good work.

7. But it was soon objected to the *bands* (as to the *classes* before), 'These were not at first. There is no Scripture for them. These are man's works, man's building, man's invention.' I reply, as before, these are also prudential helps, grounded on reason and experience, in order to apply the general rules given in Scripture according to particular circumstances.

8. An objection much more boldly and frequently urged, is that 'all these bands are mere popery'. I hope I need not pass a harder censure on those (most of them at least) who affirm this, than that they talk of they know not what, that they betray in themselves the most gross and shameful ignorance. Do not they yet know that the only popish confession is the confession made by a single person to a priest? (And this itself is in no wise condemned by our Church; nay, she recommends it in some cases.) Whereas that *we* practise is the confession of several persons conjointly, not to a priest, but to each other. Consequently, it has no analogy at all to popish confession. But the truth is, this is a stale objection, which many people make against anything they do not like. It is all popery out of hand.

VII. 1. And yet while most of these who were thus intimately joined together went on daily from faith to faith, some fell from the faith, either all at once, by falling into known, wilful sin, or gradually and almost insensibly, by giving way in what they called

[76] Cf. John 6:27.
[77] See Nahum 1:13.

little things—by sins of omission, by yielding to heart sins, or[78] by not watching unto prayer.[79] The exhortations and prayers used among the believers did no longer profit these. They wanted advice and instructions suited to their case; which as soon as I observed, I separated them from the rest, and desired them to meet me apart on Saturday evenings.

2. At this hour all the hymns, exhortations, and prayers are adapted to their circumstances; being wholly suited to those who *did* see God, but have now lost the light of his countenance; and who mourn after him, and refuse to be comforted till they know he has healed all their backsliding.[80]

3. By applying both the threats and promises of God to these real (not nominal) *penitents,* and by crying to God in their behalf, we endeavoured to bring them back to the great Shepherd and Bishop of their souls;[81] not by any of the fopperies of the Roman Church, although in some measure countenanced by antiquity. In prescribing hair-shirts and bodily austerities we durst not follow even the ancient Church; although we had unawares, both in dividing *οἱ πιστοί,*[82] the believers, from the rest of the society, and in separating the *penitents* from them, and appointing a peculiar service for them.

VIII. 1. Many of these soon recovered the ground they had lost. Yea, they rose higher than before;[83] being more watchful than ever, and more meek and lowly, as well as stronger in the faith that worketh by love.[84] They now outran the greater part of their brethren, continually walking in the light of God, and having fellowship with the Father, and with his Son, Jesus Christ.[85]

2. I saw it might be useful to give some advices to all those who thus continued in the light of God's countenance, which the rest of their brethren did not want, and probably could not receive. So I desired a small number of such as appeared to be in this state to spend an hour with me every Monday morning. My design was,

[78] 1784, 1786, omit 'by sins . . . sins, or'.
[79] See 1 Pet. 4:7.
[80] See Hos. 14:4.
[81] See 1 Pet. 2:25.
[82] Acts 10:45.
[83] All printed edns. have 'rose the higher for their fall', which Wesley thus altered in his own copy of the *Works* (1772).
[84] See Gal. 5:6.
[85] 1 John 1:3.

not only to direct them now to *press after perfection;* to exercise their every grace, and improve every talent they had received; and to incite them to love one another more, and to watch more carefully over each other; but also to have a *select company* to whom I might unbosom myself on all occasions, without reserve, and whom I could propose to all their brethren as a pattern of love, of holiness, and of all good works.[86]

3. They had no need of being encumbered with many rules, having the best rule of all in their hearts. No peculiar directions were therefore given to them, excepting only those three:

First, let nothing spoken in this society be spoken again. (Hereby we had the more full confidence in each other.)

Secondly, every member agrees to submit to his minister in all indifferent things.

Thirdly, every member will bring once a week all he can spare toward a common stock.

4. Everyone here has an equal liberty of speaking, there being none greater or less than another. I could say freely to these, when they were met together, 'Ye may all prophesy one by one' (taking that word in its lower sense), 'that all may learn and all may be comforted.'[87] And I often found the advantage of such a free conversation, and that 'in a multitude of counsellors there is safety.'[88] Any who is inclined so to do is likewise encouraged to pour out his soul to God. And here especially we have found that the effectual fervent prayer of a righteous man availeth much.[89]

IX. 1. This is the plainest and clearest account I can give of the *people* commonly called Methodists. It remains only to give you a short account of those who *serve* their brethren in love. These[90] are *Leaders* of classes and bands (spoken of before), *Assistants, Stewards, Visitors* of the sick, and *Schoolmasters.*

2. In the third part of the *Appeal* I have mentioned how we were[91] led to accept of *Lay Assistants.*[92] Their office is, in the absence of the minister:

[86] This 'select society' seems first to have been formed in London on Dec. 25, 1743 (see Wesley's MS membership records for the London Foundery).

[87] 1 Cor. 14:31.

[88] Cf. Prov. 24:6.

[89] Jas 5:16.

[90] All edns., except that of Dublin (1749), and the errata and Wesley's MS revisions in his *Works* (1772), read 'There'.

[91] All edns., except the *Works* (1772), read 'are'.

[92] *A Farther Appeal,* Pt. III, III.8-[16] (11:294-301 in this edn.).

(1). To expound every morning and evening.

(2). To meet the United Society, the Bands, the Select Society, and the Penitents once a week.

(3). To visit the Classes (London and Bristol excepted) once a month.[93]

(4). To hear and decide all differences.

(5). To put the disorderly back on trial, and to receive on trial for the Bands or Society.

(6). To see that the Stewards, the Leaders, and the schoolmasters faithfully discharge their several offices.

(7). To meet the Leaders of the Bands and Classes weekly, and the Stewards, and to overlook their accounts.

3. I think he must be no fool who has *gifts* sufficient for these things; as neither can he be void of the *grace* of God who is able to observe the rules of an Assistant, which are these that follow:

(1). Be diligent. Never be unemployed a moment. Never be triflingly employed. Never *while away* time. Neither spend any more time at any place than is strictly necessary.

(2). Be serious. Let your motto be, Holiness to the Lord. Avoid all lightness, as you would avoid hell-fire.

(3). Believe evil of no one. If you *see* it done, well; else take heed how you credit it. Put the best construction on everything. You know the judge is always supposed to be on the prisoner's side.

(4). Speak evil of no one. Else *your* word especially would eat as doth a canker. Keep your thoughts within your own breast till you come to the person concerned.

(5). Tell everyone what you think wrong in him, and that plainly and as soon as may be. Else it will fester in your heart. Make all haste to cast the fire out of your bosom.

(6). Do nothing as a gentleman. You have no more to do with this character than with that of a dancing-master. You are the servant of all. Therefore,

(7). Be ashamed of nothing but sin: not of hewing wood, if time permit, or drawing water.

(8). Take no money of anyone. If they give you food when you are hungry, or clothes when you need them, it is good; but not silver or gold. Let there be no pretence to say we grow rich by the gospel.

(9). Be punctual. Do everything exactly at the time.

(10). Act in all things, not according to your own will, but as *a son in the gospel*.[94]

[93] Dublin, 1749, 'To visit the Classes'; *Works* (1772), 'To visit the Classes once a quarter.' Wesley seems here to transcribe from his revised MS Minutes for 1744, §72(3), in Vol. 10 of this edn.

[94] These are selected and abridged from Wesley's 'Twelve Rules of a Helper' (or 'an Assistant'), first promulgated in the MS Minutes of the 1744 Conference (see Vol. 10 in this edn.), omitting rules 3 ('Touch no woman. . . .') and 10 ('Contract no debt without my knowledge').

4. In order to try these, before we can receive them as *Assistants*, we inquire,

First: Do they know in whom they have believed? Have they the love of God in their hearts? Do they desire to seek nothing but God? And are they holy in all manner of conversation?

Secondly: Have they *gifts*, as well as *grace*, for the work? Have they (in some tolerable degree) a clear, sound understanding? Have they a right judgment in the things of God? Have they a just conception of salvation by faith? And has God given them any degree of utterance? Can they express themselves justly, readily, clearly?

Thirdly: Have they *success?* Do they not only so speak (where trial was made) as to convince and affect the hearers? But have any received remission of sins by their means? A clear and lasting sense of the love of God?[95]

5. Those in whom these three marks undeniably concur we gladly receive to assist us in the work. And these we advise:

(1) Always to rise at four. (2). From four to five in the morning, and from five to six in the evening, partly to use meditation and private prayer, partly to read the Scripture, partly some close practical book of divinity, such as *The Life of God in the Soul of Man, The Christian Pattern,* Bishop Beveridge's *Private Thoughts,* Mr. Law's practical *Works,* Dr. Heylin's *Devotional Tracts, The Life of Mr. Halyburton* and of *Mr. de Renty.* (3). From six in the morning till twelve, to read, in order, slowly, and with much prayer, Bishop Pearson on the Creed, Bishop Fell on the Epistles, Mr. Boehm's and Mr. Nalson's *Sermons,* Mr. Pascal's *Thoughts,* Cave's and Fleury's *Primitive Christianity,* and Echard's *Ecclesiastical History.*[96]

And we believe, they who throughly digest only these few books will *know* enough to save both their own souls and those that hear them.[97]

X. 1. But long before this I felt the weight of a far different care, namely, care of temporal things.[98] The quarterly subscriptions amounted at a mean computation to above three hundred pounds a year. This was to be laid out, partly in repairs, partly in other necessary expenses, and partly in paying debts. The weekly contributions fell little short of eight pounds a week, which was to

[95] This is reproduced almost exactly from the disciplinary section of the MS Minutes of the 1746 Conference, *Q.* 8 (May 14), for which see Vol. 10 in this edn.

[96] Reproduced with several variations from the answer to *Q.* 15 of the MS Minutes of the 1746 Conference (see Vol. 10 in this edn.).

[97] See 1 Tim. 4:16. The whole of IX.3-5 is omitted from Wesley's *Works* (1772).

[98] All edns. read 'of "far different care, namely, care of temporal things' (with an extraneous quotation mark), except that of Dublin (1749), the errata and Wesley's MS revisions to the *Works* (1772), which substitute 'a' for the quotation mark, and the *Works* themselves, which simply omit the quotation mark.

be distributed as everyone had need.[99] And I was expected to take thought for all these things. But it was a burden I was not able to bear. So I chose out first one, then four, and after a time seven, as prudent men as I knew, and desired them to take the charge of these things upon themselves, that I might have no encumbrance of this kind.

2. The business of these *Stewards* is:

To manage the temporal things of the Society;

To receive the subscriptions and contributions;

To expend what is needful from time to time;

To send relief to the poor;

To keep an exact account of all receipts and expenses;

To inform the Minister if any of the rules of the society are not punctally observed;

To tell the Assistants[1] in love if they think anything amiss, either in their doctrine or life.

3. The rules of the Stewards are:

(1). Be frugal. Save everything that can be saved honestly.

(2). Spend no more than you receive. Contract no debts.

(3). Have no long accounts. Pay everything within the week.

(4). Give none that asks relief either an ill word or an ill look. Do not hurt them, if you cannot help.

(5). Expect no thanks from man.

4. They met together at six every Thursday morning, consulted on the business which came before them, sent relief to the sick, as every one had need, and gave the remainder of what had been contributed each week to those who appeared to be in the most pressing want. So that all was concluded within the week, what was brought on Tuesday being constantly expended on Thursday. I soon had the pleasure to find that all these temporal things were done with the utmost faithfulness and exactness. So that my cares of this kind were at an end. I had only to revise the accounts, to tell them if I thought anything might be amended, and to consult how deficiencies might be supplied from

[99] As noted above (II.3, 5, pp. 260-61), members of the Bristol classes paid one penny a week towards defraying the debt on the New Room there, and similar contributions in other societies provided a major source of income. As yet no collections were taken in the societies, except once in three months at the distribution of the quarterly class-tickets (see IV.2, p. 265). This seems to have been applied chiefly to the maintenance of the society, while the weekly contributions in general were devoted to 'the relief of the poor' [II.5(1)].

[1] *Works* (1772), 'preachers'.

time to time. For these were frequent and large (so far were we from abundance), the income by no means answering the expenses. But that we might not faint, sometimes we had unforeseen helps, in times of the greatest perplexity. At other times we borrowed, larger or smaller sums. Of which the greatest part has since been repaid. But I owe some hundred pounds to this day. So much have I *gained* by preaching the gospel!

XI. 1. But it was not long before the Stewards found a great difficulty with regard to the sick. Some were ready to perish before they knew of their illness. And when they did know, it was not in their power (being persons generally employed in trade) to visit them so often as they desired.

2. When I was apprised of this, I laid the case at large before the whole society, showed how impossible it was for the Stewards to attend all that were sick in all parts of the town, desired the leaders of classes would more carefully inquire, and more constantly inform them, who were sick, and asked, 'Who among you is willing as well as able to supply their lack of service?'[2]

3. The next morning, many willingly offered themselves. I chose six and forty of them, whom I judged to be of the most tender, loving spirit, divided the town into twenty-three parts, and desired two of them to visit the sick in each division.

4. It is the business of a *Visitor* of the sick:

To see every sick person within his district thrice a week;

To inquire into the state of their souls, and advise them, as occasion may require;

To inquire into their disorders, and procure advice for them;

To relieve them, if they are in want;

To do anything for them which he (or she) can do;

To bring in his accounts weekly to the Stewards.[b]

Upon reflection I saw how exactly in this, also, we had copied after the primitive church. What were the ancient deacons?[3] What was Phebe the deaconess, but such a visitor of the sick?[4]

[b] The leaders now do this [*Works*, 1772].

---

[2] Cf. Wesley's letter from London to his brother Charles, Apr. 21, 1741: 'I am settling a regular method of visiting the sick here. Eight or ten have offered themselves for the work, who are like to have full employment.'

[3] 1 Tim. 3:8-12; cf. Wesley's *Notes*, Vol. 6 in this edn.

[4] Rom. 16:1; cf. Wesley's *Notes* for a description of the deaconesses in the primitive church.

5. I did not think it needful to give them any particular rules, beside these[5] that follow:

(1). Be plain and open in dealing with souls.

(2). Be mild, tender, patient.

(3). Be cleanly in all you do for the sick.[6]

(4). Be not nice.[7]

6. We have ever since had great reason to praise God for his continued blessing on this undertaking. Many lives have been saved, many sicknesses healed, much pain and want prevented or removed. Many heavy hearts have been made glad, many mourners comforted. And the visitors have found from him whom they serve a present reward for all their labour.

XII. 1. But I was still in pain for many of the poor that were sick: there was so great expense, and so little profit. And first I resolved to try whether they might not receive more benefit in the *hospitals*. Upon the trial, we found, there was indeed less expense—but no more good done than before. I then asked the advice of several physicians for them; but still it profited not. I saw the poor people pining away, and several families ruined, and that without remedy.

2. At length I thought of a kind of desperate expedient. 'I will prepare and give them physic myself.' For six or seven and twenty years I had made anatomy and physic the diversion of my leisure hours; though I never properly studied them, unless for a few months when I was going to[8] America, where I imagined I might be of some service to those who had no regular physician among them. I applied to it again. I took into my assistance an apothecary, and an experienced surgeon; resolving at the same time not to go out of my depth, but to leave all difficult and complicated cases to such physicians as the patients should choose.

3. I gave notice of this to the society;[9] telling them that all who

[5] All printed edns., have 'those', which Wesley altered in his own copy of the *Works* (1772) to 'these'.

[6] Cf. Sermons 88, 'On Dress', §5, and 98, 'On Visiting the Sick', II.6, the first known examples of the printed use of the proverb, 'Cleanliness is next to godliness.' See the whole of the latter sermon for Wesley's emphasis upon the need for and practice of sick-visiting (3:249, 392-97 in this edn.).

[7] Apparently over-sensitive in performing distasteful tasks for the sick, a meaning not among the many in *OED* for this chameleon word.

[8] All other edns. except *Works* (1772), 'into'.

[9] Cf. JWJ, Dec. 4, 1746. This is apparently the point from which he reckons the

were ill of *chronical* distempers (for I did not care to venture upon *acute*) might, if they pleased, come to me at such a time; and I would give them the best advice I could, and the best medicines I had.

4. Many came. (And so every Friday since.) Among the rest was one William Kirkman, a weaver, near Old Nichol Street. I asked him, 'What complaint have you?' 'O sir', said he, 'a cough, a very sore cough. I can get no rest day nor night.' I asked, 'How long have you had it?' He replied, 'About threescore years. It began when I was eleven years old.' I was nothing glad that this man should come first; fearing our not curing him might discourage others. However, I looked up to God, and said, 'Take this[10] three or four times a day. If it does you no good, it will do you no harm.' He took it two or three days. His cough was cured, and has not returned to this day.

5. Now let candid men judge, Does humility require me to deny a notorious fact? If not, which is *vanity:* to say, *I*, by my own skill, restored this man to health? or to say, God did it, by his own almighty power? By what figure of speech this is called *boasting* I know not. But I will put no name to[11] such a fact as this. I leave that to the Rev. Dr. Middleton.[12]

6. In five months medicines were occasionally given to above five hundred persons. Several of these I never saw before; for I did not regard whether they were of the Society or not. In that time seventy-one of these, regularly taking their medicines, and following the regimen prescribed (which three in four would not do), were entirely cured, of distempers long thought to be incurable. The whole expense of medicines during this time was (nearly) forty pounds. We continued this ever since, and by the blessing of God, with more and more success.[13]

twenty-six or twenty-seven years of his medical hobby, namely from the beginning of his Oxford career in 1720.

[10] Dublin, 1749, adds 'decoction'.

[11] All other edns., except *Works* (1772), 'on'.

[12] Conyers Middleton (1683–1750), whose *Free Inquiry into the Miraculous Powers which are supposed to have subsisted in the Christian Church* (London, Manby and Cox, 1749), Wesley had attacked in an open letter of Jan. 4-24 (see *Bibliography,* No. 160, and Vol. 13 in this edn.). Wesley suspected that it was Middleton also who criticized the *Plain Account* in an open letter to the *Bath Journal* of Apr. 17, 1749, which Wesley answered in the same periodical on May 27 (see *Bibliography,* No. 166, and *Letters,* 26:358-60 in this edn.).

[13] For other accounts see JWJ, Dec. 4, 1746, which noted that by the time the *Journal* was published (1754) the dispensary became too costly to maintain, and June 6, 1747, which speaks of six hundred patients in six months, and expenses of thirty pounds.

XIII. 1. But I had for some years observed many who, although not sick, were not able to provide for themselves, and had none who took care to provide for them. These were chiefly feeble, aged widows. I consulted with the Stewards how they might be relieved. They all agreed, if we could keep them in one house it would not only be far less expensive to us, but also far more comfortable for them. Indeed we had no money to begin. But we believed he would provide who 'defendeth the cause of the widow'.[14] So we took a lease of two little houses near. We fitted them up so as to be warm and clean. We took in as many widows as we had room for, and provided them with things needful for the body; towards the expense of which I set aside, first, the weekly contributions of the bands, and then all that is[15] collected at the Lord's Supper. It is true this does not suffice. So that we are still considerably in debt, on this account also. But we are persuaded it will not always be so, seeing 'The earth is the Lord's, and the fullness thereof.'[16]

2. In this (commonly called 'The Poorhouse') we have now nine widows, one blind woman, two poor children, two upper servants, a maid and a man. I might add, four or five preachers. For I myself, as well as the other preachers who are[17] in town, diet with the poor on the same food and at the same table. And we rejoice herein as a comfortable earnest of our eating bread together in our Father's kingdom.[18]

3. I have blessed God for this house ever since it began; but lately much more than ever. I honour these widows; for they 'are widows indeed'.[19] So that it is not in vain that, without any design of so doing, we have copied after another of the institutions of the apostolic age. I can now say to all the world, 'Come, and see how these Christians love one another!'[c]

XIV. 1. Another thing which had given me frequent concern was the case of abundance of children. Some their parents could

[c] This has been since dropped for want of support. [This footnote first appeared in 1755—or possibly in the missing edn. 'D'. For the closing quotation, which Wesley elsewhere attributes to Julian the Apostate, but is also found in Tertullian, see Sermon 22, 'Sermon on the Mount, II', III.18 (1:507 in this edn.).]

---

[14] Ps. 68:5 (BCP).

[15] *Works* (1772), 'was'.

[16] Ps. 24:1; 1 Cor. 10:26, 28.

[17] 1749, Bristol and Dublin, 'were'.

[18] See Matt. 26:29; Luke 22:30.

[19] 1 Tim. 5:3.

not afford to put to school. So they remained like 'a wild ass's colt'.[20] Others were sent to school, and learned at least to read and write. But they learned all kind of vice at the same time, so that it had been better for them to have been without their knowledge than to have bought it at so dear a price.

2. At length I determined to have them taught in my own house, that they might have an opportunity of learning to read, write, and cast accounts[21] (if no more) without being under almost a necessity of learning heathenism at the same time. And after several unsuccessful trials I found two such school-masters as I wanted—men of honesty, and of sufficient knowledge, who had talents for, and their hearts in, the work.

3. They have now under their care near sixty children. The parents of some pay for their schooling, but the greater part, being very poor, do not; so that the expense is chiefly defrayed by voluntary contributions. We have of late clothed them, too, as many as wanted. The rules of the school are these that follow:[22]

First, no child is admitted under six years of age.

Second, all the children are[23] to be present at the morning sermon.

Thirdly, they are at school from six to twelve, and from one to five.[d]

Fourthly, they have no play-days.

Fifthly, no child is to speak in school, but to the masters.

Sixthly, the child who misses two days in one week, without leave, is excluded the school.

4. We appointed two stewards for the school also. The business of these is:

To receive the school subscriptions, and expend what is needful.

To talk with each of the masters weekly.

[d] Now they begin later [*Works*, 1772, struck out by Wesley in his own copy].

---

[20] Job 11:12.

[21] Orig., all edns., 'accompts', from the Latin *computare* and French *accompte,* though it was already obsolescent in English.

[22] In his own copy of his *Works* (1772) Wesley added the footnote: 'This also has been dropped for some time.' Thus what follows cannot refer to Kingswood School, founded mainly for boarders in 1748, and maintaining an uninterrupted existence until now (cf. XIV.6 below). The reference must be to one of the schools founded from 1739 onwards for day students, one of which was in the Foundery, London (where Silas Told was one of the masters), and another in the New Room, Bristol.

[23] Only Dublin (1749) and the *Works* (1772) add 'are'.

To pray with and exhort the children twice a week.

To inquire diligently whether they grow in grace and in learning, and whether the rules are punctually observed.

Every Tuesday morning, in conjunction with the masters, to exclude those children that do not observe the said rules.[24]

Every Wednesday morning to meet with, and exhort their parents to train them up at home in the ways of God.

5. An happy change was soon observed in the children, both with regard to their tempers and behaviour. They learned reading, writing, and arithmetic swiftly; at the same time they were diligently instructed in the sound principles of religion, and earnestly exhorted to fear God and work out their own salvation.[25]

6. For an account of the Grammar School in Kingswood I refer you to the tract lately published.[26]

XV. 1. A year or two ago I observed among many a distress of another kind. They frequently wanted, perhaps in order to carry on their business, a present supply of money. They scrupled to make use of a *pawnbroker*. But where to borrow it they knew not. I resolved to try if we could not find a remedy for this also. I went (in a few days) from one end of the town to the other; and exhorted those who had this world's goods to assist their needy brethren. Fifty pounds were contributed.[27] This was immediately lodged in the hands of two Stewards, who attended every Tuesday morning in order to lend to those who wanted any small sum, not exceeding twenty shillings, to be repaid within three months.[e]

2. It is almost incredible, but it manifestly appears from their accounts, that with this inconsiderable sum two hundred and fifty have been assisted within the space of one year. Will not God put it into the heart of some lover of mankind to increase this little stock? If this is not 'lending unto the Lord',[28] what is? O confer not with flesh and blood,[29] but immediately,

[e] We now lend any sum not exceeding five pounds [*Works*, 1772; in Wesley's own copy a cross shows that the footnote should be placed here rather than at the end of section 2 where the dagger was printed].

---

[24] *Works* (1772), errata, and in MS in Wesley's own copy, 'the rules'.

[25] See Phil. 2:12.

[26] This sentence occurs only in the 1749 Dublin edn. and refers to *A Short Account of the School in Kingswood, near Bristol* (Bristol, Farley, 1749), for which see *Bibliography*, No. 162, and Vol. 15 in this edn.

[27] See JWJ, July 17, 1746.

[28] Cf. Prov. 19:17.

[29] See Gal. 1:16.

Join hands with God to make a poor man live.[30]

3. I think, sir, now you know all that I know of this people. You see the nature, occasion, and design, of whatever is practised among them. And, I trust, you may be pretty well able to answer any questions which may be asked concerning them; particularly by those who inquire concerning *my revenue*, and what I do with it all.

4. Some have supposed this was no greater than that of the Bishop of London. But others computed that I received eight hundred a year from Yorkshire only. Now if so, it cannot be so little as ten thousand pounds a year[31] which I receive out of all England!

5. Accordingly a gentleman in Cornwall (the rector of R[edruth])[32] extends the calculation pretty considerably. 'Let me see', said he, 'two millions of Methodists, and each of these paying twopence a week.' If so I must have eight hundred and sixty-six thousand pounds (with some odd shillings and pence) a year.

6. A tolerable competency! But be it more or less, 'tis nothing at all to *me*. All that is contributed or collected in every place is both received and expended by others; nor have I so much as 'the beholding thereof with my eyes'.[33] And so it will be, till I turn Turk or pagan. For I look upon all this revenue, be it what I may, as sacred to God and the poor (out of which, if I want anything, I am relieved even as another poor man). So were originally all ecclesiastical revenues (as every man of learning knows). And the bishops and priests used them only *as such*. If any use them otherwise now, God help them!

7. I doubt not but if I err in this, or any other point, you will pray God to show me his truth. To 'have a conscience void of offence toward God and toward man'[34] is the desire of,

Reverend and dear sir,
Your affectionate brother and servant,
John Wesley

[30] Cf. George Herbert, *The Temple,* 'The Church Porch', ver. 63, *l.* 4, 'Join hands with God to make a man to live.'

[31] Bristol, 1749, omits 'a year'.

[32] The identification is added in Wesley's hand in his own copy of the *Works* (1772). The rector of Redruth in 1749 was the Rev. John Collins, who had been at Queen's College, Oxford (1725–31), while Wesley was there, was instituted at Redruth in 1731, rebuilt the parish church in 1768, and died in 1775.

[33] Cf. Eccles. 5:11.

[34] Cf. Acts 24:16.

12

A SHORT ADDRESS TO THE INHABITANTS OF IRELAND

(1749)

AN INTRODUCTORY COMMENT

The 'late occurrences' of the full title of the Address (dated July 6, 1749) are those described, only a few weeks after they took place, in John Wesley's letters to his brother Charles of May 30, 1749, and June 17, 1749 (pp. 360-65 and 366-72 in Vol. 26 in this ed.). Wesley gives additional details in his Journal, *July 20, 1749 (by which time he had been supplied with depositions from the principal victims of the 'occurrences'), August 1, 1749, and April 14, 1750.*

The course of events was this: On June 2, 1748, two Methodist preachers, Mr. Williams and Mr. Swindells, began to preach in Cork, and were supported by a visit from Charles Wesley, who stayed from August 20 to September 19. Until the following spring the preaching continued without actual interruption, though the clergy and the notables of the city showed their displeasure by sermons and the circulation of pamphlets and rumours and by attaching the name 'Swaddlers' to the preachers and their converts. The hostile clergy included the Rev. John Baily, Rector of Kilcully and Chaplain to the corporation (see Letter *to the Rev. Mr. Baily, pp. 288-314 below).*

In April 1749, Nicholas Butler, once a weaver, now an itinerant ballad-singer, no doubt hired for the purpose by the clergy and notables, collected several gangs of intermingled Roman Catholics and Protestants to insult and threaten the Methodists, hurl dirt and stones at them, and eventually to damage property and inflict bodily harm on the women and children. Butler led the riots, with 'his ballads in one hand and a Bible in the other', denouncing the Methodists as heretics doomed to hell.

Representations were made to the mayor, Daniel Crone, who made professions of willingness to stop the harassment but did precisely nothing. Only when soldiers were present at the preaching was there comparative quiet, and after a few weeks the soldiers were forbidden to be present.

On August 19, eight Methodists were accused before the Grand Jury as 'vagabonds', but they were acquitted, and the Judge declared that all riots were illegal. Peace seems thus to have been restored. This Address, an appeal for toleration in moderate terms, was published while the riots were in full swing.

For a summary of the four editions published during Wesley's lifetime, a stemma illustrating the transmission of the text, and a list of the substantive variant readings from the edited text (based on the 1st edn., Dublin, Powell, 1749), see Appendix A, pp. 541ff. For full bibliographical details, see Bibliography, *No. 167.*

A Short Address to the Inhabitants of Ireland

Occasioned by some late Occurrences

1. There has lately appeared (as you cannot be ignorant) a set of men preaching up and down in several parts of this kingdom who for ten or twelve years have been known in England by the title of 'Methodists'. The vulgar in Ireland term them 'Swaddlers'—a name first given them in Dublin, from one of them preaching on those words, 'Ye shall find the young child wrapped in swaddling clothes, lying in a manger.'

2. Extremely various have been the reports concerning them. Some persons have spoken favourably; but the generality of men treat them in a different manner, with utter contempt, if not detestation; and relate abundance of things in order to prove that they are not fit to live upon the earth.

3. A question then which you may naturally ask is this: In what manner ought a man of religion, a man of reason, a lover of mankind, and a lover of his country to act on this occasion?

4. Before we can properly answer this it should be inquired concerning the persons in question, what they are, what they teach, and what are the effects which are generally observed to attend their teaching.

5. It should first be inquired what they are. And in order to a speedy determination of this, we may set aside whatever will admit of any dispute (as, whether they are good men or bad, rich or poor, fools, madmen, and enthusiasts, or sober rational men).

Now waiving all this, one point is indisputable: it is allowed on all hands, they are men who spend all their time and strength in teaching those doctrines, the nature and consequences whereof are described in the following pages.

6. The doctrines they constantly teach are these: that religion does not consist in *negatives* only, in not taking the name of God in vain, in not robbing or murdering our neighbour, in bare abstaining from evil of any or every kind, but is a *real, positive* thing; that it does not consist in *externals* only, in attending the Church and sacrament (although all these things they approve and recommend), in using all the means of grace, or in works of charity (commonly so called) superadded to works of piety; but that it is properly and strictly a principle within, seated in the inmost soul, and thence manifesting itself by these outward fruits on all suitable occasions.

7. They insist that nothing deserves the name of religion but a virtuous heart, producing a virtuous life—a complication of justice, mercy, and truth, of every right and amiable temper, beaming forth from the deepest recesses of the mind in a series of wise and generous actions.

Compositum ius fasque animo, sanctique recessus
Mentis, et incoctum generoso pectus honesto.[1]

8. These are their constant doctrines. 'Tis true, they occasionally touch on abundance of other things. Thus they frequently maintain that there is an inseparable connection between virtue and happiness; that none but a virtuous (or, as they usually express it, a religious) man can be happy; and that every man is happy in the same proportion as he is truly religious; seeing a contented mind (according to them), a cheerful, thankful, joyous acquiescence in every disposal of that Sovereign Wisdom who governs both heaven and earth, if it be not an essential branch of religion, is, at least, a necessary consequence of it. On all proper occasions they strongly recommend, on the one hand, the most intense love of our country; on the other, the firmest loyalty to our Prince, abstracted from all views of private interest. They likewise take every opportunity of enforcing the absolute necessity of sobriety and temperance; of unwearied

[1] Persius, *Satires*, ii.73-74: 'A heart rightly attuned towards God and man, a mind pure in its inner depths, and a soul steeped in nobleness and honour' (Loeb Classical Library).

industry in the works of our calling; of moral honesty in all its branches, and particularly in the discharge of all relative duties, without which (they say) religion is vain. But all these they recommend on that one, single ground, the love of God and of all mankind; declaring them to be of no avail if they do not spring from this love, as well as terminate and centre therein.

9. Whoever is at the pains of hearing these preachers, or of reading what they have wrote with any degree of attention and impartiality, must perceive that these are their doctrines. And it is equally easy to discern what the effects of their preaching have been. These doctrines they spread wherever they come. They convince many in every place that religion does not consist (as they imagined once) either in negatives or externals, in barely doing no harm, or even doing good, but in the tempers of the heart; in right dispositions of mind towards God and man, producing all right words and actions.

10. And these dispositions of mind are more or less the continual consequence of their preaching (that is, if we may know the tree by its fruits;[2] which is doubtless the most rational way of judging). The lives of many who constantly attend it show that God has wrought a real change in their heart, and that the grand principle of love to God and man already begins to take root therein.

11. Hence those who were before of quite the opposite temper are now generous, disinterested lovers of their country; and faithful, loyal subjects to their Prince, his sacred Majesty King George. They are now sober and temperate in all things, and punctually honest in all their dealings. They are strict in every relative duty, and laborious and diligent in their callings. Notwithstanding the continual discouragement they receive from many who still cry out, 'Ye are idle, ye are idle; therefore ye say, Let us go and serve the Lord.'[3] They are content in every state, whether of plenty or want, and thankful to God and man.

These are plain, glaring, undeniable facts, whereof if any magistrate will be at the trouble to take them, numerous affidavits may be made, in Dublin, Cork, Limerick, and many other places.

But if these things are so, it is easy to conceive in what manner every man of religion, every man of reason, every lover of mankind, every lover of his country, ought to act on this occasion.

[2] See Matt. 12:33; Luke 6:44.

[3] Cf. Exod. 5:17.

12. For, first, ought not every *man of religion*, with all the earnestness of his soul, to praise God, who after so long a night of ignorance and error had overspread our country, has poured light on so many of those that sat in darkness and the shadow of death?[4] Has shown such numbers even of the lowest and most brutish of men wherein true religion lies; has taught them both to lay the right foundation, and to build the whole fabric thereon; has convinced them, 'Other foundation can no man lay, than that which is laid, even Jesus Christ';[5] and, 'The end of the commandment is love,'[6] of the whole commandment or law of Christ, love—the life, the soul, the spirit of religion, the river that makes glad the city of God,[7] the living water continually springing up into everlasting life.[8]

13. Admit that they do not exactly judge right as to some of the appendages of religion; that you have a clearer and juster conception than they of several things pertaining to the beauty of holiness; yet ought you not to bless God for giving these outcasts of men to see at least the essence of it? Nay, to be living witnesses of the substance of religion, though they may still mistake as to some of the circumstances of it?

14. Ought not every *man of reason* (whether he assents, or no, to that system of opinions commonly called Christianity) sincerely and heartily to rejoice in the advancement of solid, rational virtue? In the propagation, not of this or that set of opinions, but of genuine, pure morality? Of disinterested benevolence, of tender affections, to the whole of human race? Ought you not to be glad that there are any instruments found, till others appear who are more equal to the task, whose one employment it is (from whatever motive) to diffuse generous honesty throughout the land?

15. Allow that in doing this they have some particularities of opinion (for *humanum est errare et nescire*)[9] or some little, odd

[4] See Luke 1:79.

[5] Cf. 1 Cor. 3:11.

[6] 1 Tim. 1:5.

[7] See Ps. 46:4.

[8] See John 4:14.

[9] A saying which Wesley quotes four times in his *Sermons*. Although he apparently believed 'et nescire' to be an integral part of a Latin proverb, the complete phrase seems to be compounded from several sources, including Cicero, Seneca, and Augustine. See espec. Sermon 39, 'Catholic Spirit', I.4 (2:79-95 in this edn.). Wesley translates it variously, and there paraphrases: 'to be ignorant of many things, and to mistake in some, is the necessary condition of humanity.'

customs which you do not conceive to be grounded upon strict reason. Yet so long as neither those customs nor those opinions prevent the advancement of that great end, ought you not as a reasonable man to rejoice in the increase of solid virtue? Especially when you consider that they do not impose their own opinions on other men; that (whatever they are), they think and let think, and condemn no man barely for his opinion; neither blame you for not regarding those little prudential rules which many observe by their own full and free consent.[10]

16. Ought not every *lover of mankind* to have something more than a common regard for those who both labour and suffer reproach in order to promote that love in every place? And to remove every method of speaking or acting, every temper, contrary to love? Ought not you who are truly *moral men* (a lovely and venerable character) to have some value for those who spend and are spent[11] to advance genuine morality? Who spare no pains, if by any means they may induce any of their countrymen, in any part of the nation, to practise justice, mercy, and truth[12] in all their intercourse with each other? To behave in every circumstance and relation according to those eternal rules, invariably observing the royal law, 'Thou shalt love thy neighbour as thyself';[13] and, 'Whatsoever ye would that men should do unto you, even so do unto them.'[14]

17. If you are a lover of mankind, must you not sympathize with those who suffer evil in various kinds for this very thing, because they do good to mankind, looking for no reward on this side heaven?[15] As to the idle tale of their laying up treasures on earth,[16] it neither agrees with fact nor reason. Not with fact; for it is notorious that those who before piqued themselves on owing no man anything are now indebted in larger sums than humanly speaking they can ever pay. Not with reason;[17] for if riches had been their aim, they would have sought out the rich, not the poor; not the tinners in Cornwall, the colliers of Kingswood, the keelmen in Newcastle upon Tyne. At the same time they showed they were not afraid or ashamed to appear before the greatest or

[10] I.e., the *General Rules*, see pp. 69-73 above.
[11] See 2 Cor. 12:15.
[12] See Ps. 89:14.
[13] Lev. 19:18; Matt. 19:19, etc.
[14] Cf. Matt. 7:12.
[15] This paragraph clearly refers to the Wesleys rather than their followers.
[16] See Matt. 6:19.
[17] 'Not with fact. . . . Not with reason' omitted from the two London edns.

wisest of men—witness their appearing in the most public manner both at Dublin, Bristol, Oxford, and London.

18. Ought not every *lover of his country* not only [not] to oppose, but to assist with all the power and interest he has, those who continually, and not without success, recommend the love of our country? And what is so closely connected therewith, duty and loyalty to the best of princes? Ought you not to forward, so far as ever your influence will go, sobriety and temperance among your countrymen? What can be more for the interest of this poor nation, and for the good of all, whether rich or poor? You do well to promote that excellent design of spreading the linen manufacture among us.[18] None can doubt but this is admirably well calculated for the good of the whole kingdom. But are not temperance and honesty still more conducive to the good of this and of every kingdom? Nay, and how directly conducive are these virtues to that very end, the flourishing of our manufactures!

19. And what can conduce more to the general good of all the inhabitants of this land than industry joined to content? To peace with God, peace with yourselves, peace with one another? O how needful in this above all lands! For what a stranger has it been in our coasts! Ye men of Ireland, help! Come all, as one man, all men of religion and reason, all lovers of God and of mankind, all lovers of your country. O suffer not yourselves to be thus grossly abused, thus miserably imposed upon any longer. Open your eyes; look around and judge for yourselves. See plain, undeniable facts. Be convinced by the force of truth and love that the work is indeed of God. Rejoice in the good of your country, in peace [and][19] goodwill continually advanced among men. Beware you do not oppose, or speak or think evil, of what God hath done in the earth. Rather, each in the station wherein he is placed, join hearts and hands in the work, till holiness and happiness cover our land, as the waters cover the sea.[20]

Dublin, July 6th 1749

[18] The manufacture of linen in Ireland was first promoted by King William III. In 1686 he invited Louis Crommelin, a wealthy Huguenot linen merchant who had left France when he foresaw the revocation of the Edict of Nantes, to oversee the matter, and this Crommelin did successfully for twenty-five years. In 1711 the control of the industry was taken over by the official Linen Board, which continued in its operations until shortly after mechanical spinning replaced the spinning wheel in 1825. At the time of Wesley's *Address* the industry was growing rapidly and greatly helping the Irish economy. See John Horner, *The Linen Trade of Europe during the Spinning Wheel Period* (Belfast, 1920), pp. 15-213.

[19] Orig., 'of'.

[20] Isa. 11:9.

13

A LETTER TO THE REV. MR. BAILY OF CORK

(1750)

AN INTRODUCTORY COMMENT

The Rev. John Baily was rector of Kilcully, on the northern outskirts of Cork; he was born at Bandon c.*1700, and educated at Trinity College, Dublin. At the time of the* Letter *he was also chaplain to the Corporation of Cork and curate of Christ Church, Cork.*

Two open letters had been addressed to Wesley, apparently by Baily. Although some of Wesley's statements about the two are ambiguous, it seems fairly certain that the main purpose of his Letter *to Mr. Baily was to answer Baily's second* Letter, *signed 'Philalethes' and published after Wesley had left Cork on May 31, 1750, possibly about June 2, when Wesley was 'at a convenient distance' (Pref. 2). Because neither of these letters appears to have survived, not even in the National Library of Ireland, Wesley's reply remains our only source of information about them, and this information is here summarized. (See Green,* Anti-Methodist, *Nos. 218-19.)*

The first Letter *to Wesley may have been dated May 28, 1750, though this dating seems more appropriate for the second* Letter *(II.1). It was published May 30, 1750, the day Wesley arrived at Cork, and was signed 'George Fisher' (Pref. 1, 2). Wesley found it too pointless to answer (ibid.); in it the author claimed that Wesley's income was a hundred pounds a year (II.18).*

The second Letter *seems to have been dated May 28, 1750 (II.1), though probably published about June 2, when Wesley was safely in the Limerick area (Pref. 1). It was signed 'Philalethes', and Wesley found it to be a substantial challenge of at least thirty pages, which he answered in three parts, firstly giving the facts about the Cork riots of 1749/50, secondly considering both the author's charges against the Methodists and his defence of the civic and ecclesiastical opposition, and thirdly commenting on the motives behind this opposition.*

For a partial reconstruction of the letter of 'Philalethes', see Appendix B, pp. [565-66]. For a summary of the three editions published during

Wesley's lifetime, a stemma illustrating the transmission of the text, and a list of the substantive variant readings from the text, based on the first edition (Dublin, Powell, 1750), see Appendix A, pp. 541ff. For full bibliographical details see Bibliography, *No. 185.*

A Letter to the Rev. Mr. Baily[1] of Cork[2],

In Answer to a Letter to the Rev. John Wesley

Limerick, June 8, 1750

Reverend sir,

1. Why do you not subscribe your name to a performance so perfectly agreeing, both as to the matter and form, with the sermons you have been occasionally preaching for more than a year last past? As to your seeming to disclaim it by saying once and again, 'I am but a plain, simple man,' and, 'The doctrine you preach is only a revival of the old antimonian heresy, I think they call it,'[3] I presume it is only a pious fraud. But how came so plain and simple a man to know the meaning of the Greek word 'Philalethes'?[4] Sir, this is not of a piece. If you did not care to own your child, had not you better have subscribed the second (as well as the first) letter, 'George Fisher'?[a]

2. I confess you have timed your performance well. When the other pointless thing was published I came unluckily to Cork on the selfsame day. But you might now suppose I was at a convenient distance. However, I will not plead this as an excuse for taking no notice of your last favour;[5] although, to say the truth,

[a] The Letter thus subscribed was published at Cork on May 30 last.

---

[1] Although Wesley's opening paragraph implies some doubt about his opponent's identity, the title shows that this is minimal.

[2] Here, as on the title page, and as usually, Wesley spelled the name 'Corke'.

[3] These quotations are surely from one of the two open letters addressed to Wesley, apparently by Baily (see Intro. above).

[4] 'Philalethes' means 'friend of truth'.

[5] Wesley apparently uses the word 'last' here in error for 'former'. In view of the

I scarce know how to answer it, as you write in a language I am not accustomed to. Both Mr. Tucker, Mr. Church,[6] and all the other gentlemen who have wrote to me in public for some years, have wrote as gentlemen, having some regard to their own, whatever my character was. But as you fight in the dark, you regard not what weapons you use. We are not therefore on even terms. I cannot answer you in kind. I am constrained to leave this to your good allies of Blackpool and Fair Lane.[b]

I shall, first, state the facts on which the present controversy turns, and then consider the most material parts of your performance.

[I. 1.] First I am to state the facts. But here I am under a great disadvantage, having few of my papers by me. Excuse me, therefore, if I do not give so full an account now as I may possibly do hereafter, if I only give you for the present the extracts of some papers which were lately put into my hands.[7]

Thomas Jones of Cork, merchant, deposes:

That on May 3, 1749, Nicholas Butler,[8] ballad singer, came before the house of this deponent, and assembled a large mob; that this deponent went to Daniel Crone, Esq., then Mayor of Cork, and desired that he would put a stop to these riots, asking at the same time whether he gave the said Butler leave to go about in this manner; that Mr. Mayor said he neither gave him leave, neither did he hinder him; that in the evening Butler gathered a larger mob than before, and went to the house where the people called Methodists were assembled to hear the Word of God, and as they came out threw dirt and hurt several of them.

That on May 4 this deponent, with some others, went to the Mayor and told what had been done, adding, 'If your worship pleases to speak only three words

[b] Celebrated parts of Cork.

---

statement in II.18, it seems clear that he does answer the letter signed 'Philalethes', not that signed 'George Fisher'.

[6] *Works*, 1773, 'Dr. Tucker, Dr. Church'. For Josiah Tucker's *Brief History*, see pp. 47-48 above, and for Thomas Church's *Remarks* and *Farther Remarks*, pp. 80, 160-61 above.

[7] For these depositions cf. JWJ, July 20, 1749, introduced thus: 'I had now an opportunity of inquiring into the real state of the late transactions at Cork, an account of which is subjoined, being the extracts of some papers which were about this time put into my hands.' These extracts close No. 4 of Wesley's *Journal*, first published in 1754, being apparently based on the 2nd edn. of the *Letter*, 1750. The numbering of the sections is very irregular, and those in the *Journal* appear to have followed those here, the '8' missing from this document being supplied from the *Journal*. (It seems clear that Wesley did not intend to number the depositions themselves concurrently, as is done in Nehemiah Curnock's edn. of the *Journal*.)

[8] For Butler see the intro. to *A Short Address to the Inhabitants of Ireland*, p. 281 above.

to Butler it will all be [9] over'; that the Mayor gave his word and honour, there should be no more of it; he would put an entire stop to it; that notwithstanding a larger mob than ever came to the house the same evening; that they threw much dirt and many stones at the people, both while they were in the house, and when they came out; that the mob then fell upon them, both on men and women, with clubs, hangers,[10] and swords; so that many of them were much wounded, and lost a considerable quantity of blood.

That on May 5 this deponent informed the mayor of all, and also that Butler had openly declared, there should be a greater mob than ever there was that night; that the mayor promised he would prevent it; that in the evening Butler did bring a greater mob than ever; that this deponent, hearing the mayor designed to go out of the way, set two men to watch him, and when the riot was begun went to the alehouse and inquired for him; that the woman of the house denying he was there, this deponent insisted he was, declared he would not go till he had seen him, and began searching the house; that Mr. Mayor then appearing, he demanded his assistance to suppress a riotous mob; that when the mayor came in sight of them he beckoned to Butler, who immediately came down from the place where he stood; that the mayor then went with this deponent, and looked on many of the people covered with dirt and blood; that some of them still remained in the house, fearing their lives, till James Chatterton and John Reilly, Esquires, Sheriffs of Cork, and Hugh Millard, junior, Esquire, Alderman, turned them out to the mob, and nailed up the doors.

2. Elizabeth Holleran of Cork deposes:

That on May 3, as she was going down Castle Street, she saw Nicholas Butler on a table, with ballads in one hand and a Bible in the other; that she expressed some concern thereat; on which Sheriff Reilly ordered his bailiff to carry her to Bridewell; that afterward the bailiff came and said, his master ordered she should be carried to gaol; and that she continued in gaol from May 3, about eight in the evening, till between ten and twelve on May 5.

3. John Stockdale of Cork, tallow-chandler, deposes:

That on May 5, while he and others were assembled to hear the Word of God, Nicholas Butler came down to the house where they were, with a very numerous mob; that when this deponent came out they threw all manner of dirt and abundance of stones at him; that they then beat, bruised, and cut him in several places; that seeing his wife on the ground, and the mob abusing her still, he called out, and besought them not to kill his wife; that on this one of them struck him with a large stick, as did also many others, so that he was hurt in several parts, and his face in a gore of blood.

[4.] Daniel Sullivan of Cork, baker, deposes:

That every day but one from the 6th to the 16th of May, Nicholas Butler assembled a riotous mob before this deponent's house; that they abused all who came into the shop, to the great damage of this deponent's business; that on or about the 15th Butler swore he would bring a mob the next day and pull down

[9] JWJ, 'be all'.

[10] A small naval sword which hung from the belt.

his house; that accordingly on the 16th he did bring a large mob, and beat or abused all that came to the house; that the mayor walked by while the mob was so employed, but did not hinder them; that afterwards they broke his windows, threw dirt and stones into his shop, and spoiled a great quantity of his goods.

Daniel Sullivan is ready to depose farther, that from the 16th of May to the 28th the mob gathered every day before his house; that on Sunday the 28th Butler swore they would 'come the next day and pull down the house of that heretic dog', and called aloud to the mob, 'Let the heretic dogs indict you; I will bring you all off without a farthing cost.'

That accordingly, on May 29, Butler came with a greater mob than before; that he went to the mayor and begged him to come, which he for some time refused to do; but after much importunity rose up, and walked with him down the street; that when they were in the midst of the mob the mayor said aloud, 'It is your own fault for entertaining these preachers. If you will turn them out of your house I will engage there shall be no more harm done; but if you will not turn them out, you must take what you will get'; that upon this the mob set up an huzza, and threw stones faster than before; that he said, 'This is fine usage under a Protestant government; if I had a priest saying Mass in every room of it, my house would not be touched'; that the mayor replied. 'The priests are tolerated, but you are not. You talk too much; go in, and shut up your doors'; that seeing no remedy he did so, and the mob continued breaking the windows and throwing stones in, till near twelve at night.

That on May 31 the said Sullivan and two more went and informed the mayor of what the mob was then doing; that it was not without great importunity they brought him as far as the Exchange; that he would go no farther, nor send any help, though some that were much bruised and wounded came by; that some hours after, when the mob had finished their work, he sent a party of soldiers to guard the walls.

5. John Stockdale deposes farther, that on May 31 he with others was quietly hearing the Word of God, when Butler and his mob came down to the house; that as they came out the mob threw showers of dirt and stones; that many were hurt, many beat, bruised, and cut, among whom was this deponent, who was so bruised and cut that the effusion of blood from his head could not be stopped for a considerable time.

6. John M'Nerny of Cork deposes:

That on the 31st of May last, as this deponent with others was hearing a sermon, Butler came down with a large mob; that the stones and dirt coming in fast obliged the congregation to shut the doors, and lock themselves in; that the mob broke open the door, on which this deponent endeavoured to escape through a window; that not being able to do it he returned into the house, where he saw the mob tear up the pews, benches, and floor, part of which they afterwards burnt in the open street, and carried away part for their own use.

7. Daniel Sullivan is ready to depose farther:

That Butler, with a large mob, went about from street to street, and from house to house, abusing, threatening, and beating whomsoever he pleased, from June 1st to the 16th, when they assaulted, bruised, and cut Ann Jenkins; and from the 16th to the 30th, when a woman whom they had beaten miscarried, and narrowly escaped with life.

Some of the particulars were as follows:

Thomas Burnet of Cork, nailer, deposes:

That on or about the 12th of June, as this deponent was at work in his master's shop, Nicholas Butler came with a great mob to the door, and seeing this deponent told him he was an heretic dog, and his soul was burning in hell; that this deponent asking, 'Why do you use me thus?' Butler took up a stone and struck him so violently on the side that he was thereby rendered incapable of working for upwards of a week; that he hit this deponent's wife with another stone, without any kind of provocation, which so hurt her that she was obliged to take to her bed, and has not been right well since.

Ann Cooshea of Cork deposes:

That on or about the 12th of June, as she was standing at her father's door, Nicholas Butler, with a riotous mob, began to abuse this deponent and her family, called [11] them heretic bitches, saying they were damned, and all their souls were in hell; that then, without any provocation, he took up a great stone, and threw it at this deponent, which struck her on the head with such force that it deprived her of her senses for some time.

Ann Wright of Cork deposes:

That on or about the 12th of June, as this deponent was in her own house, Butler and his mob came before her door, calling her and her family heretic bitches, and swearing he would make her house hotter than hell-fire; that he threw dirt and stones at them, hit her in the face, dashed all the goods about which she had in her window, and, she really believes, would have dashed out her brains had she not quitted her shop and fled for her life.

[8.] Margaret Griffin of Cork deposes:

That on the 24th of June, as this deponent was about her business, Butler and his mob came up, took hold on her, tore her clothes, struck her several times, and cut her mouth; that after she broke from him, he and his mob pursued her to her house, and would have broke in, had not some neighbours interposed; that he had beat and abused her several times before, and one of those times to such a degree that she was all in a gore of blood, and continued spitting blood for several days after.

Jacob Connor, clothier, of Cork, deposes:

That on the 24th of June, as he was employed in his lawful business, Butler and his mob came up, and without any manner of provocation fell upon him; that they beat him till they caused such an effusion of blood as could not be stopped for a considerable time; and that he verily believes, had not a gentleman interposed, they would have killed him on the spot.

9. Ann Hughes of Cork deposes:

That on the 29th of June she asked Nicholas Butler why he broke open her house on the 21st; that hereon he called her many abusive names (being attended with his usual mob[12]) dragged her up and down, tore her clothes in pieces, and with his sword stabbed and cut her in both her arms.

Daniel Filts, blacksmith, of Cork, deposes:

That on the 29th of June Butler and a riotous mob came before his door,

[11] JWJ, 'calling'.

[12] JWJ omits 'usual'.

called him many abusive names, drew his hanger, and threatened to stab him; that he and his mob the next day assaulted the house of this deponent with drawn swords; and that he is persuaded, had not one who came by prevented, they would have taken away his life.

10. Mary Fuller of Cork deposes, that on the 30th of June, Butler, at the head of his mob, came between nine and ten at night to the deponent's shop, with a naked sword in his hand; that he swore he would cleave the deponent's skull, and immediately made a full stroke at her head; whereupon she was obliged to fly for her life, leaving her shop and goods to the mob, many of which they hacked and hewed with their swords, to her no small loss and damage.

Henry Dunkle, joiner, of Cork, deposes:

That on the 30th of June, as he was standing at the widow Fuller's shop-window, he saw Butler, accompanied with a large mob, who stopped before her shop; that after he had grossly abused her, he made a full stroke with his hanger at her head, which must have cleft her in two had not this deponent received the guard of the hanger on his shoulder; that presently after the said Butler seized upon this deponent; that he seized him by the collar with one hand, and with the other held the hanger over his head, calling him all manner of names, and tearing his shirt and clothes; and that had it not been for the timely assistance of some neighbours he verily believes he should have been torn in pieces.

Margaret Trimnell[13] of Cork deposes:

That on the 30th of June, John Austin and Nicholas Butler, with a numerous mob, came to her shop; that after calling her many names Austin struck her with his club on the right arm, so that it has been black ever since from the shoulder to the elbow; that Butler came next, and with a great stick struck her a violent blow across the back; that many of them then drew their swords, which they carried under their coats, and cut and hacked her goods, part of which they threw out into the street, while others of them threw dirt and stones into the shop, to the considerable damage of her goods and loss of this deponent.

11. It was not for those who had any regard either to their persons or goods to oppose Mr. Butler after this. So the poor people[14] patiently suffered whatever he and his mob were pleased to inflict upon them, till the assizes drew on, at which they doubted not to find a sufficient, though late relief.

Accordingly twenty-eight depositions were taken (from the foul copies of some of which the preceding account is mostly transcribed), and laid before the Grand Jury, August 19. But they did not find any one of these bills. Instead of this they made that memorable presentment, which is worthy to be preserved in the annals of Ireland to all succeeding generations:

[13] 2nd edn., London, followed by JWJ, 'Tremnell'.

[14] JWJ omits 'poor', and reconstructs this, its closing paragraph.

We find and present Charles Wesley, to be a person of ill fame, a vagabond, and a common disturber of his Majesty's peace, and we pray he may be transported.

We find and present James Williams, etc.

We find and present Robert Swindle, etc.

We find and present Jonathan Reeves, etc.

We find and present James Wheatley, etc.

We find and present John Larwood, etc.

We find and present Joseph McAuliff, etc.

We find and present Charles Skelton, etc.

We find and present William Tooker, etc.[15]

We find and present Daniel Sullivan, etc.

12. Mr. Butler and his mob were now in higher spirits than ever. They scoured the streets, day and night, frequently hollowing as they went along, 'Five pounds for a swaddler's head';[c] their chief declaring to them all, he had full liberty now to do whatever he would, even to murder if he pleased, as Mr. Swain of North Abbey and others are ready to testify.

13. The sessions held at Cork on the 5th of October following produced another memorable presentment:

'We find and present John Horton[16] to be a person of ill fame, a vagabond, and a common disturber of his Majesty's peace, and we pray that he may be transported.'

But complaint being made of this above, as wholly illegal, it vanished into air.

14. Some time after Mr. Butler removed to Dublin, and began to sing his ballads there. But having little success he returned to Cork, and in January began to scour the streets again, pursuing all 'of this way',[17] with a large mob at his heels armed with swords, staves, and pistols. Complaint was made of this to William Holmes, Esq., the present Mayor of Cork. But there was no removal of the thing complained of. The riots were not suppressed. Nay, they not only continued, but increased.

[c] A name first given to Mr. Cennick, from preaching on those words, 'Ye shall find the babe wrapped in swaddling clothes, lying in a manger.' [Luke 2:12.]

---

[15] I.e., Thomas Williams, Robert Swindells, Jonathan Reeves, James Wheatley, Samuel Larwood, Joseph Cownley, Charles Skelton, and William Tucker, eight Irish preachers in addition to Charles Wesley and Daniel Sullivan, rather than seven, as in JWJ, Aug. 19, 1749, the additional name being that of James Wheatley. Cf. II.1, p. 300 below.

[16] Apparently Wesley's preacher John Haughton, for whom see JWJ, May 21, 1750, etc., and II.1, p. 300 below.

[17] Acts 9:2.

15. From the beginning of February to the end, his Majesty's peace was preserved just as before; of which it may be proper to join two or three instances for the information of all thinking men.

William Jewell, clothier, of Shandon, Church Lane, deposes:

That Nicholas Butler, with a riotous mob, several times assaulted this deponent's house; that particularly on the 23rd of February he came thither with a large mob armed with clubs and other weapons; that several of the rioters entered the house, and swore, the first who resisted, they would blow their brains out; that the deponent's wife, endeavouring to stop them, was assaulted and beaten by the said Butler; who then ordered his men to break the deponent's windows, which they did with stones of a considerable weight.

Mary Philips of St. Peter's Church Lane deposes:

That on the 26th of February, about seven in the evening, Nicholas Butler came to her house with a large mob, and asked where her husband was; that as soon as she appeared he first abused her in the grossest terms, and then struck her on the head, so that it stunned her; and, she verily believes, had not some within thrust to and fastened the door, she should have been murdered on the spot.

It may suffice for the present to add one instance more: Elizabeth Gardelet, wife of Joseph Gardelet, Corporal, in Colonel Pawlet's regiment, Captain Charlton's company, deposes:

That on February the 28th, as she was going out of her lodgings, she was met by Butler and his mob; that Butler, without any manner of provocation, immediately fell upon her, striking her with both his fists on the side of her head, which knocked her head against the wall; that she endeavoured to escape from him, but he pursued her, and struck her several times in the face; that she ran into the schoolyard for shelter, but he followed, caught hold of her, saying, 'You whore, you stand on consecrated ground,' and threw her with such force across the lane that she was driven against the opposite wall; that when she had recovered herself a little, she made the best of her way to her lodging; but Butler still pursued, and overtook her as she was going up the stairs; that he struck her with his fist on the stomach, which stroke knocked her down backward; that falling with the small of her back against the edge of one of the stairs, she was not able to rise again; that her pains immediately came upon her, and about two in the morning she miscarried.

16. These, with several more depositions to the same effect, were in April laid before the Grand Jury. Yet they did not find any of these bills! But they found one against Daniel Sullivan the younger (no preacher, but a hearer of the people called Methodists) who, when Butler and his mob were discharging a

shower of stones upon him, fired a pistol without any ball over their heads. If any man has wrote this story to England in a quite different manner, and fixed it on 'a young Methodist preacher', let him be ashamed in the presence of God and man—unless shame and he have shook hands and parted.

17. Several of the persons presented as vagabonds in autumn appeared at the Lent assizes. But none appearing against them, they were discharged, with honour to themselves, and shame to their persecutors; who, by bringing the matter to a judicial determination, plainly showed, there is law even for Methodists; and gave his Majesty's judge a full occasion to declare the utter illegality of all riots, and the inexcusableness of tolerating (much more, causing) them on any pretence whatsoever.

18. It was now generally believed, there would be no more riots in Cork—although I cannot say that was my opinion. On May 19th I accepted the repeated invitation of Mr. Alderman Pembroke,[18] and came to his house. Understanding the place where the preaching usually was would by no means contain those who desired to hear me, at eight in the morning I went to Hammond's Marsh. The congregation was large and deeply attentive. A few of the rabble gathered at a distance; but by little and little they drew near and mixed with the congregation. So that I have seldom seen a more quiet and orderly assembly at any church in England or Ireland.[19]

19. In the afternoon, a report being spread abroad that the mayor designed to hinder my preaching on the Marsh, I desired Mr. Skelton and Jones[20] to wait upon him, and inquire concerning it. Mr. Skelton asked if my preaching there would be offensive to him, adding, 'If it would, Mr. W[esley] will not do it.' He replied

[18] Orig., 'Pembrock', and so in JWJ, May 19, 1750.

[19] For the remaining portion of this section see the parallel account in JWJ, May 19-27, 1750 (ending with his letter to the Mayor of Cork). The *Letter* probably formed the source for the *Journal*, but this contains several additions and revisions.

[20] Mr. Skelton, leader of the delegation, was presumably Charles Skelton, one of Wesley's preachers. [Mr.] Jones was probably not one of several of Wesley's preachers with that name, but 'Thomas Jones of Cork, merchant', the first deponent (and therefore of Methodist sympathies, and a person of some standing) among those giving depositions about the 1749 Cork riots. On May 3, 1749 he went to Daniel Crone, Mayor of Cork, and asked him to put a stop to the riots; he went again on May 4, and again, with others, on May 5. JWJ, June 27, 1762, says: 'So died honest Thomas Jones, *secundum artem* [i.e., in the manner in which he lived]! A man whom God raised from nothing, by a blessing on his unwearied diligence, to a plentiful fortune.' He was a successful merchant in hardware. He died in his home in Cork. JWJ, Apr. 14, 1771, speaks of him as 'the greatest benefactor of the Cork preaching-house'.

warmly, 'Sir, I'll have no mobbing.' Mr. S[kelton] said, 'Sir, there was none this morning.' He answered, 'There was. Are there not churches and meeting-houses enough? I will have no more mobs and riots.' Mr. S[kelton] replied, 'Sir, neither Mr. W[esley] nor they that heard him made either mobs or riots.' He answered plain, 'I *will have* no more preaching. And if Mr. W[esley] attempts to preach, I am prepared for him.'

I did not conceive, till now, that there was any real meaning in what a gentleman said some time since, who being told, 'Sir, King George tolerates the Methodists,' replied, 'Sir, you shall find the mayor is King of Cork.'

20. I began preaching in our own house soon after five. Mr. Mayor meantime was walking in the Change, where he gave orders to the drummers of the town and to his sergeants—doubtless to go down and keep the peace! They came down with an innumerable mob to the house. They continued drumming, and I continued preaching, till I had finished my discourse. When I came out the mob immediately closed me in. I desired one of the sergeants to protect me from the mob; but he replied, 'Sir, I have no orders to do that.' When I came into the street they threw whatever came to hand. I walked on straight through the midst of them, looking every man in the face, and they opened to the right and left, till I came near Daunt's Bridge.[21] A large party had taken possession of this, one of whom was bawling out, 'Now, hey[22] for the Romans!' When I came up these likewise shrunk back, and I walked through them into Mr. Jenkin's house.

But many of the congregation were more roughly handled; particularly Mr. Jones, who was covered with dirt, and escaped with his life almost by miracle. The main body of the mob then went to the house, brought out all the seats and benches, tore up the floor, the door, the frames of the windows, and whatever of woodwork remained, part of which they carried off for their own use, and the rest they burnt in the open street.

21. Monday the 21st I rode on to Bandon. From three in the afternoon till after seven, the mob of Cork marched in grand procession, and then burnt me in effigy near Daunt's Bridge.

Tue. 22. The mob and drummers were moving again between three and four in the morning. The same evening the mob came

[21] Orig., 'Dant's Bridge'.

[22] Orig., 'high', but 'hey' in JWJ.

down to Hammond's Marsh, but stood at a distance from Mr. Stockdale's house, till the drums beat, and the mayor's sergeant beckoned to them, on which they drew up and began the attack. The mayor, being sent for, came with a party of soldiers. Mr. Stockdale earnestly desired that he would disperse the mob, or at least leave the soldiers there to protect them from the rioters. But he took them all away with him; on which the mob went on and broke all the glass and most of the window-frames in pieces.

22. Wed. 23. The mob was still patrolling the streets, abusing all that were called Methodists, and threatening to murder them, and pull down their houses, if they did not leave 'this way'.[23]

Thur. 24. They again assaulted Mr. Stockdale's house, broke down the boards he had nailed up against the windows, destroyed what little remained of the window frames and shutters, and damaged a considerable part of his goods.

Fri. 25, and again on Sat. 26, one Roger O'Ferrall fixed up an advertisement at the Public Exchange (as he had also done for several days before) that he was ready to 'head any mob, in order to pull down any house that should dare to harbour a swaddler'.

23. Sun. 27. I wrote the following letter to the Mayor:

Mr. Mayor,

An hour ago I received *A Letter to Mr. Butler,* just reprinted at Cork. The publishers assert, 'It was brought down from Dublin to be distributed among the Society. But Mr. Wesley called in as many as he could.' Both these assertions are absolutely false. I read some lines of that letter when I was in Dublin, but never read it over before this morning. Who the author of it is I know not. But this I know; I never called in one; neither concerned myself about it, much less brought any down to distribute among the Society.

Yet I cannot but return my hearty thanks to the gentlemen who have distributed them through the town. I believe it will do more good than they are sensible of. For though I dislike its condemning the magistrates and clergy in general (several of whom were not concerned in the late proceedings), yet I think the reasoning is strong and clear. And that the facts referred to therein are not at all misrepresented will sufficiently appear in due time.

I fear God and honour the King. I earnestly desire to be at peace with all men. I have not willingly given any offence, either to the magistrates, the clergy, or any of the inhabitants of the city of Cork, neither do I desire anything of them but to be treated (I will not say as a clergyman, a gentleman, or a Christian, but) with such justice and humanity as are due to a Jew, a Turk, or a pagan. I am,

Sir, Your obedient servant, J. Wesley.[24]

[23] Acts 9:2.

[24] See *Letters,* 26:426r in this edn., for this letter reprinted from the original printed broadside.

II. 1. Your performance[25] is dated May 28, the most material parts of which I am now to consider.

It contains, first, a charge against the Methodist preachers; secondly, a defence of the Corporation and clergy of Cork.

With regard to your charge against those preachers, may I take the liberty to inquire why you drop six out of the eleven that have been at Cork, viz., Mr. Swindells, Wheatley, Larwood, Skelton, Tucker, and Haughton? Can you glean up no story concerning these? Or is it out of mere compassion that you spare them?

2. But before I proceed I must beg leave to ask, Who is this evidence against the other five? Why, one that neither dares show his face, nor tell his name, or the place of his abode; one that is ashamed (and truly not without cause) of the dirty work he is employed in; so that we could not even conjecture who he was, but that his speech bewrayeth him.[26] How much credit is due to such an evidence let any man of reason judge.

3. This worthy witness falls foul upon Mr. Cownley, and miserably murders a tale he has got by the end.[d] Sir, Mr. M.[27] is nothing obliged to you for bringing the character of his niece into question. He is perfectly satisfied that Mr. C[ownley] acted in that whole affair with the strictest regard both to honour and conscience.

You next aver that Mr. Reeves 'asked a young woman whether she had a mind to go to hell with her father'.[e] 'Tis possible. I will neither deny nor affirm it without some better proof. But suppose he did. Unless I knew the circumstances of the case, I could not say whether he spoke right or wrong.

4. But what is this to the 'monstrous, shocking, amazing blasphemy spoken by Mr. Charles Wesley', 'who one day', you say, 'preaching on Hammond's Marsh, called out, "Has any of you got the Spirit?" And when none answered, said, "I am sure some of you have got it; for I feel virtue go out of me."'[f] Sir, do you expect anyone to believe this story? I doubt it will not pass even at Cork—unless with your wise friend who said, 'Methodists? Ay,

[d] P. 13.
[e] P. 16.
[f] P. 18.

---

[25] Apparently Baily's second *Letter*, signed 'Philalethes', but possibly the first, signed 'George Fisher'; see intro. above.

[26] See Matt. 26:63.

[27] In October 1755 Joseph Cownley married Miss Massiot of Cork, whom he had met there about this time, and it seems likely that 'Mr. M.' was her uncle.

they are the people who place all their religion in wearing long whiskers.'[28]

5. In the same page you attack Mr. Williams for applying those words, 'I thy Maker am thy husband.'[29] Sir, by the same rule that you conclude, 'These expressions could only flow from a mind full of lascivious ideas,' you may conclude the forty-fifth Psalm to be only a wanton sonnet, and the Canticles[30] a counterpart to Rochester's poems.[31]

But you say, he likewise 'made use of unwarrantable expressions, particularly with regard to faith and good works. And the next day denied that he had used them.'[g] Sir, your word is not proof of this. Be pleased to produce proper vouchers of the facts; and I will then give a farther answer.

Likewise, as to his 'indecent and irreverent behavior at church, turning all the preacher said into ridicule, so that numbers asked, in your hearing, why the churchwardens did not put the profane, wicked scoundrel in the stocks', my present answer is, I doubt the facts. Will your 'men of undoubted character' be so good as to attest them?

6. Of all these, Mr. Williams, Cownley, Reeves, Haughton, Larwood, Skelton, Swindells, Tucker, and Wheatley, you pronounce in the lump that they are 'a parcel of vagabond, illiterate babblers', of whom 'everybody that has the least share of reason must know' that, though 'they amuse the populace with nonsense, ribaldry, and blasphemy, they are not capable of writing orthography or good sense.'[h] Sir, that is not an adjudged case. Some who have a little share of reason think they are capable both of speaking and writing good sense. But if they are not, if they cannot write or read, they can save souls from death;[32] they

[g] Pp. 10-11.
[h] Pp. 3-4.

---

[28] Cf. JWJ, June 5, 1749, at Rathcormack, where a gentleman had informed Colonel Barry that 'there was a people risen up that placed all religion in wearing long whiskers,' whom he equated with the Methodists.

[29] Cf. Isa. 54:5.

[30] I.e., the Song of Songs.

[31] John Wilmot, Earl of Rochester (1647–80), was a poet of eminence and power, but is generally deemed to be lascivious even by the standards of his (and the present) age. He was banished from the Court of Charles II for a satire on the king, of whom in another poem he said, 'He never said a foolish thing, nor ever did a wise one,' to which Charles II replied, 'This is very true: for my words are my own, and my actions are my ministers'.'

[32] See Jas. 5:20.

can, by the grace of God, bring sinners from darkness to light, and from the power of Satan unto God.[33]

7. But they 'made a woman plunder her poor, old husband, and another absent herself from her husband and children'.[i] Pray, what are their names? Where do they live? And how may one come to the speech of them? I have heard so many plausible tales of this kind, which on examination vanished away, that I cannot believe one word of this till I have more proof than your bare assertion.

8. So far I have been pleading for others. But I am now called to answer for myself. For '*Theophilus*[34] and *John Wesley*', say you, 'seem to me the same individual person.'[j] They may seem so to you; but not to any who knows either my style or manner of writing. Besides, if it had been mine, it would have borne my name. For I do not love fighting in the dark.

But were not 'a great number' of those books 'brought from' Dublin 'to be dispersed throughout the city'? Not by me. Not by my order; nor, to my knowledge. However, I thank you again for dispersing them.

9. But 'while charity stands in the front of Christian graces, the author of such a book can have none of that grace. For you must allow the vulgar to think.'[k] Mal-a-propo enough,[35] a lively saying. But for any use it is of, it may stand either in the front or rear of the sentence.

The argument itself is something new. A man knocks me down. I cry, 'Help! Help, or I shall be murdered.' He replies, 'While charity stands in the front of Christian graces, the author of such a cry can have none of that grace.'

[i] Pp. 24-25.
[j] P. 4.
[k] P. 26.

---

[33] Acts 26:18.

[34] 'Theophilus' was the pseudonym of the author of *A Letter to Parson B-tl-r and his Friends of Cork,* dated Jan. 21, 1750, the Cork reprint of which maintained on p. 16: 'N.B. This pamphlet was published in Dublin, and brought down to be distributed among the society. But. Mr. Wesley (finding his reception here not such as he expected) called in as many as he possibly could; but one or two falling into the hands of some gentlemen of this town, they have insisted on its being made public. Cork, May 26th, 1750.'

[35] Mrs. Malaprop, who gave rise to the term 'malapropism', did not appear in Sheridan's play, 'The Rivals', until 1775, but Wesley's 'mal-a-propo' is another to add to the various ways presented in *OED* for writing 'malapropos' (the word behind Sheridan's character), a French phrase signifying 'inappropriate' or 'inappropriately', which was gradually becoming a part of the English language.

So now you have shown to all the world 'the uncharitable and consequently unchristian spirit of Methodism'.[36] What? Because the Methodists cry out for help, before you have quite beat out their brains?

What grimace[37] is this? His Majesty's quiet, loyal, Protestant subjects are abused, insulted, outraged, beaten, covered with dirt, rolled in the mire, bruised, wounded with swords and hangers, murdered, have their house broke open, their goods destroyed, or carried away before their face—and all this in open day, in the face of the sun, yet without any remedy! And those who treat them thus are *charitable* men! Brimful of *a Christian* spirit! But if they who are so treated appeal to the common sense and reason of mankind you gravely cry, 'See the uncharitable, the unchristian spirit of Methodism!'

10. You proceed. 'But pray, what are those facts which you say are not misrepresented? Do you mean that Butler was hired and paid by the Corporation and clergy?' Or, 'that this *remarkably loyal* city is disaffected to the present government?' And that 'a Papist was supported, nay, hired by the chief magistrate to walk the streets, threatening bloodshed and murder? Declare openly, whether these are the facts.' Sir, I understand you well. But for the present I beg to be excused. There is a time and a place for all things.

11. I rejoice to hear that the city of Cork is so 'remarkably loyal', so entirely 'well-affected to the present government'. I presume you mean this chiefly of 'The Friendly Society' (in whom the power of the city is now lodged), erected some time since in opposition to that body of Jacobites commonly called, 'The Hanover Club'. I suppose that zealous anti-Methodist who some days ago stabbed the Methodist preacher in the street, and then cried out, 'Damn King George and all his armies!' did this as a specimen of his *eminent loyalty*.

It cannot be denied that this loyal subject of King George

[36] It appears that Baily's second *Letter* (signed 'Philalethes'), here quotes the passage printed in bold type on the verso of the half-title of *A Letter to Parson B-tl-r:* 'The design of publishing this pamphlet is to show the *uncharitable* and consequently the *unchristian* spirit of Methodism; in which this city, which was always remarkable for its *steady loyalty* and *firm attachment* to our *happy constitution* in *Church* and *State,* is represented not only as a *popish* and *disaffected mob,* but likewise as a set of *abandoned wretches* for whom Tophet (HELL) yawns.' Apparently Wesley thinks that Baily himself was responsible for this passage, and therefore for publishing the pamphlet.

[37] Used in the now obsolete figurative sense, implying an affectation, pretence, or sham.

(Simon Rawlins by name) was, upon oath made of those words, committed to gaol on May the 31st. And it was not till six days after that he walked in procession through the town, with drums beating, and colours flying, and declared at the head of his mob, he would never rest till he had driven all these 'false prophets' out of Cork. How sincere they were in their good wishes to King George and his armies, they gave a clear proof [of] on the tenth of this instant June, when, as ten or twelve soldiers were walking along in a very quiet and inoffensive manner, the mob fell upon them, swore they would have their lives, knocked them down, and beat them to such a degree that on June the 12th one of them died of his wounds, and another was not then expected to live many hours.

12. But you have more proofs of my uncharitableness, that is, supposing I am the author of that pamphlet. For you read there, 'Riches, ease, and honour are what the clergy set their hearts upon. But the souls for whom Christ died they leave to the tender mercies of hell.'[38] Sir, can you deny it? Is it not true, literally true, concerning some of the clergy? You ask, 'But ought we to condemn all for the faults of a few?'[l] I answer, No; no more than I will condemn all in the affair of Cork for the faults of a few. 'Tis *you* that do this. And if it were as *you* say, if they were all *concerned* in the late proceedings, then it would be no uncharitableness to say, 'They were in a miserable state indeed.' Then they would doubtless be 'kicking against the pricks, contending with heaven, fighting against God'.[39]

13. I come now to the general charge against me, independent on the *Letter to Mr. Butler.* And first, you charge me with 'a frontless assurance, and a well-dissembled hypocrisy'.[m] Sir, I thank you. This is as kind as if you was to call me (with Mr. Williams) 'a profane, wicked scoundrel'. I am not careful to answer in this matter. Shortly we shall both stand at an higher bar.

14. You charge me, secondly, with being an 'hare-brained enthusiast'.[n] Sir, I am your most obedient servant.[40]

[l] [Baily, *Letter,*] p. 20.
[m] P. 22.
[n] P. 7.

---

[38] *A Letter to Parson B-tl-r,* pp. 6-7, abr.
[39] Cf. Acts 9:5; 26:14.
[40] A rather obscure comment, but presumably an expression of mock humility ('I defer to your judgment that I am an enthusiast').

But you will prove me an enthusiast. 'For you say' (those are your words) 'you are sent of God to inform mankind' of some 'other revelation of his will' than 'what has been left by Christ and his apostles'.[o] Not so. I never said any such thing. When I do this, then call for miracles. But at present your demand is quite unreasonable. There is no room for it at all. What I advance I prove by the words of Christ or his apostles. If not, let it fall to the ground.

15. You charge me, thirdly, with being employed in 'promoting the cause of arbitrary popish power'.[p] Sir, I plead not guilty. Produce your witnesses. Prove this and I will allow all the rest.

You charge me, fourthly, with holding 'midnight assemblies'.[q] Sir, did you never see the word 'vigil' in your Common Prayer Book? Do you know what it means? If not, permit me to tell you that it was customary with the ancient Christians to spend whole nights in prayer; and that these nights were termed *vigiliae* or *vigils*. Therefore for spending a part of some nights in this manner, in public and solemn prayer, we have not only the authority of our own national church but of the universal church in the earliest ages.[41]

16. You charge me, fifthly, with 'being the cause of all that Butler has done'.[r] True; just as Latimer and Ridley (if I may dare to name myself with those venerable men) were the cause of all that Bishop Bonner did.[42] In this sense the charge is true. It has pleased God (unto him be all the glory) even by my preaching or writings to convince some of the old, Christian, scriptural doctrine, which till then they knew not. And while they declared this to others, you showed them the same love as Edmund of London did to their forefathers.[43] Only the expressions of your

[o] P. 28. [p] P. 7.
[q] P. 24. [r] P. 17.

---

[41] See Wesley's account of his watch-nights, which he claimed to be a revival of New Testament practice, in *A Plain Account of the People called Methodists*, III.1 (p. 264 above).

[42] Edmund Bonner (*c.* 1509–69) was Bishop of London from 1539, deprived under Edward VI, and restored under Mary. He enforced her laws against heresy and was responsible for the condemnation and execution of Bishops Latimer and Ridley. He refused to take the oath of allegiance to Elizabeth I under the Act of Supremacy (1559), and died in prison.

[43] I.e., Edmund Bonner.

love were not quite the same; because (blessed be God) you had not the same power.

17. You affirm, sixthly, that I 'rob and plunder the poor, so as to leave them neither bread to eat nor raiment to put on'.[s] An heavy charge, but without all colour of truth. Yea, just the reverse is true. Abundance of those in Cork, Bandon, Limerick, Dublin, as well as in all parts of England, who a few years ago, either through sloth or profaneness,[44] had not bread to eat or raiment to put on, have now, by means of the preachers called Methodists, a sufficiency of both. Since by hearing these they have learned to fear God, they have learned also to work with their hands, as well as to cut off every needless expense, to be good stewards of the mammon of unrighteousness.[45]

18. You assert, sixthly, that I am 'myself as fond of riches as the most worldly clergyman.[t] Two thousand pence a week! A fine yearly revenue from assurance and salvation tickets!'[u] I answer, (1). What do you mean by 'assurance and salvation tickets'? Is not the very expression a mixture of nonsense and blasphemy? (2). How strangely did you underrate my revenue when you wrote in the person of 'George Fisher'! You then allowed me only an hundred pounds a year! What is this to two thousand pence a week?[46] (3). 'There is not a clergyman', you say, 'who would not willingly exchange his livings for your yearly penny contributions.'[v] And no wonder. For according to a late computation they amount to no less, every year, than eight hundred, eighty-six thousand pounds, beside some odd shillings and pence[47]—in comparison of which the revenue of his Grace of Armagh, or of Canterbury, is a very trifle. And yet, sir, so great is my regard for you and my gratitude for your late services, that if you will only resign your curacy of Christ Church,[48] I will make over to you my whole revenue in Ireland.

[s] P. 8. [t] P. 26. [u] P. 8. [v] P. 21.

[44] *Works* (1773) substituted 'profaneness' for the reading of the earlier edns.—'profuseness'.

[45] Luke 16:9.

[46] This would amount to £433.6*s*.8*d*. a year. For the significance of this key passage in distinguishing between the two letters by Baily see above, p. 288.

[47] At 1*d*. per week per member this would imply a membership of over four million, while even in 1791 the reported membership was only 72,476 in the British Isles, 64,146 in America and the West Indies.

[48] Christ Church (later Holy Trinity), was one of the two ancient parishes in Cork, the church erected in 1720 standing on the south-east of Main Street.

19. But 'the honour' I gain, you think, is even 'greater than the profit'. Alas, sir, I have not generosity enough to relish it. I was always of Juvenal's mind:

Gloria quantalibet quid erit, si gloria tantum [est]?[49]

And especially while there are so many drawbacks, so many dead flies in the pot of ointment.[50] Sheer honour might taste tolerably well. But there is gall with the honey, and less of the honey than the gall. Pray, sir, what think *you?* Have I more honour or dishonour? Do more people praise or blame me? How is it in Cork? Nay (to go no farther), among your own little circle of acquaintance? Where you hear one commend, do not ten cry out, 'Away with such a fellow from the earth!'[51]

Above all, I do not love honour with dry blows. I do not find it will cure broken bones. But perhaps you may think I glory in these. O how should I have gloried, then, if your good friends at Daunt's Bridge had burnt my person, instead of my effigy!

We are here to set religion out of the question. You do not suppose I have anything to do with that. Why, if so, I should rather leave *you* the honour, and myself sleep in a whole skin. On that supposition I quite agree with the epigrammatist:

Virgilii in tumulo, divini praemia vatis,
Explicat en[52] *viridem laurea laeta comam.*
Quid te defunctum iuvat haec? Felicior olim
Sub patulae fagi tegmine vivus eras.[53]

20. Your last charge is that I 'profess myself to be a member of the Established Church, and yet act contrary to the commands of

[49] Juvenal, *Satires*, vii. 81, translated by Wesley in Vol. 32 of his *Works* (1774): 'What is glory without profit too?'

[50] See Eccles. 10:1.

[51] Acts 22:22.

[52] Orig., 'Explicuit', altered in *Works* (1773).

[53] Consultation of eminent classical scholars has failed to reveal the authorship of this epigram, which may indeed be of eighteenth-century origin. It is translated thus by Wesley in *Works* (1774), Vol. 32:

See, the green laurel rears her grateful head
O'er Virgil's tomb! But can this cheer the dead?
Happier by far thou wast of old, when laid
Beneath thy spreading beech's ample shade.

This translation fails to do justice to the epigrammatists' somewhat artificial contrast between the inability of praise to give cheer to the dead and the happiness of Virgil when he was alive.

my spiritual governors, and stab the Church to the very vitals'.[w] I answer, (1). What 'spiritual governor' has commanded me not to preach in any part of his Majesty's dominions? I know not one to this very day, either in England or Ireland. (2). What is it to stab the Church to the very vitals? Why, to deny her fundamental doctrines. And do I, or you, do this? Let any who has read her liturgy, Articles, and Homilies judge which of us two denies that 'we are justified by faith alone';[54] that every believer has 'the inspiration of God's Holy Spirit';[55] that all who are strong in faith do 'perfectly love him, and worthily magnify his holy name'.[56] He that denies this is 'the treacherous son who stabs this affectionate and tender mother'.

If you deny it, you have already disowned the Church. But as for me, I neither can nor will; I know you sincerely desire I should.

Hoc Ithacus velit, et magno mercentur Achivi.[57]

But I choose to stay in the Church, were it only to reprove those who 'betray' her 'with a kiss'.[58]

21. I come now to your defence of the Corporation and clergy. But sure such a defence was never seen before. For whereas I had said, 'I dislike the condemning the magistrates or clergy' in general, because 'several of them' (so I charitably supposed) 'were not concerned in the late proceedings';[59] you answer, 'Pray, by all means point them out, that they may be distinguished by some mark of honour above their brethren.'[x] What do you mean? If you mean anything at all it must be that they were 'all concerned in the late proceedings'. Sir, if they were (of which I own you are a better judge than I), was it needful to declare this to all the world? Especially in so plain terms as these? Did not your zeal here a little outrun your wisdom?

[w] P. 27. [x] Pp. 29-30.

[54] See Art. XI, 'Of the Justification of Man.'

[55] Cf. BCP, Communion, Collect.

[56] Cf. ibid.

[57] See Virgil, *Aeneid,* ii.104, which has Atridae (not Achivi—Achivos occurs in i.102). The passage may be translated: 'This the Ithacan (i.e., Ulysses) might wish, this the sons of Atreus (the Achaeans, in Wesley's text) would buy at a great price.'

[58] Cf. Luke 22:48.

[59] This refers to a sentence in the letter written to the Mayor by Wesley on May 27, 1750, and given above on p. 299.

22. But 'the magistrate', you say, was only 'endeavouring to secure the peace of the city'.[y] A very extraordinary way of securing peace! Truly, sir, I cannot yet believe, not even on *your* word, that 'all the magistrates except one' were concerned in 'this method'[z] of securing peace. Much less can I believe that 'all the clergy' were concerned in thus 'endeavouring to bring back their flock, led astray by these hirelings' (an unlucky word), 'into the right fold'.

23. Of the clergy you add, 'What need have they to rage and foam' at your preaching? 'Suppose you could delude the greater part of their flocks, this could not affect their temporal interest.'[a] We do not desire it should. We only desire to *delude* all mankind (if you *will* term it a delusion) into a serious concern for their eternal interest, for a treasure which none can take away.

[III.] Having now both stated the facts to which you referred, and considered the most material parts of your performance, I have only to subjoin a few obvious reflections, naturally arising from a view of those uncommon occurrences; partly with regard to the motives of those who were active therein, partly to their manner of acting.

1. With regard to the former, every reasonable man will naturally inquire on what motives could any, either of the clergy or the Corporation, ever think of opposing that preaching by which so many notoriously vicious men have been brought to an eminently virtuous life and conversation.

You supply us yourself with one unexceptionable answer: 'Those of the clergy with whom I have conversed freely own, they have not learning sufficient to comprehend your scheme of religion.'[b] If they have not, I am sorry for them. My scheme of religion is this: Love is the fulfilling of the law.[60] From the true love of God and man directly flows every Christian grace, every holy and happy temper. And from these springs uniform holiness of conversation, in conformity to those great rules, Whether ye eat or drink, or whatever you do, do all to the glory of God;[61] and,

[y] P. 6.
[z] Pp. 29-30.
[a] P. 7.
[b] P. 30.

[60] Rom. 13:10.

[61] See 1 Cor. 10:31.

Whatsoever you would that men should do unto you, even so do unto them.[62] But this, you say, 'those of the clergy with whom you converse have not learning enough to comprehend'. Consequently *their* ignorance, or not understanding our doctrine, is the reason why they oppose us.

2. I learn from you that ignorance of another kind is a second reason why some of the clergy oppose us. They (like you) think us *enemies to the Church.* The natural consequence is that in proportion to their zeal for the Church their zeal against us will be.

3. The zeal which many of them have for orthodoxy, or right opinions, is a third reason for opposing us. For they judge us heterodox in several points, maintainers of strange opinions. And the truth is, the old doctrines of the Reformation are now quite new in the world. Hence those who revive them cannot fail to be opposed by those of the clergy who know them not.

4. Fourthly, their honour is touched when others pretend to know what they do not know themselves, especially when unlearned and (otherwise) ignorant men lay claim to any such knowledge. 'What is the tendency of all this' (as you observe on another head) 'but to work in men's minds a mean opinion of the clergy?' But who can tamely suffer this? None but those who have the mind which was in Christ Jesus.[63]

5. Again, will not some say, 'Master, by thus *acting* thou reproachest us'? By preaching sixteen or eighteen times a week? And by a thousand other things of the same kind? Is not this, in effect, reproaching us as if we were lazy and indolent? As if we had not a sufficient love to the souls of those committed to our charge?

6. May there not likewise be some (perhaps unobserved) envy in the breast even of men that fear God? How much more in them that do not, when they hear of the great success of these preachers, of the esteem and honour that are paid to them by the people, and the immense riches which they acquire. What wonder if this occasions a zeal which is not the flame of fervent love?

7. Add to this a desire in some of the inferior clergy of pleasing their superiors; supposing these (which is no impossible

[62] See Matt. 7:12.

[63] See Phil. 2:5.

supposition) are first influenced by any of these motives. Add the imprudence of some that hear those preachers, and (perhaps) needlessly provoke their parochial ministers. And when all these things are considered, none need be at a loss for the motives on which many of the clergy have opposed us.

8. But from what motives can any of the Corporation oppose us? I must beg the gentlemen of this body to observe that I dare by no means lump them all together, as their awkward defender has done. But this I may say without offence: there are some even among *you* who are not so remarkably loyal as others, not so eminently well-affected to the present government. Now these cannot but observe (gentlemen, I speak plain; for I am to deliver my own soul in the sight of God) that wherever we preach, many who were his enemies before became zealous friends to his Majesty. The instances glare both in England and Ireland. Those therefore who are not so zealously his friends have a strong motive to oppose us—though it can't be expected they should own this to be the motive on which they act.

9. Others may have been prejudiced by the artful misrepresentations these have made, or by those they have frequently heard from the pulpit. Indeed this has been the grand fountain of popular prejudice. In every part both of England and Ireland the clergy, where they were inclined so to do, have most effectually stirred up the people.

10. There has been another reason assigned for the opposition that was made to me in particular at Cork, viz., 'that the mayor was offended at my preaching on Hammond's Marsh, and therefore resolved I should not preach at all; whereas, if I had not preached abroad he would have given me leave to preach in the house'. Would Mr. Mayor have given me leave to preach in my own house? I return him must humble thanks. But should he be so courteous as to make me the offer even now, I should not accept it on any such terms. Greater men than he have endeavoured to hinder me from calling sinners to repentance in that open and public manner. But hitherto it has been all lost labour. They have never yet been able to prevail. Nor ever will, till they can 'conquer King George and his armies'.[64] To *curse* them is not enough.

11. Lastly, some (I hope but a few) do cordially believe that

[64] Cf. I.19, p. 298 above.

'private vices are public benefits'.[65] I myself heard this in Cork when I was there last. These, consequently, think us the destroyers of their city by so lessening the number of those public benefactors, the gluttons, the drunkards, the dram-drinkers, the sabbath-breakers, the common swearers, the cheats of every kind, and the followers of that ancient and *honourable* trade, adultery and fornication.

12. These are the undeniable motives to this opposition. I come now to the manner of it.

When some gentlemen inquired of one of the bishops in England, 'My Lord, what must we do to stop these new preachers?' he answered, 'If they preach contrary to Scripture, confute them by Scripture; if contrary to reason, confute them by reason. But beware you use no other weapon than these, either in opposing error or defending the truth.'[66]

Would to God this rule had been followed at Cork. But how little has it been thought of there! The opposition was begun with lies of all kinds, frequently delivered in the name of God. So that never was anything so ill judged as for *you* to ask, 'Does Christianity encourage its professors to make use of lies, invective, or low, mean abuse, and scurrility, to carry on its interest?' No, sir, it does not. I disclaim and abhor every weapon of this kind. But with these have the Methodist preachers been opposed, in Cork above any other place. In England, in all Ireland, have I neither heard nor read any like those gross, palpable 'lies', those 'low', Billingsgate 'invectives', and that inexpressibly 'mean abuse', and base 'scurrility', which the opposers of Methodism, so called, have continually made use of, and which has been the strength of their cause from the beginning.

13. If it be not so, let the Right Reverend the Lord Bishop of Cork[67] (for he too has openly entered the lists against the Methodists) the Reverend Dr. Tisdall,[68] or any other whom his

[65] See the title of Bernard Mandeville's well-known book (1714), *The Fable of the Bees, or, Private Vices, Public Benefits* (London, 1714), which Wesley castigated in his *Journal*, Apr. 14, 1756, and again alluded to in his *Free Thoughts on the Present State of Public Affairs* (1770), noting that a contemporary claimed that George III lacked 'those royal vices which (with Machiavelli and Dr. Mandeville) he supposed would be public benefits'.

[66] This episcopal remark may have reached Wesley by oral transmission.

[67] Jemmet Browne, D.D. (d. 1782), who was Bishop of Cork and Ross 1745–72, when he was translated to Elphin, and in 1775 to Tuam.

[68] Orig., 'Tisdale', but this hitherto unidentified clergyman was surely a member of the prolific ecclesiastical family who spelled their name 'Tisdall', probably George Tisdall of

lordship shall appoint, meet me on even ground, writing as a gentleman to a gentleman, a scholar to a scholar, a clergyman to a clergyman. Let him thus show me wherein I have preached or written amiss, and I will stand reproved before all the world.

14. But let not his lordship, or any other, continue to put *persecution* in the place of reason; either *private persecution,* stirring up husbands to threaten or beat their wives, parents their children, masters their servants; gentlemen to ruin their tenants, labourers, or tradesmen, by turning them out of their farms or cottages, employing, or buying of them no more, because they worship God according to their own conscience; or open, barefaced, noonday, *Cork-persecution,* breaking open the houses of his Majesty's Protestant subjects, destroying their goods, spoiling or tearing the very clothes from their backs; striking, bruising, wounding, murdering them in the streets; dragging them through the mire, without any regard to age or sex; not sparing even those of tender years; no, nor women, though great with child; but, with more than pagan or Mahometan barbarity, destroying infants that were yet unborn.

15. Ought these things so to be? Are they right before God or man? Are they to the honour of our nation? I appeal unto Caesar[69]—unto his gracious Majesty King George, and to the governors under him both in England and Ireland. I appeal to all true, disinterested lovers of this their native country. Is this the way to make it a flourishing nation? Happy at home, amiable and honourable abroad? Men of Ireland, judge! Nay, and is there not some weight in that additional consideration, that this is not a concern of a private nature. Rather is it not a common cause?

If the dams are once broken down, if you tamely give up the fundamental laws of your country, if these are openly violated in the case of your fellow-subjects, how soon may the case be your own? For what protection then have any of you left for either your liberty or property? What security for either your goods or lives, if a riotous mob is to be both judge, jury, and executioner?

16. *Protestants,* what is become of that liberty of conscience for which your forefathers spent their blood? Is it not an empty shadow, a mere, unmeaning name, if these things are suffered

Dublin, who matriculated at Trinity College there on Dec. 12, 1724, aged 17, graduated B.A. in 1728, M.A. in 1737, B.D. and D.D. in 1745.

[69] Acts 25:11.

among you? *Romans*, such of you as are calm, and candid men, do *you* approve of these proceedings? I cannot think you yourselves would use such methods of convincing us, if we think amiss. *Christians* of all denominations, can you reconcile this to our royal law, 'Thou shalt love thy neighbour as thyself'?[70] O 'Tell it not in Gath!'[71] Let it not be named among those who are enemies to the Christian cause, lest that worthy name whereby we are called be still more blasphemed among the heathen!

[70] Lev. 19:18; Matt. 19:19, etc.
[71] 2 Sam. 1:20.

14–15

LETTERS TO THE REV. DR. FREE

(1758)

AN INTRODUCTORY COMMENT

John Free (1711–91) published about forty works—sermons, poems, educational text-books, and proposals, and anti-Jacobite, anti-Gallican, and anti-Methodist polemics. He was a commoner at Christ Church, Oxford, and graduated in 1730; in 1744 he was awarded the B.D. and D.D. After ordination he held the livings of Runcorn, Cheshire, and East Coker, Somerset, and paid curates to do the work. He held various lectureships in Oxford and London and was for a time vice-principal of St. Alban's Hall, Oxford. He was forced to leave Oxford after a violently anti-Jacobite sermon in the University Church and became a master at St. Saviour's Grammar School, Southwark, and then headmaster of the school.

He wrote several books with the unconcealed object of gaining preferment, but none came his way, and he died a disappointed man.

In 1758–59 nearly all his writing came from his antipathy to John Wesley and Methodism. He wrote verbosely but not without wit; but he frequently descended to scurrility and was insufferably supercilious.

In early 1758 he competed with Henry Venn, the curate of Clapham and an avowed Methodist, for the post of lecturer at St. Dunstan's-in-the-East; and in Certain Articles proposed to the Serious Consideration of the Court of Assistants of the Worshipful Company of Salters in London *(the appointing body) warned them that to appoint a Methodist would be damaging to the church and state, since the Methodists taught 'that a man shall be saved by faith alone, exclusive of good works, by which we mean virtue and morality' (see Green,* Anti-Methodist, *No. 273). Various authors came to Venn's defence, including John Wesley; and his* Letter to the Rev. Dr. Free *may be said to have disposed of Dr. Free's case. He shows without difficulty that Methodists do not contradict the Thirty-nine Articles.*

Free came back with a sermon in the University Church in Oxford, and a pamphlet, including the sermon entitled Rules for the Discovery of False Prophets; or, the Dangerous Impositions of the Methodists detected at the Bar of Scripture and Reason *(see Green,* Anti-Methodist, *No. 274). Wesley replied, in the same month of August 1758, with the* Second Letter. *Free directed three further broadsides at the Methodists, but Wesley did not trouble to reply, having decided that Dr. Free's abusiveness needed no response.*

For details of the two editions of the first Letter *published by Wesley, and the variant readings in his* Works, *see Appendix A, pp. 541ff., where also are noted the two editions of it printed by Dr. Free himself, divided by him into chapters and verses of his choosing, and annotated (see Green,* Anti-Methodist, *Nos. 275-76). For further details of Wesley's two letters see* Bibliography, *Nos. 227-28.*

A Letter to the Rev. Dr. Free

Tullamore, May 2, 1758[1]

Reverend sir,

1. A little tract appearing under your name was yesterday put into my hands. You therein call upon me to speak, 'if I have any exceptions to make to what is advanced', and promise to 'reply as fairly and candidly as I can expect', 'provided those exceptions be drawn up, *as you have set the example,* in a short compass, and in the manner wherein all *wise* and *good* people would choose to manage a *religious* dispute'.[a]

2. 'In a short compass', sir, they will certainly be drawn up, for my own sake as well as yours. For I know the value of time, and would gladly employ it all in what more immediately relates to eternity. But I do not promise to draw them up in that manner

[a] [Free, *Certain Articles proposed to the Serious Considerations of the Court of Assistants of the Worshipful Company of Salters in London* (London, Owen, 1758),] p. 22. [As usual Wesley has slightly varied some of the quoted material in order to accommodate it to his sentence structure. The page numbers vary in the 2nd edn. (London, 1759, for the author), which is entitled *A Display of the Bad Principles of the Methodists: in Certain Articles. . . .]*

[1] Wesley had been in Ireland throughout the whole of April.

whereof you 'have set the example'. I cannot; I dare not. For I fear God, and do really believe there is a judgment to come. Therefore I dare not 'return evil for evil'; neither 'railing for railing'.[2] Nor can I allow that your manner of treating this subject is that 'wherein all *wise* and *good* people would choose to manage a religious dispute'. Far, very far from it. I shall rejoice if a little more fairness and candour should appear in your future writings. But I cannot expect it; for the *nigrae sucus lolliginis*,[3] wormwood and gall,[4] seem to have infected your very vitals.

3. The quotation from Bishop Gibson, which takes up five out of nineteen pages,[5] I have particularly answered already;[b] and in a manner wherewith I have good reason to believe his lordship was entirely satisfied. With his lordship therefore I have no present concern; my business now is with you only. And seeing you are 'now ready' (as you express it) 'to run a tilt',[6] I must make what defence I can. Only you must excuse me from meeting you on the same ground, or fighting you with the same weapons. My weapons are only truth and love. May the God of truth and love strengthen my weakness!

4. I waive what relates to Mr. V[enn]'s[7] personal character, which is too well known to need my defence of it. As likewise the occurrence (real or imaginary I cannot tell) which gave birth to your performance. All that I concern myself with is your five vehement assertions with regard to the people called Methodists. These I shall consider in their order, and prove to be totally false and groundless.

5. The first is this: 'Their whole ministry is an open and avowed opposition to one of the fundamental Articles of our

[b] In *A Letter to the Right Rev. the Lord Bishop of London* [see this edn., 11:335-51. Actually this was directed against Edmund Gibson's *Observations* (1744) and his *Charge*, not against his *Pastoral Letter*].

---

[2] 1 Pet. 3:9.

[3] Horace, *Satires*, I.iv.100, 'the black ink of the cuttlefish'.

[4] Lam. 3:19.

[5] Free, *Certain Articles*, pp. 16-21, from Edmund Gibson, *The Bishop of London's Pastoral Letter to the People of his Diocese* (London, 1739).

[6] Ibid., p. 22.

[7] The Rev. Henry Venn (1725–97), who was seeking the appointment as lecturer at St. Dunstan's-in-the-East, a position held by the Rev. John Berriman, an elderly colleague of his father's. Venn had married on May 10, 1757, and thereby forfeited his income as a fellow of Queens' College, Cambridge. For the identification see Wesley's *Second Letter*, §13, and Free's edn. of this, p. 19.

religion.'[c] How so? Why, 'The 20th Article declares, we may not "so expound one Scripture that it be repugnant to another". And yet it is notorious that the Methodists do ever explain the word *faith* as it stands in some of St. Paul's writings so as to make his doctrine a direct and flat contradiction to that of St. James.'[d]

This stale objection has been answered an hundred times, so that I really thought we should have heard no more of it. But since it is required, I repeat the answer once more. By faith we mean, 'the evidence of things not seen';[8] by justifying faith, a divine evidence or conviction that Christ 'loved *me* and gave himself for *me*'.[9] St. Paul affirms that a man is justified by *this faith;* which St. James never denies, but only asserts that a man cannot be justified by a *dead faith.*[10] And this St. Paul never affirms.

'But St. James declares, "Faith without works is dead." Therefore it is clearly St. James' meaning that a faith which is without *virtue* and *morality* cannot produce salvation. Yet the Methodists so explain St. Paul as to affirm that faith without virtue or morality will produce salvation.'[11] Where? In which of their writings? This needs some proof: I absolutely deny the fact. So that all which follows is mere flourish, and falls to the ground at once; and all that you aver of their 'open and scandalous opposition to the 20th Article'[e] is no better than open and scandalous slander.

6. Your second assertion is this: 'The Methodist, for the perdition of the souls of his followers, openly gives our Saviour the lie, loads the Scripture with falsehood and contradiction. (And pray what could a Mahometan, or infidel, or the devil himself do more?) Yea, openly blasphemes[12] the name of Christ, by saying that the works of men are of no *consideration* at all; [. . .] that God makes no distinction between virtue and vice, that he does not hate vice or love virtue. [. . .] What *blasphemy* then and *impiety* are those wretches guilty of who in their diabolical frenzy dare to contradict our Saviour's authority, and that in such an essential Article of religion?"[f] Here also the Methodists plead not

[c] [Free, *Certain Articles,*] p. 4. [d] [Ibid.,] p. 5. [e] [Ibid.,] p. 6.
[f] [Ibid.,] pp. 7, 8, 9 [again slightly rephrased and rearranged in their order—'thrown together in a very irregular manner' as the notes to Free's own edn. state (p. 17)].

---

[8] Heb. 11:1. [9] Gal. 2:20.
[10] Jas. 2:17, 20, 26. [11] Free, *Certain Articles,* p. 5.
[12] Orig., 'blaspheme' (as in a different context in Free), corrected in MS to 'blasphemes' in Wesley's own copy of his *Works,* 1773.

guilty, and require you to produce your evidence, to show in which of their writings they affirm that God 'will not reward every man according to his works', 'that he makes no distinction between virtue and vice, that he does not hate vice or love virtue'. These are positions which they never remember to have advanced. If you can, refresh their memory.

7. You assert, thirdly, the Methodists, by these positions, 'destroy the essential attributes of God, and ruin his character as Judge of the world'.[13] Very true—if they held these positions. But here lies the mistake. They hold no such positions. They never did. They detest and abhor them. In arguing therefore on this supposition you are again 'beating the air'.[14]

8. You assert, fourthly, the Methodists 'teach and propagate downright atheism (a *capital* crime, and atheists in some countries have been put to death); hereby they make room for all manner of vice and villainy, by which means the bands of society are dissolved. And therefore this attempt must be considered as a sort of *treason* by *magistrates*.'[g]

Again we deny the whole charge, and call for proof—and, blessed be God, so do the magistrates in Great Britain. Bold, vehement asseverations will not pass upon them for legal evidences. Nor indeed on any reasonable men. They can distinguish between *arguing* and *calling names*. The former becomes a gentleman and a Christian. But what is he who can be guilty of the latter?

9. You assert, lastly, that any who choose a Methodist clergyman for their lecturer 'puts into that office which should be held by a minister of the Church of England an enemy who undermines not only the *legal* establishment of that Church, but also the foundation of all religion'.[h]

Once more we must call upon you for the proof, the proof of these two particulars: first, that I, *John Wesley*, am 'an enemy to the Church, and that I undermine not only the legal establishment of the Church of England, but also the very foundations of all religion'. Secondly, that 'Mr. V[enn] is an enemy to the Church, and is undermining all religion, as well as the establishment.'

10. Another word, and I have done. Are there 'certain

[g] [Ibid.,] pp. 10, 11.

[h] [Ibid.,] p. 13.

[13] Free, *Certain Articles*, p. 10.

[14] Cf. 1 Cor. 9:26.

qualifications required of all *lecturers* before they are by law permitted to speak to the people'?[i] And is a *subscription* to the Thirty-nine Articles of Religion one of these qualifications? And is a person who does not 'conform to such subscription' disqualified to be a lecturer? Or, who 'has ever *held* or *published* anything contrary to what the Church of England maintains'? Then certainly you, Dr. John Free, are not 'permitted by law to speak to the people'. Neither are you 'qualified to be a lecturer' in any church in London or England, as by law established. For you flatly deny and openly oppose more than one or two of those Articles. You do not in any wise conform to the subscription you made before you was ordained either priest or deacon. You both *hold* and *publish* (if you are the author and publisher of the tract before me) what is grossly, palpably 'contrary to what the Church of England maintains', in her Homilies as well as Articles—those Homilies to which you have also subscribed in subscribing the 36th Article. You have subscribed them, sir. But did you ever read them? Did you ever read so much as the three first Homilies? I beg of you, sir, to read these at least, before you write again about the doctrine of the Church of England. And would it not be prudent to read a few of the writings of the Methodists before you undertake a farther confutation of them? At present you know not the men or their communication. You are as wholly unacquainted both with them and their doctrines as if you had lived all your days in the islands of Japan,[15] or the deserts of Arabia. You have given a furious assault to you know not whom. And you have done it, you know not why. You have not hurt *me* thereby; but you have hurt yourself: perhaps in your character; certainly in your conscience. For this is not doing to others as you would they should do unto you.[16] When you grow cool, I trust you will see this clearly; and will no more accuse, in a manner so remote from fairness and candour,

Rev. sir,
Your servant for Christ's sake,
John Wesley

[i] P. 14.

---

[15] Cf. *The Principles of a Methodist Farther Explained,* VI.7, p. 231 and n. 41.
[16] See Matt. 7:12; Luke 6:31.

A Second Letter to the Rev. Dr. Free

Fonmon Castle,[1] August 24, 1758

Reverend sir,

1. In the Preface to your Sermon lately printed,[2] you mention your having received my former *Letter,* and add that if the proofs you have now brought do not satisfy me 'as to the validity of your former assertions', if I am not yet convinced that such 'positions are held by people who pass under the denomination of *Methodists,* and will signify this by a private letter', I shall have a more 'particular answer'.[3] I desire to live peaceably with all men;[4] and should therefore wish for no more than a private answer to a private letter, did the affair lie between you and me. But this is not the case. You have already appealed to the archbishop, the university, the nation. Before these judges you have advanced a charge of the highest kind, not only against me, but a whole body of people. Before these, therefore, I must either confess the charge, or give in my answer.

2. But you say: 'I charge blasphemy, impiety, etc., upon the profession of *Methodism* in general. I use no *personal* reflections upon *you,* nor any invective against you, but in the character of a *Methodist.*'[5] That is, you first say, 'All Methodists are pickpockets, rebels, blasphemers, atheists'; and then add, 'I use no reflections upon *you,* but in the character of a Methodist'—but in the character of a pickpocket, blasphemer, atheist. None but? What can you do more?

3. But this, you say, 'is the practice of all honest men, and a

[1] This was the home of Wesley's frequent correspondent, Mary Jones, whom he continued to visit almost annually after the death of her husband in 1742. John Wesley had returned from Ireland only two weeks earlier and had set out for Wales after a week in Bristol.

[2] *Rules for the Discovery of false Prophets, . . . A Sermon preached before the University at St. Mary's in Oxford, on Whitsunday, 1758. With a Preface in vindication of Certain Articles proposed to the serious Consideration of the Company of Salters in London: and an Appendix containing authentic Vouchers from the Writings of the Methodists, etc., in support of the Charge which has been brought against them* (London, Owen, 1758). A 2nd edn. was published the same year, and a 3rd in 1759, with the material spreading over different pages.

[3] Ibid., Pref., p. xviii.

[4] Rom. 12:18.

[5] Free, *Rules,* Pref., p. v, where Free referred to 'Mr. V[enn]', not Wesley—a point on which he made great play in his edn. of Wesley's *Second Letter.*

part of the liberty wherewith Christ hath made you free'.[a] Nay, surely there are some honest men who scruple using their opponents in this manner. At least, I do. Suppose *you* was an atheist, I would 'not bring against' you 'a railing accusation'. I would still endeavour to 'treat you with gentleness and meekness', and thus to 'show the sincerity of my faith'.[6] I leave to *you* that exquisite 'bitterness of spirit, and extreme virulence of language',[7] which you say 'is your duty', and term 'zeal'.[8] And certainly 'zeal', fervour, heat, it is. But is this heat from above? Is it the offspring of heaven? Or a smoke from the bottomless pit?[9]

4. O sir, whence is that zeal which makes you talk in such a manner to his Grace of Canterbury? 'I lay before you the disposition of an *enemy* who threaten our Church with a general *alteration* or total *subversion;* who interrupt us as we walk the streets' (Whom? When? Where?), 'in that very dress which distinguishes us as *servants of the state*' (*Altogether* servants of the state?), 'in the now *sad* capacity of ministers of the *falling* Church of England. [. . .] Such being the *prostrate, miserable* condition of the Church, and such the *triumphant* state of its *enemies,* none of the English priesthood can expect better *security* or longer *continuance* than the rest. They all subsist at mercy. . . . Your Grace and those of your Order will fare no better than those of our own.'[b] Sir, are you in earnest? Do you really believe Lambeth[10] is on the point of being blown up?

5. You go on. 'In the remote counties of England I have seen a whole troop of these divines on horseback, travelling with each a sister behind him.'[c] O sir, 'What should be great, you turn to farce.'[11] Have you forgot that the Church and nation are on the brink of ruin? But pray when and where did you see this? In what year? Or in what county? I cannot but fear, you take this story on

[a] Preface, p. 5. Dr. free's words throughout are printed in italic. [In this present edn. quotations are placed within quotation marks.]

[b] Dedication, p. 2.

[c] [Ibid.,] p. 3.

---

[6] Cf. Free, *Rules,* Pref., p. iv, where he had apparently been alluding to 2 Cor. 10:1 and Tit. 2:7.

[7] Ibid., quoting one of the replies to his *Certain Articles*.

[8] Ibid.

[9] Rev. 9:2.

[10] I.e., Lambeth Palace, the headquarters of Dr. Thomas Secker, the Archbishop of Canterbury.

[11] Prior, 'The Ladle', *l.* 139.

trust—for such a sight, I will be bold to say, was never seen.[12]

6. With an easy familiarity you add, 'My lord, permit me here to whisper a word' (Is not this *whispering in print* something new?) 'that may be *worth remembering*. In our memory some of the priesthood have not proved so good subjects as might have been expected till they have been *brought over with preferments that were due to other people.*' Meaning, I presume to yourself. Surely his Grace will remember this, which is so well 'worth remembering', and dispose of the next preferment in his gift where it is so justly *due*. If he does not, if he forgets either this, or your other directions, you tell him frankly what will be the consequence. 'We must apply to Parliament.'[d] Or to his Majesty. And indeed how can you avoid it? For 'it would be using him', you think, '*extremely ill*, not to give him proper information that there are now a set of people offering such indignity to his Crown and Government.'

7. However, we are not to think your opposing the Methodists was owing 'to self-interest alone'. Though, what if it was? 'Was I to depart from my duty because it happened to be my interest? Did these saints ever forbear to *preach* to the *mob* in the *fields* for fear lest they should get the pence of the mob? Or do not the *pence* and the *preaching* go hand in hand together?'[e] No, they don't. For many years neither I nor any connected with me have 'got' any 'pence', as you phrase it, 'in the fields'. Indeed, properly speaking, they *never* did. For the collections which Mr. Whitefield made, it is well known, were not for his own use, either in whole or in part. And he has long ago given an account in print of the manner wherein all that was received was expended.[13]

8. But it is not my design to examine at large either your Dedication, Preface, or Sermon. I have only leisure to make a few cursory remarks on your *definition* of the Methodists (so called), and on the account you give of *their* first *rise*, of their *principles* and *practice*—just premising that I speak of those alone who began (as

[d] [Ibid.,] p. 6.

[e] Preface, pp. 2-3.

[12] Free replied that on October 8 or 9, 1753, in Gisburn, Yorkshire, he saw 'a cavalcade of men and women preachers', and that 'the Mercury, or chief speaker of this company of deaconesses and travelling apostles, was a man who had lost an arm.' Wesley himself was not in Yorkshire at that time, and this was several years before Sarah Crosby and Mary Bosanquet began to preach for him, and their group did not remove to Leeds until 1768. The kernel of fact in Free's statement may have been a gathering of Inghamites.

[13] See George Whitefield, *An Account of Money Received and Disbursed for the Orphan-House in Georgia* (London, Strahan, 1741).

you observe) at Oxford. If a thousand other sets of men 'pass under that denomination',[14] yet they are nothing to me. As they have no connexion with *me,* so I am no way concerned to answer either for their principles or practice, any more than you are to answer for all who 'pass under the denomination' of Church of England men.

9. The account you give of their rise is this: 'The Methodists began at Oxford. The name was first given to a few persons who were so uncommonly *methodical* as to keep a diary of the most trivial actions of their lives, as how many slices of bread and butter they ate,[15] how many dishes of tea they drank, how many country dances they danced at their dancing club, or after a fast how many pounds of mutton they devoured. For upon these occasions they eat like lions, having made themselves uncommonly voracious.'[f] Of this not one line is true. For, (1), it was from an ancient sect of physicians, whom we were supposed to resemble in our regular diet and exercise, that we were originally styled Methodists.[16] (2). Not one of us ever kept a diary of 'the most trivial' actions of our lives. (3). Nor did any of us ever set down what or how much we ate[17] or drank. (4). Our dancing club never existed—I never heard of it before. (5). On our fast days we used no food but bread; on the day following we fed as on common days. (6). Therefore our 'voraciousness' and 'eating like lions' is also pure, lively invention.

10. You go on: 'It was not long before these gentlemen began to *dogmatize* in a public manner, feeling a strong inclination to

[f] Preface, p. 6.

---

[14] Free, *Certain Articles,* p. 22; cf. *Rules,* Pref., pp. vi, ix-x.

[15] Orig., 'eat', both in Free and Wesley.

[16] In *The Character of a Methodist* (1742, §3) Wesley had given the same probable derivation of the name, though adding, 'or from their more regular *method* of study and behaviour'. In *A Short History of Methodism* (1765, §5) he again omits any alternative to the 'ancient physicians'. Yet Free may well have had some justification for complaining: 'The person who gave you this name knew nothing in all probability of any such ancient sect of physicians as you mention. Nor was there any similitude between your profession and theirs that could induce him to distinguish you by that title. Neither did you ever at that time of the day pretend to derive the origin of your name from that occasion *yourselves.* But having since dipped into Dr. Freind's *History of Physick,* and met with such a sect of physicians, you thought it would look better if you affected to be their relations . . . than that the world should remember your being nick-named from the whimsical *method* of keeping a diary of all your actions.' (*Dr. Free's Edition of the Rev. Mr. John Wesley's Second Letter,* p. 39. In fact there seems to be no evidence of Wesley having read Dr. John Freind's *History of Physick* [2 vols., London, 1725–26], though his brother Dr. Robert Freind was an acquaintance of the Wesley family.)

[17] Orig., 'eat'.

new-model almost every circumstance or thing in the system of our *national* religion.'[g] Just as true as the rest. These gentlemen were so far from feeling any inclination at all to 'new-model' any circumstance or thing, that during their whole stay at Oxford they were High-Churchmen in the strongest sense—vehemently contending for every circumstance of Church order according to the *old model.* And in Georgia too we were rigorous observers of every *rubric* and *canon,* as well as (to the best of our knowledge) every tenet of the Church. Your account, therefore, of the rise of the Methodists, is a mistake from beginning to end.

11. I proceed to your definition of them: 'By the Methodists was then and is now understood, a set of *enthusiasts* who, pretending to be members of the Church of England, either offend against the order and discipline of the Church, or pervert its doctrine relating to faith and works, and the terms of salvation.'

Another grievous mistake. For whatever 'is now', 'by the Methodists then was' *not* 'understood' any 'set of enthusiasts', or not enthusiasts 'offending against the order and discipline of the Church'. They were tenacious of it to the last degree, in every the least jot and tittle. Neither were they 'then understood to pervert its doctrines relating to faith and works, and the terms of salvation'. For they thought and talked of all these just as you do now, till some of them, after their return from Georgia, were 'perverted' into different sentiments by reading the Book of Homilies. Their perversion therefore (if such it be) is to be dated from this time. Consequently, your definition by no means agrees with the persons defined.

12. However, 'as a shibboleth to distinguish them at present, when they pretend to conceal themselves, [one may] throw out this or suchlike proposition, "Good works are necessary to salvation."' You might have spared yourself the labour of proving this. For who is there that denies it? Not I. Not any in connexion with me. So that this 'shibboleth' is just good for nothing.

And yet we firmly believe 'that a man is justified by faith, without the works of the law';[18] that to him that worketh not, but believeth on him that justifieth the ungodly, his faith, without any good work preceding, is counted to him for righteousness.[19] We

[g] [Pref.,] p. 7.

---

[18] Cf. Rom. 3:28.
[19] See Rom. 4:5.

believe (to express it a little more largely) that we are accounted righteous before God, only for the merit of Christ, by faith, and not for our own works or deservings. Good works follow after justification, springing out of true, living faith, so that by them living faith may be as evidently known as a tree discerned by the fruit.[20] And hence it follows that as the body without the soul is dead, so *that* faith which is without works is dead also. This therefore, properly speaking, is not faith—as a dead man is not properly a man.

13. You add: 'The original Methodists affect to call themselves Methodists of the Church of England. By which they plainly inform us, there are others of their body who do not profess to belong to it. Whence we may infer that the Methodists who take our name do yet by acknowledging them as namesakes and brethren, give themselves the lie when they say they are of our communion.'[h] *Our* name! *Our* communion! *Apage cum ista tua magnificentia!*[21] How came it, I pray, to be *your* name any more than Mr. *Venn*'s?[22] But waiving this: Here is another train of mistakes. For (1), we do not 'call ourselves Methodists' at all. (2). That we call ourselves members of the Church of England is certain. Such we ever were, and such we are at this day. (3). Yet we do not 'by this plainly inform' you that there are others of our body who do not belong to it. By what rule of logic do you infer this conclusion from those premises? (4). You have another inference full as good: 'Hence one may infer that by acknowledging them as namesakes and brethren, they give themselves the lie when they say they are of our communion.' As we do not take the name of Methodists at all, so we do not acknowledge any 'namesakes' in this. But we acknowledge as 'brethren' all Dissenters (whether they are called Methodists or not) who labour to have a conscience void of offence toward God and toward man.[23] What lies upon you to prove is this: whoever acknowledges any Dissenters as brethren does hereby give himself the lie when he says he is a member of the Church of England.

[h] [Pref.,] p. 9.

---

[20] See Matt. 12:33.

[21] Cf. Terence, *Phormio*, 930 (V.vii.37): 'In hinc malam rem cum ista magnificentia'—'Away with you and your grandiloquence!'

[22] See above, p. 317.

[23] Acts 24:16.

14. However, you allow, there may be place for repentance. For 'if any of the founders of this sect renounce the opinions they once were charged with, they may be permitted to lay aside the name.'[i] But what are the opinions which you require us to renounce? What are, according to you, the *principles* of the Methodists?

You say, in general, 'they are *contradictory* to the gospel, *contradictory* to the Church of England, full of *blasphemy and impiety*, and ending in downright *atheism*.'[j]

For '(1). They expound the Scripture in such a manner as to make it contradict itself.

(2). With blasphemy, impiety, and diabolical frenzy they contradict our Saviour, by denying that he will judge men according to their works.

(3). By denying this they destroy the essential attributes of God, and ruin his character as Judge of the world.'[k]

In support of the first charge you say, 'It is notorious, and few men of common sense attempt to prove what is "notorious" till they meet with people of such notorious *impudence* as to deny it.'

I must really deny it. Why then, you will 'prove' it by Mr. Mason's[24] own words. Hold, sir! Mr. Mason's words prove nothing. For we are now speaking of *original* Methodists. But he is not one of them. Nor is he in connexion with them, neither with Mr. Whitefield nor me.[25] So that what Mr. Mason speaks, be it right or wrong, is nothing to the present purpose. Therefore unless you can find some better proof, this whole charge falls to the ground.

Well, here it is—Roger Balls.[l] Pray, who is Roger Balls? No

[i] [Pref.,] p. 10. [The pages for this note and the next but one were transposed by the printer.]

[j] P. 11.

[k] P. 12.

[l] [Free, *Rules*,] Dedication, p. 5 [viz., a quotation from '*The Mystery of Christ Crucified*, etc., by Roger Balls, Minister of the Gospel, from Sandwich in Kent, Newcastle: printed for and sold by the publisher'].

---

[24] William Mason, clockmaker of Rotherhithe Wall, who wrote *Remarks and Observations on the Morality and Divinity contained in Dr. Free's Certain Articles* . . . (signed 'W.M.' [1758]; for excerpts see 2nd edn., of Free, *Certain Articles* [i.e., *A Display* . . .], pp. 20-22, and the 'almost anonymous pamphlet' in the preface to Free's *Rules*, pp. x-xii, though Mason is not named therein).

[25] Free replied (in his edn. of Wesley's *Second Letter*, pp. 68-69), 'He says he is a Methodist of the Church of England, [and] had so far connections as to be one of your hearers at Mrs. Gin's meeting-house in Southwark.'

more a Methodist than he is a Turk. I know not one good thing he ever said or did beside the telling all men, I am no Methodist, which he generally does in the first sentence he speaks, when he can find any to hear him. He is therefore one of your own allies. And a champion worthy of his cause![26]

If then you have no more than this to advance in support of your first charge, you have alleged what you are not able to prove. And the more heavy that allegation is, the more unkind, the more unjust, the more unchristian, the more inhuman it is [to] bring it without proof.

15. In support of the second charge you say, 'Our Saviour declares our *works* to be the object of his judgment. But the Methodist, for the perdition of the souls of his followers, says our works are of *no consideration* at all.'[m]

Who says so? Mr. Whitefield? Or my brother? Or I? We say the direct contrary. But 'one of my *anonymous correspondents*'[27] says so. Who is he? How do you know he is a Methodist? For aught [that] appears, he may be another of your allies, a brother to Roger Balls.

Three or threescore *anonymous* correspondents cannot yield one grain of proof, any more than an hundred anonymous Remarkers on *Theron and Aspasio*.[28] Before these can prove what the Methodists hold you must prove that these are Methodists—either that they are *original* Methodists, or in connexion with them.

16. Will you say, 'If these were not Methodists themselves they would not defend the Methodists?' I deny the consequence. Men may be far from being Methodists, and yet willing to do the Methodists justice. I have known a clergyman of note say to another, who had just been preaching a very warm[29] sermon: 'Sir, I do not thank you at all for this. I have no acquaintance with Mr.

[m] [Free, *Rules*, Pref.,] p. 14.

---

[26] To Wesley's disavowal of Balls as a Methodist, Free replied (edn. of *Second Letter*, pp. 67-68) that all he knew of Balls was from a sermon sent to him along with Wesley's Assize Sermon, but that he must be 'a *methodistical* fellow, if not a Methodist'.

[27] Pref., p. 14, referring to one of Free's correspondents.

[28] Cf. Free's edn. of Wesley's *Second Letter*, pp. 61-62, where Free quoted from 'the anonymous Remarker on *Theoren and Aspasio*' (London, 1765), whose author Free described as 'the weak and crazy Mr. Hervey, one of the reputed Fathers of Methodism, whose laboured antichristian theology and religious blasphemy have been so zealously propagated through the land, and revered as the Bible by the Methodists'.

[29] For 'warm' cf. *Advice to the People called Methodists*, §16, n. 21.

Whitefield or Mr. Wesley. And I do not agree with them in opinion. But I will have no more railing in my pulpit.'

17. From the principles of the Methodists you proceed to their practice. 'They hunt', say you, 'for *extraordinary marks* and *revelations* whereby to know the state of the soul.'[n] The *marks* by which I know the state of any soul are the inward fruit of the spirit—love, joy, peace, meekness, gentleness, goodness, long-suffering, temperance, patience[30]—shown not by words only, but by the genuine fruit of outward holiness.

Again, 'They magnify their office beyond the truth, by high pretences to miraculous inspiration.'[o] To this assertion we have answered over and over, we pretend to no other 'inspiration' than that which not only every true gospel minister, but every real Christian enjoys.

Again, 'the end of all impostors is some kind of worldly gain. And it is difficult for them to conceal their views entirely. The love of filthy lucre will appear, either by the *use* they *make* of it, or the *means* of *getting* it.'[p] As to the 'use' made of it, you are silent. But as to the 'means' of getting it, you say: 'Besides inhumanity wringing from the poor, the helpless widows, the weeping orphans' (the proof! the proof!), 'they creep into houses, and lead captive silly women, laden with divers lusts.' 'Tis easy to *say* this, and ten times more. But can you *prove* it? And ought you to *say* it till you can?

I shall not concern myself with anything in your Appendix[31] but what relates to me in particular. This premised, I observe on No. 1:[32] There are several instances in my *Journals* of persons that were in *agonies* of grief or fear, and *roared* for the disquietness of their heart;[33] of some that exceedingly *trembled* before God, perhaps *fell down* to the ground, and of others whom God in his adorable Providence suffered to be *lunatic* and sore vexed.[34] The particular instances hereof to which you refer have been largely

[n] Sermon, p. 9.
[o] P. 23.
[p] P. 29.

[30] Gal. 5:22-23.
[31] 'The Appendix: containing some specimens of the blasphemous doctrines and delusions of Methodists, and Methodistical writers, noted and censured in the foregoing Sermon', pp. 32-40.
[32] 'Of Mock Possession and Inspirations'.
[33] See Ps. 38:8 (BCP).
[34] Matt. 17:15.

vindicated already, in the two letters to the Rev. Dr. Church,[35] as well as that to the late Bishop of London.[36]

In the six following Numbers I am not concerned. The eighth contains those words from my second *Journal*, 'The rest of the day we spent in hearing the *wonderful work* which God is *beginning* to work all over the earth.'[37] On this likewise I have spoken at large to Dr. Church and Bishop Gibson. The sum is: It is *a great work* when one notorious sinner is throughly changed in heart and life. It is wonderfully great when God works this entire change in a large number of people, particularly when it is done in a very short time. But so he hath wrought in Kingswood, Cornwall, Newcastle. It is therefore a truly *wonderful* work which God hath now more than *begun* to work upon earth.

I have now sir, briefly answered for myself, which if required I will do more at large. But I trust it does already appear to every impartial reader, that of the many and heavy allegations you have brought, with an unparalleled bitterness of spirit, and an acrimony of language almost without precedent, you have not yet proved one. How far you are to be commended for this (unless by Messrs. Balls and the *Monthly Reviewers*) it is not for me to judge. Let all lovers of truth, of humanity, and candour determine. At present I have no more to add than that I beseech the Father of everlasting compassion to show more mercy to you than you have shown to,

Reverend sir,
Your servant for Christ's sake,
John Wesley

[35] See above, pp. 80-122, 160-237.
[36] See 11:335-51 in this edn.
[37] JWJ, June 17, 1738.

REASONS
AGAINST A
SEPARATION
FROM THE
CHURCH of ENGLAND.

By JOHN WESLEY, A.M.

Printed in the Year 1758.

WITH

HYMNS for the PREACHERS among the METHODISTS (so called),

By CHARLES WESLEY, A.M.

THE SECOND EDITION.

LONDON:

Printed by W. STRAHAN, and Sold at the Foundery in Upper-Moorfields.

MDCCLX.

16

REASONS AGAINST A SEPARATION FROM THE CHURCH OF ENGLAND

(1758)

AN INTRODUCTORY COMMENT

The publication of this writing followed a critical period in the discussions of John Wesley with his brother Charles and with his preachers on the issue of separation from the Church of England. In October 1754, Charles Wesley recorded that two lay preachers, Charles Perronet in London, and Thomas Walsh in Reading, had administered the sacrament of Holy Communion. Charles suspected that John was on the point of ordaining some of his preachers; he argued strongly against this and sought as much support as he could muster for the debate in the ensuing Conference of 1755 in Leeds. John probably had no intention at that time of ordaining (though he maintained later that ordination by him did not constitute separation from the Church of England); and he wrote a powerful treatise against separation (which is not preserved) when he found himself in complete opposition to Micaiah Towgood's statement of the Nonconformist position, A Dissent from the Church of England fully justified, *which he studied at the time.*

At the Conference, John read a paper in which he argued that it was in law perfectly possible to continue Methodist practices, and indeed to criticize the canons and other parts of the Book of Common Prayer, without separating from the church; he contended that it was not expedient for him to ordain anyone to administer the sacraments (though he defended his practice of appointing preachers), and he urged all his preachers to demonstrate their loyalty to the Church and set a good example to the Methodists by regularly attending worship in the parish church and by absenting themselves from dissenting meetings.

After three days' debate his views prevailed, though Charles's fears of later separation were not entirely laid to rest (see Frank Baker, John Wesley and the Church of England, *pp. 164-67, for this whole series of events). In 1758, when the fierceness of argument had largely abated, John Wesley, in publishing* A Preservative against Unsettled Notions in Religion, *included the main points of the paper which he had read to the 1755 Conference, and this digest is the present writing. For the paper itself, see Appendix C, 'Ought we to Separate from the Church of England?'*

In 1760, Charles republished it with closing comments of his own and the addition of seven hymns calling on Methodist preachers to be loyal to the Church of England. This version of the work reached ten thousand copies and was reprinted in 1785. John included the seven hymns when he published the treatise in his Works *of 1773, thus endorsing their intent and content.*

Beneath the arguments here and elsewhere (see also Some Thoughts upon an Important Question *and* Farther Thoughts on Separation from the Church, *pp. 518-19, 538-40 below; and the sermons 'Of the Church' and 'On Schism' in Vol. 3 of this edn. lay Wesley's profound conviction, which he shared with his brother, that the church of Christ is one church, that the Church of England is its embodiment in England, and that to divide the Church of England would be a sin of terrible magnitude, unless it had committed the prior sin of commanding things contrary to the Word of God—which the Church of England had not done.*

For a summary of the six editions published during Wesley's lifetime, a stemma illustrating the transmission of the text, and a list of the substantive variant readings from the edited text (based on that in the Preservative, *1758), see Appendix A, pp. 541ff. For full bibliographical details see* Bibliography, *No. 240.*

Reasons against a Separation from the Church of England

'Printed in the year 1758'[1]

Whether it be *lawful* or no (which itself may be disputed, being not so clear a point as some may imagine) it is by no means *expedient* for us to separate from the established Church:

[I.] 1. Because it would be a contradiction to the solemn and repeated declarations which we have made in all manner of ways, in preaching, in print, and in private conversation.

2. Because (on this as well as many other accounts) it would give huge occasion of offence to those who seek and desire occasion, to all the enemies of God and his truth.

3. Because it would exceedingly prejudice against us many who fear, yea, who love God, and thereby hinder their receiving so much, perhaps any farther, benefit from our preaching.

4. Because it would hinder multitudes of those who neither love nor fear God from hearing us at all, and thereby leave them in the hands of the devil.[2]

5. Because it would occasion many hundreds, if not some thousands, of those who are now united with us, to separate from us; yea, and some of those who have a deep work of grace in their souls.

6. Because it would be throwing balls of wild-fire among them that are now quiet in the land. We are now sweetly united together in love. We mostly think and speak the same thing. But this would occasion inconceivable strife and contention between those who left and those who remained in the Church, as well as between those who left us and those who remained with us—nay, and between those very persons who remained, as they were variously inclined one way or the other.

7. Because, whereas controversy is now asleep, and we in great

[1] Inserted on title-page of the two 1760 edns.

[2] All except the two edns. of the *Preservative* omit 'and thereby . . . devil'.

measure live peaceably with all men,[3] so that we are strangely at leisure to spend our whole time and strength in enforcing plain, practical, vital religion (O what would many of our forefathers have given to have enjoyed so blessed a calm!), this would utterly banish peace from among us, and that without hope of its return. It would engage me for one in a thousand controversies, both in public and private (for I should be in conscience obliged to give the reasons of my conduct, and to defend those reasons against all opposers), and so take me off from those more useful labours which might otherwise employ the short remainder of my life.

8. Because to form the plan of a new Church would require infinite time and care (which might be far more profitably bestowed), with much more wisdom and greater depth and extensiveness of thought than any of us are masters of.

9. Because from some having barely entertained a distant thought of this, evil fruits have already followed, such as prejudice against the clergy in general, an aptness to believe ill of them; contempt (not without a degree of bitterness) of clergymen as such, and a sharpness of language toward the whole order, utterly unbecoming either gentlemen or Christians.

10. Because the experiment has been so frequently tried already, and the success never answered the expectation. God has since the Reformation raised up from time to time many witnesses of pure religion. If these lived and died (like John Arndt,[4] Robert Bolton,[5] and many others) in the churches to which they belonged, notwithstanding the wickedness which overflowed both the teachers and people therein, they spread the leaven of true religion far and wide, and were more and more useful, till they went to paradise. But if upon any provocation or consideration whatever they separated and founded distinct parties, their influence was more and more confined; they grew less and less useful to others, and generally lost the spirit of religion themselves in the spirit of controversy.

11. Because we have melancholy instances of this even now before our eyes. Many have in our memory left the Church, and formed themselves into distinct bodies. And certainly some of

[3] Rom. 12:18.

[4] John Arndt (1555–1611), whose *True Christianity*, abridged by Wesley from Anthony W. Boehm's English translation from the German, Wesley had inserted in his *Christian Library* (1749–51), Vols. I-II.

[5] The Puritan Robert Bolton (1572–1631), several of whose works Wesley included in his *Christian Library* (1751), Vols. VII-IX.

them from a real persuasion that they should do God more service. But have any separated themselves and prospered? Have they been either more holy or more useful than they were before?

12. Because by such a separation we should not only throw away the peculiar glorying which God has given us, that we do and will suffer all things for our brethren's sake, though the more we love them the less we be loved; but should act in direct contradiction to that very end for which we believe God hath raised us up. The chief design of his Providence in sending us out is undoubtedly to quicken our brethren. And the first message of all our preachers is to the lost sheep of the Church of England. Now would it not be a flat contradiction to this design to separate from the Church? These things being considered, we cannot apprehend, whether it be lawful in itself or no, that it is lawful for us—were it only on this ground, that it is by no means expedient.

II. It has indeed been objected that till we do separate we cannot be a compact, united body.

It is true we cannot till then be a 'compact united body', if you mean by that expression a body distinct from all others. And we have no desire so to be.

It has been objected, secondly, 'It is mere cowardice and fear of persecution which makes you desire to remain united with them.'

This cannot be proved. Let everyone examine his own heart, and not judge his brother.

It is not probable. We never yet, for any persecution, when we were in the midst of it, either turned back from the work or even slackened our pace.

But this is certain, that although persecution many times proves an unspeakable blessing to them that suffer it, yet we ought not wilfully to bring it upon ourselves. Nay, we ought to do whatever can lawfully be done in order to prevent it. We ought to avoid it so far as we lawfully can—when persecuted in one city, to flee into another.[6] If God should suffer a general persecution, who would be able to abide it we know not. Perhaps those who talk loudest might flee first. Remember the case of Dr. Pendleton.[7]

[6] See Matt. 10:23.

[7] Dr. Henry Pendleton (d. 1557), after preaching against Lutheranism under Henry VIII, himself became a Protestant under Edward VI, but after boasting of his courageous fidelity, once more turned Roman Catholic under Queen Mary.

III. [1.] Upon the whole one cannot but observe how desirable it is that all of us who are engaged in the same work should think and speak the same thing, be united in one judgment, and use one and the same language.

Do we not all now see *ourselves*, the *Methodists* (so called) in general, *the Church*, and *the clergy* in a clear light?

We look upon *ourselves*, not as the authors or ringleaders of a particular sect or party (it is the farthest thing from our thoughts), but as messengers of God to those who are Christians in name, but heathens in heart and in life, to call them back to that from which they are fallen, to real, genuine Christianity. We are therefore debtors to all these, of whatever opinion or denomination; and are consequently to do all that in us lies to please all, for their good, to edification.[8]

We look upon the *Methodists* (so called) in general, not as any particular party (this would exceedingly obstruct the grand design for which we conceive God has raised them up), but as living witnesses in and to every party of that Christianity which we preach; which is hereby demonstrated to be a real thing, and visibly held out to all the world.

We look upon *England* as that part of the world, and *the Church* as that part of England, to which all we who were born and have been brought up therein owe our first and chief regard. We feel in ourselves a strong *στοργή*,[9] a kind of natural affection for our country, which we apprehend Christianity was never designed either to root out or to impair. We have a more peculiar concern for our brethren, for that part of our countrymen to whom we have been joined from our youth up, by ties of a religious as well as a civil nature. True it is that they are in general 'without God in the world'.[10] So much the more do our bowels yearn over them. They do lie 'in darkness and the shadow of death'.[11] The more tender is our compassion for them. And when we have the fullest conviction of that complicated wickedness which covers them as a flood,[12] then do we feel the most (and we desire to feel yet more) of that inexpressible emotion with which our blessed Lord beheld Jerusalem, and wept and lamented over it.[13] Then are we the most

[8] See Rom. 15:2.

[9] Natural affection; the word does not occur in the Greek New Testament, although *ἄστοργος* does in Rom. 1:31 and 2 Tim. 3:3, in contexts which imply approval of *στοργή*.

[10] Eph. 2:12.

[11] Ps. 107:10.

[12] See Amos 8:8.

[13] See Matt. 23:37, etc.

willing 'to spend and to be spent'[14] for them, yea, to 'lay down our lives for our brethren'.[15]

We look upon *the clergy*, not only as a part of these our brethren, but as that part whom God by his adorable Providence has called to be watchmen over the rest, for whom therefore they are to give a strict account. If these then neglect their important charge, if they do not watch over them with all their power, they will be of all men most miserable,[16] and so are entitled to our deepest compassion. So that to feel, and much more to express, either contempt or bitterness toward them, betrays an utter ignorance of ourselves and of the spirit which we especially should be of.

Because this is a point of uncommon concern, let us consider it a little farther.

The clergy, wherever we are, are either friends to the truth, or neuters, or enemies to it.

If they are friends to it, certainly we should do everything and omit everything we can with a safe conscience, in order to continue, and, if it be possible, increase their goodwill to it.

If they neither further nor hinder it, we should do all that in us lies, both for their sakes and for the sake of their several flocks, to give their neutrality the right turn, that it may change into love rather than hatred.

If they are enemies, still we should not despair of lessening, if not removing, their prejudice. We should try every means again and again. We should employ all our care, labour, prejudice, joined with fervent prayer, to overcome evil with good,[17] to melt their hardness into love.

It is true that when any of these openly wrest the Scriptures, and deny the grand truths of the gospel, we cannot but declare and defend, at convenient opportunities, the important truths which they deny. But in this case especially we have need of all gentleness and meekness of wisdom.[18] Contempt, sharpness, bitterness, can do no good. 'The wrath of man worketh not the righteousness of God.'[19] Harsh methods have been tried again and again (by two or three unsettled railers)—at Wednesbury, St.

[14] 2 Cor. 12:15.
[15] Cf. 1 John 3:16.
[16] 1 Cor. 15:19.
[17] Rom. 12:21.
[18] Jas. 3:13.
[19] Jas. 1:20.

Ives, Cork, Canterbury. And how did they succeed? They always occasioned numberless evils, often wholly stopped the course of the gospel. Therefore, were it only on a prudential account, were conscience unconcerned therein, it should be a sacred rule to all our preachers, 'No contempt, no bitterness to the clergy.'

2. Might it not be another (at least prudential) rule, for every Methodist preacher 'not to frequent any Dissenting Meeting'? (Though we blame none who have been always accustomed to it.) But if *we* do this, certainly our people will. Now this is actually separating from the Church. If therefore it is (at least) not expedient to separate, neither is this expedient. Indeed we may attend our assemblies and the Church too, because they are at different hours. But we cannot attend both the Meeting[20] and the Church, because they are at the same hours.

If it be said, 'But at the Church we are fed with chaff, whereas at the Meeting we have wholesome food,' we answer: (1). The Prayers of the Church are not chaff—they are substantial food for any who are alive to God. (2). The Lord's Supper is not chaff, but pure and wholesome for all who receive it with upright hearts. Yea, (3), in almost all the sermons we hear there we hear many great and important truths. And whoever has a spiritual discernment may easily separate the chaff from the wheat therein. (4). How little is the case mended at the Meeting! Either the teachers are *New Light Men,*[21] denying the Lord that bought them,[22] and overturning his gospel from the very foundations; or they are predestinarians, and so preach predestination and final perseverance, more or less. Now whatever this may be to them who are educated therein, yet to those of our brethren who have lately embraced it, repeated experience shows it is not wholesome

[20] I.e., of course, the 'Dissenting Meeting'. Cf. Johnson's *Dictionary* (1755), under 'Meeting': '3. A conventicle; an assembly of Dissenters'. Wesley attempted to confine his use of this proper noun to these and steered his people away from the term 'meeting-house' for a Methodist place of worship to 'preaching-house'.

[21] It does not seem that there was a religious group which used this as its official title, but Wesley was no doubt referring to the High-Calvinist near-antinomian party in contemporary Dissent. 'New Light' was a familiar term, as Wesley knew, in New England Dissent; the movement which claimed this name there was anti-Arminian and stood for enthusiasm and the guidance of the Holy Spirit rather than the formal and the rational, for free grace rather than good works, and for the church as consisting solely of those clearly converted ('visible saints'). It reached its peak in 1754 and was beginning to decline when Wesley wrote, but he was sensitive on the matter because of the defection of John Edwards, John Whitford, and others to Dissent. (I owe the substance of this note to Dr. Geoffrey Nuttall. Ed.)

[22] 2 Pet. 2:1.

food—rather to them it has the effect of deadly poison. In a short time it destroys all their zeal for God. They grow fond of opinions and strife of words. They despise self-denial and the daily cross; and to complete all, wholly separate from their brethren.

3. Nor is it expedient for any *Methodist* preacher to imitate the Dissenters in their manner of praying. Either in his *tone*—all particular tones, both in prayer and preaching, should be avoided with the utmost care. Nor in[23] his *language*—all his words should be plain and simple, such as the lowest of his hearers both use and understand. Or in the *length* of his prayer, which should not usually exceed four or five minutes, either before or after sermon. One might add, neither should we sing, like them, in a slow, drawling manner—we sing swift, both because it saves time, and because it tends to awake and enliven the soul.

4. Fourthly, if we continue in the Church, not by chance, or for want of thought, but upon solid and well-weighed reasons, then we should never speak contemptuously of the Church, or anything pertaining to it. In some sense it is the mother of us all who have been brought up therein. We ought never to make her blemishes matter of diversion, but rather of solemn sorrow before God. We ought never to talk ludicrously of them; no, not at all, without clear necessity. Rather we should conceal them, as far as ever we can without bringing guilt upon our own conscience. And we should all use every rational and scriptural means to bring others to the same temper and behaviour. I say, *all;* for if some of us are thus minded, and others of an opposite spirit and behaviour, this will breed a real schism among ourselves. It will of course divide us into two parties, each of which will be liable to perpetual jealousies, suspicions, and animosities against the other. Therefore on this account likewise it is expedient in the highest degree that we should be tender of the Church to which we belong.

5. In order to secure this end, to cut off all jealousy and suspicion from our friends, and hope from our enemies, of our having any design to separate from the Church, it would be well for every Methodist preacher who has no scruple concerning it to attend the Service of the Church as often as conveniently he can. And the more we attend it, the more we love it, as constant experience shows. On the contrary, the longer we abstain from it, the less desire we have to attend it at all.

[23] 1770 reads, 'Nor is his language', an error; cf. p. 578, v. 3, line 3.

6. Lastly, whereas we are surrounded on every side by those who are equally enemies to us and to the Church of England; and whereas these are long practised in this war, and skilled in all the objections against it—while our brethren on the other hand are quite strangers to them all, and so on a sudden know not how to answer them—it is highly expedient for every preacher to be provided with sound answers to those objections, and then to instruct the societies where he labours how to defend themselves against those assaults. It would be therefore well for you carefully to read over the foregoing *Preservative*,[24] together with *Serious Thoughts concerning Perseverance*[25] and *Predestination Calmly Considered.*[26] And when you are masters of them yourselves, it will be easy for you to recommend and explain them to our societies, that they may 'no more be tossed to and fro by every wind of doctrine', but being settled in one mind and one judgment, by solid scriptural and rational arguments, 'may grow up in all things into him who is our head, even Jesus Christ'.[27]

John Wesley[28]

I think myself bound in duty to add my testimony to my brother's. His twelve reasons against our ever separating from the Church of England are mine also. I subscribe to them with all my heart. Only with regard to the first *I* am quite clear that it is neither expedient nor LAWFUL for *me* to separate—and I never had the least inclination or temptation so to do. My affection for the Church is as strong as ever. And I clearly see my calling, which is to live and to die in her communion. This, therefore, I am determined to do, the Lord being my helper.

I have subjoined the HYMNS for the Lay Preachers, still farther 'to secure this end, to cut off all jealousy and suspicion from our friends, or hope from our enemies, of our having any design of

[24] All edns. except the *Preservative* read: 'to read over the *Preservative against unsettled Notions in Religion*'.

[25] *Serious Thoughts upon the Perseverance of the Saints* (1751); see *Bibliography*, No. 192, and Vol. 12 in this edn.

[26] *Predestination Calmly Considered* (1752); see *Bibliography*, No. 194, and Vol. 12 in this edn.

[27] Cf. Eph. 4:14-15.

[28] Wesley's name is not present in the *Preservative*, but was clearly added by Charles to point out their individual responsibilities in the work, more especially his own addition of the following two paragraphs.

ever separating from the Church'.[29] I have no secret reserve, or distant thought of it. I never had. Would to God all the Methodist preachers were, in this respect, like minded with

Charles Wesley

Hymns For the Use of the Methodist Preachers[30]

Hymn I

1 O Lord, our strength and righteousness,
   Our base, and head, and corner-stone,
Our peace with God, our mutual peace,
   Unite, and keep thy servants one,
That while we speak in Jesu's name,
We all may speak, and think, the same.

2 That spirit of love to each impart,
   That fervent mind which was in thee;
So shall we all our strength exert,
   In heart, and word, and deed agree
T' advance the kingdom of thy grace,
And spread thine everlasting praise.

3 O never may the fiend steal in,
   Or one unstable soul deceive.
Assailed by our besetting sin,
   And tempted sore the work to leave,
Preserve us, Lord, from self and pride,
And let nor life, nor death divide.

4 Pride, only pride, can cause divorce,
   Can separate 'twixt our souls and thee:
Pride, only pride, is discord's source,
   The bane of peace and charity.
But us it never more shall part,
For thou art greater than our heart.

5 Wherefore to thine almighty hand
   The keeping of our hearts we give,
Firm in one mind and spirit stand,
   To thee and to each other cleave,
Fixed on the Rock which cannot move,
And meekly safe in humble love.

[29] See III.5 above.

[30] Most if not all of these seven hymns appear to have been written by Charles to meet the emergency of preachers whom he believed were seeking to improve their status by becoming ordained clergy or Dissenting ministers. None were republished during his

Hymn II

1 Forth in thy strength, O Lord, we go,
Forth in thy steps and loving mind,
To pay the gospel debt we owe
(The word of grace for all mankind),
To sow th' incorruptible seed,
And find the lost, and wake the dead.

2 The wand'ring sheep of England's fold
Demand our first and tenderest care,
Who under sin and Satan sold
Usurp the Christian character,
The Christian character profane,
And take thy Church's name in vain.

3 Or shameless advocates for hell
Their crimes they Sodom-like confess,
Or varnished with a specious zeal,
An empty form of godliness,
The power they impiously blaspheme,
And call our hope a madman's dream.

4 Haters of God, yet still they cry,
'The temple of the Lord are we!
The Church, the Church!'—who dare defy
Thy self-existent deity,
Proudly oppose thy righteous reign,
And crucify their God again.

5 'Gainst these by thee sent forth to fight,
A suffering war we calmly wage,
With patience meet their fierce despite,
With love repay their furious rage,
Reviled, we bless; defamed, entreat;
And spurned, we kiss the spurner's feet.

6 Armed with thine all-sufficient grace,
Thy meek unconquerable mind,
Our foes we cordially embrace
(The filth and refuse of mankind)
We gladly all resign our breath,
To save one precious soul from death.

lifetime. For each of them at least one MS version is available in Charles Wesley's hand, and all of them appear in his MS 'Miscellaneous Hymns' (*c.* 1786), 316 pages containing 211 items, of which these seven are to be found on pp. 115-27 (see Methodist Archives, Manchester). In this printed appearance no account has been taken of variants between the original and either the other edns. or the MS versions, unless it is to show alterations made by John Wesley in his *Works*.

Hymn III

1 So be it, Lord! If thou ordain,
We come to suffer all thy will,
The utmost violence to sustain
Of those that can the body kill,
But having pushed us to the shore
The feeble worms can do no more.

2 We come, depending on thy name,
For we have counted first the cost.
Let ease, and liberty, and fame,
And friends, and life itself be lost,
We come our faithfulness t' approve,
And pay thee back thy dying love.

3 Not in a confident conceit
Of our own strength, and virtuous power,
We offer up ourselves to meet
The fierceness of that fiery hour:
Left to ourselves we all shall fly,
And I shall first my Lord deny.

4 I first, of ill o'ercome, shall yield,
Apostate from thy glorious cause,
Shall vilely cast away my shield,
And hate the haters of thy cross,
Retort the sharp opprobrious word,
Or smite with the offensive sword.

5 Strange fire will in this bosom burn
Unless thou quench it with thy blood;
Impatient of their cruel scorn
My spirit will throw off the load,
'And Baal's priests with wrath repel,
And send th' accursed brood to hell.'

6 Or I shall gall the *mitred* race
By satire keen, and railings rude,
By proud contempt, and malice base,
Scurrilous wit, and laughter lewd,
Laughter which soon itself bemoans,
And ends in everlasting groans.

7 But do not, Lord, from us remove,
While sin and Satan are so near;
But arm us with thy patient love,
That, only to ourselves severe,
The world we may, like thee, oppose,
And die a ransom for our foes.

Hymn IV

1 Master, at thy command we rise,
No prophets we, or prophets' sons,
Or mighty, or well-born, or wise;
But quickened clods, but breathing stones,
Urged to cry out, constrained to call,
And tell mankind—He died for all!

2 We speak because *they* hold their peace
Who *should* thy dying love proclaim.
We *must* declare thy righteousness,
Thy truth, and power, and saving name,
Though the dumb ass with accent clear
Rebuke the silence of the seer.

3 But shall we e'er ourselves forget,
And in our gifts and graces trust,
With wild contempt the prophets treat,
Proudly against the branches boast,
Or dare the rulers vilify,
Or mock the priests of God most high?

4 'Let them alone,' thy wisdom cries,
If blind conductors of the blind!
Let them alone, our heart replies,
And draws us to the work assigned,
The work of publishing the word,
And seizing sinners for our Lord.

5 Here let us spend our utmost zeal,
Here let us all our powers exert,
To testify thy gracious will,
Inform the world how kind thou art,
And nothing know, desire, approve,
But Jesus—and thy bleeding love.

Hymn V

1 Jesu, thy waiting servants see
Assembled here with one accord,
Ready to be sent forth by thee,
To preach, when thou shalt give, the word:
Now, Lord, our work, our province show,
For lo! we come thy will to do.

2 O what a scene attracts our eyes!
What multitudes of lifeless souls!
An open vale before us lies,
A place of graves, a place of skulls,

The desolate house of England's sons,
A Church—a charnel of dry bones!

3 The slaves of pride, ambition, lust,
Our broken pale, alas, receives!
The world into the temple thrust,
And make our Church a den of thieves,
Her grief, her burden, and her shame;
Yet all assume the Church's name.

4 Her desolate state too well we know,
But neither hate her, nor despise:
Our bosoms bleed, our tears o'erflow;
We view her, Saviour, with thine eyes
(O might she know in this her day!)
And still we weep, and still we pray.

5 We pray that these dry bones may live:
We see the answer of our prayer!
Thou dost a thousand tokens give,
That England's Church is still thy care;
Ten thousand witnesses appear,
Ten thousand proofs that God is here!

6 Here then, O God, vouchsafe to dwell,
And mercy on our Zion show;
Her inbred enemies expel,
Avenge her of her hellish foe,
Cause on her wastes thy face to shine,
And comfort her with light divine.

7 O Light of life, thy spirit shed,
In all his cheering, quick'ning power.
Thy word that raised *us* from the dead
Can raise ten thousand, thousand more,
Can bring them up from nature's grave,
And the whole house of Israel save.

Hymn VI

1 Great Guardian of Brittania's land,
To thee we here present our blood,
Set forth the last, a desperate band
Devoted for our country's good:
Our brethren dear, our flesh and bone,
We live, and die, for them alone.

2 *Our brethren*—tho' they still disclaim,
And us despitefully intreat,

With scornful rage cast out our name,
  Trample as dirt beneath their feet,
Out of their synagogues expel,
And doom us to the hottest hell.

3 If thou preserve our souls in peace
  Our brethren shall afflict in vain:
Most patient when they most oppress,
  We all their cruel wrongs sustain,
And strengthened by thy meek'ning power,
The more they hate, we love the more.

4 No, never shall their rage prevail,
  Or force us the dry bones to leave:
The more they push us from the pale,
  The closer we to Zion cleave,
And, daily in the temple found,
Delight to kiss the sacred ground.

5 If some defile the hallowed place,
  The truth, and us, with slanders load,
Or fiercely from their altars chase,
  And rob us of the children's food,
We will not quit thy house and Word,
Or loathe the offerings of the Lord.

6 Should those who sit in Moses' seat
  Conspire thy little flock to harm,
Judge in their courts, and scourge, and beat,
  And bruise us with the ruler's arm,
Matter of joy our shame we make,
And bear it, Saviour, for thy sake.

7 Or should they stir the people up
  Our goods to spoil, our limbs to tear,
Sustained by that immortal hope
  Their lawless violence we bear;
Or laid in bonds our voices raise,
And shake the dungeon with thy praise.

8 A gazing-stock to fiends and men,
  When armed with thine all-patient power,
As sheep appointed to be slain,
  We wait the last, the fiery hour,
And ne'er from England's Church will move,
Till torn away—to that above.

Hymn VII

The Preacher's Prayer for the Flock

1 Shepherd of souls, the great, the good,
For the dear purchase of thy blood
To thee in faith we pray:
The lambs and sheep of England's fold,
Now in thy book of life enrolled,
Preserve unto that day.

2 Whom thou by us hast gathered in,
Defend the little flock from sin,
From error's paths secure:
Stay with them, Lord, when we depart,
And guard the issues of their heart,
And keep their conscience pure.

3 Soon as their guides are taken home
We know the grievous wolves will come,
Determined not to spare;
The stragglers from thy wounded side
The wolves will into sects divide,
And into parties tear.

4 Ev'n of ourselves shall men arise,
With words perverse, and soothing lies,
Our children to beset,
Disciples for themselves to make,
And draw, for filthy lucre's sake,
The sheep into their net.

5 What then can their protection be?
The virtue that proceeds from thee,
The power of humble love:
The strength of all-sufficient grace,
Received in thine appointed ways,
Can land[31] them safe above.

6 Now, Saviour, clothe them with thy power,
And arm their souls against that hour
With faith invincible;
Teach them to wield the Spirit's sword,
And mighty in the written Word
To chase both earth and hell.

7 When I, from all my burdens freed,
Am numbered with the peaceful dead
In everlasting rest,

[31] Orig., 'lead', altered in *Works* to 'land'.

Pity the sheep I leave behind,
My God, unutterably kind,
And lodge them in thy breast.

8 Ah! never suffer them to leave
The Church, where thou art pleased to give
Such tokens of thy grace!
Confirm them in their calling here,
Till ripe by holiest love t' appear
Before thy glorious face.

9 Whom I into thy hands commend,
Wilt thou not keep them to the end,
Thou infinite in love?
Assure me, Lord, it shall be so,
And let my quiet spirit go
To join the Church above.

10 Zion, my first, my latest care,
The burden of my dying prayer,
Now in thine arms I see;
And sick on earth of seeing more,
I hasten home, my God t' adore
Through all eternity.

17

A LETTER TO THE REV. MR. DOWNES

(1759)

AN INTRODUCTORY COMMENT

The Letter *is a reply to* Methodism Examined and Exposed: or, the Clergy's Duty of guarding their Flocks against False Teachers. A Discourse lately delivered in four parts. By the Rev. Mr. Downes, Rector of St. Michael, Wood-Street, and Lecturer of St. Mary le Bow, London: Printed for John Rivington at the Bible and Crown in St. Paul's Churchyard, 1759 *(see Green,* Anti-Methodist, *No. 282).*

Mr. Downes in his discourse used as his text Acts 20:28-30, and applied it to the Church of England, 'first, to give some account of these "grievous wolves which have entered in among us"' (pp. 6-27); 'secondly, to show that they . . . "[speak] perverse things, etc.,"' (pp. 29-60); and 'thirdly [to caution the Church of England], "Take heed therefore unto yourselves, and to all the flock, etc."' (pp. 61-106, Parts III and IV).

Wesley was in Bristol on October 16, 1759, when Methodism Examined *was advertised in the* London Chronicle, *but from October 27 he spent most of the winter in London and dated his reply November 17, 1759.*

John Downes (c. 1691–1759) was a Londoner who went from Merchant Taylors' School to St. John's College, Cambridge, where he graduated B.A. in 1713, and was ordained deacon by the Bishop of Llandaff later that year. From 1739–45 he was vicar of St. Paul's, Sheffield, and from 1745 until his death, rector of St. Michael's, Wood Street, London.

Downes died on November 25, 1759, just after Wesley's Letter *appeared, and further controversy was thus obviated. His widow Anne, daughter of Henry Balguy of Darwent Hall, published a pamphlet, dated April 1, 1760,* The Widow Downes' Answer to the Rev. Mr. John Wesley's Letter, which was addressed to her late husband the Rev. Mr. Downes, just at the time of his decease. London,

Printed for the Benefit of the Widow, *16 pp. (see Green,* Anti-Methodist, *No. 283). Wesley noticed this only briefly in a letter to* Lloyd's Evening Post *for November 24, 1760, as 'wrote or procured to be wrote, by Mrs. Downes': 'The letter which goes under Mrs. Downes's name scarcely deserves any notice at all, as there is nothing extraordinary in it but an extraordinary degree of virulence and scurrility. Two things only I remark concerning it (which I suppose the writer of it knew as well as me): (1) That my letter to Mr. Downes was both wrote and printed* before Mr. Downes died, *(2) That when I said,* Tibi parvula res est *('Your ability is small'), I had no view to his fortune, which I knew nothing of; but (as I there expressly say) to his wit, sense, and talents as a writer' (JWJ, November 22, 1769, mistakenly speaks of this letter as written to the* Monthly Review*).*

It will be observed that the style of Wesley's reply to Downes is less restrained than usual and that he was not inclined to speak more kindly of him after his death. But no doubt the provocation was also greater than usual.

For details of the two editions of this work see Bibliography, *No. 238; for the major variants between the one here presented and the version given in Wesley's* Works, *Vol. 17 (1773) pp. 31-54, see Appendix A, pp. 541ff.*

A Letter to the Rev. Mr. Downes,

Rector of St. Michael, Wood-Street: Occasioned by his Late Tract, entitled *Methodism Examined and Exposed*

Rev. sir,

1. In the tract which you have just published concerning the People called Methodists you very properly say, 'Our first care should be, candidly and fairly to examine their doctrines. For, as to censure them *unexamined* would be unjust, so to do the same without a *fair and impartial examination* would be ungenerous.'[1] And again, 'We should, in the first place, carefully and candidly

[1] Downes, *Methodism Examined,* p. 63.

examine their doctrines.'[a] This is undoubtedly true. But have you done it? Have you ever examined their doctrines yet? Have you examined them *fairly?* Fairly and *candidly?* Candidly and *carefully?* Have you read over so much as the *Sermons* they have published? Or the *Appeal to Men of Reason and Religion?*[2] I hope you have not—for I would fain make some little excuse for your uttering so many senseless, shameless falsehoods. I hope you know nothing about the Methodists, no more than I do about the Cham of Tartary, that you are ignorant of the whole affair, and are so *bold* only because you are *blind.* Bold enough! Throughout your whole tract you speak *satis pro imperio*[3]—as authoritatively as if you was not an archbishop only, but apostolic vicar also; as if you had the full *papal power* in your hands, and *fire and faggot* at your beck! And blind enough. So that you blunder on, through thick and thin, bespattering all that come in your way. According to the old, laudable maxim, 'Throw dirt enough, and some will stick.'[4]

2. I hope, I say, that this is the case, and that you do not knowingly assert so many palpable falsehoods, You say, 'If I am mistaken, I shall always be ready and desirous to retract my error.'[b] A little candour and care might have prevented those mistakes. This is the first thing one would have desired. The next is, that they may be removed; that you may see wherein you have been mistaken, and be more wary for the time to come.

3. You undertake to give an account, first, of the rise and principles, then of the practices, of the Methodists.

On the former head you say: 'Our Church has long been infested with these *grievous wolves,* who though no more than two when they entered in, and they so young, they might rather be called *Wolflings,*' (That is lively and pretty!) 'have yet spread their ravenous kind through every part of this kingdom. Where what havoc they have made, how many of the sheep they have torn—I need not say.'[c] 'About twenty-five years ago these two bold,

[a] [Downes, *Methodism Examined,*] p. 68.
[b] P. 56.
[c] Pp. 4-5.

---

[2] *An Earnest Appeal* (1743; see 11:37-94 in this edn.), and the supplementary treatises entitled *A Farther Appeal.*

[3] Terence, *Phormio, l.* 195; 'as if you had imperial power'.

[4] In Wesley's writings there are many examples of this proverb (orig. Latin, 'Calumniare fortiter, aliquid adhaerebit'), as in 11:365, 500 in this edn.; cf. 11:426(26).

though beardless divines' (Pity, sir, that you had not taught me twenty-five years ago *sapientem pascere barbam,*[5] and thereby to avoid some part of your displeasure) 'being lifted up with spiritual pride, were presumptuous enough to become founders of the sect called Methodists.'[d] 'A couple of young, raw, aspiring twigs of the ministry dreamed of a special and supernatural call to this.'[e] No, sir, it was *you* dreamed of this, not *we*. We dreamed of nothing twenty-five years ago but instructing our pupils in religion and learning, and a few prisoners in the common principles of Christianity. You go on. 'They were ambitious of being accounted missionaries, immediately delegated by heaven to correct the errors of bishops and archbishops, and reform their abuses, to instruct the clergy in the true nature of Christianity, and to caution the laity not to venture their souls in any such unhallowed hands as refused to be initiated in all the mysteries of Methodism.'[f] Well *asserted* indeed! But where is the *proof* of any one of these propositions? I must insist upon this: clear, cogent proof. Else they must be set down for so many glaring falsehoods.

4. 'The Church of Rome (to which on so many accounts they were much obliged, and as gratefully returned the obligation) taught them to set up for *infallible* interpreters of Scripture.'[g] Pray on what accounts are we 'obliged to the Church of Rome'? And how have we 'returned the obligation'? I beg you would please, (1), to explain this, and (2), to prove that we ever yet (whoever taught us) 'set up for *infallible* interpreters of Scripture'.[6] So far from it that we have over and over declared, in print as well as in public preaching: 'We are no more to expect *any living man* to be *infallible* than to be omniscient.'[h]

5. 'As to other *extraordinary gifts, influences,* and *operations* of the Holy Ghost, no man who has but once dipped into their Journals, and other *ostentatious trash* of the same kind, can doubt their looking upon themselves as not coming one whit behind the greatest of the apostles.'[i]

[d] P. 6. [e] P. 25. [f] Pp. 20-21. [g] P. 54.
[h] *Sermons,* Vol. III, p. 207 [i.e., No. 40, *Christian Perfection,* I.5 (2:102 in this edn.)].
[i] P. 21.

---

[5] Horace, *Satires,* II.iii.35; 'to grow a wiseacre's beard'.

[6] The italicizing of 'infallible' in the quotation was carried out by Wesley, not Downes. In most of these quotations Wesley rearranged, paraphrased, or introduced minor variations to fit the context or the purposes of his argument, while remaining true to the main intent and language of his source.

I acquit you, sir, of ever having 'once dipped into that ostentatious trash'. I do not accuse you of having read so much as the titles of my Journals. I say, *my* journals; for (as little as you seem to know it) my brother has published none.[7] I therefore look upon this as simple ignorance. You talk thus because you know no better. You do not know that in these very Journals I utterly disclaim the '*extraordinary gifts* of the Spirit', and all other 'influences and operations of the Holy Ghost', than those that are common to all real Christians.

And yet I will not say this ignorance is blameless. For ought you not to have known better? Ought you not to have taken the pains of procuring better information, when it might so easily have been had? Ought you to have publicly advanced so heavy charges as these without knowing whether they were true or no?

6. You proceed to give as punctual an account of us, *tanquam intus et in cute nosses*.[8] 'They outstripped, if possible, even Montanus for external sanctity and severity of discipline. They condemned all regard for temporal concerns. . . .[j] They encouraged their devotees to take no thought for any one thing upon earth. The consequence of which was a *total neglect* of their affairs, and *impoverishment* of their families.'[k] Blunder all over! We had no room for any discipline, severe or not, five and twenty years ago—unless College discipline, my brother then residing at Christ Church, and I at Lincoln College. And as to our 'sanctity' (were it more or less), how do you know it was only *external?* Was you intimately acquainted with us? I do not remember where I had the honour of conversing with you. Or could you (as the legend says of St. Pachomius)[9] 'smell an heretic ten miles' off?

[j] P. 22 [Wesley's own references to Montanus are uniformly favourable, though he does not take up Mr. Downes's point here. See 'The Real Character of Montanus' (1785) in Vol. 12 of this edn.; cf. also Sermon 68, 'The Wisdom of God's Counsels', §9, 2:555 in this edn., and n. 31 there].

[k] P. 23.

---

[7] Charles Wesley's *Journals* were first published in 1849. Downes is probably making the error in part because the other member of the Methodist triumvirate, George Whitefield, had become notorious for publishing his *Journals*.

[8] Cf. Persius, *Satires*, iii.30, 'ego te intus et in cute novi' (correctly quoted in JW's letter to Charles Wesley, Sept. 25, 1749, §28; *Letters*, 26:385 in this edn.), translated by Wesley in his *Works*, Vol. 32 (1774), 'As if you knew us inside and out.'

[9] Pachomius (*c.* 290–346) is generally recognized as the founder of Christian monasticism of the cenobitic sort. His first monastery on communal lines was in the Thebaid near the Nile in A.D. 320. By the time of his death he was abbot-general of nine monasteries for men and two for women.

And how came you to dream again that we 'condemned all regard for *temporal* concerns, and encouraged men to take no thought for any one thing upon *earth*'? Vain dream! We on the contrary severely condemn all who neglect their *temporal* concerns, and who do not take care of everything on earth wherewith God hath entrusted them. The consequence of this is that the Methodists, so called, do not 'neglect their affairs and impoverish their families', but by diligence in business 'provide things honest in the sight of all men'.[10] Insomuch that multitudes of them, who in time past had scarce food to eat or raiment to put on, have now 'all things' needful for 'life and godliness',[11] and that for their families as well as themselves.

7. Hitherto you have been giving an account of two 'wolflings' only. But now they are grown into perfect *wolves*. Let us see what a picture you draw of them in this state, both as to their principles and practice.

You begin with a home stroke: 'In the Montanist you may behold the *bold* lineaments and *bloated countenance* of the Methodist.'[l] I wish you do not squint at the *honest countenance* of Mr. Venn,[12] who is indeed as far from fear as he is from guile. But if it is somewhat *bloated*, that is not his fault—sickness may have the same effect on yours or mine.

But to come closer to the point. 'They have darkened religion with many ridiculous fancies, tending to confound the head and to corrupt the heart.'[m] 'A thorough knowledge of them would work in every rightly disposed mind an abhorrence of those doctrines which directly tend to distract the head, and to debauch the heart, by turning faith into frenzy, and the grace of God into wantonness.'[n] 'These doctrines are unreasonable and ridiculous, clashing with our natural ideas of the divine perfections, with the end of religion, with the honour of God, and man's both present and future happiness. . . . Therefore we pronounce them *filthy dreamers*, turning faith into fancy, the gospel into farce, thus adding blasphemy to enthusiasm.'[o]

[l] P. 17.
[m] P. 13.
[n] P. 27.
[o] Pp. 66, 68.

---

[10] Rom. 12:17.
[11] 2 Pet. 1:3.
[12] See above, p. 317.

Take breath, sir; there is a long paragraph behind.

The abetters of these wild and whimsical notions are: (1), close friends to the Church of Rome, agreeing with her in almost everything but the doctrine of merit. (2). They are no less kind to *infidelity*, by making the Christian religion a mere creature of the imagination. (3). They cut up Christianity by the roots, frustrating the very end for which Christ died, which was that by holiness we might be 'made meet for the inheritance of the saints'. (4). They are enemies, not only to Christianity, but to *every religion whatsoever*, by labouring to subvert or overturn the whole system of morality. (5). Consequently they must be *enemies of society*, dissolving the bands by which it is united and knit together.[p]

In a word, 'All ancient heresies have in a manner *concentered* in the Methodists,' particularly those of 'the Simonians, Gnostics, Antinomians' (as widely distant from each other as Predestinarians from Calvinists!), Valentinians, Donatists, and Montanists.[13] While your hand was in, you might as well have added Carpocratians, Eutychians, Nestorians, Sabellians.[14] If you say, 'I never heard of them,' no matter for that—you may find them as well as the rest in Bishop Pearson's *Index*.[15]

Well, all this is mere flourish—raising a dust to blind the eyes of the spectators. Generals,[16] you know, prove nothing. So leaving this as it is, let us come to particulars.

[p] Pp. 101-2 [highly compressed].

---

[13] Cf. Downes, *Methodism Examined*, pp. 9, 26; in the intervening pages Downes deals with each at some length.

[14] Carpocrates was a Gnostic of the second century, teaching that Jesus was the son of Joseph, but became especially righteous; that matter, including the human body, was created by inferior angels, and that sexual license was therefore a matter of indifference; and that souls are reincarnated until they have committed all sins. (This is Irenaeus' account of him.)

Eutyches (*c.* 378–454) was accused of confounding the two natures in Christ while attempting to confute Nestorius. He was deposed from his monastic office, reinstated, and finally condemned at the Council of Chalcedon (451).

Nestorius (died *c.* 451), Archbishop of Constantinople and opponent of Eutyches, distinguished the two natures in Christ, but asserted his oneness, and rejected the notion that Mary was the 'Mother of God'. He was accused (wrongly, as is now widely believed) of teaching that there were two persons in Christ, and condemned and deposed by the Council of Ephesus (431).

Sabellius, who taught in Rome in the third century, held that the Father, Son, and Holy Spirit were not distinct persons, but successive modes of being within the one God. His followers were called Modalist Monarchians.

[15] John Pearson (1613–86, Bishop of Chester). Wesley refers, not to one of Pearson's lesser known or lost works, but to the index to his *Exposition of the Creed* (London, 1659), which, however, does not mention Antinomians, Gnostics, or Carpocratians, though there is a lavish supply of other heretics.

[16] I.e., general statements; the *OED* offers no use before 1761 of the term 'generalization', which might have been appropriate.

But first give me leave to transcribe a few words from a tract published some years ago: 'Your Lordship premises, "It is not at all needful to charge the particular tenets upon the particular persons among them." Indeed it is needful in the highest degree. Just as needful as it is not to put a stumbling[-block] in the way of our brethren; not to lay them under an almost insuperable temptation of condemning the innocent with the guilty.'[q]

And it is now far more needful than it was then, as that title of reproach, 'Methodist', is now affixed to many people who are not under my care, nor ever had any connexion with me. And what have I to do with these? If you give me a nickname, and then give it to others whom I know not, does this make *me* accountable for *them?* Either for their principles or practice? In no wise. I am to answer for myself, and for those that are in connexion with me. This is all that a man of common sense can undertake, or a man of common humanity require.

Let us begin then upon even ground. And if you can prove upon *me, John Wesley,* any one of the charges which you have advanced, call me not only a *wolf,* but an *otter*, if you please.

8. Your first particular charge (which indeed runs through your book, and is repeated in twenty different places) is that we make the way to heaven *too broad,* teaching, Men may be saved by faith, without works. Some of your words are: 'They *set out* with forming a *fair and tempting* model of religion, so *flattering* the follies of degenerate man that it could not fail to gain the hearts of multitudes, especially of the loose and vicious, the lazy and indolent.'[r] 'They want to get to heaven the *shortest way,* and with the *least trouble.* Now a reliance on Christ and a disclaiming of good works are *terms as easy* as the merest libertine can ask. They persuade their people that they may be saved by the righteousness of Christ, without any holiness of their own; nay, that good works are not only unnecessary, but also dangerous';[s] 'that we may be saved by faith, without any other requisite' such as 'gospel obedience and an holy life'.[t] Lastly, 'The Valentinians pretended that if good works were necessary to salvation, it was only to *animal* men, that is, to all who were not of their clan; and that

[q] [John Wesley,] *Letter to the Bishop of London,* pp. 4-5 [§§4, 6; see 11:336-37, 388 in this edn.].

[r] P. 52 [abr., Wesley's italics].

[s] P. 38.

[t] P. 31 ['an' added only in the errata and Wesley's own copy of his *Works*].

although sin might damn *others,* it could not hurt *them.* In consequence of which they lived in all lust and impurity, and wallowed in the most unheard-of bestialities. The Methodists distinguish much after the same manner.'[u]

Sir, you are not awake yet. You are dreaming still, and fighting with shadows of your own raising. The 'model of religion with which the Methodists *set out*' is perfectly well known, if not to you, yet to many thousands in England who are no Methodists. I laid it before the University of Oxford, at St. Mary's, on January 1, 1733. You may read it when you are at leisure, for it is in print, entitled, 'The Circumcision of the Heart'.[17] And whoever reads only that one discourse, with any tolerable share of attention, will easily judge whether *that model of religion* 'flatters the follies of degenerate man', or is likely to 'gain the hearts of multitudes, especially of the loose and vicious, the lazy and indolent'. Will a man choose this as 'the *shortest way* to heaven, and with the *least trouble*'? Are these 'as *easy terms* as any libertine or infidel can desire'? The truth is, we have been these thirty years continually reproached for just the contrary to what you dream of: with making the way to heaven *too strait;* with being ourselves *righteous overmuch,* and teaching others, they could not be saved without *so many works* as it was impossible for them to perform. And to this day, instead of teaching men that they may be saved by a faith which is without good works, without 'gospel obedience and holiness of life', we teach exactly the reverse, continually insisting on all *outward* as well as all *inward holiness.* For the notorious truth of this we appeal to the whole tenor of our Sermons, printed and unprinted, in particular to those upon our Lord's Sermon on the Mount, wherein every branch of gospel obedience is both asserted and proved to be indispensably necessary to eternal salvation.

Therefore as to the rest of the 'antinomian trash' which you have so carefully gathered up, as, 'that the regenerate are as pure as Christ himself, that it would be criminal for them to pray for pardon; that the greatest crimes are no crimes in the saints',[v] etc., etc., I have no concern therewith at all, no more than with any that teach it. Indeed I have confuted it over and over, in tracts published many years ago.

[u] P. 14.

[v] Pp. 16-17.

[17] Sermon 17 in Vol. 1 of this edn., first published in Vol. 2 of Wesley's *Sermons,* 1748.

9. A second charge which you advance is that 'we suppose every man's final doom to depend on God's sovereign will and pleasure' (I presume you mean on his absolute, unconditional decree); that we 'consider man as a mere machine'; that we suppose believers 'cannot fall from grace'.[w] Nay, I suppose none of these things. Let those who do answer for themselves. I suppose just the contrary, in *Predestination Calmly Considered*, a tract published ten years ago.[18]

10. A third charge is: 'They represent faith as a supernatural principle, altogether precluding the judgment and understanding, and discerned by some internal signs; not as a firm persuasion, founded on the evidence of reason, and discernible only by a conformity of life and manners to such a persuasion.'[x]

We do not represent faith 'as altogether precluding' or at all precluding 'the judgment and understanding'; rather as enlightening and strengthening the understanding, as clearing and improving the judgment. But we do represent it as 'the gift of God',[19] yea, and a 'supernatural gift'; yet it does not preclude 'the evidence of reason', though neither is this its whole foundation. 'A conformity of life and manners' to that persuasion, Christ 'loved *me* and gave himself for *me*',[20] is doubtless *one* mark by which it is discerned, but not the *only* one. It is likewise discerned by *internal signs*, both by the witness of the Spirit, and the fruit of the Spirit, namely 'love, peace, joy, meekness, gentleness',[21] by all 'the mind which was in Christ Jesus'.[22]

11. You assert, fourthly: 'They speak of grace, that it is as perceptible to the heart as sensible objects are to the senses; whereas the Scriptures speak of grace, that it is conveyed imperceptibly, and that the only way to be satisfied whether we have it or no is to appeal, not to our inward feelings, but our outward actions.'[y]

We do speak of grace (meaning thereby that power of God which worketh in us both to will and to do of his good pleasure),[23]

[w] P. 31 [cf. also pp. 32-33 for the last phrase, which is not present in this section of *Methodism Examined*].

[x] P. 32 [orig., '11'].

[y] P. 32.

---

[18] See p. 341 above.

[19] Eph. 2:8.

[20] Gal. 2:20.

[21] Cf. Gal. 5:22-23.

[22] Cf. Phil. 2:5.

[23] See Eph. 3:20; Phil. 2:13.

that it is 'as perceptible to the heart' (while it comforts, refreshes, purifies, and sheds the love of God abroad[24] therein) 'as sensible objects are to the senses'. And yet we do not doubt but it may frequently be 'conveyed to us imperceptibly'. But we know no Scripture which speaks of it as *always* conveyed, and *always working,* in an imperceptible manner. We likewise allow that outward actions are *one way* of satisfying us that we have grace in our hearts. But we cannot possibly allow that 'the only way to be satisfied of this is to appeal to our *outward actions,* and not our *inward feelings*'. On the contrary, we believe that love, joy, peace are *inwardly felt,* or they have no being; and that men are satisfied they have grace, first by feeling these, and afterward by their outward actions.

12. You assert, fifthly: 'They talk of regeneration in every Christian as if it was as sudden and miraculous a conversion as that of St. Paul and the first converts to Christianity, and as if the signs of it were frightful tremors of body, and convulsive agonies of mind; not as a work graciously begun and gradually carried on by the blessed Spirit, in conjunction with our rational powers and faculties, the signs of which are sincere and universal obedience.'[z]

This is part true, part false. We do believe regeneration, or in plain English, the new birth, to be as miraculous or supernatural a work now as it was seventeen hundred years ago. We likewise believe that the spiritual life which commences when we are born again must, in the nature of the thing, have a *first moment,* as well as the natural. But we say again and again, We are concerned for the *substance* of the work, not the *circumstance.* Let it be wrought at all, and we will not contend whether it be wrought gradually or instantaneously. 'But what are the signs that it is wrought?' We never said or thought that they were either 'frightful tremors of body' or 'convulsive agonies of mind'—I presume you mean agonies of mind attended with bodily convulsions. Although we know many persons who *before* this change was wrought felt much fear and sorrow of mind, which in some of these had such an effect on the body as to make all their bones to shake. Neither did we ever deny that it is a 'work graciously begun by the Holy Spirit', enlightening our understanding (which I suppose you call 'our rational powers and faculties') as well as influencing our

[z] P. 33.

---

[24] See Rom. 5:5.

affections. And it is certain he 'gradually carries on this work', by continuing to influence all the powers of the soul, and that the *outward sign* of this inward work is 'sincere and universal obedience'.

13. A sixth charge is, 'They treat Christianity as a wild, enthusiastic scheme, which will bear no *examination*.'[a] Where or when? In what Sermon? In what tract, practical or polemical? I wholly deny the charge. I have myself closely and carefully *examined* every part of it, every verse of the New Testament, in the original, as well as in our own and other translations.

14. Nearly allied to this is the threadbare charge of *enthusiasm*, with which you frequently and largely compliment us. But as this also is *asserted* only, and not *proved*, it falls to the ground of itself. Meantime your asserting it is a plain proof that you know nothing of the men you talk of. Because you know them not you so boldly say, 'One advantage we have over them, and that is *reason*.'[25] Nay, that is the very question. I appeal to all mankind whether you have it or no. However, you are sure, we have it not, and are never likely to have. For 'Reason', you say, 'cannot do much with an enthusiast, whose first principle is to have nothing to do with reason, but resolve all his religious opinions and notions into immediate inspiration.'[26] Then by your own account I am no enthusiast, for I resolve none of my notions into immediate inspiration. I have something to do with reason—perhaps as much as many of those who 'make no account of my labours'.[27] And I am ready to give up every opinion which I cannot by calm, clear reason defend. Whenever therefore you 'will try what you can do by *argument*',[28] which you have not done yet, I wait your leisure, and will follow you step by step, which way soever you lead.

15. 'But is not this a plain proof of the enthusiasm of the Methodists, that they despise human learning, and make a loud and terrible outcry against it?'[29] Pray, sir, when and where was this

[a] P. 30.

---

[25] Downes, p. 105.
[26] Ibid.
[27] Cf. Job 33:13.
[28] Downes, p. 105.
[29] Cf. Downes, pp. 56-59, where he speaks of the supposed alliance of the Methodists with the followers of John Hutchinson, saying: 'For besides his joining with them in their loud and terrible outcry against human learning and natural religion, he hath by his critical

done? Be so good as to point out the time and place, for I am quite a stranger to it. I believe indeed, and so do you, that many men make an ill use of their learning. But so they do of their Bibles. Therefore this is no reason for despising or crying out against it. I would use it just as far as it will go. How far I apprehend it may be of use, how far I judge it to be expedient, at least, if not necessary for a clergyman, you might have seen, in the Earnest Address to the Clergy.[30] But in the meantime I bless God that there is a more excellent gift than either the knowledge of languages or philosophy. For tongues and knowledge and learning will 'vanish away'; but 'love never faileth'.[31]

16. I think this is all you have said which is any way material concerning the *doctrines* of the Methodists. The charges you bring concerning their *spirit* or practice may be dispatched in fewer words.

And, first, you charge them with *pride* and *uncharitableness*. 'They talk as proudly as the *Donatists* of their being the only true preachers of the gospel, and esteem themselves, in contradistinction to others, as the regenerate, the children of God, and as having arrived at sinless perfection.'[b]

All of a piece. We neither talk nor think so. We doubt not but there are many true preachers of the gospel, both in England and elsewhere, who have no connexion with, no knowledge of us. Neither can we doubt but that there are many thousand children of God who never heard our voice or saw our face. And this may suffice for an answer to all the assertions of the same kind which are scattered up and down your work. Of sinless perfection, here brought in by head and shoulders, I have nothing to say at present.

17. You charge them, secondly, with boldness and blasphemy, 'who, triumphing in their train of credulous and crazy followers, the *spurious* (should it not be rather the *genuine*) offspring of their *insidious craft*, ascribe the glorious event to divine grace, and in

[b] P. 15.

skill and acumen in the Hebrew language . . . struck out for them a new revelation . . .' (p. 57). A footnote on p. 59 adds: 'If this should seem inconsistent with the true character of the Methodists, who are known to despise human learning, let it be remembered that so did Mr. Hutchinson, notwithstanding his wonderful proficiency in it. Besides, in whom do the Methodists despise it? Not in themselves, but in others. . . .'

[30] I.e., *An Address to the Clergy* (1756); see *Bibliography*, No. 216, and Vol. 14 in this edn.

[31] 1 Cor. 13:8 *(Notes)*.

almost every page of their *paltry harangues* invoke the Blessed Spirit to go along with them in their soul-awakening work, that is, to continue to assist them in seducing the simple and unwary'.[c]

What we ascribe to divine grace is this, the convincing sinners of the errors of their ways, and the 'turning them from darkness to light, from the power of Satan to God'.[32] Do not you yourself 'ascribe this to grace'? And do not *you* too 'invoke the Blessed Spirit to go along with you in every part of your work'? If you do not, you lose all your labour.—Whether we 'seduce men into sin', or by his grace save them from it, is another question.

18. You charge us, thirdly, with 'requiring a blind and implicit trust from our disciples',[d] who accordingly 'trust as implicitly in their preachers as the Papists in their Pope, Councils, or Church'.[e] Far from it. Neither do we require it; nor do they that hear us place any such trust in any creature. They 'search the Scriptures',[33] and hereby try every doctrine, whether it be of God.[34] And what is agreeable to Scripture they embrace; what is contrary to it they reject.

19. You charge us, fourthly, with injuring the clergy in various ways. First, 'They are very industrious to dissolve or break off that spiritual intercourse which the relation wherein we stand requires should be preserved betwixt us and our people.'[f] But can that spiritual intercourse be either preserved or broke off which never existed? What spiritual intercourse exists between *you*, the *Rector* of St. Michael, and the people of your parish? I suppose you preach to them once a week, and now and then read Prayers. Perhaps you visit one in ten of the sick. And is this all the *spiritual intercourse* which you have with those 'over whom the Holy Ghost hath made you an overseer'?[35] In how poor a sense then do you 'watch over the souls' for whom you are to 'give an account'[36] to God! Sir, I wish to God there were a truly spiritual intercourse between you and all your people! I wish you 'knew all your flock

[c] P. 41.
[d] P. 10.
[e] P. 51.
[f] P. 44.

---

[32] Acts 26:18 *(Notes)*.
[33] John 5:39.
[34] See John 7:17; 1 John 4:1.
[35] Cf. Acts 20:28.
[36] Cf. Heb. 13:17 *(Notes)*.

by name, not excepting the men-servants and women-servants'![37] Then you might 'cherish' each, 'as a nurse her own children',[38] and 'train them up in the nurture and admonition of the Lord'.[39] Then might you 'warn every one and exhort every one', till you should 'present every one perfect in Christ Jesus'.[40]

'But they say our sermons contradict the Articles, Homilies, and Liturgy of our own Church. Yea, that we contradict ourselves, saying one thing in the desk and another in the pulpit.'[41] And is there not cause to say so? I myself have heard several sermons preached in churches which flatly contradicted both the Articles, Homilies, and Liturgy, particularly on the head of justification. I have likewise heard more than one or two persons who 'said one thing in the desk and another in the pulpit'. In the desk they prayed God to 'cleanse the thoughts of their hearts by the inspiration of his Holy Spirit'.[42] In the pulpit they said there was 'no such thing as *inspiration* since the time of the apostles'.

'But this is not all. You poison the people by the most peevish and spiteful invectives against the clergy, the most rude and rancorous revilings, and the most invidious calumnies.'[g] No more than I poison them with *arsenic*. I make no peevish or spiteful invectives against any man. Rude and rancorous revilings (such as your present tract abounds with) are also far from me. I dare not 'return railing for railing',[43] because (whether you know it, or no) I fear God. Invidious calumnies likewise I never dealt in. All such weapons I leave to *you*.

20. One charge remains, which you repeat over and over, and lay a peculiar stress upon. (As to what you talk about 'perverting Scripture', I pass it by as mere unmeaning, commonplace declamation.) It is the poor old, worn-out tale of 'getting money by preaching'. This you only intimate at first. 'Some of their followers had an *inward call* to sell all that they had, and lay it *at their feet*.'[h] Pray, sir, favour us with the name of one, and we will

[g] P. 51.
[h] P. 22 [cf. Acts 4:34-35, etc.].

---

[37] The fact that this 'quotation' is not to be found in Scripture, or the Book of Common Prayer, or in Downes's own work, may indicate that the quotation marks were inserted by mistake.

[38] Cf. 1 Thess. 2:7.

[39] Cf. Eph. 6:4.

[40] Cf. Col. 1:28.

[41] Downes, p. 47.

[42] BCP, Communion, Collect.

[43] Cf. 1 Pet. 3:9.

excuse you as to all the rest. In the next page you grow bolder, and roundly affirm, 'With all their heavenly-mindedness, they could not help casting a sheep's eye at the unrighteous Mammon. Nor did they pay their court to it with less cunning and success than Montanus. Under the specious appearance of gifts and offerings, they raised contributions from every quarter. Besides the weekly pensions squeezed out of the poorer and lower part of their community, they were favoured with very large oblations from persons of better figure and fortune, and especially from many *believing* wives, who had learned to practise pious frauds on their *unbelieving* husbands.'[44]

I am almost ashamed (having done it twenty times before) to answer this stale calumny again. But the bold, frontless manner wherein you advance it obliges me so to do. Know then, sir, that you have no authority either from Scripture or reason to judge of other men by *yourself.* If *your own* conscience convicts you of loving money, of 'casting a sheep's eye at the unrighteous Mammon', humble yourself before God, if haply the thoughts and desires of your heart may be forgiven you. But, blessed be God, my conscience is clear. My heart does not condemn me in this matter. I know, and God knoweth, that I have no desire to 'load' myself 'with thick clay';[45] that I love money no more than I love the mire in the streets; that I seek it not. And I have it not—any more than suffices for food and raiment, for the plain conveniences of life. I pay no court to it at all, or to those that have it, either with cunning or without. For myself, for my own use, I raise no contributions, neither great nor small. The weekly contributions of our community (which are freely given, not *squeezed* out of any) as well as the gifts and offerings at the Lord's table, never come into my hands. I have no concern with them, not so much as 'the beholding them with my eyes'.[46] They are received every week by the stewards of the society, men of well-known character in the world, and by them constantly distributed within the week to those whom they know to be in real necessity. As to the 'very large oblations wherewith I am favoured by persons of better figure and fortune', I know nothing of them. Be so kind as to refresh my memory by mentioning a few of their names. I have the happiness of knowing some of great figure and

[44] Downes, pp. 23-24.
[45] Cf. Hab. 2:6.
[46] Cf. Eccles. 5:11.

fortune, some Right Honourable persons. But if I were to say that all of them together had given me seven pounds in seven years I should say more than I could make good. And yet I doubt not but they would freely give me anything I wanted—but by the blessing of God I want nothing that they can give. I want only more of the spirit of love and power, and of[47] an healthful mind.—As to those 'many *believing* wives who practise pious frauds on their *unbelieving* husbands', I know them not, no, not one of that kind. Therefore I doubt the fact. If you know any such, be pleased to give us their names and places of abode. Otherwise you must bear the blame of being the 'lover', if not 'the maker of a lie'.[48]

Perhaps you will say, 'Why, a great man said the same thing but a few years ago.' What if he did? Let the frog swell as long as he can, he will not equal the ox.[49] *He* might say many things, all circumstances considered, which will not come well from *you*, as *you* have neither his wit, nor sense, nor learning, nor age, nor dignity.

Tibi parvula res est.[50]
Metiri se quemque suo modulo ac pede verum est.[51]

If *you* fall upon people that meddle not with you, without either fear or wit, you may possibly find they have a little more to say for themselves than you was aware of. I 'follow peace with all men',[52] but if a man set upon me without either rhyme or reason, I think it my duty to defend myself, so far as truth and justice permit. Yet still I am (if a poor enthusiast may not be so bold as to style himself your brother),

Reverend sir,
Your servant for Christ's sake,
John Wesley

London, Nov. 17, 1759

[47] Added in *Works* (1773).
[48] Cf. Rev. 22:15.
[49] A reference, of course, to the fable by Aesop.
[50] Horace, *Epistles*, I.xviii.29, 'Your means are slight.' (Cf. n. 51 below.)
[51] Horace, *Epistles*, I.vii.98, 'It is right for a man to measure himself by his own rule and standard.' In his *Works*, Vol. 32, Wesley presents these two passages separated by a comma only, and offers the translation: 'You are not upon a level with Bishop W[arburto]n. Let every man know his own size.'
[52] Heb. 12:14.

18

A SHORT HISTORY OF METHODISM

(1765)

AN INTRODUCTORY COMMENT

This is not so much what its title announces it to be as a description of the theological differences within Methodism, prefaced by a brief account of Methodist origins. It is best read in conjunction with the fuller narrative 'A Short History of the People called Methodists' (1781) which is to be found on pp. 425-503 below, with annotations which throw light on this writing also.

For a stemma depicting the transmission of the text through the five editions published during Wesley's lifetime and noting the very few variants from the edited text (based on the 1st edn. of 1765), see Appendix A, pp. 541ff. For fuller details see Bibliography, *No. 264.*

A Short History of Methodism

1. It is not easy to reckon up the various accounts which have been given of the People called Methodists. Very many of them as far remote from truth as that given by the good gentleman in Ireland. '*Methodists!* Ay, they are the people who place all religion in *wearing long beards*.'[1]

2. Abundance of the mistakes which are current concerning them have undoubtedly sprung from this—men lump together under this general name many who have no manner of connexion with each other, and then whatever any of these speaks or does is of course imputed to all.

3. The following short account may prevent persons of a calm and candid disposition from doing this, although men of a warm

[1] See JWJ, June 5, 1749, and *A Letter to the Rev. Mr. Baily*, II.4, p. 301 above.

or prejudiced spirit will do just as they did before. But let it be observed, this is not designed for a *defence* of the Methodists (so called), or any part of them. It is a bare *relation* of a series of naked facts, which alone may remove abundance of misunderstandings.

[4.] In November 1729 four[2] young gentlemen of Oxford, Mr. John Wesley, Fellow of Lincoln College, Mr. Charles Wesley, Student of Christ Church, Mr. Morgan, Commoner of Christ Church, and Mr. Kirkham, of Merton College, began to spend some evenings in a week together, in reading, chiefly[3] the Greek Testament. The next year two or three of Mr. John Wesley's pupils desired the liberty of meeting with them, and afterwards one of Mr. Charles Wesley's pupils. It was in 1732 that Mr. Ingham, of Queen's College, and Mr. Broughton, of Exeter, were added to their number. To these, in April, was joined Mr. Clayton, of Brasenose,[4] with two or three of his pupils. About the same time Mr. James Hervey was permitted to meet with them, and in 1735 Mr. Whitefield.

5. The exact regularity of their lives, as well as studies, occasioned a young gentleman of Christ Church to say, 'Here is a new set of *Methodists* sprung up'—alluding to some ancient physicians who were so called. The name was new and quaint, so it took immediately, and the 'Methodists' were known all over the university.

6. They were all zealous members of the Church of England, not only tenacious of all her doctrines, so far as they knew them, but of all her discipline, to the minutest circumstances. They were likewise zealous observers of all the university statutes, and that for conscience' sake. But they observed neither these nor anything else any further than they conceived it was bound upon them by their one book, *the Bible*, it being their one desire and design to be downright *Bible Christians*—taking the Bible, as interpreted by the primitive Church and our own, for their whole and sole rule.

7. The one charge then advanced against them was that they were 'righteous overmuch',[5] that they were abundantly too scrupulous, and too strict, carrying things to great extremes. In particular, that they laid too much stress upon the rubrics and

[2] 1789, 'some'.
[3] 1789 omits 'chiefly'.
[4] Orig., 'Brazen-nose'.
[5] Eccles. 7:16.

canons of the Church; that they insisted too much on observing the statutes of the university, and that they took the Scriptures in too strict and literal a sense—so that if they were right, *few* indeed would *be saved*.[6]

8. In October 1735 Mr. John and Charles Wesley, and Mr. Ingham, left England, with a design to go and preach to the Indians in Georgia. But the rest of the gentlemen continued to meet, till one and another was ordained and left the university. By which means, in about two years' time, scarce any of them were left.

9. In February 1738 Mr. Whitefield went over to Georgia, with a design to assist Mr. John Wesley; but Mr. Wesley just then returned to England. Soon after he had a meeting with Messrs. Ingham, Stonehouse, Hall, Hutchings, Kinchin, and a few other clergymen, who all appeared to be of one heart, as well as of one judgment, resolved to be Bible-Christians at all events, and, wherever they were, to preach with all their might, plain, old, Bible-Christianity.

10. They were hitherto perfectly regular in all things, and zealously attached to the Church of England. Meantime they began to be convinced that 'by grace we are saved through faith',[7] that justification by faith was the doctrine of the Church, as well as of the Bible. As soon as they *believed*, they *spake*, salvation by faith being now their standing topic. Indeed this implied three things: (1). That men are all by nature 'dead in sin',[8] and consequently 'children of wrath'.[9] (2). That they are 'justified by faith'[10] alone. (3). That faith produces inward and outward holiness. And these points they insisted on, day and night. In a short time they became popular preachers. The congregations were large wherever they preached. The former name was then revived. And all these gentlemen, with their followers, were entitled 'Methodists'.

11. In March 1741, Mr. Whitefield being returned to England, entirely separated from Mr. Wesley and his friends 'because he did not hold *the decrees*'.[11] Here was the first breach,

[6] Luke 13:23.
[7] Cf. Eph. 2:8.
[8] Cf. Eph. 2:5, etc.
[9] Eph. 2:3.
[10] Rom. 3:28, etc.
[11] According to John Calvin, God's 'eternal decrees' predestined some of his creatures to eternal salvation and some to eternal damnation.

which warm men persuaded Mr. Whitefield to make, merely for a difference of opinion. Those indeed who believed *universal redemption* had no desire at all to separate. But those who held *particular redemption* would not hear of any accommodation, being determined to have no fellowship with men that 'were in so dangerous errors'.[12] So there were now two sorts of Methodists, so called, those for *particular*, and those for *general*, redemption.

12. Not many years passed before William Cudworth[13] and James Relly[14] separated from Mr. Whitefield. These were properly *antinomians*, absolute, avowed enemies to the law of God, which they never preached or professed to preach, but termed all *legalists* who did. With them 'preaching the law' was an abomination. They had 'nothing to do' with the law. They would 'preach Christ', as they called it, but without one word either of holiness or good works. Yet these were still denominated Methodists, although differing from Mr. Whitefield, both in judgment and practice, abundantly more than Mr. Whitefield did from Mr. Wesley.[15]

13. In the meantime Mr. Venn and Mr. Romaine[16] began to be spoken of, and not long after, Mr. Madan[17] and Mr. Berridge,[18] with a few other clergymen, who, although they had no connexion with each other, yet preaching salvation by faith, and endeavouring to live accordingly, to be Bible-Christians, were soon included in the general name of Methodists. And so indeed were

[12] The words quoted here seem to be a summary of the view held by Whitefield's supporters about Wesley's.

[13] Cudworth was regarded by Wesley as an absolutely inflexible opponent, though he was approved of by the Countess of Huntingdon.

[14] Relly was a Welshman converted through Whitefield's preaching; he became a minister among the Calvinistic Methodists, and the pastor of a meeting-house in Bartholomew Close, London; he died in 1778.

[15] See the appendix on 'The Controversy with Antinomianism' in *The History of the Methodist Church in Great Britain*, ed. R. E. Davies and G. Rupp (London, Epworth Press, 1965), I.176-79.

[16] The Rev. William Romaine was successively lecturer at St. Dunstan-in-the-West, preacher at St. George's, Hanover Square, curate of St. Olave's, Southwark, and then (1766–90) rector of St. Anne's, Blackfriars. He was supporter and friend of Benjamin Ingham.

[17] The Rev. Martin Madan (a cousin of William Cowper), converted through Wesley's preaching, was chaplain of the Lock Hospital in London, 1750–80. He excited fierce opposition by advocating polygamy in one of his books.

[18] The Rev. John Berridge was presented by his college, Clare Hall, Cambridge, to the living of Everton in 1755, and served there until his death in 1793. He became friendly with Wesley in 1758, and from his parish headquarters became an enthusiastic and eccentric itinerant preacher on the Calvinist wing of the revival.

all others who preached 'salvation by faith', and appeared more *serious* than their neighbours. Some of these were quite *regular* in their manner of preaching; some were quite *irregular* (though not by choice; but necessity was laid upon them—they must preach *irregularly*, or not at all); and others were between both, regular in *most*, though not in *all* particulars.

14. In 1762 George Bell,[19] and a few other persons, began to speak great words. In the latter end of the year they foretold that the world would be at an end on the 28th of February. Mr. Wesley, with whom they were then connected, withstood them both in public and private. This they would not endure. So in January and February 1763 they separated from him, under the care of Mr. Maxfield,[20] one of Mr. Wesley's preachers. But still Mr. Maxfield and his adherents, even the wildest enthusiasts among them, go under the general name of Methodists, and so bring a scandal upon those with whom they have no connexion.[21]

15. At present those who remain with Mr. Wesley are mostly Church of England men. They love her Articles, her Homilies, her Liturgy, her discipline, and unwillingly vary from it in any instance. Meantime, all who preach among them declare, 'We are all by nature children of wrath.'[22] But 'by grace we are saved through faith'[23]—saved both from the guilt and from the power of sin. They endeavour to *live* according to what they preach, to be plain, Bible-Christians. And they meet together at convenient times to encourage one another therein. They tenderly love many that are Calvinists, though they do not love their opinions. Yea, they love the antinomians themselves; but it is with a love of compassion only. For they hate their doctrines with a perfect hatred; they abhor them as they do hell-fire. Being convinced

[19] George Bell, a corporal in the King's Life Guard, associated himself with Thomas Maxfield and, in Wesley's judgment, helped him to disturb the societies in London, largely by utterances of a wild nature, asserting, e.g., that man can be as perfect as the angels and that once we are pure in heart we cannot fall into sin. See Wesley's account of his activities in §§97-98 of 'A Short History of the People called Methodists', pp. 481-82 below. Bell left the Methodists in 1763.

[20] For Thomas Maxfield, Wesley's first lay preacher, but later his opponent, see the intro. to *A Letter to the Rev. Mr. Thomas Maxfield*, pp. 416-18 below.

[21] The 2nd edn., 1765, followed by Wesley's *Works*, 1772, altered this section to read: 'So in January and February 1763 they separated from him. Soon after Mr. Maxfield, one of Mr. Wesley's preachers, and several of the people, left Mr. Wesley. But still Mr. Maxfield and his adherents go under the general name of Methodists.'

[22] Cf. Eph. 2:3.

[23] Cf. Eph. 2:8.

nothing can so effectually destroy all faith, all holiness, and all good works.

16. With regard to these, Mr. Relly and his adherents, it would not be strange if they should grow into reputation. For they will never shock the world either by the harshness of their doctrine or the singularity of their behaviour. But let those who determine both to preach and to live the gospel expect that men will 'say all manner of evil of them'.[24] 'The servant is not above his Master, nor the disciple above his Lord. If then they have called the Master of the house Beelzebub, how much more them of his household?'[25] It is their duty indeed, 'as much as lieth in them to live peaceably with all men'.[26] But when they labour after peace, the world will 'make themselves ready for battle'.[27] It is their constant endeavour to 'please all men, for their good, to edification'.[28] But yet they know it cannot be done. They remember the word of the Apostle, 'If I yet please men, I am not the servant of Christ.'[29] They go on therefore, 'through honour and dishonour, through evil report and good report',[30] desiring only that their Master may say in that day, 'Servants of God, well done.'[31]

[24] Cf. Matt. 5:11.
[25] Cf. Matt. 10:24-25.
[26] Rom. 12:18.
[27] Cf. Ps. 120:6 (BCP).
[28] Cf. Rom. 15:2.
[29] Cf. Gal. 1:10.
[30] 2 Cor. 6:8 *(Notes)*.
[31] Although the Scripture of Matt. 25:21 lies in the background, this seems to be only indirectly, for unlike most of Wesley's scriptural quotations, which are italicized, this is enclosed within quotation marks. Almost certainly he is thinking of a line from one of Charles Wesley's poems; cf. the opening line of his elegy for George Whitefield, 1770: 'Servant of God, well done!'

19

A LETTER TO THE REV. DR. RUTHERFORTH

(1768)

AN INTRODUCTORY COMMENT

Thomas Rutherforth (1712–71) was the son of the similarly named rector of Papworth Everard, Cambridge; he entered St. John's College, Cambridge, when he was still thirteen, and graduated B. A., at sixteen. He was elected a fellow of the Royal Society in 1743, and Regius Professor of Divinity at Cambridge in 1745, when he was also awarded D.D. He held various livings in plurality, and in 1752 was presented to the archdeaconry of Essex. He died October 5, 1771. He wrote extensively on biblical, theological, philosophical, and scientific themes, and several of his publications led to controversy.

In 1763 he published Four Charges to the Clergy of the Archdeaconry of Essex *(Cambridge, Bentham; see Green,* Anti-Methodist, *No. 343). The themes were:*

'Charge I. Some plain arguments to prove that Christianity does not reject the aid of human learning' (pp. 1-14).

'Charge II. An examination of the doctrine of the Methodists concerning inward feelings' (pp. 15-38).

'Charge III. An examination of the doctrine of the Methodists concerning assurances' (pp. 39-60).

'Charge IV. An inquiry whether the Article of the resurrection of the body, or flesh, was not inserted into the public creeds before the middle of the fourth century; and whether the language of it is not agreeable to the language of the Scriptures: in answer to a posthumous pamphlet of the late Dr. Sykes' (pp. 61-95).

Dr. Rutherforth's academic standing was so high that Wesley felt that he should issue a reply, though he did so somewhat belatedly. His manner of reply is much more respectful to his opponent than in other cases. His first section (pp. 374-76) deals with Part III, his second (pp. 376-81) with Part I, and his third (pp. 381-88) with Part II.

The year of writing must be 1768, in spite of the 'M.DCC.LXVII' on the title-page, both because Wesley was riding around Ireland in March

1767, and (especially) because of his statement in the opening sentence about Rutherforth's work having been published 'five years ago'.

Dr. Rutherforth's criticisms give Wesley in this Letter *an opportunity to clarify his teaching on assurance, and he does this succinctly on pp. 375-76. Even more valuable, since it is not so easily available elsewhere in his writings, is the precise statement of his position in the matter of 'bodily emotions' and 'inward feelings' (pp. 384-87).*

For details of the two editions of this work and variants introduced in Wesley's Works *(1773, Vol. XVII) see Appendix A, pp. 541ff. For further historical and bibliographical details see* Bibliography, *No. 308.*

A Letter to the Rev. Dr. Rutherforth

March 28, 1768

Rev. sir,

I. 1. Your *Four Charges*, published five years ago, I did not see till yesterday. In the fourth I am unconcerned. The three former I purpose now to consider: and I do it the more cheerfully because they are wrote with such seriousness as becomes the importance of the subject, and with less tartness than I am accustomed to expect from opponents of every kind.

2. But before I enter on the subject, suffer me to remove a stumbling-block or two out of the way. You frequently charge me with *evasion:* and others have brought the same charge. The plain case is this: I have wrote on various heads, and always as clearly as I could. Yet many have misunderstood my words, and raised abundance of objections. I answered them by explaining myself, showing what I did not mean, and what I did. One and another of the objectors stretched his throat, and cried out, 'Evasion! Evasion!' And what does all this outcry amount to? Why, exactly thus much. They imagined they had tied me so fast that it was impossible for me to escape. But presently the cobwebs were swept away, and I was quite at liberty. And I bless God I can unravel truth and falsehood, although artfully twisted together.

Of *such* 'evasion' I am not ashamed. Let them be ashamed who constrain me to use it.

3. You charge me likewise, and that more than once or twice, with *maintaining contradictions.* I answer, (1). If all my sentiments were compared together, from the year 1725 to 1768, there would be truth in the charge: for during the latter part of this period I have relinquished several of my former sentiments. (2). During these last thirty years I may have varied in some of my sentiments or expressions without observing it. (3). I will not undertake to defend all the expressions which I have occasionally used during this time, but must desire men of candour to make allowance for those,

> *Quas aut incuria fudit,*
> *Aut humana parum cavit natura.*[1]

(4). It is not strange if among these inaccurate expressions there are some *seeming* contradictions, especially considering I was answering so many different objectors, frequently attacking me at once, and one pushing this way, another that, with all the violence they were able. Nevertheless, (5), I believe there will be found few, if any, *real* contradictions in what I have published for near thirty years.

4.[2] I come now to your particular objections. I begin with the subject of your third charge, *assurances*—because what I have to say on this head will be comprised in few words. Some are fond of the *expression;* I am not—I hardly ever use it. But I will simply declare (having neither leisure nor inclination to draw the saw of controversy[3] concerning it), what are my present sentiments with regard to the *thing* which is usually meant thereby.

I believe a few, but very few, Christians have an *assurance* from God of *everlasting salvation;* and that this is the thing which the Apostle terms 'the plerophory, or full assurance of hope'.[4]

[1] Horace, *Art of Poetry,* 352-53, translated by Wesley in the Appendix to Vol. 32 of his *Works* (1774): 'Such as escaped my notice; or such as may be placed to the account of human infirmity.' A better translation may perhaps be: 'Such as either carelessness missed or human nature was not wary of.' Cf. Wesley's *Letter to the Rev. Mr. Horne,* II.10 (1762), 11:458, in this edn.

[2] Orig., '5', altered in *Works* to '4'.

[3] A proverbial expression frequent with Wesley. Cf. his letters of May 22, 1750; Oct. 11, 1764; Sept. 20, 1776, etc.

[4] Heb. 6:11. Cf. *A Second Letter to the Author of The Enthusiasm of the Methodists,* 1751 (11:398 in this edn.).

I believe more have such an *assurance* of being *now in the favour of God* as excludes all doubt and fear. And this, if I do not mistake, the Apostle means by 'the plerophory' or 'full assurance of faith'.[5]

I believe a *consciousness* of *being in the favour of God* (which I do not term 'plerophory', or 'full assurance', since it is frequently weakened, nay perhaps interrupted, by returns of doubt or fear), is the common privilege of Christians fearing God and working righteousness.[6]

Yet I do not affirm, there are no exceptions to this general rule. Possibly some may be in the favour of God, and yet go mourning all the day long. (But I believe this is usually owing either to disorder of body, or ignorance of the gospel promises.)

Therefore I have not for many years thought a consciousness of acceptance to be essential to justifying faith.

And after I have thus explained myself, once for all, I think without any evasion or ambiguity, I am sure without any self-contradiction, I hope all reasonable men will be satisfied. And whoever *will* still dispute with me on this head must do it for disputing['s] sake.

II. 1. In your first charge you undertake to prove that 'Christianity does not reject the aid of human learning.'[a]

Mr. B[erridge][7] thinks it does. But I am not accountable for him, for whom in this I totally differ. Yet you certainly include *me* when you say, 'these *new reformers* maintain that every believer who has the gift of utterance is qualified to preach the gospel.'[b] I never maintained this. On many occasions I have maintained quite the contrary. I never said, 'Human learning is an impediment to a divine, which will keep him from the knowledge of the truth.'[c] When therefore you say, 'The contempt with which *these men* treat human learning', you do me much injustice; as likewise when you say, 'They agree that human learning is of no use at all to a preacher of the gospel.'[d] I do not agree with any who

[a] [Rutherforth, *Four Charges*,] p. 1.
[b] P. 2.
[c] P. 3.
[d] Ibid.

[5] Heb. 10:22. Cf 11:398 in this edn.

[6] See Acts 10:35.

[7] On pp. 2-3 Rutherforth had quoted from 'Mr. B———'s letters printed in *A Fragment of the True Religion*'. The author of the *Fragment* (1760) described himself as 'a Methodist Preacher in Cambridgeshire', and was in fact the well-known (and somewhat eccentric) evangelical clergyman, the Rev. John Berridge of Everton.

speak thus. Yet you cite my own writings to prove it.[e] If I say any such thing either there or anywhere else, let me bear the blame for ever.

2. For my deliberate thoughts on human learning I appeal to my *Serious Address to the Clergy*.[8] I there lay down *ex professo*[9] the qualifications, the learning in particular, which (as I apprehend) every clergyman who *can* have *ought* to have. And if any who are educated at the university have it not, they are inexcusable before God and man.

To put this matter beyond dispute, I appeal to something more than words. Can any man seriously think I despise learning who has ever heard of the school at Kingswood? Especially if he knows with how much care, and expense, and labour, I have kept it on foot for these twenty years! Let him but read 'the rules of Kingswood school'[10] and he will urge this objection no more.

3. But you 'employ illiterate preachers'.[11] I cannot answer this better, than by transcribing the very page to which you refer:

> It will easily be observed that I do not depreciate learning of any kind. The knowledge of the languages is a valuable talent; so is the knowledge of the arts and sciences. Both the one and the other may be employed to the glory of God and the good of men. But yet I ask, Where hath God declared in his Word that he cannot or will not make use of men that have it not? Has Moses or any of the prophets affirmed this? Or our Lord? Or any of his apostles? You are sensible all these are against you. You know the apostles themselves, all except St. Paul, were ἄνδρες ἀγράμματοι καὶ ἰδιῶται, common, unphilosophical, unlettered men.[f]

[e] *Farther Appeal*, Pt. III, p. 106 [i.e., III.8 (11:294-95 in this edn.), which in fact Rutherforth quotes and cites as evidence that 'whatever they may do in private amongst their own people, (they) have not ventured to carry this matter quite so far in their public writings,' though Wesley's 'Yet' implies incorrectly that Rutherforth uses the passage to show the contrary. In addition to this fundamental error, in most of his quotations Wesley follows the course normal for both himself and many of his contemporaries, of summarizing the general sense adequately, but frequently deserting the actual words].

[f] My words are marked with single commas [here given as a quotation, in smaller type. See *A Farther Appeal*, Pt. III, p. 106, cited above by Rutherforth; cf. 11:294-95 in this edn.].

---

[8] I.e., *An Address to the Clergy* (1765), see *Bibliography*, No. 216; cf. above, p. 362, where also Wesley quoted the title incorrectly, on that occasion prefixing the adjective 'Earnest' rather than 'Serious'.

[9] 'Professedly, by open acknowledgment'. Cf. *A Second Letter to the Author of The Enthusiasm of the Methodists* (1751), 11:387 in this edn.

[10] Apparently Wesley has in mind *A Short Account of the School in Kingswood, near Bristol* (1749), for which see *Bibliography*, No. 162 (Vol. 15 in this edn.).

[11] Rutherforth, *Four Charges*, p. 3.

4. Suffer me to add that paragraph from which you strangely infer that I hold learning to be of 'no use at all to a preacher':[12]

> I am bold to affirm that these unlettered men have help from God for that great work, the saving souls from death; seeing he hath enabled, and doth enable them still, to turn many to righteousness. Thus hath he destroyed the wisdom of the wise, and brought to nought the understanding of the prudent. When they imagined they had effectually shut the door, and blocked up every passage whereby any help could come to two or three preachers, weak in body as well as soul, who they might reasonably believe would, humanly speaking, wear themselves out in a short time; when they had gained their point by securing (as they supposed) all the men of learning in the nation—He that sitteth in heaven laughed them to scorn, and came upon them by a way they thought not of. Out of the stones he raised up those who should beget children to Abraham. We had no more foresight of this than you. Nay, we had the deepest prejudices against it; until we could not but own that God gave wisdom from above to these unlearned and ignorant men; so that the work of the Lord prospered in their hand, and sinners were daily converted to God.
>
> Indeed in the one thing which they profess to know they are not ignorant men. I trust there is not one of them who is not able to go through such an examination in substantial, practical, experimental divinity, as few of our candidates for holy orders, even in the university (I speak it with sorrow and shame, and in tender love) are able to do. But Oh! what manner of examination do most of those candidates go through! And what proof are the testimonials commonly brought (as solemn as the form is wherein they run) either of the piety or knowledge of those to whom are entrusted those sheep which God hath purchased with his own blood![13]

5. Yet you cite this very paragraph to prove that I 'intimate the help which these illiterate men receive from God is such as will enable them to preach Christ's gospel without reading the Scriptures. Adding St. Paul's command to Timothy is a sufficient confutation of this groundless, or rather impious pretence.'[g] I cannot conceive how you could imagine those words to intimate any such thing. Be this *pretence* whose it will, it is none of mine—it never entered into my thoughts.

6. But 'there are in the Scriptures "things hard to be understood". And is *every unlettered mechanic* able to explain them?'[h] No surely. But may we not likewise ask: is *every clergyman* able to explain them? You will not affirm it. However, 'they are the

[g] [Rutherforth, *Four Charges,*] p. 9 [citing Wesley, *A Farther Appeal,* Pt. III, pp. 106-7—actually pp. 107-8 in all three edns. available to Rutherforth].
[h] [Ibid.,] p. 11.

---

[12] Rutherforth, p. 3.
[13] *A Farther Appeal,* Pt. III, III.10 (11:296-97 in this edn.).

safest guides, who from their childhood have known the Holy Scriptures, and have diligently and faithfully made use of all the helps to understand them which a liberal education has put into their hands; who have “given attendance to reading”, have “meditated on those things”, and have “given themselves wholly to them”.’[i]

Certainly these are the safest guides. But how many, sir, do you know of *these?* Suppose there are thirty thousand clergymen in England, can you vouch this for ten thousand of them? I remember his late Grace of Canterbury (I mean Archbishop Potter)[14] was occasionally saying that on searching the records he could find only three hundred of the clergy who stood out against popery in Queen Mary’s reign. Do you think the other twenty-nine thousand seven hundred were ‘the safest guides’? I hope indeed things are mended now. I see no reason to doubt but there are among the present clergy a far greater number both of learned and pious men. And yet I fear we cannot count many thousands now that answer your strong description. May our good Lord increase their number, how many so ever they be!

7. Now I beg leave to ask a question in my turn. Which do *you* think is the safest guide—a cursing, swearing, drinking clergyman (that such there are you know), or a tradesman, who has in fact ‘from his childhood known the Holy Scriptures’, and has for five years (to say no more) ‘faithfully and diligently made use of all the helps which the English tongue has put into his hands; who has “given attendance to reading”, has “meditated on these things”, and “given himself wholly to them”’? Can any reasonable man doubt one moment which of these is the safest guide?

Certainly ‘those who want *these* qualifications’, who do not give attendance to reading, who do not meditate on those things, yea and give themselves wholly to them, are ‘ignorant and unstable men’, in a very bad sense of the words. And let them understand philosophy ever so well, and be ever such critics in Greek and Hebrew, ‘they will pervert the Scriptures when they pretend to interpret them,’[j] and that not only to *their own* destruction.[15]

[i] Ibid.

[j] [Ibid.,] p. 12.

[14] John Potter (1674?–1747), formerly Bishop of Oxford, who had ordained Wesley.

[15] See 2 Pet. 3:16, ‘wrest . . . the . . . scriptures unto their own destruction’. Wesley’s point, of course, is that a clergyman’s false interpretation of Scripture harms not only

8. But 'many of these strolling preachers are so ignorant as not to know that the Scriptures were not written in their mother tongue.'[k] Indeed they are not. Whoever gave you that information abused your credulity. Most of the travelling preachers in connexion with me are not ignorant men. As I observed before, they know all which they profess to know. The languages they do not profess to know—yet some of them understand them well. Philosophy they do not profess to know—yet some of them tolerably understand this also. They understand both one and the other better than great part of my pupils at the university did. And yet these were not inferior to their fellow collegians of the same standing (which I could not but know, having daily intercourse with all the undergraduates, either as Greek lecturer or moderator). Nor were these inferior to the undergraduates of other colleges.

9. You conclude this charge. For 'those whose minds are not stored with useful literature [. . .] the wisdom of the public has provided such guides as are both able and willing to show them the right way.'[l] Would to God it had! But is it really so? Is there such a guide in every parish in England! Are then all the rectors, vicars, and curates therein 'both able and willing' to guide all their parishioners to heaven? Do not both you, and I, and all the world, know that this is not the case? Are there not many who are utterly unable to guide others, having neither learning nor understanding to guide themselves? Are there not more, who, if they are able, are not willing, taking no care or thought about it? They eat, and drink, and rise up to play,[16]

> And leave to tattered crape the drudgery of prayer.[17]

Once more. Are there not too many of those guides 'whom the wisdom of the public has provided' who are neither able nor willing to guide others in the right way, being equally void of knowledge and piety? Is it then 'the duty of the people to continue in the things which they have learned'[18] from these guides? And

[k] P. 8.

[l] P. 13.

---

himself but his parishioners. This point was missing in the 1768 original, which omitted 'not'; this was restored in the *Works* (1773).

[16] See Exod. 32:6; 1 Cor. 10:7.

[17] Samuel Garth, *The Dispensary*, i.142.

[18] Cf. Rutherforth, p. 13 (quoted above), citing 2 Tim. 3:14.

'to hold fast the faithful word as they have been taught'?[19] Why, what have they been taught? Just nothing. From these guides they have learned nothing, nor could learn anything, either from their precept or example. And are they 'then only in danger when they do not follow these guides'?[20] If they do follow them, they must follow them to hell. O sir, why will you constrain me to show the nakedness of the land?[21] I would far rather spread a veil over it. And I heartily wish, I may never more be laid under a necessity of touching on this unpleasing subject.

10. Upon the whole, what I believe concerning learning, as I have again and again declared, is this: That it is *highly expedient* for a guide of souls, but not *absolutely necessary*. What I believe to be absolutely necessary is, a faith unfeigned, the love of God and our neighbour, a burning zeal for the advancement of Christ's kingdom, with an heart and life wholly devoted to God. These I judge to be necessary in the highest degree. And next to these, a competent knowledge of Scripture, a sound understanding, a tolerable utterance, and a willingness to be as 'the filth and offscouring of the world'.[22]

III. 1. You entitle your second charge, 'An examination of the doctrine of the Methodists concerning *inward feelings*.'

I have explained myself so frequently and so largely upon this head already that I flattered myself I should scarce have occasion to do it any more. But as I am still totally misunderstood and misrepresented I am under a necessity of doing it yet again.

You state the question thus: 'Have we any reason to believe that the mind has an *inward feeling*, which will enable it to perceive the ordinary influences of God's Spirit, so as to discern from whence they come?'[m]

I answer, (1). The fruit of his *ordinary influences* are love, joy, peace, long-suffering, gentleness, meekness.[23] (2). Whoever has these, *inwardly feels* them. And if he understands his Bible, he discerns from whence they come. Observe, what he inwardly feels is *these fruits themselves: whence they come* he learns from the Bible.

[m] [Rutherforth,] p. 15.

---

[19] Ibid., p. 14, citing Titus 1:9.
[20] Ibid.
[21] Gen. 42:9, 12.
[22] Cf. 1 Cor. 4:13.
[23] Gal. 5:22-23.

This is my doctrine concerning 'inward feelings', and has been for above these forty years. And this is clear to any man of common sense—I appeal to all the world if it is not. Only do not puzzle the cause by a cloud of words, and then lay the blame on *me*.

2. You state the question again: 'What I mean to affirm is, that while the soul is united to such a body, the operations of external things' (Say, the operations of the Holy Spirit, for of these we are talking, and of these alone) 'upon some one or more of these organs, excite no *inward feeling*.'[n] Nay, nor outward neither. He must be a bold man that will affirm the contrary. If this be all that you mean to affirm, we agree to an hair's breadth.

3. You afterwards open yourself farther. 'The mind in its present situation has no *inward sense* by which the influence of external causes' (the influence of the Holy Spirit) 'or the causes themselves' (this is quite another question) 'may be felt or discerned. It then only perceives them when they affect the organs of the body, so as to raise a sensation in it by their means.'[o]

Did ever the most illiterate Methodist talk in such a manner as this? 'The mind then only perceives the influences of the Holy Spirit when they affect the organs of the body!'

If you say, 'I do not mean the Holy Spirit by "external causes",' then you mean and say what is nothing to the purpose. For your very title confines you to the influences of the Holy Spirit; and you are, or should be, speaking of nothing else.

4. You go on. 'It is a fundamental principle in the Methodist school that all who come into it must renounce their reason.'[24] Sir, are you awake? Unless you are talking in your sleep, how can you utter so gross an untruth! It is a fundamental principle with *us*, that to renounce reason is to renounce religion; that religion and reason go hand in hand, and that all irrational religion is false religion. I therefore speak quite 'consistently with my [own standing] doctrines'[25] when I caution my followers 'against

[n] [Ibid.,] p. 17.
[o] P. 22.

---

[24] Cf. Rutherforth, pp. 22-23.

[25] Cf. Rutherforth, p. 23: 'One of them, he best knows how consistently with his standing doctrine of convictions and assurances, cautions his followers "against judging of the spirit. . . ."' Wesley's MS apparently read, 'consistently with my own standing doctrines', which the printer mistakenly composed as '. . . my understanding doctrines'; in his *Works* he improved the sense by changing 'understanding' into 'own'.

judging of the spirit by which anyone speaks by their own *inward feelings*, . . . because these, being of a doubtful nature, may come from God, or may not'.[26] You add: 'What therefore shall we think of these *inward feelings?* They cannot be clear perceptions of the cause from which these affections or sentiments are derived.'[27] Who says they are? I never did. *You* cite the words wherein I say just the contrary. *Whom then doth your arguing reprove?* Do you not 'fight as one that beateth the air'?[28]

5. 'Mr. W[esley]' indeed 'endeavours to explain away the doctrine of the Methodists concerning *inward feelings*.'[p] That is, I plainly tell what I mean by those expressions. My words run thus: 'By "feeling" I mean being inwardly conscious of. By the "operations of the Spirit" I do not mean *the manner* in which he operates, but *the graces* which he operates in a Christian.'[29] And again: 'We believe that love, joy, peace are inwardly felt, or they have no being; and that men are satisfied they have grace, first by feeling these, and afterwards by their outward actions.'[30]

One might imagine the controversy was now at an end. No: I am not a jot the nearer. For you go on: 'If he and his brethren' (away with 'his brethren'—the point lies between *you* and *me*) 'mean no more than this, why do they speak of this matter in such a language as makes their disciples pretend to have an inward sense, by which they feel, sometimes the power of God, sometimes the Holy Ghost, sometimes Jesus Christ, and by which they can as clearly discern each of these while he acts upon them as they can discern outward objects by their bodily senses.'[q] So now the matter is out! But who are the men? What are their names? And where do they live? If *you* know any who pretend to this, I do not—but I know, they are none of *my* disciples. They never learned it of *me*. I have three grains of common sense, whether you believe it or not.

6. But you will pin it upon me whether I will or no; and that by

[p] [Rutherforth,] p. 25 [n.].
[q] [Rutherforth,] p. 26 [n.].

---

[26] Rutherforth, p. 23, citing JWJ, June 22, 1739—quoted in a similarly selective manner to Wesley's own quotations from Rutherforth.

[27] Ibid.

[28] Cf. 1 Cor. 9:26.

[29] *A Farther Appeal*, Pt. I, V.2, quoted and cited by Rutherforth, p. 26n. (cf. 11:139-40 in this edn.).

[30] *A Letter to the Reverend Mr. Downes*, §11, quoted and cited by Rutherforth, ibid. (cf. p. 360 above).

three passages of my own writings. (1). 'Lucy Godshall felt the love of God *in an unusual manner*.'[31] She did. I mean, *in an unusual degree*. And what will you make of this? (2). 'When he examined some of his disciples, and they related their "*feeling* the blood of Christ running upon their arms, or going down their throats, or poured like water upon their breast and heart", did he tell them that "these circumstances" were all the dreams of an heated imagination?'[32] I did: I told them that *these* three *circumstances*, and *several* others of the same kind, were mere dreams, though *some* which they then related *might be* otherwise. I will tell you more: I was so disgusted at them for those dreams that I expelled them out of our society.

The third passage is this. 'We do speak of grace (meaning thereby the power of God which worketh in us both to will and to do of his good pleasure), that it is as perceptible to the heart (while it confirms, refreshes, purifies, and sheds the love of God abroad therein) as sensible objects are to the senses.'[r] I do speak thus. And I mean thereby that the *comfort* which God administers, not his *power* distinct from it, the *love* and *purity* which he works, not his *act* of working distinguished from it, are as clearly discernible by the soul as outward objects by the senses. And I never so much as dreamed that anyone could find any other meaning in the words.

7. I cannot close this subject of *inward feelings* without recurring to the 20th page of your tract. Here you attempt to prove that 'these preachers confine the influences of God's Holy Spirit to themselves and their followers,' because, say you, 'no one else feels its workings'[33]—none but they and their followers. Observe: it is not *I* affirm this but *you*, that 'none but Methodists *feel the workings of the Spirit*.' But how will you reconcile this assertion with the seventeenth Article of our Church, which teaches that all 'godly persons *feel in themselves the working of the Spirit* of Christ, mortifying the works of the flesh, and drawing up their mind to high and heavenly things'? It is in this sense, and this only, that I did and do assert, all good men 'feel the working of

[r] [Rutherforth,] p. 27 [citing *A Letter to the Reverend Mr. Downes*, §11 (see above, pp. 359-60)].

---

[31] Rutherforth, p. 27n., citing JWJ, Sept. 9, 1742.
[32] Ibid., pp. 26-27n., citing JWJ, Sept. 6, 1742.
[33] Rutherforth, p. 21, conflating two passages.

the Holy Spirit'. If any can prove they do not, I stand condemned: if not, none can condemn me concerning *inward feelings.*

8. You subjoin some reflections on another subject, *bodily emotions* of various kinds. Before we reason upon it, let us state the fact. These outward symptoms are not at all times, nor in all places; for two or three years they were (not constant but) frequent in London, Bristol, Newcastle upon Tyne, and in a few other places. They sometimes occur still, but not often. And we do not regard whether they occur or not, knowing that the essence of religion, righteousness, peace, and joy in the Holy Ghost,[34] is quite independent upon them.

Upon this you ask, 'Are these the fruits of the Spirit?'[s] I answer, no. Whoever thought they were? You ask, (2), 'Are these the marks whereby we may be assured that they who are thus affected discern its workings?' You answer for me: 'They themselves do not believe it. Nay, Mr. W[esley] declares, it is his opinion, "*Some of these agonies are from the devil*"; . . . and makes no doubt but it was *Satan tearing them,* as they were coming to Christ.'[t] But if I myself declare this, what room was there for the preceding questions? Now certainly you must be quite satisfied. No. You are as far from it as ever! You gravely ask, 'What experienced physicians of the soul must these be, who are unable to distinguish the influence of the Holy Ghost from the tearing of Satan.'[35] Why, sir, you this instant repeated the very words wherein I *do* distinguish them. 'But you ascribe the same symptoms sometimes to the one, and sometimes to the other.'[36] Indeed I do not. I always ascribe *these* symptoms to 'Satan tearing them'.

9. You add in a marginal note, 'Mr. W[esley] sometimes denies that he considers these fits as signs of the new birth.'[37] I always deny it, if you mean by *signs* anything more than 'something which may accidentally attend it'. Yet 'in some of his writings he calls these fallings and roarings by the name of *convictions.*' He says, 'Many were wounded deeply; but none were delivered from that painful conviction.' 'Monday 30, two more were in strong pain, both their souls and bodies being wellnigh

[s] [Rutherforth,] p. 31.
[t] Pp. 31-33.

---

[34] See Rom. 14:17.
[35] Rutherforth, p. 33.
[36] Ibid.
[37] Ibid., p. 30n.

torn asunder.'[38] Very true: but in which of these passages do I 'call *fallings* and *roarings* by the name of *convictions*'? Excuse me. If I cannot distinguish God from the devil, I can at least distinguish the soul from the body. For do I ever confound *bodily disorders* with sorrow or *pain of mind?*

10. However, 'Mr. W[esley] speaks of these at least as outward signs that the new birth "is *working* in those that have them".'[u] I speak of them as 'outward symptoms which have often accompanied the inward work of God'.[39] A peculiar instance of this I relate in the first Journal, which you are at the pains to transcribe. And, as you observe, 'there are many instances in the same Journal in which I express myself in the same manner.'[40] But what does all this prove? Just what I said before, and not one jot more—I speak of them as 'outward symptoms which have often accompanied the inward work of God'. *Often,* I say, not *always;* not *necessarily;* they may, or they may not. This work may be without those symptoms; and those symptoms may be without this work.

11. But you say: 'The following account which he writes to one of his correspondents will make the matter clear. "I have seen very many persons changed in a moment from the spirit of fear, horror, despair, to the spirit of love, joy, peace; and from sinful desires, till then reigning over them, to a pure desire of doing the will of God. That such a change was then wrought appears, not from their shedding tears only, or falling into fits, or crying out (these are not the fruits, or signs, whereby I judge) but from the whole tenor of their lives." '[v]

Now I should really imagine, this passage proves just the contrary of what you intend. Yea, that it is full and decisive. 'But, say you, though he denies these to be the fruits by which he judges that this inward change is wrought, yet he looks upon them as

[u] [Rutherforth,] p. 23 [i.e., 33n., citing JWJ, May 20, 1739].
[v] [Rutherforth,] p. 33 [citing JWJ, May 1739].

---

[38] Ibid., pp. 30-31n., quoting JWJ, July 23, 30, 1739.

[39] Ibid., p. 33, citing JWJ, Mar. 12, 1743. In this paragraph Wesley seems a little at odds with Rutherforth because pp. 26-33 contain voluminous footnotes below a scanty text and the references to Wesley's writing in each differ, as well as being in the more awkward form of 'Wesley's Journal from Sept. 3, 1741, to Oct. 27, 1743, p. 91', etc.

[40] Cf. ibid., p. 32n., although in fact Rutherforth's reference is not to *Journal* 1 but *Journal* 3.

signs that it is *working*.'[41] Yes, in the sense above explained. While God was inwardly *working*, these outward signs *often* appeared—nay, almost daily in Bristol, during the first summer which I spent there.

12. Upon the whole, I declare once for all (and I hope to be troubled no more upon the subject), I look upon some of those bodily symptoms to have been preternatural or diabolical, and others to have been effects which in some circumstances naturally followed from strong and sudden emotions of mind. Those emotions of mind, whether of fear, sorrow, or joy, I believe were chiefly supernatural, springing from the gracious influences of the Spirit of God, which accompanied his word.

13. I believe this is all the answer I need give to the severe accusation you have brought against me: for which I trust men of candour will discern, there was not the least foundation. With respect to the first point, 'despising learning', I am utterly clear. None can bring any proof, or shadow of proof, that I do not highly esteem it. With regard to the 'assurance of faith and hope' I have spoken as clearly as I can; and I trust serious men who have some experience in religion will not find much to condemn therein. And with respect to 'inward feelings', whoever denies them in the sense wherein alone I defend them must deny all the life and power of religion, and leave nothing but a dead, empty form. For take away the love of God and our neighbour, the peace of God, and joy in the Holy Ghost,[42] or (which comes to the same) deny that they are felt, and what remains but a poor, lifeless shadow?

14. This is what I do, and must contend for. 'I thought you had contended for quite another thing.'[43] If you had only thought so, or only said so in private conversation, it had been of no great consequence. But it was of consequence when you not only brought a false accusation against your brother, before so venerable an assembly, but also published it to all the world. Surely the first step was enough, and more than enough. Was there nothing more important wherewith to entertain the 'stewards of the mysteries of God'[44] than the mistakes, if they really had been such, of the Methodists, so called? Had they no enemies more dangerous than these? Were they not in more

[41] Rutherforth, p. 33n.

[42] See Rom. 14:17.

[43] Wesley does not appear to be quoting Rutherforth, but summarizing the gist of his incorrect inferences in his extended footnotes, pp. 26-33.

[44] 1 Cor. 4:1.

imminent danger, if of no outward sin, nothing in their behavior or conversation unworthy of their calling, yet of neglect, of remissness, of not laying out all their time, and care, and pains, in feeding the sheep which Christ hath purchased with his own blood?[45] Were none of them in danger of levity, of pride, of passion, of discontent, of covetousness? Were none of them seeking the praise of men more than the praise of God?[46] O sir, if this was the case with any of them, I will not say how trifling, how insignificant, but how mischievous to these, how fatal, how destructive, must a charge of this kind be! By which they were led, not to examine themselves, to consider either their own hearts or ways, but to criticize on[47] others, on those with whom nine in ten had no manner of concern? Surely so solemn an opportunity might be improved to far other purposes! Even to animate everyone present, to offer up himself a living sacrifice to God,[48] that so he may be ready to be offered up on the sacrifice and service of his faith. To have one thing only in his eye, to desire, to aim at nothing else; not honour, not ease, not money, not preferment—but to save his own soul, and them that hear him.[49]

I am,
Reverend sir,
Your brother and servant for Christ's sake,
John Wesley

[45] See Acts 20:28.

[46] John 12:43.

[47] The form 'criticize on' (or 'upon') implied to discuss critically, with no connotation of an adverse judgment; it became obsolete early in the 19th century (see *OED*).

[48] See Rom. 12:1.

[49] A favourite expression of Wesley, from 1 Tim. 4:16. In describing the first Methodist Conference he spoke of it as a conference with brethren 'who desire nothing but to save their own souls, and those that hear them' (JWJ, June 25, 1744).

20

A LETTER TO THE REV. MR. FLEURY

(1771)

AN INTRODUCTORY COMMENT

Methodism was introduced to Waterford, a cathedral city on the south-east coast of Ireland, by Robert Swindells, in or about the year 1748, and a preaching-house was built in 1759. The society was a struggling one, but strengthened by Wesley's almost biennial visits from 1752 onwards. The cathedral clergy did all they could to disrupt the work. After Wesley's visit of almost five days in June 1769, the Rev. George Lewis Fleury attacked the Methodists from the cathedral pulpit. Two years later, when Wesley again stayed for nearly five days, it was known in advance that Mr. Fleury was about to attack the Methodists in cathedral sermons, and Wesley was able to attend the cathedral twice in order to hear them. He records: 'At eleven, and again in the afternoon, I went to the cathedral, where a young gentleman most valiantly encountered the "grievous wolves", as he termed the Methodists. I never heard a man strike more wide of the mark. However, the shallow discourse did good, for it sent abundance of people, rich and poor, to hear and judge for themselves. So that the court, at the top of which I stood, was filled from end to end' (JWJ, April 28, 1771).

The subsequent events are set out in the Letter. *After writing it, Wesley dropped the issue and made no effort to advertise the pamphlet or to keep it in print, and he omitted it from his* Works.

Fleury (1742–1825) was a pensioner at Trinity College, Dublin, from 1759 until he became a scholar in 1761; he graduated B.A. in 1763 and was later ordained. He was one of the clergy preaching in the cathedral in 1769 and 1771; in December 1771 he was collated to the prebend of Kilgobinet. He became Archdeacon of Waterford in 1773 and remained in that office for fifty-two years. He confessed in later years when referring to this controversy with Wesley: 'I was but a novice and a greenhorn then' (Crookshank, I.246).

His sermons attacking Wesley were published anonymously and have disappeared. They can be partially reconstructed from Wesley's Letter, *which uses brief replies to each as a sandwich in which to incorporate* A Letter to a Clergyman *of 1748 (pp. 247-51 above); for the reconstructed sermons see Appendix D (pp. 581-82). This appears to be the only edition of this pamphlet. For further details see* Bibliography, *No. 329.*

A Letter to the Rev. Mr. Fleury

I labour for peace; but when I speak thereof
they make themselves ready for battle. Psa. 120:7.

[Limerick, May 18, 1771]

Rev. sir,

1. In June 1769 I spent two or three days at Waterford.[1] As soon as my back was turned you valiantly attacked me, I suppose both morning and afternoon. Hearing when I was there two or three weeks ago[2] that you designed me the same favour, I waited upon you at the Cathedral on Sunday, April 28. You was as good as your word—you drew the sword, and in effect threw away the scabbard.[3] You made a furious attack on a large body of people of whom you knew just nothing. Blind and bold, you laid about you without fear or wit, without any regard either to truth, justice, or mercy. And thus you entertained, both morning and evening, a large congregation, who came to hear 'the words of eternal life'.[4]

2. Not having leisure myself,[5] I desired Mr. Bourke[6] to wait upon you the next morning. He proposed our writing to each other. You said: 'No. If anything can be said against my Sermons, I expect it shall be printed. Let it be done in a public, not a private

[1] June 9-14, 1769.

[2] Apr. 25-29, 1771.

[3] For this allusion to Clarendon's *History of the Rebellion,* vii. 84, a phrase used also by the Young Pretender before the Battle of Prestonpans, Aug. 20, 1745, see Wesley's letter of Nov., 27, 1750 (26:447 in this edn.).

[4] John 6:68.

[5] Wesley seems to have left early on Monday morning *en route* to Cork, preaching at Clonmel that evening.

[6] Richard Bourke (also spelled 'Burke') was one of Wesley's itinerant preachers from 1766, and died in 1778 (see JWJ, Feb. 15, 1778). At this time he was the assistant of the Athlone Circuit and apparently accompanying Wesley during his itinerary through that circuit.

way.' I did not desire this. I had much rather it had been done privately. But since you will have it so, I submit.[7]

3. Your text was: 'I know this, that after my departure shall grievous wolves enter in among you, not sparing the flock. Also of your own selves shall men arise, speaking perverse things to draw away disciples after them.'[a] Having shown that St. Paul foresaw these false teachers, you undertake to show, (1), the mischiefs which they occasioned; (2), the character of them, and how nearly this concerns a set of men called 'Methodists'.[b]

4. Against these false teachers, you observe, St. Paul warned the Corinthians, Galatians, Colossians, and Hebrews.[c] Very true. But what is this to the point? Oh, much more than some are aware of. The insinuation was all along just as if you had said, 'I beseech you, my dear hearers, mark the titles he gives to these, "grievous wolves", "false apostles, deceitful workers",[8] and apply them to the Methodist teachers. There I give them a deadly thrust.'

5. 'These are well styled by Christ "ravening wolves",[9] by St. Paul "grievous wolves", from the mischiefs they do, rending the Church of Christ, and perverting the true sense of the gospel for their own private ends. They ever did, and to this day [do,][10] pretend to extraordinary inspiration.'[d]

Round assertions! Let us consider them one by one. 'These are styled by Christ "ravening wolves", by St. Paul "grievous wolves".' True; but how does it appear that these names are applicable to the Methodists? Why, they rend the Church of Christ. What is the Church of Christ? According to our Article,[11] a Church is 'a company of faithful people', of true believers, who have 'the mind that was in Christ',[12] and 'walk as Christ

[a] Acts 20:29-30.
[b] *First Sermon,* pp. 1-4.
[c] Pp. 5-7.
[d] P. 8.

---

[7] From the outset it seems to have been Fleury's intention to publish his sermons against the Methodists, and in fact he did so, though no copy appears to have survived. From the evidence of Wesley's references, the two sermons were paged separately, the first almost certainly of sixteen pages, the second probably of twenty. Because of the speed with which Wesley was able to prepare his reply they must surely have been printed locally, possibly as a unit. See Appendix D.

[8] 2 Cor. 11:13.

[9] Matt. 7:15.

[10] Orig., 'to'.

[11] Art. XIX of the Thirty-nine Articles.

[12] Cf. Phil. 2:5.

walked'.[13] Who then are the Church of Christ in Waterford? Point them out, sir, if you know them, and then be pleased to show how the Methodists rend this Church of Christ. You may as justly say they rend the walls or the steeple of the Cathedral Church. 'However, they pervert the true sense of the gospel for their own private ends.' Wherein do they pervert the true sense of the gospel? I have published *Notes* both on the Gospels and the other Scriptures.[14] But wherein do those *Notes* pervert the sense? None has yet attempted to show. But for what *private ends* should I pervert it? For ease or honour? Then I should be sadly disappointed. Or for money? This is the silliest tale of all. You may easily know, if you are willing to know it, that I did not leave Waterford without being some pounds lighter than I was when I came thither.

6. 'But they pretend to *extraordinary* inspiration.' They do not. They expressly disclaim it. I have declared an hundred times, I suppose ten times in print, that I pretend to no other inspiration than that which is common to all real Christians, without which no one can be a Christian at all. 'They denounce hell and damnation to all that reject their pretences.'[e] This is another charge; but it is as groundless as the former—it is without all shadow of truth. You may as well say, the Methodists denounce hell and damnation to all that reject Mahometanism. As groundless, as senselessly, shamelessly false, is the assertion following: 'To reject their ecstasies and fanatic pretences to revelation is cried up as a crime of the blackest die.' It cannot be that we should count it a crime to reject what we do not pretend to at all. But I pretend to no ecstasies of any kind, nor to any other kind of revelation that you yourself, yea, and every Christian enjoys, unless he is 'without God in the world'.[15]

7. 'These grievous wolves pretended to greater mortification and self-denial than the apostles themselves.'[f] This discovery is spick-and-span new—I never heard of it before. But pray, sir, where did you find it? I think not in the canonical Scriptures! I doubt you had it from some apocryphal writer. 'Thus also do the

[e] P. 9.

[f] P. 11.

[13] Cf. 1 John 2:6.

[14] *Explanatory Notes upon the New Testament* (1755, etc.), and *Explanatory Notes upon the Old Testament* (1765); see *Bibliography*, Nos. 209, 294; and Vols. 5-6 in this edn.

[15] Eph. 2:12.

modern false teachers.' I know not any that do. Indeed I have read of some such, among the Mahometan dervishes,[16] and among the Indian Brahmins.[17] But I doubt whether any of these outlandish creatures have been yet imported into Great Britain or Ireland.

8. 'They pretend to know the mind of Christ better than his apostles.'[g] Certainly the Methodists do not: this is another sad mistake, not to say slander. 'However, better than their successors do.' That is another question. If you rank yourself among their successors, as undoubtedly you do, I will not deny that some of these poor, despised people, though not acting in a public character, do know the mind of Christ, that is, the meaning of Scripture, better than you do yet. But perhaps, when ten years more are gone over your head, you may know it as well as they.

9. You conclude this Sermon, 'Let us not be led away by those who represent the comfortable religion of Christ as a path covered over with thorns.'[h] This cap does not fit *me*. I appeal to all that have heard me at Waterford or elsewhere, whether I represent religion as an uncomfortable thing. No, sir. Both in preaching and writing I represent it as far more comfortable than *you* do, or are able to do. 'But you represent *us* as lovers of pleasures more than lovers of God.'[18] If any do this, I doubt they touch a sore spot—I am afraid the shoe pinches. 'They affirm pleasure in general to be unlawful, grounding it on, "They that are in the flesh cannot please God".'[i] Wrong, top and bottom. Did we hold the conclusion, we should never infer it from such premises. But we do not hold it. We no more affirm pleasure in general to be unlawful than eating and drinking. This is another invention of your own brain, which never entered into our thoughts. It is really curious when you add, 'This is bringing men *after the principles of the world, and not after Christ.*' What, the affirming that pleasure is unlawful! Is this 'after the principle of the world'? Was ever text[19] so unhappily applied?

[g] P. 12.
[h] P. 14.
[i] P. 15 [quoting Rom. 8:8].

---

[16] Orig., 'Dervises'.
[17] Orig., 'Bramins'.
[18] 2 Tim. 3:4.
[19] The scriptural text which is nearest to the quotation from Fleury is Gal. 4:3: 'Even so we . . . were in bondage under the elements of the world' (AV), and Fleury may have been referring loosely to this. The word στοιχεῖα, translated 'elements' in the Authorized Version, could be translated 'principles', in the sense of 'elementary teachings'.

10. So much for your first Sermon, wherein, though you do not seem to want goodwill, yet you are marvelously barren of invention, having only retailed two or three old, threadbare objections, which have been answered twenty times over. You begin the second, 'I shall now consider some of their many *absurd doctrines*, the first of which is, "The pretending to be divinely inspired"'[j]—an odd 'doctrine' enough—'and called in an extraordinary manner to preach the word of God.'[k]

This is all harping upon the same string, the grand objection of *lay preachers*. We have it again and again, ten, twenty times over. I shall answer it once for all. Not by anything new—that is utterly needless—but barely by repeating the answer which convinced a serious clergyman many years ago.[20]

Rev. sir, Tullamore, May 4, 1748

I have at present neither leisure nor inclination to enter into a formal controversy; but you will give me leave just to offer a few loose hints relating to the subject of our last night's conversation.

[I.] 1. Seeing life and health are things of so great importance, it is without question highly expedient, that physicians should have all possible advantages of learning and education.

2. That trial should be made of them by competent judges before they practise publicly.

3. That after such trial they be authorized to practise by those who are empowered to convey that authority;

4. And that while they are preserving the lives of others they should have what is sufficient to sustain their own.

5. But supposing a gentleman bred at the university in Dublin, with all the advantages of education; after he has undergone all the usual trials, and then been regularly authorized to practise;

6. Suppose, I say, this physician settles at——for some years, and yet makes no cures at all; but after trying his skill on five hundred persons cannot show that he has healed one; many of his patients dying under his hands, and the rest remaining just as they were before he came.

7. Will you condemn a man who, having some little skill in physic, and a tender compassion for those who are sick or dying all round him, cures many of those, without fee or reward, whom the doctor could not cure?

8. At least, *did* not (which is the same thing as to the case in hand)—were it only for this reason, because he did not go to them, and they would not come to him.

9. Will you condemn him because he has not learning? Or has not had an university education?

[j] *Second Sermon*, p. 1.
[k] Pp. 2-4.

[20] See *A Letter to a Clergyman*, pp. 247-51 above, repeated almost verbatim.

What then? He cures those whom the man of learning and education cannot cure.

10. Will you object that he is no physician, nor has any authority to practise? I cannot come into your opinion. I think he is a physician who heals—*medicus est qui medetur*— and that every man has authority to save the life of a dying man. But if you only mean, he has no authority to take fees, I contend not—for he takes none at all.

11. Nay, and I am afraid it will hold, on the other hand, *medicus non est qui non medetur:* I am afraid, if we use propriety of speech, he is no physician who works no cure.

12. 'Oh, but he has taken his degree of Doctor of Physic, and therefore has authority.'

Authority to do what? 'Why, to heal all the sick that will employ him.' But (to waive the case of those who will not employ him—and would you have even *their* lives thrown away?) he does not heal those that do employ him. He that was sick before is sick still; or else he is gone hence, and is no more seen.

Therefore his authority is not worth a rush; for it serves not the end for which it was given.

13. And surely he has not authority to kill them, by hindering another from saving their lives!

14. If he either attempts or desires to hinder him, if he condemns or dislikes him for it, 'tis plain to all thinking men he regards his own fees more than the lives of his patients.

II. Now to apply. 1. Seeing life everlasting and holiness, or health of soul, are things of so great importance, it is highly expedient that ministers, being physicians of the soul, should have all advantage of education and learning.

2. That full trial should be made of them, in all respects, and that by the most competent judges, before they enter on the public exercise of their office, the saving souls from death.

3. That after such trial they be authorized to exercise that office by those who are empowered to convey that authority. (I believe, bishops are empowered to do this, and have been so from the apostolic age.)

4. And that those whose souls they save ought meantime to provide them what is needful for the body.

5. But suppose a gentleman bred at the university in Dublin, with all the advantages of education, after he has undergone the usual trials, and been regularly authorized to save souls from death;

6. Suppose, I say, this minister settles at——for some years, and yet saves no souls at all; saves no sinners from their sins, but after he has preached all this time to five or six hundred persons, cannot show that he has converted one from the error of his ways; many of his parishioners dying as they lived, and the rest remaining just as they were before he came.

7. Will you condemn a man who, having compassion on dying souls, and some knowledge of the gospel of Christ, without any temporal reward saves many from their sins whom the minister could not save?

8. At least *did* not—nor ever was likely to do it, for he did not go to them, and they would not come to him.

9. Will you condemn such a preacher because he has not learning? Or has not had an university education?

What then? He saves those sinners from their sins whom the man of learning and education cannot save.

A peasant being brought before the College of Physicians at Paris, a learned doctor accosted him, 'What, friend, do you pretend to prescribe to people that have agues? Dost thou know what an ague is?'

He replied, 'Yes, sir. An ague is what I can cure, and you can't.'

10. Will you object, 'But he is no minister, nor has any authority to save souls'?

I must beg leave to dissent from you in this. I think he is a true evangelical minister, διάκονος, servant of Christ and his church, who *οὕτως διακονεῖ*, so ministers as to save souls from death, to reclaim sinners from their sins; and that every Christian, if he is able to do it, has authority to save a dying soul.

But if you only mean he has no authority to take tithes, I grant it. He takes none. As he has freely received, so he freely gives.

11. But to carry the matter a little farther, I am afraid it will hold, on the other hand, with regard to the soul as well as the body, *medicus non est qui non medetur.* I am afraid reasonable men will be much inclined to think, he that saves no souls is no minister of Christ.

12. 'Oh, but he is ordained, and therefore has authority.'

Authority to do what? To save all the souls that will put themselves under his care. True. But (to waive the case of them that will not—and would you desire that even those should perish?) he does not, in fact, save them that are under his care. Therefore, what end does his authority serve? He that was a drunkard is a drunkard still. The same is true of the sabbath-breaker, the thief, the common swearer. This is the best of the case. For many have died in their iniquity, and their blood will God require at the watchman's hand.

13. For surely he has no authority to murder souls, either by his neglect, by his smooth if not false doctrine, or by hindering another from plucking them out of the fire, and bringing them to life everlasting.

14. If he either attempts or desires to hinder him, if he condemns or is displeased with him for it, how great reason is there to fear that he regards his own profit more than the salvation of souls!

11. 'But why do you not prove your mission by *miracles*?' This likewise you repeat over and over. But I have not leisure to answer the same stale objection an hundred times. I therefore give this also the same answer which I gave many years ago.

12. What is it you would have us prove by *miracles*? That the doctrines we preach are true? This is not the way to prove that. We prove the doctrines we preach by Scripture and reason. Is it [(1),] that A. B. was for many years without God in the world, a common swearer, a sabbath-breaker, a drunkard? Or, (2), that he is not so now? Or, (3), that he continued so till he heard us preach, and from that time was another man? Not so. The proper way to prove these facts is by the testimony of competent witnesses. And these witnesses are ready, whenever required, to give full evidence of them. Or would you have us prove by

miracles, (4), that this was not done 'by our own power or holiness'? That God only is able to raise the dead, those who are dead in trespasses and sins? Nay, 'if you hear not Moses and the prophets' and the apostles on this head, 'neither' will you believe, 'though one rose from the dead'. It is therefore utterly unreasonable and absurd to require or expect the proof of miracles in questions of such a kind as are always decided by proofs of quite another nature.[l]

If you will take the trouble of reading that little tract you will find more upon the same head.

13. If you say, But those who lay claim to *extraordinary* inspiration and revelation ought to prove that claim by miracles, we allow it. But this is not our case. We lay claim to no such thing. The apostles did lay claim to extraordinary inspiration, and accordingly proved their claim by miracles. And our blessed Master claimed to be Lord of all, the eternal Son of God. Well therefore might he be expected to do 'the works which no other man did',[21] especially as he came to put an end to that dispensation, which all men knew to be of God. See then how idly and impertinently you require the Methodists to work miracles, 'because Christ and his apostles did'!

14. You proceed. 'They pretend to be as free from sin as Jesus Christ.'[m] You bring three proofs of this. (1). 'Mr. Wesley, in his answer to a divine of our Church, says, "Jesus Christ stands as our regeneration, to help us to the same holy undefiled nature which he himself had. And if this very life and identical nature is not propagated and derived on us, he is not our Saviour."'[n] When I heard you read these words, I listened and studied, and could not imagine where you got them. I knew they were not mine—I use no such queer language—but did not then recollect that they are Mr. Law's words, in his answer to Dr. Trapp, an extract from which I have published.[22] But be they whose they will, they by no means imply that we are to be 'as righteous as

[l] *Farther Appeal to Men of Reason and Religion*, p. 122, etc. [i.e., Pt. III, III.28 (11:310 in this edn.)].
[m] P. 6.
[n] P. 7.

[21] John 15:24.
[22] *A Serious Answer to Dr. Trapp's four Sermons on the Sin, Folly, and Danger of being Righteous overmuch. Extracted from Mr. Law* (Cork, Harrison, 1748, reprinted by Powell of Dublin in 1749); see *Bibliography*, No. 147. This was abridged from William Law, *An Earnest and Serious Answer* . . . , 1740. The quotation consists of two passages from pp. 31 and 30, in Law's lengthy, rhapsodical exposition of his creed, §§25, 24, reversed and conflated.

Christ was', but that we are to be (which St. Peter likewise affirms) 'partakers of the divine nature'.[23] (2). 'A preacher of yours declared, he was as free from sin as Christ ever was.' I did not hear him declare it. Pray did you? If not, how do you know he declared it at all? Nay, (3), 'Another declared, he believed it was impossible for one whom he named to sin, for the Spirit of God dwelt in him bodily.'[o] Pray, sir, did you hear this yourself? Else the testimony is nothing worth. Hearsay evidence will not be admitted by any court in the kingdom.

What you say of that good man Mr. Whitefield, now with God, I leave with Mr. H———'s remark, 'I admire your prudence, though not your generosity; for 'tis much safer to cudgel a dead man that a living one.'[24]

15. You next descant upon 'the disorders which the spirit of enthusiasm created in the last age'. Very likely it might. But, blessed be God, that is nothing at all to *us*. For he hath given us, not the spirit of enthusiasm, but of love and of a sound mind.[25] In the following page you quaintly compare your hearers to sheep, and yourself and friends to the dogs in the fable; and seem much afraid lest the silly sheep should be 'persuaded to *give you up to these ravening wolves*'. Nay, should not you rather be ranked with the sheep than the dogs? For your teeth are not so sharp as razors.

16. 'Another fundamental error of the Methodists is the asserting that laymen may preach; yea, the *most ignorant* and illiterate of them, provided they have the *inward call* of the Spirit.'[p]

The former part of this objection we had before. The latter is a total mistake. They do not allow the 'most ignorant' men to preach, whatever 'inward call' they pretend to. Among them none are allowed to be stated preachers but such as (1), are truly alive to God; such as experience the 'faith that worketh by love';[26] such as

[o] P. 8.
[p] P. 10.

---

[23] 2 Pet. 1:4.

[24] Whitefield had died at Newburyport, Massachusetts, on Sept. 30, 1770. News of his death reached London on Nov. 5, and Wesley preached a funeral sermon for him on Sunday, Nov. 18. Even after this news had arrived Samuel Foote's burlesque on him, *The Minor* (1760), continued to be performed in the theatre at Edinburgh, which led to a public outcry 'against ridiculing the man after he was dead' (see Luke Tyerman, *Life of Whitefield* [London, 1890], 2:428-39). The identity of 'Mr. H', however, is unknown. It is entirely possible that 'Mr. H's remark', though contemporary, was made in reference to someone other than Whitefield.

[25] See 2 Tim. 1:7.

[26] Gal. 5:6.

love God and all mankind; (2), such as have a competent knowledge of the Word of God, and of the work of God in the souls of men; (3), such as have given proof that they are called of God, by converting sinners from the error of their ways.[27] And to show whether they have these qualifications or no they are a year, sometimes more, upon trial. Now I pray, what is the common examination either for Deacon's or Priest's Orders, to this?

17. 'But no ambassador can act without a commission from his king, consequently, no preacher without a commission from God.'[q] This is a tender point. But you constrain me to speak. I ask then, Is *he* commissioned from God to preach the gospel who does not know the gospel? Who knows little more of the Bible than of the Koran? I fear not. But if so, what are many of our brethren? Sent of man, but not of God!

'However, these laymen are not sent of God to preach. For does not St. Paul say, "No man taketh this honour to himself, but he that is called of God, as was Aaron." '[r] Another text most unhappily applied—for Aaron did not preach at all. But if these men are not sent of God, how comes God to confirm their word by convincing and converting sinners? He 'confirms the word of his messenger',[28] but of none else. Therefore if God owns their word, it is plain that God has sent them.

'But the earth opened and swallowed up those intruders into the priestly office, Korah, Dathan, and Abiram.'[s] Such an intruder are *you,* if you convert no sinners to God. Take heed lest a deeper pit swallow *you* up!

18. 'But the Church of Rome has sent out preachers among us, such as Thomas Heath, a Jesuit, and Faithful Commin,[29] a

[q] P. 11. [r] P. 13 [quoting Heb. 5:4]. [s] P. 14.

---

[27] See Jas. 5:20. [28] Cf. Isa. 44:26.

[29] Mr. Fleury, to show that the Wesley brothers are impostors, cites two proven cases of imposture, not from Irish history, as might have been expected, but from Elizabethan England. He borrows his examples from Bishop Lavington's *The Enthusiasm of Methodists and Papists Compared.* In this work (Pt. II [London, 1749], p. 187), quoting from *Foxes and Firebrands* (p. 7) and the Registry of Rochester, Lavington narrates that 'Thomas Heath, a Jesuit', preached against Popery, 'laboured to refine the Protestants' and purify the Church—and then was discovered to be a Jesuit through a letter from the Society of Jesus dropped accidentally in the pulpit. He was found to have a license from the Jesuits, and a Bull of Pope Pius V giving him authority to preach 'whatever doctrine the Society of Jesus pleased, for dividing Protestants'.

Earlier in the same work (pp. 180-84) Lavington cites the case of Faithful Cummin, a Dominican Friar, and includes a long transcript (the genuineness of which has been questioned, but not successfully) of his trial for being a 'sower of sedition among H. M.

Dominican friar.'[t] And what do you infer from hence? That my brother, who was thought a Student of Christ Church in Oxford, was really a Jesuit? And that while I passed for a Fellow of Lincoln College I was in fact a Dominican friar? Even to hint at such absurdities as these is an insult on common sense.

19. We have now done with the argumentative part of your Sermons, and come to the exhortation. 'Mark them that cause divisions and offences among you, for they serve not the Lord, but their own bellies.'[u] Who 'serve their own bellies'? The Methodists, or ———? Alas, how terribly might this be retorted! 'And by fair speeches deceive the hearts of the simple.'[30] Deceive them into what? Into the knowledge and love of God! The loving their neighbour as themselves![31] The walking in justice, mercy, and truth;[32] the doing to all as they would be done to.[33] *Felices errore suo!*[34] Would to God all the people of Waterford, rich and poor, yea, all the men, women, and children in the three kingdoms, may be thus 'deceived'!

20. 'Do not credit those who tell you that we must judge of our regeneration by sensible impulses, impressions, ardours, and ecstasies.'[v] Who tells them so? Not I. Not Mr. Bourke. Not any in connexion with me. Sir, you yourself either do or ought to know the contrary. Whether therefore these are or are not 'signs of the Spirit',[w] see *you* to it; it is nothing to *me,* any more than whether the Spirit does or does not 'show itself in groanings and sighings, in fits and starts'. I never affirmed it did; and when you represent

[t] Pp. 16-17.
[u] P. 18 [quoting Rom. 16:17].
[v] P. 19.
[w] P. 20.

———

faithful subjects' by the Queen and her Council. Cummin had claimed that he preached 'even in the wide world, among the flock of Christ scattered over the whole earth'; he was later discovered in secret talks and prayers with Roman Catholics. When the trial was going against him, he 'jumped bail' and fled to the Continent, where he was rewarded by the Pope with two thousand ducats.

From these instances Lavington argues that denunciation of the Pope by an enthusiast is no proof of sincerity. 'And' he writes, 'we may still have reason to suspect of Methodism that the Marks of the Beast are upon it.' Mr. Fleury's argument is similar. In replying to Lavington, Wesley mentioned Cummin but not Heath (see 11:427 in this edn.).

[30] Rom. 16:18, presumably quoted by Fleury, ibid.

[31] See Lev. 19:18, etc.

[32] Ps. 89:14.

[33] See Matt. 7:12, etc.

[34] Lucan, *Civil War,* i.459, which Wesley quotes in Sermon 76, 'On Perfection', III.12, adding his translation, 'happy in their mistake' (3:87 in this edn.).

me as so doing, you are a sinner against God, and me, and your own soul.

21. If you should see good to write anything more about the Methodists, I beg you would first learn who and what they are. Be so kind as at least to read over my *Journals*, and the *Appeals to Men of Reason and Religion*. Then you will no longer 'run' thus 'uncertainly', or 'fight as one that beateth the air'.[35] But I would rather hope you will not fight at all. For whom would you fight with? If you *will* fight, it must be with your friends; for such we really are. We wish all the same happiness to *you* which we wish to our own souls. We desire no worse for you than that you may 'present' yourself 'a living sacrifice, holy, acceptable to God'.[36] That you may watch over the souls committed to your charge as he 'that must give account';[37] and that in the end you may receive 'the crown which the Lord, the righteous Judge, will give to all that love his appearing'![38] So prays,

Rev. sir,
Your affectionate brother,
John Wesley

Limerick, May 18, 1771

[35] Cf. 1 Cor. 9:26.
[36] Rom. 12:1.
[37] Heb. 13:17.
[38] Cf. 2 Tim. 4:8.

21

AN ANSWER TO MR. ROWLAND HILL'S TRACT (1777)

AN INTRODUCTORY COMMENT

A month after John Wesley had laid the foundation stone of his New Chapel in City Road, London, on April 21, 1777, and preached a sermon for the occasion from Num. 23:23, the tract of Rowland Hill appeared under the title of Imposture Detected, and the dead vindicated; in a letter to a friend, containing some gentle strictures on the false and libellous harangue lately delivered by Mr. John Wesley, upon his laying the first stone of his new Dissenting House, near the City Road *(see Green,* Anti-Methodist, *No. 496).*

Hill maintained, in strictures which could certainly not be described as gentle, that Wesley had made excessive and boastful claims for himself and the Methodists, denied the truths of Calvinism (which was for him the gospel), and traduced the character of George Whitefield. He roundly proclaimed that Wesley was Whitefield's inferior in spiritual influence, a rebel against the Church of England, and in character a hypocrite, a cheat, a crafty slanderer, 'as unprincipled as a rook', and, in brief, 'an enemy to all righteousness'.

This wild and savage assault, prompted surely as much by jealousy as by conviction, provoked many replies from Wesley's friends, such as Thomas Olivers, who rebutted the criticisms, and also from some of his critics who deplored Hill's calumnious and abusive style.

Wesley was on his travels when the tract appeared and did not read it until six weeks after its publication. 'I read the truly wonderful performance of Mr. Rowland Hill. I stood amazed! Compared to him, Mr. Toplady is a very civil, fair-spoken gentleman.' He wrote his Answer *at once and dated it London, June 28, 1777.*

Hill, reacting to the furor which his tract had created, acknowledged that it was far 'too ludicrous and severe', and explained that he had not been able to correct it while it was being printed as he was itinerating in Devon and Cornwall; he had tried to make emendations when he saw the proof, but he was too late; and therefore he withdrew all copies from sale. He added that he was distressed to find that a second edition had been issued without his authority.

This account of the matter appears in a second tract, published in Bristol on October 1, 1777: A Full Answer to the Rev. J. Wesley's Remarks upon a Late Pamphlet, published in Defence of the Characters of the Rev. Mr. Whitefield and Others *(see Green,* Anti-Methodist, *No. 497). In this, after making the acknowledgements given above, he repeated his general accusations against Wesley, but in a lower key. Wesley did not reply to the second tract in print and made no revisions of his original* Answer. *He was eager to end the controversy as soon as possible.*

The Rev. Rowland Hill (1744–1833) was the sixth son of Sir Rowland Hill, first baronet, and younger brother of another antagonist of Wesley, Sir Richard Hill (1732–1808). While at St. John's College, Cambridge, he had carried out 'Methodist' practices by visiting the sick and preaching without authority. He was ordained deacon in 1773 but was never admitted to the priesthood. A chapel at Wotton-under-Edge, Gloucestershire, was built for him, and here he exercised what was in effect a Dissenting ministry; in 1783 he moved to Surrey Chapel in London. His Village Dialogues *(1810) were widely read, and he was known for unorthodox good works.*

For details of the four editions of Wesley's Answer, *a stemma showing the probable transmission of the text, and an account of the few variant readings, see Appendix A, pp. 541ff., and for further details see* Bibliography, *No. 368.*

An Answer to Mr. Rowland Hill's Tract, entitled, Imposture Detected[1]

Jealousy, cruel as the grave! Cant. 8:6.

Michael, the archangel, when contending with the Devil, durst not bring a railing accusation against him. Jude 9.

In the tract just published by Mr. Rowland Hill there are several *assertions* which are *not true*. And the whole pamphlet is wrote in an *unchristian* and *ungentlemanlike manner*. I shall first set down the *assertions* in order, and then proceed to the *manner*.

I. 1. 'Throughout the whole of Paul's epistles he can scarcely write *a single line* without mentioning Christ.'[a] I just opened on the fifteenth chapter of the First Epistle of the Corinthians. In the last thirty verses of this chapter, how often does he 'mention Christ'? In every 'single line'?

2. 'In that *wretched harangue* which he calls a Sermon he makes *himself* the *only* subject of *his own panegyrics*.'[b]

Being aware of this charge I had said, 'I am in one respect an improper person to give this information; as it will oblige me frequently to speak of myself, which may have the appearance of ostentation. But with regard to this I can only cast myself upon the candour of my hearers, being persuaded they will put the most favourable construction upon what is not a matter of choice, but of necessity. For there is no other person, if I decline the task, who can supply my place, who has a perfect knowledge of the work in question from the beginning of it to this day.'[c]

[a] [Hill, *Imposture Detected*,] p. 3.

[b] P. 4. [As usual the quotations are often inexact, abridged, or paraphrased, sometimes with italics added, yet faithful to the general sense of the original.]

[c] [Wesley,] *Sermon on Numbers xxiii.23* [1st edn., London, Fry, 1777], p. 9 [i.e., No. 112, *On Laying the Foundation of the New Chapel*, §4; see 3:580 in this edn.].

---

[1] *Imposture Detected, and the Dead Vindicated: in a Letter to a Friend. Containing some gentle Strictures on the false and libellous Harangue, lately delivered by Mr. John Wesley upon his laying the first Stone of his new Dissenting Meeting-House, near the City-Road (London, 1777).* The title page also contained the following quotation:

> Fain would he make the earth his pedestal;
> Mankind the gazers, the sole figure He.
> So, stilted dwarfs their littleness betray!
>
> Young.

I give an account of the rise of this work at Oxford, from 1725 to 1735, pages 10-14, at London and elsewhere, pages 16-19. In all this there is not a line of 'panegyric upon myself', but a naked recital of facts. Nor is there any panegyric on anyone in the following pages, but a plain account of the Methodist doctrines.

It may be observed (if it is worth observing), that I preached *in the open air* in October 1735. Mr. Whitefield was not then ordained.[2]

3. 'Not a single line tending to vindicate or illustrate any one fundamental doctrine of the gospel appears throughout the whole.'[d] Yes. 'Thou shalt love the Lord thy God' is one fundamental doctrine of the gospel; 'Thou shalt love thy neighbour as thyself' is another. And both these are vindicated and illustrated for several pages together.[3]

4. 'His sacrilegious hand violates the ashes of the dead, traduces the character of Mr. Whitefield, insinuates that he was the first who preached *in the open air;* with the *greatest bitterness of speech* traduces the dead as a dissenter from the Church.'[e]

My words are 'A good man who met with us at Oxford, while he was absent from us, conversed much with Dissenters, and contracted a strong prejudice against the Church. And not long after he totally separated from us'[f]—from my brother and me. This is every word I say about Mr. Whitefield. And is this 'violating the ashes of the dead'? Is this 'traducing his character'? Certainly not traducing him as 'a Dissenter from the Church'. Much less 'with the *greatest bitterness of speech*'. Where is the bitterness? And this is the whole ground for pouring out such a flood of abuse, obloquy, and calumny! But Mr. Hill goes on: 'With ungodly *craft* he *claws* up the ashes of the dead. He says Mr. Whitefield, by conversing with the Dissenters' (I mean chiefly the Presbyterians in New England) 'contracted a strong prejudice

[d] [Hill,] p. 4.
[e] [Hill,] p. 16 [the opening phrase is from p. 5].
[f] *Sermon,* p. 42 [i.e., No. 112, II.16 (3:590-91 in this edn.)].

---

[2] Hill had made great play of the fact that Wesley followed Whitefield's lead in field-preaching and also insinuated that 'he was the *first* champion who went forth into the highways and hedges to call sinners to repentance'—'a downright untruth' (p. 6). Wesley cannot deny the first fact, but points out that he had at least preached in the open air at an earlier date, *en route* to Georgia (§4). This Hill ridiculed at length in his *Full Answer,* pp. 6-13. See also I.4 below.

[3] Sermon 112, II.1-5, 17 (3:585-87, 591-92 in this edn.).

against the Church.'[g] I say so still. And how will Mr. Hill disprove it? Why, 'he manifested his strong attachment to the Church by erecting Tottenham Court Chapel for the celebration of the Church Service; yea, and reading the liturgy himself.' Nay, if this proved *his* strong attachment to the Church, it will equally prove mine. For I have read the liturgy as often as he. And I am now erecting a chapel *(hinc illae lachrymae!)*[4] for the celebration of the Church Service.

5. 'He cast lots for his creed.'[h] Never in my life. 'That paltry story is untrue.' They who tell it cast no honour upon him who published a private letter, wrote in confidence of friendship.[5]

6. 'He gives up *the righteousness of Christ*.'[i] No more than I give up his Godhead. But I renounce both the *phrase* and *thing* as it is explained by antinomian writers.

7. 'He gives up the *atonement* of Christ. The atonement, and the righteousness of Christ, he considers as mere words.'[j] Nothing can be more false. It is not concerning these I advise,

Proiicere ampullas et sesquipedalia verba.[6]

'But a man cannot *fear God*, and *work righteousness* evangelically, without living faith.' Most certainly. And who denies this? I have proved it an hundred times.

8. 'He RENOUNCED the grand Protestant doctrine of justification by faith alone, in those *horrid Minutes*.' I never renounced it yet, and I trust, never shall. The *'horrid Minutes'*[7] Mr. Fletcher[8]

[g] [Hill,] p. 18.
[h] [Ibid.,] p. 8.
[i] [Ibid.,] p. 9.
[j] P. 10.

---

[4] Terence, *The Lady of Andros*, *l.* 126, 'That's the source of those tears!'

[5] In his *Letter to the Reverend Mr. John Wesley: in answer to his Sermon, entitled, Free Grace* (1741), Whitefield had castigated Wesley for casting lots as to whether he should 'preach and print' that sermon, a fact of which Wesley had informed him in a letter. This passage Hill (as he admitted in his *Full Answer*, pp. 5-6) had twisted into a story about 'casting lots for his Creed', and continued: 'Pelagianism turned up as the doctrine he was *doomed* to preach.' (*Imposture*, pp. 8-9.) It was to this which Wesley referred in the sentence (in error placed within quotation marks by Wesley's printer): 'That paltry story is untrue.'

[6] Cf. Horace, *The Art of Poetry*, *l.* 97, 'to reject bombast and abnormally long words'; translated by Wesley in his *Works*, Vol. 32 (1774), 'to lay aside big words that have no determinate meaning'. Cf. JWJ, Dec. 1, 1767.

[7] Wesley's controversy with the Calvinists over predestination came to a head with the publication in the *Minutes* of his 1770 Conference of a somewhat carelessly worded anti-Calvinist document which contained this (among similar) passages: 'God does in fact justify those who by their own confession neither feared God nor wrought righteousness' (see Vol. 10 of this edn.).

[8] One of the by-products of the controversy over the 1770 *Minutes* was the stepping

has so effectually vindicated that I wonder Mr. Hill should mention them any more.

9. 'After all possible *candour* and *forbearance* had been shown to him.' By whom? By Mr. Toplady?[9] Mr. Richard Hill?[10] Or Mr. Rowland (who has excelled them all)? 'This *interloper*' (a pretty word, but what does it mean?) 'has *totally renounced the gospel of Christ*.'[k] Totally false—unless by the gospel be meant antinomian Calvinism.

10. 'In his last year's *Minutes* he speaks of the *doctrines* of grace' (Calvinism) 'with as *much venom* as ever.' Just as much. Let the reader judge. The words occur page 11:

> Q[uestion] 26. Calvinism has been the greatest hindrance of the work of God. What makes men swallow it so greedily?
>
> A[nswer]. Because it is so pleasing to flesh and blood, the doctrine of final perseverance in particular.
>
> Q. 27. What can be done to stop its progress?
>
> A. (1). Let all our preachers carefully read our tracts, and Mr. Fletcher's and Sellon's.
>
> (2). Let them preach universal redemption frequently and explicitly; but in love and gentleness, taking care never to return railing for railing. Let the Calvinists have all this on their side.[11]

Ecce signum![12]

11. 'He is most marvellously curious in forbidding his preachers to say, "My Lady".'

Were ever words so distorted and misrepresented! The words in the *Minutes* are, page 12: 'Do not imitate them' (the Calvinists,

[k] P. 11.

---

forward of the Rev. John Fletcher as Wesley's champion in the controversy with the Calvinists. Wesley himself edited and published the first of Fletcher's several 'Checks to Antinomianism', entitled *A Vindication of the Rev. Mr. Wesley's Last Minutes*, 1771 (see *Bibliography*, No. 333).

[9] Augustus Montague Toplady (1740–78), the hymn writer, who first came under Wesley's influence, but developed into one of his most implacable opponents, both in pamphlets and in *The Gospel Magazine*, of which he was the editor. Cf. Vol. 13 of this edn. for Wesley's reply to Toplady in *The Consequence Proved* (1771), *Bibliography*, No. 335.

[10] Richard (later Sir Richard) Hill (1732–1808), Rowland's eldest brother, one of Wesley's most prolific opponents since the 1770 *Minutes*, from two of whose major attacks Wesley had defended himself; in 1772, *Some Remarks on Mr. Hill's Review of all the Doctrines taught by Mr. John Wesley* (*Bibliography*, No. 341), and 1773, *Some Remarks on Mr. Hill's Farrago Double-Distilled* (*Bibliography*, No. 345), for both of which see Vol. 13 in this edn.

[11] See *Minutes*, 1776, in Vol. 10 of this edn. The original *Minutes* end, 'all this to themselves'.

[12] 'Here is the proof!'

of Trevecka in particular) 'in screaming, allegorizing, calling themselves ordained, boasting themselves of their *learning,* the *college,* or "my lady".' Is this 'forbidding them to say "my lady"'?[13] No more than forbidding them to make a bow.

12. 'A vast number of *sluts* had taken possession of the preaching-houses' (No: the preaching-houses were not in question), 'and *female servants* by courtesy called maids' (civil and kind! But neither were servants in question) 'are *filthy slovens* in their persons, dress, and *manoeuvres.*' (See, Mr. Hill understands French!)[14] 'So Mr. John gives the public to understand.' No, not Mr. John, but Mr. Hill. He goes on. 'And how is this mighty grievance to be redressed? Why, says this Solomon in a cassock' (Is not that witty?), 'sluts are to be kept out, by not letting them in.'[l] And is all this wit bestowed upon three poor lines! The words are just these:

> 'Complaint is made that sluts spoil our houses.
> How then can we prevent this?'
> 'Let no known slut live in any of them.'[15]

What a colour does Mr. Hill put upon this! But meantime where is conscience? Where is honour?

13. 'He denies the doctrines of the Church of England.'[m] That is, absolute predestination. Mr. Sellon has abundantly proved that this is no doctrine of the Church of England.[16] When Mr. Hill has answered his arguments I will give him some more. The

[l] P. 12.

[m] P. 13. [This is not in fact a quotation, but a summary of the charges made on pp. 12-14.]

---

[13] The context (in the 1776 *Minutes*) and Wesley's use of quotation marks for the title make it clear that Wesley was indeed warning his preachers against name-dropping.

[14] *OED* shows that the word *manoeuvre* was only slowly being accepted into English, and even then was usually italicized as a foreign borrowing. Wesley seems never to have used it except in this quotation, according to the Rev. Dr. George Lawton.

[15] *Minutes,* p. 1776, *Q.* 23.

[16] Walter Sellon (1715–92), whom Wesley had appointed classical master for Kingswood School in 1748, and who was sponsored for an evangelical ministry a few years later by the Countess of Huntingdon. In various curacies he came into his own as a writer in defence of the Christian faith (usually signing himself simply 'A Clergyman'), especially from 1765 onwards. He defended Wesley against James Hervey's *Eleven Letters* in his *Answer to Aspasio Vindicated* (1767), but the treatise which Wesley here has in mind is *The Church of England Vindicated from the Charge of Absolute Predestination* (1771), a reply to Toplady's *The Church of England Vindicated from the Charge of Arminianism* (1769).

objections against lay preachers (which come ill from Mr. Hill[17]) I have largely answered in the *Third Appeal to Men of Reason and Religion*.[18] But I know not that any lay preachers in connexion with me either baptize children or administer the Lord's Supper. I never *entreated* anything of Bishop Erasmus (who had abundant, unexceptionable credentials as to his episcopal character). Nor did he ever 'reject any overture' made by me.[n] Herein Mr. Hill has been misinformed. I deny the fact: let him produce his evidence. The *perfection* I hold is so far from being contrary to the doctrine of our Church[19] that it is exactly the same which every clergyman prays for every Sunday: 'Cleanse the thoughts of our hearts by the inspiration of thy Holy Spirit, that we may *perfectly love thee,* and *worthily magnify* thy holy name.'[20] I mean neither more nor less than this. In doctrine therefore I do not dissent from the Church of England.

14. However, 'he renounces the *discipline* of the Church.'[o] This objection too I have answered at large, in my letters to Dr. Church[21]—another kind of opponent than Mr. Rowland Hill—a gentleman, a scholar, and a Christian; and as such he both spoke and wrote.

15. 'He falsely says, almost all who were educated at Trevecka, except those that were ordained, and some of them

[n] P. 14. [According to Hill this 'long-bearded foreigner, who styled himself a Greek bishop, . . . positively *refused* Mr. John's pressing entreaties' that Erasmus should 'procure episcopal ordination' for him, 'and *rejected* all his overtures'. For the impact of Erasmus on English Methodism, and his status, see Baker, *John Wesley and the Church of England*, pp. 200-201, 380-81. Hill's *Full Answer* (pp. 17-18) adds another piece of evidence, 'in an extract from a letter received from a friend': 'One Mr. Arvin, of the Borough, near London, a bigoted devotee to Mr. John Wesley, owned it to me as an incontrovertible fact, and it is not *three* months ago since the Rev. Mr. R——n assured me that he was told by Erasmus himself, that Mr. Charles Wesley offered him forty guineas if he would consecrate his brother John a bishop.' Apart from the fact that the documentation for this evidence is less than convincing, it certainly does not provide the proof of his own implication for which Wesley asked.]

[o] P. 15. [In fact this is not a quotation, but a summary of the arguments of that page.]

---

17 Because he himself had functioned in this way before his ordination.

18 I.e., *A Farther Appeal*, Pt. III, III.7-16 (11:294-301 in this edn.).

19 See Hill, *Imposture*, pp. 14-15: 'To add no more, his favourite doctrine of *perfection* . . . shows to *what* Church he *really* belongs; for . . . the Church of England . . . expressly disclaims and reprobates this wretched and pernicious tenet in her XVth Article, and in various parts of her Homilies and Liturgy.'

20 BCP, Communion, Collect. This Wesley had also quoted in Sermon 112, II.4 (3:586 in this edn.).

21 The reference is to *The Principles of a Methodist Farther Explained*, III.2-5 (pp. 186-92 above).

too, disclaimed the Church, nay, and spoke of it upon all occasions with exquisite bitterness and contempt.'[22] This is a terrible truth. If Lady Huntingdon requires it, I can procure affidavits both concerning the time and place.

16. 'He professes he stands in no need of Christ's righteousness.'[p] I never professed any such thing. The very sermon referred to, the fifth in the first volume, proves the contrary.[23] But I flatly deny *that sense* of *imputed righteousness* which Mr. Hill contends for.

17. 'He *expressly* maintains the *merit* of *good works* in order to justification.'[q] Neither *expressly* nor implicitly. I *hope* Mr. Hill has not read Mr. Fletcher's *Checks*, nor my sermons on the subject. If he has not, he has a *poor* excuse for this assertion; if he has, he can have no excuse at all.

18. 'He contradicts himself concerning Enoch and Elijah. See his notes, the former edition.'[r] Wisely directed! For Mr. Hill *knew* the mistake was corrected in the next edition.

[p] P. 23 [i.e., pp. 22-23: 'Mr. John says that "we are to work *for* life", or in other words, we are "to do good works *in order* to find favour with God". Consequently this staunch friend to the religion of Rome, . . . who has no need of Christ's righteousness, can stand excellently alone.' Cf. Sermon 112, II.17 (3:591-92 in this edn.)].

[q] P. 24.

[r] P. 28. [In his *Explanatory Notes upon the New Testament* (1755), on John 3:13, 'For no one hath gone up to heaven but he that came down from heaven,' Wesley had written, 'Then Enoch and Elijah are not in heaven, but only in paradise,' which was toned down in the 2nd ed. (1757) to, 'Are then Enoch and Elijah in heaven, or only in paradise?' and

[22] Hill, *Imposture,* p. 20, quoting (with the same kind of accuracy as Wesley) from pp. 42-43 of Sermon 112, II.16 (3:591 in this edn.): 'She has, it seems, established a college in Wales, where, says Wesley, she patronizes a set of young men who, together with some of her clergy, "disclaim the Church, nay, speak against it upon all occasions, with exquisite bitterness and contempt".' Hill's footnote claims that here 'the crafty slanderer is taken in his own net; for the many thousands of Mr. Whitefield's still surviving friends can . . . convict him . . . as a liar of the most *gigantic* magnitude.'

In 1768 the Countess of Huntingdon founded a college at Trevecka (usually now spelled Trevecca) for the training, free of charge, of young men from any Protestant denomination who wished to enter the ministry. John Fletcher, vicar of Madeley, became president, without giving up his incumbency. In 1770 Wesley issued the *Minutes* of his Conference refuting Calvinism. Lady Huntingdon called on all the students at Trevecka to renounce the *Minutes* or be expelled. Fletcher resigned his post and shortly afterwards began to write his *Checks to Antinomianism* (see *History of the Methodist Church in Great Britain,* 1:176-79).

[23] I.e., 'Justification by Faith', first published 1746 (see Sermon 5, in this edn.). Hill quoted from II.4 what he termed 'this truly Socinian, truly heathen, and truly infernal passage': 'It can never consist with God's unerring wisdom to think that *I* am innocent, to judge that *I* am righteous, because *another* is so. He can no more in this manner confound *me* with Christ than with David or Abraham' (see 1:188-89 in this edn.).

19. 'He is ever raising malicious accusation against the *lives* and doctrines of *all* Calvinists, whether Churchmen or Dissenters, throughout all the kingdom.'[s]

Thousands of Calvinists know the contrary, both Churchmen and Dissenters.

20. 'He exerts all his art to irritate the civil powers against *all the people of God*.'[t] 'He says the Dissenters *revile* and *lightly esteem* the sacred person of the king.' I answer, (1). Are the Dissenters, are the Calvinists, 'all the people of God'? (2). If you think they are, do *all* these defend the American rebels? Who affirms it? [24] I hope, not a quarter, not a tenth part of them. (3). Do I say, 'all' the Dissenters 'revile' the king? I neither say so, nor think so. Those that do are guilty of what you impute to *me*. They 'irritate the civil powers' against themselves.

21. 'He says he will no more continue in fellowship with Calvinists than with thieves, drunkards, or common swearers.'[u] No: I say I will have no fellowship with those 'who rail at their governors' (be they Calvinists or Arminians) who '"speak all manner of evil" of them in *private*, if not in *public* too'.[25] 'Such is the character he gives of the Calvinistic Methodists.'[v] I do not; no more than of the Arminians. But I know there have been such

dropped altogether from the 1760 edn. onwards. In his note on Rev. 19:20 he had written in 1755: 'There were *two* that went alive into heaven. . . . Enoch and Elijah entered at once into the highest degree of glory.' In the 2nd edn. this was changed to: '. . . It may be Enoch and Elijah entered at once into the highest degree of glory, without first waiting in paradise.' See in this edn., Vols. 5-6. The footnote thus illustrating Wesley's lack of perfection ends: 'See Mr. John's *New Testament*, Edition of 1755.' In his *Full Answer*, p. 22, Hill adds a footnote: 'I own I knew the mistake was corrected concerning Enoch and Elijah. Nor did I know of the note charging this mistake again upon Mr. Wesley till I saw it in print. Here then I set Mr. Wesley the example of recantation; may he learn from his various inconsistencies to follow it.']

[s] P. 29.

[t] Pp. 29-30 [citing Wesley's *Calm Address to the Inhabitants of England*, §23 (1777, *Bibliography*, No. 365, Vol. 15 in this edn.)].

[u] P. 31.

[v] [Ibid.]

---

[24] One of the four edns. of Wesley's *Answer*, that 'sold at the Foundery', omits this sentence, which was probably a part of Wesley's original text and therefore more probably contained in the earlier edn., but omitted (surely by accident) from the second.

[25] Wesley's quotations come from *A Calm Address to the Inhabitants of England*, §23, but not in the same order: 'And dare *you* bring or retail an hundred railing accusations against your lawful governors? . . . Permit me to add a few more words to you . . . who are vulgarly called Methodists. Do any of *you* 'blaspheme God or the king"? None of you, I trust, who are in connexion with *me*. I would no more continue in fellowship with those who continued in such a practice than with whoremongers, or sabbath-breakers, or

among them: if they are wiser now I am glad. In the meantime let him wear the cap whom it fits, be it Mr. Wilkes[26] or Mr. Hill himself.

22. 'This *apostate miscreant*' (civil!) 'invites the king and his ministers to fall upon'—Whom? Those who '"rail at their governors", who "speak all manner of evil" of them, in *private,* if not in *public* too'. I am glad they cry out, though before they are hurt; and I hope they will cease to 'speak evil of dignities',[27] before those who 'bear not the sword in vain'[28] 'fall upon them',[29] not for their opinion, but their evil practices.

23. 'He says, Calvinists and *all* Dissenters are rebels.'[w] I never said or thought so. 'But a few years ago he himself thought the Americans were in the right.' I did; for then I thought that they sought nothing but legal *liberty;* but as soon as I was convinced they sought *independency,* I knew they were in the wrong. Mr. Evans's low and scurrilous tracts have been confuted over and over.[30]

24. 'He trumpets himself forth as *the greatest man that has ever lived since Constantine the Great.*'[x] *This too* is in *italics*.[31] It might have been in *capitals;* but it is an utter falsehood. Mr. Hill might as well have said, 'He trumpets himself forth as the King of Great Britain.' The passage to which I suppose he alludes, and the only one he can allude to, is this: 'When has true religion, since the time of Constantine the Great, made so large a progress within so

[w] P. 32.
[x] P. 37.

---

thieves, or drunkards, or common swearers. But there are not a few who go under that name though they have no connexion with *us*; . . . who hate the king and all his ministers only less than they do—an Arminian; and who speak all manner of evil of them in private, if not in public too.' A footnote in the 2nd edn. adds, 'But many of them are of a better mind.'

[26] John Wilkes (1727–97), the politician, the Opposition Member of Parliament for Middlesex.

[27] 2 Pet. 2:10; Jude 8.

[28] Rom. 13:4.

[29] Jer. 6:21.

[30] For Wesley's change of mind over the grievances of the Americans, and the part played by the Rev. Caleb Evans as their Bristol supporter and Wesley's antagonist, see Wesley, *A Calm Address to our American Colonists* (1775), *Bibliography,* No. 354, Vol. 15 in this edn.

[31] Wesley possibly says this as if the italics carried the implication that it was a quotation from his writings, which is implied by many other italicized passages; in fact, however, this is no such quotation, but Hill's description of him.

small a space?'[y] Is this '*trumpeting myself forth as the greatest man that has ever lived* since then'?

25. 'All his disciples are commanded *not to read* what is wrote against him.'[z] No; it is the Tabernacle disciples [who] are commanded 'not to read Mr. Fletcher'. And reason good; for there is no resisting the force of his arguments. Thousands, if they read them with any candour, would see that 'God willeth all men to be saved.'[32]

26. Mr. Hill concludes: 'I should have been glad to have addressed him in the softest and most tender style. But those are weapons he turns to ridicule.'[a] When? Show me a single instance. Indeed, I never was tried. What Calvinist ever addressed me in a soft and tender style? And which of them did I 'turn to ridicule'? I am utterly guiltless in this matter.

II. 1. I have now done with the merits of the cause, having refuted the charge *in every article*. And as to the *manner*, let any man of candour judge whether I have not 'spoken the truth in love'.[33] I proceed now to take some notice of the *manner* wherein Mr. Hill speaks, to illustrate which I need only present a few of his flowers to the impartial reader.

2. 'All the divinity we find in this "wretched harangue which he calls a sermon" are a few *bungling scraps* of the religion of nature, namely, love to God and love to man, which an heathen might have preached as well as Mr. John' (Polite!), 'and probably in a much better manner. Erase half a dozen lines, and I defy anyone to discover whether *the lying apostle of the Foundery* be a Jew, a Papist, a pagan, or a Turk.'[b]

'Else I should have treated *his trumpery* with the silence and *contempt* it deserves. But to see Mr. Whitefield scratched out of his grave by the claws of this *designing wolf*' (There is metaphor for you!) 'is enough to make the very stones cry out, or (which would be a greater miracle still) redden even a Wesley's forehead with a blush.'[c] I think it would be a greater miracle still to make *a wolf blush*!

[y] [Wesley,] *Sermon,* p. 28 [i.e., No. 112, II.6 (3:587 in this edn.)].
[z] [Hill, *Imposture Detected,* cf.] p. 38.
[a] P. 39.
[b] P. 4. [The 'wretched harangue' passage is inserted out of order.]
[c] P. 5.

[32] 1 Tim. 2:4 *(Notes).*

[33] Cf. Eph. 4:15.

'The dictatorial Mr. John *lyingly* maintains . . . argument enough for the *gaping dupes* whom he *leads by the nose*.'[d]

'He and his *lay-lubbers* go forth to poison the minds of men.'[e] Are not then the 'lay-lubbers' and the 'gaping dupes' just fit for each other?

But who are these 'lay-lubbers'? They are 'Wesley's ragged legion of preaching tinkers, scavengers, draymen, and chimney-sweepers.'[f]

3. 'No man would do this, unless he were as *unprincipled* as a ROOK, and as silly as a JACKDAW.'[34]

'His own people say he "is a very poor preacher", and that most of his laymen, raw and ignorant as they are, preach much more to the purpose. Indeed the old gentleman has *lost his teeth*. But should he not then cease *mumbling* with his gums?'[g]

'Why do they not keep the *shatter-brained old gentleman* locked up in a garret?'[h]

4. 'I doubt not but for *profit['s] sake* he would profess himself a staunch Calvinist.'[i]

'The Revd. Mr. John, Mr. Whitefield's *quondam understrapper*.'[j] How sadly then did he mistake when he so often subscribed himself, 'Your dutiful, your obliged and affectionate *son*'!

'Mark the venom that now distils from his *graceless* pen';[k] 'the venomous quill of this *grey-headed enemy to all righteousness*'.[l]

5. 'The *wretch* thought himself safe, but the *crafty slanderer* is taken in his own net.'[m]

'This truly Socinian, truly heathen, truly *infernal* passage is found in that *heretic's* sermon.'[n]

'The most rancorous pretences that ever actuated the *prostituted* pen of a *venal profligate*.'[o]

'With him *devils* and *Dissenters* are terms synonymous. If so what a *devil* must he be!'[p]

[d] P. 6. [The ellipsis (shown as usually by a dash) between 'maintains' and 'argument' in the edn. 'Sold at the Foundery' is a strong argument in favour of its priority, for it is the kind of typographical feature which might readily be dropped, but was unlikely to be inserted by an over-zealous compositor.]

[e] P. 11.
[f] P. 21.
[g] P. 25.
[h] Pp. 35-36.
[i] P. 16.
[j] Ibid.
[k] P. 17.
[l] P. 19.
[m] P. 20.
[n] P. 23.
[o] P. 30.
[p] Ibid.

[34] P. 7.

'The sole merit of the disappointed Orlando Furioso' (How pretty and quaint that is!) 'is seeking to enkindle a flame of ecclesiastical and civil discord.' No: to put it out, which I bless God is done already, to a great degree. 'And his sole perfection consists in his perfect hatred of all goodness and all good men.'[q]

6. Now let all the world judge between Mr. Hill and me. I do not say all the religious world, but all that have the smallest portion of common sense and common humanity. Setting everything else aside, suppose him to be my superior in rank, fortune, learning, and understanding: is this treatment for a *young* man to give to an *old* one, who at least is no fool, and who, before Mr. Hill was born, was in a more honourable employ than he is ever likely to be? What can inspire this young hero with such a spirit, and fill his mouth with such language? Is it any credit to his person, or to his cause? What can men think either of one or the other? If he does not reverence me, or common decency, should he not reverence himself? Why should he place himself on a level with 'the ragged legion of tinkers, scavengers, draymen, chimney-sweepers'?[35] Nay, there are many of these who would be ashamed to let such language come out of their mouth. If he writes any more, let him resume the scholar, the gentleman, and the Christian. Let him remember him who 'left us an example, that we might tread in his steps',[36] 'in meekness instructing those that oppose themselves, if peradventure God may bring them to the knowledge of the truth'.[37]

London, June 28, 1777

[q] P. 31.

---

[35] Hill, *Imposture,* p. 21, quoted by Wesley above, II.2.
[36] Cf. 1 Pet. 2:21.
[37] Cf. 2 Tim. 2:25.

22

A LETTER TO THE REV. MR. THOMAS MAXFIELD

(1778)

AN INTRODUCTORY COMMENT

Born in Bristol, Thomas Maxfield as a young man gained his first taste of evangelical religion while listening to George Whitefield in the open air there on February 17, 1739. On May 21 of that year he was dramatically convicted of sin under Wesley's preaching at the Nicholas Street Society, Bristol, and was converted later that evening. In 1740 he went with Charles Wesley to London, became assistant leader in the Foundery Society there, and then was accepted, somewhat reluctantly, on the strong advice of Susanna Wesley, as a full-time lay itinerant preacher by John Wesley—the first such, termed by Wesley his first 'son in the gospel'. He continued as a trusted preacher for over twenty years and was ordained by Dr. William Barnard, Bishop of Derry, 'to assist that good man (Wesley), that he may not work himself to death'. In the early 1760s, however, he took over the leadership of a group of visionaries which broke away from Wesley, and in 1763 he set up as an independent minister in London. In 1767 he published a lengthy Vindication *of his conduct and doctrine both before and after leaving Wesley. His introductory letter to Whitefield included this sentence: 'To many I owe this account, but to none so much as you, whose sermon first preached in the open air in Kingswood was the means, under God, of my conversion.'*[1] *This rather surprising change in his view of his spiritual pilgrimage had become a set part of his thinking, and he developed it further after the death of his wife, who had herself been one of Whitefield's first converts. She died November 23, 1777, and early the following year Maxfield published* A Short Account of God's Dealings with Mrs. Elizabeth Maxfield.[2] *Having dealt with the influence of Whitefield upon her life, Maxfield turned to Whitefield's influence upon his own, and to the original rift between Wesley and Whitefield and the more recent one between Wesley and himself. Wesley*

[1] *Vindication* (Green, *Anti-Methodist,* No. 390), p. iii.
[2] See Green, *Anti-Methodist,* No. 512.

felt that Maxfield had completely distorted the facts, which was likely enough in view of the heavily charged atmosphere of apocalyptic expectation in which Maxfield had been living.

In fact, however, there had been substance to Maxfield's charges, though their manner of presentation awakened no memory in Wesley. There were four points which Wesley felt that he must publicly refute. The first was that Maxfield was 'some of the first fruits of Mr. Whitefield's ministry' rather than of his own, and Wesley may well have been correct in implying that Maxfield had garbled the facts, even though he admittedly had first heard the preaching of Whitefield. The second, that Whitefield had committed huge numbers of his own followers to Wesley before leaving for America in 1739, did have some substance. The third and fourth arose out of the second, the third implying Wesley's treachery in proselytizing Whitefield's followers, with Whitefield's doctrinal excesses a mere subterfuge, and the fourth that the breach between Calvinist and Arminian Methodists had never been healed. Answering the third, Wesley demonstrated that the main fault was Whitefield's, not for holding *Calvinist views, but for attacking Wesley's teaching publicly, even from Wesley's own Foundery pulpit. As to the fourth, he claimed that he remained a great friend of Whitefield and his societies, and prayed for their increase, even though he did indeed defend himself against those Calvinists who made calumnious attacks upon him personally.*

The second charge, however, was indeed based on facts, though because Wesley had misunderstood the charge he had completely forgotten these. When Whitefield left the second time for America—not in 1741, as Wesley misremembered the event, but in August 1739—he did indeed ask his former tutor to take care of—not any societies of his, but—his thousands of hearers, now hearers of the Wesleys also, in the open air. That the changed loyalties of many of these hearers deeply grieved Whitefield upon his return is made clear by two of his letters. To James Habersham, his agent in charge of the Georgia Orphan-house, he wrote sadly, shortly after landing in England: 'Congregations at Moorfields and Kennington Common on Sunday were as large as usual. On the following weekdays, quite contrary: twenty thousand dwindled down to two or three hundred. . . . Many, many of my spiritual children . . . are so prejudiced by the dear Messrs. W[esley]s' dressing up the doctrine of election in such horrible colours that they will neither hear, see, nor give me the least assistance. . . . I am now constrained, on account of our differing in principles, publicly to separate from my dear,

dear old friends Messrs. J——— and C——— W——y, whom I still love as my own soul.'[3]

It is against this background of festering embitterment in the mind of Maxfield, utilizing long-forgotten wounds to Whitefield, that Wesley's shocked and puzzled protestations must be read.[4] *Wesley dated his open letter to Maxfield February 14, 1778. Before his death on March 18, 1784, however, Maxfield seems to have become a little more reconciled to his former Methodist colleagues.*

Wesley's Letter *to him was never reprinted. Further details of the only edition may be found in* Bibliography, *No. 385.*

A Letter to the Rev. Mr. Thomas Maxfield

Occasioned by a late Publication

I was a little surprised to read, in a late publication of yours,[1] the following assertions:

1. Thomas Maxfield was 'some of the first fruits of Mr. Whitefield's ministry.'[a]

[a] P. 18 [Maxfield describes how Whitefield himself said, pointing to Maxfield, about 1769—he died in 1770: 'He and his wife are two—he some of the first fruits of my ministry at Bristol, and she at London,' whereon Maxfield added, 'I could only be silent, for I knew it was true'].

---

[3] Whitefield, *Works*, Vol. I (1771), pp. 256-57, March 25, 1741. A similar letter about the loss of his 'spiritual children' was written to the Rev. Gilbert Tennent on Feb. 2, 1742 (I. 362), and the general situation was confirmed by a 1748 autobiographical reminiscence of Howell Harris (see Tom Beynon, *Howell Harris's Visits to London,* Aberystwyth, Cambrian News Press, 1960, pp. 192-93).

[4] In Maxfield's *Vindication,* also dedicated to Whitefield (1767), he wrote (p. iv): 'For though your wounds are healed, which you received so many years ago in the house of your friends, you know that mine are still bleeding, therefore I humbly beg a kind Samaritan's compassion.'

---

[1] *A Short Account of God's Dealings with Mrs. Elizabeth Maxfield, wife of the Rev. Thomas Maxfield; from the time of her being awakened at the beginning of Mr. Whitefield's Preaching till her death. Who died of an Asthma, November 23, 1777* (London, Pasham, 1778).

2. 'When he went abroad he delivered me, and many thousands more, into the hands of those he thought he could have trusted them with, and who would have given *them back to him again,* at his return. But, *alas! it was not so.*'[b]

'I heard Mr. Whitefield say, at the Tabernacle, in the presence of five or six ministers, to Mr. [Wesley], a little before he left England the last time, "I delivered thirty thousand people into the hands of your brother and you, when I went abroad. And by the time I came back you had so turned their hearts against me that not three hundred of them would come to hear me." [. . .] I knew this was true.'[c]

3. 'I heard Mr. Whitefield say, "When I came first from Georgia there was no speaking evil of each other. O what would I not give, or suffer, or do, to see such times again! But O that division, that division! What slaughter it has made!"'[2]

'It was doctrine that caused the difference; or, at least, it was so pretended.'[d]

'He preached a few times in connexion with his old friends. But ah! how soon was the sword of contention drawn!'[e]

4. 'Where can you now find any loving ones, of *either* party? [. . .] They have no more love to each other than Turks.'[f]

'Read their vile contentions, and the *evil characters* they give of *each other,* raking the filthiest ashes to find some black story against their fellow-preachers.'[g]

They 'slay with the sword of bitterness, wrath, and envy. Still more [to] their shame is what they have sent out into the world against each other, on *both sides,* about five or six years ago, and till this very day.'[h]

To satisfy both friends and foes I propose a few queries on each of these four heads.

[b] Ibid. [Actually pp. 17-18, beginning, 'And when he went abroad again he delivered her, me, and many thousands more. . . .' This was in August 1739.]

[c] Ibid. [As may be seen from note 'a' above, the last phrase apparently referred to Maxfield's being the fruit of Whitefield's ministry rather than to Wesley's stealing of Whitefield's sheep.]

[d] Ibid.

[e] P. 19.

[f] Ibid. [and p. 22].

[g] P. 20.

[h] P. 21.

---

[2] Maxfield, *Short Account,* p. 17, paraphrased and conflated.

I. As to the first, I read a remarkable passage in the Third *Journal*, page 50, the truth of which may be still attested by Mr. Durbin,[3] Mr. Westell,[4] and several others then present, who are yet alive: 'A young man who stood behind sunk down, as one dead; but soon began to roar out, and beat himself against the ground, so that six men could scarce hold him. This was *Thomas Maxfield*.'[5] Was this *you*? If it was, how are you 'the first fruits of Mr. Whitefield's ministry'? And how is it that neither I, nor your fellow-labourers, ever heard one word of this during all those years wherein you laboured in connexion with us?

II. 'When he went abroad again he delivered *me*, and many thousands, into the hands of Mr. [Wesley].'[6]

When? Where? In what manner? This is quite new to *me*! I never heard one word of it before!

But stay! Here is something more curious still! 'I heard Mr. Whitefield say, at the Tabernacle, in the presence of five or six ministers, a little before he left England the last time, "I delivered thirty thousand people into the hands of you and your brother, when I went abroad."'

Mr. Whitefield's going abroad which is here referred to was in the year 1741.[7] Did he then deliver *you* into my hands? Was you not in my hands before? Had you not then, for above a year, been a member of the Society under my care? Nay, was you not at that very time one of *my* preachers? Did you not *then* serve me, as a son, in the gospel? Did you not eat my bread, and lodge in my house?[8] Is not this then a *total* misrepresentation? Would to God it be not a *wilful* one!

[3] Henry Durbin (*c.* 1719–99), a young apothecary who was made a freeman of Bristol in 1747, a highly respected member of St. Thomas's Church and one of the leading members of Wesley's Methodist Society.

[4] Thomas Westell (*c.* 1719–94), a joiner of Bristol who became one of Wesley's first three full-time itinerant preachers (along with Thomas Maxfield and Thomas Richards) and the only one of the three who remained in connexion with Wesley to the end of his life.

[5] See JWJ, May 21, 1739.

[6] Cf. §2. Actually Wesley's 'Mr.———' represents Maxfield's orig., 'one of the gentlemen concerned'.

[7] As noted above, the date was in fact August 1739. Whitefield returned from America early in 1741 and did not leave for America again until August 1744.

[8] As so frequently, Wesley's recollection of events is good, but of dates very faulty. Maxfield was *not* a preacher in August 1739, but about that time became a band-leader in Bristol, leaving for London about six months later, where most probably that summer, or possibly the following spring, his calling as a preacher was recognized by Wesley. (For the problem of ascertaining the date see Frank Baker, 'Thomas Maxfield's First Sermon', *Proceedings of the Wesley Historical Society* (1949), 27:7-15.) For independent confirmation

'I heard', you say, 'Mr. Whitefield say, at the Tabernacle, in the presence of five or six ministers, a little before he left England the last time'—Who then can doubt the truth of what follows? For here is chapter and verse! Here both the time, the place, and the persons present are specified. And they ought to be; seeing the crime alleged is one of a very heinous nature. Many a man has been justly sentenced to death for sins which, in the sight of God, were not equal to this. The point therefore requires a little more examination. And first I desire to know, What are the names of those five or six ministers? And which of them heard Mr. Whitefield say, 'When I went abroad (in 1741) I delivered thirty thousand people into the hands of you and your brother'? Thirty thousand people! Whence did they come? Did they spring out of the earth? Why, there were not at that time five thousand Methodists in England, or in the world. The societies in London, Bristol, and Kingswood (the only ones I had), contained fourteen or fifteen hundred members. I believe not so many were in *his* societies. But were they fewer or more, they were nothing to *me*. He never entrusted *me* with them. He never delivered into mine, or my brother's hands, either his society at the Tabernacle in London, or that in Bristol, or in Kingswood, or any other place whatever. He never delivered (that I remember) one single society into my hands. I bless God I needed it not. I did not need to build upon another man's foundation. 'A dispensation of the gospel was given me'[9] also; and my labour was not in vain. I was constrained to cry out (and *you* yourself used the same words to God, in *my* behalf):

> O the fathomless love
> Which has deigned to approve
> And prosper the work of my hands!
> With my pastoral crook
> I went over the brook,
> And, behold! I am spread into bands![10]

of Whitefield's entrusting many adherents to Wesley in 1739 and missing them in 1741, see his letters of March 25, 1741, to Habersham, and Feb. 1, 1742, to Tennent. Cf. a somewhat ambiguous autobiographical reminiscence by Howell Harris in 1748 (Tom Beynon, *Howell Harris's Visits to London*, p. 192. The general fact of this handing over by Whitefield to Wesley of a spiritual trust was clear in Whitefield's mind, but it was distorted from uncommitted hearers into committed members, and it is not surprising that Wesley failed to recognize the incident as recorded by an embittered Maxfield nearly forty years later.

[9] Cf. 1 Cor. 9:17.

[10] Charles Wesley, *Hymns and Sacred Poems* (2 vols., Bristol, Farley, 1749), II.257-59, entitled 'On his Birthday', beginning, 'Away with my fears', and (the beginning changed to

With what view then can you charge me with that perfidy which I am no more guilty of than of high treason? For what end can you affirm, 'When he went abroad he delivered many thousands into the hands of those he thought he could have trusted them with.'—Delivered! When? Where? How? What can you mean? I flatly deny that ever he delivered one thousand, or one hundred, souls into *my* hands. Do you mean, 'He spoke honourably of you to them at Kennington Common[11] and Rose Green'?[12] True: but not so honourably as I spoke of *you,* even at London—yea, as late as the year 1763! Yet was this the same thing with 'delivering the people at London "into your hands"'? Nay, but 'Mr. Whitefield trusted that you would have given them back at his return.' Them! Whom? His society at London, or Bristol? I had them not to give. He never entrusted me with them. Therefore I could not 'give them back'.

But how *melancholy* is the exclamation that follows: 'Alas! It was not so!' Was not how? Why, I did not give back what I never had received, but went straight on my way, taking the best care I could of those who *entrusted themselves* to me.

III. So much for the second article. As to the third, your words are: 'I heard Mr. Whitefield say, 'O that division, that division! What slaughter it has made!'

But who made that division? It was not I: it was not my brother. It was Mr. Whitefield himself: and that notwithstanding all admonitions, arguments, and entreaties. Mr. Whitefield first wrote a treatise against me by name. He sent it to my brother, who endorsed it with these words, 'Put up again thy sword into its place.'[13] It slept awhile; but after a time he published it. I made no reply. Soon after Mr. Whitefield preached against my brother and me, by name. This he did constantly, both in Moorfields, and in all other public places. We never returned railing for railing;[14] but spoke honourably of him at all times, and in all places. But is it any wonder that those who loved us should no longer choose to

'Away with our fears') No. 221 in the 1780 *Collection of Hymns* (see 7:357-60 in this edn.), of which this forms ver. 8.

[11] In London, a favourite site for preaching in the open air.

[12] In Bristol, another favourite place for field preaching.

[13] Matt. 26:52 *(Notes)*. The 'treatise' was in fact *A Letter to the Reverend Mr. John Wesley: In Answer to his Sermon entitled,* Free Grace. Wesley had attacked a doctrine; Whitefield attacked a person, and that one his friend.

[14] See 1 Pet. 3:9.

hear him? Meantime was it *we* that 'turned their hearts against him'? Was it not *himself?*

But you say, 'It was doctrine that caused the difference' (oddly enough expressed!)—'at least, it was so pretended!' It was so *pretended!* What do you mean? That difference of doctrine was only *pretended?* That we were agreed at the bottom, and only fought, like prize-fighters, to show our skill? Nay, here was no pretence: the thing was as plain as the sun at noonday. Did not Mr. Whitefield proclaim, upon the housetop, the difference between us and him? And yet it was not merely the *difference* of *doctrine* that caused the division. It was rather the *manner* wherein he maintained his doctrine, and treated us in every place. Otherwise, difference of doctrine would not have created any difference of affection, but he might *lovingly* have held *particular* redemption, and we *general,* to our lives' end.

He did indeed 'preach a few times in connexion with his old friends. But how soon was the sword of contention drawn'![15] By whom? Truly, by himself. Do not you know (thousands do, if you do not) that, when he preached in the very Foundery, and my brother sat by him,[16] he preached the absolute decrees, in the most peremptory and offensive manner? What was this but drawing the sword, and throwing away the scabbard?[17] Who then is chargeable with the contention and division that ensued?

IV. 'But where, you ask, can you now find any loving ones, of either party?' Blessed be God, I can find many thousands, both in London, in Bristol, in Kingswood, and in various parts, not only of England, but also of Scotland and Ireland—persons as full of love, both to God and man, as any I knew forty years ago.

Some of these I find (and much rejoice to find) in Mr. Whitefield's societies. And I pray God they may increase a thousandfold, both in number and in strength. 'Nay, they have no more love to *each other* than Turks.' They! Who? This is not the case with our societies. They not only love each other, but love their enemies, even those that still despitefully use them.[18] But

[15] See §3.

[16] See Charles Wesley's letter of Mar. 16-17, 1741, from London, to JW in Bristol, 26:54-55 in this edn.

[17] See above p. 390.

[18] See Matt. 5:44.

'read their vile contentions, and the *evil character* they give *each other,* raking the filthiest ashes to find some black story.' I will answer for one: I give no '*evil character* of my fellow preachers'. I rake into no 'filthy ashes for black stories'—let him who does take it to himself. 'They slay with the sword of bitterness, wrath, and envy.' I do not. I plead, Not guilty. As I envy no man, so neither my wrath nor bitterness slays any human creature. 'Still more to their shame is what they have sent out into the world against each other, *on both sides,* about five or six years ago, and till this very day.'

'What they have sent out against each other, *on both sides,* about five or six years ago'. Within five or six years I have been vehemently called to answer for myself; twice by Mr. Richard Hill,[19] and afterwards by his brother.[20] Have you read what we 'have sent out into the world against each other, *on both sides*'? If you have not, how can you so peremptorily affirm what *both sides* have done? You cannot possibly be a judge of what you have not read—and if you *had* read you could not have passed such a sentence. Three tracts I have wrote; but in none of these do I 'slay with the sword of bitterness, or wrath, or envy'. In none of them do I speak one bitter, or passionate, or disrespectful word. Bitterness and wrath, yea, low, base, virulent invective, both Mr. Richard and Mr. Rowland Hill (as well as Mr. Toplady) have poured out upon me, in great abundance. But where have I, in one single instance, returned them railing for railing? I have not so learned Christ.[21] I dare not rail, either at them, or you. I return not cursing, but blessing. That the God of love may bless both them and you is the prayer of

Your injured,
Yet still affectionate brother,
John Wesley

February 14, 1778

[19] See above, pp. 357-58.

[20] See *An Answer to Mr. Rowland Hill's Tract, entitled* Imposture Detected, above, pp. 402-15.

[21] Eph. 4:20.

23

A SHORT HISTORY OF THE PEOPLE CALLED METHODISTS

(1781)

AN INTRODUCTORY COMMENT

This is the closing section of John Wesley's Concise Ecclesiastical History, *which was based on Archibald Maclaine's English translation of Mosheim's* Ecclesiastical History *(1765). Although he found Maclaine's work very useful, he took exception to the chronological table which it contained, for the good reason that it listed Wesley and George Whitefield as heretics. He therefore subjoined this* Short History *to his* Concise Ecclesiastical History *as a corrective of Maclaine's error.*

It should be compared with A Short History of Methodism *(pp. 367-72 above), and contains his considered judgment that the essence of Methodism was its emphasis upon the gathering for fellowship of like-minded people, in addition to their attendance at public worship. He distinguishes three stages in the development of the movement, in Oxford, in Savannah, and in London, before he was called to preach in the open air in Bristol and to the colliers of Kingswood and to set up societies in both places.*

By the time that he came to write this work, at the age of 78, Wesley clearly believed that Methodism was an important phenomenon in the history of the church, likely to become permanent and deserving a chapter in an Ecclesiastical History.

The four volumes of A Concise Ecclesiastical History *extend over 347, 316, 332, 281 pages (apart from the index), a total of 1276 pages, while the account of Methodism occupies pp. 169-281, i.e., 112 pages, or over 11 percent of the whole. It comprises the closing feature of Vol. IV, apart from the lengthy index, in which neither 'Methodism' nor 'Wesley' occurs.*

It was reprinted once during Wesley's lifetime as a separate item (in Halifax, Nova Scotia, by J. Howe) for his followers in British North America. As it seems certain that the forty-two stylistic variants there introduced do not represent Wesley's revisions, they are not listed in Appendix A. For further details see Bibliography, *No. 420.*

This Short History *consists largely of extracts, taken almost verbatim, from John Wesley's* Journal. *The necessary footnotes to the text are therefore largely to be found in the* Journal *at the appropriate places (vols. 18–23 of this edn.).*

A Short History of the People called Methodists

1.[1] As no other person can be so well acquainted with Methodism, so called, as I am, I judge it my duty to leave behind me, for the information of all candid men, as clear an account of it as I can. This will contain the chief circumstances that occurred for upwards of fifty years, related in the most plain and artless manner before him whose I am, and whom I serve.[2]

I do this the rather because under the article of Heretics, Dr. Maclaine,[3] in his chronological tables, is pleased to place Mr. Whitefield and me. Mr. Whitefield has given a large account of himself. And so indeed have I. But as that account is too large to be soon read over, it may be a satisfaction to many serious persons to see it contracted into a narrower compass. Those who desire to have a fuller account of these things may at their leisure read all my Journals.

It will easily be observed that I nearly confine myself to the things of which I was an eye- or ear-witness. If any wish to be more largely informed of other things, they may consult the *Arminian Magazine*.[4]

2. In November 1729, at which time I came to reside at Oxford, my brother and I, and two young gentlemen more,

[1] This closing section of the *Concise Ecclesiastical History* is numbered I-CXXXII, which is here altered to 1-132.

[2] Acts 27:23.

[3] Orig., 'M'Lane', i.e., Archibald Maclaine (1722–1804), Scots Presbyterian minister, upon whose English translation of Mosheim's *Ecclesiastical History* (1765) Wesley's *Concise Ecclesiastical History* was based. For Maclaine's categorization of the Methodists see the 2nd edn., Vol. 5 (1768), p. 257, where among 'Heretics or Enemies of Revelation' during the eighteenth century he closes with: 'Among the sects of this century we may reckon the Herrnhuters or Moravian Brethren, and the followers of Whitefield, Wesley, and others of the same stamp.'

[4] Founded by Wesley in 1778: see extracts therefrom following this *History*.

agreed to spend three or four evenings in a week together.[a] On Sunday evening we read something in divinity; on other nights, the Greek or Latin classics. In the following summer we were desired to visit the prisoners in the Castle. And we were so well satisfied with our conversation there that we agreed to visit them once or twice a week. Soon after we were desired to call upon a poor woman in the town that was sick. And in this employment, too, we believed it would be worth while to spend an hour or two in every week. Being now joined by a young gentleman of Merton College,[5] who willingly took part in the same exercises, we all agreed to communicate as often as we could (which was then once a week at Christ Church), and to do what service we could to our acquaintance, the prisoners, and two or three poor families in the town.

3. In April 1732[6] Mr. Clayton of Brasenose College began to meet with us. It was by his advice that we began to observe the fasts of the ancient Church, every Wednesday and Friday. Two or three of his pupils, one of my brother's, two or three of mine, and Mr. Broughton, of Exeter College, desired likewise to spend six evenings in a week with us, from six to nine o'clock, partly in reading and considering a chapter of the Greek Testament, and partly in close conversation. To these were added the next year Mr. Ingham, with two or three other gentlemen of Queen's College; then Mr. Hervey, and in the year 1735 Mr. George Whitefield. I think at this time we were fourteen or fifteen in number, all of one heart and of one mind.[7]

4. Having now obtained what I had long desired, a company of friends that were as my own soul,[8] I set up my rest, being fully determined to live and die in this sweet retirement. But in spring 1735 I was suddenly called to attend my dying father, who a little before his death desired me to present a book he had just finished to Queen Caroline.[9] Almost as soon as I returned to Oxford I was

[a] *Works*, Vol. 26 [1774], p. 88 and sequel [i.e., *Journal* 1, Pref., §4 (Vol. 18 in this edn.)].

---

[5] Robert Kirkham, son of the Rev. Lionel Kirkham, rector of Stanton, Gloucestershire.

[6] This narrative of the beginnings and development of the 'Holy Club' is a brief summary of Wesley's account of the matter in numerous passages of JWJ. Here he introduces the chief members.

[7] See Acts 4:32.

[8] See 1 Sam. 18:1, etc.

[9] *Dissertationes in Librum Jobi.* Wesley's father died Apr. 25, 1735, and upon John Wesley fell a large share of seeing the volume through the press. A few copies were hastily bound, and he presented a copy to Queen Caroline on Sunday, Oct. 12, 1735, two days before he embarked for Georgia; the title-pages of the regular copies were dated 1736 (see *Bibliography,* No. 7).

obliged on this account to go to London, where I was strongly solicited to go over to Georgia, in order to preach to the Indians. This, at first, I peremptorily refused; but many providential incidents followed, which at length constrained me to alter my resolution, so that on October 14, 1735, Mr. Ingham, Mr. Delamotte,[10] my brother, and I embarked for America.[b] We were above three months on board, during which time our common way of living was this. From four in the morning till five each of us used private prayer. From five to seven we read the Bible together. At seven we breakfasted. At eight was the public service. From nine to twelve I learned German, Mr. Delamotte, Greek; my brother wrote sermons, and Mr. Ingham instructed the children. At twelve we met together. About one we dined. The time from dinner to four we spent in reading to those of whom each of us had taken charge, or in speaking to them severally, as need required. At four were the Evening Prayers, when either the Second Lesson was explained (as it always was in the morning), or the children were catechized and instructed before the congregation. From five to six we again used private prayer. From six to seven I read in our cabin, to two or three of the passengers (we had eighty English on board), and each of my brethren to a few more in theirs. At seven I joined with the Germans (of whom we had twenty-six on board) in their public service, while Mr. Ingham was reading between the decks to as many as desired to hear. At eight we met again, to instruct and exhort each other, and between nine and ten went to bed.

5. Sunday, March 7, 1736, finding there was not yet any opportunity of going to the Indians, I entered upon my ministry at Savannah,[c] officiating at nine, at twelve, and in the afternoon. On the week-days I read prayers, and expounded the Second Lesson, beginning at five in the morning and seven in the evening. Every Sunday and holiday I administered the Lord's Supper. My brother followed the same rule, whether he was at Frederica or

[b] [*Works*, Vol. 26,] p. 106 and sequel [i.e., JWJ, Oct. 14, 1735].
[c] [Ibid.,] p. 125, and sequel [i.e., JWJ, Mar. 27, 1736].

---

[10] Charles Delamotte was not a member of the Holy Club, although Wesley met him in Oxford. He did not please Wesley very much by his activities and demeanour in Georgia, where he stayed on for six months after Wesley's departure. Wesley shows himself as no better pleased with Delamotte in a letter to him late 1738 (25:597 in this edn.). He lived subsequently in Hull, Barrow upon Humber, and Aylesby, Lincolnshire, and died at the age of 82 in 1796.

Savannah. Sunday, April 4, I embarked for Frederica, hearing my brother was ill, and brought him with me to Savannah on Tuesday the 20th.

I now advised the serious part of the congregation to form themselves into a sort of little society, and to meet once or twice a week in order to instruct, exhort, and reprove one another. And out of these I selected a smaller number for a more intimate union with each other: in order to which I met them together at my house every Sunday in the afternoon.

6. Monday, May 10, I began visiting my parishioners in order from house to house, for which I set apart the time when they could not work because of the heat, namely from twelve to three in the afternoon.

Monday, July 26. My brother, not having his health, left Savannah in order to embark for England.[d] Saturday, February[11] 26, 1737, Mr. Ingham set out for England. By him I wrote to Dr. Bray's Associates,[12] who had sent a parochial library to Savannah. It is expected of the ministers who receive these, to send an account to their benefactors of the method they use in catechizing the children, and instructing the youth of their respective parishes. Part of my letter was:

> Our general method is this. A young gentleman who came with me teaches between thirty and forty children to read, write, and cast accounts. Twice a day he catechizes the lowest class. In the evening he instructs the larger children. On Saturday I catechize them all; as also on Sunday before the evening service. And in the church, immediately after the Second Lesson, a select number of them having repeated the Catechism, and been examined in some part of it, I endeavour to explain at large, and to enforce that part both on them and the congregation.
>
> After the evening service as many of my parishioners as desire it meet at my house (as they do also on Wednesday evening) and spend about an hour in prayer, singing, and mutual exhortation. A small number (mostly those who design to communicate the next day) meet here on Saturday evening. And a few of these come to me on the other evenings, and pass half an hour in the same employment.[e]

[d] [Ibid.,] p. 145 [i.e., JWJ, July 26, 1736].
[e] [Ibid.,] p. 155 [actually pp. 155-56, i.e., Feb. 26, 1737].

---

[11] Orig., in error, 'January'.
[12] Dr. Bray's Associates was the name from 1723 of those who administered the libraries set up in connection with the Society for Promoting Christian Knowledge, which was founded by Thomas Bray in 1698.

I cannot but observe that these were the first rudiments of the Methodist Societies. But who could then have even formed a conjecture whereto they would grow?

7. But my work at Savannah increased more and more, particularly *on the Lord's day*. The English service lasted from five to half hour past six. The Italian (with a few Vaudois) began at nine. The second service for the English (including the Sermon and the Holy Communion) continued from half an hour past ten till about half an hour past twelve. The French service began at one. At two I catechized the children. About three began the English service. After this was ended I joined with as many as my largest room would hold in reading, prayer, and singing praise. And about six the service of the Germans began—at which I was glad to be present, not as a teacher, but as a learner.[f]

8. On Friday, December 2, finding there was no possibility of preaching to the Indians, I left Savannah, and going through Carolina on Saturday [the] 24th sailed over Charlestown bar. After a pleasant voyage, on February 1, 1738, early in the morning [I] landed at Deal. And on Friday [the] 3rd I came once more to London, after an absence of two years and near four months.

Within three weeks following (while I remained in town at the request of the Trustees for the Colony of Georgia) I preached in many churches, though I did not yet see the nature of saving faith.[g] But as soon as I saw this clearly, namely on Monday, March 6, I declared it without delay. And God then began to work by my ministry as he never had done before.

9. On Monday, May 1, our little society began in London.[13] But it may be observed, the first rise of Methodism (so called) was in November 1729, when four of us met together at Oxford; the second was at Savannah, in April 1736, when twenty or thirty persons met at my house; the last was at London, on this day, when forty or fifty of us agreed to meet together every Wednesday evening, in order to a free conversation, begun and ended with singing and prayer. In all our steps we were greatly assisted by the advice and exhortations of Peter Böhler,[14] an excellent young

[f] [Ibid.,] p. 211 [i.e., JWJ, Oct. 30, 1737].

[g] [*Works*, Vol. 26,] p. 249 and sequel [i.e., JWJ, Feb. 4-15, etc., 1738].

---

[13] I.e., the Fetter Lane Society, organized that day by Wesley and Peter Böhler jointly.

[14] For Böhler's formative influence upon Wesley after he had returned from Georgia see JWJ, Feb. 7, 17; Mar. 4-6, 23; Apr. 22-23, 26; and May 1-4, 10, 24 (§§11-12), 1738.

man, belonging to the society commonly called Moravians.

10. In summer I took a journey into Germany, and spent some time at Herrnhut,[15] a little town where several Moravian families were settled. I doubt such another town is not to be found upon the earth. I believe there was no one therein, young or old, who did not fear God and work righteousness.[16] I was exceedingly comforted and strengthened by the conversation of this lovely people, and returned to England more fully determined to spend my life in testifying the gospel of the grace of God.

11. It was still my desire to preach in a church, rather than in any other place. But many obstructions were now laid in the way. Some clergymen objected to this *new doctrine*, 'Salvation by faith'. But the far more common (and indeed more plausible) objection was, 'The people crowd so, that they block up the church, and leave no room for the best of the parish.' Being thus excluded from the churches, and not daring to be silent, it remained only to preach in the open air—which I did at first, not out of choice, but necessity. But I have since seen abundant reason to adore the wise providence of God herein, making a way for myriads of people who never troubled any church, nor were likely so to do, to hear that word which they soon found to be the power of God unto salvation.[17]

12. In January 1739 our society consisted of about sixty persons. It continued gradually increasing all the year. In April I went down to Bristol.[h] And soon after a few persons agreed to meet weekly, with the same intention as those in London. These were swiftly increased, by the occasion of several little societies, which were till then accustomed to meet in diverse parts of the city, but now agreed to unite together in one. And about the same time several of the colliers of Kingswood, beginning to awake out of sleep, joined together, and resolved to walk by the same rule. And these likewise swiftly increased. A few also at Bath began to help each other in running the race set before them.[18]

13. In the remaining part of the summer my brother and I, and two young men who were willing to spend and be spent[19] for God,

[h] [*Works*, Vol. 27,] pp. 64-65, etc. [i.e., JWJ, Apr. 1-2, 1739].

---

15 Orig., 'Hernuth'.

16 See Acts 10:35.

17 Rom. 1:16.

18 See Heb. 12:1.

19 2 Cor. 12:15.

continued to call sinners to repentance,[20] in London, Bristol, Bath, and a few other places. But it was not without violent opposition, both from high and low, learned and unlearned. Not only all manner of evil[21] was spoke of us, both in private and public, but the beasts of the people[22] were stirred up almost in all places 'to knock these mad dogs on the head at once'.[23] And when complaint was made of their savage, brutal violence, no magistrate would do us justice. Yet by the grace of God we went on, determined to testify as long as we could the gospel of God our Saviour, and not counting our lives dear unto ourselves, so we might finish our course with joy.[24]

14. In October, upon a pressing invitation, I set out for Wales,[i] and preached in several parts of Glamorganshire and Monmouthshire, chiefly in the open air, as I was not permitted to preach in the churches, and no private house would contain the congregations. And the word of God did not fall to the ground. Many 'repented and believed the gospel'.[25] And some joined together, to strengthen each others' hands in God, and to provoke one another to love and to good works.[26]

15. In November I wrote to a friend a short account of what had been done in Kingswood.[j] It was as follows:

> Few persons have lived long in the West of England who have not heard of the colliers of Kingswood, a people famous for neither fearing God nor regarding man; so ignorant of the things of God that they seemed but one remove from the beasts that perish; and therefore utterly without desire of instruction, as well as without the means of it.
>
> Many last winter used to say of Mr. Whitefield, 'If he will convert heathens, why does he not go to the colliers of Kingswood?' In spring he did so. And as there were thousands who resorted to no place of worship, he went after them into their own wilderness, 'to seek and save that which was lost'. When he was called away others went 'into the highways and hedges' to 'compel them to come in'. And by the grace of God their labour was not in vain. The scene is already

[i] [Ibid.,] p. 146, etc. [i.e., JWJ, Oct. 13, 1739].
[j] [Ibid.,] p. 175 [i.e., JWJ, Nov. 27, 1739].

---

[20] Matt. 9:13, etc.
[21] Matt. 5:11.
[22] Ps. 68:30 (BCP).
[23] Cf. Wesley's letter to Samuel Sparrow, Dec. 28, 1773, about the early preaching of the two brothers: 'And for this it was that they carried their lives in their hands, that both the great vulgar and the small looked upon them as mad dogs, and treated them as such, sometimes saying (in terms), "Will nobody knock that mad dog on the head?"'
[24] Acts 20:24.
[25] Cf. Mark 1:15.
[26] Heb. 19:24 *(Notes).*

changed. Kingswood does not now, as a year ago, resound with cursing and blasphemy. It is no more filled with drunkenness and uncleanness, and the idle diversions that naturally lead thereto. It is no longer full of wars and fightings, of clamour and bitterness, of wrath and envyings. Peace and love are there. Great numbers of the people are mild, gentle, and easy to be entreated. They do not cry, neither strive, and hardly is 'their voice heard in the streets'; or indeed in their own wood, unless when they are at their usual diversion, singing praise unto God their Saviour.

16. April 1, 1740, the rioters in Bristol, who had long disturbed us, being emboldened by impunity, were so increased as to fill, not only the court, but a considerable part of the street. The mayor sent them an order to disperse. But they set him at defiance. At length he sent several of his officers, who took the ringleaders into custody.[k] The next day they were brought into court, it being the time of the quarter-sessions. There they received a severe reprimand; and we were molested no more.

17. Sunday, Sept. 13, 1741, Mr. Deleznot, a French clergyman in London, desiring me to officiate at his chapel in Hermitage Street, Wapping, I administered the Lord's Supper there to about two hundred persons of our society (as many as the place would well contain) which then consisted of about a thousand members.[l] The same number attended the next Lord's day, and so every Sunday following. By this means all the society attended in five weeks. Only those who had the sacrament at their parish churches I advised to attend there.

18. It was on the last day of this year that Sir John Ganson[27] called upon me,[m] and informed me, 'Sir, you have no need to suffer these riotous mobs to molest you, as they have done long. I and all the other Middlesex magistrates have orders from above to do you justice whenever you apply to us.' Two or three weeks after we did apply.[28] Justice was done, though not with rigour. And from that time we had peace in London.

19. Feb. 15, 1742, many met together at Bristol to consult

[k] [*Works*, Vol. 27,] p. 201, etc. [i.e., JWJ, Apr. 1, 1740].

[l] Vol. 29 [i.e., 28], p. 4 [i.e., JWJ, Sept. 13, 1741].

[m] [Ibid.,] p. 26 [i.e., JWJ, Dec. 31, 1741, mentions meeting Sir John, but not his offer of legal protection for the Methodists].

---

[27] Sir John Ganson was Chairman of the Middlesex magistrates. He had been successful over eighteen months earlier in quashing a charge that the Foundery was a seditious assembly (Jackson, ed., *Journal of Charles Wesley*, May 31, 1740).

[28] Wesley's diary records several visits of Sir John to Wesley, but this source of information is not available from Aug. 9, 1741 to Dec. 2, 1782.

concerning a proper method of paying the public debt, contracted by building.[n] And it was agreed, (1), that every member of the society that was able should contribute a penny a week; (2), that the whole society should be divided into little companies or classes, about twelve in each class; and (3), that one person in each should receive that contribution of the rest, and bring it in to the stewards weekly. Thus began that excellent institution, merely upon a temporal account—from which we reaped so many spiritual blessings that we soon fixed the same rule in all our societies.

20. In May, on the repeated invitation of John Nelson,[29] who had been for some time calling sinners to repentance at Birstall and the adjoining towns in the West Riding of Yorkshire, I went to Birstall, and found his labour had not been in vain.[o] Many of the greatest profligates in all the country were now changed. Their blasphemies were turned to praise. Many of the most abandoned drunkards were now sober; many sabbath-breakers remembered the sabbath to keep it holy.[30] The whole town wore a new face, such a change did God work by the artless testimony of one plain man. And from thence his word sounded forth to Leeds, Wakefield, Halifax, and all the West Riding of Yorkshire.

21. I had long had a desire to visit the poor colliers near Newcastle upon Tyne. And being now so far in my way I went forward, and on Friday 28 came to Newcastle. On Sunday morning I preached at the end of Sandgate, the poorest and most contemptible part of the town. In the evening I preached on the side of the adjoining hill, to thousands upon thousands. I could only just make a beginning now. But on November 13 I came again, and preached morning and evening till the end of December. And it pleased God so to bless his word that above eight hundred persons were now joined together in his name, besides many, both in the towns, villages, and lone houses within

[n] [*Works,*] Vol. 28, p. 38 [i.e., pp. 37-38, JWJ, Feb. 15, 1741. This and the following footnote were transposed on p. 179 of 'A Short History'].

[o] [Ibid.,] p. 62, and sequel [i.e., JWJ, May 26, 1742. For Nelson see also pp. 438, 506 below].

[29] John Nelson (1707–74) was born in Birstall, Yorkshire, and was by trade a stonemason. He was converted through a sermon by John Wesley in Moorfields, London, and soon became one of his itinerant preachers—one of the most effective and courageous of them all.

[30] See Exod. 20:8.

ten or twelve miles of the town. I never saw a work of God in any other place so evenly and gradually carried on. It continually rose step by step. Not so much seemed to be done at any one time as had frequently been at Bristol or London, but something at every time. It was the same with particular souls. I saw few in that ecstatic joy which had been common at other places. But many went on calm and steady, increasing more and more in the knowledge of God.

22. In this year many societies were formed in Somersetshire, Wiltshire, Gloucestershire, Leicestershire, Warwickshire, and Nottinghamshire, as well as the southern parts of Yorkshire. And those in London, Bristol, and Kingswood were much increased.

23. In the beginning of January 1743, after my brother had spent a few days among them, I went to the poor colliers in and about Wednesbury, in Staffordshire, and preached both in the town hall morning and evening, and in the open air.[p] Many appeared to be exceeding deeply affected, and about a hundred desired to join together. In two or three months these were increased to between three and four hundred. But in the summer following there was an entire change. The minister of Wednesbury, Mr. Egginton, with several neighbouring justices, Mr. Lane of Bentley Hall, and Mr. Persehouse of Walsall in particular, stirring up the basest of the people, such outrages followed as were a scandal to the Christian name. Riotous mobs were summoned together by sound of horn; men, women, and children abused in the most shocking manner, being beaten, stoned, covered with mud; some, even pregnant women, treated in a manner that cannot be mentioned. Meantime their houses were broke open, by any that pleased, and their goods spoiled or carried away, at Wednesbury, Darlaston, West Bromwich, etc., some of the owners standing by, but not daring to gainsay, as it would have been at the peril of their lives.[31]

24. Nevertheless I believed it my duty to call once more on this poor, harassed, persecuted people. So on October 20 I rode over from Birmingham to Wednesbury, and preached at noon in a

[p] [Ibid.,] p. 145, etc. [in fact, pp. 127-28, JWJ, Jan. 8-9, 1743].

[31] For fuller accounts of the anti-Methodist rioting in the Wednesbury area see JWJ, *Modern Christianity, exemplified at Wednesbury* (1743), pp. 132-58 above, and *A Farther Appeal,* Pt. III, II.6-14 (11:282-89 in this edn.); for further details see Waddy, *The Bitter Sacred Cup.*

ground near the middle of the town, to a far larger congregation than was expected, on 'Jesus Christ, the same yesterday, and today, and for ever'.[q] And no creature offered to molest us, either going or coming. But in the afternoon the mob beset the house. The cry of all was, 'Bring out the minister.' I desired one to bring their captain into the house. After a few words the lion became a lamb. I then went out among the people, and asked, 'What do you want with me?' They said, 'We want you to go with us to the justice.' I said, 'Shall we go tonight or in the morning?' Most of them cried, 'Tonight, tonight.' So I went before, and two or three hundred followed.

When we came to Bentley Hall, two miles from Wednesbury, a servant came out and said, 'Mr. Lane is in bed.' One then advised to 'go to Justice Persehouse at Walsall.' All agreed, and about seven we came to his house. But Mr. Persehouse likewise sent word that he was in bed. They then thought it would be best to go home. But we had not gone a hundred yards when the mob of Walsall came, pouring in like a flood. In a short time, many of the Darlaston mob being knocked down, the rest ran away, and left me in their hands. They dragged me along through the main street, from one end of the town to the other. At the west end of the town, seeing a door half open, I would have gone in. But a gentleman in the shop would not suffer me. However, I stood at the door, and after speaking a few words, broke out into prayer. Presently the man who had headed the mob turned and said, 'Sir, I will spend my life for you. Follow me, and not one soul here shall touch a hair of your head.' Two or three of his fellows confirmed his words, and got close to me immediately. The people then fell back to the right and left, while those three or four men carried me through them all; and a little before ten God brought me safe to Francis Ward's at Wednesbury, having lost only one flap of my waistcoat, and a little skin from one of my hands.

25. There was now no more place for any Methodist preacher in these parts. The mob were lords paramount. And they soon began to know their own strength, and to turn upon their employers. They required money of the gentlemen, or threatened to serve them as they had done the Methodists. This opened their eyes. And not long after, a grave man riding through Wednesbury, the mob swore he was a preacher, pulled him off his horse, dragged him to a coal-pit, and were hardly restrained from

[q] [Ibid.,] p. 175, etc. [i.e., JWJ, Oct. 20, 1742; the text is from Heb. 13:8].

throwing him in. But the Quaker (such he was) not being so tame as a Methodist, indicted the chief of them at the assizes. The cause was tried at Stafford and given against them. And from that time the tumults ceased.

26. On May 29, 1743, being Trinity Sunday, I began officiating at the chapel in West Street near the Seven Dials, London (built about sixty years ago by the French Protestants), which by a strange chain of providences fell into my hands.[32] After reading prayers and preaching, I administered the Lord's Supper to some hundreds of communicants. I was a little afraid at first that my strength would not suffice for the business of the day, when a service of five hours (for it lasted from ten to three) was added to my usual employment.[r] But God looked to that. So I must think, and they that will call it enthusiasm, may. I preached at the Great Gardens in Whitechapel, to an immense congregation. Then the leaders met, and after them the bands. At ten at night I was less weary than at six in the morning. The next Sunday the service at the chapel lasted till near four in the afternoon. So that I found it needful for the time to come to divide the communicants into three parts, that I might not have above six hundred at once.

27. On August 26, 1743 (my brother and one or two of our preachers having been there before), I set out for Cornwall, but made no considerable stop till I came to St. Ives on Tuesday [the] 30th. Some time since Captain Turner[33] of Bristol put in here, and was agreeably surprised to find a little society formed upon Dr. Woodward's plan,[34] who constantly met together. They were much refreshed and strengthened by him, as he was by them. This was the occasion of our first intercourse with them. I now spoke severally with those of the society, who were about a hundred and twenty, near a hundred of whom had found peace with God. But they were very roughly handled both by the rector, the curate, and the gentry, who set the mob upon them on all occasions.[s] I spent

[r] [Ibid.,] pp. 149-50 [i.e., JWJ, May 29, 1743].
[s] [Ibid.,] p. 160 [i.e., JWJ, Aug. 26-31, 1743].

[32] The event is significant because the chapel in West Street was the first building acquired by Wesley in London for the administration of Holy Communion.

[33] Captain Turner's ship seems to have put into St. Ives in the year 1743. On July 16 Charles Wesley visited the society there.

[34] This plan is the one set out by Josiah Woodward in his description of Anthony Horneck's societies. See Introduction to this volume, p. 5 and n. 9.

three weeks in preaching here, and in Zennor, Morvah,[35] St. Just, Sennen,[36] St. Mary's (one of the Isles of Scilly), Gwennap,[37] and on several of the downs throughout the west of Cornwall. And it pleased God, the seed which was then sown has since produced an abundant harvest. Indeed I hardly know any part of the three kingdoms where there has been a more general change. *Hurling,* their favourite diversion, at which limbs were usually broke, and very frequently lives lost, is now hardly heard of: it seems in a few years it will be utterly forgotten. And that scandal of humanity, so constantly practised on all the coasts of Cornwall, the plundering [of] vessels that struck upon the rocks, and often murdering those that escaped out of the wreck, is now wellnigh at an end; and if it is not quite, the gentlemen, not the poor tinners, are to be blamed. But it is not harmlessness, or outward decency alone, which has within few years so increased, but the religion of the heart, faith working by love, producing all inward as well as outward holiness.

28. In April 1744 I took a second journey into Cornwall, and went through many towns I had not seen before.[t] Since my former visit there had been hot persecution, both of the preachers and the people. The preaching-house at St. Ives was pulled down to the ground; one of the preachers pressed and sent for a soldier, as were several of the people; over and above the being stoned, covered with dirt, and the like, which was the treatment many of them met with from day to day. But notwithstanding this, they who had been eminent for hurling, fighting, drinking, and all manner of wickedness, continued eminent for sobriety, piety, and all manner of goodness. In all parts more and more of the lions became lambs, continually praising God, and calling their old companions in sin to come and magnify the Lord together. About the same time John Nelson and Thomas Beard[38] were pressed and sent for soldiers, for no other crime, either committed or pretended, than that of calling sinners to repentance. The case of John Nelson is well known. Thomas Beard also was nothing

[t] [Ibid.,] p. 214 [i.e., JWJ, Apr. 1-2, 1744; he remained in Cornwall until April 17].

---

[35] Orig., 'Morva'.
[36] Orig., 'Sennan'.
[37] Orig., 'Gwenap'.
[38] Thomas Beard was one of the first of Wesley's lay preachers; after he was impressed into the army, he continued to preach in uniform. He died in 1744.

terrified by his adversaries. Yet the body after awhile sunk under its burden. He was then lodged in the hospital at Newcastle, where he still praised God continually. His fever increasing, he was let blood. His arm festered, mortified, and was cut off, two or three days after which God signed his discharge, and called him up to his eternal home.

29. All this year the alarms were uninterrupted, from the French on the one hand and the rebels on the other; and a general panic ran through the nation, from the east to the west, from the north to the south. I judged it the more needful to visit as many places as possible, and avail myself of the precious opportunity. My brother and our other preachers were of the same mind—they spoke and spared not. They rushed through every open door,

> And cried, Sinners, behold the Lamb![39]

And their word did not fall to the ground: they saw abundant fruit of their labour.[40] I went through many parts of Wales; through most of the midland counties; and then through Lincolnshire and Yorkshire, to Newcastle upon Tyne. In every place the generality of the people seemed to have ears to hear. And multitudes who were utterly careless before did now 'prepare to meet' their 'God'.[41]

30. Monday, June 25, and the five following days, we spent in Conference with our preachers,[u] seriously considering by what means we might the most effectually save our own souls and them

[u] [Ibid.,] p. 229 [i.e., JWJ, June 25, 1744].

---

[39] See John 1:29, upon which this line of verse—surely written by Charles Wesley and misquoted by John Wesley—was based. The nearest lines of Charles Wesley to John's version seem to be:

> O that I was as heretofore,
> When first sent forth in Jesu's name
> I rush'd through every open door,
> And cried to all, 'Behold the Lamb!'
> Seized the poor trembling slaves of sin
> And forced the outcasts to come in.

This is the first verse of No. 12 in a group of hymns, 'For a preacher of the Gospel' (*Hymns and Sacred Poems,* Charles Wesley, 1749, I.300). The hymn has eight verses. Many modern Methodist hymn books include it, but only ver. 3, 5, 6, and 7, starting, 'Give me the faith that can remove'. (I owe this reference to Wilfrid Little. Ed.).

[40] See Phil. 1:22.

[41] Amos 4:12.

that heard us.[42] And the result of our consultations we set down, to be the rule of our future practice.

Friday, August 24, St. Bartholomew's Day, I preached for the last time before the University of Oxford. I am now clear of the blood of these men. I have fully delivered my own soul.[v] And I am well pleased that it should be the very day on which, in the last century, near two thousand burning and shining lights[43] were put out at one stroke. Yet what a wide difference is there between their case and mine! They were turned out of house and home, and all that they had: whereas I am only hindered from preaching, without any other loss; and that in a kind of honourable manner, it being determined that when my next turn to preach came they would pay another person to preach for me. And so they did twice or thrice, even to the time that I resigned my fellowship.[44]

31. All this summer our brethren in Cornwall had hard service, the war against the Methodists being carried on more vigorously than that against the Spaniards. I had accounts of this from all parts, one of which was as follows:

Rev. sir, Sept. 16, 1744

The word of God has free course here: it runs and is glorified. But the devil rages horribly. Even at St. Ives we cannot shut the door of John Nance's house to meet the society, but the mob immediately threatens to break it open. And in other places it is worse. I was going to Crowan on Tuesday, and within a quarter of a mile of the place where I was to preach some met me and begged me not to go up, saying, 'If you do, there will surely be murder, if there is not already; for many were knocked down before we came away.' By their advice I turned back to the house where I had left my horse. We had been there but a short time when many of the people came in very bloody. But the main cry of the mob was, 'Where is the preacher?', whom they sought for in every corner of the house, swearing bitterly, 'If we can but knock him on the head, we shall be satisfied.'

Not finding me they said, 'However, we shall catch him on Sunday at Camborne.'[45] But it was Mr. Westell's[46] turn to be there. While he was preaching at Mr. Harris's a tall man came in and pulled him down. Mr. Harris demanded his warrant. But he swore, 'Warrant or no warrant, he shall go with

[v] [Ibid.,] p. 233 [JWJ, Aug. 24, 1744].

[42] See 1 Tim. 4:16.

[43] See John 5:35. Both Wesley's grandfathers and one of his paternal great-grandfathers were ejected from their livings on 'Black Bartholomew' , August 24, 1662, the day of implementation of the Act of Uniformity. See 'Wesley's Puritan Ancestry', by Frank Baker, *London Quarterly Review* 187 (July 1962): 180-86.

[44] As became necessary upon his marriage; see his letter of resignation, June 1, 1751 (26:462-63 in this edn.).

[45] Orig., 'Cambourn'.

[46] Orig., 'Westall's'.

me.' So he carried him out to the mob, who took him away to the church town. They kept him there till Tuesday morning, and then carried him to Penzance, when Dr. Borlase wrote his *Mittimus,* by virtue of which he was to be committed to the House of Correction at Bodmin as a vagrant. So they took him as far as Camborne that night, and the next day to Bodmin.

I desire your continual prayer for me, your weak servant in Christ,

Henry Millard[w]

Henry Millard did not long continue in these troubles. A short time after this he took the smallpox, and in a few days joyfully resigned his spirit up to God.

The justices who met at the next quarter-sessions in Bodmin, knowing a little more than Dr. Borlase, declared Mr. Westell's commitment to be contrary to all law, and immediately set him at liberty.

32. All this year God was carrying on the same work in the English army abroad, some account of which is given by one of their preachers in the following letter:

Rev. sir, Ghent, Nov. 12, 1744

We make bold to trouble you with this, to acquaint you with some of the Lord's dealings with us here. We have hired two rooms: one small, wherein a few of us meet every day, and another large one, wherein we meet for public service twice a day, at nine and at four. And the hand of the omnipotent God is with us, to the pulling down of the strongholds of Satan.

The seventh instant, when we were met together in the evening, as I was in prayer, one that was kneeling by me cried out, like a woman in travail, 'My Redeemer! my Redeemer!' which continued about ten minutes. When he was asked what was the matter, he said he had found that which he had often heard of, an heaven upon earth. And several others had much ado to forbear crying out in the same manner.

Dear sir, I am a stranger to you in the flesh. I know not if I have seen you above once, when I saw you preaching on Kennington Common. And I then hated you as much as by the grace of God I love you now. The Lord pursued me with convictions from my infancy, and I made many good resolutions. But finding I could not keep them, I at length gave myself over to all manner of profaneness. So I continued till the battle of Dettingen. The balls then came very thick about me, and my comrades fell on every side. Yet I was preserved unhurt. A few days after the Lord was pleased to visit me. The pains of hell gat hold upon me; the snares of death encompassed me. I durst no longer commit any outward sin, and I prayed God to be merciful to my soul. Now I was at a loss for books. But God took care for this also. One day I found an old Bible in one of the train waggons. This was now my only companion, and I believed myself a very good Christian, till we came to winter quarters, where I met with John Haime. But I was soon sick of his company, for he robbed me of my treasure, telling me I and my works

[w] [Ibid.,] pp. 237-39 [JWJ, Sept. 16, 1744].

were going to hell together. This was strange doctrine to me, and as I was of a stubborn temper, he sometimes resolved to forbid my coming to him any more.

When the Lord had at length opened my eyes, and shown me that 'by grace we are saved, through faith,' I began immediately to declare it to others, though I had not yet experienced it myself. But October 23, as William Clements was at prayer, I felt on a sudden a great alteration in my soul. My eyes overflowed with tears of love. I knew I was through Christ reconciled to God, which inflamed my soul with love to him, whom I now saw to be my complete Redeemer.

O the tender care of Almighty God, in bringing up his children! Dear sir, I beg you will pray for him who is not worthy to be a doorkeeper to the least of my Master's servants.

John Evans[x]

He continued both to preach and to live the gospel till the battle of Fontenoy. One of his companions saw him there laid across a cannon, both his legs having been taken off by a chain-shot, praising God, and exhorting all that were round about him; which he did till his spirit returned to God.

33. Many persons still representing the Methodists as enemies to the clergy, I wrote to a friend the real state of the case, in as plain a manner as I could:

March 11, 1745

1. About seven years since we began preaching *inward, present* salvation, as attainable by *faith alone*.

2. For preaching *this doctrine* we were forbidden to preach in most churches.

3. We then preached in *private houses*, and when the houses could not contain the people, in the *open air*.

4. For *this* many of the clergy *preached* or *printed* against us, as both heretics and schismatics.

5. Persons who were convinced of sin begged us to advise them more particularly how to flee from the wrath to come. We desired them (being many) to come at one time, and we would endeavour it.

6. For *this* we were represented, both from the pulpit and the press, as introducing *popery* and raising sedition. Yea, all manner of evil was said both of us and of those that used to assemble with us.

7. Finding that some of these *did* walk disorderly, we desired them not to come to us any more.

8. And some of the others were desired to overlook the rest, that we might know whether they walked worthy of the gospel.

9. Several of the clergy now stirred up the people to treat us as outlaws or mad dogs.

10. The people did so, both in Staffordshire, Cornwall, and many other places.

11. And they do so still, wherever they are not restrained by fear of the magistrates.

[x] [Ibid.,] pp. 245-48 [JWJ, Dec. 3, 1744].

Now what can *we* do, or what can *you* our brethren do, towards healing this breach?

Desire of *us* anything which we can do with a safe conscience, and we will do it immediately. Will *you* meet us here? Will you do what we desire of you, so far as you can with a safe conscience?

Do you desire us, (1), to preach another, or to desist from preaching this doctrine?

We cannot do this with a safe conscience.

Do you desire us, (2), to desist from preaching in *private houses*, or *in the open air*?

As things are now circumstanced, this would be the same as desiring us not to preach at all.

Do you desire us, (3), not to advise those who meet together for that purpose? To dissolve our societies?

We cannot do this with a safe conscience; for we apprehend many souls would be lost thereby.

Do you desire us, (4), to advise them one by one?

This is impossible because of their number.

Do you desire us, (5), to suffer those that walk disorderly still to mix with the rest?

Neither can we do this with a safe conscience: for evil communications corrupt good manners.

Do you desire us, (6), to discharge those leaders (as we term them) who overlook the rest?

This is, in effect, to suffer the disorderly walkers still to remain with the rest.

Do you desire us, lastly, to behave with tenderness both to the characters and persons of our brethren, the clergy?

By the grace of God, we can and will do this—as indeed we have done to this day.

If you ask what we desire of *you* to do we answer:

1. We do not desire any of you to let us preach in your church, either if you believe us to preach false doctrine, or if you have the least scruple. But we desire any who believes us to preach true doctrine, and has no scruple in the matter, not to be either publicly or privately discouraged from inviting us to preach in his church.

2. We do not desire that any who thinks it his duty to preach or print against us should refrain therefrom. But we desire that none will do this till he has calmly considered both sides of the question; and that he would not condemn us unheard, but first read what we say in our own defence.

3. We do not desire any favour if either popery, sedition, or immorality be proved against us.

But we desire you would not credit without proof any of those senseless tales that pass current with the vulgar; that if you do not credit them yourselves you will not relate them to others; yea, that you will discountenance those who still retail them abroad. Now these things you certainly can do, and that with a safe conscience. Therefore till these things be done, if there be any breach, it is chargeable on you only.[y]

[y] [Ibid.,] pp. 263-67 [JWJ, Mar. 11, 1745, slightly abr.].

34. In June I paid another visit to Cornwall, where our preachers were in danger of being discouraged, being continually persecuted, only not unto death, both by the great vulgar and the small.[z] They showed a little more courtesy to me, till Thursday, July 4, when I went to see a gentlewoman in Falmouth who had been long indisposed. I had scarce sat down when the house was beset with an innumerable multitude of people. A louder or more confused noise could hardly be at the taking of a city by storm. The rabble roared, 'Bring out the Canorum! Where is the Canorum?' (A Cornish nickname for a Methodist.) They quickly forced open the outer door and filled the passage, there being now only a wainscot partition between us. Among them were the crews of some privateers, who being angry at the slowness of the rest thrust them away, and setting their shoulders to the inner door cried out, 'Avast, lads, avast!' Away went all the hinges at once, and the door fell back into the room. I stepped forward into the midst of them and said, 'Here I am. Which of you has anything to say to me?' I continued speaking till I came into the middle of the street, though I could be heard by few only. But all that could hear were still, till one or two of their captains turned and swore, 'Not a man shall touch him.' A clergyman then came up, and asked, 'Are you not ashamed to use a stranger thus?' He was seconded by some gentlemen of the town, who walked with me to Mrs. Maddern's. They then sent my horse before me to Penryn, and sent me thither by water, the sea running close by the backdoor of the house in which we were.

I never saw before, no not even at Walsall, the hand of God so clearly shown as here. There I received blows, was covered with dirt, and lost part of my clothes. Here, although the hands of hundreds of people were lifted up to strike or throw, yet they were one and all stopped in the midway, so that not a man touched me with his fingers. Neither was anything thrown from first to last, so that I had not a speck of dirt upon my clothes. Who can deny that God heareth the prayer? Or that he hath all power in heaven and earth?

35. October 31 I preached upon Newcastle town moor, at a small distance from the English camp, where were several thousands both of English and Germans, till they marched for Scotland. None attempted to make the least disturbance, from

[z] [Ibid.,] p. 284 [JWJ, June 16, 1745, etc.].

the beginning to the end. Yet I could not reach their hearts. The words of a scholar did not affect them like those of a dragoon or grenadier.[a]

November 1, a little after nine, just as I began to preach on a little eminence before the camp, the rain (which had continued all the morning) stayed, and did not begin till I had finished. A lieutenant endeavoured to make some disturbance. However, when I had done he tried to make some amends, by standing up and telling the soldiers, all I had said was very good.

November 2, also, the rain which fell before and after was stayed while I preached. And I began to perceive some fruit of my labour, not only in the number of hearers, but in the power of God, which was more and more among them, both to wound and to heal.

Sunday 30th, I preached about half hour after eight to a larger congregation than any before, on, 'The Kingdom of God is at hand; repent ye, and believe the gospel.'[47] And were it only for the sake of this hour I should not have thought much of staying at Newcastle longer than I intended. Between one and two in the afternoon I went to the camp once more. Abundance of people now flocked together, horse and foot, rich and poor, to whom I declared, 'There is no difference; for all have sinned, and come short of the glory of God.'[48] I observed many Germans standing disconsolate in the skirts of the congregation. To these I was constrained (though I had discontinued it so long) to speak a few words in their own language. Immediately they gathered up close together, and drank in every word.

36. In the beginning of December I received some further account from the army, the substance of which was as follows:

Rev. sir,

I shall acquaint you with the Lord's dealings with us since April last. We marched from Ghent to Allest[49] on the 14th, where I met with two or three of our brethren in the fields, and we sung and prayed together, and were comforted. On the 15th I met a small company about a mile[50] from the town, and the Lord filled our hearts with love and peace. On the 17th we marched to the camp near Brussels. On the 18th I met a small congregation on the side of a hill, and opened on those words, 'Let us go forth therefore to him without the camp,

[a] [Ibid.,] p. 328 and sequel [JWJ, Oct. 31, 1745].

[47] Mark 1:15.

[48] Rom. 3:22-23.

[49] Orig., 'Allost'.

[50] JWJ, 'about three miles'.

bearing his reproach.' On the 28th I spoke from those words of Isaiah. 'Thus saith the Lord concerning the house of Jacob, Jacob shall not now be ashamed, neither shall his face now wax pale.' On the 29th we marched close to the enemy, and when I saw them in their camp, my bowels moved towards them, in love and pity for their souls. We lay on our arms all night. In the morning, April 30th, the cannon began to play at half an hour after four. And the Lord took away all fear from me, so that I went into the field with joy. The balls flew on either hand, and men fell in abundance; but nothing touched me till about two o'clock. Then I received a ball through my left arm, and rejoiced so much the more. Soon after I received another in my right, which obliged me to quit the field. But I scarce knew whether I was on earth or in heaven. It was one of the sweetest days I ever enjoyed.

William Clements[b]

Another letter (from Lierre,[51] near Antwerp) adds:

On April 30th the Lord was pleased to try our little flock, and to show them his mighty power. Some days before, one of them standing at his tent door, broke out into raptures of joy, knowing his departure was at hand, and was so filled with the love of God that he danced before his comrades. In the battle, before he died, he openly declared, 'I am going to rest from my labours in the bosom of Jesus.' I believe nothing like this was ever heard of before, in the midst of so wicked an army as ours. Some were crying out in their wounds, 'I am going to my Beloved'; others, 'Come, Lord Jesus! Come quickly!' And many that were not wounded were crying to the Lord to take them to himself. There was such boldness in the battle among this little despised flock that it made the officers as well as common soldiers amazed. As to my own part, I stood the fire of the enemy for above seven hours. Then my horse was shot under me, and I was exposed both to the enemy and our own horse. But that did not discourage me at all; for I knew that the God of Jacob was with me. I had a long way to go, the balls flying on every side. And thousands lay bleeding, groaning, dying, and dead, on each hand. Surely I was as in the fiery furnace; but it never singed one hair of my head. The hotter it grew, the more strength was given me. I was full of joy and love, as much as I could bear. Going on, I met one of our brethren, with a little dish in his hand, seeking water. He smiled and said he had got a sore wound in his leg. I asked, Have you got Christ in your heart? He answered, 'I have, and I have had him all this day. Blessed be God that I ever saw your face.' Lord, what am I, that I should be counted worthy to set my hand to the gospel plough! Lord, humble me, and lay me in the dust!

John Haime

37. All this year the work of God gradually increased in the southern counties, as well as the north of England. Many were awakened in a very remarkable manner; many were converted to

[b] [Ibid.,] pp. 324-43 [JWJ, Dec. 2, 1745].

---

[51] Orig., 'Leare'.

God. Many were enabled to testify that 'the blood of Jesus Christ cleanseth from all sin.'[52] Meantime we were in most places tolerably quiet, as to popular tumults. Where anything of the kind appeared the magistrates usually interposed, as indeed it was their duty to do. And wherever the peace officers do their duty no riot can long subsist.

38. In February 1747 I set out for Newcastle upon Tyne, my brother being just returned from thence. The wind was full north, and blew so exceeding hard and keen that when we came to Hatfield neither my companions nor I had much use of our hands or feet. After we left it, the large hail drove so vehemently in our faces that we could not see, nor hardly breathe. However, we made shift to get on to Potton,[53] whence we set out in the morning, as soon as it was well light. But it was hard work to get forward, for the ice would not well bear or break. And the untracked snow covering all the road, we had much ado to keep our horses on their feet. Meantime the wind rose higher and higher, till it was ready to overturn both man and beast. However, after a short bait at Buckden,[54] we pushed on, and were met in the middle of an open field with so violent a storm of rain and hail as we had not had before. It drove through our coats, great and small, boots and everything, and yet froze as it fell, even upon our eyelashes; so that we had scarce either strength or motion left when we came into the inn at Stilton. However, we took the advantage of a fair blast, and made the best of our way towards Stamford. But on the heath the snow lay in such large drifts that sometimes horses and men were nigh swallowed up. Yet we pushed through all, and by the help of God on Thursday evening came safe to Epworth.[c]

39. The Monday following I set out for the eastern parts of Lincolnshire. On Tuesday I examined the little society at Tetney. I have not seen such another in England, no, not to this day. In the class-papers (which gives an account of the contribution for the poor), I observed, one gave eightpence, often tenpence a week; another, thirteen, fifteen, or eighteenpence; another, sometimes one, sometimes two shillings. I asked Micah Ellmoor, the leader (an Israelite indeed, who now rests from his labour), 'How is this? Are you the richest society in England?' He answered, 'I suppose

[c] [*Works*,] Vol. 29, pp. 10-15 [JWJ, Feb. 16-24, 1747].

---

[52] Cf. 1 John 1:7.

[53] Orig., 'Potten'.

[54] Orig., 'Bugden'.

not. But as we are all single persons we have agreed together to give ourselves, and *all we have,* to God. And we do it gladly, whereby we are able to entertain all the strangers that from time to time come to Tetney, who often have no food to eat, or any friend to give them a lodging.'

40. In the following spring and summer we were invited into many parts of Yorkshire, Lancashire, Derbyshire, and Cheshire, where we had not been before. In June my brother spent some time at Plymouth and Plymouth Dock, and was received by the generality of the people with the utmost cordiality. But before I came, June 26th, there was a surprising change. Within two miles of Plymouth one overtook and informed us that all the Dock was in an uproar. Another met us and begged we would go the back way, for there were thousands of people at Mr. Hide's door. We rode up straight into the midst of them. They saluted us with three huzzas, after which I alighted, took several of them by the hand, and begged to talk with them. I would gladly have talked with them for an hour, and believe if I had, there had been an end of the riot. But it being past nine o'clock I was persuaded to go in. The mob then recovered their spirits, and fought valiantly with the doors and windows. But about ten they were weary and went away.

About six in the evening I went to the head of the town. While we were singing, 'The Lieutenant', a famous man, came with a large retinue of soldiers, drummers, and mob. They grew fiercer and fiercer as their numbers increased. After a while I walked down into the thickest of them, and took the captain of the mob by the hand. He immediately said, 'Sir, I will see you safe home. Sir, no man shall touch you. Gentlemen, stand off. Give back. I will knock the first man down that touches him.' We walked in great peace till we came to Mr. Hide's door, and then parted in much love. I stayed in the street after he was gone near half an hour, talking with the people, who had now quite forgot their anger, and went away in high good humour.[d]

41. Hitherto God had assisted us (my brother and me, and a handful of young men) to labour as we were able (though frequently at the peril of our lives) in most parts of England. But our line was now stretched a little farther. On Tuesday, August 4th, I set out from Bristol for Ireland. I reached Holyhead on

[d] [Ibid.,] p. 41 [JWJ, June 27, 1747].

Saturday 8th, and finding a vessel ready, went on board, and on Sunday morning landed at St. George's Quay in Dublin.[e] About three I wrote a line to the curate of St. Mary's, who sent me word, he should be glad of my assistance. So I preached there (another gentleman reading prayers), to as gay and senseless a congregation as ever I saw. Monday 10th at five in the morning I met our own society (gathered by Mr. Williams,[55] who had been there some weeks) and preached at six to many more than our room would contain, on 'Repent ye, and believe the gospel.'[56] In the evening I went to Marlborough Street. The house wherein we preached was originally designed for a Lutheran church, and contains about four hundred people. But abundantly more may stand in the yard. Many of the rich were there, and ministers of every denomination. If my brother or I could have been here for a few months, I know not but there might have been as large a society as that in London.

I continued preaching morning and evening to many more than the house could contain; and had more and more reason to hope, they would not all be unfruitful hearers. On Saturday I purposely stayed at home, and spoke to all that came. But I scarce found any Irish among them. I believe ninety-nine in a hundred of the native Irish remain still in the religion of their forefathers. The Protestants, whether in Dublin or elsewhere, are all transplanted from England.

42. Monday 17th I began examining the society, which I finished the next day. It contained about two hundred and fourscore members, many of whom had found peace with God. The people in general are of a more teachable spirit than in most

[e] [Ibid.,] p. 51 [JWJ, Aug. 6, 1747].

---

[55] The early Methodist preacher Thomas Williams does not appear in the *Dictionary of Welsh Biography*, and it is difficult to be sure that we are always dealing with the same man in his frequent appearances in John Wesley's *Letters* (26:182, 322, 338, 351, 354, 376, 378, 395, 399, 402, 449, 453, 636 in this edn.) and his sole appearance in the *Journal*, on Aug. 2, 1744, as severed from the Methodist Society. He seems to have been brought into the Methodist itinerancy about 1741 by the Wesleys, but fell foul of them when he unsuccessfully sought ordination in 1744, then redeemed himself by his evangelical labours in Ireland, to which he introduced John Wesley in 1747. He left them again in 1754. He is perhaps to be distinguished from the preacher of the same name who worked with the Calvinistic Methodists from 1743 onwards, to whom there are many references in Charles Wesley's *Journal*. See A. H. Williams, ed., *John Wesley in Wales* (Cardiff, 1971), pp. xxiv, xxv, and Gomer M. Roberts, *Selected Trevecka Letters, 1742–1747* (Caernarvon, 1956), p. 162.

[56] Mark 1:15.

parts of England. But on that very account they must be watched over with the more care, being equally susceptible of good and ill impressions.

Sunday 23rd I began in the evening before the usual time; yet were a multitude of people got together in the house, yard, and street, abundantly more than my voice could reach. I cried aloud to as many as could hear, 'All things are ready. Come ye to the marriage.'[57] Having delivered my message, about eleven I took ship for England, leaving J. Trembath (then a burning and shining light,[58] and a workman that needed not to be ashamed)[59] to water the seed which had been sown.[60] Saturday 29th I met my brother at Garth in Brecknockshire, in his way to Ireland. He spent several months there, chiefly in Dublin, Athlone, Cork, and Bandon, and had great reason to bless God that in every place he saw the fruit of his labours.

43. Tuesday, March 8, 1748, Mr. Meriton,[61] Swindells,[62] and I embarked at Holyhead, and reached Dublin in the afternoon. We went directly to our house in Cork Street (vulgarly called Dolphin's Barn Lane), and came thither while my brother was meeting the society. The remaining days of the week I dispatched all the business I could. Sunday 13th he preached both morning and evening, expecting to sail at night; but before night the wind turned east, and so continued all the week. Monday 14th I began preaching at five in the morning, an unheard-of thing in Ireland! I expounded part of the first chapter of the Acts, which I purposed, God willing, to go through in order. Sunday 20th I preached at eight on Oxmantown Green, where the whole congregation was still as that at London. About three I preached at Marlborough Street, and in the evening at our own house in Cork Street. Wednesday 23rd I preached to the prisoners in Newgate, but without any present effect. Friday 25th, at two, I began in Ship Street, to many rich and genteel hearers. The next day I finished

[57] Matt. 22:4 *(Notes)*.

[58] See John 5:35.

[59] 2 Tim. 2:15.

[60] John Trembath, of St. Gennys, Cornwall, had been one of Wesley's preachers since 1743 but left the itinerancy in 1760.

[61] The Rev. John Meriton, a non-parochial clergyman who had accepted Wesley's invitation to the first Methodist Conference in 1744 and who had accompanied Wesley on his first visit to Ireland.

[62] Robert Swindells, one of Wesley's first itinerant preachers, who spent most of his ministry in Ireland. He died in 1782.

meeting the classes, and was glad to find there was no loss. I left three hundred and ninety-four members in the society—and they were now three hundred and ninety-six.[f]

44. Wednesday 30th[63] I rode to Philipstown, the shire town of the King's County. The street was soon filled with those that flocked from every side. And even at five in the morning I had a large congregation. After preaching I spoke severally to those of the society, of whom forty were troopers. At noon I preached to a larger congregation than any in Dublin. And I am persuaded, God did then make an offer of life to all the inhabitants of Philipstown.

In the following days I preached at Tullamore, Tyrrellspass,[64] Clyro,[65] Templemacateer,[66] Moate,[67] and on Saturday, April 2nd, came to Athlone. My brother was here some time before, although it was with the imminent hazard of his life. For within about a mile of the town he was waylaid by a very numerous popish mob, who discharged a shower of stones, which he very narrowly escaped by setting spurs to his horse. This had an exceeding happy effect, prejudicing all the Protestants in our favour. And this seemed to increase every day. The morning I went away most of the congregation were in tears. Indeed almost all the town seemed to be moved, full of goodwill and desires of salvation. But the waters were too wide to be deep. I found not one under strong conviction, much less had anyone attained the knowledge of salvation, in hearing above thirty sermons. After re-visiting the towns I had seen before, on Tuesday 16th I returned to Dublin. Having spent a few days there I made another little excursion through the country societies. Saturday, May 14th, I returned to Dublin, and had the satisfaction to find that the work of God not only spread wider and wider, but was also much deepened in many souls. Wednesday 18th we took ship, and the next morning landed at Holyhead.

45. Saturday, April 15, 1749, I embarked again at Holyhead for Ireland, and after spending a few days in Dublin visited all our societies in Leinster. I then went to Limerick, in the province of Munster. Mr. Swindells had prepared the way, and a society was

[f] [Ibid.,] pp. 88-89 [JWJ, Mar. 7-16, 1748].

---

[63] I.e., Mar. 30, 1748.

[64] Orig., 'Tyrrelpass'.

[65] Orig., 'Claro'.

[66] Orig., 'Temple-Macqueker'.

[67] Orig., 'Moat'.

formed already. So that I found no opposition, but everyone seemed to say, 'Blessed is he that cometh in the name of the Lord!'[68] But the more I conversed with this friendly people, the more I was amazed. That God had wrought a great work among them was manifest. And yet the main of the believers and unbelievers were not able to give a rational account of the plainest principles of religion. 'Tis clear, God begins his work at the heart; then the inspiration of the Highest giveth understanding. On Tuesday 29 I set out for Cork; but the next day Mr. Skelton[69] met me, just come from thence, and informed me, it was impossible for me to preach there while the riotous mob filled the street. They had for some time done what they listed; broke into the houses of all that were called Methodists, or (as their elegant term was, Swaddlers), and beat or abused them just as they pleased. The worthy mayor, Daniel Crone, Esq., encouraged them so to do, and told them, 'You may do anything but kill them, because that is contrary to law.' So I rode through Cork to Bandon, and having spent a few days there, returned to Dublin nearly the same way I came, only touching at Portarlington and a few other places which I had not seen before.[g]

46. In all this journey I had the satisfaction to find that ever since I was in Ireland first my fellow-labourers had been fully employed in watering the seed that had been sown. And it had pleased God exceedingly to bless their labours in Munster, as well as in Leinster. In various parts of both these provinces considerable numbers were brought, not from one opinion or mode of worship to another, but from darkness to light, from serving the devil to serve the living God.[70] This is the point, the only point, for which both I and they think it worth our while to labour, desiring no recompense beside the testimony of our conscience, and what we look for in the resurrection of the just.

I have purposely placed together in one view what was transacted in Ireland for three years, and shall now mention a few things done in England during that period.

47. During all this time the work of God (it is no cant word—it

[g] [Ibid.,] p. 164 and sequel [i.e., to p. 183, Apr. 15–July 20, 1749].

---

[68] Matt. 21:9, etc.

[69] Charles Skelton was one of Wesley's pioneer preachers in Ireland, who later became an Independent minister in Southwark. See above, p. 288, etc., for the persecution he suffered in Cork alongside Charles Wesley.

[70] See Acts 26:18.

means the conversion of sinners from sin to holiness) was both widening and deepening, not only in London and Bristol, but in most parts of England; there being scarce any county, and not many large towns, wherein there were not more or fewer witnesses of it. Meantime the greatest numbers were brought to the great Shepherd of their souls[71] (next to London and Bristol) in Cornwall, the West Riding of Yorkshire, and Newcastle upon Tyne. But still we were obliged in many places to carry our lives in our hands. Several instances of this have been related already. I will mention one more.

Friday, February 12,1748, after preaching at Oakhill (a village in Somersetshire), I rode on to Shepton [Mallet], but found all the people under a strange consternation. A mob, they said, was hired and made sufficiently drunk to do all manner of mischief. Nevertheless I preached in peace, the mob being assembled at another place where I used to alight. And they did not find their mistake till I had done preaching. They then attended us to William Stone's house, throwing dirt, stones, and clods in abundance; but they could not hurt us. Mr. Swindells had only a little dirt on his coat, and I a few specks on my hat. After we were gone into the house they began throwing large stones, in order to break the door. But finding this would require some time, they first poured in a shower of stones at the windows. One of their captains, in his great zeal, had thrust into the house, and was now shut in with us. He would fain have got out; but it was not possible. So he kept as close to me as he could, thinking himself safest when he was near me. But staying a little behind when I went up two pairs of stairs, a large stone struck him on the forehead, and the blood spouted out like a stream. He cried out, 'O sir, are we to die tonight? What must I do?' I said, 'Pray to God.' He took my advice, and began praying as he had scarce ever done before.

Mr. Swindells and I then went to prayer, after which I told him, 'We must not stay here.' He said, 'Sir, we cannot stir; you see how the stones fly about.' I walked straight through the room, and down the stairs, and not a stone came in till we were at the bottom. The mob had just broke open the door when we came into the lower room; and while they burst in at one door, we walked out at the other. Nor did one man take any notice of us, though we were

[71] See 1 Pet. 2:25.

within five yards of each other. They filled the house at once, and proposed setting it on fire. But one of them would not consent, his house adjoining to it. Hearing one of them cry out, 'They are gone over the grounds,' I thought the hint was good. So we went over the grounds to the far end of the town, where one waited and guided us safe to Oakhill.[h]

48. Friday, June 24th, being the day we had appointed for opening the school at Kingswood, I preached there on, 'Train up a child in the way that he should go, and when he is old he will not depart from it.'[72] My brother and I then administered the Lord's Supper to many who came from far. We then agreed on the general rules of the school, which we published soon after.[i]

49. On July 18th I began my journey northward from Newcastle. Having appointed to preach in Morpeth at noon, I accordingly went to the cross. But I had scarce begun when a young man appeared at the head of his troop, and told me very plainly and roughly, 'You shall not preach here.' I went on, upon which he gave the signal to his companions. But they quickly fell out among themselves. So I went on without any considerable interruption, the multitude softening more and more till, towards the close, the far greater part appeared exceeding serious and attentive.

In the afternoon we rode to Widdrington. The people flocked from all parts, and every man hung upon the word. None stirred his head or hand, or looked to the right hand or the left, while I declared in strong terms, 'The grace of our Lord Jesus Christ'.[73]

Tuesday 19th I preached at Alnmouth,[74] a small seaport town, and then rode to Alnwick, one of the largest inland towns in Northumberland. At seven I preached at the cross to a multitude of people, much resembling those at Athlone. All were moved a little, but none much. The waters spread wide, but not deep.

On Wednesday I went to Berwick-upon-Tweed, and preached both that and the next evening, as well as the following morning, in a large, green space near the Governor's house. A little society had been formed there before, which was not considerably increased; and several members of it (most of whom are now in

h [Ibid.,] pp. 78-81 [JWJ, Feb. 12, 1748].
i [Ibid.,] p. 111 [JWJ, June 24, 1748].

72 Prov. 22:6.
73 Rom. 16:20.
74 Orig., 'Alemouth'.

Abraham's bosom)[75] walked worthy of the vocation wherewith they were called.[76] After preaching at several other places in the way, on Saturday 23rd I returned to Newcastle.[j]

50. During the summer there was a large increase of the work of God both in Northumberland, the county of Durham, and Yorkshire. As likewise in the most savage part of Lancashire, though here in particular the preachers carried their lives in their hands. A specimen of the treatment they met with there may be seen in the brief account following.

On August 26th, while I was speaking to some quiet people at Roughlee, near Colne[77] in Lancashire, a drunken rabble came, the captain of whom said he was a deputy constable, and I must go with him. I had scarce gone ten yards when a man of his company struck me in the face with all his might. Another threw his stick at my head. All the rest were like as many ramping and roaring lions. They brought me, with Mr. Grimshaw,[78] the minister of Haworth, Mr. Colbeck[79] of Keighley, and Mr. Mackford[80] of Newcastle (who never recovered the abuse he then received), into a public house at Barrowford, a neighbouring village, where all their forces were gathered together.

Soon after Mr. Hargrave, the high constable, came, and required me to promise, I would come to Roughlee no more. This I flatly refused. But upon saying, 'I will not preach here now,' he undertook to quiet the mob. While he and I walked out at one door, Mr. Grimshaw and Colbeck went out at the other. The mob immediately closed them in, tossed them to and fro with the utmost violence; threw Mr. Grimshaw down, and loaded them both with dirt and mire of every kind. The other quiet, harmless people, who followed me at a distance, they treated full as ill. They poured upon them showers of dirt and stones, without any regard to age or sex. Some of them they trampled in the mire, and dragged by the hair of the head. Many they beat with their clubs

[j] [Ibid.,] pp. 116-18 [JWJ, July 18-23, 1748].

---

[75] Luke 16:22.

[76] See Eph. 4:1.

[77] Orig., 'Coln'.

[78] The Rev. William Grimshaw (1708–63), who had just become Wesley's clerical lieutenant in the north of England.

[79] Thomas Colbeck (1723–79), grocer of Keighley (orig., 'Kighley') and pillar of the Methodist society there. See JW's letter of Aug. 26, 1748 (26:325 in this edn.).

[80] William Mackford, one of the trustees of Wesley's Orphan-House at Newcastle upon Tyne.

without mercy. One they forced to leap from a rock ten or twelve feet high into the river. And when he crept out, wet and bruised, were hardly persuaded not to throw him in again. Such was the recompense we frequently received from our countrymen for our labour of love![k]

51. April 7, 1750, I embarked in the morning at Holyhead, and in the evening landed in Dublin. Here I received a full account of the shocking outrages which had been committed in Cork,[81] for several months together, which the good magistrates rather encouraged than opposed, till at the Lent assizes several depositions were laid before the grand jury. Yet they did not find any of these bills! But they found a bill against Daniel Sullivan, a baker, who when the mob were discharging a shower of stones upon him discharged a pistol (without ball) over their heads, which put them into such bodily fear that they all ran away, without looking behind them.

Being desirous of giving the poor, desolate sufferers, all the assistance I could, I made a swift journey through the inland societies, and on Saturday, May the 19th, came to Cork. The next day, understanding the house was small, about eight I went to Hammond's Marsh. It was then a large open space; but is now built over. The congregation was large and deeply attentive. I have seldom seen a more orderly assembly at any church in England or Ireland.

In the afternoon Mr. Skelton and Jones waited on the mayor, and asked if my preaching on the Marsh would be disagreeable to him. He answered, 'Sir, I will have no more mobs and riots.' Mr. Skelton replied, 'Sir, Mr. Wesley has made none.' He answered plain, 'Sir, I will have no more preaching. And if Mr. Wesley attempts it, I am prepared for him.'

I would not therefore attempt to preach on the Marsh, but began in our own house about five. The good mayor meantime was walking in the Change, and giving orders to his sergeants and the town drummers, who immediately came down to the house, with an innumerable mob attending them. They continued drumming, and I continued preaching, till I had finished my discourse. When I came out the mob presently closed me in.

[k] [Ibid.,] p. 126. [In fact this event took place on Aug. 25, and Wesley is quoting from the letters which he wrote on the following day, pp. 127-29.]

[81] See above, pp. 290-99.

Observing one of the sergeants standing by, I desired him to keep the King's peace. But he replied, 'Sir, I have no orders to do that.' As soon as I came into the open street the rabble threw whatever came to hand. But all went by me, or over my head, nor do I remember that anything touched me. I walked straight through the midst of the rabble, looking every man before me in the face, and they opened to the right and left till I came near Daunt's[82] Bridge. A large party had taken possession of this: but when I came up they likewise shrunk back, and I walked through them to Mr. Jenkins' house. But a stout Papist woman stood just within the door, and would not let me come in till one of the mob (aiming, I suppose, at *me*, but missing me) knocked *her* down flat. I then went in, and God restrained the wild beasts, so that not one attempted to follow me.

But many of the congregation were more roughly handled; particularly Mr. Jones, who was covered with mud, and escaped with his life almost by miracle. Finding the mob were not inclined to disperse, I sent to Alderman Pembroke,[83] who immediately desired Alderman Wenthrop, his nephew, to go down to Mr. Jenkins', and with whom I walked up the street, none giving me an unkind or disrespectful word.

All the following week it was at the peril of his life if any Methodist stirred out of doors. And the case was much the same during the whole mayoralty of Mr. Crone. But the succeeding mayor declared in good earnest, 'There shall be no more mobs or riots in Cork.' And he did totally suppress them. So that from that time forward even the Methodists enjoyed the same liberty with the rest of his Majesty's subjects.

52. In the meantime the work of God went on with little opposition both in other parts of the county of Cork, and at Waterford, and Limerick, as well as in Mountmellick, Athlone, Longford, and most parts of the province of Leinster. In my return from Cork I had an opportunity of visiting all these. And I had the satisfaction of observing how greatly God had blessed my fellow-labourers, and how many sinners were saved from the error of their ways.[84] Many of these had been eminent for all manner of sins; many had been Roman Catholics. And I suppose the number of these would have been far greater had not the good

[82] Orig., 'Dant's'.
[83] Orig., 'Pembrook'.
[84] See Jas. 5:20.

Protestants, as well as the popish priests, taken true pains to hinder them.

53. It was on April 24, 1751, that Mr. Hopper[85] and I set out for Scotland. I was invited thither by Captain (afterwards Colonel) Gallatin,[86] who was then quartered at Musselburgh.[87] I had no intention to preach in Scotland, not imagining there were any that desired I should. But I was mistaken. Curiosity (if nothing else) brought abundance of people together in the evening. And whereas in the kirk (Mrs. Gallatin informed me) there used to be laughing and talking, and all the marks of the grossest inattention, it was far otherwise here. They remained as statues from the beginning of the sermon to the end. I preached again, at six the next evening, on, 'Seek ye the Lord while he may be found.'[88] I used great plainness of speech towards high and low, and they all received it in love, so that the prejudice which the devil had been several years planting was torn up by the roots in one hour. After preaching one of the bailiffs of the town, with one of the elders of the kirk, came to me, and begged I would stay with them awhile, nay, if it were but two or three days, and they would fit up a far larger place than the school, and prepare seats for the congregations. Had not my time been fixed, I should gladly have complied. All that I could now do was to give them a promise that Mr. Hopper would come back the next week and spend a few days with them. He did accordingly come, and spent a fortnight, preaching every day. And it was not without a fair prospect. The congregations were very numerous. Many were cut to the heart, several joined together in a little society. Some of these are now removed to Abraham's bosom, and some remain to this day.

54. February 28, 1753, I looked over Mr. Prince's *Christian History*. What an amazing difference is there in the manner wherein God has carried on his work in England and in America! There, above a hundred of the established clergymen of age and experience, and of the greatest note for sense and learning of any in those parts, were zealously engaged in the work. Here, almost

[85] Christopher Hopper, who died in 1802, one of Wesley's most trusted itinerant preachers from 1747.

[86] Bartholomew Gallatin (here spelled 'Galatin') was a naturalized Swiss career officer in the army, whose wife was a strong supporter of the Methodists after first meeting George Whitefield in Manchester (where Gallatin was then quartered) in 1749. See JW's letter to her July 19, 1750 (26:432-33 in this edn.).

[87] Orig., 'Musselborough'.

[88] Isa. 55:6.

the whole body of the aged, experienced, learned clergy are zealously engaged against it; and but a handful of raw, young men engaged in it, without name, learning, or eminent sense! And yet by that large number of honourable men the work seldom flourished above six months at a time. And then followed a lamentable and general decay, before the next revival of it. Meantime that which God has wrought by these despised instruments has continued increasing for fifteen years together. Yea, we may now say (Blessed be the God of all grace!), for three and forty years together. And at whatever time it has declined in any one place, it has more eminently flourished in another.[1]

55. April 15th, I set out for Scotland again, not indeed for Musselburgh, but Glasgow, to which place I was invited by Mr. Gillies, the minister of the college kirk.[89] I came thither the next evening, and lodged at his house. Thursday 19th, at seven, I preached about a quarter of a mile from the town, and at four in the afternoon to a far larger congregation. I had designed to preach at the same place on Friday morning. But as it rained Mr. Gillies desired me to preach in his church. At four in the afternoon we had a far larger congregation than the church could have contained. At seven Mr. Gillies preached a home, affectionate sermon. Had not God still a favour for this city? It was long eminent for religion. And he is able to repair what is now decayed, and to build up the waste places.[90]

On Saturday, both in the morning and evening, I preached to numerous congregations. Sunday 22nd it rained much. Nevertheless upwards (I suppose) of a thousand people stayed with all willingness while I explained and applied, 'This is life eternal, to know thee the only true God, and Jesus Christ whom thou hast sent.'[91] I was desired to preach afterwards at the prison, which I did about nine o'clock. All the felons, as well as debtors, behaved with the utmost decency. It may be some, even of these poor sinners, will occasion 'joy in heaven'.[92]

The behaviour of the people at church, both morning and afternoon, was beyond anything I ever saw but in *our*

[1] [Ibid.,] p. 244 [JWJ, Feb. 28, 1753].

---

[89] John Gillies (1712–96) was minister of the college church, Glasgow, from 1742 until his death. He and Wesley remained in friendly correspondence for several years. Later Dr. Gillies became the biographer of George Whitefield and the editor of his *Works*.

[90] See Isa. 58:12.

[91] John 17:3 *(Notes)*.

[92] Luke 15:17.

congregations: none bowed or curtsied to each other, either before or after service, from the beginning to the end of which none talked, or looked at any but the minister. Surely much of the *power* of religion *was* here, where so much of the *form* still remains.[93] The meadow where I stood in the afternoon was full from side to side. I spoke as closely as ever I did in my life. Many of the students, and many of the soldiers, were there. And they could indeed bear sound doctrine.[94] Having now delivered my own soul,[95] I rode on Monday to Tranent,[96] and the next day to Berwick.[m]

56. Sunday, June 23rd, that blessed man, Mr. Walsh, preached at Short's Gardens, in Irish.[97] Abundance of his countrymen flocked to hear, and some were cut to the heart. Sunday, July 1st, he preached in Irish in Moorfields. The congregation was exceeding large. And all behaved seriously, though probably many of them came purely to hear what manner of language it was. For the sake of these he preached afterwards in English, if by any means he might gain some.[98] And wherever he preached, whether in English or Irish, the word was sharper than a two-edged sword.[99] So that I do not remember ever to have known any preacher who, in so few years as he remained upon earth, was an instrument of converting so many sinners from the error of their ways.[1]

57. Tuesday, July 10th, after one of our preachers had been there for some time, I crossed over from Portsmouth into the Isle of Wight. From Cowes we rode straight to Newport, the chief town in the isle, and found a little society in tolerable order. Several of them had found peace with God,[2] and walked in the light of his countenance.[3] At half hour after six I preached in the

[m] [Ibid.,] p. 251 [i.e., pp. 250-55 in JWJ, Apr. 15-24, 1753].

[93] See 2 Tim. 3:5.

[94] See. 2 Tim. 4:3.

[95] See Ezek. 3:19, etc.

[96] Orig., 'Traneat', but 'Tranent' in JWJ, Apr. 23, 1753.

[97] Thomas Walsh (1730–59), an Irish Roman Catholic who became a Methodist preacher in 1750 and visited London three times, on the last occasion (preceding his death) staying almost two years. Short's Gardens was one of Wesley's favourite open-air preaching places in London.

[98] See 1 Cor. 9:22.

[99] Heb. 4:12.

[1] See Jas. 5:20.

[2] Rom. 5:1.

[3] See Ps. 89:15.

market-place to a numerous congregation. But many of them were remarkably ill-behaved. The children made much noise; and many grown persons were talking aloud almost all the time I was preaching. There was a large congregation again at five in the morning, and every person therein seemed to know that this was the word whereby God would judge him in the last day. In the evening the congregation was more numerous, and far more serious than the night before. Only one drunken man made a little disturbance. But the mayor ordered him to be taken away.[n] In October I visited them again, and spent three or four days with much comfort, finding those who had before professed to find peace had walked suitably to their profession.

58. August 6, 1755, I mentioned to our congregation in London a means of increasing serious religion, which had been frequently practised by our forefathers, the joining in a *covenant* to serve God with all our heart and with all our soul. I explained this for several mornings following, and on Friday many of us kept a fast unto the Lord, beseeching him to give us wisdom and strength, that we might 'promise unto the Lord our God and keep it'.[4] On Monday at six in the evening we met for that purpose, at the French church in Spitalfields. After I had recited the tenor of the covenant proposed, in the words of that blessed man, Richard Alleine,[5] all the people stood up, in token of assent, to the number of about eighteen hundred. Such a night I scarce ever knew before. Surely the fruit of it shall remain for ever.[o]

59. January 1, 1756. How much were men divided in their expectations concerning the ensuing year! Some believed that it would bring a large harvest of temporal calamities. Others that it would be unusually fruitful of spiritual blessings. Indeed, the general expectation of those calamities spread a general seriousness over the nation. This was a means of abundant spiritual blessings. We endeavoured in every part of the kingdom to avail ourselves of the apprehensions which we frequently found

[n] [Ibid.,] p. 268, etc. [JWJ, Oct. 3-5, 1753].
[o] [*Works*,] Vol. 30, pp. 31-32 [orig., in error, 'p. 54'; see JWJ, Aug. 6-7, 1755].

---

[4] Ps. 76:11 (BCP).
[5] The Puritan minister, Richard Alleine, in *Vindiciae Pietatis* (London, 1663), set out the directions to accompany the form of prayer for joining in a covenant with God composed by his son-in-law, also a Puritan minister, Joseph Alleine, probably between 1658 and 1660. Wesley used both the prayer and the directions (see David Tripp, *The Renewal of the Covenant in the Methodist Tradition* [London, 1969], espec. pp. 11-32).

it was impossible to remove, in order to make them conducive to a nobler end, to that 'fear of the Lord, which is the beginning of wisdom'.[6] And at this season I wrote *An Address to the Clergy*,[7] which, considering the situation of public affairs, I judged would be more seasonable and more easily borne at this time than at any other.[p]

60. March 30th I visited Ireland again, and after seeing the societies in Leinster and Munster, in the latter end of June went with Mr. Walsh into the province of Connaught. We went through the counties of Clare and Galway to Castlebar, the chief town of the county of Mayo. The rector having left word that I should have the use of his church, I preached morning and evening to a very large congregation. Mr. Walsh afterwards preached in the court-house, to another numerous and serious congregation. On Tuesday I rode over to Newport, eleven miles from Castlebar, on the very extremity of the land. The rector had before given me an invitation. Between seven and eight I preached to (I suppose) more than all the Protestants in the town. Deep attention sat on every face; and surely God touched some of their hearts. On Wednesday I returned to Castlebar. There was just such a work here as that at Athlone some years ago, and afterwards at Limerick. All were *pleased*, but very few *convinced*. The stream ran very wide, but very shallow.[q]

61. July 12th, after preaching at many of the intermediate places, I went on to Longford. I began at five in the Old Barrack. A huge crowd soon flocked in; but most of the Papists stood at the gate, or just without the wall. They were all as still as night, nor did I hear an uncivil word while I walked from one end of the town to the other.

But how is it that almost in every place, even where there is no lasting fruit, there is so great an impression made at first upon a considerable number of people? The fact is this: everywhere the work of God rises higher and higher, till it comes to a point. Here it seems for a short time to be at a stay, and then it gradually sinks again.

All this may easily be accounted for. At first curiosity brings

[p] [Ibid.,] p. 54 [JWJ, Jan. 1-5, 1754].
[q] [Ibid.,] p. 67 and sequel [i.e., JWJ, Mar. 30, June 27–July 1, 1756].

---

[6] Ps. 111:10.
[7] See *Bibliography*, No. 216 (1756), and Vol. 14 in this edn.

many hearers; at the same time God draws many by his preventing grace to hear his word, and comforts them in hearing. One then tells another. By this means, on the one hand curiosity spreads and increases; and on the other the drawings of God's Spirit touch more hearts, and many of them more powerfully than before. He now offers grace to all that hear, most of whom are in some measure affected, and more or less moved with approbation of what they hear, have a desire to please God, with goodwill to his messenger. And these principles, variously combined and increasing, raise the general work to its highest point. But it cannot stand here, in the nature of things. Curiosity must soon decline. Again, the drawings of God are not followed, and thereby the Holy Spirit is grieved: he strives with this and that man no more, and so his drawings end. Thus the causes of the general impression declining, most of the hearers will be less and less affected. Add to this that in process of time 'it must be that offences will come.'[8] Some of the hearers, if not teachers also, will act contrary to their profession. Either their follies or faults will be told from one to another, and lose nothing in the telling. Men once curious to hear will hear no more; men once drawn, having stifled their good desires, will disapprove what they approved of before, and feel dislike instead of goodwill to the preachers. Others who were more or less convinced will be afraid or ashamed to acknowledge that conviction. And all these will catch at ill stories, true or false, in order to justify their charge. When by that means all who do not savingly believe have quenched the Spirit of God, the little flock that remain go on from faith to faith; the rest sleep and take their rest.[9] And thus the number of hearers in every place may be expected, first to increase, and then to decrease.

62. Monday, [July] 19th, [1756], I first set foot in the province of Ulster. But several of our preachers had been labouring in various parts of it for some years. And they had seen much fruit of their labour. Many sinners had been convinced of the error of their ways;[10] many, truly converted to God. And a considerable number of these had united together, in order to strengthen each others' hands in God. I preached in the evening at Newry to a large congregation, and to a great part of them at five in the

[8] Cf. Matt. 18:7; Luke 17:1.
[9] See Matt. 26:45, etc.
[10] See Jas. 5:20.

morning. Afterwards I spoke to the members of the society, consisting of Churchmen, Dissenters, and (late) Papists. But there is no striving among them, unless 'to enter in at the straight gate'.[11]

On Tuesday I preached at Terryhoogan,[12] near Scarva; on Wednesday in the market-house at Lisburn. Here the rector and curate called upon me, candidly proposed their objections, and spent about two hours in free, serious, friendly conversation. How much evil might be prevented or removed would other clergymen follow their example!

63. I preached in the evening at Belfast, the largest town in Ulster, to as large a congregation as at Lisburn, and to near the same number in the morning. Hence we rode along the shore to Carrickfergus, said to be the most ancient town in the province. I preached in the session-house at seven, to most of the inhabitants of the town. Sunday 25th, at nine, I preached in the upper court-house, which was much larger, and at eleven went to church. After dinner one of our friends asked if I was ready to go to the Presbyterian meeting. I told him, 'I never go to a meeting.' He seemed as much astonished as the old Scot at Newcastle, who left us 'because we were mere *Church of England men*'. We are so, although we condemn none *who have been brought up* in another way.

64. Monday 26th Mr. Walsh met me at Belfast, and informed me that the day before he was at Newtown[ards] intending to preach; but while he was at prayer one Mr. Mortimer came with a drunken mob, seized him by the throat, and dragged him along till a stout man seized him and constrained him to quit his hold. Mr. Walsh, having refreshed himself at a friend's house, began a second time. But in a quarter of an hour Mr. Mortimer, having rallied his mob, came again, on which Mr. Walsh gave him the ground, and walked away over the fields.

On Tuesday evening I preached in the market-house at Lurgan. Many of the gentry were met in the room over this, it being the time of the assembly. The violins were just tuning. But they ceased till I had done; and the novelty (at least) drew and fixed the attention of the whole company. Having visited most of the societies in Ulster, I returned to Dublin August 5th. On

[11] Luke 13:24.

[12] Orig., 'Terryuagan'.

Tuesday evening I preached my farewell sermon. But it was still a doubt (though I had bespoken the cabin of the packet for myself and my friends) whether we should sail or no, Sir Thomas Prendergast having sent word to the captain that he would go over, and it being his custom *(hominis magnificantiam!)*[13] to keep the whole ship to himself. But the wind turning foul, he would not go; so about noon Mr. Walsh, Haughton,[14] Morgan,[15] and I went on board, and fell down to the mouth of the harbour. The next evening we landed at Holyhead.

65. Thursday 26th, about fifty of the preachers being met at Bristol, the *Rules* of the Society[16] were read over, and carefully considered one by one. But we did not find any that could be spared. So we agreed to retain and enforce them all.

The next day the *Rules* of the Bands[17] were read over, and considered one by one, which after some verbal alterations we all agreed to observe and enforce.

On Saturday the *Rules* of Kingswood School[18] were read over, and considered one by one. And we were fully satisfied that they were all agreeable both to Scripture and reason.

My brother and I closed the Conference by a solemn declaration of our purpose never to separate from the Church. And all our brethren cheerfully concurred therein.[r]

66. February 28, 1757, one of our preachers wrote me the following letter:

> Rev. and dear sir,
>
> At Bradford, on the 30th January last, I was pressed for a soldier, and carried to the inn where the gentlemen were. Mr. Pearse offered bail for my appearance the next day. They said they would take his word for a thousand pounds, but not for *me*—I must go to the round-house, the little stone room on the side of the bridge. So thither I was conveyed by five soldiers. I found nothing to sit on but a stone, and nothing to lie on but a little straw. But soon after a friend sent me a chair, on which I sat all night. I had a double guard, twelve soldiers in all, two without, one in the door, and the rest within. I passed the night without sleep, but, blessed be God, not without rest, for my peace was not broken a moment.

[r] [Ibid.,] pp. 111-12 [i.e., JWJ, Aug. 26-28, 1756, describing the annual Conference].

---

[13] 'The ostentation of the man!'

[14] The preacher, John Haughton (orig., 'Houghton').

[15] The preacher, James Morgan.

[16] See above, pp. 68-73.

[17] See above, pp. 77-79.

[18] See *A Short Account of Kingswood School*, 1749 (*Bibliography*, No. 162, presented in Vol. 15 of this edn.).

My body was in prison: but I was Christ's freeman; my soul was at liberty. And even there I found some work to do for God. I had a fair opportunity of speaking to them that durst not leave me. And I hope it was not in vain.

The next day I was carried before the Commissioners, and part of the Act read which empowered them to take such able-bodied men as 'had no business, and had no lawful or sufficient maintenance'. Then I said, 'But I have a lawful calling, being in partnership with my brother, and have also an estate. Give me time, and you shall have full proof of this.' They agreed. The next day I set out for Cornwall. After staying at home a few days, on Saturday I came to Bradford. On Monday I appeared before the Commissioners, with the writings of my estate. When they had perused them, they set me at liberty. I hope you will give thanks to God for my deliverance out of the hands of unreasonable and wicked men.

William Hitchens[s]

67. March 13th, finding myself weak at Snowsfields,[19] I prayed that God, if he saw good, would send me help at the chapel.[20] He did so. As soon as I had done preaching, Mr. Fletcher[21] came, who had just then been ordained priest, and hastened to the chapel on purpose to assist me, as he supposed me to be alone. How wonderful are the ways of God! When my bodily strength failed, and no clergyman in England was able and willing to assist me, he sent me help from the mountains of Switzerland! And a helpmeet for me in every respect! Where could I have found such another![t]

68. Monday, April 11th, at five in the evening about twelve hundred of the society met at Spitalfields. I expected two clergymen to help me; but none came. I held out till between seven and eight. I was then scarce able to walk or speak. But I looked up and received strength. At half hour after nine God broke in mightily upon the congregation. 'Great' indeed 'was our glorying in him'; we were 'filled with consolation'.[22] And when I returned home between ten and eleven I was no more tired than at ten in the morning.[u]

69. Tuesday, October 25th, as I was returning from Bath, a

[s] [Ibid.,] pp. 126-28 [JWJ, Feb. 28, 1757. In 'A Short History' the name is spelled, 'Hichins'].

[t] [Ibid.,] p. 129 [JWJ, Mar. 13, 1757]. [u] [Ibid.,] p. 132 [JWJ, Apr. 11, 1757].

---

[19] Orig., 'Snow-fields', i.e., Snowfields Chapel, formerly Maze Pond Chapel, which Wesley acquired in 1743 (see JWJ, Aug. 6, 1743).

[20] Namely West Street Chapel, his main centre for sacramental worship.

[21] John William Fletcher (1729–85), who was ordained deacon on Sunday, Mar. 6, and priest on Sunday, Mar. 13, in the Chapel Royal in Whitehall.

[22] 2 Cor. 7:4.

man met me at Hanham,[23] and told me, 'The school-house in Kingswood is burnt down.' When I came thither I was informed, about eight the night before two or three boys went into the gallery up two pair of stairs. One of them heard a strange crackling[24] in the room above. Opening the staircase door, he was beat back by smoke, on which he cried out, 'Fire, murder, fire!' Mr. Baynes hearing this, ran immediately down, and brought up a pail of water. But going in and seeing the blaze, he had not presence of mind to go up to it, but threw the water upon the floor. The room was quickly all in a flame, the deal partitions taking fire, and spreading to the upper rooms of the house. Water enough was now brought, but none could come near the place where it was wanted, the room being so filled with flame and smoke. At last a long ladder was reared up against the wall of the house. But it was then observed that one of the sides of it was broke in two, and the other quite rotten. However, John How,[25] a young man that lived next door, ran up it with an axe in his hand. But he then found the ladder was so short that as he stood on the top of it he could but just lay one hand over the battlements. How he got over them to the leads none can tell; but he did so, and immediately made a hole through the roof, on which, a vent being made, the smoke and flame issued out as from a furnace. Those who brought water, but were stopped before by the smoke, then got upon the leads and poured it down through the tiling. By this means the fire was quickly quenched, having only consumed part of the partition, with some clothes, and a little damaged the roof, and the floor beneath. It is amazing that so little hurt was done. For the fire (which began in the middle of the room, none knew how) was so violent that it broke every pane of glass but two in the window, both at the east and west end. What was more amazing still, was that it did not hurt either the beds (which seemed all covered with flame) or the deal partitions on the other side of the room, though it beat against them for a considerable time. What can we say to these things, but that God had fixed the bounds which it could not pass![v]

70. Having before visited most other parts of Ireland, on May

[v] [Ibid.,] pp. 187-88 [JWJ, Oct. 25, 1757. The closing sentence alludes to Job 14:5].

[23] Orig., 'Hannam'.
[24] Orig., 'cracking', but 'crackling' in JWJ.
[25] 'A Short History', 'Haw', but 'How' in JWJ.

27, 1758, I entered the county of Sligo, bordering on the western ocean, I think the best peopled that I have seen in the kingdom. I believe the town is above half as large as Limerick. Sunday 28th, at nine, I preached in the market-house to a numerous congregation. But they were doubled at five in the afternoon, and God made his 'word quick and powerful, and sharper than a two-edged sword.'[26] And from that time there have never been wanting a few in Sligo who worship God in spirit and in truth.[27] In many other parts of the county likewise many sinners have been truly converted to God.[w]

71. June 17th I met Thomas Walsh once more in Limerick, alive, and but just alive. Three of the best physicians in these parts had attended him, and all agreed that it was a lost case—that by violent straining of his voice he had contracted a true, pulmonary consumption, which was then in the last stage, and beyond the reach of any human help. O what a man, to be snatched away in the strength of his years! Surely thy 'judgments are a great deep'![x]

72. I rode over to Courtmatrix,[28] a colony of Germans, whose parents came out of the Palatinate in Queen Anne's region. Twenty families of them settled here; twenty more at Killiheen,[29] a mile off; fifty at Ballingrane,[30] two miles eastward, and twenty at Pallas,[31] four miles farther. Each family had a few acres of ground, on which they built as many little houses. They are since considerably increased, not indeed in families, but in number of souls. Having no minister, they were become eminent for drunkenness, cursing, swearing, and an utter contempt of religion. But they are changed since they heard, and willingly received, the truth as it is in Jesus.[32] An oath is now rarely heard among them, or a drunkard seen in their borders. They have built

[w] [Ibid.,] p. 216 [JWJ, May 27-28, 1758].
[x] [Ibid.,] pp. 222-23 [JWJ, June 17, 1758. The closing quotation is from Ps. 36:6].

---

[26] Heb. 4:12. [27] John 4:24.

[28] Courtmatrix (orig., 'Courtmattress') is about twenty miles south-west of Limerick, beside Castle Matrix where Wesley is said to have stayed on at least one occasion.

[29] Killiheen is a hamlet near Courtmatrix, and there are still Methodist families there.

[30] Ballingranne (as it is now usually spelled, but there are many variants) is the only village of those mentioned by Wesley where there is still a Methodist chapel.

[31] Pallas is sometimes thought to be Pallaskerry, close to the estuary of the Shannon, but its name is, apparently, never shortened, and Pallas Green, south-east of Limerick, fourteen miles out on the road to Tipperary, is a much more likely identification. An area nearby is called Palatine Street, and many Methodist families in the whole neighbourhood are descendants of the immigrants from the Palatinate.

[32] See Eph. 4:21.

a pretty large preaching-house, in the middle of Courtmatrix. But it would not contain one half of the congregation. So I stood in a large yard. Many times afterwards I preached at Ballingrane and Pallas; so did my fellow-labourers, and with lasting effect. So did God at last provide for these poor strangers, who for fifty years had none that cared for their souls!

The plain, old Bible religion had now made its way into every county in Ireland, save Kerry. And many in each county, and in most large towns, were happy witnesses of it. But I doubt not there would have been double the number had not true pains been taken by Protestants (so called) as well as Papists, either to prevent their hearing, or at least to prevent their laying to heart, the word that is able to save their souls.[33]

73. March 3, 1759, I rode to Colchester, and found that out of the hundred and twenty-six I had left here last year we had lost only twelve, in the place of whom we had gained forty. Such is the fruit of visiting from house to house![y]

Having at length submitted to the importunity of my friends, and consented to hire James Wheatley's Tabernacle at Norwich, I went on thither on Tuesday, and inquiring the next day found that neither any society nor any subscribers were left. So that everything was to be wrought out of the ore, or rather out of the cinders. In the evening I desired those who were willing to join would speak to me the next day. About twenty did so; but the greater part of them appeared like frighted sheep. On Saturday and Sunday about forty more came, and thirty or forty on Monday. Two-thirds of them seemed to have known God's pardoning love. Doth he not send by whom he *will* send?[34] In a week or two more, having joined the new members with those of the old society, all together amounted to four hundred and twenty, and by April 1st to above five hundred and seventy. A hundred and five of these were in no society before, although many of them had found peace with God. I believe they would have increased to a thousand if I could have stayed a fortnight longer. But which of these will hold fast their profession?[35] The fowls of the air will devour some. The sun will scorch more, and

[y] [Ibid.,] p. 253 [JWJ, Mar. 3-5, 1759].

---

[33] See Jas. 1:21.
[34] See Exod. 4:13.
[35] See Heb. 4:14.

others will be choked by the thorns springing up. I wonder we should ever expect that half of those that at first 'hear the word with joy' will 'bring forth fruit unto perfection'![z]

74. In May the work of God exceedingly increased at and near Everton in Huntingdonshire. I cannot give a clearer view of this than by transcribing the journal of an eye witness:

> Sunday, May 20th, several fainted and cried out while Mr. Berridge was preaching. Afterwards at church many cried out, especially children, whose agonies were amazing. One of the eldest, a girl ten or twelve years old, was in violent contortions of body and wept aloud, I think incessantly, during the whole service. And several much younger children were agonizing as this did. The church was crowded within and without, so that Mr. Berridge was almost stifled by the breath of the people. I believe there were three times more men than women, a great part of whom came from far. The text was, 'Having the form of godliness, but denying the power of it'. When the power of religion came to be spoken of, the presence of God filled the place. And while poor sinners felt the sentence of death in their souls, what sounds of distress did I hear! The greatest number of them that cried out were men; but some women, and several children, felt the power of the same Almighty Spirit, and seemed just sinking into hell. This occasioned a mixture of various sounds, some shrieking, some roaring aloud. The most general was a loud breathing, like that of persons half strangled and gasping for life. And indeed most of the cries were like those of dying creatures. Great numbers wept without any noise. Others fell down as dead, some sinking in silence, some with extreme pain and violent agitation. I stood on the pew seat, as did a young man in the opposite pew, an able-bodied, healthy countryman. But in a moment, while he seemed to think of nothing less, down he dropped with a violence inconceivable. And the beating of his feet were ready to break the boards as he lay in strong convulsions at the bottom of the pew. Among the children who felt the arrows of the Almighty I saw a sturdy boy, about eight years old, who roared above his fellows, and seemed to struggle with the strength of a grown man. His face was red as scarlet, and almost all on whom God laid his hand turned either very red or almost black. When I returned to Mr. Berridge's house, after a little walk, I found it full of people. He was fatigued, yet said he would give them a word of exhortation. I stayed in the next room, and saw a girl lying as dead. In a few minutes a woman was filled with peace and joy. She had come thirteen miles, and had dreamed Mr. Berridge would come to her village on that very day whereon he did come, though without either knowing the place or the way to it. She was convinced at that time. Just as we heard of her deliverance, the girl on the floor began to stir. She was then set in a chair, and after sighing awhile, suddenly rose up, rejoicing in God. She frequently fell on her knees, but was generally running to and fro, speaking these and the like words: 'O what can Jesus do for lost sinners! He has forgiven me all my sins.' Meantime I saw a thin, pale girl weeping with joy for her companion, and with sorrow for herself. Quickly the smiles of heaven came likewise on her face, and her praises joined with those of the other.

[z] [Ibid.,] pp. 254-58 [JWJ, Mar. 6–Apr. 1. For the closing sentence cf. Luke 8:5-7, 13-14].

75. Two or three well-dressed young women, who seemed careless before, now cried out with a loud and bitter cry. We continued praising God with all our might; and his work went on. I had for some time observed a young woman all in tears; but now her countenance changed; her face was as quick as lightning, filled with smiles, and became of a crimson colour. Immediately after, a stranger who stood facing me fell backward to the wall, then forward on his knees, wringing his hands and roaring like a bull. His face at first turned quite red, then almost black; he rose and ran against the wall, till two persons held him. He screamed, 'O what shall I do? O for one drop of the blood of Christ!' As he spoke, God set his soul at liberty, and the rapture he was in seemed almost too great to be borne. He had come forty miles to hear Mr. Berridge, and was to leave him the next morning, which he did with a glad heart, telling all who came in his way what God had done for his soul.

76. About the time Mr. Coe (that was his name) began to rejoice, a girl about twelve years old, exceeding poorly dressed, appeared to be as deeply wounded as any. But I lost sight of her, till I heard of another born in Zion, and found upon inquiry, it was her. And now I saw such a sight as I do not expect to see again on this side of eternity. The faces of three children, and I think of all the believers, did really shine. And such a beauty, such a look of extreme happiness, and of divine love and simplicity, I never saw in human faces till now. The newly justified eagerly embraced one another, weeping on each other's necks for joy. Then they saluted all of their own sex, and besought all to help them in praising God.

77. Thursday 24th I went to hear Mr. Hickes at Wrestlingworth, four miles from Everton. We were glad to hear that he had given himself up to the work of God, and that the power of the Highest fell on his hearers, as on Mr. Berridge's. While he was preaching, fifteen or sixteen persons felt the arrows of the Almighty, and dropped down. A few of these cried out with the utmost violence, and with little intermission, for some hours; while the rest made no great noise, but continued struggling, as in the pangs of death. Besides these, one little girl was deeply convinced, and a boy, nine or ten years old. Both these, and several others, when carried into the parsonage-house, either lay as dead, or struggled with all their might. But in a short time their cries increased above measure. I prayed, and for a time all were calm. But the storm soon rose again. Mr. Hickes then prayed, and afterwards Mr. Berridge. But still, though some received consolation, others remained in deep sorrow of heart.

Upon the whole I remark that few ancient people experience anything of this work of God, and scarce any of the rich. These generally show either an utter contempt of it, or an enmity to it. Indeed so did Mr. Hickes himself some time since, even denying the sacrament to those who went to hear Mr. Berridge. As neither of these gentlemen have much eloquence, the Lord hereby more clearly shows that it is his own work. It extends into Cambridgeshire, to within a mile of the university; and about as far into Huntingdonshire; but flourishes most of all in the eastern and northern parts of Bedfordshire. The violent struggling of many in the above-mentioned churches has broke several pews and benches. Yet it is common for people to remain unaffected there, and afterwards drop down in their way home. Some have been found lying as dead in the road; others in Mr. Berridge's garden; not being able to walk from the church to his house, though it is not two hundred yards.[a]

[a] [Ibid.,] pp. 278-85 [JWJ, May 30, 1759].

78. Saturday, November 24th, I rode to Everton (having been there some months before). On Sunday afternoon God was eminently present with us, though rather to comfort than convince. But I observed a remarkable difference since I was here as to the manner of the work. None now were in trances; none cried out; none fell down, or were convulsed. Only some trembled exceedingly; a low murmur was heard; and many were refreshed with the multitude of peace. The danger *was* to regard *extraordinary* circumstances too much, such as outcries, convulsions, visions, trances, as if these were *essential* to the inward work, so that it *could not* go on without them. Perhaps the danger *is* to regard them too little; to condemn them altogether; to imagine they had nothing of God in them, yea, were a hindrance to the work. Whereas the truth is: (1). God suddenly and strongly convinced many that they were undone, lost sinners, the *natural* consequences whereof were sudden outcries, and strong bodily convulsions. (2). To strengthen and encourage them that believed, and to make his work more apparent, he favoured several of them with divine dreams, others with trances or visions. (3). In some of these instances, after a time, nature mixed with grace. (4). Satan likewise mimicked *this part of the work of God*, in order to discredit the *whole* work. And yet it is not wise to give up *this part*, any more than to give up *the whole*. At first it was doubtless wholly from God. It is partly so at this day; and he will enable us to discern how far in every case the work is *pure*, and how far *mixed*.[b]

79. On Thursday 29th, the day appointed for a General Thanksgiving, I preached at West Street, Seven Dials, London, both morning and afternoon. I believe the oldest man in England has not seen a Thanksgiving Day so observed before. It had the solemnity of the General Fast. All the shops were shut up. The people in the streets appeared, one and all, with an air of seriousness. The prayers, lessons, and whole public service, were admirably suited to the occasion. The prayer for our enemies, in particular, was extremely striking—perhaps it is the first instance of the kind in Europe. There was no noise, hurry, bonfires, fireworks, in the evening, and no public diversions. This is indeed a *Christian holy-day*, a 'rejoicing unto the Lord'.[36] The next day

[b] [Ibid.,] pp. 343-44 [JWJ, Nov. 24-25, 1759].

---

[36] Cf. Ps. 2:11 (BCP).

came the news that Admiral Hawke had dispersed the French fleet.[c]

80. In the beginning of the year 1760 there was a great revival of the work of God in Yorkshire.

On January 13th (says a correspondent), about thirty persons were met together at Otley (a town ten miles north-east of Leeds) in the evening, in order (as usual) to pray, sing hymns, and to provoke one another to love and to good works. When they came to speak of the several states of their souls, some with deep sighs and groans complained of the heavy burden they felt from the remains of inbred sin, seeing in a clearer light than ever before the necessity of a deliverance from it. When they had spent the usual time together, a few went to their own houses; but the rest remained upon their knees, groaning for the 'great and precious promises'. When one of them was desired to pray, he no sooner lifted up his voice to God than the Holy Ghost made intercession in all that were present, 'with groanings that could not be uttered'. And in a while they expressed the travail of their souls by loud and bitter cries. They had no doubt of the favour of God; but they could not rest while they had anything in them contrary to his nature. One cried out in an agony, 'Lord, deliver me from my sinful nature!' Then a second, a third, a fourth. And while he that prayed first was uttering those words, 'Thou God of Abraham, Isaac, and Jacob, hear us for the sake of thy son Jesus,' one broke out, 'Blessed be the Lord forever, for he has purified my heart!' Another, 'Praise the Lord with me; for he has cleansed my heart from sin.' Another cried, 'I am hanging over the pit of hell!' Another shrieked out, 'I am in hell. O save me, save me!' While another said, with a far different voice, 'Blessed be the Lord, for he hath pardoned all my sins!' Thus they continued for the space of two hours, some praising and magnifying God; some crying to him for pardon or purity of heart, with the greatest agony of spirit. Before they parted, three believed God had fulfilled his word, and 'cleansed them from all unrighteousness'. The next evening they met again, and the Lord was again present to heal the broken in heart. One received remission of sins, and three more believed God had 'cleansed them from all sin'. And it is observable, these are all poor, illiterate creatures, incapable of counterfeiting, and unlikely to attempt it. But 'when his word goeth forth, it giveth light and understanding to the simple.'[d]

81. Here began that glorious work of sanctification which had been nearly at a stand for twenty years. But from time to time it spread, first through various parts of Yorkshire, afterwards in London; then through most parts of England; next through Dublin, Limerick, and all the south and west of Ireland. And wherever the work of sanctification increased, the whole work of God increased in all its branches. Many were convinced of sin, many justified, many backsliders healed. So it was in the London

[c] [Ibid.,] pp. 345-46 [JWJ, Nov. 29-30, 1759].
[d] [Ibid.,] pp. 352-54 [JWJ, Feb. 16, 1760].

society in particular. In February 1761 it contained upwards of three and twenty hundred members—in 1763 above eight and twenty hundred.

82. February 27, 1761, I met about thirty persons who had experienced a deep work of God. And whether they are 'saved from sin' or no, they are certainly full of faith and love.

Wednesday, March 4th, I was scarce come into the room where a few believers were met together when one began to tremble exceedingly. She soon sunk to the floor. After a violent struggle she burst out into prayer, which was quickly changed into praise. And she then declared, 'The Lamb of God has taken away all my sins.'[e] Wednesday 28th. By talking with several in Wednesbury I found God was carrying on his work here as at London. We had ground to hope one prisoner was set at liberty under the sermon on Saturday morning, another on Saturday evening. One or more received remission of sins on Sunday. On Monday morning another, and on Wednesday yet another believed 'the blood of Christ' *had* 'cleansed' *them* 'from all sin'.[37] In the evening I could scarce think, but more than one heard him say, 'I will; be thou clean.'[38] Indeed, so wonderfully was he present till near midnight, as if he would have healed the whole congregation.[f]

Monday 23rd. Many preachers meeting me at Leeds, I inquired into the state of the northern societies, and found the work of God was increasing on every side. Afterwards I talked with several of those who believed they were saved from sin. And after a close examination I found reason to believe that fourteen of them were not deceived.[g]

83. Saturday, May 2nd. After Mr. Hopper had spent some time there, and formed a little society, I went to Aberdeen. I preached there morning and evening, either in the College hall or the Close, to very numerous and attentive congregations, on Sunday and the three following days. Thursday 7th, leaving near ninety members in the society, I rode over to Sir Archibald Grant's, near Monymusk, about twenty miles north-west from

[e] [*Works*,] Vol. 31, p. 79 [JWJ, Feb. 27–Mar. 4, 1761. The closing quotation is from John 1:29].

[f] [Ibid.,] p. 83 [JWJ, Mar. 18, 1761].

[g] [Ibid.,] p. 88 [i.e., pp. 84-85, JWJ, Mar. 23, 1761].

[37] 1 John 1:7.

[38] Matt. 8:3, etc.

Aberdeen. About six I preached in the church, pretty well filled with such persons as we did not look for, so near the highlands. I was much comforted among them; and setting out early on Friday, on Saturday reached Edinburgh.[h]

84. Thursday 21st,[i] inquiring how it was that in all these parts we had so few witnesses of full salvation, I constantly received one and the same answer: 'We see now, we sought it by our *works*. We thought it was to come *gradually*. We never expected it to come in a moment, by simple *faith*, in the very same manner as we received justification.' What wonder is it then that you have been fighting all these years 'as one that beateth the air'?[39] Monday, June 22nd, I spoke one by one to the society at Hutton Rudby, near Yarm. Of about eighty members near seventy were believers, and I think sixteen renewed in love. Here were two bands of children, one of boys and one of girls, most of whom were walking in the light.[40] Four of those who seemed to be saved from sin were of one family, and all of them walked holy and umblameable.[41] And many instances of the same kind I found in every part of the county.

85. August 22nd, I returned to London, and found the work of God swiftly increasing. The congregations in every place were larger than they had been for several years. Many were from day to day convinced of sin. Many found peace with God. Many backsliders were healed, and filled with love. And many believers entered into such a rest as it had not before entered into their hearts to conceive. Meantime the enemy was not wanting to sow tares among the good seed.[42] I saw this clearly, but durst not use violence, lest in plucking up the tares I should root up the wheat also.[j] On Monday, September 21st, I came to Bristol. And here likewise I found a great increase of the work of God. The congregations were exceeding large, and the people longing and thirsting after righteousness.[43] And every day afforded us fresh instances of persons convinced of sin or converted to God. So that it seems he was pleased to pour out his Spirit this year on every part both of England and Ireland, in a manner we never had

[h] [Ibid.,] pp. 90-93 [JWJ, May 2-9, 1761].
[i] [Ibid.,] p. 103 [JWJ, May 21, 1761].
[j] [Ibid.,] p. 110 [JWJ, Aug. 22, 1761].

[39] Cf. 1 Cor. 9:26.
[40] See 1 John 1:7.
[41] JWJ, June 22, 1761.
[42] See Matt. 13:25-27.
[43] See Matt. 5:6.

seen before, at least not for twenty years. O what pity that so many of the children of God did not know the day of their visitation![44]

86. December 26th I made a particular inquiry into the case of Mary Special, a young woman then living at Tottenham Court Road. She said, 'Four years since I found much pain in my breasts, and afterwards hard lumps. Four months ago my left breast broke, and kept running continually. Growing worse and worse, after some time I was recommended to St. George's Hospital. I was let blood many times, and took hemlock thrice a day; but I was no better. The pain and lumps were the same, and both my breasts were quite hard, and black as soot. Yesterday sennight I went to Mr. Owen's, where there was a meeting for prayer. Mr. B[ell] saw me and asked, "Have you faith to be healed?" I said, "Yes." He then prayed for me, and in a moment all my pain was gone. But the next day I felt a little pain again. I clapped my hands on my breasts and cried out, "Lord, if thou wilt, thou canst make me whole." It was gone; and from that hour I had no pain, no soreness, no lumps or swelling, but both my breasts were perfectly well, and have been so ever since.'

Now here are plain facts. (1). She *was* ill. (2). She *is* well. (3). She became so in a moment. Which of these can with modesty be denied?[k]

87. All January 1762 God continued to work mightily, not only in and about London, but in most parts of England and Ireland. February 5th I met at noon, as usual, those who believed they were saved from sin, and warned them of the enthusiasm that was breaking in, by means of two or three weak, though good men, who through a misconstrued text in 'the Revelations' inferred that they should not die. This gave great occasion of triumph to those that sought occasion, who rejoiced as though they had found great spoil.[l] This year, from the beginning to the end, was a year never to be forgotten. Such a season I never saw before! Such a multitude of sinners were converted from the error of their ways, in all parts both of England and Ireland, and so many were filled with pure love.

88. In April I crossed over to Ireland,[m] and in every part of the

[k] [Ibid.,] p. 126 [actually p. 133, i.e., JWJ, Dec. 26, 1761].
[l] [Ibid.,] p. 135 [actually pp. 139-40, i.e., JWJ, Feb. 5, 1762].
[m] [Ibid.,] p. 156 [actually p. 144, i.e., JWJ, Apr. 2, 1762].

[44] See Luke 19:44.

kingdom, north, west, and south, found cause to bless God for the abundant increase of his work. On July 24th I returned to Dublin, and found the flame still increasing. The congregation was as large this evening as it used to be on Sunday evening. Monday 26th it was larger at five in the morning than it used to be in the evening. And in two days and a half four persons gave thanks for a sense of God's pardoning mercy. And seven (among whom were a mother and her daughter) for being 'perfected in love'.[45] The person by whom chiefly it pleased God to work was John Manners, a plain man, of middling sense, and not elegant, but rather slow of speech—one who had never before been eminently useful, but seemed to be raised up for this single work. And as soon as it was done he fell into a consumption, languished awhile, and died.[n]

89. I found he had not at all exceeded the truth in the accounts he had sent me from time to time. In one of his first letters he says:

> The work here is such as I never expected to see. Some are justified or sanctified almost every day. This week three or four were justified, and as many, if not more, renewed in love. The people are all on fire. Such a day as last Sunday I never saw before. While I was at prayer in the society the power of the Lord overshadowed us, and some cried out, 'Lord I *can* believe!' The cry soon became general, with strong prayers. Twice I attempted to sing; but my voice could not be heard. I then desired them to restrain themselves, and in stillness and composure to wait for the blessing; on which all but two or three who could not refrain came into a solemn silence. I prayed again, and the softening power of grace was felt in many hearts. Our congregations increased much, and I have no doubt but we shall see greater things than these.

Four days after he writes:

> The work of God increases every day. There is hardly a day but some are justified, or sanctified, or both. On Thursday three came and told me, 'The blood of Christ had cleansed them from all sin.' One of them told me, she had been justified seven years, and had been five years convinced of the necessity of sanctification. But this *easy* conviction availed not. A fortnight since she was seized with so keen a conviction as gave her no rest till God had sanctified her, and witnessed it to her heart.
>
> The fire catches all that come near. An old soldier, in his return from Germany to the North of Ireland, fell in, one night, with these wrestling Jacobs, to his great astonishment. As he was going to Germany, in the beginning of the

[n] [Ibid.,] pp. 176-77 [JWJ, July 24, 1762. Cf. the following two sections for Wesley's abridged account of his itinerant preacher John Manners].

[45] Cf. 1 John 4:12, 18.

war, the Lord healed him in Dublin; and in spite of all the distresses of a severe campaign he walked in the light continually. On his return through London he was convinced of the necessity of full sanctification. And soon after he came hither his heart was broken in pieces, while he was with a little company who meet daily for prayer. One evening, as they were going away, he stopped them and begged they would not go till God had blessed him. They kneeled down again, and did not cease wrestling with God till he had a witness that he was saved from all sin.

90. In his last letter he says:

> I had much fear about the children, lest our labour should be lost upon them. But I find we shall reap, if we faint not. Margaret Roper, about eight years old, has been thoughtful for some time. The other day, while they were at family prayer, she burst into tears and wept bitterly. They asked what was the matter. She said she was 'a great sinner, and durst not pray'. They bade her go to bed. She no sooner went into the chamber than she began crying and clapping her hands, so that they heard her across the street. But God soon bound up her broken heart. Being asked how she felt herself she said: 'Ten times better. Now I can love God. I wish you would sit up and sing with me all night.' She has been happy ever since, and is as serious as one of forty. July 3rd. Our joy is now quite full. The flame rises higher and higher. Since Saturday eight sinners were justified, and two more renewed in love. Our house was once large enough; now it is scarce sufficient to contain us. And we have not many in the society who are not either wrestling with God for his love, or rejoicing therein.

91. Upon examination I found three or four and forty in Dublin who enjoyed the pure love of God. At least forty of these had attained it in four months. The same number had received remission of sins. Nor was the hand of the Lord shortened yet;[46] he still wrought as swiftly as ever. In some respects the work of God in this place was more remarkable than even that at London. (1). It is far greater in proportion to the time and to the number of the people. This society is scarce a fifth part of that. Yet six months after this flame broke out [t]here we had about thirty witnesses of the great salvation; here were above forty in four months. (2). The work here was more pure. In all this time there were none of them headstrong or unadvisable, none who dreamed of being immortal, or infallible, or incapable of temptation—in short, no whimsical or enthusiastic persons. All were calm and sober-minded. I know, several of these were in process of time 'moved from their steadfastness'.[47] I am nothing

[46] See Isa. 59:1.
[47] Cf. 2 Pet. 3:17.

surprised at this. It was no more than was to be expected. I rather wonder that more were not moved. Nor does this in any degree alter my judgment concerning the great work which God then wrought, the greatest, I believe, that has been wrought in Europe since the Reformation.

92. The same work was now carrying on in Limerick, of which I had several accounts. The last ran thus: 'Blessed be God, since you was here his word runs swiftly. Last night his power was present indeed, and another was assured that God had "cleansed him from all unrighteousness".[48] There are now ten women and thirteen men who witness the same confession. And their lives agree thereto. Eight have lately received the remission of their sins. And many are on the full stretch for God, and just ready to step into the pool.' Hence it appears that in proportion to the time, which was only three or four weeks, and the number of hearers (not one half, if a third part), the work of God was greater in Limerick than even in Dublin itself.

93. Sunday, August 1st, I landed at Parkgate, and rode on to Chester. Never was the society in such a state before. There was nothing but peace and love among them. About twelve believed they were saved from sin. Most of the rest were strongly athirst for God, and looking for him continually.[o] Wednesday 4th I rode to Liverpool, where also was such a work of God as had never been known there before. There was a surprising congregation in the evening, and had been for some months. A little before I went nine were justified in one hour. The next morning I spoke severally with those who believed they were sanctified. They were fifty-one in all: twenty-one men, twenty-one widows or married women, and nine young women or children. In one of these the change was wrought three weeks after she was justified; in three, seven days after it; in one, five days; and in Samuel Lutwich,[49] aged fourteen, two days only. I asked Hannah Blakeley, aged eleven, 'What do you want now?' She said, with amazing energy, the tears running down her cheeks, 'Nothing in this world; nothing but more of my Jesus!'

94. One wrote thus from Bolton in Lancashire: 'Glory be to God, he is doing wonders among us. Since Mr. Furz left us there

[o] [Ibid.,] p. 187 [JWJ, Aug. 1, 1762].

---

[48] Cf. 1 John 1:9.
[49] JWJ, 1767, 1791, 'Sus. Lutwich'; *Works* (1774), 'S. Lutwich'.

have been seven (if not more) justified, and six sanctified at one meeting. Two of these were, I think, justified and sanctified in less than three days. O what a meeting was our last class-meeting! In three minutes or less God quite unexpectedly convinced an old opposer of the truth, and wounded many more. I never felt the abiding presence of God so exceeding powerful before.'[50]

Inquiring how the revival began at Macclesfield, I received the following account. In March last, after a long season of dryness and barrenness, one Monday night John Oldham preached. When he had done, and was going away, a man dropped down, and cried aloud for mercy. In a short time so did several others. He came back, and wrestled with God in prayer for them. About twelve he retired, leaving some of the brethren in prayer for them, who resolved to wrestle on till they had an answer of peace. They continued in prayer till six in the morning, and nine prisoners were set at liberty.

They met again the next night, and six or seven more were filled with peace and joy in believing. So were one or two more every night till the Monday following, when there was another general shower of grace. And many believed that 'the blood of Christ had cleansed them from all sin.'[51] I spoke to these (forty in all) one by one. Some of them said, they received that blessing ten days, some seven, some four, some three days, after they found peace with God. What marvel! Since 'one day is with God as a thousand years!'[52]

95. The case of Ann Hooly was peculiar. She had often declared, 'The Methodist God shall not be *my* God. I will sooner go to hell than I will go to heaven in *their* way.' She was standing in the street with two young men, when John Oldham passing by, spoke to one and the other, and went on. She burst into tears, and said, 'What, am I such a sinner that he will not speak to me?' About twelve he was sent for in haste. He found her in deep distress, but continued in prayer till all her trouble was gone, and her spirit rejoiced in God her Saviour.[53] Yet three nights after she was in much distress again, crying, 'I have a wicked heart till God takes it away.' He did so in a few hours. She was ever after a pattern to all the young people in the town. She was thirteen years old. In about a year her spirit returned to God.

[50] See JWJ, Aug. 6, 1762.

[51] Cf. 1 John 1:7.

[52] Cf. 2 Pet. 3:8.

[53] See Luke 1:47.

On Saturday I spoke to those at Manchester who believed God had cleansed their hearts. They were sixty-three in number, to about sixty of whom I could not find there was any reasonable objection.

96. Many years ago my brother frequently said, 'Your day of Pentecost is not fully come. But I doubt not it will. And you will then hear of persons sanctified as frequently as you do now of persons justified.' Any unprejudiced person might observe that it was now fully come. And accordingly we did hear of persons sanctified, in London, and most other parts of England, and in Dublin, as well as most other parts of Ireland, as frequently as of persons justified—although instances of the latter were far more frequent than they had been for twenty years before. That many of these did not retain the gift of God is no proof that it was not given them. That many do retain it to this day is matter of praise and thanksgiving. And many of them are gone to him whom they loved, praising him with their latest breath—just in the spirit of Ann Steed, the first witness in Bristol of the great salvation, who, being worn out with sickness and racking pain, after she had commended to God all that were round her, lifted up her eyes, cried aloud, 'Glory! Hallelujah!' and died.[54]

97. Monday, December 6th, I heard George Bell[55] pray at the Foundery. I believe part of what he said was from God, part from a heated imagination. But as he did not speak anything dangerously wrong I did not yet see cause to hinder him. Many of our brethren were now taking much pains to propagate that principle, 'that none can teach those who are renewed in love unless he be in that state himself'. I saw the tendency of this, but I durst take no violent step. I mentioned this to some of my friends, and told them what would be the consequence. But they could not believe it. So I let it rest, only desiring them to remember I had told them before.[p]

Sunday 26th. That I might do nothing hastily, I permitted George Bell to be once more at West Street Chapel, and once more (on Wednesday evening) at the Foundery. But it was worse and worse. He now spoke as from God what I knew God had not

[p] [Ibid.,] pp. 211-12 [JWJ, Dec. 6-13, 1762].

[54] See JWJ, Oct. 28, 1762.

[55] Cf. *A Short History of Methodism*, §14 (p. 371 above).

spoken. I therefore desired he would pray there no more. I well hoped this would repress the impetuosity of a few good but mistaken men; especially considering the case of Benjamin Harris, the most impetuous of them all. A week or two before, as he was working in his garden, he was struck raving mad. He continued so till Tuesday, December 21st, when he lay still and sensible, but could not speak, till on Wednesday morning his spirit returned to God. I now stood and looked back on the past year, a year of uncommon trials and uncommon blessings. Abundance have been convinced of sin. Very many have found peace with God. And in London only I believe full two hundred have been brought into glorious liberty. And yet I have had more care and trouble in six months than in several years preceding.

98. Friday, January 7th, 1763, I desired George Bell to meet me, and took much pains to convince him of his mistakes, particularly that which he had lately adopted, that the end of the world was to be on February the 28th. But I could make no impression upon him. He was as unmoved as a rock.

Sunday 23rd, in order to check a growing evil, I preached on, 'Judge not, that ye be not judged.'[56] But it had quite the contrary effect on many, who construed it all into a satire on George Bell, one of whose friends said, 'If the devil himself had been in the pulpit he would not have preached *such a sermon*!' All this time I had information from all quarters that there would soon be a division in the society. But I was still in hopes that by bearing all things I should overcome evil with good;[57] till on Tuesday evening the 15th Mrs. Coventry came in, and threw down her ticket, with those of her husband, daughters, and servants, saying they would 'hear such doctrines no longer. Mr. ——— preached perfection; but Mr. Wesley pulled it down.' So I did—the perfection of George Bell, and all that abetted him. So the breach is made, the water is let out. Let those who can gather it up. More and more persons threw up their tickets every day. And all these were zealous to gain converts to their party, chiefly by speaking all manner of evil, whereby many that did not join *them*, left us. So in a few months above two hundred members left the society.

99. Monday, February 22nd, observing the terror occasioned by that wonderful prophecy to spread far and wide, I endeavoured

[56] Matt. 7:1.
[57] Rom. 12:21.

to draw some good therefrom by enforcing those words at Wapping, 'Seek ye the Lord while he may be found: Call upon him while he is near'[58]—but declaring at the same time (as I had frequently done before), 'It *must* be false, if the Bible is true.' The next three days I spent in transcribing the names of the society. I found about thirty of those who were saved from sin had left us. But above four hundred of those that witnessed the same confession were more united than ever. Monday the 28th, preaching in the evening at Spitalfields, on 'Prepare to meet thy God',[59] I largely showed the utter absurdity of the supposition that the world was to end that night. But notwithstanding all I could say, many were afraid to go to bed; and some wandered about in the fields, being persuaded that if the world did not end, at least London would be swallowed up by an earthquake. I went to bed at my usual time, and was fast asleep at ten o'clock.

The greatest part of this spring I was fully employed in visiting the society, and settling the minds of those who had been confused and distressed by a thousand misrepresentations. Indeed a flood of calumny and evil-speaking (as was easily foreseen) had been poured out on every side. My point was still to go straight forward in the work whereto I am called.

100. I did not leave London till the 16th of May.[q] After spending a few days in Scotland, I returned through Newcastle to Barnard Castle, in the county of Durham, and preached there to an exceeding numerous and deeply serious congregation. I intended after preaching to meet the society, but the bulk of the people were so eager to hear more that I could not forbear letting in near as many as the room would contain. Thursday, June 6th, even at five in the morning, I was obliged to preach abroad by the numbers that flocked to hear. There is something remarkable in the manner wherein God revived his work in this place. A few months ago the generality of the people in this circuit were exceeding lifeless. Samuel Meggot (now with God)[60] perceiving this, advised the society in Barnard Castle to observe every Friday as a day of fasting and prayer. The very first Friday they met together God broke in upon them in a marvellous manner.

[q] [Ibid.,] pp. 228-29 [JWJ, May 16–June 6, 1763].

---

[58] Isa. 55:6.

[59] Amos 4:12.

[60] Wesley's preacher, stationed in the Dales, died in 1764. JWJ, 1762–65, was not published until 1768.

And his work has been increasing among them ever since. The neighbouring societies heard of this, agreed to follow the same rule, and soon experienced the same blessing. Is not the neglect of this plain duty (I mean fasting, ranked by our Lord with thanksgiving and prayer) one general occasion of deadness among Christians? Can anyone willingly neglect it and be guiltless?

101. I had desired Samuel Meggot to give me some further account of the work of God at Barnard Castle. Part of his answer was as follows:

June 7, 1763

Within ten weeks at least twenty persons have found peace with God, and twenty-eight the great salvation. This morning before you left us one found peace, and one the second blessing; and after you was gone two more received it. One of these had belonged to the society before, but after he turned back had bitterly persecuted his wife, particularly after she professed the being saved from sin. On the 29th of May he came in a furious rage to drag her out of the society. One cried out, 'Let us go to prayer for him.' Presently he ran away, and his wife went home. Not long after he came in like a madman, and swore he would be the death of her. One said, 'Are you not afraid lest God should smite you?' He answered, 'No. Let God do his worst, I will make an end of her and the brats, and myself too, and we will go to hell together.' His wife and children fell down and broke out into prayer. His countenance changed, and he was quiet as a lamb. But it was not long before a horrible dread overwhelmed him—he was sore distressed. The hand of God was upon him, and gave him no rest day or night. On Tuesday in the afternoon he went to her who prayed for him when he came to drag his wife out, begging her, with a shower of tears, to pray for his deliverance. On Thursday he wrestled with God till he was as wet all over with sweat as if he had been dipped in water. But that evening God wiped away his tears, and filled him with joy unspeakable. This morning while he was at prayer God gave him a witness in himself that he had purified his heart. When he rose from his knees he could not help declaring it. He now ran to his wife, not to kill her, but to catch her in his arms, that they might weep over one another with tears of joy and love.

102. Wednesday, October 12th, I went to Norwich, resolved either to mend or end the society.[r] On Friday I read the *Rules* of our society to the congregation, adding: 'Those who will keep these rules, and these only, may continue with us. For many years I have had more trouble with this society than with half the societies in England put together. With God's help I will try you one year longer, and if you bring any better fruit I shall rejoice.' The Sunday following I met the society for the first time

[r] [Ibid.,] p. 261 [JWJ, Oct. 12, 1763].

immediately after morning preaching. Afterwards I went to church with a considerable number of the people, several of whom I suppose had not been within those walls for many years. In the evening God made bare his arm,[61] and his word was sharp as any two-edged sword.[62] And from this time I had more and more proof that our labour at Norwich had not been in vain.

103. Friday, November 18th, I finished the visitation of the classes in London. Here I stood and looked back on the late occurrences. Before Mr. Walsh left England, God began that great work which has continued ever since without any considerable intermission. During the whole time, many have been convinced of sin, many justified, and many backsliders healed. But the peculiar work of this season has been what St. Paul calls 'the perfecting of the saints'.[63] Many persons in London, Bristol, York, and in various parts both of England and Ireland, have experienced so deep and universal a change as it had not before entered into their hearts to conceive. After a deep conviction of inbred sin, they have been in an instant filled with faith and love; sin vanished, and they found from that time no pride, anger, desire, or unbelief. They could 'rejoice evermore, pray without ceasing, and in everything give thanks'.[64] Now whether we call this the *destruction of sin* or not, it was a glorious work of God—such a work as, considering both the depth and extent of it, we never saw in these kingdoms before. 'Tis possible some who spoke of this were mistaken, and 'tis certain some have lost what they then received. A few (very few compared to the whole number) first gave way to enthusiasm, then to pride; next to prejudice and offence; and at last separated from their brethren. But although this laid a huge stumbling-block in the way, yet the work of God went on. Nor has it ceased to this day in any of its branches. God still convinces, justifies, sanctifies. We lost only the dross, the enthusiasm, the prejudice, and offence. The pure gold remained, 'faith working by love':[65] yea, and increased daily.[s]

104. Friday, March 30, 1764, I met those in Sheffield who believed God had 'redeemed them from all their sins'.[66] They were about sixty in number, I could not learn that any among

[s] [Ibid.,] pp. 269-70 [JWJ, Nov. 18, 1763].

---

[61] See Isa. 52:10.
[62] See Heb. 4:12.
[63] Eph. 4:12.
[64] 1 Thess. 5:16-18.
[65] Cf. Gal. 5:6.
[66] Cf. Titus 2:14.

them walked unworthy of their profession.[67] Many watched over them for evil: but they overcame evil with good.[68] I found nothing of self-conceit, stubbornness, impatience of contradiction, or enthusiasm among them. They had learned better of him that was meek and lowly of heart,[69] and 'adorned the doctrine of God our Saviour'.[70]

105. Friday, June 8th, having visited the southern parts of Scotland, I set out for Inverness, but I could not reach it till eight on Sunday morning. It rained much, so that I could not preach abroad; and as I knew no one in the town, and could hear of no convenient room, I knew not which way to turn. At ten I went to the high kirk. After service Mr. Fraser, one of the ministers, invited me to dinner, and then to drink tea. As we were drinking tea he asked at what hour I would please to preach. I said, 'At half hour past five.' The kirk was filled in a very short time; and I have seldom found greater liberty of spirit. The other minister came afterwards to our inn, and showed the most cordial affection. I preached in the morning once more, and I think the kirk was fuller than before. And I could [not][71] but observe the remarkable behaviour of the whole congregation after service. Neither man, woman, nor child spoke one word all the way down the main street! About eleven we took horse. While we were dining at Nairn the innkeeper said, 'Sir, the gentlemen of the town have read the little book you gave me on Saturday, and would be glad if you would please to give them a sermon.' On my consenting, the bell was immediately rung, and a large congregation assembled. What a difference is there between South and North Britain! Everyone here at least loves to *hear* the word of God. And none takes it into his head to speak one uncivil word to any for endeavouring to save his soul.[t] Not long after a little society was formed at Inverness, which continues to this day.

106. All this, as well as the preceding year, there was a remarkable increase in most of our societies, both in England and in Ireland. I crossed over from Scotland to the north of Ireland in the beginning of May, and having traversed Ulster and Connaught, on Wednesday, June 19th, reached Cork.[u] On the

[t] [Ibid.,] pp. 311-13 [JWJ, June 8-11, 1764].
[u] [*Works*,] Vol. 32, p. 12 [JWJ, June 19-25, 1765].

[67] See Eph. 4:1.
[68] See Rom. 12:21.
[69] See Matt. 11:29.
[70] Titus 2:10.
[71] Present in JWJ.

Monday and Tuesday following I spoke, one by one, to the members of the society. They were two hundred and ninety-five, fifty or sixty more than they had been for several years. This was owing partly to the preaching abroad, and partly to the meetings for prayer in several parts of the city. These had been the means of awakening many gross sinners, of recovering many backsliders, and bringing many that never thought of it before to attend the preaching at the new room. After visiting the intermediate societies, on Thursday, July 18th, I reached Dublin, and having spent a little time very comfortably there, in the beginning of August returned to England.

107. Sunday 8th, having heard a strange account, as soon as I came to Redruth I sent for the person herself, Grace Paddy, a sensible young woman. I can speak of her now without restraint, as she is safe in Abraham's bosom. She said:

> I was harmless, as I thought, but quite careless about religion, till about Christmas, when my brother was saying, 'God has given me all I want. I am as happy as I can live.' This was about ten in the morning. The words struck me to the heart. I went into my chamber and thought, Why am not I so? O, I cannot be, because I am not convinced of sin. I cried out vehemently, 'Lord, lay as much conviction upon me as my body can bear.' Immediately I saw myself in such a light that I roared for the disquietness of my heart. The maid running up, I said, 'Call my brother.' He came, and rejoiced over me, and said, 'Christ is just ready to receive you; only believe'; and then went to prayer. In a short time all my trouble was gone, and I did believe. All my sins were blotted out. But in the morning I was thoroughly convinced of the want of a deeper change. I felt the remains of sin in my heart, which I longed to have taken away. I longed to be saved from all sin, to be cleansed from all unrighteousness. And all the time Mr. Rankin was preaching this desire increased exceedingly. Afterwards he met the society. During his last prayer I was quite overwhelmed with the power of God. I felt an inexpressible change, in the very depth of my heart. And from that time I have felt no anger, no pride, no wrong temper of any kind, nothing contrary to the pure love of God, which I feel continually. I desire nothing but Christ: and I have Christ always reigning in my heart. I want nothing. He is my sufficient portion, in time and in eternity.

Such an instance I never knew before: such an instance I never read! A person convinced of sin, converted to God, and renewed in love, within twelve hours! Yet it is by no means incredible, seeing one day is with God as a thousand years.[v]

108. Sunday, November 24th, I preached in London, on those

[v] [Ibid.,] pp. 26-28 [JWJ, Sept. 8, 1765].

words in the lesson for the day, 'The Lord is our righteousness.'[72] I said not one thing which I have not said at least fifty times within this twelvemonth. Yet it appeared to many entirely new, who much importuned me to print my sermon, supposing it would stop the mouths of all gainsayers. Alas for their simplicity! In spite of all I can print, say, or do, will not those who *seek* occasion, *find* occasion?[w]

109. I went into Ireland again, in the latter end of March 1767.[73] It was my desire to know the real state of the work of God throughout that kingdom. And the sum of my observations was (after visiting every part of it): There is a considerable increase of the work of God, throughout the province of Ulster. There is some increase in Connaught, particularly in Sligo, Castlebar, and Galway. In some parts of Leinster there is an increase. But in Munster, a land flowing with milk and honey, how amazing a change is there for the worse within a year or two. At some places the god of this world has wholly prevailed, and those who were changed are returned as a dog to his vomit;[74] in others there is but a spark of the first love left. And in Limerick itself I found only the remembrance of the fire which was kindled two years ago![x]

110. In Cork society I left two years before above three hundred members. I now found one hundred and eighty-seven. What occasioned so considerable a decrease? I believe the real cause was this. Between two and three years ago T. Taylor and W. Penington went to Cork, who were zealous men and sound preachers. They set up meetings for prayer in several places, and preached abroad at both ends of the city. Hearers swiftly increased. The society increased; so did the number both of the convinced and the converted. I went when the flame was at the height, and preached abroad at both ends of the city. More and more were stirred up, and there was a greater awakening here than in any part of the kingdom. But misunderstandings crept in between the leaders, and between some of them and the preachers. A flame of anger succeeded the flame of love, and

[w] [Ibid.,] p. 34 [JWJ, Nov. 24, 1765].
[x] [Ibid.,] p. 104 [i.e., p. 105, i.e., JWJ, May 9, 1767].

---

[72] Sermon 20, 'The Lord Our Righteousness', on Jer. 23:6, was published early the following year. (See *Bibliography*, No. 295, and 1:444-65 in this edn.)
[73] Orig., '1762'.
[74] See 2 Pet. 2:22.

many were destroyed by it. Then some of our brethren learnt a new opinion, and passionately contended for it. The Spirit of God was grieved, his blessing was withheld, and of course the flock was scattered. When they are convinced of their sin, and humbled before him, then he will return.

111. In the latter end of April 1768, there was a remarkable work among the children at Kingswood School. One of the masters sent me a short account as follows:[y]

April 27, 1768

Rev. and dear sir,

On Wednesday the 20th God broke in upon our boys in a surprising manner. A serious concern has been observable in some of them for some time past. But that night, while they were in their private apartments, the power of God came upon them, even as a mighty rushing wind, which made them cry aloud for mercy. Last night, I hope, will never be forgotten, when about twenty were in the utmost distress. But God quickly spoke peace to two of them, J. Glascot and T. M[aurice]. A greater display of his love I never saw; they indeed rejoice with joy unspeakable. We have no need to exhort them to prayer, for the spirit of prayer runs through the whole school. While I am writing the cries of the boys from their several apartments are sounding in my ears. There are many still lying at the pool, who wait every moment to be put in. They are come to this: 'Lord, I will not, I cannot rest without thy love.' Since I began to write, eight more are set at liberty, and rejoice in God their Saviour, viz., John Coward, John Lyon,[75] John Maddern, John Boddily, John Thurgar, Charles Brown, William Higham, and Robert Hindmarsh. Their age is from eight to fourteen. There are but few that withstand the work, nor is it likely they should do it long. For the prayers of those that believe seem to carry all before them. Among the colliers likewise the work of God now increases greatly. The number added to the society since the conference is a hundred and thirty.

I had sealed my letter, but have opened it to inform you that two more of our children have found peace. Several others are under deep conviction. Some of our Bristol friends are here, who are thunderstruck. This is the day we have wished for so long, the day you have had in view, which has made you go through so much opposition for the good of these poor children.

James Hindmarsh

112. A few days after one wrote thus: 'I cannot help congratulating you on the happy situation of your family here. The power of God continues to work, with almost irresistible force; and there is good reason to hope, it will not be withdrawn till every soul is converted to God. I have had frequent opportunities of conversing alone with the boys, and find that the

[y] [Ibid.,] p. 174 [JWJ, May 5, 1768].

---

[75] Orig., 'Lion'.

work has taken deep root in many hearts. The house rings with prayer and praise, and the whole behaviour of the children strongly speaks for God. The number of the newborn is increased since you received your last information. I have been a witness of part; but the whole exceeds all that language can paint.' Another writes, May 18th: 'The work of God still goes on at Kingswood. Of the hundred and thirty members that have been added to the society since the last conference, the greater part have received justifying faith, and are still rejoicing in God their Saviour. And (what is the most remarkable) I do not know of one backslider in the place. The outpouring of the Spirit on the children in the school has not been exceeding great. I believe, there is not one among them who has not been affected more or less. Twelve of them have found peace with God, and some in a very remarkable manner. These have no more doubt of the favour of God than of their own existence. And the Lord is still with them, though not so powerfully as he was some weeks ago.' Indeed I cannot doubt but at first he wrought irresistibly, at least on some of them; but afterwards they might resist the grace of God, which several of them did, till they had wellnigh quenched his Spirit.[76] I fear some of them have done it altogether. 'Tis well if their last state be not worse than the first.[77]

113. Tuesday, August 1, 1769, our conference began at Leeds. On Thursday I mentioned the case of our brethren at New York. For some years past several of our brethren from England and Ireland (and some of them preachers) had settled in North America, and had in various places formed societies, particularly in Philadelphia and New York. The society at New York had lately built a commodious preaching-house, and now desired our help, being in great want of money, but much more of preachers. Two of our preachers, Richard Boardman and Joseph Pilmore,[78] willingly offered themselves for the service, by whom we determined to send over fifty pounds, as a token of our brotherly love.[z] Several others of our preachers went over in the following years. As they taught the same doctrine with their brethren here, so they used the same discipline. And the work of

[z] [Ibid.,] p. 266 [JWJ, Aug. 3, 1769].

[76] See 1 Thess. 5:19.
[77] See Matt. 12:45.
[78] Orig., 'Pillmoor'.

God prospered in their hands; so that a little before the Rebellion broke out about two and twenty preachers (most of them Americans) acted in concert with each other, and near three thousand persons were united together in the American societies. These were chiefly in the provinces of Maryland, Virginia, Pennsylvania, and New York.

114. June 17, 1770, I met the Select Society in Whitby, consisting of sixty-five members. I believe all of these were saved from sin, and most of them still walked in glorious liberty. Many of them spoke with admirable simplicity; and their word was like fire. Immediately the fire kindled, and spread from heart to heart. At nine I met the children, most of whom *had* known the love of God. And several of them were able still to rejoice in God their Saviour.[79] Almost as soon as I began to speak, God spoke to their hearts, and they were ill able to contain themselves. I observed one little maid in particular, who heaved and strove for some time, till at length she was constrained to yield, and broke out into strong cries and tears. In the evening I met those children only who had tasted that the Lord is gracious.[80] I asked her that cried so violently in the morning what was the reason of it. She said, 'I was so overwhelmed with the power and love of God that I could not hide it. A quarter of a year ago, one Saturday night, I was quite convinced I was a sinner, and afraid of dropping into hell; but on Sunday I felt the pardoning love of God. Yet I had many doubts till Monday evening, when they were all taken away in a moment. After this I saw and felt the wickedness of my heart, and longed to be delivered from it. And on Sunday I was delivered, and had as clear a witness of this as of my justification. But I was some time off my watch; then it was not so clear. And people commended me, till by little and little I lost it. Indeed I still feel the love of God—but not as I did then.'[a]

115. Saturday, Sept. 15th, I observed a very uncommon concern in the children at Kingswood School, while I was explaining and enforcing upon them the first principles of religion.[b] Tuesday 18th, most of them went to see the body of

[a] [Ibid.,] pp. 312-14 [JWJ, June 17, 1770].

[b] Journal 16, p. 4 [i.e., JWJ, Sept. 2, 1770–Sept. 12, 1773, which was published in 1777. Journal 15 was the last to appear in the *Works*, 1771–74. The lengthy extracts depicting the religious revival among the children of Kingswood School cover pp. 4-9 of the original *Journal*, Sept. 15-30, and §§115-20 of 'A Short History'].

[79] See Luke 1:47.

[80] 1 Pet. 2:3.

Francis Evans, one of our neighbours, who died two or three days before. About seven Mr. Hindmarsh met them all in the school, and gave an exhortation suited to the occasion. It was with great difficulty they contained themselves till he began to pray. Then Alexander Mather, and Richard N[oble] cried aloud for mercy; and quickly another and another, till all but two or three were constrained to do the same. And as long as he continued to pray they continued the same loud and bitter cry. One of the maids, Elizabeth Nutt, was as deeply convinced as any of them. After prayer Mr. Hindmarsh said, 'Those of you that are resolved to serve God may go and pray together.' Fifteen of them did so, and continued wrestling with God, with strong cries and tears, till nine o'clock.

116. Wednesday 19th, at the morning prayer, many of them cried out again, though not so violently. From this time their whole spirit and behaviour were changed: they were all serious and loving to each other. The same seriousness and mildness continued on Thursday, and they walked together, talking only of the things of God. On Friday evening their concern greatly increased, so that they broke out again into strong cries. And they seemed to lose none of their concern, and spent all their spare time in prayer.

Sunday 23rd, fifteen of them gave me their names, 'being resolved', they said, 'to serve God'. On Tuesday, during the time of prayer in the evening, they were affected just as the Tuesday before. The two other maids were then present, and were both cut to the heart.

117. Wednesday 26th, 'I rode', says Mr. Rankin,

> to Kingswood, and going upstairs, heard one of the children praying in the next room. When he ceased I went in, and found two others with him. Just then three more came in. I went to prayer. The power of God seemed to rest upon them, and pierced their hearts with deep conviction. The next morning I spent some time with all the children, and then desired those that were resolved to save their souls to come upstairs. Nine of them did so. While I prayed the power of God came down, so that my voice was drowned by their cries. When I concluded, one of them broke out into prayer, in a manner that quite astonished me. And during the whole day a peculiar spirit of seriousness rested on all the children.

118. On Friday 28th, says Mr. Hindmarsh,

> when I came out into the ground, ten of the children quickly gathered round about me, earnestly asking what they must do to be saved. Nor could I disengage myself from them till the bell rung for dinner. All this time we observed that the

children who were most affected learned faster and better than any of the rest. In the evening I explained to them the nature of the Lord's Supper. I then met twelve of them apart, and spoke to each particularly. When I asked one of them (Simon Lloyd), 'What do you want, to make you happy?', after a little pause, he answered 'God.' We went to prayer. Presently a cry arose from one and another, till it went through all, vehemently calling upon God, and refusing to be comforted without the knowledge and love of God. About half an hour after eight I bade them good night, and sent them up to bed. But Lloyd, Brown, and Robert Hindmarsh slipped aside, being resolved not to sleep till God revealed himself to them. Some of the rest heard them pray, and one and another stole down, some half dressed, some almost naked. They continued praying by turns, near three-quarters of an hour, in which time four of them found peace with God. After I had prayed with them, and praised God, till half an hour past nine, I desired them to go to bed. The rest did; but those three slipped away, and stayed with Richard Piercy, who was in deep agony of soul, and would by no means be persuaded to rise from his knees. The children, hearing them pray, in a few minutes ran down again. They continued wrestling, with still increasing agonies and tears, till three more found peace with God. About a quarter past ten I went to them again, and insisted upon their going to bed, which all of them did. But quickly one and another stole out of bed, till in a quarter of an hour they were all at prayer again. And the concern among them was deeper than ever, as well as more general; there being only four or five and twenty that were not cut to the heart. However, fearing they might hurt themselves, I sent one of our maids to persuade them to go up. But Jacky Brown, catching hold of her said, 'O Betty, seek the salvation of your soul! Seek it in earnest! It is not too late. And it is not too soon.' Immediately she fell upon her knees, and burst out into tears and strong cries. The two other maids, hearing this, ran in, and were presently seized as violently as her. Jacky Brown then began praying for Betty, and continued in prayer near three quarters of an hour. By that time there was a general cry from all the maids and all the boys. This continued till past eleven. We then, with much difficulty, persuaded them to go to bed. The maids continued below in much distress. But in a quarter of an hour Betty broke out into thanksgiving. The other two remained on their knees, praying as in an agony. I desired them to go into their own room. Yet they would not go to bed, but continued in prayer!

119. On Saturday I was waked between four and five by the children, vehemently crying to God. The maids went to them at five. And first one of the boys, then another, then one and another of the maids, poured out their souls before God. They continued weeping and praying till near nine o'clock, not thinking about meat or drink. Nay, Richard Piercy took no food all the day, but remained in words and groans calling upon God. About nine Diana went into her own room and prayed, partly alone, and partly with Betty. About ten (as Betty was praying) she sunk down as dead. But after some minutes, while Betty was praying on, she started up, praising God with all her might.

120. Mary, hearing her, broke off her work, and ran in to her in haste. They all remained praying by turns till twelve, when she lay like one at the point to die. But there was not any answer to prayer, nor any deliverance. About one all the maids and three of the boys went upstairs, and began praying again. And between two and three Mary likewise rejoiced with joy unspeakable. They all

continued till after four, praising the God of *their* salvation. Indeed they seemed to have forgotten all things else, and thought of nothing but God and heaven.

In the evening all the maids, and many of the boys, were so hoarse they were scarce able to speak. But they were strong in the Spirit, full of love, and of joy, and peace in believing.

Sunday 30th, eight of the children, and three maids, received the Lord's Supper for the first time. And hitherto they are all rejoicing in God, and walking worthy of the gospel.

121. Thursday, Jan. 16, 1772, I set out for Luton. Here I was offered the use of the church. The frost was exceeding sharp, and the glass was taken out of the windows. However, for the sake of the people I accepted the offer, though I might as well have preached in the open air. There were four or five times as many people as used to come to the room. So I did not repent of my labour. It was with great difficulty that we got through the deep snow to Hertford the next day, and I found the poor children whom Mr. A[ndrews] kept at school were increased to about thirty boys and thirty girls. I went in immediately to the girls. Almost as soon as I began to speak some of them burst into tears, and their emotion rose higher and higher. But it was kept within bounds till I began to pray. A cry then arose, which spread from one to another, till almost all cried aloud for mercy, and would not be comforted. But how was the scene changed when I went to the boys! They seemed as dead as stones, and scarce appeared to mind anything that was said. Nay, some of them could ill refrain from laughing. However, I spoke on, and set before them the terrors of the Lord. Presently one was cut to the heart; soon after, another and another; and in ten minutes the far greater part of them were little less affected than the girls. Except at Kingswood, I have seen no such work of God upon children for above thirty years.

122. Wednesday, June 3rd, I desired to speak with those in Weardale[81] (a valley in the county of Durham) who believed God had saved them from inward sin.[c] They were twenty in all: ten men, eight women, and two children. Of one man and two women I stood in doubt. The experience of the rest was clear, particularly that of the children, Margaret Sp[enser], aged fourteen, and Sally Bl[ackburn], a year younger. Lord, let neither of these live

[c] [Ibid.,] p. 466.

---

[81] Orig., throughout this section, 'Wardale'.

to dishonour thee! Rather take them unspotted to thyself!

In this part of Weardale the people in general are employed in the lead-mines. In the year 1749 Mr. Hopper and John Brown came and preached among them. None opposed, and none asked them to eat or drink. Nevertheless, Mr. Hopper made them several more visits. In autumn four found peace with God, and agreed to meet together. At Christmas two young men of Allendale determined to visit Weardale. Before they entered it they kneeled down on the snow, and besought the Lord that he would incline someone to receive them into his house. At the first house where they called they were bid welcome; and they stayed there four days. Many were convinced, and some converted to God. One of the young men was Jacob Rowell. They made them several more visits during the winter. In summer twenty lively people were joined together. From that time they increased gradually to thirty-five, and so continued for ten years. They increased by means of Samuel Meggot to eighty, but four years since sunk to fifty-three. From that time they increased again, and were in August a hundred and twenty.

123. In two respects this society has always been peculiarly remarkable: the one, they have been liberal in providing everything needful for the preachers; the other, they have been careful to marry with each other, and that not for the sake of money, but virtue. Hence they assisted each other in bringing up their children; and God has eminently blessed them therein. For in most of their families the greatest part of their children above ten years old are converted to God. It was observed, too, that the leaders were upright men, and truly alive to God. And even when they had no preacher with them they met every night for singing and prayer.

124. Last summer the work of God revived and gradually increased till the end of November. Then God made bare his arm.[82] Those who were strangers to God felt as it were a sword in their bones.[83] Those who knew God were filled with joy unspeakable.[84] The convictions that seized the unawakened were generally exceeding deep; so that their cries drowned every other voice, and no other means could be used than the speaking to the distressed one by one, and encouraging them to lay hold on

[82] See Isa. 52:10.
[83] See Ps. 42:10.
[84] 1 Pet. 1:8.

Christ. And this was not in vain. Many that were either on their knees, or prostrate on the ground, suddenly started up, and their very countenance showed that the Comforter was come. Immediately these began to go about from one to another of those that were still in distress, praying to God, and exhorting them without delay to come to so gracious a Savior. Many who then appeared quite unconcerned were thereby cut to the heart, and suddenly filled with such anguish as extorted loud and bitter cries. By such a succession of persons mourning and rejoicing they were frequently detained great part of the night.

125. On Sunday afternoon, Dec. 1st, as William Hunter was preaching (this is the account given by the leader), the power of God fell on the congregation in a wonderful manner. Many, being cut to the heart, cried aloud for mercy, and ten were added to the society. On Tuesday evening we met at six, but could not part till ten. Four found peace with God, and ran from one to another, exhorting them to believe in Christ. On Wednesday night many were deeply distressed, but none set at liberty. While we were meeting on Thursday night two were enabled to rejoice in God their Saviour.[85] On Saturday night we met at six, and three of us sung and prayed. But before the third had done his voice could not be heard for the cries of the people. Seven of these soon arose, blessing and praising God, and went about encouraging others. Many hardened sinners were much affected thereby, and began to cry as loud as they had done; so that we had nothing to do but to stand and see the wonderful work of God.[86] And Oh! how dreadful, yet pleasing was the sight! All this time many were crying for mercy. Among these were four young men who remained on their knees five hours together. We endeavoured to break up the meeting at ten, but the people would not go, so that we were constrained to continue till twelve. Near this time one was asked what he thought of this. He answered, 'I wish it may be all real.' He then turned to go home, but after taking a few steps began to cry aloud for mercy. He cried till his strength was quite gone; and then lay as one dead till about four o'clock in the morning; then God revealed his Son in his heart. During this meeting eleven persons found peace with God.

126. On Sunday morning we met at the common hour, and three of us sung and prayed as usual, till our voice was drowned by the thanksgiving of the new converts, and the cries of convinced sinners. Among the rest an ancient woman was so struck that she vehemently cried out, 'Mercy, mercy! O what a sinner am I! I was the first that received them into my house in Weardale, and have heard them almost these thirty years. O pray for me! Mercy, mercy!' It was not long before she found mercy, and mightily rejoiced in God her Saviour.[87] And about the same time another mourner passed from death unto life.[88]

We met again at two, and abundance of people came from various parts, being alarmed by some confused reports. We sung and prayed; and the power of God

[85] See Luke 1:47.
[86] See 1 Sam. 12:16.
[87] See Luke 1:47.
[88] John 5:24.

descended. A young man who had been deeply wounded in the morning now found One mighty to heal. We then concluded; but many of the people came in again, and others stayed at the door. Among those who came in was one who had been remarkably profligate. He cried for mercy with all his might; several crowded about to see him. And before we parted not only he but five more were rejoicing and praising God together. We met together on Monday, Tuesday, and Wednesday, and by that time nine more found peace.

Mr. Rowell came on Tuesday, stayed three days, and joined many new members. Three and thirty of these had found peace with God, as did five more in the week following. When Mr. Watson came he joined many more, eleven of whom were justified. At our meeting on Tuesday, eleven more were filled with the peace of God. Yet one young man seemed quite unconcerned. But suddenly the power of God fell upon him. He cried for two hours with all his might, and then the Lord set his soul at liberty. On Saturday a few met at Mr. Hunter's room who were athirst for full sanctification. For this they wrestled with God, till a young man found the blessing, as several others have done since. We have ever since continued our meetings, and God has continued his loving-kindness toward us. So that above a hundred and twenty are added to the society, above a hundred of whom are believers.

127. I left John Fenwick on Friday, June 5th, [1772,] to examine the society one by one. This he did on Friday and Saturday. The account of what ensued he gave in the following words:

On Saturday evening God was present through the whole service, but especially towards the conclusion. Then one and another dropped down, till six lay on the ground together, roaring for the disquietude of their hearts. Observing many to be quite amazed at this, I besought them to stand still, and see the salvation of God. But the cry of the distressed soon drowned my voice, so I dismissed the congregation. About half of them went away. I continued to pray with the rest, when my voice could be heard; when it could not I prayed without a voice, till after ten o'clock. In this time four of those poor mourners were clothed with the robes of praise.

The society now consists of a hundred and sixty-five members; of whom there are but twenty that have not found peace with God. Surely such a work of God has not been seen before in any part of the three kingdoms.

Forty-three of these are children, thirty of whom are rejoicing in the love of God. The chief instrument God has used among these is Jane Salkeld, a young woman, a school-mistress, who is a pattern to all that believe. A few of her children are: Phoebe Fetherstone, nine years and a half old, a child of uncommon understanding; Hannah Watson, ten years old, full of faith and love; Aaron Ridson, not eleven years old, but wise and stayed as a man; Sarah Smith, eight years and a half old, but as serious as a woman of fifty. Sarah Morris, fourteen years of age, is as a mother among them, always serious, always watching over the rest, and building them up in love.

Mention was made of four young men who were affected on the second Wednesday in December. These, hearing of the roaring of the people, came out of mere curiosity. That evening six were wounded, and fell to the ground, crying aloud for mercy. One of them hearing the cry, rushed through the crowd, to see what was the matter. He was no sooner got to the place than he dropped down himself, and cried as loud as any. The other three rushing on, one after another, were struck just in the same manner. And indeed all of them were in such agonies that many feared they were struck with death. But all the ten were fully delivered before the meeting concluded, which indeed was not till four in the morning.

128. I waited a few days before I set down what had lately occurred among the children at Kingswood. From the time God visited them last several of them retained a measure of the fear of God. But they grew colder and colder, till Ralph Mather[d] met them in the latter end of August. Several then resolved to meet in class again, and appeared to have good desires. On Saturday, Sept. 4th, he talked with three of them, about four in the afternoon. These freely confessed their besetting sins, and appeared to be greatly humbled. At five all the children met in the school. During an exhortation then given first one, then two or three, were much affected. Afterwards two more were taken apart, who were soon deeply distressed; and one of them (James Whitestone), in less than half an hour found a clear sense of the love of God. Near seven they came down to the boys in the school; and Mr. Mather asked, 'Which of you will serve God?' They all seemed to be thunderstruck, and ten or twelve fell down upon their knees. Mr. Mather prayed, and then James Whitestone. Immediately one and another cried out, which brought in the other boys, who seemed struck more and more, till about thirty were kneeling and praying at once. Before half past nine, ten of them knew that they were accepted in the beloved.[89] Several more were brought to the birth; and all the children but three or four were affected more or less.

Sunday 5th I examined sixteen of them who desired to partake of the Lord's Supper. Nine or ten had a clear sense of the pardoning love of God. The others were fully determined never to rest till they could witness the same confession.

Eighteen of the children from this time met in three bands,

[d] Poor Ralph Mather! What is he now? [*Concise History*, IV.274n. Ralph Mather was admitted as a preacher on trial at the Conference of 1773, but Wesley described him on Jan. 29, 1774, as 'a devoted young man, but almost driven out of his senses by mystick divinity'. He later became a Quaker.]

---

[89] Eph. 1:6.

besides twelve who met in trial bands. These were remarkable for their love to each other, as well as for steady seriousness. They met every day, beside which all the children met in class.

Those who found peace were: James Whitestone, Alexander Mather, Matthew Lowes, William Snowdon, John Keil, Charles Farr, John Hamilton, Benjamin Harris, and Edward Keil.

Monday 6th. After Mr. Mather had preached at Pensford he met the children there. Presently the spirit of conviction fell upon them, and then the spirit of grace and of supplication, till the greater part of them were crying together for mercy, with a loud and bitter cry.[90] And all Miss Owen's children but one (two and twenty in number) were exceedingly comforted.[91]

129. Friday 10th I went over to Kingswood, and inquired into the present state of the children. I found part of them had walked closely with God; part had not, and were in heaviness. Hearing in the evening that they were got to prayer by themselves in the school, I went down; but not being willing to disturb them I stood at the window. Two or three had gone in first; then more and more, till above thirty were gathered together. Such a sight I never saw before, or since. Three or four stood and stared as if affrighted. The rest were all on their knees, pouring out their souls before God, in a manner not easy to be described. Sometimes one, sometimes more, prayed aloud. Sometimes a cry went up from them all, till five or six of them who were in doubts before saw the clear light of God's countenance.

Saturday 12th, four of Miss Owen's children desired leave to partake of the Lord's Supper. I talked with them severally, and found they were all still rejoicing in the love of God. And they confirmed the account, that 'there was only one of their whole number who was unaffected on Monday, but all the rest could then say with confidence, Lord, thou knowest that I love thee.'[92] I suppose such a visitation of children has not been known in

[90] Esther 4:1.

[91] See JWJ, Sept. 3-6, 1773. The children had no doubt come from Publow, a very short distance away. Here Mrs. Owen and her daughters had set up a girls' boarding school, limited to twenty girls, with Wesley's encouragement and support. 'Such mistresses and such a company of children as I believe all England cannot parallel' is Wesley's comment when he visited the school in 1772 (JWJ, Sept. 16). When the Anglican evangelical reformer, Hannah More, set up schools in Cheddar and the neighbouring villages, not far from Publow, in the late 1780s, her first headmistress in Cheddar was a Wesleyan, and Miss More complained that the only people capable of staffing her schools were of the Methodist persuasion. The educational influence of Wesley is apparent.

[92] See above, §128; the closing quotation is from John 21:15-17.

England these hundred years! In so marvellous a manner 'out of the mouths of babes and sucklings, God has perfected praise.'[93]

130. Tuesday, June 13, 1775. I was not very well in the morning, but supposed it would soon go off. In the afternoon, the weather being extremely hot, I lay down on the grass in Mr. Lark's orchard, at Cockhill. This I had been accustomed to do for forty years, and never remember to have been hurt by it. Only I never before lay on my face, in which posture I fell asleep. I waked, a little, and but a little, out of order, and preached with ease to a multitude of people. Afterwards I was a good deal worse. However the next day I went on a few miles to The Grange. The table was placed here in such a manner that all the time I was preaching a strong and sharp wind blew full on the left side of my head. And it was not without a good deal of difficulty that I made an end of my sermon. I now found a deep obstruction in my breast; my pulse was exceeding weak and low. I shivered with cold, though the air was sultry hot, only now and then burning for a few minutes. I went early to bed, drank a draught of treacle and water, and applied treacle to the soles of my feet. I lay till seven on Thursday the 15th, and then felt considerably better. But I found nearly the same obstruction in my breast; I had a low, weak pulse; I burned and shivered by turns, and if I ventured to cough it jarred my head exceedingly. In going to Derryanvil,[94] I wondered what was the matter, that I could not attend to what I was reading; no, not for three minutes together, but my thoughts were perpetually shifting. Yet all the time I was preaching in the evening (although I stood in the open air, with the wind whistling round my head), my mind was as composed as ever. Friday 16th, in going to Lurgan, I was again surprised that I could not fix my attention on what I read. Yet while I was preaching in the evening on the Parade I found my mind perfectly composed, although it rained a great part of the time, which did not well agree with my head. Saturday 17th I was persuaded to send for Dr. Laws, a sensible and skilful physician. He told me I was in a high fever, and advised me to lay by. But I told him that could not be done, as I had appointed to preach at several places, and must preach as long as I could speak. He then prescribed a cooling draught, with a grain or two of camphire, as my nerves were universally agitated.

93 Cf. Matt. 21:16.

94 Orig., 'Derry-Anvill'.

This I took with me to Tandragee; but when I came there I was not able to preach, my understanding being quite confused, and my strength entirely gone. Yet I breathed freely, and had not the least thirst, nor any pain from head to foot.

I was now at a full stand whether to aim at Lisburn or to push forward for Dublin. But my friends doubting whether I could bear so long a journey, I went straight to Derryaghy, a gentleman's seat on the side of a hill, three miles beyond Lisburn. Here nature sunk, and I took my bed, but I could no more turn myself therein than a new-born child. My memory failed as well as my strength, and wellnigh my understanding. Only those words ran in my mind when I saw Miss Gayer on one side of the bed, looking at her mother on the other:

> She sat like patience on a monument
> Smiling at grief.[95]

But still I had no thirst, no difficulty of breathing, no pain from head to foot.

I can give no account of what followed for two or three days, being more dead than alive. Only I remember it was difficult for me to speak, my throat being exceeding dry. But Joseph Bradford tells me, I said on Wednesday, 'It will be determined before this time tomorrow'; that my tongue was much swollen, and as black as a coal; that I was convulsed all over, and that for some time my heart did not beat perceptibly, neither was there any pulse discernible.

In the night of Thursday 22nd Joseph Bradford came to me with a cup and said, 'Sir, you must take this.' I thought, 'I will, if I can swallow, to please him; for it will do me neither harm nor good.' Immediately it set me a vomiting; my heart began to beat, and my pulse to play again. And from that hour the extremity of the symptoms abated. The next day I sat up several hours, and walked four or five times across the room. On Saturday I sat up all day, and walked across the room many times without any weariness. On Sunday I came downstairs, and sat several hours in the parlour. On Monday I walked out before the house; on Tuesday I took an airing in the chaise; and on Wednesday, trusting in God, to the astonishment of my friends, I set out for Dublin.

[95] Shakespeare, *Twelfth Night,* II.iv.117-18.

I did not determine how far to go that day, not knowing how my strength would hold out. But finding myself no worse at Banbridge, I ventured on to Newry. And after travelling thirty (English) miles, I was stronger than in the morning.

Thursday 29th I went to The Man of War, forty (Irish) miles from the Globe at Newry.

Friday 30th we met Mr. Simpson (with several other friends), coming to meet us at Drogheda, who took us to his country seat at Jamestown, about two miles from Dublin.

Tuesday, July 4th, finding myself a little stronger, I preached for the first time; and I believe most could hear. I preached on Wednesday again, and my voice was clear, though weak. So on Sunday I ventured to preach twice, and found no weariness at all. Monday 10th I began my regular course of preaching morning and evening.

131. From this time I have by the grace of God gone on, in the same track, travelling between four and five thousand miles a year, and once in two years going through Great Britain and Ireland, which, by the blessing of God, I am as well able to do now as I was twenty or thirty years ago. About a hundred and thirty of my fellow-labourers are continually employed in the same thing. We all aim at one point (as we did from the hour when we first engaged in the work): not at profit, any more than at ease, or pleasure, or the praise of men; but to spread true religion through London, Dublin, Edinburgh, and, as we are able, through the three kingdoms; that truly rational religion which is taught and prescribed in the Old and New Testament; namely, the love of God and our neighbour, filling the heart with humility, meekness, contentedness; and teaching us on the one hand, whatever we do, to do it all to the glory of God;[96] and on the other, to do unto every man what we would they should do unto us.[97] This is our point. We leave every man to enjoy his own opinion, and to use his own mode of worship, desiring only that the love of God and his neighbour be the ruling principle in his heart, and show itself in his life by an uniform practice of justice, mercy, and truth.[98] And accordingly we give the right hand of fellowship[99] to every lover of God and man, whatever his opinion or mode of worship be; of which he is to give an account to God only.

[96] See 1 Cor. 10:31.

[97] See Matt. 7:12.

[98] See Ps. 89:14.

[99] Cf. above, *The Character of a Methodist,* §18, and parallels noted.

132. This is 'the way' (called 'heresy' by Dr. Maclaine[1] and others) 'according to which we worship the God of our fathers'.[2] And we have known some thousands who walked therein, till their spirits returned to God.[3] Some thousands likewise we now know who are walking in the same path of love, and studying to have a conscience void of offence towards God and towards man.[4] All these, as they fear God, so they honour the King,[5] who 'is the minister of God unto them for good'.[6] They submit themselves to every ordinance of man, for the Lord's sake.[7] Meantime they expect that men should 'say all manner of evil against them, for' their Master's 'sake'.[8] But they have counted the cost, and are willing to be'as the filth and offscouring of the world'.[9] Yea, they have many times shown that they 'counted not their lives dear unto themselves, so they might finish their course with joy, and testify the gospel of the grace of God'.[10]

London, November 16, 1781

[1] Orig., 'M'Lean'; see §1, n. 3 above.
[2] Cf. Acts 24:14.
[3] See Eccles. 12:7.
[4] See Acts 24:16.
[5] 1 Pet. 2:17.
[6] Rom. 13:4.
[7] 1 Pet. 2:13.
[8] Matt. 5:11.
[9] Cf. 1 Cor. 4:13.
[10] Cf. Acts 20:24.

24–27

METHODIST PREACHING-HOUSES

AN INTRODUCTORY COMMENT

In these writings John Wesley deals with problems and conflicts that arose from the powers given to trustees when Methodist preaching-houses were built. The development of legal processes in this matter is described in the Introduction to this volume, pp. 17-20.

The cases of the preaching-houses in Birstall and Dewsbury were exceptionally awkward. In Birstall, John Nelson had innocently agreed in 1751 to a deed of trust 'in the Presbyterian form', according to which the trustees had power to 'place and displace' the preachers; this had been Wesley's original plan for the New Room in Bristol, but he had quickly changed it. When a new and larger house was needed in Birstall in 1782, Wesley was unable to prevent the deed from being in the same form as the old; and consequently brought the matter before the Conference.

Wesley hoped that the Deed of Declaration of 1784, establishing the Conference as a legal entity which was entitled to own property and to station the preachers, would solve such problems once and for all. But in Dewsbury a year or two later a deed of trust was drawn up giving the trustees powers over the preachers which Wesley thought intolerable, and in consequence the Conference agreed to build another preaching-house nearby on an acceptable deed.

Wesley was entirely convinced that the powers which the trustees of Birstall and Dewsbury wished to hold represented a threat to the future of Methodism, and to the itinerancy in particular.

24

The Case of Birstall House[1]

(1783)

[I]. 1. As many persons have spoke much upon this subject, without well understanding it, I believe it is my duty to throw all the light upon it that I can. And in order to this, I will,

First, endeavour to state the case;

Secondly, argue a little upon it.

2. In order to state the case fully I must look back to ancient times. As soon as the heat of persecution was over, and Christians increased in goods, some built preaching-houses, afterwards called churches. In following times those that built them were termed *patrons,*[2] and appointed whom they pleased to preach in them. And when they annexed lands to them, they disposed of houses and lands together.

3. At the Reformation many rich men built new churches, and disposed of them at their pleasure. And when many Presbyterians and Independents in England built preaching-houses, they placed in them whom they pleased; which power they *entrusted* when they died, to a few friends they could confide in.[3]

4. I built the first Methodist preaching-house so called at Bristol, in the year 1739. And knowing no better, I suffered the

[1] Wesley used the spelling 'Birstal', but in accordance with present-day practice, in this edn., the spelling used is 'Birstall'.

The Case of Birstall House was first issued as a folio printed letter, at the foot of which was printed, 'London, 178—', leaving blanks for Wesley to sign and fill in the current date. The surviving copy, at Duke University, is dated Jan. 3, 1783, and addressed on the blank cover 'To Mr. Thompson at the Methodist Chapel in Hull' (see *Bibliography,* No. 430). The document seems to have been based substantially on Wesley's letter to Joseph Benson of Nov. 29, 1782, of which a copy in the hand of an amanuensis but signed by Wesley is extant in Victoria University, Toronto. Wesley's trustees continued to represent a threat, as he believed, to the future of Methodism, and seven years later he reprinted the *Case* in the *Arminian Magazine* (1788), XI.148-59, 205-8, adding the sub-heading: 'Recommended to the serious consideration of the People called Methodists'.

[2] Orig., *'Pastors'*. In the margin of the broadsheet someone has written, 'Should it not be *Patrons?*' and in Wesley's own copy of the 1788 *Arminian Magazine* he did in fact alter the word to 'patrons'; cf. [II.]4.

[3] 1788, 'which power they left to their heirs'. The italicizing of 'entrusted' is apparently a reference to the legal nature of this appointment.

Deed of Trust to be drawn up in the Presbyterian form. But Mr. Whitefield hearing of it, wrote me a warm letter, asking, 'Do you consider what you do? If the trustees are to *name* the preachers, they may exclude even *you* from preaching in the house you have built. Pray let this deed be immediately cancelled.'[4] To this the trustees readily agreed. Afterwards I built the preaching-houses in Kingswood, and at Newcastle upon Tyne. But none beside myself had any right to appoint the preachers in them.[5]

5. About this time a preaching-house was built at Birstall, by contributions and collections. And John Nelson, knowing no better, suffered a deed to be drawn in the Presbyterian form, giving twelve or thirteen persons power not only of *placing,* but even of *displacing* the preachers *at their pleasure.*[6] Had Mr. Whitefield or I known this, we should have insisted on its either being cancelled, like that at Bristol, or so altered as to insure the application of the house to the purpose for which it was built, without giving so dangerous a power to any trustees whatever.

6. But a considerable difficulty still remained. As the houses at Bristol, Kingswood, and Newcastle were *my* property, a friend reminded me that they were all liable to descend to my heirs. (Pray let those consider this who are so fond of having preaching-houses vested in them and *their heirs* for ever!) I was struck, and immediately procured a form to be drawn up by three of the most eminent counsellors in London, whereby not only these houses, but all the Methodist houses hereafter to be built, might be settled on such a plan as would secure them, so far as

[4] The date of the letter from which Wesley quotes is not known, nor does the original appear to be extant in any form.

[5] JWJ for May 23, 1746, states: 'I made over the houses in Bristol and Kingswood, and the next week that at Newcastle, to seven trustees, reserving only to my brother and myself the liberty of preaching and lodging there.' In fact the deeds are dated Mar. 5, 1746—at least those for Bristol and Newcastle (see Methodist Archives, Manchester, and W. W. Stamp, *The Orphan-House of Wesley* [London, 1863], pp. 267-71).

[6] Nelson, the stonemason preacher of Birstall, was named as one of the trustees in the Bristol and Newcastle deeds. Another was Henry Thornton, the Yorkshire lawyer who was apparently chiefly responsible for drawing up the 1746 deeds. In August 1750, while the Birstall house was being built, Nelson asked Wesley's advice about a suitable legal form upon which the building could be settled, and the Birstall deed of 1751 was apparently drawn up at least roughly along the same lines as those of 1746 approved by Wesley. During the thirty years' interval, however, Wesley had come to realize one of the flaws in those early documents—that after his death and those of his named successors the responsibility for continuing Methodist worship passed into the hands of the trustees themselves. See E. Benson Perkins, *Methodist Preaching Houses and the Law,* (London, Epworth Press, 1952), pp. 25-28.

human prudence could, *from the heirs* of the proprietors, for the purpose originally intended.

7. In process of time the preaching-house at Birstall became abundantly too small for the congregation. It was then proposed to build a new one. And a new deed was prepared, which, like the old, gave a few persons the power of *placing* and *displacing* the preachers *at their pleasure.* This was brought and read to me at Dawgreen.[7] As soon as ever I heard it, I vehemently objected to it, and positively refused to sign it. I now thought I had done with it: but in the evening several persons came again, and importunately urged me to sign it; averring that it was the same in effect with the old deed, and that the old deed *could not be altered.* Not adverting that it *was altered* in the new one, I at length unwillingly complied.

But observe. Whether I did right or wrong herein, or in any other instance, it does not affect the merits of the cause. The dwelling upon this is mere finesse to divert us from the one question, 'Is that deed right or wrong?'

8. These things were mentioned at the ensuing Conference, and it was asked, What can be done? The answer was: 'If the trustees still refuse to settle it on the Methodist plan, if they still insist that they will have the right of *placing* and *displacing* the preachers *at their pleasure,* then,

First, Let a plain state of the case be drawn up.

Secondly, Let a collection be made throughout England, in order to purchase ground, and build another preaching-house, as near the present as may be.'[8]

9. This I take to be a plain state of the case, separating it from all unimportant circumstances of what this or the other person said or did, all which only puzzle the cause. Now this, neither more nor less, being the naked fact, I proceed,

[II]. Secondly, to argue a little upon it.

I. If it be asked, Why should not the Birstall preaching-house, or any other, be settled according to that deed? I answer:

Because whenever the trustees exert their power of *placing* and *displacing* preachers, then,

1. Itinerant preaching is no more. When the trustees in any

[7] That is, Dawgreen where the Dewsbury preaching-house was built, which caused similar trouble for Wesley. See below, *The Case of Dewsbury House,* 1789, pp. 512-14.

[8] See *Minutes,* 1782, *Q.* 22, in which Wesley has made a few verbal changes, and added the clause, 'if they still insist . . . *pleasure*'.

place have found and fixed a preacher they like, the rotation of preachers is at an end—at least till they are tired of their favourite preacher, and so turn him out.

2. While he stays, is not the bridle in his mouth? How dares he speak the full and the whole truth, since whenever he displeases the trustees he is liable to lose his bread? How much less will he dare to put a trustee, though ever so ungodly, out of the society?

If you say, 'But though they have this power, they will not exert it. They never have exerted it at Birstall.' Reason good; because they have it not till my death. And if they had, prudence, if not gratitude, would restrain them, till I am out of the way. But it does not follow that neither they nor *their heirs* will exert it by and by.

3. But suppose any beside the Conference (who as long as they subsist will be the most impartial judges) name the preachers, should it be thirty or forty men, or the whole society? Nay, why not the entire congregation? Or at least all the subscribers?

4. The power of the trustees is greater than that of any nobleman; yea, or of the king himself. Where he is patron, he can *put in* a preacher, but he cannot *put him out.*

But you ask, 'Since this power will not commence till your death, why should *you* oppose it? Why should not you keep yourself out of the broil, and let them fight it out when you are at rest? Why should you pull an old house upon your own head, when you are just going out of the world? Peace will be in *your* days. Why should you take upon yourself the burden which you may leave to your successors?'

I answer, In this very respect I have an advantage which my successors cannot have. Everyone sees, I am not pleading my own cause. I have already all that I contend for. No. I am pleading for Mr. Hopper,[9] Mr. Bradburn, Mr. Benson, and for every other travelling preacher, that you may be as free after I am gone hence as you are now I am at your head; that you may never be liable to be turned out of any or all of our houses, without any reason given but that so is *the pleasure* of twenty or thirty men.

I say, *any*—for I see no sufficient reason for giving up *any* house

[9] 1788, 'Taylor'. Christopher Hopper (1722–1802) was the grand old man of the itinerant preachers, who began preaching in 1747, but even in 1788 he was not yet superannuated, being last stationed in 1789. Thomas Taylor began to itinerate in 1761, Joseph Benson in 1771, and Samuel Bradburn in 1744.

in England. Indeed if one were given up, more would follow; it would be 'as the letting out of the water'.[10]

I insist upon that point, and let everything else go. No Methodist trustees, if I can help it, shall after my death, any more than while I live, have the power of *placing* and *displacing* the preachers.

Observe. *Placing* and *displacing* the preachers! This is the one point. Do not ramble from the question. Do not puzzle it by a multitude of words. If the trustees will not give it up, we must proceed according to the Minute of the Conference.

'But why should we not wait till another Conference?'

First, because that will not alter the merits of the cause. To lodge the power of *placing* and *displacing* the preachers in trustees would be as wrong then as it is now.

Secondly, because you cannot ensure my life till another Conference. Therefore whatever is done should be done quickly.

'But then, it is said, you occasion endless strife, animosity, confusion, and destroy the work of God.' No; not I. It is these trustees that occasion all the strife, animosity, and confusion, by insisting upon a right to *place* and *displace* preachers. I go on in the old way, as I did at Bristol, Kingswood, and Newscastle. It is they that by obstinately going out of it hinder, yea, destroy the work of God. And I charge *them* with the blood of all those souls that are destroyed by this contention. I sit down with the loss, leave them the house, and go on as if it were not in the world.[11] It is they that do the wrong that *will place* and *displace* preachers, who bawl and pour out bitter words. But let them take care; for God heareth. And he will arise and maintain his own cause![12]

London, 178—[13]

[10] Cf. Prov. 17:14.

[11] This sentence is omitted from the 1788 reprint.

[12] See Ps. 140:12.

[13] The reprint in the *Arminian Magazine* closes: 'London, reprinted Jan. 12, 1788. John Wesley.' See n. 1 above.

25

[A Letter to the Methodists][1]

Redruth, August 23, 1789

Some years since Mr. Valton wrote to me from Yorkshire informing me there was great want of a larger preaching-house at Dewsbury, and desiring leave to make subscriptions and collections in order to build one. I encouraged him to make them. Money was subscribed and collected, and the house built, which the trustees promised to settle in the usual form. But when it was finished they refused to settle it unless a power was given them to displace any preacher they should object to.

[1] In *The Case of Birstall House* (pp. 505-9 above) the question at issue was the danger of trustees gaining power over Wesley's itinerant preachers. This was largely resolved by the Deed of Declaration of 1784 (see Vol. 10 in this edn.), whereby the Conference was incorporated as a legal entity in which was vested the right to station the preachers after Wesley's death. A similar trouble arose in the preaching-house at Dawgreen, Dewsbury, where the trustees sought to retain complete power over its use for themselves. Wesley brought the matter before his preachers in Conference, who agreed that a new building should be erected controlled only by Wesley and his preachers. To that end the 1789 Conference (*Q.* 19) agreed that no other preaching-house should be built that year except this new one at Dewsbury, in addition to 'those which have already been begun or set on foot'. Those *Minutes* listed the preachers who approved of 'settling the preaching-houses upon the Methodist Plan' on pp. 18-19, and on pp. 20-21 furnished a subscription list of the amounts so far given 'towards a new preaching-house at Dewsbury', from 125 preachers, a total of £206.6*s*.0*d*. (N.B. Neither *Minutes* nor the Conference Journal make any reference to a discussion of the Dewsbury case.)

Wesley followed this up with two printed circulars seeking understanding and help more especially from his lay followers, the first being this letter dated Aug. 23, 1789 (*Bibliography*, No. 448), of which no original appears to have survived, the primary source being Thomas Jackson's edition of Wesley's *Works* (1831), XIII.245. In view of the preachers' subscription list in the *Minutes*, the title which Jackson supplied for this (almost certainly untitled) letter is surely incorrect—'A Letter to the Methodist Preachers'. (It was quite normal for Wesley's circulars to his followers not to have any title.)

The second circular was dated Sept. 11, 1789, and was printed on p. (1) of the foolscap sheet folded into four, leaving room for one page to be used to address it to Methodist leaders—as was almost certainly the case with the first circular. Of this two copies have survived (see *Bibliography*, No. 449). It was entitled *the Case of Dewsbury House*, and like the previous *Case* it was reprinted in the *Arminian Magazine* with the addition of the same sub-title, 'Recommended to the consideration of the People called Methodists'—in this instance in the *Arminian Magazine* (1790), XIII.103-4. About this Wesley wrote to Henry Moore on Sept. 5, 1789: 'I am glad you delayed the making of the collection for Dewsbury. I suppose you have now my second paper, which should be printed and sent to every Assistant. Herein I show them more plainly what my sentiments are than I have ever done.'

After all possible means had been used to bring them to a better mind, the case was referred to the Conference; and it was unanimously agreed to build another house, as soon as possible, that the flock might not be scattered.

I therefore entreat everyone that wishes well to Methodism, especially to the itinerant plan, to exert himself on this important occasion, that a work so absolutely necessary may be finished as soon as possible. I say, absolutely necessary; for if the trustees of houses are to displace preachers, then itinerancy is at an end.

I am, my dear brother,
Your affectionate brother
and servant for Christ's sake,
John Wesley

N.B. Make this collection immediately. Lose not one day.

26

The Case of Dewsbury House[1]

(1789)

1. When, about fifty years ago, one and another young man[2] offered to serve me as Sons in the Gospel, it was on these terms, 'that they would labour where I appointed'; otherwise we should have stood in each other's way. Here began itinerant preaching *with us*. But we were not the first itinerant preachers in England. Twelve were appointed by Queen Elizabeth, to travel continually in order to spread true religion through the kingdom.[3] And the

[1] See opening note to previous item.

[2] Orig., 'men'.

[3] Wesley was writing from memory, of course, and his memory in this as in many instances was inaccurate. He knew at least some of the ecclesiastical compilations of John Strype (1643–1737), and he may well have been remembering an entry in his *Ecclesiastical Memorials* (1721) for December 1551:

'In this month of December it was thought fit the King should retain six chaplains in ordinary; who should not wait upon him, but be itineraries, and preach the gospel all the nation over. Two of these six to be ever present at court, and four absent abroad in preaching. One year, two in Wales, two in Lancashire and Derby. The next year, two in the marches of Scotland, two in Yorkshire. The third year, two in Devonshire, two in Hampshire. The fourth year, two in Norfolk and Essex, and two in Kent and Sussex. And these six to be, Bill, Harley, Pern, Grindal, Bradford, and the sixth dashed out in the journal, but probably was Knox.' (Oxford edn., 25 vols., 1812-28, *Memorials*, ii.521-22.) This was in the time of King Edward VI, of course, not that of Queen Elizabeth. Wesley might indeed have been trying to recall instead a passage which he may have seen at the end of Bishop Burnet's *History of the Reformation*, which reprinted a similar paragraph from King Edward VI's journal for Dec. 18, 1551, beginning: 'It was appointed, I should have six chaplains ordinary, of which two ever to be present, and four always absent in preaching. . . .' Their salary was £40, paid by the Privy Council (see Knox, *Dictionary of National Biography*, p. 310).

Not only was the future Archbishop Edmund Grindal one of these royal itinerant chaplains, but so also were John Bradford (martyred 1555) and the Scots reformer, John Knox. So also was Hugh Latimer, claiming that his right to preach anywhere came not from a bishop's license but because 'The University of Cambridge hath authority apostolic to admit twelve yearly, of whom I am one.' (Latimer's *Works*, Parker Society, ed. G. E. Corrie, Vol. 28, II.324, 329; the editor adds: 'The University of Cambridge . . . still [1845] has the power to license twelve persons to preach in any part of the realm.') It seems fairly clear that the number of royal chaplains was indeed eventually increased to twelve, corresponding with the number whom Cambridge was empowered to license. The only serious research on this subject seems to have been carried out by the Lancashire antiquarian, Ernest Axon, who concluded that: 'at the beginning of the eighteenth century

office and *salary* still continues, though their work is little attended to. Mr. Milner,[4] late vicar of Chipping in Lancashire, was one of them.

2. As the number of preachers increased, it grew more and more difficult to fix the places where each should labour from time to time. I have often wished to transfer this work of stationing the preachers once a year to one or more of themselves. But none were willing to accept of it. So I must bear the burden, till my warfare shall be accomplished.[5]

3. When preaching-houses were built, they were vested immediately in trustees, who were to see that those preached in them whom I sent, and none else. This, we conceived, being the only way whereby itinerancy could be regularly established. But lately, after a new preaching-house had been built at Dewsbury,[6] by the subscriptions and contributions of the people (the trustees alone not contributing one quarter of what it cost), they seized upon the house, and though they had promised the contrary positively refused to settle it on the Methodist plan, requiring that they should have a power of refusing any preacher whom they disliked. If so, I have no power of stationing the Dewsbury preachers, for the trustees may object to whom they please. And they themselves, not I, are finally to judge of those objections.

4. Observe. Here is no dispute about the right of *houses* at all. I have no right to any preaching-house in England. What I claim is a right of stationing the preachers. This these trustees have robbed me of in the present instance. Therefore only one of these two ways can be taken: either to sue for this house, or to build another. We prefer the latter, being the most friendly way.

I beg therefore, my brethren, for the love of God, for the love of me, your old and wellnigh worn-out servant, for the love of

a King's Preachership was merely a useful perquisite for a beneficed clergyman or a bishop's chaplain. Its most serious duty was the preaching of a sermon a year, probably the same sermon, in each of a number of country chapels.' Ernest Axon, 'The King's Preachers in Lancashire', *Transactions of the Lancashire and Cheshire Antiquarian Society*, Vol. 56 (1911–12), pp. 67-101, espec. p. 103.

[4] The Rev. John Milner (*c.* 1710–77, educated at Jesus College, Cambridge, was vicar of Chipping, Lancashire, from 1739 until his death. Wesley preached for him on several occasions, for which Milner suffered persecution, and he was present at Wesley's 1753 Conference. Cf. Wesley's *Letters*, Jan. 11, 1750, and June 30, 1751 (26:397-98, 467, in this edn.). Venn's entry on him in *Alumni Cantabrigienses* notes the confirmation of Wesley's statement: 'King's Preacher, 1748', but Axon does not mention him.

[5] See Isa. 40:2.

[6] *Arminian Magazine*, 'Dewsbury, in Yorkshire'.

ancient Methodism (which if itinerancy is interrupted will speedily come to nothing), for the love of justice, mercy, and truth, which are all so grievously violated by the detention of this house, that you will set your shoulders to the necessary work. Be not straitened in your own bowels.[7] We have never had such a cause before. Let not then unkind, unjust, fraudulent men have cause to rejoice in their bad labour. This is a common cause. Exert yourselves to the utmost. I have subscribed fifty pounds. So has Dr. Coke.[8] O let you that have much,[9] give plenteously. Perhaps this is the last labour of love I may have occasion to recommend to you. Let it then stand as one more monument of your real gratitude to,

My dear brethren,
Your old, affectionate brother,
John Wesley

Bristol, Sept. 11, 1789[10]

[7] 2 Cor. 6:12.

[8] Wesley and Coke, with these amounts, head the subscription list printed in the 1789 *Minutes*. At this point the version in the *Arminian Magazine* adds (bearing in mind the same subscription list): 'The preachers have done all they could.'

[9] 'you that have much' in the circular is altered in the *Arminian Magazine* to 'them that have much'.

[10] *Arminian Magazine* omits the place and date.

27

A Word to Whom it may Concern[1]

In August 1788 Mr. Atlay[2] wrote me word, I 'must look out for another servant', for he would 'go to Dewsbury on September the 25th'. So far was I from 'bidding him go', that I knew nothing of it till that hour. But I then told him, 'Go and serve them,' seeing I found he would serve me no longer.

He sent me word that I had in London £13,751. 18*s*. 5*d*. stock in books. Desiring to know exactly, I employed two booksellers to take an account of my stock. The account they brought in, October 31, 1788, was:

'Value of stock, errors excepted, £ 4,827. 10*s*. 3½*d*.
John Parsons,
Thomas Scollick.'

Why did John Atlay so wonderfully overrate my stock? Certainly to do me honour in the eyes of the world.

I never approved of his going to Dewsbury; but I submitted to what I could not help.

With regard to Dewsbury house, there never was any dispute about the *property of preaching-houses*—that was an artful misrepresentation—but merely the *appointing of preachers* in them.

[1] *Arminian Magazine* (1790), XIII.328.

[2] John Atlay had been one of Wesley's itinerant preachers since 1762. From 1773 he was stationed in London, with the special note in 1776, 'John Atlay keeps his [i.e., Wesley's] accounts,' and from 1777 onwards, 'John Atlay is the Book Steward.' In 1784 he became a supernumerary in London, but continued to serve as Book Steward. On Aug. 19, 1788, he wrote to Wesley stating that he felt constrained to accept the invitation offered by the malcontent trustees at Dewsbury to be their preacher, since Wesley had withdrawn the Conference preachers from them. From that time to Sept. 24, 1788, when Atlay left London for Dewsbury, nine letters passed between him and Wesley, mainly about a successor and the final stocktaking. Clearly Wesley was unhappy about his departure, especially to lead a recalcitrant society. A number of Wesley's preachers were more outspoken in their criticism, and Atlay felt that behind all this were Wesley's machinations. Accordingly in January 1790 he published their correspondence, with a lengthy introduction depicting the circumstances, and an epilogue hinting that Wesley did not live up to his own *Character of a Methodist* in not speaking evil of his neighbour. Wesley penned this public reply and published it in his *Arminian Magazine,* emphasizing the disruption and apparent deception which had been associated with the recalcitrant trustees at Dewsbury and underlining points made in the previous two documents.

If John Atlay has a mind to throw any more dirt upon me, I do not know I shall take any pains to wipe it off. I have but a few days to live; and I wish to spend those in peace.

John Wesley

London, City Road, Feb. 25, 1790

28–34

EXTRACTS FROM THE *ARMINIAN MAGAZINE*

AN INTRODUCTORY COMMENT

These seven writings, all of them dating from the last decade of Wesley's life and all of them reprinted from the Arminian Magazine, *are in the strict sense 'occasional', dealing with problems and situations which had arisen during the growth of Methodism. All but one deal with issues which had arisen among the Methodists; the exception ('Some Remarks on Article X of Mr. Maty's* New Review*') is concerned with a particular critic's distortions of Methodist history.*

The two themes which run through the remaining six are the essence of Methodism as pure Christianity and the necessity of remaining within the Church of England in spite of provocations, frustrations, and dilemmas (see Introduction to Reasons against a Separation from the Church of England *pp. 332-33 above).*

28

Some Thoughts upon an Important Question[1]

(1781)

1. For many years I have earnestly advised, both in public and in private, all in connexion with me who have been brought up in the Established Church to continue therein; and of consequence to attend the Public Service of the Church, at all opportunities. And my reason for so doing I published to all the world more than twenty years ago.[2]

2. But a few months ago I was favoured with a letter which required me to review my sentiments. It is signed by several members of our Society, men of a loving spirit, and of an unblameable conversation. And it is worthy of the greater regard as they speak not only in their own name, but in the name of many who wish to have a conscience void of offence, both towards God and towards man.[3]

3. Part of it runs thus:

> Having read many of your books, and heard many of your preachers, and being in connexion with you, we have from time to time been advised by them and you constantly to attend the church. But we find that neither you nor your preachers have given any countenance to the doctrines of Calvinism. This induces us humbly to ask the following questions.
>
> First, Whether you would have us to go to that church where the doctrines of Calvinism are continually inculcated? And where the doctrines taught by you, Christian perfection in particular, are continually exploded?
>
> Secondly, Whether you think we shall be profited in any degree by hearing such preaching?
>
> Thirdly, Whether it is not a means of filling our hearts with prejudice either against those preachers or against the truth?
>
> Fourthly, Whether hearing them does not expose us to temptation from those who continually ask, How did you like the sermon today? We cannot dissemble; and if we do not, we offend them.

[1] *Arminian Magazine* (1782), V.92-93.

[2] *Reasons against a Separation from the Church of England* (1758). See pp. 332-42 above.

[3] See Acts 24:16.

If you please, you may give us your sentiments in the *Arminian Magazine*.

Baildon,
Near Bradford,
July 24, 1781

John W——
Nathan O——
John R——[4]

Francis B——
Joseph B——

4. It is a delicate, as well as important point, on which I hardly know how to answer. I cannot lay down any general rule. All I can say at present is, 'If it does not hurt you, hear them; if it does, refrain.' Be determined by your own conscience. Let every man in particular act 'as he is fully persuaded in his own mind'.[5]

John Wesley

Nov. 19, 1781

[4] The names have not been identified.
[5] Cf. Rom. 14:5.

29

On Hearing Ministers who Oppose the Truth[1]

(1782)

1. Last summer I received a letter from Yorkshire signed by several serious men, who proposed a difficulty they were under, wherein they knew not how to act. And indeed I did not well know how to advise them. So I delayed giving them a determinate answer till I could lay the matter before our brethren at the ensuing Conference.

2. Their difficulty was this. 'You advise all the members of our societies constantly to attend the Service of the Church. We have done so for a considerable time. But very frequently Mr. R., our minister, preaches not only what we believe to be false, but dangerously false doctrine. He asserts, and endeavours to prove, that we cannot be saved from our sins in this life, and that we must not hope to be perfected in love on this side eternity. Our nature is very willing to receive this; therefore it is very liable to hurt us. Hence we have a doubt whether it is our duty to hear this preaching, which experience shows to weaken our souls.'

3. This letter I laid before the Conference, and we easily perceived, the difficulty therein proposed concerned not only the Society at Baildon, but many others in various parts of the kingdom. It was therefore considered at large, and all our brethren were desired to speak their sentiments freely. In the conclusion, they unanimously agreed: (1). That it was highly expedient, all the Methodists (so called) who had been bred therein, should attend the Service of the Church as often as possible; but that, secondly, if the minister began either to preach the absolute decrees, or to rail at and ridicule Christian perfection, they should quietly and silently go out of the church, yet attend it again the next opportunity.

4. I have since that time revolved this matter over and over in my own mind. And the more I consider it, the more I am convinced, this was the best answer that could be given. I still

[1] *Arminian Magazine* (1782), V.152-53.

advise all our friends, when this case occurs, quietly and silently to go out. Only I must earnestly caution them not to be critical, not to make a man an offender for a word; no, nor for a few sentences, which any who believe the decrees may drop without design. But if such a minister should at any time deliberately and of set purpose endeavour to establish absolute predestination, or to confute scriptural perfection, then I advise all the Methodists in the congregation quietly to go away.

John Wesley

Lewisham, Jan. 9, 1782

30

Some Remarks on Article X of Mr. Maty's *New Review*, for December, 1784[1]

(1785)

1. A day or two ago this *Review* fell into my hands, which contains a letter from the Rev. Mr. Badcock. I have not the pleasure of knowing this gentleman. But I esteem him for his useful and ingenious publications. And I think it my duty to inform both him and the public better of some points wherein they have been misinformed.

2. He says: 'Mr. Samuel Wesley, of Epworth, in Lincolnshire, was sent to the university.'[2] This is not accurate. He was educated for some years at a dissenting academy, from which he then privately retired, and entered himself at Exeter College in Oxford. 'His heroic poem, *The Life of Christ*, excited the ridicule of the wits.'[3] His own account of it was: 'The cuts are good; the

[1] See *Arminian Magazine* (1785), VIII.151-55. Paul Henry Maty (1745–87) published his *New Review* from 1782 to 1786, and prepared most of the monthly issues himself. Article X for December 1784 (pp. 460-69), dealt with 'An Account of the Gentlemen's Society at Spalding. Being an Introduction to the *Reliquiae Galeanae,* Nichols, 4to'. Maty devoted all except his opening paragraph to what he termed 'the most interesting part', which he quoted at length, an account of the Wesley family written by the Rev. Samuel Badcock (1747–88), a dissenting minister of South Molton, Devon, where it was penned on Dec. 5, 1782. Badcock had been a close friend of John Wesley's brother Samuel, possessed several Wesley family documents, and had seen many more. A discussion of John Wesley, 'a singular man' who 'had all Whitefield's zeal and perseverance, with double his understanding, and ten times more learning', appears on pp. 463-69. Badcock especially paid tribute to his 'dexterity in debate', which led a 'celebrated preacher' to say of him: 'I know him of old. He is an eel; take him where you will, he will slip through your fingers' (p. 465). He assessed Wesley's mission thus: 'Such schemes of reformation as were so extensive and complicated as his were not the transient visions of an overheated fancy, but the deep projects of a subtle mind, and called for the most determined efforts of a warm, resolute, and yet cautious spirit' (pp. 467-68). Badcock testified: 'At the age of fourscore Mr. Wesley is still active and cheerful. . . . He is an excellent companion; and, in spite of censure, I believe he is an honest man' (p. 468). His article is very discursive, but contains many points of interest, including an account of Wesley's dining with the Bishop of Exeter after receiving the sacrament at the cathedral in the summer of 1782. Wesley, however, felt that there were too many errors and unjustified criticisms for the essay to pass unnoticed, and therefore used his own monthly magazine as the vehicle for a reply.

[2] P. 460.

[3] Ibid.

notes pretty good; the verses so so.' 'At a very advanced age he published a Latin work on the Book of Job, which was never held in any estimation by the learned.'[4] I doubt that. It certainly contains immense learning; but of a kind which I do not admire.

3. 'He married a woman of extraordinary abilities, the daughter of Dr. Samuel Annesley.'[5] (Dr. Annesley and the then Earl of Anglesey were brother's sons.) 'Samuel, his eldest son, was a noted Jacobite.'[6] Nay, he was no more a Jacobite than he was a Turk. And what amends can Mr. Badcock or Mr. Maty make for publishing this egregious falsehood? 'Many of his political satires remain unpublished, on account of their treasonable tendency.'[7] Here is a double mistake. For, (1). He never published anything political, whether satirical or not. (2). He never wrote anything of a treasonable tendency; he sacredly avoided it. 'In his rage of Jacobitism, he poured out the very dregs of it on royalty itself.'[8] No, never. He never wrote, much less published, one line against the King. I speak it from personal knowledge, having often heard him say, 'If it reflects on the King, it is none of mine.' His constant practice may be learnt from those lines, in *The Battle of the Sexes:*

> Forgive the voice that useful fiction sings;
> Not impious tales of deities impure,
> Not faults of breathless Queens, or living Kings,
> In open treason, or in veil[s] obscure.[9]

'Time, however, changed the satirist against Sir Robert into an humble suppliant.' Nay, I do not believe he ever wrote a line to Sir Robert, either in verse or prose.[10]

4. 'Mrs. Wesley lived long enough to deplore the extravagance[s] of her two sons, John and Charles, considering them as "under strong delusions to believe a lie."'[11] By vile misrepresentations she was deceived for a time. But she no sooner heard them

[4] P. 461. [5] Ibid.
[6] P. 462. [7] Ibid.
[8] Ibid.
[9] *Poems,* 1736, p. 46, *ll.* 491-94.
[10] John Wesley was misinformed or forgetful. Badcock had apparently seen the twenty-four manuscript poems satirizing Sir Robert Walpole's administration which did not appear in print until James Nichols's edn. of Samuel Wesley's *Poems* (London, Simpkin Marshall, 1862), pp. 610-37.
[11] Cf. 2 Thess. 2:11. See her letter to her son Samuel, Mar. 8, 1738/39, given in Joseph Priestley, *Original Letters by the Rev. John Wesley and his Friends* (Birmingham, Pearson, 1791), espec. pp. 91-92, and Samuel to John Wesley, Apr. 16, 1739 (ibid., p. 96). On Oct. 20, 1739, Samuel Wesley wrote to his mother lamenting the fact that she had

speak for themselves than she was thoroughly convinced, they were in no delusion, but spoke 'the words of truth and soberness'.[12] She afterwards lived with *me* several years, and died rejoicing and praising God.

5. I was born in June 1703, and was between six and seven years old[13] when I was left alone in my father's house, being then all in flames; till I was taken out of the nursery window by a man strangely standing on the shoulders of another. Those words in the picture, 'Is not this a brand plucked out of the burning?' chiefly allude to this.[14]

6. 'He had early a very strong impression of his designation to some extraordinary work.'[15] Indeed, not I. I never said so. I never thought so. I am guiltless in this matter. The strongest impression I had till I was three or four and twenty was,

> *Inter sylvas academi quaerere verum;*[16]

and afterwards (while I was my father's curate) to save my own soul and those that heard me.[17] When I returned to Oxford it was my full resolve to live and die there, the reasons for which I gave in a long letter to my father, since printed in one of my Journals.[18] In this purpose I continued till Dr. Burton, one of the Trustees for Georgia, pressed me to go over with General Oglethorpe (who is still alive, and well knows the whole transaction) in order to preach to the Indians.[19] With great difficulty I was prevailed upon to go, and spent upwards of two years abroad. At my return I was

'countenanced a spreading delusion so far as to be one of Jack's congregation' (ibid., p. 109).

[12] Acts 26:25.

[13] Actually 'between five and six', for the fire occurred on Feb. 9, 1709. Oddly enough, Wesley has here made a mistake about his age at the time of the fire. He was born on June 17, 1703; the fire was on Feb. 9, 1709 (this is established by a letter of his mother Susanna dated Aug. 1709). Many historians have been misled by Wesley's error here.

[14] Badcock had recounted the story of Wesley's rescue from the burning rectory, with some inaccuracies, adding: 'This extraordinary incident explains a certain device in some of the earlier prints of John Wesley. . . . Many have supposed this device to be merely *emblematical* of his spiritual deliverance . . .' (p. 463). The text quoted is from Zech. 3:2.

[15] P. 464.

[16] Horace, *Epistles,* II.ii.45, 'to search for truth in the groves of learning'. Cf. his letter to 'John Smith', June 25, 1746: 'To this day I have abundantly more temptation to lukewarmness than to impetuosity; to be a saunterer *inter sylvas academicas,* a philosophical sluggard, than an itinerant preacher' (26:197 in this edn.).

[17] See 1 Tim. 4:16.

[18] Dec. 10, 1734; see *Letters,* 25:397-410 in this edn.

[19] See *Letters,* 25:432, 434-37 in this edn., presenting letters from James Oglethorpe and John Burton, Sept. 9 and 28, 1735.

more than ever determined to lay my bones at Oxford. But I was insensibly led, without any previous plan or design, to preach, first in many of the churches in London, then in more public places, afterwards in Bristol, Kingswood, Newcastle, and throughout Great Britain and Ireland. Therefore all that Mr. Badcock adds of the incidents that 'gave an additional force' to an impression that never existed is very ingenious, yet is in truth a castle in the air.

7. It is true that for a while I admired the mystic writers.[20] But I dropped them even before I went to Georgia—long before I knew or suspected any [such] thing as justification by faith. Therefore all that follows, of my 'making my system of divinity more commodious for general use', and of 'employing myself to search for some common bond, whereby the most dissonant sects might have a centre of union', having no foundation to stand upon, falls to the ground at once. I had quite other work while I was at Oxford, being fully engaged, partly with my pupils, and partly with my little offices, being Greek Lecturer, and Moderator of both the classes.

8. 'His dexterity in debate has been so long known that it is almost become proverbial.' It has been my first care for many years to see that my cause was good, and never, either in jest or earnest, to defend the wrong side of a question. And shame on me if I cannot defend the right, after so much practice; and after having been so early accustomed to separate truth from falsehood, how artfully so ever they were twisted together.

9. If the poem on Religious Discourse 'delineates the disposition and character of the author', it does not delineate mine; for I was not the author, but Mr. John Gambold.[21] What becomes then of that good-natured remark: 'The wonder is not that *John Wesley* should have shown an inclination to insult the memory of a sober divine, but that *Samuel Wesley* should have been disposed to

[20] See p. 464: 'The dawn of Mr. Wesley's public mission was clouded with mysticism. . . .'

[21] See pp. 465-66: 'A poem intitled "Religious Discourse", and published by him in one of his earlier collections, was pointed out to me by his own niece as a very striking delineation of his disposition and characters. She said her father regarded it in the same unfavourable light. I have some doubt of this, for I have the original copy now before me, with marginal corrections (chiefly verbal) in the handwriting of Samuel Wesley. . . .' One of these, referring to Tillotson, he quotes. This poem was first published in the Wesley's *Hymns and Sacred Poems* (London, Strahan, 1739), pp. 58-63. John Gambold (1711–71), of course, was an Oxford Methodist who later became a Moravian bishop.

show lenity to a Whig of the Revolution'? Mistake upon mistake! (1). Those marginal notes were not wrote by *Samuel*, but *Charles Wesley*. He told me so this very day. (2). Both my father and all his sons have always praised God for the happy Revolution. I let Bishop Warburton alone.[22] He is gone to rest. I well hope, in Abraham's bosom.

10. 'Mr. *Wesley* had a very important end in view.'[23] What end, but to save sinners? What other end could I possibly have in view? Or can have at this day? 'Deep projects of a subtle mind'.[24] Nay, I am not subtle, but the veriest fool under the sun, if I have any earthly project at all now! For what do I want which this world can give? And, after the labour of fourscore years,

> No foot of land do I possess,
> No cottage in the wilderness:
> A poor, wayfaring man
> I dwell awhile in tents below,
> Or gladly wander to and fro,
> Till I my Canaan gain.[25]

John Wesley

City Road, Jan. 11, 1785

[22] See p. 467, where Badcock relates Bishop William Warburton's satire on Wesley (see 11:459-538 in this edn., Wesley's *Letter* to the Bishop of Gloucester, 1763).

[23] P. 467.

[24] Ibid.

[25] [Charles Wesley], *Hymns for those that seek, and those that have Redemption* (London, Strahan), p. 67, st. 6 of 'The Pilgrim' (*Poetical Works*, IV.279). Orig., 'this wilderness', and 'I lodge awhile'.

31

Thoughts upon Methodism[1]

(1786)

1. I am not afraid that the people called Methodists should ever cease to exist either in Europe or America. But I am afraid lest they should only exist as a dead sect, having the form of religion without the power.[2] And this undoubtedly will be the case unless they hold fast both the doctrine, spirit, and discipline with which they first set out.

2. What was their fundamental doctrine? That the Bible is the whole and sole rule both of Christian faith and practice. Hence they learned: (1). That religion is an inward principle; that it is no other than the mind that was in Christ;[3] or in other words, the renewal of the soul after the image of God,[4] in righteousness and true holiness.[5] (2). That this can never be wrought in us but by the power of the Holy Ghost.[6] (3). That we receive this and every other blessing merely for the sake of Christ;[7] and, (4), that whosoever hath the mind that was in Christ, the same is our brother, and sister, and mother.[8]

3. In the year 1729 four young students in Oxford agreed to spend their evenings together. They were all zealous members of the Church of England, and had no peculiar opinions, but were distinguished only by their constant attendance on the church and sacrament. In 1735 they were increased to fifteen, when the

[1] *Arminian Magazine* (1787), X.100-102, 155-56. In his later years Wesley made frequent attempts to summarize the history and effects of the revival, of which we may note the following, with their disposition in this edition:

Apr. 1777: Sermon 112, *On Laying the Foundation of the New Chapel* (3:577-92).
Apr. 1783: Sermon 63, *The General Spread of the Gospel* (2:485-99).
Aug. 1786: 'Thoughts upon Methodism' (this item).
Oct. 1787: Sermon 107, 'On God's Vineyard' (3:502-17).
July 1788: 'Thoughts upon a Late Phenomenon' (see below).

[2] See 2 Tim. 3:5.

[3] See Phil. 2:5.

[4] See Col. 3:10.

[5] Eph. 4:24.

[6] Rom. 15:13.

[7] See Eph. 4:32.

[8] See Matt. 12:50.

chief of them embarked for America, intending to preach to the heathen Indians. Methodism then seemed to die away; but it revived again in the year 1738. Especially after Mr. Wesley (not being allowed to preach in the churches) began to preach in the fields. One and another then coming to inquire what they must do to be saved,[9] he desired them to meet him all together, which they did, and increased continually in number. In November a large building, the Foundery, being offered him, he began preaching therein morning and evening—at five in the morning, and seven in the evening, that the people's labour might not be hindered.

4. From the beginning the men and women sat apart, as they always did in the primitive church. And none were suffered to call any place their own, but the first-comers sat down first. They had no pews, and all the benches for rich and poor were of the same construction. Mr. Wesley began the service with a short prayer; then sung a hymn and preached (usually about half an hour), then sang a few verses of another hymn, and concluded with prayer. His constant doctrine was, salvation by faith, preceded by repentance, and followed by holiness.

5. But when a large number of people was joined, the great difficulty was to keep them together. For they were continually scattering hither and thither, and we knew no way to help it. But God provided for this also, when we thought not of it. A year or two after Mr. Wesley met the chief of the society in Bristol, and inquired, 'How shall we pay the debt upon the preaching-house?' Captain Foy[10] stood up and said, 'Let everyone in the society give a penny a week and it will easily be done.' 'But many of them', said one, 'have not a penny to give.' 'True', said the captain, 'then put ten or twelve of them to me. Let each of these give what they can weekly, and I will supply what is wanting.' Many others made the same offer. So Mr. Wesley divided the societies among them; assigning a *Class* of about twelve persons to each of these, who were termed *Leaders*.

6. Not long after, one of these informed Mr. Wesley that calling on such an one in his house he found him quarrelling with his wife. Another was found in drink. It immediately struck into Mr. Wesley's mind, This is the very thing we wanted. The *leaders*

[9] See Acts 16:30.

[10] This appears to be the only place where Captain Foy is identified by name as the one who 'stood up' and made the proposal here given. The event is described in *A Plain Account of the People called Methodists*, II.3; see p. 260 above and n. 46.

are the persons who may not only receive the contributions, but also watch over the souls of their brethren. The society in London being informed of this, willingly followed the example of that in Bristol. As did every society from that time, whether in Europe or America. By this means it was easily found if any grew weary or faint, and help was speedily administered. And if any walked disorderly, they were quickly discovered, and either amended or dismissed.

7. For those who knew in whom they had believed,[11] there was another help provided. Five or six, either married or single men, met together at such an hour as was convenient, according to the direction of St. James, 'Confess your faults one to another, and pray one for another, and ye shall be healed.' And five or six of the married or single women met together for the same purpose. Innumerable blessings have attended this institution, especially in those who were 'going on to perfection'.[12] When any seemed to have attained this, they were allowed to meet with a select number who appeared, so far as man could judge, to be partakers of the same 'great salvation'.[13]

8. From this short sketch of Methodism (so called) any man of understanding may easily discern that it is only plain scriptural religion, guarded by a few prudential regulations. The essence of it is holiness of heart and life; the circumstantials all point to this. And as long as they are joined together in the people called Methodists, no weapon formed against them shall prosper. But if even the circumstantial parts are despised, the essential will soon be lost. And if ever the essential parts should evaporate, what remains will be dung and dross.

9. It nearly concerns us to understand how the case stands with us at present. I fear, wherever riches have increased (exceeding few are the exceptions) the essence of religion, the mind that was in Christ,[14] has decreased in the same proportion. Therefore do I not see how it is possible, in the nature of things, for any revival of true religion to continue long. For religion must necessarily produce both industry and frugality. And these cannot but produce riches. But as riches increase, so will pride, anger, and love of the world in all its branches.

[11] See 2 Tim. 1:12.
[12] Cf. Heb. 6:11.
[13] 1 Sam. 14:45.
[14] Phil. 2:5.

10. How then is it possible that Methodism, that is, the religion of the heart, though it flourishes now as a green bay-tree,[15] should continue in this state? For the Methodists in every place grow diligent and frugal; consequently they increase in goods. Hence they proportionably increase in pride, in anger, in the desire of the flesh, the desire of the eyes, and the pride of life.[16] So, although the form of religion remains, the spirit is swiftly vanishing away.

11. Is there no way to prevent this? This continual declension of pure religion? We ought not to forbid people to be diligent and frugal. We *must* exhort all Christians to gain all they can, and to save all they can—that is, in effect to grow rich! What way then (I ask again) can we take that our money may not sink us to the nethermost hell? There is one way, and there is no other under heaven. If those who *gain all they can,* and *save all they can,* will likewise *give all they can,*[17] then the more they gain, the more they will grow in grace, and the more treasure they will lay up in heaven.

London, Aug. 4, 1786

[15] See Ps. 37:35.
[16] See 1 John 1:16.
[17] See Sermon 50, 'The Use of Money' (2:263-80 in this edn.), the headings of the three parts.

32

Thoughts on the Consecration of Churches and Burial-Grounds[1]

(1788)

1. It has been a custom for some ages in Roman Catholic countries to have a particular form of consecration for all churches and chapels; and not for these only, but for everything pertaining to them, such as fonts, chalices, bells, sacerdotal vestments, and churchyards in particular. And all these customs universally prevailed in England as long as it was under the papal power.

2. From the time of our Reformation from popery most of these customs fell into disuse. Unconsecrated bells were rung

[1] *Arminian Magazine* (1788), XI.541-42. At the beginning of the Methodist revival both Wesley brothers seem to have accepted the conventional view that worship—especially sacramental worship—was most appropriate in a duly consecrated building, though valid elsewhere in any emergency. Both encouraged the Methodists to worship and communicate in their own parish churches wherever possible. In the face of church harassment, however, even Charles—much the more rigid churchman in the long run—administered communion occasionally in the open air in Kingswood (1740) and in the schoolroom there (1741), as well as utilizing the expedient of extending sick-bed communions to large groups of visitors. In London the problem was readily solved by using the consecrated Huguenot chapel in West Street (1743; see John C. Bowmer, *The Lord's Supper in Early Methodism* [London, Epworth Press, 1951], pp. 62-68). John Wesley publicly nailed his colours to the mast in his *Journal* entry for Aug. 20, 1764: 'I went to Canterbury and opened our new chapel by preaching on, "One thing is needful." How is it that many Protestants, even in England, do not know that no other consecration of church or chapel is allowed, much less required, in England, than the performance of public worship therein? . . . Let this be remembered by all who talk so idly of preaching in unconsecrated places!' (Cf. JWJ, Mar. 28, 1772, where he equated opening a preaching-house with 'consecrating' it.)

John Wesley had been disturbed by the fact that his brother Charles nevertheless did not wish to be buried near his mother in Bunhill Fields nor near his brother behind their New Chapel in City Road, both of which were 'unconsecrated'. In accordance with his wishes, therefore, on Apr. 5, 1788, Charles Wesley was interred in Marylebone churchyard—which ironically turned out itself not to have been consecrated. On Apr. 8 John wrote to the Rev. Peard Dickinson: ''Tis pity but the remains of my brother had been deposited with me. Certainly that *ground* is as *holy* as any in England.' On Apr. 27 he wrote again to Dickinson: 'I really think it will be proper to publish something in the magazine on that idle popish conceit of "Consecrated Ground". The ground of Bunhill Fields is full as well consecrated as that in St. Luke's churchyard.' This was the genesis, of course, of the present article.

without scruple, and unconsecrated vestments worn. But some of them remained still—the consecration of churches and churchyards in particular—and many scrupled the performing divine service in an *unconsecrated church*, and could not consent that their bodies should be buried in *unconsecrated ground.*

3. Accordingly the consecrating of churches and churchyards has been practised in England ever since. But it is a thing purely indifferent, being neither forbidden nor established by law. The case is different in Ireland. While the Earl of Strafford[2] was Lord Lieutenant of that kingdom a law was made for the consecration, not only of churches, but of churchyards also. And a form of consecration for both was inserted in the Common Prayer Book, which is used at this day, much resembling that which Archbishop Laud used in the consecration of St. Katherine Cree Church[3] in London.

4. But such a law has never passed in England, much less [been] inserted in our Common Prayer Book. However, such consecration has been generally practised, though not authorized by the legislature. 'Is it then illegal?' That word is capable of a twofold meaning. It may mean either without any law in its favour, or against law. I do not conceive it to be illegal in the latter sense. Perhaps it is in the former. I do not know any law that enjoins or even permits it.

5. And certainly, as it is not enjoined by the law of the land, so it is not enjoined by the law of God. Where do we find one word in the New Testament enjoining any such thing? Neither do I remember any precedent of it in the purest ages of the Church. It seems to have entered, and gradually spread itself, with the other innovations and superstitions of the Church of Rome. 'Do you think it then a superstitious practice?' Perhaps it is not, if it be practised as a thing indifferent. But if it be done as a *necessary* thing, then it is flatly superstitious.

6. For this reason I never wished that any bishop should consecrate any chapel or burial-ground of mine. Indeed I should not dare to suffer it, as I am clearly persuaded, the thing is wrong in itself, being not authorized either by any law of God, or by any law of the land. In consequence of which I conceive that either the clerk or the sexton may as well consecrate the church or the churchyard as the bishop.

[2] The First Earl of Strafford, Sir Thomas Wentworth (1593–1641).

[3] Orig., 'St. Katherine-Creed's Church'.

7. With regard to the latter, the churchyard, I know not who could answer that plain question: You say, 'This is *consecrated ground*, so many feet *broad*, and so many *long*.' But pray, how *deep* is the consecrated ground? 'Deep! What does that signify?' Oh, a great deal! For if my grave be dug too *deep*, I may happen to get out of the *consecrated ground!* And who can tell what unhappy consequences may follow from this!

8. I take the whole of this practice to be a mere relic of Romish superstition. And I wonder that any sensible Protestant should think it right to countenance it, much more that any reasonable man should plead for the necessity of it! Surely it is high time now that we should be guided, not by custom, but by Scripture and reason.

J. W.

Dumfries, May 14, 1788

33

Thoughts upon a Late Phenomenon[1]

(1788)

1. A glorious work of God began upon the earth on the day of the descent of the Holy Ghost, on the day of Pentecost; which *so swiftly* increased that in a very short time, in Jerusalem alone, thousands of sinners were brought from darkness to light, and from the power of Satan to God. Those were effectually changed from all vice to all holiness; indeed, being 'all filled with the Holy Ghost [. . .] they were all of one heart and one mind'.[2] And their life was suitable thereto: 'they continued steadfastly in the apostles' doctrine, in the breaking of bread, in prayers';[3] and 'having all things in common, there was none among them that lacked, but distribution was made to everyone as he had need.'[4]

2. But in the meantime the god of this world[5] was not idle; he did not fail to sow tares among the wheat.[6] The mystery of iniquity[7] began to work almost as soon as the mystery of godliness.[8] This grew up to a considerable height, even in the days of the apostles, insomuch that before St. John had finished his course the fine gold was become dim;[9] and iniquity had overspread the Christian Church as well as the heathen world. Although it did not come to its height till the fatal time when Constantine called himself a Christian.[10]

1 *Arminian Magazine* (1789), XII.46-49; cf. above, 'Thoughts upon Methodism', pp. 527-30 and n. 1.

2 Cf. Acts 4:31-32.

3 Cf. Acts 2:42.

4 Cf. Acts 4:32, 34, 35.

5 2 Cor. 4:4.

6 See Matt. 13:25.

7 2 Thess. 2:7.

8 1 Tim. 3:16.

9 See Lam. 4:1.

10 The Emperor Constantine was baptized only on his deathbed, but he gave powerful support to the Christian Church throughout his reign (A.D. 307–37), publishing the Edict of Milan (which gave freedom to all religions and ended the persecution of Christians) in 313, and presiding at the Council of Nicaea in 325. Wesley held that by associating Christianity with the Roman State, Constantine had begun the process of turning the church into a secular institution.

3. Yet God never left himself without witness.[11] In every age and in every nation there were a few that truly feared God and wrought righteousness. And these were raised up in their several generations that they might be lights shining in a benighted world. But few of them answered the design of Providence for any considerable time. In every age most of the excellent ones of the earth, being weary of the contradiction of sinners,[12] separated from them, and retired, if not into deserts, yet into distinct churches or religious bodies. So their light no longer shone among men, among those that needed them most; but they contentedly gave up the world to the service of its old master.

4. Again and again this has been the case, for fifteen or sixteen hundred years. And it has chiefly been by this means that many revivals of religion have been of so short a continuance; seldom lasting (as Martin Luther observes) longer than a generation, that is, thirty years.[13] Generally in that time a considerable number of men, being awakened, thought they could stand alone. So they formed themselves into a distinct body, and left the world to themselves. Hence the world received no more benefit from them; and by degrees their own 'love waxed cold',[14] till either their memorial perished from the earth,[15] or they remained a dry, cold sect.

5. But between fifty and sixty years ago a new phenomenon appeared in the world. Two or three young men, desiring to be scriptural Christians, met together for that purpose. Their number gradually increased. They were then all scattered. But fifty years ago two of them met again, and a few plain people joined them, in order to help one another in the way to heaven. Since then they increased to many thousands, both in Europe and America. They are still increasing in number, and as they humbly hope, in the knowledge and love of God;[16] yea, and in what they neither hoped for nor desired, namely, in worldly substance.

6. All of these were, when they first set out, members of the established Church: and a great majority of them, probably nine in ten, continue such at this day. But they have been solicited

[11] Acts 14:17.

[12] Heb. 12:3.

[13] Cf. Sermon 63, *The General Spread of the Gospel*, §16 (2:492 in this edn.), where Albert C. Outler points to the source in Luther's *Fastenpostillen*.

[14] Cf. Matt. 24:12.

[15] See Pss. 9:6; 109:14 (BCP).

[16] BCP, Communion, Blessing.

again and again from time to time to separate from it, and to form themselves into a distinct body, independent of all other religious societies. Thirty years ago this was seriously considered among them, at a general Conference.[17] All the arguments urged on one side and the other were considered at large; and it was determined, without one dissenting voice, that they 'ought not to separate from the Church'.

7. This is a new thing in the world: this is the peculiar glory of the people called Methodists.[18] In spite of all manner of temptations, they will not separate from the Church. What many so earnestly covet, they abhor: they will not be a distinct body. Now what instance of this have we before, either in ancient or modern history, of a body of people, in such circumstances, who will not be a distinct party, but choose to remain in connexion with their own Church, that they may be more effectually the servants of all?

8. This, I say again, is an utterly new phenomenon![19] I never saw, heard, or read of anything like it. The Methodists will not separate from the Church, although continually reproached for doing it. Although it would free them from abundance of inconveniences, and make their path much smoother and easier; although many of their friends earnestly advise and their enemies provoke them to it, the clergy in particular; most of whom, far from thanking them for continuing in the Church, use all the means in their power, fair and unfair, to drive them out of it.

9. One circumstance more is quite peculiar to the people called Methodists, that is, the terms upon which any person may be admitted into their society. They do not impose, in order to their admission, any opinions whatever. Let them hold particular or general redemption, absolute or conditional decrees; let them be Churchmen or Dissenters, Presbyterians or Independents, it is no obstacle. Let them choose one mode of worship[20] or another, it is no bar to their admission. The Presbyterian may be a Presbyterian still, the Independent or Anabaptist use his own mode of worship. So may the Quaker; and none will contend with

[17] That of 1755. See Appendix C.

[18] See Sermon 112, *On Laying the Foundation of the New Chapel,* II.14 (3:590 in this edn.).

[19] In his own copy of the *Arminian Magazine* Wesley added in MS, 'a', to read 'an utterly a new phenomenon', either overlooking the presence of the earlier 'an' or wishing to change the wording and forgetting to strike out that earlier 'an'.

[20] In his own copy of the *Arminian Magazine* Wesley altered 'worship' to 'baptism'.

him about it. They think and let think. One condition, and one only is required, a real desire to save their soul.[21] Where this is, it is enough. They desire no more. They lay stress upon nothing else. They ask only, 'Is thy heart herein as my heart? If it be, give me thy hand.'[22]

10. Is there any other society in Great Britain or Ireland that is so remote from bigotry? That is so truly of a Catholic spirit? So ready to admit all serious persons without distinction? Where then is there such a society in Europe? In the habitable world? I know none. Let any man show it me that can. Till then let no one talk of the bigotry of the Methodists.

Nottingham, July 13, 1788

[21] See *General Rules*, §4, p. 70 above.

[22] 2 Kgs. 10:15. See Sermon 39, 'Catholic Spirit', for which this is the text (2:79-95 in this edn.).

34

Farther Thoughts on Separation from the Church[1]

(1789)

1. From a child I was taught to love and reverence the Scripture, the oracles of God, and next to these to esteem the primitive Fathers, the writers of the three first centuries. Next after the primitive Church I esteemed our own, the Church of England, as the most scriptural national church in the world. I therefore not only assented to all the doctrines, but observed all the rubric[s][2] in the Liturgy, and that with all possible exactness, even at the peril of my life.

2. In this judgment and with this spirit I went to America, strongly attached to the Bible, the primitive Church, and the Church of England, from which I would not vary in one jot or tittle on any account whatever. In this spirit I returned, as regular a clergyman as any in the three kingdoms; till, after not being permitted to preach in the churches, I was constrained to *preach in the open air.*

3. Here was my first *irregularity.* And it was not voluntary, but constrained. The second was *extemporary* prayer. This likewise I believed to be my bounden duty, for the sake of those who desired me to watch over their souls. I could not in conscience refrain from it; neither from accepting those who desired to serve me *as sons in the gospel.*

4. When the people joined together, simply to help each other to heaven, increased by hundreds and thousands, still they had no more thought of leaving the Church than of leaving the kingdom.

[1] *Arminian Magazine,* XIII.214-16 (Apr. 1790). As in his tributes to God's blessings upon Methodist progress (noted above, pp. 535-36, so in other distinct pronouncements he continued to protest his own fundamental loyalty to the Church of England, in spite of his seemingly unorthodox methods. This was one of the preoccupations of his failing years, as evidenced in this apologia, in which (faulty memory and all) he sought to emphasize this point above all in a capsulated history of Methodism, within which he claimed that to the end he would 'live and die a member of the Church of England'.

[2] This use of 'rubric' as a collective noun may possibly be deliberate rather than an error for the plural which he normally uses.

Nay, I continually and earnestly cautioned them against it, reminding them that we were a part of the Church of England, whom God had raised up, not only to save our own souls, but to enliven our neighbours, those of the Church in particular. And at the first meeting of all our preachers in conference, in June 1744, I exhorted them to keep to the Church, observing that this was our peculiar glory, not to form any new sect, but abiding in our own Church to do to all men all the good we possibly could.

5. But as more Dissenters joined with us, many of whom were much prejudiced against the Church, these, with or without design, were continually infusing their own prejudices into their brethren. I saw this, and gave warning of it from time to time, both in private and in public. And in the year 1758[3] I resolved to bring the matter to a fair issue. So I desired the point might be considered at large, whether it was expedient for the Methodists to leave the Church. The arguments on both sides were discussed for several days; and at length we agreed, without a dissenting voice, 'It is by no means expedient that the Methodists should leave the Church of England.'

6. Nevertheless the same leaven continued to work, in various parts of the kingdom. The grand argument (which in some particular cases must be acknowledged to have weight) was this: 'The minister of the parish wherein we dwell neither lives nor preaches the gospel. He walks in the way to hell himself, and teaches his flock to do the same. Can you advise them to attend his preaching?' I cannot advise them to it. 'What then can they do on the Lord's day, suppose no other church be near? Do you advise them to go to a dissenting meeting? Or to meet in their own preaching-house?' Where this is really the case, I cannot blame them if they do. Although therefore I earnestly oppose the *general* separation of the Methodists from the Church, yet I cannot condemn such a *partial* separation, in this particular case. I believe to separate thus far from these miserable wretches who are the scandal of our Church and nation would be for the honour of our Church, as well as to the glory of God.

7. And this is no way contrary to the profession which I have made above these fifty years. I never had any design of separating

[3] This should be 1755. Wesley's error was probably due to the fact that he first published an abridgement of his paper on separation for his Conference three years later (see Appendix C; and Baker, *John Wesley and the Church of England* [London, 1970], pp. 162-67).

from the Church. I have no such design now. I do not believe the Methodists in general design it when I am no more seen.[4] I do and will do all that is in my power to prevent such an event. Nevertheless, in spite of all that I can do, many of them will separate from it (although I am apt to think not one half, perhaps not a third of them). These will be so bold and injudicious as to form a separate party, which consequently will dwindle away into a dry, dull, separate party. In flat opposition to these I declare once more that I live and die a member of the Church of England, and that none who regard my judgment or advice will ever separate from it.

John Wesley

London, Dec. 11, 1789

[4] See Acts 20:25.

APPENDIX A

Wesley's Text: Editions, Transmission, Presentation, and Variant Readings

The problems of identifying and dealing with the most reliable text of Wesley's publications has been discussed at some length in the final volume of his *Sermons* (4:421-30). Here there is little need to do more than summarize.

Between them John Wesley and his younger brother Charles published some 450 items, a large proportion edited from the writings of others, ranging from multi-volume works to tiny pamphlets and a few broadsheets, and passing through some two thousand separate editions. The first editions usually present and most reliable text, though later editions sometimes contain both the correction of errors and deliberate revisions. In general, however, the reprints display a gradual deterioration of the text through the errors of printers, Wesley's editorial helpers, and even his own over-hasty attempts at making sense of garbled passages. (He seems speedily to have destroyed his manuscripts and normally to have prepared a new edition by touching up the most recent printed version that was readily available.)

This makes it all the more important to secure the history of the text of each separate work as it passed through a few or many editions prepared by the many printers employed by Wesley in the major cities of the British Isles, especially of those versions which may appear to have been corrected by him personally. The numbering of the editions is often quite unreliable, based upon the often imperfect knowledge of the local printer alone, so that of the nineteen editions of *The Character of a Methodist* there are three described as 'third', two as 'seventh', and two as 'ninth'. The editions are designated, therefore, by successive capital letters, and for most works a stemma is furnished showing the descent of the successive editions in each family of text.

The relationships between the editions in the stemmata are traced by solid lines linking the letter symbols representing them, the occasional doubtful dependencies being indicated by dotted lines. A capital letter followed by an arrow (e.g., D) denotes that the variant reading is present in D and also in the editions which stem from it, and in those only. If there are several branches of textual descent from D, then it may be assumed that the same variant occurs in them all, though further accidental errors do inevitably occur. The capital letter at the end of the formula represents the last edition printed during Wesley's lifetime.

In order to prepare the stemmata it is often necessary to follow minute errors which may bear little direct relevance to the major alterations in the text, yet occasionally may reveal either subtle or striking variations in Wesley's thought. For the full history of the text we need to follow Wesley's itineraries as he delivers new text or corrected text from printer to printer. We must also study the varying relations between him and his different printers, when and how he employed them, their idiosyncrasies, strengths, and weaknesses. And especially we must watch out for the telltale continuing misprints which offer clues and often proof of the reproduction by one compositor of another's error or alteration. Only by such careful study of apparently insignificant clues are we able to trace the sometimes complex trail of the text through various presses.

Good examples of minor changes which reveal or confirm the identity of specific families of text may be seen in Wesley's *General Rules.* This pamphlet went through thirty-six surviving editions (and four deduced editions) from at least fourteen printers. On page 71, note 16 refers to lines 6-7 of the text, whose explication may be followed in greater detail in the variant readings for those lines. Wesley's standard of conduct to demonstrate Methodist sincerity was, 'by doing no harm'. He gave as one illustration the avoidance of 'uncharitable and unprofitable conversation'. This was sufficient for the first four Bristol editions in 1743. In the London edition of 1744, however, he added: 'especially speaking evil of ministers or those in authority'. This became more specific in the edition printed in Dublin in 1747—which Wesley first visited in August that year: 'especially speaking evil of magistrates or of ministers'. From this edition another London printer in 1750 omitted the second 'of'. Probably Wesley himself again altered this phrase in Bristol in 1762, which culminated in the final reading: 'particularly speaking evil of magistrates or of ministers'. Each of these changes was incorporated into at least two later editions. These family identifications are outlined in the stemma and may be documented in general by such substantive variants, relatively unimportant though they may be—and supported by the evidence of dozens of other minute stylistic details of insufficient importance to reproduce.

In the *Rules of the Band Societies* the evidence of stylistic details, typographical variants, and printers' flowers, becomes still more important in securing a reasonably defensible stemma, for of the eighteen English editions known, specific dates are given for only three, and printers' names for only two. The first omission of one searching question, however, in J, 'Have you nothing you desire to keep secret?' divides the series neatly into two. The fact that this particular edition actually speaks of 'five' questions yet in fact omits the fifth, further marks it clearly as the edition inaugurating the group having four questions only (p. 78, l. 17). And the 1791 American edition, which still retained Q.5, affords a demonstration (together with other evidence) of a further interesting feature: that the band rules urged by Asbury and Coke on the American Methodists was based on a text long outmoded in England itself.

In the presentation of the text the large number of nonsubstantive minutiae in spelling, punctuation, the use of capitals, etc., although often important in preparing the stemmata, are ignored in the text, as are obvious errors and variant forms of words and phrases. From the outset of this project the Directors decided that it was not to be an antiquarian presentation. In spelling, the use of capitals and italics, in punctuation, this edition is made as easily readable as possible, though without the omission, addition, or substantive alteration of any word without informing the reader by means of square brackets or footnotes. In the relatively few instances where Wesley's English usage is outmoded—as in 'you was', 'this was wrote'—we have made no attempt to change it to a modern equivalent, though in rare instances we have added an explanatory footnote. During the 1770s there was a reformation in British spelling and typography, bringing it very close to present day usage. This we have attempted to standardize and slightly extend throughout this edition. We follow, for example, his own alteration from 'burthen' and 'murther' (found in his own early letters) to 'burden' and 'murder' in his later years—and follow such later spellings wherever either 'burthen' or 'murther' occur, the results of Wesley's own changed practice in his later years.

For the sake of future scholars who may well discover new editions to fit into the background of those now known, as also for those who in any case wish to check the researches of this present generation, all the collated texts of the thousands of varying editions are being preserved in the archives of the project, and will be made available to bona fide researchers.

F.B.

Key to abbreviations: *e* = errata; *m* = MS errata; *a, b, c,* etc. = notes

The Character of a Methodist

A		Bristol, Farley, 1742
B	2	Bristol, Farley, 1743
C	3	Newcastle, Gooding, [1742?]
D	3	Bristol, Farley, 1743
E	3	Newcastle, Gooding, 1743
F	French	London, Strahan, 1743
G	5	London, Strahan, 1745
H	6	Bristol, Farley, 1747
I		Dublin, Powell, 1747
J		Cork, Harrison, [1748?]
K		Belfast, Joy, [1750?]
L	7	London, Cock, 1751
M	7	Bristol, Farley, 1751
N	8	Bristol, Pine, 1763
O	9	London, 1766
P	9	Bristol, Pine, 1769
Q		*Works*, 15:359-73, Bristol, Pine, 1772
R	10	London, Paramore, 1786
S	11	London, New Chapel, 1791

Stemma

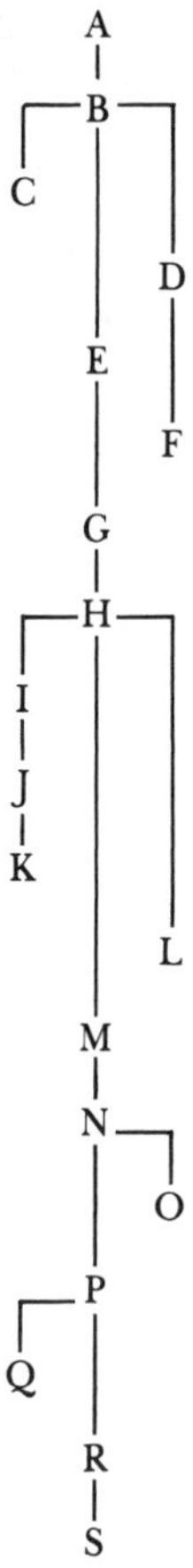

```
      A
      |
  ┌───B───┐
  C   |   |
      |   D
      E   |
      |   F
      G
      |
  ┌───H───┐
  I   |   |
  |   |   |
  J   |   |
  |   |   |
  K   |   L
      M
      |
      N───┐
      |   O
      P
  ┌───┘
  Q   |
      R
      |
      S
```

(For fuller details see *Bibliography*, No. 57)

Variants

page	*line*	
32	30	B→ 'by a student'
33	6	G-L 'I shall still rejoice', but M 'I shall rejoice', and N→ 'I should rejoice'; B→ 'be at the head'
	8	H→ 'but be buried'
	9	L 'those that *will*'
	14	I,K add 'John Wesley', J 'John Westley'
	19-20	I-L 'of such and such'

page	*line*	
34	1	P→ 'by the inspiration'; C,E→ 'herein we are'
	2	N→ 'We believe the written Word'
	3	G→ '*only and sufficient rule*'
	6	P→ 'herein we are distinguished'
	13	Q 'or common set', corrected in Q*e,m*
	29	C 'or in the covering our heads'; G→ 'or the covering of our heads'; N→ 'nor yet abstaining'
	32	A 'the marks'
35	3	Q 'he distinguished'
	4	L 'on a *single part*'
	12	Q 'No, not in all'
	14	R→ 'Much less any one'
36	20	H→ 'hath this hope'
37	2	Q omits second 'careful'
	14	Q*e,m*, 'is my heart'
	16-17	Q omits 'the lifting up the heart to God. This is the essence of prayer'
	20	R→ 'in business'
	21	L 'lieth down or riseth up'
	22-23	E-M 'mind still fixed'
	26	N→ 'by praying without ceasing'
38	11	H,L,M omit 'pride and haughtiness of spirit, whereof alone cometh'
	15	I→ 'as God for Christ's sake hath forgiven'
	16	H,L,M 'ground for pride and haughtiness of spirit, whereof alone cometh contention' (apparently inserting by error the phrase omitted from the same three edns. in 11)
	28	L 'the loving eye of his soul'
	33	L 'and is obedient to the law'
39	10	E-M 'It is glory and joy so to do'; N→ omit 'and joy'
	30	Q omits 'to'
40	8	M→ 'the race that is set'
	14	A-S 'no more than', altered to 'any more than', in Q*e,m*
41	8-9	M,Q omit 'and to provoke those who have peace with God'; restored in Q*e,m*. (It seems almost certain that this error in Q was coincidental rather than due to the use of M in preparaing the *Works* text, for the other major omission from M in 40:19-20 was not followed by Q, and using P would be much more natural)
	9-10	L 'in love and good works'
	10	M→ 'and be spent'
	17	A 'Why are these', corrected in B→ to, 'Why, these are'
	19-20	M omits 'I would to God both thou and all men knew that'
	27-28	A 'as revealed in his written Word'
42	3	A 'and whose minds'
	5-6	N→ 'Not from'
	19	O 'love, and endeavouring'
	21	A-D, 'with hope of our one calling' (surely in continued error); E,G,H,M 'with hope of our calling'; F 'comme il y a une esperance de notre seule vocation' ('as there is one hope of our one calling'); L 'with the hope of our calling'; I-K, N-U (including Wesley's own copy of his *Works*) 'with one hope of our calling'

The Whole Armour of God

(*The Whole Armour of God,* a poem by Charles Wesley on Ephesians 6, No. 56 in the Wesley *Bibliography,* was appended to editions A,B, and D of the *Character.* It had probably also been printed in Bristol earlier in 1742. We add here a stemma of its first four editions, and the variants therein, ignoring the variants which arose later.)

A		[? Bristol, Farley, 1742], broadsheet	A
B		Bristol, Farley, 1742, pp. [18-20]	B
C	2	Bristol, Farley, 1743, pp. [18-20]	C
D	3	Bristol, Farley, 1743, pp. [21-24]	D

Variants

page	*line*	
43	24	A 'And righteousness'
45	102	A 'Nor from his table move'

The Principles of a Methodist

A		Bristol, Farley, 1742	A
B	2	Bristol, Farley, 1746	B
C		Dublin, Powell, 1747	C
D	3	London, n.p., 1756	D
E		*Works,* 16:17-40, Bristol, Pine, 1772	E
F	4	London, Hawes, 1777	F
G		London, for the author, 1789	G

(For fuller details see *Bibliography,* No. 67)

Variants

page	*line*	
49	2	F→ 'one man (or but one)'
	17	F→ 'hit every blow'
	24	F→ 'in everything I say'
51	8	E omits 'and fulfilling . . . perfectly'
	19	F→ 'they justify not altogether'
	26	E omits 'his law fulfilled'
	28-30	E omits 'He for them . . . of the law.'
52	6	F→ 'do ever so'
	23	E 'merit and virtue'

page	*line*	
53	24	D,F→ 'published a few years since'
	31-55:20	E omits subsections (2)-(5)
54	16-17	F 'not essential to salvation, or salvation, or from manifold'; G 'not essential to salvation, or salvation from manifold'
56	6	A-C, and even E, read 'suffered 1541'
59	4	G omits 'both'
	27	E 'I believe when a man is justified, he is born of God.'
60	6	B→ (but not C) 'were necessarily *previous*'
61	33	E 'after the full'
	35	E 'I believe a man is justified at the same time that he is born of God.'
62	8	B→ omit 'indeed'
	11	D,F→ 'necessarily'
	16-17	E omits 'and generally long after'
	21	F→ omit 'that'
63	4	D, F→ 'necessarily'—and this time E also (cf. 60:6,62:11); E, F→ 'no, nor on anything else'
	10	E 'a strong assurance'
	28-29	E 'a clear heart', and omits 'neither the . . . Spirit', but adds 'Not in the full sense of the word.'
64	10	A→ 'considered and distinctly'; E only omits 'and', erroneously added to Tucker's text.
	20-21	E omits 'He has Christ . . . *in* him.'
	22	E omits 'or the indwelling of the Spirit'
65	2-3	E omits 'Then have . . . of the Spirit' and for 'clean' reads 'clear'
	13	E 'For no other proof'
66	5-8	E omits 'And that Christ . . . them ourselves.'
	21-22	E 'towards the inconsistencies'
	34	G 'of this subject'

The Nature, Design, and General Rules of the United Societies

A		Newcastle, Gooding, 1743
B		n.p., n.p., 1743
C	2	Bristol, Farley, 1743
D	3	Bristol, Farley, 1743
E	4	London, Strahan, 1744
[F	4	Bristol, Farley, 1745?]
G	5	Bristol, Farley, 1747
[H	5	London, 1747?]
I	5	Dublin, Powell, 1747
J	5	Cork, Harrison, [1748?]

K	5	Limerick, Welsh, [1749?]
L	6	London, Cock, 1750
M	6	Belfast, Joy, 1750
N	7	London, Pasham, 1755
O	8	London, n.p., 1756
P	6	Dublin, Powell, 1758
Q	10	Cork, Harrison, 17[5?]8
R	Welsh	Bala, Rowland, 1761
S	7	Bristol, Pine, 1762
T	8	London, n.p., 1764
U	9	London, n.p., 1766
V	9	Bristol, Pine, 1769
W	10	Bristol, Pine, 1770
X	10	London, n.p., 1772
Y		*Works* 15:231-36, Bristol, Pine, 1772
Z	11	London, Hawes, 1774
2A	16	London, Hawes, 1776
2B	17	London, Paramore, 1781
2C	18	London, Paramore, 1782
[2D		New York, 1784?]
[2E	French	London, Strahan, 1784?]
2F	19	London, Paramore, 1785
2G	19	London, Paramore, 1787
2H	18	New York, Ross, 1788
2I	19	*Discipline,* Elizabeth Town, Kollock, 1788, pp. 49-54
2J		*Discipline,* New York, Ross, 1789, pp. 47-50
2K	21	London, New Chapel, 1790

2L	*Discipline*, Philadelphia, Aitken, 1790, pp. 48-51	2L
2M	*Discipline*, Philadelphia, Crukshank, 1791, pp. 53-56	2M

(For fuller details see *Bibliography*, No. 73.)

N.B. Only limited notice is taken of variants in the American editions, since they were clearly not prepared by Wesley and did not apply to the British scene. On page 69, for instance, in the second line of the text of 2H, 'came to me' was altered to 'came to Mr. Wesley', and in other passages 'I' was changed to 'he'. In general, however, the *General Rules* were only minimally Americanized, and from 1788 became an integral feature of the annual *Discipline.*

Variants

page	*line*	
69	6-20	2I→ replaced by: 'Our Society is nothing more than "a company . . ." '; the section numbers were correspondingly lowered from 2-6, though in 2I itself '7' was retained, and not altered to '6' until 2J.
	20	2H 'first in Europe, and then in America'
70	1	2H 'There are but twelve' (an error, corrected 2I→
	3	E,J→,T→ omit 'the'
	6	I,M,P add 'and the necessary expenses of the Society'; 2H reads 'relief of the church and poor', and adds the footnote: 'These parts refer wholly to towns and cities, where the poor are generally numerous, and church expenses considerable.' 2I→ 'the relief of the preachers, church, and poor', and the footnote opens, 'This part refers'.
	8	Y omits 'may', restored in Y*e,m*
	12-13	C→ 'pay to'; B 'received in their'; C→ (except 2H) alter the order of the paragraphs to: 'To inform . . . ; To pay . . . ; And/To show . . .'
	14-15	2H→ omit this paragraph.
	18	O,P 'There is only one condition'; X→ 'of those'
	20	2H→ 'i.e. a desire to be saved'
	24-25	2H→ 'evil of every kind . . . Such as'
	27	Q 'the profaning of the day of the Lord'
	30	2H-2I '(unless in cases of necessity)', omitted from 2J; 2L-2M 'drunkenness, or drinking spirituous liquors, unless [in] cases of necessity'. 2I→ add the following lines: 'especially the buying or selling the bodies and souls of men, women, or children, with an intention to enslave them.' In 2J→ 'especially the' was omitted, and this became a separate paragraph.
72	1	A-Q 'going to law'; S-2M 'brother *going to law* with brother'
	4	2I→ 'The buying or selling goods that have not paid the duty'
	5	S→ add, 'i.e. unlawful interest'
	6	A-D,G,Q 'Uncharitable or unprofitable conversation', to which was later added, E,J,K 'Especially speaking evil of ministers or those in authority'; I,M,P 'Especially speaking evil of magistrates or of ministers' (L,N,O omit the second 'of'); S→ 'Particularly speaking evil of magistrates or of ministers'
	11-12	A-K,2G,2K 'The putting on of gold or costly apparel'; L-Q,Y omit 'of'; S-2C,2H read 'gold and costly apparel'. In 1781 new text was added (2B→, except 2H→): 'particularly the wearing of calashes, high-heads, or enormous bonnets'.
	18	X→ 'treasure'

page	*line*	
72	1-2	S→ In 1762 Wesley added a new prohibition: 'Borrowing without a probability of paying, or taking up goods without a probability of paying them', which latter phrase was corrected in X→ to 'paying for them'.
	11	A-D,G→,I→,Q,S-X,Z-2M 'exhorting all we have', so that the only known edns. corrected to 'they have' are E,J,K,Y
	13	2H→ omit 'of devils'; X,Z→ 'our hearts'
	17	C→ omit 'that'; 2H→ add after 'buying one of another': '(unless you can be served better elsewhere)', changed in 2M to 'better served'
	26	T→ 'for the Lord's sake'
73	6	A-D,G,I,L-Q 'Private prayer', which in E,J,K,S-2K was preceded by 'Family and'; M adds after 'Private Prayer', 'Family Prayer'
	10	2H→ 'word, which is the only rule'
	14	T→ 'break any of them'
	14-15	A,B 'unto him who watches over that soul as one that must give account'; C 'unto them who watch over that soul, as they that must give an account'
	15-16	A-B 'I will admonish. . . . I will bear . . .'; C→ 'We will admonish. . . . We will bear . . .'
	17	C→ 'But then if'
	20	A 'Feb. 23, 1742-3' after 'John Wesley' (only) in previous line; B→ 'May 1, 1743' and 'Charles Wesley' after 'John Wesley' in previous line. The date was changed to 'May 1, 1764' in T-X, Z-2A, and in 2H→ both signatures and date were changed to 'Thomas Coke, Francis Asbury. May 28, 1787.' These signatures were continued in 2I-2J, but omitted 2L-2M.
	21	The following edns. omit the 'Prayer', with various replacements: E,J,K, M,R,Y,2H→

Rules of the Band Societies

[N.B. Eighteen distinct English editions have so far been identified, as well as several minor states or issues of those editions, and the likelihood remains that other editions existed and may be discovered. Specific dates can be given for three only, however, specific printers for two only. It is impossible to furnish a stemma of which the complete sequence may be firmly established, let alone its accurate dating. In order to envisage the possible descent of the text, however, a table was created enumerating the minor textual and typographical variants of over forty-six brief passages. A midway change in the numbering of five searching questions to found divided them neatly into two groups, one early, one late, with one edition clearly transitional between them. These two groups were then subdivided with a fair amount of likelihood to make an outline that is at least defensible, though most of the dates remain conjectural within some narrow limits.

The inferred numbers of unnumbered pages are shown underlined; the inferred numbers of blank pages are shown underlined within parentheses; the actual format of printed page numbers are shown within quotation marks alone, or in addition to parentheses or square brackets.]

A London, Strahan, 1744, *General Rules*, pp. *8*, 9 (10) 11-12

B [London, Strahan, c. 1746], pp. *1*, '(2)', (3)', (*4*)

C Newcastle, Gooding, 1748, pp. *1-2*, 3 (*4*), 5-6, *7-8*

D [London?], 1750, half-sheet, two columns

E [London, 1756?], pp. *1*, '(2)', '(3)', (*4*)

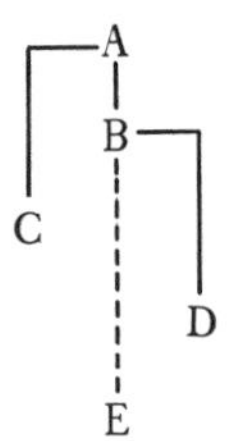

F	[Bristol, Pine, 1763?], pp. *1*, '(2)' '(3)', (*4*)
G	[Bristol, Pine, 1766?], pp. *1*, '[2]'-'[4]'
H	London, Hawes, [1773?], pp. *i*, '(ii)'-'(iv)'
I	[London, Hawes, 1774?], pp. *1*, '(2)'-'(4)'
J	[London, Hawes, 1780?], pp. *1*, '(2)'-'(4)'
K	[London, Paramore, 1782?], pp. *1*, '(2)'-'(4)'
L	[London, Paramore, 1783?], pp. *1*, '(2)'-'(4)'
M	[London, Paramore, 1784?], pp. *1*, '(2)'-'(4)'
N	[London, Paramore, 1786?], pp. *1*, '(2)'-'(4)'
O	[London, Paramore, 1787?], pp. *1*, '(2)'-'(4)'
P	[London, Paramore, 1788?], pp. *1*, '(2)'-'(4)'
Q	[London, Paramore, 1789?], pp. *1*, '(2)'-'(4)'
R	[London, Paramore, 1790?], pp. *1*, '(2)'-'(4)'
S	Philadelphia, Crukshank, 1791, *Discipline*, pp. 14-16

(For fuller details see *Bibliography*, No. 81.)

Variants

page	*line*	
77	4-5	L,P,Q 'for one another that ye may'; E-K,M-O, 'that you may'
78	16-24	C omits, possibly by error, because of the peculiar format
	17	A,B,D-I,S 'five following'; J retains this text, but omits Q.5; K-R 'four following'
	18	A 'What known sin'
	23	A,B,D 'a sin'
	24	J-R omit Q.5
79	6	B-R 'buy or sell'; A,S only read 'nor'
	22	O 'and self-denial'
	24	O 'attend to all'
	32	J-R 'meditate therein'

Answer to the Rev. Mr. Church's Remarks

A		Bristol, Farley, [1745]
B	2	London, Strahan, 1745
C		*Works* 16:41-107, Bristol, Pine, 1772

(For fuller details see *Bibliography*, No. 97)

Variants

page	*line*	
82	2	C (note) N.B. The sentences quoted from the *Remarks* are all printed in *italics.*
84	13	B 'first of all these'
92	15	C omits 'with', restored in C*e,m*
96	6-7	C omits 'Not in the same degree'
99	30	C 'which is wrought in us'
100	9,15	A,B 'Once you hold', revised in C
105	1	C 'wretchedness', revised back to 'wretchlessness' in C*e,m*
107	21	A 'self-murther'
109	29	C 'nothing to your purpose'
111	22	C 'Having spoken'
112	16	C 'Yes are witnesses'
114	13-14	C 'the directions of God's Spirit'
115	28	C*e,m* 'resisting the Spirit'
116	6	C 'the works of God'
	13	A→ 'their *original* meaning' altered in C*e,m*
119	15	C 'both the disorders and removals'

Advice to the People called Methodists

A		[Newcastle, Gooding], 1745
B	2	London, [Strahan], 1746 (*sic*)
C	3	Bristol, Farley, 1745
D	4	Bristol, Farley, 1746
E	5	Bristol, Farley, 1746
F		Dublin, Powell, 1748
G		London, Cock, 1751
H		*Works,* 16:3-16, Bristol, Pine, 1772
I		London, Paramore, 1787

(For fuller details see *Bibliography,* No. 108.)

Variants

page	*line*	
123	8	A,F,G 'in uniform resemblance'
124	23	B→ 'mortal eye'
	25	B-D 'to *me* a sinner'
	29	B-D 'that *his* sins are forgiven'
126	19-20	A,F-H, 'unless in cases of necessity'
	34	I omits 'either'

page	line	
127	13-14	H omits 'and' in 14, which Wesley corrected in H*e*, *m* by changing the opening 'Consider' to 'Considering'
128	12	B→ add 'King George'
	26-27	D→ 'rank yourself'
129	9	I adds 's' to 'acquaintance', which Wesley had treated as a collective noun.
	14	A,F-H, 'to persons'
	24-25	A→ 'Keep . . . tread' in roman, perhaps in order to throw the emphasis forward to *'Be true to your principles.'*
131	16	I omits 'anger'

Modern Christianity exemplified at Wednesbury

A		Newcastle, Gooding, 1745
B	2	London, Strahan, 1745
C		*Works* 18:16-51, Bristol, Pine, 1773
D		London, New Chapel, 1790

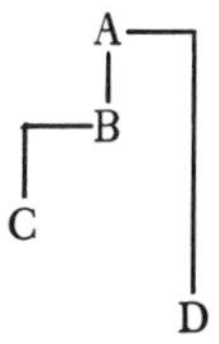

(For fuller details see *Bibliography*, No. 110.)

Variants

page	line	
137	13	B,C 'John Fletcher'
	29	B 'with club' (error, mistakenly corrected by C 'a club')
138	33	C 'On the 10th of June'
	34	C 'On the 10th of June'
139	13	C 'On the 20th of June'
	14	C 'John Baker by name, first'
	17	C 'casement' (surely an error)
149	5	C 'whosoever did not'
143	16	C omits 'of' from 'off of'
	34	C 'removing the goods'
147	8	A 'Tuesday, Jan. 31, 1742/3'; B-C 'Jan. 31, 1743/4', D' Jan. 31, 1743'. A and D were incorrect, B and C correct: Jan. 31, 1744 (by modern reckoning) was indeed a Tuesday.
	14	D, 'They said', surely an editorial attempt to correct the apparent discrepancy of the unintroduced 'she' speaking.
	18-19	B,C 'came in part'
148	11	C omits 'iron'
	35	D 'beside a hedge'
149	19-20	B,C, 'some iron'
	33	A 'March 5, 1742/3'; B 'March 5, 1743/4'; C 'March 25, 1743/4'; D 'March 5, 1743'. Cf. 147:8 above. Again A,D are incorrect, B-C correct for the year, though C's day is apparently a misprint—the date was March 5, 1744. Again this is confirmed by the fact that Feb. 7 was Shrove Tuesday in 1744, but not in 1743.

page	*line*	
150	17	C 'They that came to my house first'
	31	D omits 'I'
151	6	C only adds 'provided'
	8	D 'But they then said'; C 'I must set my hand to this paper'
	34	A-D 'what they were come for'; D inserts 'here'.
152	11	D 'John Sheldon was at this time helping'
154	5-6	D 'the foregoing account'
	11	D omits 'him'
	35-36	D omits 'that he should have no warrant; and farther said'
	38	D 'warrant'
155	4-5	C This is Wesley's closing comment, for from his *Works* he omits the account of his own experience with the Staffordshire rioters.
	7	A-B 'Wednesday, Oct. 19, 1743', but D, 'Wednesday, Oct. 19, 1744', the earlier date being proved correct from Wesley's *Journal.*
156	24	D 'done to you'
	38	B 'bitterly professing'
157	8	D 'overruling him'
	21	D omits 'once'

The Principles of a Methodist Farther Explained

A London, Strahan, 1746

B *Works* 16:108-221, Bristol, Pine, 1771

A
|
B

(For fuller details see *Bibliography*, No. 123.)

Variants

page	*line*	
167	14	A→ 'in any ways', corrected in B*e,m*
170	24-25	A→ 'the justness of . . . your remarks . . . have been', corrected in B*e,m*
172	2	A→ 'August 8, 1741': see the letter, 26:24-31 in this edn.
175	36	B omits 'have'
179	29	A 'state is thus begun'
181	21	B 'I begin thus'
	26	B 'the severest frost'
182	3	A '(you said)'
	35	B 'the opposite revelations'
183	33	B 'You make'
189	11	B omits 'part', which is reinseted B*e,m*
197	10	A 'was false persuasion', 'a' added in B
201	18	B omits 'my'
203	19	B omits 'to'
207	19	A 'in the hope'; Wesley's omission of 'the' echoes Rom. 5:2.
208	13	B erroneously alters to 'of the kind'; cf. p. 119 above, l. 25.
	23	B 'I suppose that you'; B*e,m* remove the added 'that'.
212	20	B omits 'quite'

page	line	
213	28	B 'but hence you'; 'since' is restored in B*e,m*
219	26	B omits 'shall'
220	28	B omits 'not', then restores by B*e,m*
222	20	B *'natural cause'*
224	19	B 'the work of the Lord'
229	12	A 'hearts'
	21-24	B omits
230	10	B 'generality of Methodists'
	11	B 'regular, and well-disposed'
231	22	B adds 'at'
	23	B Wesley does not add 'and' here, as in 230:11
233	8	B omits 'even'
234	24	B 'How long will you'
	31	B 'of their own holiness'

Gair i'r Methodist—A Word to a Methodist

A	Dublin, [Powell?], 1748	A
B	Dublin, [Powell?], 1751	B

(For fuller details see *Bibliography*, No. 145.)

Variants

page	line	
240	6	A 'Roedd', altered in B to 'Yr oedd'
	27	A 'gida', altered in B to 'gyd a'
241	21-22,36	A 'tuac' (three times in this sentence), altered in B to 'tuag'
	25	A 'drwg-sariad', altered in B to 'drwg-siarad'

A Letter to a Clergyman

A		Dublin, Powell, 1748	A
B		London, [Strahan, 1748]	B
C	3	Bristol, Pine, 1766	C
D		*Letter to . . . Fleury,* pp. 7-11, Dublin, [Kidd], 1771	D
E		*Works* 16:247-53, Bristol, Pine, 1772	E

(For fuller details see *Bibliography*, No. 146)

Variants

page	*line*	
248	6	D adds 'our'
	26	E 'all around'
249	22	E 'he has no authority'
250	10	E 'saves no soul at all'
251	25-27	D omits

A Plain Account of the People called Methodists

A		Bristol, Farley, 1749
B	2	London, Strahan, 1749
C		Dublin, Powell, 1749
[D?	4	Newcastle, Gooding, 1749??. See note below]
E	5	London, Cock, 1755
F	6	Bristol, Pine, 1764
G		*Works* 15:194-230, Bristol, Pine, 1772
H	7	London, Paramore, 1784
I	8	London, Paramore, 1786

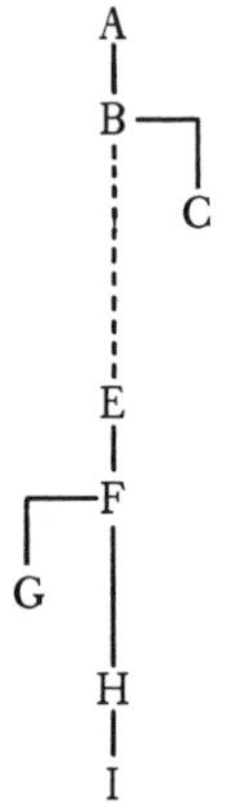

A
B
C
E
F
G
H
I

(For fuller details see *Bibliography.* No. 156.)

N.B. Wesley was in Newcastle Sept. and Oct. 1749, but searches in local newspapers show a tailing off in Gooding's advertisements of single items. Possibly a further Bristol edition has disappeared.

Variants

page	*line*	
254	4	G adds after title, '(Written in the Year 1748)'
	24	E→ 'About ten years ago'
255	3	G*m* (only) 'in doing good, in using'
	23	H→ omit 'as well as . . . determined', possibly a compositorial error.
256	11	G omits 'the'
	15	E→ 'you desire this'
257	2	G omits 'and', as does the original *Rules.*
	2-22	G omit 'But wherever . . . fasting or abstinence', and adds a footnote, 'See the Rules of the United Societies.'
	8	A→ 'Such as', apparently a continued misprint for orig., 'Such is'.
	11	H→ omit 'particularly'
	18-19	I 'of you falsely'; F,H→ 'for the Lord's sake'
	20	A-B (in error) 'Be attending'
	23-24	E 'as had an opportunity'

page	*line*	
259	4	C adds after 'toward them': 'And they (generally speaking) continue to join in the same public worship they did before.'
	7-8	I omits 'But the fellowship . . . cannot be destroyed.'
260	12	E→ 'under those inconveniences' but G*e* reverted to 'these'
261	32	C 'who were not averse'; E→ 'they often had no opportunity'
	36	G*m* 'cleared up'; E→ omits 'both'
262	16	H→ 'And by speaking'
	17	C→ 'they grew up into'; G 'who is the head'
	37	C,G 'another, is not'
263	3-4	E→ 'formal or dead'
	9	H→ 'text that forbids'
	29	B,E→ 'several Scripture Rules'
	33	F→ 'gifts nor graces'
264	1-2	C 'both from experience and observation, from the advices'
265	29-30	G 'of the community'
266	4-5	H→ omit 'frequently to read . . . to hear'
	13	H→ 'folly of man'
	31	F→ 'pour out their hearts'
267	23-24	B,E,F,I→ 'necessities shall require'
	27-28	G adds 'in band'
268	24	G 'what, they betray'
	37	E,F,H,I 'they call'
269	1-2	H→ omit 'by sins of . . . heart sins, or'; H varies the residue to 'giving way in what they call little things, by sins not watching unto prayer'; from this I omits 'sins'.
	23	A→ 'they rose the higher for their fall'; G*m* alters to 'they rose higher than before'
	28	H→ 'some advice'
270	7	G omits 'all'
	22	E→ 'in the multitude'
	29	A,B,E→ have 'There are Leaders'; C altered this to 'These are Leaders', which was later noted by Wesley, who added the same reading in G*e,m*—though it may well have been an error in C.
	31-32	A-F,H→, 'how we are'
271	1	C 'To expound the Scripture every'
	4-5	C omits '(London . . . excepted) once a month'; G reads 'quarter' for 'month'
	13-272:28	G omits the rules and qualifications of the Assistants.
	38	E,F,H→ omit 'Act', surely in continued error.
272	29	C (only) inserts 'a', but does so instead of an opening quotation mark, which is closed only in I. G removes this opening quotation mark, but does not realize that C's 'a' was almost certainly a genuine correction, not a conjectural addition. When this was at length realized, G*e,m* added 'a'.
273	16	G 'preachers'
274	30	H→ 'his account'; G, footnote, 'The leaders now do this.'
275	2	A→ 'beside those', altered in G*m* to 'these'
276	13	C 'Take this decoction three'
	20	G 'name to such'
277	8	F,H→ 'who defended the cause'
	13	G 'then all that was'
	21	A,C 'who were in town'
	30	E→ add footnote, 'This has been since dropped for want of support.'
278	8	A→ 'cast accompts'

page	line	
	17	G 'The rules of the school are these that follow'; this is cancelled by a footnote in G*m*: 'This also has been dropped for some time.'
	19	A-B, E-F,H→ 'children to be present; C,G add 'are'
	22	G footnote, 'Now they begin later', is deleted in G*m*
	27	E→ 'We appoint two stewards'; G*e,m* restore 'appointed'
279	5	G*e,m* strike out 'said'
	8	H→ 'A happy change'
	10	E→ 'They learned . . . swiftly; and at the same time'
	13-14	C only adds section 6.
	26	G adds footnote, 'We now lend any sum, not exceeding five pounds.'
280	10	B→ add 'a year' to A's 'ten thousand pound which I receive'
	15-16	E→ 'eight hundred and sixty thousand pounds'
	17	G 'Tolerable competence!'; G*m* restores 'A'

A Short Address to the Inhabitants of Ireland

A		Dublin, Powell, 1749	A—┐
B	2	London, Cock, 1749	| B
C	3	London, Cock, 1749	| C
D		Dublin, Powell, 1750	D

(For fuller details see *Bibliography*, No. 167.)

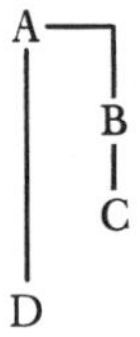

Variants

page	line	
285	28	B→ 'only'
286	28-31	B→ omit 'Not with fact . . . reason; for'
287	28	B→ 'continually advancing'

A Letter to the Rev. Mr. Baily of Cork

A		Dublin, Powell, 1750	A
B	2	London, [Strahan], for Robinson, 1750	B
C		*Works* 18:99-139, Bristol, Pine, 1773	C

(For fuller details see *Bibliography*, No. 185.)

Variants

page	*line*	
290	2	C 'Dr. Tucker, Dr. Church'
	20	C 'stop to those'
293	29	C 'would have broken in'
294	23	B 'Tremnell', followed by JWJ.
295	34	C 'from his first preaching'
296	6	A 'yet particularly'
	17	C 'thrust and fastened'
297	9	C 'their prosecutors'
298	3	C 'churches and meetings enough'
300	26	C 'I know the circumstances of the cause'
306	8	A-B "sloth or profuseness', corrected to 'profaneness' in C.
307	1-2	C 'greater than profit'
	22	A-B *'Explicuit'*
310	23	C 'mind that was'

A Letter to the Rev. Dr. Free

A		Bristol, Farley, 1758	A
B		*Dr. Free's Edition*, London, for the author, 1759	B (from A)
C	2	*Dr. Free's Edition*, London, for the author, 1759	C (from B)
D		*Works*, 17:23-30, Bristol, Pine, 1773	D (from A)

(For fuller details see *Bibliography*, No. 227.)

Variants

page	*line*	
318	27	A 'Mahomedan', altered in D to 'Mahometan'
	28	B*m* alters A's 'blaspheme' to 'blasphemes'
319	22	D 'evidence'
	35	D 'foundation'

A Second Letter to the Reverend Dr. Free

A	Bristol, Farley, 1758	A
B	*Dr. Free's Edition*, London, for the author, 1759	B (from A)

(For fuller details see *Bibliography*, No. 228.)

Variants

N.B. There are many minor errors in the text of the *Works*, but no substantive variants worth recording.

Reasons against a Separation from the Church of England

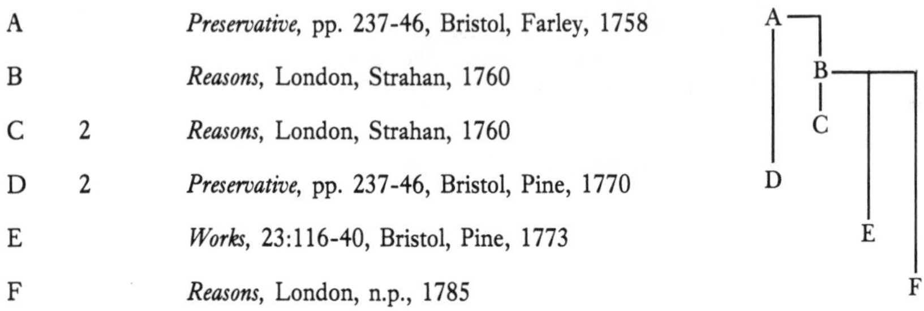

A		*Preservative*, pp. 237-46, Bristol, Farley, 1758
B		*Reasons*, London, Strahan, 1760
C	2	*Reasons*, London, Strahan, 1760
D	2	*Preservative*, pp. 237-46, Bristol, Pine, 1770
E		*Works*, 23:116-40, Bristol, Pine, 1773
F		*Reasons*, London, n.p., 1785

(For fuller details see *Bibliography*, Nos. 226, 240.)

Variants

page	*line*	
334	3	E*e,m* add 'Written in the year 1758'
	17-18	B,C,E,F omit 'and thereby . . . the devil'
335	17	B,C,E,F 'and aptness' (surely an error)
337	22	B,C,E,F 'who are born'
338	1	C,F 'and be spent'
340	8	D 'Nor is his language' (surely in error)
341	10	All except A,D have 'to read over the *Preservative against unsettled Notions in Religion*'.
	18	A,D omit John Wesley's name, as he alone was responsible for the *Preservative*. Nor does that volume contain Charles Wesley's added note nor his hymns, though John does add these to his *Works*, i.e., E.
348	30	E,F 'land them safe' instead of Charles's 'lead them safe'.

A Letter to the Rev. Mr. Downes

A	London, n.p., for Foundery, 1759	A
B	*Works* 17:31-54, Bristol, Pine, 1773	B

(For fuller details see *Bibliography*, No. 238.)

Variants

page	*line*	
356	10	B reads 'the band', whereas Downes (p. 102) had 'those bands or ligaments'. (There seem to be somewhat more minor errors than usual in the *Works* version of the text. Most of these are ignored, where the correct text was available in A.)
357	34	A,B 'obedience and holy life'; B*e*,*m* supply 'an'
363	10	B omits 'is', though a large space is left for it.
	36	A (p. 19) misplaced an incorrect footnote cue to 'P. 44'; B omits both cue and note completely
365	27	B 'either great or small'
366	6	B adds 'of' to 'an healthful mind'

A Short History of Methodism

A		London, [Bowyer], 1765
B	2	London, [Bowyer?], 1765
C		*Works* 15:374-81, Bristol, Pine, 1772
D		London, Hawes, 1774
E		London, New Chapel, 1789

(For fuller details see *Bibliography*, No. 264.)

Variants

page	*line*	
368	5	E 'some young gentlemen'
	9	E omits 'chiefly'
	15	A-D 'Brazen-nose', E 'Brazen nose'
369	1	E omits 'on'
370	5-6	E 'such dangerous errors'
371	12-16	B,C revise and abridge the paragraph after 'under him': 'Soon after Mr. Maxfield, one of Mr. Wesley's preachers, and several of the people, left Mr. Wesley. But still Mr. Maxfield and his adherents go under the general name of Methodists.'

A Letter to the Rev. Dr. Rutherforth

A	Bristol, Pine, 1767 [i.e., 1768]
B	*Works* 17:87-109, Bristol, Pine, 1773

(For fuller details see *Bibliography*, No. 308.)

Variants

page	*line*	
374	2	A 'March 24, 1768', altered in B to March 26
378	28	A 'illusterate men', though Pine had no difficulty with 'illiterate' when he met it on 377:16, nor with the correction in B.
379	36	A 'and that only to *their own* destruction'; B adds 'not'
382	32-33	A ' "consistently with my understanding doctrines" ', a misprint discussed in note 25, and amended in B by ' "consistently with my own doctrines" '
384	12	B 'out of the society'
388	7	B 'the case of any of them'

A Letter to the Rev. Mr. Fleury

N.B. There is no stemma in this instance, because the letter was not even reprinted in Wesley's *Works,* probably because its substance had already been incorporated in *A Letter to a Clergyman* of 1748 (pp. 247-51). Therefore, of course, there are no variants. (For fuller details see *Bibliography,* No. 329.)

An Answer to Mr. Rowland Hill's Tract, entitled, Imposture Detected

A		London, [Fry], 1777	A
B		London, Fry, 1777	B
C	3	London, Fry, 1777	C
D		London, Hawes, 1777	D

(For fuller details see *Bibliography,* No. 368.)

Variants

page	*line*	
404	17	C→ 'I have said'
411	10	B→ add 'Who affirms it?' [Actually this omission, rather than being an oversight in a second edition, seems more likely to have been an error in a first edition, anonymously printed, and advertised only as 'Sold at the Foundery'—which in fact all four editions were. Therefore this, which was originally thought to have been the first edition, seems now more probably to have been the second edition.]

A Letter to the Rev. Mr. Thomas Maxfield

As in the case of *A Letter to the Rev. Mr. Fleury* above, there is no stemma, simply the single edition, and thus no variants.

(For fuller details see *Bibliography,* No. 385.)

Short History of the People called Methodists

As pointed out in the introduction (p. 425) this work was reprinted in Halifax, Nova Scotia, apparently in 1787. There is no evidence, however, that Wesley himself had any hand in that reprint, so that the forty or so stylistic variants therein are of no real importance in the history of Wesley's text. No stemma nor variant readings are therefore given except some parallels with the passages of his own *Journal*, which is his main literary source.

Excerpts from the Arminian Magazine

Eleven occasional writings appeared during Wesley's last decade and dealt with the present problems and future destiny of the Methodist Societies, whether as an entity within the Church of England or in some form of cooperation or separation. Most had their sole or major appearance in the pages of Wesley's monthly, *The Arminian Magazine*, though one or two appeared as broadsheets or printed letters. None seemed to have a wide circulation, and there seems no point in attempting to prepare stemmata nor variant readings.

APPENDIX B

'Philalethes' to John Wesley
A partial reconstruction based upon Wesley
A Letter to the Rev. Mr. Baily (1750)
[see above, pp. 289-314]

pp. [1-2?]. The author claims, 'I am but a plain, simple man' [Pref. 1].

pp. [2-3?]. He asks for the facts about the Cork riots [I.1; I.11].

pp. 3-4. The author criticizes the Methodist preachers, Williams, Cownley, Reeves, Haughton, Larwood, Skelton, Swindells, Tucker, and Wheatley, as 'a parcel of vagabond, illiterate babblers' of whom 'everybody that has the least share of reason must know' that, though 'they amuse the populace with nonsense, ribaldry, and blasphemy, they are not capable of writing orthography or good sense' [II.6].

p. 4. He accuses Wesley of being 'Theophilus', the author of *A Letter to Parson B[u]tl[e]r and his friends in Cork: 'Theophilus* and *John Wesley* seem to me the same individual person' [II.8].

p. [5?]. 'The doctrine you teach is only a revival of the old antinomian heresy, I think they call it' [Pref. 1].

p. 6. 'The magistrate' [mayor] was only 'endeavouring to secure the peace of the city' [II.22].

p. 7. He charges Wesley with being a 'hare-brained enthusiast' [II.13].

p. 7. He charges Wesley with 'promoting the cause of arbitrary popish power' [II.15].

p. 7. The clergy are really unaffected by Wesley: 'What need have they to rage and foam' at his preaching? 'Suppose you could delude the greater part of their flocks, this could not affect their temporal interest' [II.23].

p. 8. He charges Wesley with 'rob[bing] and plunder[ing] the poor, so as to leave them neither bread to eat nor raiment to put on' [II.17].

p. 8. He calculates Wesley's income from the class-money of the poor: 'Two thousand pence a week! A fine yearly revenue from assurance and salvation tickets!' [II.18].

p. [9?]. 'The honour' is 'greater than the profit' [II.19].

pp. 10-11. The Methodist preacher Thos. Williams 'made use of unwarrantable expressions, particularly with regard to faith and good works. And the next day denied that he had used them.' Author also speaks of his 'indecent and irreverent behaviour at church, turning all the preacher said into ridicule, so that numbers asked, in your hearing, why the churchwardens did not put the profane, wicked scoundrel in the stocks' [II.5].

p. 13[-16]. A witness falls foul upon Mr. Cownley, and miserably murders a tale he has got by the end, and Mr. M. will not thank Philalethes for bringing the character of his niece into question in relation to Cownley [II.3].

p. 16. Wesley says, 'You next aver that Mr. Jonathan Reeves' (his preacher) 'asked a young woman whether she had a mind to go to hell with her father' [II.3].

p. 17. Author charges Wesley with 'being the cause of all that Butler has done' [II.16].

p. 18. Author relates the 'monstrous, shocking, amazing blasphemy spoken by Mr. Charles Wesley, who one day, preaching on Hammond's Marsh, called out, "Has any of you got the Spirit?" And when none answered, said, "I am sure some of you have got it; for I feel virtue go out of me"' [JW does not believe this; II.4].

p. 18. Author attacks Thos. Williams for applying the words, 'I thy Maker am thy husband,' author concluding, 'These expressions could only flow from a mind full of lascivious ideas' [II.5].

p. 20. Re: clergy, 'But ought we to condemn all for the faults of a few?' [II.12].

p. 21. Author says Wesley himself is 'as fond of riches as the most worldly clergyman' [II.18].

p. 21. 'There is not a clergyman who would not willingly exchange his living for your yearly penny contribution' [II.18].

p. 22. Wesley says, 'independent on the *Letter to Mr. Butler,* you charge me with "a frontless assurance, and a well-dissembled hypocrisy"' [II.13].

p. 24. Author charges Wesley with holding 'midnight assemblies' [II.15].

pp. 24-25. Preachers 'made a woman plunder her poor, old husband, and another absent herself from her husband and children' [II.7].

p. 26. 'While charity stands in the front of Christian graces, the author of such a book [apparently Theophilus, *Letter to Butler*] can have none of that grace. For you must allow the vulgar to think' [II.9].

p. 27. Wesley says, 'Your last charge is, that I "profess myself to be a member of the Established Church, and yet act contrary to the commands of my spiritual governors, and stab the Church to the very vitals", [and am] "the treacherous son who stabs this affectionate and tender mother"' [II.20].

p. 28. 'You say you are sent of God to inform mankind of some other relevation of his will' than 'what has been left by Christ and his apostles' [II.14].

pp. 29-30. Wesley, 'I come now to your defence of the Corporation and clergy.' Philalethes asks for names of those concerned in riots: 'Pray by all means point them out, that they may be distinguished by some mark of honour above their brethren' [II.21].

pp. 29-30. 'All the magistrates except one' were concerned in 'this method' of securing peace, and 'all the clergy' in thus 'endeavouring to bring back their flock, led astray by these hirelings, into the right fold' [II.22].

p. [30?]. 'What is the tendency of all this but to work in men's minds a mean opinion of the clergy?' [III.4].

p. 30. 'Those of the clergy with whom I have conversed freely own they have not learning sufficient to comprehend your scheme of religion' [III.1].

p. [?]. 'Does Christianity encourage its professors to make use of lies, invectives, or low, mean abuse, and scurrility, to carry on its interest?' [III.12].

APPENDIX C

Ought we to Separate from the Church of England?

[see above, pp. 334-42]

The correspondence between John and Charles Wesley shows that during the winter of 1754–55 the danger of Methodism separating from the Church of England because of ambitious preachers was a constant threat. (See Frank Baker, *John Wesley and the Church of England*, pp. 164-67.) To meet the controversy which was likely at the 1755 Conference, John prepared a document to read at that Conference, which was eventually revised to become *Reasons against a Separation from the Church of England*. There are, however, many interesting and important points of difference, and in any case the *Reasons* only utilizes sections III.(IV)–V.6 of this document.

We do not have Wesley's own manuscript, but a transcript made by his preacher John Nelson on pp. 1-45 of a duodecimo notebook owned by Charles Wesley, now in the Methodist Archives, Manchester. Nelson's obvious spelling errors have been corrected, abbreviations have been extended, and the whole has been styled in accordance with the general principles adopted for this edition. Because Wesley's organization of the material leaves several dangling series of numbers within sections II and III, each of these has been divided into sub-sections, (I)–(III) and (I)–(IV), to which Wesley's own numberings are attached as sub-sub-sections. This is a normal use by Wesley himself of (I)–(III), but in each instance they are enclosed within [ ] to demonstrate that they are editorial interventions.

'Ought we to Separate from the Church of England?'[1]

I. This is a question which has been proposed to us many times, and indeed many years since. It has been moved by very serious and pious men, zealous for God and the salvation of men, to whose minds it has frequently been brought at the times of their nearest approach to God, in private and in public prayer, at the Lord's Supper, and at seasons of solemn humiliation. I in particular have had many thoughts concerning it, which were chiefly occasioned by a serious man who, when I was in Dublin, pressed me upon the head, and urged several reasons for it.[2]

[1] MS 170, Methodist Archives, The John Rylands University Library of Manchester, reproduced by permission of the Archivist of The Methodist Church.

[2] Because of illness Wesley had not been in Dublin since 1752. The 'serious man' may have been the Huguenot banker William Lunell (1699–1774), who had been a leading Methodist but had come strongly under the influence of Whitefield's Calvinism, which proved a disruptive force in Dublin.

It is evidently a question of vast importance, as affecting so great a number of people called Methodists who[3] (whether they joined in it or not) would be deeply concerned in such a separation, but likewise the whole body of people commonly termed the Church of England. It concerns all these in a very tender point. With many it is touching the apple of their eye. It appears to them to be like removing ancient landmarks and throwing all things into disorder and confusion.

It is therefore highly necessary to be considered, and that with the utmost care and exactness—the rather because it has been so much canvassed already both by our friends and our enemies. But with how little effect! And that for a plain reason: scarce any of the disputants on either side understood in any tolerable degree the question of which they disputed. Nor is this any wonder, seeing the terms of it are extremely complex and ambiguous.

II.[(I).] Wherefore before any reasonable answer can be given it is necessary to fix the meaning of these terms. What then do we here mean by the 'Church of England', and what by 'separating from it'? As to the former, 'A Church' (according to our Nineteenth Article) 'is a congregation or company of faithful (believing) people, in which the pure Word of God is preached and the Sacraments duly administered, in all that essentially pertains thereto.'[4]

It has been questioned whether according to this definition the Church of England, so called, be any Church at all. But waiving this, let us take that term in the usual sense, meaning thereby, 'that body of people, nominally united, which profess to hold the doctrine contained in the Articles and Homilies, and to use Baptism, the Lord's Supper, and Public Prayer, according to the Common Prayer Book'. Perhaps some would add, 'And to submit to the governors of the Church, and obey the laws of it'.

By the *laws* of the Church I mean the *rubrics*. Whether the *Canons* are laws of the Church of England is doubtful, seeing it is a question whether they were ever confirmed by any competent authority.

Many affirm that we have separated from the Church already, to whom we answer plainly:

We do not *separate* from the *people* of the Church as such. We were bred up with them, and we remain with them. We are now as much united with them as ever we were, and as the rest of them are with one another.

We do not *separate* from the *doctrine* of the Church. We receive both the Articles and Homilies as excellent compendiums of Christian doctrine, and can make it appear that we keep closer thereto than any other body of people in England.

We do not *separate* from the *Sacraments* or *Prayers* of the Church, but willingly attend them at all opportunities.

We submit to the *governors* and *laws* of the Church in all things not contrary to Scripture.

But we dare not so submit to those governors or those laws as to omit: (1)

[3] Orig., 'w^c' [i.e., 'which']. Nelson, the amanuensis, may have been representing Wesley's 'wch', but it may in fact have been an error (at least in some instances) for Wesley's 'w^o', which Nelson sometimes does reproduce, as he also reproduces 'who'; see II.(II).3, *ll.* 5, 17. We therefore present it here in eight following instances as '[who]'.

[4] As usual Wesley abridges and to a small extent paraphrases Art. XIX.

preaching the gospel in all places; (2) using sometimes extemporary prayer; (3) assisting those which desire to forward each others' salvation; (4), encouraging others to do the same, though they are not episcopally ordained. If any *will* call this 'separating from the Church' they are at liberty so to do.

[(II).1.] Ought we to *separate* from the Church any farther? Should we renounce all religious intercourse with the *people* of the Church? It is not clear to us that this is lawful. Certainly it is not expedient.

2. Ought we to renounce the *doctrine* of the Church, contained in the Articles and Homilies? We cannot in conscience. For though we take knowledge that the writers of them were fallible men, though we will not undertake to defend every particular expression in them, yet we cannot but very highly esteem them as yielding to few human compositions.

3. Ought we to refrain from the *public service* of the Church? The Prayers, sermons, and Lord's Supper? This would amount to a formal separation from the Church. This properly constitutes a Dissenter.

And it may be pleaded for it, 'That the ministers are wicked men. They not only know not, but flatly deny the truth. They rail at those who either teach it or hold it. Therefore no blessing can attend their ministrations. Nay, we should receive more harm than good therefrom. Therefore we scruple to attend them. Yea, we sometimes doubt, after hearing a railing sermon, whether we should not openly protest against it!'

Suppose they are wicked men (though this is not true of all, nor should you think it of any without full proof), had you this scruple when you received the love of God first? Perhaps some had; but many had not. In some doubtless it may have proceeded from tenderness of conscience; but I fear not in all. Let each of you, then, consider when and how came this scruple into your mind. Perhaps you heard a railing sermon, and instead of the tenderest pity toward him, you felt your heart rise against the preacher. Was it not then first that thought arose, 'Hear these blind guides no more'? And who, think you, suggested it? I fear, not the God of love. Had you been full of his spirit it could have found no place. It did find none while you simply waited on God in lowliness and meekness of wisdom. But 'can no blessing attend the ministration[s] of a wicked minister?'[5] You yourself can witness the contrary. You attended them many years, and you know you not only received no harm, but received many blessings thereby. So have I myself, even under a very bad sermon, and much more in the prayers and at the Lord's table. So have hundreds, yea, thousands of the people. And so they do to this very day, God hereby witnessing that the virtue of the ordinance does not depend on him that ministers but him that ordains it, and calling us to continue in the Church for our own sake as well as for [an] example to others. Although therefore it is highly to be desired that all [who] either preach or administer the sacraments were holy men (nay, and all [who] receive it—for it is a grievous thing to see servants of the devil at the table of the Lord) yet that the ministers are not so is no reason for your scrupling to attend the Church, much less for openly protesting against them, even when they rail against the truth. Neither our blessed Lord himself nor any of his apostles ever gave us a precedent of this.

5 Cf. Art. XXVI, 'Of the Unworthiness of the Ministers, which hinder not the effects of the Sacraments'.

This would indeed do infinitely more harm than good, and bring numberless difficulties both on ourselves and our brethren.

But how is it that you are grown so impatient? This is not the temper which you had once. What spirit are you of? If you cannot bear this, how would you bear the spoiling of your goods? How, when smitten on the [one] cheek, turn the other also? How resist unto blood? Be not overcome of evil, but overcome evil with good.[6]

Indeed while you have a scruple, which may sometimes be very innocent, you must act accordingly. But beware that your scruple be not your sin—as it certainly is if it springs from anger, impatience, resentment, or any wrong temper, or if you have not used and do not still use all possible means to remove it.

4. Ought we, lastly, to renounce all submission to the governors and laws of the Church? It is not plain to us that it is either expedient or lawful, seeing the rubrics are laws confirmed by Parliament, and the bishops are constituted (in some measure) governors by the same authority. Therefore we hold ourselves obliged in things indifferent to submit to both, and that by virtue of God's command: 'Submit yourself to every ordinance of man for the Lord's sake.'[7]

[(III).] Indeed some affirm, 'We may not submit to any ordinance of man relating to the worship of God: (1). Because Christ is the only lawgiver in his Church, (2). Because the Bible is the only rule of Christian worship. (3). Because Christ himself has said, "Call no man Rabbi, Master, Father,"[8] on earth; and again: "In vain do they worship me, teaching for doctrines the commandments of men." '[9]

[1.] We answer, first, The Jewish Church was Christ's as really as the Christian. And he was the only lawgiver in the Jewish as well as in the Christian Church. Yet King Jehoshaphat proclaimed a fast without any derogation to Christ's authority.[10] Yet King Josiah commanded the law to be read, and gave many other directions to that church.[11] Yet Nehemiah ordained the whole form of divine worship, and Christ was honoured, not injured, thereby. Yea, himself honoured with his presence the yearly Feast of the Dedication, instituted long before by Judas Maccabeus.[12]

It plainly follows that magistrates may regulate divine worship without any infringement of his supreme authority, and that although Christ is the only *supreme* lawgiver therein, yet magistrates are *subordinate* lawgivers, even to the Church.

2. 'But is not the Bible the only rule of Christian worship?' Yes, the only *supreme* rule. But there may be a thousand rules *subordinate* to this, without any violation of it at all. For instance the supreme rule says, 'Let all things be done decently and in order.'[13] Not repugnant to, but plainly flowing from this, are the subordinate rules concerning the time and place of divine service. And so are

[6] Rom. 12:21. (N.B. In this paragraph, as commonly throughout Wesley's writings, there are several scriptural allusions, including those to Heb. 10:34; Matt. 5:39; and Heb. 12:4. In this appendix, however, we are only footnoting lightly, and do not attempt fully to document such allusions.)

[7] 1 Pet. 2:13.

[8] Cf. Matt. 23:8-10.

[9] Matt. 15:9; Mark 7:7.

[10] 2 Chr. 20:3.

[11] 2 Kgs. 23:1-25; 2 Chr. 34:29-33; 35:1-19.

[12] See Neh., chs. 7–13.

[13] 1 Cor. 14:40.

many others observed in Scotland, Geneva, and in all other Protestant churches.

3. Therefore that text, 'Call no man Rabbi, Father, Master', is absolutely wide of the point. This has no relation at all to modes of worship, but means this and nothing else: do not pay any such *implicit* faith or obedience to any mere man as the Jews pay to their Rabbis, whom they generally call 'Father' or 'Master'.

As wide of the point is that other, 'In vain do they worship me, teaching for doctrines the commandments of men'—that is, *such* commandments of men as 'make void the commandments of God'.[14] Our Lord immediately instances in that commandment of men which made void the Fifth Commandment.

It remains, it is not a sin but our bounden duty, in all things indifferent, of whatever kind, to 'submit to every ordinance of man for the Lord's sake'.[15]

4. But is it not our duty to separate from it because, 'The Church is only a creature of the state'? If you mean only that King Edward the Sixth required several priests in the then Church of England to 'search into the law of God and teach it the people';[16] that afterwards he restored the scriptural worship of God to the utmost of his knowledge and power, and (like Josiah and Nehemiah) gave several rules for the more decent and orderly performance of it—if you mean this only by saying 'the Church is a creature of the state'—we allow it is, and praise God for it. But this is no reason at all why we should separate from it.

5. Neither is this, that 'the king is the supreme governor of the Church of England.' We think the king ought to be the supreme governor of his subjects. And all of the Church of England are his subjects. Therefore (unless he should command anything contrary to the law[17] of God) we willingly obey him as our supreme (visible) governor.

6. 'But can you defend the *spiritual courts,* so called?' No. They call aloud for a reformation. But we cannot reform them. Neither need we on this account separate from our brethren, many thousands of whom, as well as we, esteem them the scandal of our nation.

7. No more can we defend several of the *Canons*. Yet neither for this need we separate from our brethren, many of whom groan under the same burden, and patiently wait for deliverance from it.

8. Nay, there are some things in the *Common Prayer Book* itself which we do not undertake to defend.

As, in the *Athanasian Creed* (though we firmly believe the doctrine contained therein), the *damnatory clauses,* and the speaking of *this faith* (that is, these opinions) as if it were the ground term of salvation.

That expression, first used concerning King Charles the Second, 'our most religious king'.

The answers in the *Office of Baptism* which are appointed to be made by the sponsors.

[14] Mark 7:9; cf. ver. 8. The Authorized Version reads, 'reject the commandments of God'; in his *Explanatory Notes upon the New Testament* (published in the same year of 1755 during which this document was prepared) Wesley translated ἀθετεῖτε as 'abolish'. His 'make void' here probably comes from the ἀκυροῦντες of ver. 13, which the Authorized Version renders, 'making . . . of none effect', and Wesley's *Notes,* 'abrogating'.

[15] 1 Pet. 2:13.

[16] Cf. Ezra 7:10, 25.

[17] 'Word' is given as an alternative for 'law'.

The Office of *Confirmation*.

The *absolution* in the Office for Visiting the Sick.

The thanksgiving in the *Burial Office*.

Those parts of the Office for *Ordaining Bishops, Priests, and Deacons,* which assert or suppose an essential difference between bishops and presbyters.

The use of those words in *Ordaining Priests,* 'Whose soever sins ye remit, they are remitted.'

One might add (though these are not properly a part of the Common Prayer) Hopkins' and Sternhold's *Psalms*.

But supposing these are blemishes in that book, which is the general rule of public worship to that body of men [who] are termed the Church of England, still we do not see that this is a sufficient cause to separate from them. We can leave the evil and keep the good. And so may every private member of this body. We could not indeed 'declare our unfeigned assent and consent to *all and everything* prescribed and contained in that book'. But this is not required of us, nor of any ministers but those [who] are inducted to a benefice.

Therefore it does not yet appear to be either lawful or expedient (much less necessary) to separate from the Church.

'But ought you not to do this one thing—to appoint persons to baptize and administer the Lord's Supper?'

III. [(I).] It must be acknowledged this would answer many good ends. It would save our time and strength, and probably prolong our lives.[18] It would prevent abundance of trouble and much expense to several of our preachers, as well as the hazard of losing either in part or in whole the assistance of our most useful fellow-labourers, who after they are ordained seldom give themselves to the work so entirely as they did before.

But notwithstanding these great advantages which might result from it, we doubt whether it be either lawful or expedient. And, indeed, were the thing in itself lawful, yet if it is not expedient it is not now lawful to us.

If it be said, 'The doubt comes too late. You have done it already in appointing to preach,' we answer: we have not (in the sense in question) *appointed* any man to preach. There is not one of you [who] did not preach more or less antecedent to any appointment of ours. The utmost we have ever done is this: after we were convinced that God had *appointed* any of you an extraordinary preacher of repentance, we *permitted* you to act in connexion with us. But from our *permitting* you to preach with us it does not follow that we either did or can *appoint* you to administer the sacraments. We always acknowledged that nothing but absolute necessity could justify your preaching without being ordained in the scriptural manner by the 'laying on of the hands of the presbytery'.[19] Without your preaching numberless souls must have perished. But there is no such necessity for your administering the sacraments. It does not appear that one soul will perish for want of your doing this.

'But you *have allowed* [them] to administer the sacraments in permitting them to preach. For everyone [who] has authority to preach has authority to administer them.'

[18] Wesley here speaks, of course, of himself and his brother as ordained clergy, not of the preachers in general.

[19] 1 Tim. 4:14.

We cannot believe that all who have authority to preach have authority to administer the sacraments.

[(II).]1. Because from the beginning of the Jewish Church it was not so. Quite from the giving of the Law by Moses to the destruction of Jerusalem, the preachers (anciently called 'prophets', afterwards 'scribes') were one order, the *priests* another. Nor during all that time did the highest prophet as such, no, not Moses himself, meddle with the priestly office.

It is true, *extraordinary prophets* were frequently raised up, who had not been educated in the 'schools of the prophets', neither had the outward, ordinary call. But we read of no *extraordinary priests*. As none took it to himself, so none exercised this office but he that was outwardly 'called of God, as was Aaron'.[20]

2. Because from the beginning of the Christian Church it was not so. Both the evangelists and deacons preached. Yea, and women when under extraordinary inspiration. Then both their sons and their daughters prophesied, although in ordinary cases it was not permitted to 'a woman to speak in the Church'.[21] But we do not read in the New Testament that any evangelist or deacon administered the Lord's Supper; much less that any woman administered it, even when speaking by extraordinary inspiration, that inspiration which authorized them for the one not authorizing them for the other. Meantime we do read in all the earliest accounts (whatever were the case with baptism, which deacons it seems did frequently administer by the appointment of superior ministers) that none but the president or ruling presbyter ever administered the Lord's Supper. Nor is there now any one Christian Church under heaven, Greek, Latin, Lutheran, Calvinist, or any other, that affirms or allows every preacher as such to have a right of administering it.

3. Because this supposition absolutely destroys the different orders of Christian ministers, and reduces them to one, contrary both to the New Testament and to all antiquity. It is evident these always describe, if not more, at least two orders distinct from each other, the one having power only to preach and (sometimes) baptize, the other to ordain also and administer the Lord's Supper.

(III). 'But is there any priest or any sacrifice under the New Testament?' As sure as there was under the Old. The 'unbloody sacrifice' of wine and oil and fine flour was one of the most solemn which was then offered, in the place of which and [of] all the other Jewish sacrifices is the one *Christian sacrifice* of bread and wine. This also the ancients termed 'the unbloody sacrifice', which is as proper a sacrifice as was the *minchah* or 'meal offering' (not the 'meat offering', as it is stupidly falseprinted).[22] And he that offers this as a memorial of the death of Christ is as proper a priest as ever Melchisedek was.

[20] Heb. 5:4.

[21] 1 Cor. 14:35. Wesley correctly alters the 'women' of the Authorized Version to 'woman'. Cf. Acts 2:17.

[22] This mistranslation of the Authorized Version was corrected in Wesley's *Explanatory Notes upon the Old Testament,* 3 vols. (Bristol, Pine, 1765); see espec. his note on Lev. 2:1. As opposed to the sacrifice of meat, that of grain was bloodless, and the phrase, 'unbloody sacrifice', was transferred also to the Lord's Supper in the early years of the English Reformation. Wesley read John Johnson's *Unbloody Sacrifice* (1714) on his voyage to Georgia.

If it be asked, 'But is this a propitiatory sacrifice?' I answer, 'No'. Nor were there ever any such among the Jews. There never was or can be more than one such sacrifice, that offered by 'Jesus Christ the righteous.'[23]

But to proceed. It has been said, 'If you do not ordain ministers, who can? Not wicked bishops, for they are no ministers themselves.' We answer:

1. Are you assured, have you full proof, that all the bishops in England are wicked men? Dare you make the supposition without full proof? Who art thou that thus judgest of another's servants? Is it a little breach either of wisdom, justice, or love, to pass so harsh a sentence on a considerable number of persons without any proof at all against a great part, perhaps against any one of them?

2. If a wicked bishop, and consequently a wicked priest (the reason being the same) is no minister, then there were no priests in the whole Jewish Church for many hundred years together. And if they had no priests, then (their administrations being null and void) they had no sacraments for so many ages. But is it possible any should believe this who reads over the Epistle to the Hebrews? Did St. Paul ever dream while he was writing it that those priests were no priests and their sacrifices no sacrifices? Does he ever charge the inefficacy of those ministrations upon the wickedness of the ministers?

3. If a wicked bishop is no bishop, and his ordination by consequence is no ordination, then the sacraments administered by him whom such a bishop ordains are no sacraments. It follows, if we suppose two or three bishops of London successively are wicked men (by whom the ministers of London in general are ordained), that there are no ministers and so no sacraments there, that there is neither baptism nor the Lord's Supper administered in any Church in London. Come closer yet. Are *you* baptized? Are you sure of it? Are you sure the minister who baptized you was an holy man? If you are, that is not enough. Was the bishop likewise who ordained him a real Christian? If not, your baptism is no baptism. You are unbaptized to this day.

4. The Papists maintain that 'a pure intention in him that administers is necessary to the very being of a sacrament,'[24] and consequently that wherever this is wanting that which is administered is no sacrament. You have therefore these on your side. But you flatly contradict every other Church in the world. All these maintain that the unworthiness of the minister does not destroy the effect, much less the nature, of the sacrament, seeing this depends not on the character of the administrator but the truth, love, and power of the Ordainer.

[(IV).] We cannot therefore allow that sacraments administered by unholy men are no sacraments, or that wicked ministers are no ministers at all, or that every preacher has a right to administer the sacraments.[25] Nor yet that it is expedient for us (suppose it were lawful) to ordain ministers, seeing it would be little less than a formal separation from the Church, which we cannot judge to be expedient:

1. Because it would at least be a seeming contradiction to the solemn and

[23] 1 John 2:1.

[24] See the Council of Trent, Session 7, Canon II. Cf. *The Advantage of the Members of the Church of England over those of the Church of Rome* (1753), §10, and *Popery Calmly Considered* (1779), IV.2, in Vol. 13 of this edn.

[25] It is at this point that Wesley begins his slightly revised extract from the document which he published as *Reasons against a Separation from the Church of England;* see above, pp. 334-41, for fuller annotation.

repeated declarations which we have made in all manner of ways, in preaching, in print, and in private conversation.

2. Because (on this as well as many other accounts) it would give huge occasion of offence to those who seek and desire occasion, to all the enemies of God and his truth.

3. Because it would exceedingly prejudice against us many who fear, yea, who love God, and thereby hinder their receiving so much, perhaps any farther, benefit from our preaching.

4. Because it would hinder multitudes of those who neither love nor fear God from hearing us at all, and thereby leave them in the hands of the devil.

5. Because it would occasion many hundreds, if not some thousands, of those who are now united with us, to separate from us; yea, and some of those who have a work of grace in their souls.

6. Because it would be throwing balls of wild-fire among them that are now quiet in the land. We are now sweetly united together in love. We mostly think and speak the same thing. But this would occasion inconceivable strife and contention between those who left and those who remained in the Church, as well as between those very persons who remained, as they were variously inclined one way or the other.

7. Because, whereas controversy is now asleep, and we in great measure live peaceably with all men, so that we are strangely at leisure to spend our whole time and strength in enforcing plain, practical, vital religion (O what would many of our forefathers have given to have enjoyed so blessed a calm!), this would utterly banish peace from among us, and that without any hope of its return. It would engage me for one in a thousand controversies, both in public and private (for I should be in conscience obliged to give the reasons of my conduct, and to defend those reasons against all opposers), and so take me off from those more useful labours which might otherwise employ the short remainder of my life.

8. Because to form the plan of a new Church would require infinite time and care which might be far more profitably bestowed, with much more wisdom and greater depth and extensiveness of thought than any of us are masters of.

9. Because from the bare entertaining a distant thought of this, evil fruits have already followed, such as prejudice against the clergy in general, an aptness to believe ill of them, contempt (and not without a degree of bitterness) of clergymen as such, and a sharpness of language toward the whole order, utterly unbecoming either gentlemen or Christians.

10. Because the experiment has been so frequently tried already, and the success never answered the expectation. God has since the Reformation raised up from time to time many witnesses of pure religion. If these lived and died (like John Arndt, Robert Bolton, and many others) in the churches to which they belonged, notwithstanding the wickedness which overflowed both the teachers and people therein, they spread the leaven of true religion far and wide, and were more and [more] useful, till they went to paradise. But if upon any provocation or consideration whatever they separated and founded distinct parties, their influence was more and more confined; they grew less and less useful to others, and generally lost the spirit of religion themselves in the spirit of controversy.

11. Because we have melancholy instances of this even now before our eyes. Many have in our memory left the Church, and formed themselves into distinct bodies. And certainly some of them from a real persuasion that they should do God more service. But have any separated themselves and prospered? Have they been either more holy or more useful than they were before?

12. Because by such a separation we should only throw away the peculiar glorying which God has given us, that we do and will suffer all things for our brethren's sake, though the more we love them the less we be loved; but should act in direct contradiction to that very end for which we believe God hath raised us up. The chief design of his Providence in sending us out is undoubtedly to quicken our brethren, and the first message of all our preachers is to the lost sheep of the Church of England. Now would it not be a flat contradiction to this design to separate from the Church? These things being considered, we cannot apprehend (whether it be lawful in itself or no) that it is lawful for us—were it only on this ground, that it is by no means expedient.

IV. It has indeed been *objected*, that till we do separate, at least so far as to *ordain*, that our helpers may administer the sacraments, we cannot be a compact, united body. It is true we cannot till then be a 'compact united body' if you mean by that expression a body of people distinct from and independent on all others. And we do not desire so to be. Nay, we earnestly desire not to be so, but to remain united as far as is possible with the rest of the Church of England, till either a little leaven leaven the whole or they violently cast us out.

It has been objected, secondly, 'It is mere cowardice and fear of persecution which makes you desire to remain united with them.' This cannot be proved. Let everyone examine his own heart, and not judge his brother.

It is not probable. We never yet, for any persecution, when we were in the midst of it, either turned back from the work or even slackened our pace.

But this is certain, that although persecution many times proves an unspeakable blessing to them that suffer it, yet we ought not willfully to bring it upon ourselves; nay, we ought to do whatever can lawfully be done in order to prevent it. We ought to avoid it so far as we lawfully can—when persecuted in one city to flee into another. If God should suffer a general persecution, who would be able to abide it we know not. Perhaps those who talk loudest might flee first. Remember the case of Dr. Pendleton.[26]

V. [1.] Upon the whole one cannot but observe how desirable it is that all of us who are engaged in the same work should think and speak the same thing, be united in one judgment, and use one and the same language.

To this it may contribute not a little, by the blessing of God, that we have now throughly considered this great point; and the far greater part of us more nearly agree than ever we did before.

Do we not all now see *ourselves*, the *Methodists* in general, the *Church*, and the *clergy* in a clear light?

[26] Dr. Henry Pendleton preached against Lutheranism under Henry VIII, became a Protestant under Edward VI, but became a Roman Catholic once more under Mary. He died in 1557 (according to Foxe's *Acts and Monuments*), repenting his popish errors, and was buried in St. Stephen's, Walbrook.

We look upon *ourselves*, not as the authors or ringleaders of a particular sect or party (it is the farthest thing from our thoughts!), but as messengers of God to those who are Christians in name but heathens in heart and life, to call them back to that from which they are fallen, to real, genuine Christianity. We are therefore debtors to all these, of whatever opinion or denomination, and are consequently to do all that in us lies to please all, for their good, to edification.

We look upon the *Methodists* in general, not as any particular party (this would exceedingly obstruct the Grand Design for which we conceive God has raised them up), but as living witnesses in and to every party of that Christianity which we preach, which is hereby demonstrated to be a real thing, and visibly held out to all the world.

We look upon *England* as that part of the world, and the *Church* as that part of England, to which all we who were born and have been brought up therein owe our first and chief regard. We feel in ourselves a strong στοργή, a kind of natural affection for our country, which we apprehend Christianity was never designed either to root out or to impair. We have a more peculiar concern for our brethren, for that part of our countrymen to whom we have been joined from our youth up, by ties of a religious as well as a civil nature. True it is that they are in general 'without God in the world'. So much the more do our bowels yearn over them. They do lie 'in darkness and the shadow of death'. The more tender is our compassion for them. And when we have the fullest conviction of that complicated wickedness which covers them as a flood, then do we feel the most (and we desire to feel yet more) of that inexpressible emotion with which our blessed Lord beheld Jerusalem, and wept and lamented over it. Then are we the most willing 'to spend and to be spent' for them, yea, to 'lay down our lives for our brethren'.

We look on the *clergy*, not only as a part of these our brethren, but as that part whom God by his adorable Providence has called to be watchmen over the rest, for whom therefore they are to give a strict account. If these then neglect their important charge, if they do not watch over them with all their power, they will be of all men most miserable, and so are entitled to our deepest compassion. So that to feel, and much more to express, either contempt or bitterness toward them, betrays an utter ignorance of ourselves and of the spirit which we especially should be of.

Because this is a point of uncommon concern, let us consider it in another view. The clergy, wherever we are, are either friends to the truth, or neuters, or enemies to it.

If they are friends to it, certainly we should do everything and omit everything we can with a safe conscience, in order to continue, and, if it be possible, increase their goodwill to it.

If they neither further nor hinder it, we should do all that in us lies, both for their sakes and for the sake of their several flocks, to give their neutrality the right turn, that it may change into love rather than hatred.

If they are enemies, still we should not despair of lessening, if not removing their prejudice. We should try every means again and again. We should employ all our care, labour, prudence, joined with frequent prayer, to overcome evil with good, to melt their hardness into love.

It is true that when any of these openly wrest the Scriptures and deny the grand truths of the gospel, we cannot but declare and defend, at convenient opportunities, the important truths which they deny. But in this case especially we have need of all gentleness and meekness of wisdom.

Contempt, sharpness, bitterness, can do no good. 'The wrath of man worketh not the righteousness of God.' Harsh methods have been tried again and again—at Wednesbury, St. Ives, Cork, Canterbury.[27] And how did they succeed? They always occasioned numberless evils, often wholly stopped the course of the gospel. Therefore were it only on a prudential account, were conscience unconcerned therein, it should be a sacred rule to all our preachers—'No contempt, no bitterness to the clergy.'

2. Might it not be another (at least prudential) rule for every Methodist preacher, 'Not to frequent any Dissenting Meeting'? (Though we blame none who have been always accustomed to it.) But if *we* do this, certainly our people will. Now this is actually separating from the Church. If therefore it is (at least) not expedient to separate, neither is this expedient. Indeed we may attend our assemblies and the Church too, because they are at different hours; but we cannot attend both the Meeting and the Church, because they are at the same hours.

If it be said, 'But at the Church we are fed with chaff, whereas at the meeting we have wholesome food,' we answer: (1). The Prayers of the Church are not chaff—they are substantial food for any who are alive to God. (2). The Lord's Supper is not chaff, but pure and wholesome food for all who receive it with upright hearts. Yea, (3), in almost all the sermons we hear there we hear many great and important truths, and whoever has a spiritual discernment may easily separate the chaff from the wheat therein. (4). How little is the case mended at the Meeting! Either the teachers are 'new light men', denying the Lord that bought them, and overturning his gospel from the very foundations; or they are predestinarians, and so preach predestination and final perseverance, more or less. Now whatever this may be to them who are educated therein, yet to those of our brethren who have lately embraced it, repeated experience shows it is not wholesome food—rather to them it has the effect of deadly poison. In a short time it destroys all their zeal for God. They grow fond of opinions and strife of words. They despise self-denial and the daily cross; and to complete all, wholly separate from their brethren.

Which then is the safer way, to attend that place where you have good food though it is often mixed with chaff, or that where it is generally mixed with poison? Indeed there may be poison at Church too, but it is gross, fulsome poison, such as *we* can in no wise swallow, whereas that at the Meeting is sweet to your taste, though to you it proves death to your soul.

3. Nor is it expedient for any Methodist preacher to imitate the Dissenters in their manner of praying: either in his *tone*—all particular tones both in prayer and preaching should be avoided with the utmost care; nor in his *language*—all his words should be plain and simple, such as the lowest of his hearers both use and understand; or in the *length* of his prayer, which should not usually exceed four or five minutes, either before or after sermon. One might add: neither should we sing like them, in a slow drawling manner—we sing swift, both because it saves time and because it tends to awaken and enliven the soul.

[27] See JWJ, Oct. 20, 1743; Apr. 4-7, 1744; July 20, 1749; Apr. 14, 1750—all examples, however, of successive anti-Methodist persecution at those places, not of Methodist 'harsh methods'.

4. Fourthly, if we continue in the Church, not by chance, or for want of thought, but upon solid and well-weighed reasons, then we should never speak contemptuously of the Church or anything pertaining to it. In some sense it is the mother of us all who have been brought up therein. We ought never to make her blemishes matter of diversion, but rather of solemn sorrow before God. We ought never to talk ludicrously of them; no, not at all, without clear necessity. Rather we should conceal them, as far as ever we can without bringing guilt upon our own conscience. And we should all use every rational and scriptural means to bring others to the same temper and behaviour. I say, *all;* for if some of us are thus minded, and others of an opposite spirit and behaviour, this will breed a real schism among ourselves. It will of course divide us into two parties, each of which will be liable to perpetual jealousies, suspicions, and animosities against the other. Therefore on this account likewise it is expedient in the highest degree that we should be tender of the Church to which we belong.

5. In order to secure this end, to cut off all jealousy and suspicion from our friends, and hope from our enemies, of our having any design to separate from the Church, it would be well for every Methodist preacher who has no scruple concerning it to attend the Service of the Church as often as conveniently he can. And the more we attend it, as constant experience shows, the more we desire to attend it. On the contrary, the longer we abstain from it, the less desire we have to attend it at all.

6. Lastly, whereas we are surrounded on every side by those who are equally enemies to us and to the Church of England; and whereas these are long practised in this war, and skilled in all the objections against it—while our brethren on the other hand are quite strangers to them all, and so on a sudden know not how to answer them—it is highly expedient for every preacher to be provided with sound answers to those objections, and then to instruct the societies where he labours how to defend themselves against those assaults. It would therefore be well for you carefully to read over the controversial tracts which we have published, in particular, *A Word to a Protestant,*[28] with *The Advantage of the [Members of the] Church of England over [those of] the Church of Rome,*[29] *A Letter to a Quaker,*[30] *Thoughts concerning Infant Baptism,*[31] *[Serious] Thoughts concerning Godfathers and Godmothers,*[32] *Serious Thoughts concerning Perseverance,*[33] and *Predestination Calmly Considered.*[34] And when you are masters of them yourselves, it will be easy for you to recommend and explain them to our

[28] *A Word to a Protestant* (1745), see *Bibliography,* No. 113, and Vol. 14 in this edn.

[29] *The Advantage . . .* (1753), see *Bibliography,* No. 205, and Vol. 13 in this edn.

[30] *A Letter to a Person lately joined with the People called Quakers* (1748), see *Bibliography,* No. 144, and Vol. 13 in this edn.

[31] *Thoughts upon Infant Baptism* (Bristol, 1751), extracted from William Wall's *History of Infant Baptism,* and published anonymously, see *Bibliography,* No. 191.

[32] *Serious Thoughts concerning Godfathers and Godmothers* (1752), see *Bibliography,* No. 197, and Vol. 12 in this edn.

[33] *Serious Thoughts upon the Perseverance of the Saints* (1751), see *Bibliography,* No. 192, and Vol. 12 in this edn.

[34] *Predestination Calmly Considered* (1752), see *Bibliography,* No. 194, and Vol. 12 in this edn.

societies, that they may 'no more be tossed to and fro by every wind of doctrine,' but being settled in one mind and one judgment, by solid scriptural and rational arguments, 'may grow up in all things into him who is our head, even Jesus Christ'.[35]

[35] Eph. 4:14, 15.

APPENDIX D

George L. Fleury, Two Sermons
A partial reconstruction based upon Wesley
A Letter to the Rev. Mr. Fleury (1771)
(see above, pp. 389-90)

These two sermons were preached on April 28, 1771, in Waterford Cathedral, attacking the Methodists from the text, Acts 20:29-30, and were published very soon afterwards, though no copies are extant. An outline may be reconstructed from Wesley's *Letter*. In this text quotations from Wesley are given in single quotation marks, from Fleury in double.

First Sermon, pp. 1-4. 'Your text was, "I know this, that after my departure shall grievous wolves enter in among you, not sparing the flock. Also of your own selves shall men arise, speaking perverse things, to draw away disciples after them. Acts 20:29-30."' 'Having shown that St. Paul foresaw these false teachers, you undertook to show, (1), the mischiefs which they occasioned; (2), the character of them, and how nearly this concerns a set of men called "Methodists".' (§3)

pp. 5-7. 'Against these false teachers, you observe, St. Paul warned the Corinthians, Galatians, Colossians, and Hebrews.' (§4)

p. 8. "These are well styled by Christ 'ravening wolves', by St. Paul 'grievous wolves', from the mischiefs they do, rending the Church of Christ, and perverting the true sense of the gospel for their own private ends. They ever did, and to this day do, pretend to extraordinary inspiration." (§5)

p. 9. "They denounce hell and damnation to all that reject their pretences." (§6) "To reject their ecstasies and fanatic pretences to revelation is cried up as a crime of the blackest dye." (§6)

p. 11. "These grievous wolves pretended to greater mortification and self-denial than the apostles themselves." (§7) "However, better than their successors." (§8) "Thus also do the modern false teachers." (§8)

p. 12. "They pretend to know the mind of Christ better than his apostles." (§8) "However, better than their successors do." (§8)

p. 14. 'You conclude this Sermon, "Let us not be led away by those who represent the comfortable religion of Christ as a path covered over with thorns."' (§9)

"But you represent *us* as lovers of pleasure more than lovers of God." (§9)

p. 15. "They affirm pleasure in general to be unlawful, grounding it on, 'They that are in the flesh cannot please God.'" (§9) "This is bringing men *after the principles of the world, and not after Christ.*" (§9)

Second Sermon, p. 1. 'You begin the second, "I shall now consider some of their many *absurd doctrines*, the first of which is, 'the pretending to be divinely inspired'."' (§10)

pp. 2-4. "and called in an extraordinary manner to preach the word of God". (§10)

p. [5?]. "This is . . . the grand objection of *lay preachers*." (§10)
"But why do you not prove your mission by miracles?" (§11)
"Those who lay claim to *extraordinary* inspiration and revelation ought to prove that claim by miracles." (§13) "Because Christ and his apostles did." (§13)

p. 6. "They pretend to be as free from sin as Jesus Christ." (§14)

p. 7. 'You bring three proofs of this: "(1). Mr. Wesley, in his answer to a divine of our Church, says, 'Jesus Christ stands as our regeneration, to help us to the same holy, undefiled nature which he himself had. And if this very life and identical nature is not propagated and derived on us, he is not our Saviour.'" 'But be they whose they will, they by no means imply that we are to be "as righteous as Christ was".' (§14)

p. 8. "(2). A preacher of yours declared, he was as free from sin as Christ ever was." (§14)
"(3). Another declared, he believed it was impossible for one whom he named to sin, for the Spirit of God dwelt in him bodily." (§14)
'What you say of that good man Mr. Whitefield, now with God, I leave. . . .' (§14)

p. [9] 'You next descant upon "the disorders which the spirit of enthusiasm created in the last age". . . . In the following page you quaintly compare your hearers to sheep, and yourself and friends to the dogs in the fable; and seem much afraid lest the silly sheep should be "persuaded to *give you up to these ravening wolves*".' (§15)

p. 10. "Another fundamental error of the Methodists is the asserting that laymen may preach, yea, the *most ignorant* and illiterate of them, provided they have the *inward call* of the Spirit." (§16)

p. 11. "But no ambassador can act without a commission from his king; consequently, no preacher without a commission from God." (§17)

p. 13. "However, these laymen are not sent of God to preach. For does not St. Paul say, 'No man taketh this honour to himself, but he that is called of God as was Aaron'?" (§17)

p. 14. "But the earth opened and swallowed up those intruders into the priestly office, Korah, Dathan, and Abiram." (§17)

pp. 16-17. "But the Church of Rome has sent out preachers among us such as Thomas Heath, a Jesuit, and Faithful Commin, a Dominican friar." (§18)

p. 18. 'We have now done with the argumentative part of your Sermons, and come to the exhortation. "Mark them that cause divisions and offences among you, for they serve not the Lord, but their own bellies. And by fair speeches deceive the hearts of the simple."' (Rom. 16:17-18; §19)

p. 19. "Do not credit those who tell you that we must judge of our regeneration by sensible impulses, impressions, ardours, and ecstasies." (§20)

p. 20. 'Whether therefore these are or are not "signs of the Spirit", see *you* to it; it is nothing to *me*, any more than whether the Spirit does or does not "show itself in groanings and sighings, in fits and starts". I never affirmed it did; and when you represent me as so doing you are a sinner against God. . . .' (§20)

INDEX
OF SCRIPTURAL REFERENCES

This index covers all references to Scripture, whether cited by Wesley himself or identified by the present editor. More then one citation of a text on the same page is indicated by a figure in parentheses immediately after the page number.

Where Wesley is quoting the Psalms from the Book of Common Prayer the numbering of verses sometimes differs from that of the Authorized Version. These cases are distinguished by adding (BCP) to the reference.

OLD TESTAMENT

NEW TESTAMENT

GENERAL INDEX

The alphabetical arrangement of entries is on a word-by-word basis. Foreign words and phrases are listed under the appropriate language, preceded in the case of Greek by a transliteration and arranged accordingly. Definite and indefinite articles are ignored in the titles of publications.

The abbreviation 'W' is used throughout for the surname 'Wesley', either alone when the reference is to John Wesley himself or following the Christian name of other members of the family. The entry under 'Wesley, John' is confined to personal characteristics and major periods and events in his life. For his publications and sermons (of which lists are given) see under titles.

Footnote references are indicated by the addition of 'n' or 'nn' to the page numbers; '(n)' indicates a reference in the main text which is made explicit by a footnote. A figure in brackets after a page number draws attention to more than one reference on a page.